Artists don't seek reason
They are all by definition c
and vice versa

Daisy Bell 6

Al Borboleta

Cookbook

Butterfly Wings and Culinary Happenings

23/8/97.

The Bield,
Gifford,
East Lothian,
Scotland, United Kingdom. Tel 01620 810232.
EH41 4QL

Dear Karl, Jutta and Christiane,

This year's visit seems even better than last year's – our visits here to your lovely restaurant are the highlight of the holiday. Tonight I was honoured to become "Lady Ann of the Butterflies" – an honour beyond my dreams!! Thank-you for everything & please come and see us in Scotland – we mean it, most sincerely, but don't expect the same cuisine!

Lots of love,

"Lady" Ann

Not forgetting the "Old Man"

An Drambuideache

Jeffreys

continued on next page . . . .

Thank you very much for all the meat skewers and peanut sauce! Please send us a copy of your book

lots of love

Amy

EB

Al Borboleta

Cookbook

Butterfly Wings and Culinary Happenings

A COLLECTION OF RECIPES AND CHILDREN'S DRAWINGS PRESENTED BY JUTTA HINRICHS AND FAMILY

The Book Guild Limited
Sussex, England

First published in Great Britain in 2001 by:
The Book Guild Ltd, 25 High Street, Lewes,
East Sussex BN7 2LU

Origination, printing and binding in Singapore
under the supervision of MRM Graphics Ltd, Winslow, Bucks.

A catalogue record for this book is available from
The Britsh Library.

ISBN 1 85776 501 X

Dedication

A word (or two) of thanks:
My special gratitude goes to my loving family and friends who enabled me to survive and triumph over ten years of Al Borboleta: especially to Alice and Dieter Schaupp for their financial support and Helen Rodda for her incessant help prior to the opening of the restaurant, Papa Fritz and Tante Marlies, my sister Sylvia and her family; my dear friends Bärbel and Hans, Marei, Inge, Duldi, Wendy, Heido (can't thank you enough for being by my side as my art support!!) and Roy, and last but not least my husband Karl and my children Christiane and Dirk (Christiane, you and I were a great team, and thank you especially for all the translations from German into English and the typing job). Words do not suffice. To all of you, and anyone that I may have forgotten, a huge 'thank you'!

Our warmest thanks have to go to our 'regulars' – residents and 'semis' – who loyally and faithfully stood by us over all the years, helping us to survive the difficult times and share the good times (!) in the Algarve. This of course includes the hitches, putting up with Karl and last but not least Teddy's barking...

And of course a massive thank you to all the kids right across the globe for their butterfly designs, which really were the initiator for this book – we felt they were by far too precious to just put in a drawer. Unfortunately we were not able to use all of them, of course, but they were all fantastic. Thank you!

Jutta Hinrichs

Contents

Long, long ago he had
Discovered that the most
Beautiful and delicate of things
Were the hardest to touch.

Herman Hesse

Not only is this observation a true reflection of the nature of butterflies, but it is equally true for the art of blending the flavours of raw ingredients and creating dishes to excite our demanding palate.

During a wonderful ten–year period of managing a country restaurant named Al Borboleta (the Portuguese translation of butterfly) in a beautiful area in the Algarve, both my own passion for cookery developed, along with a precious collection of the drawings made by the children of many families who came to dine with us and also became our friends. The innocence of children's art, especially when depicting the magical, almost illusive quality of one of the world's most beautiful creatures, is for me both wonderful and worth preserving. This, combined with my recipes resulting from the process of experimentation, refinement and the ultimate satisfaction of serving to the restaurant's visitors, is the reason and inspiration for this book.

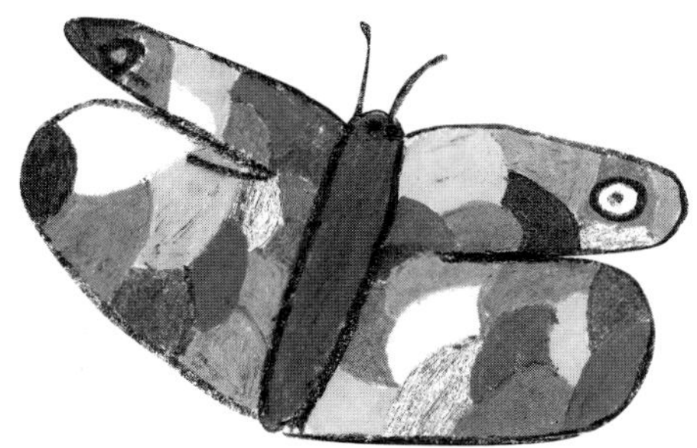

For Starters...

When my mother asked me to write an introduction to her 'dream', I tried to ignore those Freudian anecdotes creeping into my subconscious – I also had to undo a few buttons as I sat down to write! One of the problems associated with being a 'son' is that you *have* to eat everything your mother cooks – to the last morsel – 'hell hath no fury like a woman spurned'! Fortunately I have never had a problem with 'the last morsel' and hence my mother is of a very sunny disposition – which brings me back to this book. 'Float like a butterfly, sting like a bee' Muhammed Ali is reputed to have once said. Alas, after wallowing in my mother's cooking pots for more than a third of a century, I am no longer able to do either (except on the few occasions, perhaps, when she has been a little heavy–handed with the chilli – then I do the latter!)

Officially this collection of culinary and artistic delights serves as a testament and a farewell (touched with *saudade*) to an adventurous decade in the Algarve, and in Al Borboleta in particular, our own restaurant. It is also meant as a tribute to all our guests over the years, both occasional and regular, and especially their children, who so lovingly and, unbeknown to them, illustrated this book for us. Amongst the drawings you will find a pot–pourri of, until now, closely guarded recipes to awaken even the most dormant of taste buds and tickle the most spoilt of gums. In other words, something for everyone. At this point, before the meal gets cold, there only remains for me to say 'farewell' on behalf of Karl, stern barman, chief 'Borboleta' and father; Christiane, life and soul of Al Borboleta as well as head waitress and sister; Jutta, chief cook, mother and perpetrator of this historical work; and last as well as least my good self, washer–upper, son, brother, scribe and chief taster.

Dirk Bandele Hinrichs

PS Now enjoy!

The Recipes

This is by no means meant to be a conventional cookery book – I am just giving away my recipes of ten years, for which I have been asked so many times by guests. It leaves some room for imagination and adjustment according to your personal taste and, of course, to the inventive cook.

Not every ingredient is given in its exact weight or liquid measure – in Al Borboleta every dish turned out a bit different every day (a bit of this, oh, why not a bit of that today, that might taste good!...)

I even had comments on that from guests: 'But last week the curry tasted more of coconut,' etc.

That's human for you.

Jutta Hinrichs

Notes:

Spoon measures are always level, unless otherwise stated

Cream is single, flour is plain, sugar is caster.

A lot of the recipes use garlic – do be careful not to overfry or burn garlic, as this will make it taste bitter.

The Al Barbaleta Story

All stories have a beginning. Ours was Africa, the amazing continent where my father had spent many happy years. It was also the place where I was born. After some years in England, the old yearnings for the sight of blue skies, the feeling of sun on his face and the memories of living amongst friendly, warm people became too strong. Fuelled by these memories and the desire to build his family a new home and indeed a new life in such a place, brought us to the Algarve. More precisely, to a beautiful valley at the base of the Monchique mountains, surrounded by hills of pine and eucalyptus trees and teeming with colourful butterflies. With my mother, who had always been a passionate cook, my sister involved in catering and our dog and myself, who are equally passionate about eating, we had the ideal location and the raw recruits to roll up our sleeves and start living out the great adventure of running our own family restaurant.

Much preparation on everybody's behalf had preceded this momentous event. Friends were recruited and uprooted, bars and restaurants belonging to others terrorised in the quest for experience, recipes chosen and discarded, staff employed locally, a *casita*, or bungalow, built behind the restaurant, the list is endless... Eventually my mother became 'cook', Christiane, my sister, was in charge of everything in the restaurant, her best friend Jo grilled everything there was to grill, my father was firmly entrenched behind the bar and Teddy, our dog, assumed responsibility for all left-over disposals. In addition, three ladies from the local village, led by Gracinda, carried out all other duties. In the following years many others, myself included, helped at different times.

Our guests helped too – by coming to sample our cooking, the unique atmosphere, and the 'amateur' approach, which seemed to appeal to many! After a few years it became apparent that many people from all over the world shared our love of the Algarve and visited it, and us, on a regular basis. Many of these, as well as others, had (and still have!) young children. In order to keep them occupied (and allow their parents to dine in peace) my mother initially started a competition involving the drawing of butterflies. These artistic impressions soon adorned the walls of the restaurant, and the request for pens and paper became part and parcel of ordering! The art work was then admired on subsequent visits; the grown–ups joined in too, with a little more sophisticated contributions, and the restaurant came to be decorated with tiles, ceramics, metal ornaments, plates, mounted frames and ashtrays – just to mention a few – all depicting butterflies! The cocoon had truly hatched; over the years Al Borboleta emerged from an abstract name that meant little to our guests to a firm favourite with its own true butterfly identity. A dream had sprouted wings and had taken to the air. Today the name remains – but the soul is contained in this book. Cooking, my mother feels, is a form of art too; so, in order to commemorate the spirit of Al Borboleta, she decided to create a cookery book with a difference: children's drawings, facts and information about butterflies and unusual international recipes – so please join in our celebration of colour, taste and thought–provoking ideas!

Dirk Bandele Hinrichs

Soups

American Potato Soup

Ingredients:

1 KG POTATOES, PEELED • CHICKEN STOCK TO COVER
125G STREAKY BACON • 1 TSP DRIED MARJORAM • SEASONING
2 TSP FRESH CHOPPED PARSLEY • 25G FRESHLY GRATED
PARMESAN CHEESE • 2 EGG YOLKS

Method:

Boil the potatoes in the stock until tender. Dice the bacon and fry until golden and crisp. Mash the potatoes or put through a blender, stir in the marjoram and Parmesan and season. Beat the egg yolks and use to bind the soup. To serve, stir in the bacon and parsley.

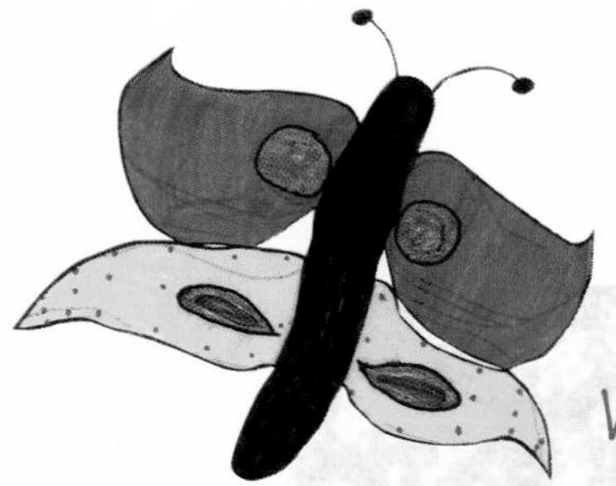

While resting, butterflies fold their wings over their heads.

Carrot and Orange Soup

Ingredients:

450G CARROTS • JUICE OF 3 ORANGES AND ZEST OF 1 MEDIUM ORANGE • 1 LARGE ONION • 3 CLOVES GARLIC • 1 TSP GINGER, PEELED AND GRATED • 3 TBS OLIVE OIL • SEASONING VEGETABLE STOCK TO COVER

Method:

Peel the carrots if they have tough skin and slice thickly. Peel the onion and cut into large chunks. Peel and slice the garlic. Heat the olive oil in a saucepan, sauté the onions, garlic, ginger and carrots for 10 minutes. Add the orange juice and zest and stock to cover. Bring to the boil, reduce heat and simmer, covered, for 20 minutes. Blend in a food processor until smooth and adjust seasoning.

Chilled Curry and Apricot Soup

Serves 6

Ingredients:

3 SPRING ONIONS, PEELED • 2 TBS VEGETABLE OIL • 2–3 TBS MILD CURRY POWDER • 2 TBS FLOUR • 250ML CHICKEN STOCK 300G FRESH APRICOTS • 750ML BUTTERMILK • SALT FRESHLY GROUND BLACK PEPPER

Method:

Wash the spring onions and slice finely. Heat the oil and fry the onion rings until soft. Stir in the curry powder and flour, and slowly add the stock. Bring to the boil, reduce the heat and simmer, covered, for five minutes. Meanwhile, wash the apricots, halve and remove the stones. Cut into wedges and add to the soup. Remove the saucepan from the heat. Once it has cooled down, stir in the buttermilk and season well. Chill overnight before serving.

Cream of Pepper Soup

Serves 4–6

Ingredients:

6–8 PEPPERS, DE-SEEDED • 1 LARGE ONION • 2–3 LARGE CARROTS • 1 APPLE, PEELED AND CORED • OIL FOR FRYING • 2 TBS FRESH CORIANDER • VEGETABLE STOCK TO BARELY COVER • JUICE OF 1 LARGE LEMON • SEASONING • 125ML SINGLE CREAM (OPTIONAL)

Method:

Roughly chop the peppers, onion, carrots and apple. Heat the oil and fry until soft and golden. Add the fresh coriander, lemon juice and enough stock to cover. Bring to the boil, cover and simmer for 15 minutes. Blend until smooth in a food processor. Adjust the seasoning. Stir in cream if using.

Butterflies are the only insects who are able to roll up their 'trunk' spirally when they are not using it for the intake of food.

Cream of Pumpkin Soup

Serves 6

Ingredients:

½ LARGE PUMPKIN • 1 LARGE ONION • 2 TOMATOES, COARSELY CHOPPED • 1 LARGE TBS FINELY DICED GINGER • 1 TSP MILD CURRY POWDER • 1 STICK OF CELERY • 4 CLOVES GARLIC • SEASONING VEGETABLE STOCK • 4 TBS OLIVE OIL FOR FRYING • 1 BUNCH PORTUGUESE CABBAGE LEAVES OR 200G GREEN CABBAGE (SUMMER SAVOY) • 125ML SINGLE CREAM (OPTIONAL)

Method:

Remove the skin from the pumpkin, scrape out the seeds and cut into large chunks. Peel and chop the onion and radish coarsely. Peel the garlic and slice. Heat the olive oil in a saucepan and sauté the onion, garlic, pumpkin and ginger for 10 minutes. Add the spices and fry for another 5 minutes. Season and add the tomatoes and enough stock to cover. Bring to the boil, reduce the heat and simmer for 20 minutes, covered. Blend in a food processor and stir in the cream if using. Adjust the seasoning.

Cream of Watercress Soup with Pernod

Ingredients:

2 LARGE BUNCHES OF WATERCRESS, LEAVES ONLY • 1 LARGE ONION
3 CLOVES GARLIC • 3 TBS VEGETABLE OIL • 250G POTATOES, PEELED AND DICED • SEASONING • CHICKEN STOCK TO BARELY COVER • 125ML SINGLE CREAM (OPTIONAL) • 20ML PERNOD

Method:

Wash the watercress. Peel the onion and chop into large chunks. Peel the garlic and slice. Heat the oil in a saucepan and sauté the onion and garlic until soft. Add the watercress and potatoes and sauté for a further 5 minutes. Season and cover with stock. Bring to the boil and simmer for 15–20 minutes. Blend in a food processor and add cream if using. Adjust seasoning and stir in the Pernod.

The Bengali propagate for butterfly is the scienscript word pragapati (Lord of the Creatures) given to Brahmas and the old Richis.

Garlic Soup

Serves 6

Ingredients:

2 LARGE ONIONS • 6 BULBS OF GARLIC • 3 TBS OLIVE OIL
250 ML MILK • ½ TSP DRIED OREGANO • ½ TSP DRIED MARJORAM
¼ TSP DRIED THYME • 25G BUTTER OR MARGARINE
2 TBS FLOUR • 1 CHICKEN STOCK CUBE • 200ML WHITE WINE
500–750ML MILK • SEASONING

Method:

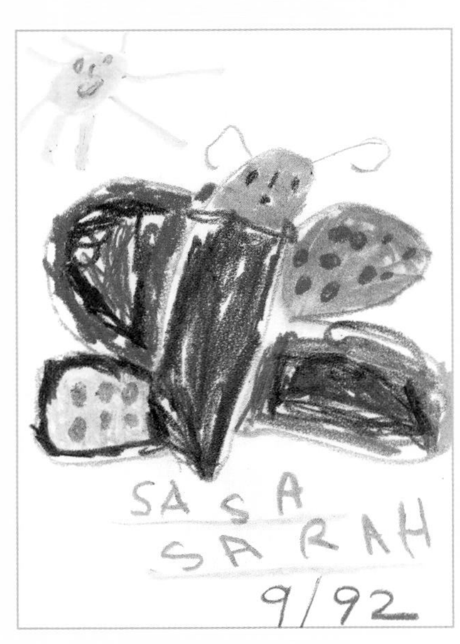

Peel the onions and cut into large chunks. Peel the garlic. Heat the olive oil in a saucepan and fry the onion and garlic for about 3 minutes. Add enough milk to just cover (about 250ml), the mixed herbs and some salt and pepper. Boil on a high heat for 5–10 minutes. Set aside. Melt the butter in a saucepan, remove from the heat and stir in the flour. Add the white wine a bit at a time, stirring constantly, then stir in 500ml of milk. Crumble in the stock cube and season with some salt and freshly ground black pepper. Return to the heat and bring to the boil, simmer until thickened. If the consistency is too thick, add more milk to taste. Blend in a food processor until everything is smooth. Adjust the seasoning and add some lemon juice if you wish it more pungent.

Goat's Cheese Soup

Serves 4–6

Ingredients:

100G LEEKS • 100G CELERIAC • 100G SHALLOTS, PEELED
1 MEDIUM POTATO, PEELED • 1/4 TSP FRESHLY GROUND NUTMEG
20 G BUTTER • 100ML DRY WHITE WINE • 1 LITRE VEGETABLE STOCK
200ML CREAM • 1 TBS SOURED CREAM • 200G FRESH GOAT'S CHEESE • SALT • FRESHLY GROUND BLACK PEPPER
1/2 TSP DRIED THYME • 1 TBS BALSAMIC VINEGAR • FRESH PARSLEY • CROUTONS

Method:

Chop and wash the leeks and celery. Dice the shallots and potato. Melt the butter and sauté the potato and vegetables with the ground nutmeg until soft. Add the wine and stock and bring to the boil. Reduce the heat, cover and simmer for 20 minutes. Place in a food processor and purée until smooth. Add the cream, soured cream, cheese, seasoning and thyme. Heat through and finally add the vinegar. Serve sprinkled with fresh parsley and croutons.

The minute scales that butterflies are covered in contain dyes, which sparkle in many different colours when hit by light.

Leek and Apple Soup

Serves 6

Ingredients:

4 MEDIUM LEEKS • 3 LARGE COOKING APPLES • 1 LARGE ONION 1 LARGE POTATO • 3 TBS VEGETABLE OIL • PINCH OF GRATED NUTMEG • SEASONING • CHICKEN STOCK TO COVER • 125ML SINGLE CREAM (OPTIONAL)

Method:

Slice the leeks lengthwise and wash under plenty of cold running water to remove any dirt. Peel, core and roughly chop the apples. Peel the onion and potato and cut into chunks. Heat some oil in a saucepan, fry the leeks, apples and onion until soft. Add the potato and sauté for another 3 minutes. Add the nutmeg and seasoning. Cover with stock, bring to the boil, reduce the heat, cover and simmer for 15–20 minutes. Blend in a food processor and adjust the seasoning. Stir in the cream if using and serve.

Melon, Cucumber and Tomato Soup

Serves 4

Ingredients:

3 TBS VEGETABLE OIL • ¼ MEDIUM MELON • 1 SMALL CUCUMBER • 4 MEDIUM TOMATOES, PEELED • 1 LARGE ONION
3 CLOVES GARLIC • 1 TSP DRIED OREGANO • SEASONING
VEGETABLE STOCK TO COVER

Method:

Peel the garlic and onion. Slice the garlic and cut the onion into large chunks. Peel the cucumber, cut into half lengthways and remove the seeds. Peel, de–seed and chop the melon. Chop the tomatoes into quarters. Heat the oil in a saucepan and sauté the onion and garlic until soft. Add the cucumber and melon and fry for another few minutes. Add the rest of the ingredients plus enough stock to cover. Bring to the boil and simmer, covered, for 20 minutes. Purée in a food processor until smooth. Check the seasoning and chill.

The Greeks called the butterfly psyche (soul) or also petomene psyche (flying soul).

Pea and Coconut Soup

- with Quark Dumplings -

Ingredients:

3 TBS VEGETABLE OIL • 1 ONION, PEELED AND DICED
3 LARGE CLOVES GARLIC, DICED • 1 MEDIUM HEAD LETTUCE, WASHED AND DICED • CAYENNE PEPPER TO TASTE • SEASONING
800ML STOCK • 9 TBS COCONUT MILK • 250G QUARK (GERMAN SOFT CHEESE) • 3 LARGE EGG YOLKS • 2 SMALL RED CHILLIES, FINELY DICED • 1 1/2 TSP SALT • 1 TBS CORNFLOUR • FRESH MINT

Method:

Sauté the onion and garlic for about 10 minutes on a very low heat. Add the lettuce, peas, cayenne pepper and coconut milk. Cover with stock, bring to the boil and simmer, covered for 15 minutes. Blend in a food processor and season. Mix the quark, egg yolks, chillies, cornflour and 1/2 the salt. Bring 1 litre of water to the boil, add the remaining salt. With the help of a teaspoon form walnut–size dumplings and place in the water. Leave to poach for 3–4 minutes, remove with a slotted spoon and add to the soup. Garnish with mint.

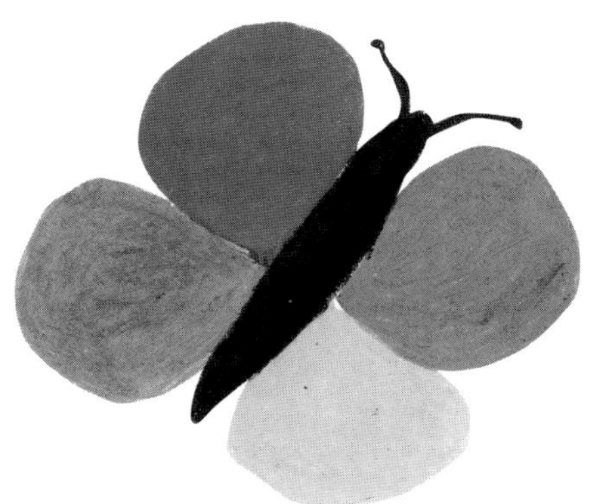

Tomato Soup à la Angel'

Serves 6

Ingredients:

25G MARGARINE • 1 LARGE ONION • 400G LEAN MINCED BEEF SEASONING • 2 TBS FLOUR • 2 X 800G TIN TOMATOES, CHOPPED 2 TBS TOMATO PURÉE • 500ML BEEF STOCK • 50ML BRANDY CAYENNE PEPPER TO TASTE • 3 TBS MARINATED GREEN HOT CHILLIES OUT OF A JAR • 125ML CRÈME FRAÎCHE

Method:

Dice the onion. Sauté in the margarine, together with the minced beef until the mince is brown – about 5 minutes. Take off the heat and stir in the flour. Season. Add the tomatoes and purée, bring to the boil and simmer for 10 minutes. Add the stock and simmer for a further 10 minutes. Stir in the chillies and brandy and adjust seasoning, adding cayenne pepper to taste. Serve with a dollop of crème fraîche on top.

Soup Suggestions

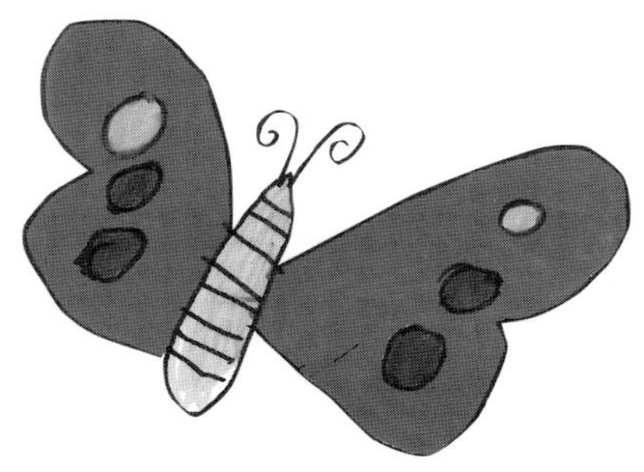

Italian Cabbage and Bacon

Lettuce and Peas
(with a little Broccoli)

Chick Pea and Smoked Ham

Asparagus (with the tips left whole)
and Broccoli

Curried Pea and Tomato

Cream of Cannellini Beans and Ham

Cream of Vegetable, Bean Sprouts
and Fennel

Cream of Cheese and Herbs

Cream of Cabbage with cream
and cumin

Cream of Prawn and Broccoli
(with some prawns left whole)

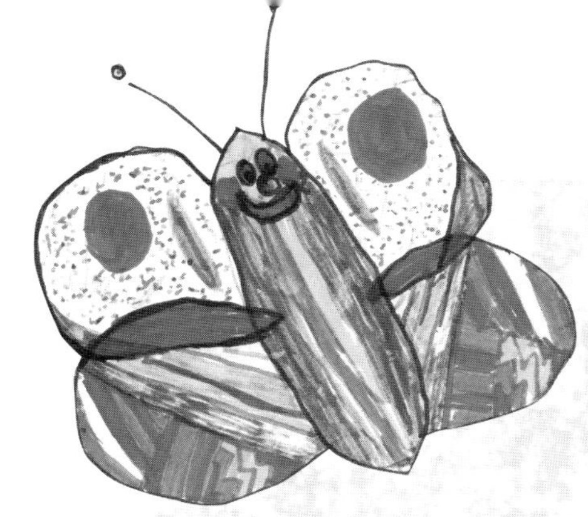

The incredible transition from caterpillar to butterfly must be one of the greatest wonders of nature.

General Tip:

Always start your soup by sautéing the onion and garlic (if using). Add the vegetables plus some potatoes to thicken the soup. Sauté these for another few minutes to bring out the flavours. Add the spices and enough stock to cover, bring to the boil and simmer for 15–20 minutes. Put through the food processor – and Bob's your uncle!

Tip for an easy home-made stock (for 1.5 litres):

For chicken stock use three carcasses – for beef use any offcuts or cheap cuts, about 500g. Wash the meat or chicken, place in a large saucepan, add a large sprig of parsley, one medium carrot chopped into large chunks, 1 onion peeled and quartered spiked with four cloves, 4 cloves garlic, peeled, 1 tsp paprika, 1 tsp each of coarse salt and whole black peppercorns. Cover generously with water – about 2 litres, bring to the boil, reduce heat and simmer, covered for at least 30 minutes. The longer you boil it the more intense the flavour. For a vegetable stock, substitute the meat with vegetables such as leeks, broccoli, cauliflower or any other preferred vegetable. Strain through a sieve and use.

NB: For people with little time: I often produce a 'quick stock' while I am frying, e.g. chicken pieces. I boil the carcasses in some salt water for 20 minutes and use this immediately for the sauce.

Starters

Tuna Fish Salad

Serves 4

Ingredients:

2 X 120G TINS TUNA FISH • 2 EGGS • 2 MEDIUM TOMATOES
1 MEDIUM ONION • 4 TBS MAYONNAISE • 2 TSP FRESH
PARSLEY, CHOPPED • SEASONING • TOMATO OR EGG QUARTERS
TO GARNISH

Method:

Hard-boil the eggs and rinse under cold water. Peel and chop roughly. Peel and dice the onion finely and chop the tomatoes. Drain the tuna and flake. Mix with the onion and tomato. Spoon the mayonnaise into the salad and finally add the chopped parsley and eggs. Check the seasoning. Chill the salad for a few hours or overnight and garnish with tomato or egg quarters. Ideal as a first course or a late evening snack, served with French bread.

Liptauer Cheese

Serves 4

Ingredients:

300G QUARK OR CURD CHEESE • 100G BUTTER, SOFTENED
½ TBS CAPERS, FINELY CHOPPED • 1 SMALL ONION, MINCED
½ TBS PAPRIKA POWDER • 1 TSP MUSTARD
½ TSP WHOLE CARAWAY SEEDS • SEASONING • CHOPPED PARSLEY TO GARNISH

Method:

With an electric hand mixer beat together all the ingredients apart from the quark and the seasoning. Thoroughly blend in the quark and season. Chill overnight before serving and arrange on a wooden board sprinkled with chopped parsley and paprika. This may be served as a starter or as the cheese course at the end of the meal.

Starters

Sardine Pâté

Serves 4

Ingredients:

350G TINNED SARDINES, DRAINED • 1 MEDIUM ONION, ROUGHLY CHOPPED • 1 TSP CHILLI POWDER • 1 TSP SALT • 1/2 TSP MIXED HERBS • 1 TBS LEMON JUICE • 25G MARGARINE • 200G CREAM CHEESE • 25ML BRANDY

Method:

Place the sardines in a food processor and mix with the onion until smooth. Add the spices, lemon juice and margarine and process until well mixed. Then blend all together with the soft cheese and brandy. Chill for several hours.

Butterflies are just like flowers, a very special part of creation – an object dear and made to awake a certain awe. They seem to have been invented by friendly, loving and fun-loving geniuses – just like the flowers – as a decoration, as jewels, as little glittering pieces of art and songs of praise...

Chicken Liver Pâté

Ingredients:

250G CHICKEN LIVERS • 1 TBS OLIVE OIL • 2 CLOVES GARLIC, CRUSHED • DRIED OREGANO TO TASTE • SEASONING • APPROX. 100ML RED WINE • 50G BUTTER

Method:

Clean and wash the chicken livers. Pat dry with kitchen paper. Heat the olive oil in a frying pan or wok and fry the chicken livers, with the garlic, until brown on all sides. Add the oregano, seasoning and enough red wine so that the livers are three–quarters covered. Cover and simmer for 5–8 minutes until cooked but tender. Place in a food processor without the liquid. Purée, adding the liquid a little at a time – it may not need all of it. While mixing, add the cold butter a little at a time. Chill for several hours or preferably overnight before serving.

Chickpea Dip

Serves 6

Ingredients:

545G TIN CHICKPEAS, DRAINED WITH SOME OF THE JUICE RESERVED • JUICE OF 1 LEMON • 2–4 CLOVES GARLIC, PEELED AND CRUSHED • 2 TSP LIGHT TAHINI PASTE • 1–2 TBS ROASTED SESAME SEEDS • SEASONING • A LITTLE OLIVE OIL

Method:

Place the chickpeas in a food processor with the lemon juice, crushed garlic, tahini paste and seasoning. Blend until mushy. Add a few tablespoons of the chickpea liquid and slowly add some oil while the mixer is still running. Once a fairly thick and creamy consistency has been reached, adjust the seasoning and stir in the sesame seeds. Chill before serving. Tahini is a sesame paste sold in most delicatessen or health food shops.

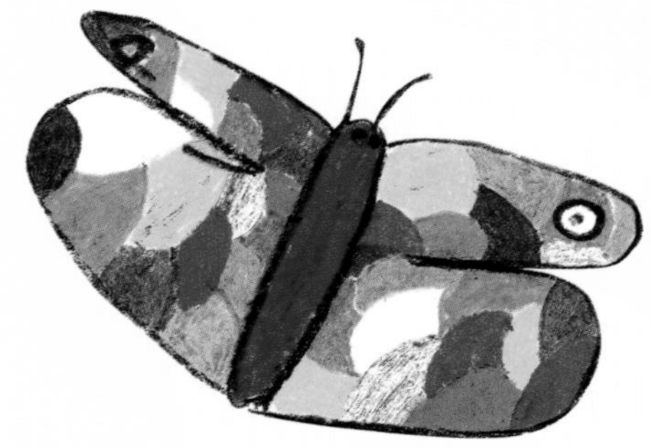

Marinated Greek Mushrooms

Serves 4

Ingredients:

900G BUTTON MUSHROOMS • SALT • FRESHLY GROUND BLACK PEPPER • 6 TBS OLIVE OIL • 2 TBS SHERRY VINEGAR • 1 1/2 TBS CORIANDER SEEDS, CRUSHED • 3 BAY LEAVES • 2 TBS CHOPPED FRESH CORIANDER • 1 LEMON, HALVED AND THINLY SLICED
450G TOMATOES, CHOPPED (OPTIONAL)

Method:

Wash and dry the mushrooms. Season with salt and pepper. Heat the oil and the vinegar in a pan with the crushed coriander seeds. When hot, drop in all the ingredients apart from the tomatoes. Cook on a high heat for 10–15 minutes. Lift out the mushrooms and add the tomatoes, if using. Boil the sauce rapidly until reduced by half. Pour back over the mushrooms, cover and chill before serving.

The amount of time a caterpillar needs from the egg to the chrysalis depends on the type. It can take anything from two weeks to two years.

Stuffed Tomatoes

Serves 4

Ingredients:

4 LARGE TOMATOES • 125G SEMI–MATURED GOAT'S CHEESE 50G BREADCRUMBS • 25G FRESH BASIL OR SIMILAR • 1 CLOVE GARLIC • 30G BLACK OLIVES, CHOPPED • SEASONING • 50ML OIL

Method:

Wash tomatoes and cut off lids. Scoop out insides and lightly salt. Mix crumbled cheese, breadcrumbs, basil, crushed garlic, finely chopped olives and seasoning. Stuff the tomatoes with the mixture and sprinkle with the oil. Bake in the oven for about 20 minutes at 180°C/Gas 4 with lids off.

The butterfly has four wings, covered in fine scales that resemble fine feathers. The caterpillar has sixteen feet and feeds itself with green leaves – it then transforms itself into a smooth and shiny golden chrysalis, which clings to a fixed place, surviving without feet and without nourishment. This turns into a lively butterfly with six legs, sucking the sweet honey of the blossoms.

Garlic Mushrooms

Serves 4

Ingredients:

750G MUSHROOMS • 1 1/2 TBS MINCED GARLIC • 3 TBS OLIVE OR VEGETABLE OIL • 20G BUTTER • SALT AND PEPPER CHOPPED PARSLEY TO GARNISH • 1/2 LEMON

Method:

Wipe the mushrooms and slice (leave whole if they are very small). Heat the oil and butter in a pan until very hot and add the mushrooms. Fry on a high heat until starting to brown. Add the minced garlic and continue to fry, stirring constantly, until the mushrooms are brown all over. Squirt over some lemon juice and season. Serve immediately with fresh bread or toast. (Together with the garlic soup our biggest runner)

Starters

Gravlax with a Mustard and Dill Sauce

- Swedish Marinated Salmon -

Serves 8–10 as a starter, 6–8 as a light main meal

For the marinated Salmon:

1KG MIDDLE CUT OF SALMON, IN 2 FILLETS • 4 TBS SALT 2 TSP ROUGHLY CRUSHED PEPPER • 2-4 TBS SUGAR • 2 TBS DRIED DILL • A PLASTIC BAG LARGE ENOUGH TO HOLD THE SALMON

For the Mustard and Dill Sauce:

2 LARGE EGG YOLKS • 2 TBS CASTER SUGAR • 4 TBS STRONG FRENCH MUSTARD • 4 TBS WHITE WINE VINEGAR • 175ML SUNFLOWER OIL • 50ML OLIVE OIL • SEASONING • LETTUCE AND WEDGES OF LEMON TO SERVE

Method:

For the marinated Salmon: Make sure that all bones have been removed from the fillets. Mix all the other ingredients together and rub half of the mixture into the inside of the fillets. Sandwich them together, skin side out, ensuring that a thick part covers each of the thin parts. Rub some more of the spice into the outside – then place the salmon in the bag with plenty of mixture around it and seal. Place between two wooden boards and weigh down with a heavy object before putting it into the fridge for two days. NB: If possible, it is easier to buy the salmon already filleted.

For the Mustard and Dill Sauce: Beat the egg yolks, sugar and mustard together - this can best be done in a food processor – add the vinegar. Then gradually blend in the oils, and season to taste with salt and freshly ground black pepper. Serve separately. Before serving, scrape off the spices and dill, then carve the fish in very thin slices exactly as though carving smoked salmon, leaving the skin intact. Arrange on a bed of lettuce and garnish with wedges of lemon. NB: Serve with wholemeal crackers or bread as a starter or hot new potatoes steamed in their skins and thin cucumber slices as a light main meal.

Filled Eggs

Serves 4

Ingredients:

4 LARGE EGGS • 1 SMALL ONION, PEELED • 1 ½ TBS MAYONNAISE • 1 TSP GREEK–STYLE YOGHURT • 2 LARGE GHERKINS 75G COOKED HAM, FINELY DICED (OPTIONAL) • ½ TSP PAPRIKA 1 LEVEL TSP CURRY POWDER • SEASONING • LETTUCE AND CHOPPED PARSLEY TO SERVE

Method:

Boil the eggs for 8–10 minutes until the centres are firm but not grey. Rinse under cold water, peel and cut in half. Scoop the egg yolks from 2 eggs into a bowl and mash with a fork. Stir in the mayonnaise and yoghurt, mixing well. Add the paprika and curry powder. Chop the onion and gherkins very finely and stir into the mixture together with the ham (if using). Scoop out the other egg yolks and discard. Season the filling and spoon generously into the egg halves. Chill for several hours before serving. Arrange on a bed of lettuce and sprinkle with parsley.

Poultry Dishes

Chicken 'Creole'

Serves 4

Ingredients:

8 SMALL CHICKEN BREASTS OR 4 LARGE ONES • FLOUR FOR COATING • 4 TBS VEGETABLE OIL • 6 WHOLE CLOVES • 1 CHICKEN STOCK CUBE (OPTIONAL) • 1½ TBS HONEY • JUICE AND RIND OF 1 ORANGE • 3 CLOVES GARLIC, CRUSHED • 1 TBS PAPRIKA PASTE OR 1 TSP PAPRIKA POWDER • 50ML WHITE RUM • 350G SLICED MUSHROOMS • 1 TSP GROUND CINNAMON • ½ TSP CAYENNE PEPPER • 2 TSP GROUND CORIANDER • 1 TSP PAPRIKA • 250ML WATER (OR STOCK) • 200ML CREAM • 2 HEAPED TBS CORNFLOUR CHOPPED FRESH CORIANDER OR PARSLEY

Method:

Trim the chicken breasts and cut them in half. Heat the oil. Roll the chicken pieces in the flour and fry until golden brown on all sides. Place the chicken in a casserole dish and add all the other ingredients.

Heat some oil in the same frying pan and add all the spices. Fry for 2 minutes, then add the sliced mushrooms and fry until soft. Loosen the sediment by adding a little water or stock. Add to the casserole. Add enough water or stock to barely cover the chicken and season with salt. Bring to the boil, reduce heat and simmer for 20 minutes. Mix the cream, rum and cornflour to a paste and add to the chicken once it is cooked. Leave to thicken for a few minutes and serve sprinkled with fresh chopped coriander or parsley.

Chicken in Almond and Port Wine Sauce

Ingredients:

4 EGGS • 2 TBS CHOPPED FRESH PARSLEY • 2 CHICKENS, JOINTED • 6 TBS FLOUR • 3 TBS OLIVE OIL • 2 MEDIUM ONIONS, PEELED AND DICED • SEASONING • 200ML RUBY PORT 250–400 ML CHICKEN STOCK • 200G ALMONDS, SHELLED

Method:

Hard–boil the eggs and remove the egg yolks. Mix them with the parsley to make a smooth paste. Discard the whites. Wash and dry the chicken pieces and turn in flour. Fry golden brown in the olive oil. Place in a casserole. Sauté the onions and add to the chicken. Season. Add the port and the stock to the casserole and bake in a medium pre–heated oven for 30 minutes. Meanwhile, roast the almonds in a dry pan or in the oven until golden. Grind finely. Add to the chicken together with the egg paste and cook for a further 15 minutes, adding more stock if necessary. This may also be replaced by a little cream. Season to taste and serve with fresh bread and a green salad.

Poultry Dishes

Chicken Curry 'Dona Jutta'

Serves 4–6

Ingredients:

3 CHICKENS, CUT INTO PIECES, SKIN REMOVED • 6 TBS VEGETABLE OIL • FLOUR FOR COATING • 4 LARGE BAY LEAVES 2 THICK SLICES OF LEMON • CHICKEN STOCK TO COVER • 1 LARGE APPLE • 1 LARGE ONION, PEELED • 3 CLOVES GARLIC, PEELED (OPTIONAL) • 5 ROUNDED TBS CURRY POWDER • 4 HEAPED TBS FLOUR • 1/2 PACKET DESICCATED COCONUT, ROASTED • 800G TIN TOMATOES, CHOPPED

Method:

Coat the chicken pieces in flour and fry in hot oil until golden on all sides. Remove with a fork and place in a casserole dish, together with the thick lemon slices and the bay leaves. Barely cover with stock, bring to the boil. Reduce the heat and simmer, covered, for 20 minutes. Meanwhile, peel and core the apple. Chop both the apple and onion finely. Crush the garlic, if using. Fry in the same oil as the chicken pieces until soft and golden brown. Remove the chicken pieces and keep warm, discard bay leaves and lemon slices and keep the stock on the side. Now add the curry powder to the fried onion mixture and fry gently on the lowest heat possible for 7 minutes. Add the flour and fry for a further 2 minutes. Remove from the heat and gradually add half the stock. Stir in the chopped tomatoes and roasted coconut, then add the rest of the stock, stirring constantly. Return to the heat, bring to the boil and simmer, uncovered, for a couple of minutes until the sauce has thickened. Check the seasoning and pour over the chicken to serve.

NB: It is nice to make this dish a day in advance to allow the spices to yield their full flavours.

Chicken in Spicy Peach Sauce

Ingredients:

1KG CHICKEN BREASTS • SALT • FRESHLY GROUND BLACK PEPPER FLOUR TO COAT • 4 TBS VEGETABLE OIL TO FRY • 2 STICKS CINNAMON • 1 TBS TURMERIC • JUICE AND ZEST OF 2 LEMONS 1 LARGE ONION, ROUGHLY DICED • 1 TSP CAYENNE PEPPER 2 TBS SUGAR • 300ML CHICKEN STOCK, OR TO COVER • 100ML WHITE PORT • 4 RIPE PEACHES • 100ML SINGLE CREAM (OPTIONAL)

Method:

Cut the chicken breasts in half, roll in the flour and seasoning, and fry golden brown in the vegetable oil. Place in a casserole dish. Fry the onion until soft, add the spices and continue to fry for another 2 minutes. Add to the casserole together with the lemon rind and juice, the sugar and enough stock to cover. Cover, bring to the boil and simmer for 15 minutes. Meanwhile, remove the stones from the peaches and cut into segments. Add to the casserole after 15 minutes together with the port and continue to simmer for another quarter of an hour. Adjust the seasoning and add a little cream if you like.

NB: You may use oranges instead of peaches, and mixed spice, garlic and fresh ginger instead of cinnamon and turmeric for a different taste. Serve with rice or a French loaf.

Butterflies regulate their body temperature by using their wings to absorb or reflect the sun's heat. Once warm, the males search for their mates.

Braised stuffed Chicken Thighs with Lentils

Ingredients:

3 TBS OLIVE OIL • 1 ONION, PEELED • 2 GARLIC CLOVES, PEELED • 175G MUSHROOMS • 50G COOKED HAM, CHOPPED 25G GRUYERE, GRATED • 8 LARGE CHICKEN THIGHS • 25G BUTTER OR MARGARINE • 300ML WHITE WINE • 350G GREEN LENTILS 600ML CHICKEN STOCK • SEASONING • STRING FOR TYING

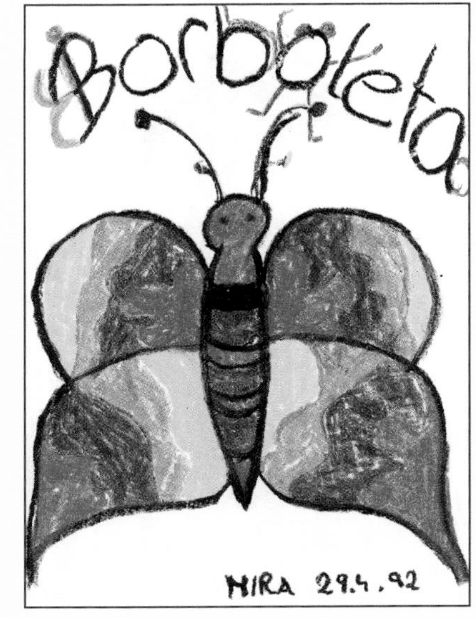

Method:

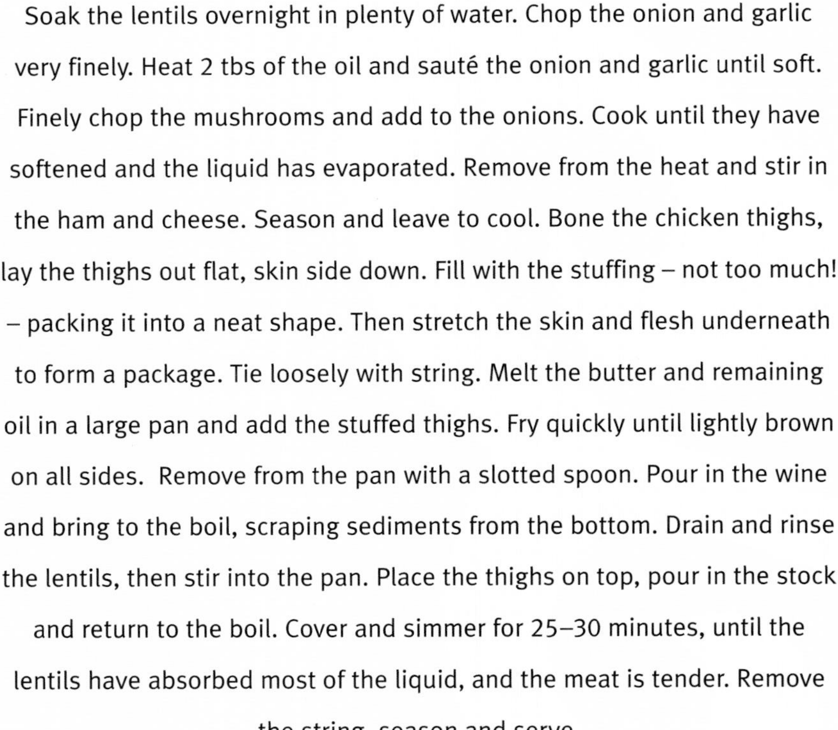

Soak the lentils overnight in plenty of water. Chop the onion and garlic very finely. Heat 2 tbs of the oil and sauté the onion and garlic until soft. Finely chop the mushrooms and add to the onions. Cook until they have softened and the liquid has evaporated. Remove from the heat and stir in the ham and cheese. Season and leave to cool. Bone the chicken thighs, lay the thighs out flat, skin side down. Fill with the stuffing – not too much! – packing it into a neat shape. Then stretch the skin and flesh underneath to form a package. Tie loosely with string. Melt the butter and remaining oil in a large pan and add the stuffed thighs. Fry quickly until lightly brown on all sides. Remove from the pan with a slotted spoon. Pour in the wine and bring to the boil, scraping sediments from the bottom. Drain and rinse the lentils, then stir into the pan. Place the thighs on top, pour in the stock and return to the boil. Cover and simmer for 25–30 minutes, until the lentils have absorbed most of the liquid, and the meat is tender. Remove the string, season and serve.

NB: This is very nice with crisp potato croquettes and a salad.

Groundnut Casserole

Ingredients:

2 CHICKENS, JOINTED • 6 TBS VEGETABLE OIL FOR FRYING • FLOUR FOR COATING • CHICKEN STOCK • 1 LARGE ONION, PEELED • 1 LARGE APPLE, PEELED AND CORED • 3 CLOVES GARLIC, PEELED • 150ML THICK COCONUT MILK • JUICE AND ZEST OF 1 ORANGE • 340G JAR PEANUT BUTTER • SALT • CAYENNE PEPPER TO TASTE

Method:

Remove the skin from the chicken pieces and turn them in flour. Heat the oil and fry the chicken pieces until golden brown on all sides. Place in a large saucepan and cover with chicken stock. Bring to the boil, covered, and simmer for 20 minutes. Dice the onion and apple and chop the garlic finely. Heat 2 tbs of vegetable oil and fry the onion, garlic and apple until soft. Add cayenne pepper to taste and stir in the peanut butter together with the juice and zest of the orange. Stir in enough stock and the coconut milk to form a creamy sauce. Season with salt and add the chicken pieces. Heat through thoroughly and adjust seasoning. Serve with rice, steamed okras, boiled eggs (optional) and a crispy green salad.

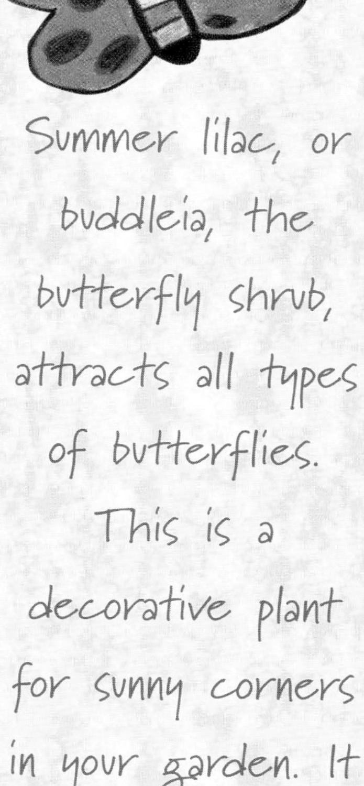

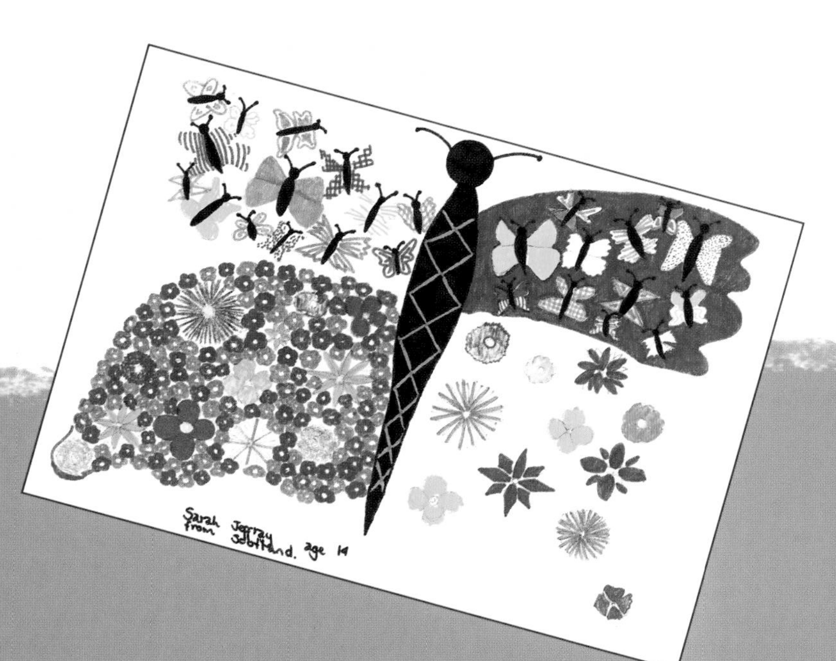

Frango na Púcara

Serves 4

Ingredients:

1 LARGE CHICKEN, JOINTED • 75G SMOKED HAM (PRESUNTO)
4 LARGE TOMATOES, PEELED • 2 CLOVES GARLIC, PEELED
10 SMALL ONIONS, PEELED • 100G RAISINS • 2 TBS BUTTER, MELTED
• 1 TBS DIJON MUSTARD • 20ML WHITE PORT • 20ML OLD BRANDY •
100ML WHITE WINE • SEASONING

Method:

Pre–heat the oven to 180°C/Gas 4. Place the chicken pieces in a greased ovenproof dish. Cut the presunto and tomatoes into cubes. Slice the garlic. Layer all the ingredients onto the chicken and add the liquids. Season well and cover. Bake in the oven for about 45 minutes until the chicken is cooked. Remove the lid and continue to bake until the sauce has reduced. Serve with rice and preferably a bean salad.

Breast of Turkey Casserole

Serves 6

Ingredients:

$1\frac{1}{2}$ KG TURKEY BREASTS • FLOUR FOR COATING • 6 TBS VEGETABLE OIL FOR FRYING • 500G SHALLOTS OR ONIONS, PEELED • 4 CLOVES OF GARLIC, PEELED • 200G BACON, DICED • 1 TSP DRIED THYME 1 TBS CHUTNEY (OPTIONAL) • 1 TBS SUGAR • ZEST AND JUICE OF 1 ORANGE • 1 LITRE DRY RED WINE • 1 STOCK CUBE • SEASONING

Method:

Coat the meat in flour and fry until golden. Place in a casserole. Dice and sauté the onions and garlic, add the bacon and fry. Add all ingredients to the casserole and cook for 20 minutes. Adjust seasoning and reduce until thick and creamy.

Meat Dishes

Mexican Beef

Serves 4

Ingredients:

4 SPRING ONIONS • 4 TBS WHITE WINE • 2 TBS WINE VINEGAR SEASONING • ½ TSP TARRAGON • 4 THICK BEEFBURGERS 2 AVOCADOS • 1 TBS VEGETABLE OIL • ½ TSP CHILLI POWDER 25G BUTTER • 1 LARGE ONION, SLICED • 1 TSP FLOUR • 2 TBS LEMON JUICE • FRESH TARRAGON TO GARNISH

Method:

Wash and chop the spring onions. Make a marinade with the spring onions, wine, vinegar, seasoning and tarragon. Marinate the beef burgers for several hours or overnight. Halve the avocados, remove the stones and peel. Dice one of them and thinly slice the other. Stir the diced avocado into the marinade. Heat the oil in a casserole, sprinkle with chilli powder and brown the beefburgers quickly on each side. Add the butter and onion and sweat for a few minutes, sprinkle with flour and brown. Pour in the strained marinade and cook for 15 minutes. Add the diced avocado and stir in gently. Taste and adjust the seasoning. Arrange the slices of avocado on top of the meat, sprinkle with lemon juice and cook for a further 10 minutes. Garnish with fresh tarragon and serve with a tomato salad and creamed potatoes.

For the Scandinavians a butterfly is drangr Larve (ghost) and for the Slavs veja (butterfly, deceiving light and witch).

Beef in Guinness with Orange Zest

Serves 6

Ingredients:

$1\frac{1}{2}$ KG GOOD BEEF, CUBED • 2 TBS OLIVE OIL • 1 LARGE ONION, CHOPPED • 4 CLOVES GARLIC, CRUSHED • 3 BAY LEAVES ZEST AND JUICE OF 1 ORANGE • 2 STICKS CELERY, CHOPPED 150G MUSHROOMS, SLICED • 1 TSP SUGAR • 1 TSP DRIED THYME SEASONING • 2 X 500ML CANS OF GUINNESS • VEGETABLE STOCK, IF NEEDED • 2 TBS CORNFLOUR • 200ML CREAM

Method:

Fry the beef in the olive oil. Place in a casserole dish. Sauté the onions and garlic for a few minutes and add to the beef, together with the bay leaves, orange zest and juice. Sauté the celery and mushrooms and add to the casserole together with the thyme, sugar and seasoning. Add the Guinness, and stock to cover if needed. Simmer, covered, for 30 minutes until tender. Mix together the cornflour and cream. Remove the meat and vegetables from the casserole and thicken the sauce with the cream and cornflour. Serve with rice or boiled potatoes.

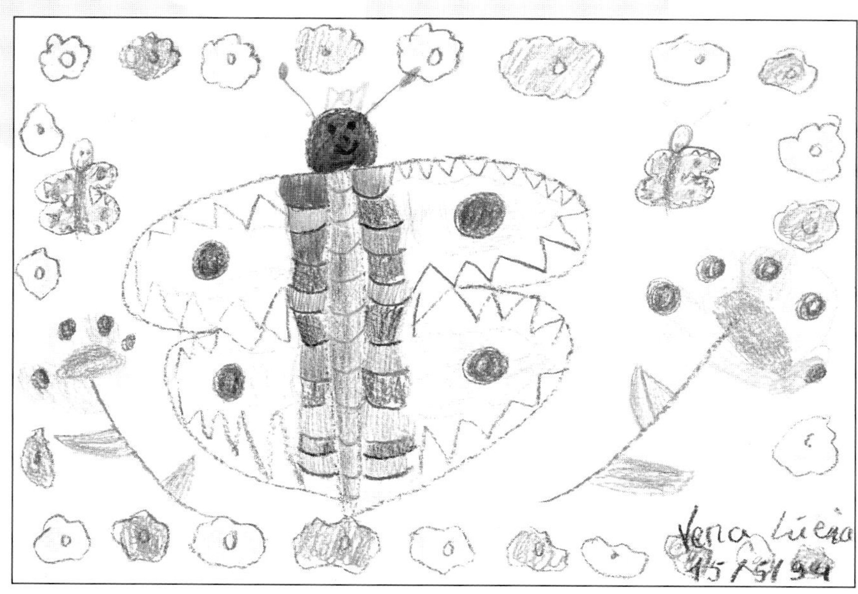

Cajun Chilli Alabama à la Dirk

Serves 4

Ingredients:

2 TBS VEGETABLE OIL • 1 TBS OLIVE OIL • 350G MINCED BEEF
1 MEDIUM ONION, PEELED AND DICED • 1 MEDIUM CARROT, DICED
1 GREEN PEPPER, DE-SEEDED AND DICED • 1 FRESH CHILLI,
DE-SEEDED AND DICED • 100G SMALL MUSHROOMS, HALVED
3 CLOVES GARLIC, PEELED • 125G SPICY SAUSAGE, DICED
100G SMOKED HAM, DICED • 1 X 400G TIN CHOPPED TOMATOES
2-3 TBS TOMATO PURÉE • 150ML VEGETABLE STOCK • 1 BAY LEAF
SEASONING • 200G FROZEN SWEET CORN • 200G TINNED KIDNEY
BEANS • 2 TSP CHILLI POWDER • 1 TSP MIXED HERBS
2 TBS PAPRIKA POWDER • 1 TSP GROUND CINNAMON • TABASCO
SAUCE TO TASTE • 1 EGG • 200G GRATED HARD CHEESE
200ML CREAM • 150G WHITE RICE • 125G PLAIN YOGHURT

Method:

Finely dice the garlic and prepare all ingredients for cooking. Heat the oil in a pan, brown the mince and transfer to a casserole dish. Sauté the onion, carrot, green pepper, chilli, mushrooms and garlic, add the tabasco and then add to the mince. Simmer for 10 minutes. Add the sausage and smoked ham, diced tomatoes, tomato purée, bay leaf and stock. Season with chilli powder, mixed herbs, paprika, seasoning, cinnamon and more tabasco if wished. Bring to the boil and simmer for 45 minutes. Prepare and boil the rice. Mix together the egg, cream and cheese in a small bowl. Add the sweet corn and kidney beans to the stew and simmer for a further 15 minutes. Pour the egg mixture into the casserole slowly and stir. Take out the bay leaf and adjust the spices to taste. Serve with a bowl of seasoned yoghurt or crème fraîche.

Lamb and Apricot Casserole

Serves 4

Ingredients:

750G LEAN LAMB, CUBED • 2 TBS OLIVE OIL • 2 MEDIUM ONIONS, PEELED AND DICED • 4 CLOVES GARLIC, PEELED AND FINELY SLICED
1 CINNAMON STICK, BROKEN INTO 2 • 1 TSP GROUND CORIANDER
2 TBS TOMATO PURÉE • 800G TINNED TOMATOES, CHOPPED
175G DRIED APRICOTS • 1 TSP SUGAR • 150ML VEGETABLE STOCK
150ML WHITE WINE

Method:

Fry the cubes of lamb in very hot olive oil. Place in a casserole dish. Sauté the onions and garlic until soft. Add the spices and fry for a further 2–4 minutes. Add to the lamb. Add the tomatoes and purée to the meat, together with the remaining ingredients. Season and simmer for 1¼ hours. Remove the cinnamon sticks.

Meat Dishes

Oriental Lamb

Serves 4

Ingredients:

450G MINCED LAMB • SEASONING • 1/4 TSP DRIED MIXED HERBS • 1 LARGE ONION, PEELED • 2 TBS VEGETABLE OIL 1 LARGE LEEK, WASHED AND FINELY SLICED • 1 AUBERGINE, WASHED AND DICED ROUGHLY 1CM X 1CM • 400G TIN TOMATOES 1 CINNAMON STICK • 1/2 TSP GROUND CORIANDER 1/2 TSP CUMIN SEEDS • 4 TBS WATER • 150ML WHITE WINE

Method:

Pre–heat the oven to 160°C/Gas 3. Mix the lamb in a bowl with the seasoning and mixed herbs. Make into small balls. Slice the onion and sauté in the oil until soft. Add the leek and leave the pan on a low heat. Coat the balls of lamb with seasoned flour. Remove the leeks and onions to a casserole and fry the lamb until golden brown, lift into the casserole. Place the aubergine, tomatoes, cinnamon, herbs and spices in the pan with the wine and water. Bring to the boil and pour over the lamb. Cook for one hour in the oven. Taste and adjust seasoning before serving. Serve with sauté potatoes and a yoghurt dip.

Veal Paprika

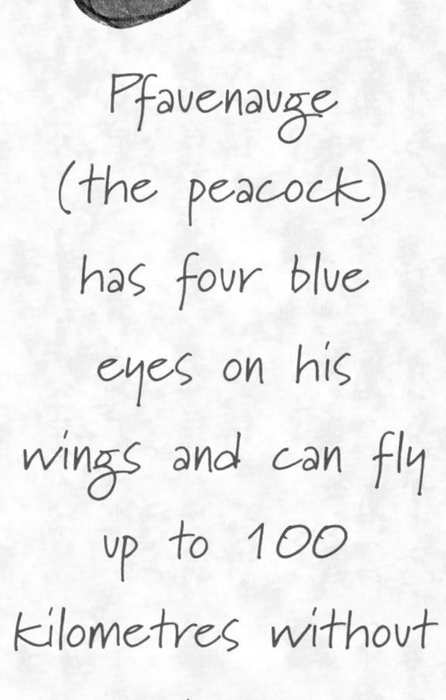

Ingredients:

450G PIE VEAL, CUBED • 1 TBS FLOUR • 1 TBS PAPRIKA
1 TBS MARGARINE • 2 TBS OLIVE OIL • 1 MEDIUM ONION, PEELED AND SLICED • 150ML CHICKEN STOCK • 225G TOMATOES, SKINNED, SEEDED AND CHOPPED • 1 TBS TOMATO PURÉE
1 TBS CHOPPED FRESH PARSLEY • ½ TSP PAPRIKA
3 TBS SOUR CREAM

Method:

Pre-heat the oven to 180°C/Gas 4. Toss the veal in flour, paprika and seasoning. Heat the fat in a large frying pan and add the veal. Fry with the onion for 5 minutes. Stir in the stock and bring to the boil, stirring, and add all the remaining ingredients except the last three. Transfer to a casserole. Bake in the centre of the oven for 1½ – 1¾ hours until the meat is tender. Taste and adjust the seasoning. Sprinkle with chopped parsley and paprika, and pour over sour cream. Serve with boiled or jacket potatoes.

Pork Curry

Serves 4–5

Ingredients:

1 KG PORK, CUBED • 6 TBS VEGETABLE OIL • 1 LARGE ONION, PEELED • 1 APPLE, PEELED AND CORED • 2 CLOVES GARLIC, PEELED • 4 LARGE TBS HOT CURRY POWDER • 3 TBS FLOUR 250ML VEGETABLE STOCK • 100ML COCONUT MILK • 1 TSP DRIED ROSEMARY • SEASONING • 125 ML CREAM

Method:

Heat the oil in a large saucepan and fry the pork until crisp and brown on all sides. Remove with a slotted spoon and place in a casserole dish. Dice the onion and apple and finely chop the garlic. Sauté in the oil until soft. Add the curry powder and sauté for another 5 minutes. Add the flour, stir and remove from the heat. Form a sauce together with the stock. Add the coconut milk, rosemary and seasoning and bring to the boil. Pour onto the meat and simmer with the lid on for 20–30 minutes until the pork is tender. Stir in the cream and reduce the sauce if necessary. Serve with fried bananas and rice, or with creamed potatoes and a salad.

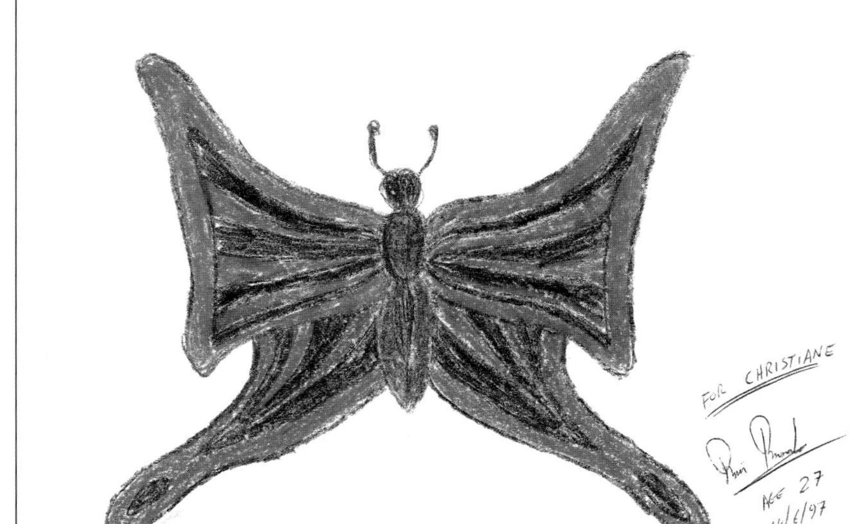

Wendy's Pork, Mushroom and Orange Casserole

Ingredients:

2 ORANGES • 1–2 FRESH GREEN CHILLIES • 3 CLOVES GARLIC
1 LARGE RED PEPPER • 2 TBS WHITE WINE VINEGAR
1 TBS HONEY • 2 PINCHES CAYENNE PEPPER • 25G BUTTER
2 TBS SUNFLOWER OIL • 750G STEWING PORK, CUT INTO CUBES
2 TSP GROUND CORIANDER OR 2 TBS FRESH CORIANDER
200G MUSHROOMS SLICED (OPTIONAL) • SALT

To Serve:

250ML SOUR CREAM OR NATURAL YOGHURT

Method:

First boil the whole washed oranges in a covered pan of water for 2 hours (30 minutes in a pressure cooker). Meanwhile, under running water cut open the green chillies and discard the seeds. Peel the garlic and chop finely, together with the chillies. Cut the pepper in half, then quarters, discarding the seeds, and slice across fairly thinly. When the oranges are ready, cool a little under cold water until easier to handle, and then cut open and pick out the pips. Put into a food processor with the vinegar, the honey and the cayenne pepper and whiz until smooth. Then whiz in 4 tbs of water and season to taste with salt. Preheat the oven to 180°C/Gas 4. On top of the cooker heat the butter with the oil in a flameproof casserole. Over a high heat add the pork and stir round to seal all over. Then stir in the chopped garlic chillies and ground coriander. Stir around for a minute and then add the orange purée and sliced peppers. Cover the dish and cook in the centre of the oven for 30 minutes, then turn down the oven to the lower setting of 140°C/Gas 1, for another hour or until very tender. After this add the sliced mushrooms if using and cook for 10–15 minutes more. Before serving, spoon over the sour cream or yoghurt.

Rustic Stews

Hungarian Gulasch Soup

Serves 4–6

Ingredients:

500G LEAN PORK AND BEEF, FINELY CUT • 150G LEAN BACON, FINELY CUT • VEGETABLE OIL FOR FRYING • 2 LARGE ONIONS • 2 POTATOES, PEELED • 2 LARGE CARROTS • 250G TOMATOES, PEELED AND CHOPPED • 2 CLOVES GARLIC, CRUSHED • 1 TSP WHOLE CARAWAY SEEDS • 1 TSP DRIED THYME • 2 BAY LEAVES • 2 TBS PAPRIKA ZEST OF ½ LEMON • 1–1½ LITRES STOCK • 200ML SOUR CREAM PINCH OF SUGAR • SALT

Method:

Heat the oil and fry the meat and bacon until brown on all sides. Place in a casserole. Add the onions and garlic to the frying pan and cook for a further few minutes. Dice the carrots and potatoes finely and add to the onion and garlic. Sauté for a further 5 minutes. Stir in the tomatoes, herbs and spices and cook until the liquid has reduced. Add to the meat, together with the lemon zest. Add enough stock to cover well and bring to the boil. Reduce the heat and simmer, covered, for 30–45 minutes until the meat is tender. Adjust the seasoning and add the sugar and sour cream. Heat through and serve.

Bean Stew 'Dona Jutta'

Serves 6–8

Ingredients:

400G PIECE STREAKY BACON • 2 LARGE SMOKED SAUSAGES
1 PARSNIP, DICED • 1 TURNIP, DICED • 2 LARGE CARROTS, DICED
1 ONION, DICED • 1 LARGE LEEK, DICED • 2 DRIED CHILLIES, FINELY MINCED • 4 CLOVES GARLIC, DICED • 800G TIN TOMATOES, CHOPPED
800G TIN CANNELLINI BEANS • 800G TIN KIDNEY BEANS
1–2 TSP DRIED OREGANO • SEASONING • 1 LARGE POTATO, PEELED AND GRATED

Method:

Cover the bacon and sausages with water and boil for 20 minutes. Remove to cool, but reserve the stock. When cold, cut the meat into small cubes. Meanwhile, heat some vegetable oil in a large saucepan and sauté the vegetables together with the garlic and chillies. The quantities of garlic and chillies may be varied according to taste. Add all other ingredients to the vegetables including the diced meat. Simmer for 20 minutes and adjust seasoning. The tins of beans may be replaced by soaked and cooked pulses. Finally, add the grated potato to thicken.

NB: I use the beans undrained.

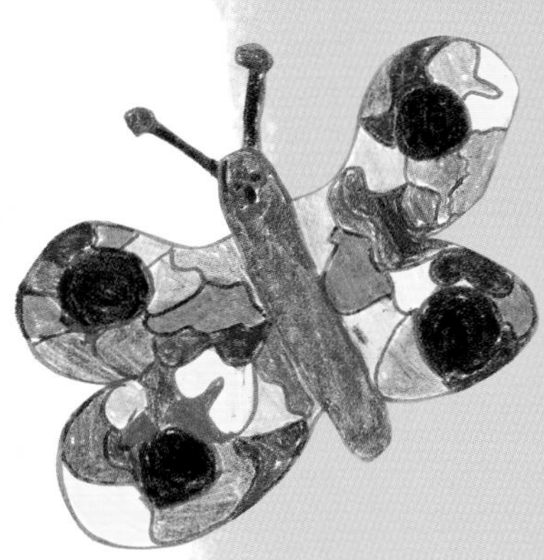

Pears, Beans and Bacon (Bohnen, Birnen und Speck)

Serves 6

Ingredients:

1KG GREEN BEANS, FRENCH OR RUNNER • 8 SMALL FIRM PEARS
1 LARGE ONION, PEELED • 1 LITRE WATER • 500G PIECE STREAKY BACON • 6 WHOLE PEPPERCORNS • 3 TBS CHOPPED FRESH PARSLEY • SEASONING • 2 HEAPED TBS FLOUR

Method:

Boil the bacon, together with the onion and peppercorns, covered, in the water for 30 minutes. Remove the onion and peppercorns. Wash and trim the beans and the pears, removing the cores from the pears, and add to the stock, together with the bacon for a further 20 minutes. Season the vegetables with salt and pepper. Slice the bacon. Make the flour into a paste by adding a little of the stock. Slowly add the rest of the stock and bring to the boil to thicken. Sprinkle with parsley and serve with boiled potatoes.

Lentil Tureen 'Al Borboleta'

Serves 6–8

Ingredients:

500G WHOLE RED LENTILS • 125G LARD • 1 LARGE ONION, PEELED
250G LEEKS, WASHED • 4 CLOVES GARLIC, PEELED • 500G PIECE SMOKED BACON • 2 BAY LEAVES • 250ML RED WINE • 2 TBS SHERRY VINEGAR • SEASONING

Method:

Soak the lentils overnight in water Finely chop the onions, garlic, leeks and bacon. Melt the lard and fry everything for a few minutes. Add the lentils, the red wine and vinegar plus extra water if needed to cover. Bring to the boil and simmer with the lid on for an hour until all the ingredients are well integrated and the lentils are soft. Serve with a dollop of crème fraîche.

Curry Soup with Chicken

Serves 4

Ingredients:

1.5KG CHICKEN • 1 TURNIP, PEELED • 1 LARGE CARROT, PEELED
1 LARGE SPRIG PARSLEY • 2 LARGE ONIONS, PEELED
1 TSP BLACK PEPPERCORNS • 2 BAY LEAVES • SALT • 2 CLOVES
GARLIC • 2 TBS VEGETABLE OIL • 2 TBS MEDIUM CURRY POWDER
60G FLOUR • FRESHLY GROUND BLACK PEPPER • 125–200ML
CONDENSED MILK • 300G FROZEN OR TINNED PEAS
200G MUSHROOMS, SLICED • 150G COOKED HAM, DICED
125ML SOUR CREAM

Method:

Chop the vegetables. Boil the chicken for 45 minutes in a covered pan, together with the carrot, turnip, parsley, an onion, the peppercorns, bay leaves and cloves in $1\frac{1}{2}$ litre of salted water. Pour the stock through a sieve and leave the chicken to cool a little until fit to handle. Heat the oil and sauté the chopped garlic and remaining onion. Add the curry powder and the flour and stir in the stock. Bring to the boil and season. Add the remaining ingredients and simmer for 15 minutes. De–bone the chicken and discard the skin. Chop roughly. Stir in the chicken and heat through. Adjust seasoning. Serve with a dollop of sour cream.

Butterflies are truly the 'jewels of creation', celebrated by poets. Sadly they are threatened by habitat destruction almost everywhere.

Vegetarian Dishes

Egg Creole

Serves 4

Ingredients:

25G BUTTER, PLUS A LITTLE EXTRA FOR BAKING • 2 MEDIUM ONIONS, PEELED AND FINELY DICED • 1 CLOVE GARLIC, PEELED AND CHOPPED • 1 SWEET RED PEPPER, DE-SEEDED AND CHOPPED
1 SWEET GREEN PEPPER, DE-SEEDED AND CHOPPED
½ COURGETTE, FINELY DICED • 110G MUSHROOMS, CHOPPED
100ML THICK COCONUT CREAM • HOT PEPPER TO TASTE
SEASONING • 400G TIN TOMATOES, CHOPPED • ½ BUNCH CHIVES, FINELY CHOPPED • 4 LARGE EGGS

Method:

Preheat the oven to 190°C/Gas 5. Melt the butter in a saucepan, add the onions, garlic, sweet peppers and courgette, and cook gently for about 3–4 minutes. Do not brown. Add the mushrooms, coconut cream, hot pepper and seasoning to taste. Simmer, slightly covered, for about 5 minutes. Mix in very carefully the chopped tomatoes and chives. Taste for seasoning. Pour the mixture into a shallow ovenproof dish large enough to contain the eggs as well. Make 4 holes in the mixture. Break an egg into each hole, and place a knob of butter on each egg. Bake for about 10–12 minutes or until the eggs are set. Serve with avocados and baked yams or hot buttered bread.

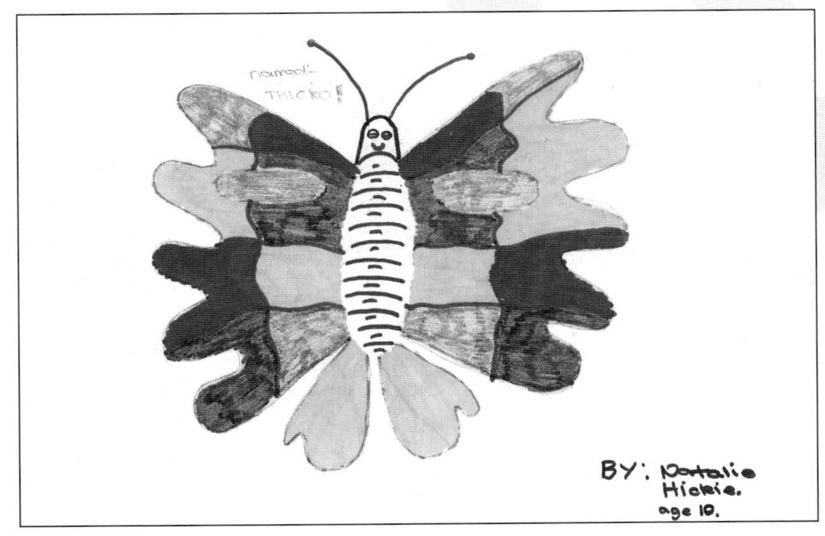

Lentil Roast

Serves 4–6

Ingredients:

225G BROWN OR GREEN LENTILS • 2 TBS VEGETABLE OIL 2 ONIONS • 2 CLOVES GARLIC • 1 LARGE COOKING APPLE, PEELED AND CORED • 2 LARGE TOMATOES, CHOPPED • 50G FRESH BREADCRUMBS • 1 LARGE EGG, BEATEN • 1 TSP DRIED SAGE OR MIXED HERBS • SEASONING • 1–2 TOMATOES, SLICED

Method:

Soak the lentils overnight. Next day, cook them in the same water until soft. Finely chop the onion, garlic and apple and fry in the oil until soft. Add the chopped tomatoes and fry for a further 2 minutes. Stir into the lentils with the breadcrumbs, egg, sage and seasoning. Grease a loaf tin (30cm x 10cm), sprinkle with breadcrumbs. Layer with the tomato slices. Press the lentil mixture on top and cover tightly with foil. Bake in a moderately hot oven for 40 minutes until firm. Leave to stand for a few minutes before turning out.

Pea and Potato Curry

Serves 4

Ingredients:

1 KG POTATOES • SALT • 1 LARGE ONION, PEELED • 3 CLOVES GARLIC, PEELED • 25G FRESH GINGER, PEELED • 4 TBS SUNFLOWER OIL • 5 TBS TOMATO PURÉE • 2–3 TBS MILD CURRY POWDER • 300G FROZEN PEAS, DEFROSTED • 1 TBS SESAME OIL • SMALL BUNCH FRESH CORIANDER

Method:

Boil the potatoes in their skins in boiling salt water until they are just tender. Peel and dice. Grate the onion, garlic and ginger finely. Heat the oil and sauté until soft. Add the tomato purée and curry powder. Fry for another few minutes. Stir in the diced potatoes, and season with salt. Cover and bring to the boil. Reduce the heat to a minimum and simmer for 10 minutes. If necessary, add a little water during this time. Stir in the peas and simmer for a further 5 minutes. Check the seasoning, roughly chop the fresh coriander. Stir into the casserole together with the sesame oil.

Sweet and Sour Chickpea and Potato Stew

Serves 4

Ingredients:

1 TBS OLIVE OIL • 2 GARLIC CLOVES, PEELED • 1 LARGE ONION, PEELED • 2 TSP GROUND CORIANDER • 1 TSP GROUND CUMIN 1 TSP GROUND CINNAMON • 350G LARGE NEW POTATOES, SCRUBBED AND CUT INTO LARGE CUBES • 400G CAN CHICKPEAS • 400G CAN TOMATOES, CHOPPED • 2 TBS RED WINE VINEGAR 1 TBS LIGHT BROWN SUGAR • 50G SULTANAS • 50G PITTED GREEN OLIVES, CHOPPED • 2 TBS CHOPPED FRESH CORIANDER SEASONING • 150ML SINGLE CREAM (OPTIONAL)

Method:

Crush the garlic and dice the onion. Heat the oil and fry, together with the spices, for 5 minutes. Add the potatoes and continue to fry gently for 10 minutes, stirring from time to time. Stir in the chickpeas including the liquid, tomatoes, vinegar and sugar. Bring to the boil, cover and simmer for 20 minutes. Stir in the sultanas, green olives, coriander, seasoning and cream (if using). Simmer gently, uncovered, for a further 10 minutes until the potatoes are tender and the sauce has thickened slightly.

NB: This may be served as a main course on its own with salad or with meat or chicken.

Courgette Quiche with a Lentil and Oat Base

Ingredients:

125G RED LENTILS • 125G PORRIDGE OATS • 1 MEDIUM ONION, PEELED • 2 LARGE CLOVES GARLIC, PEELED • 2–3 TBS LEMON JUICE 2 TBS TOMATO PASSATA • SALT • FRESHLY GROUND BLACK PEPPER • MARGARINE TO GREASE THE TIN • 2 TBS MARGARINE FOR FRYING • 2 MEDIUM COURGETTES • 250ML MILK • 4 LARGE EGGS • 150G GRATED HARD CHEESE • 1 TSP DRIED OREGANO

Method:

Cook the lentils until they are very soft. Meanwhile finely dice the onion and mince the garlic, and fry in a little margarine. Mash the lentils to a thick paste and mix with the oats, lemon juice, tomato passata and onion mixture. Preheat the oven to 180°C/Gas 4. Line a loose–bottomed quiche tin (approx. 24cm) with greaseproof paper and grease well with margarine or butter. Press the lentil mixture into the tin, ensuring that an edge is formed. Coarsely grate the courgettes. Lightly sprinkle the base with a little cheese. Season the courgettes well with salt, pepper and some oregano and put into the flan case. Beat the eggs, stir in the milk and pour over the courgettes. Sprinkle with the rest of the cheese and bake in a moderately hot oven for 30–40 minutes until set and golden.

Aubergine and Tomato Gratin

Zitronenfalter (the brimstone) can deep-freeze itself during the winter. The first rays of sun thaw it – and it is the first to flutter through the garden in spring.

Serves 4

Ingredients:

1 LARGE ONION • 4 CLOVES GARLIC • 200G MUSHROOMS, THINLY SLICED • 2 AUBERGINES, CUT INTO CHUNKS • 3 TBS OLIVE OIL • BASIL, OREGANO, PAPRIKA • 1 X 400G TIN TOMATOES 100G MOZZARELLA • SEASONING • 50G FRESHLY GRATED PARMESAN • 6 FRESH TOMATOES • 150ML WHITE WINE 4 LARGE EGGS

Method:

Finely slice both the onion and garlic. Heat a little olive oil and sauté together with the mushrooms until soft. Remove from the pan. Heat the remaining oil until very hot and fry the aubergine until soft and brown, drain on kitchen paper. Add the herbs and spices during the last few minutes. Pre–heat the oven to 190°C/Gas 5. Chop the tinned tomatoes and place at the base of an ovenproof dish. Season. Add half the aubergine chunks. Sprinkle with half the cheeses and cover with the onion and mushroom mixture. Cut the tomatoes in quarters and place on top with the remaining aubergine. Season. Sprinkle with the other half of the cheese and pour over the wine. Bake in the oven for 40 minutes. Remove and make four indents with a spoon, breaking an egg into each indent. Bake for a further 10–15 minutes until the eggs are set. Serve with baguette and a green salad.

Mixed Vegetable Curry

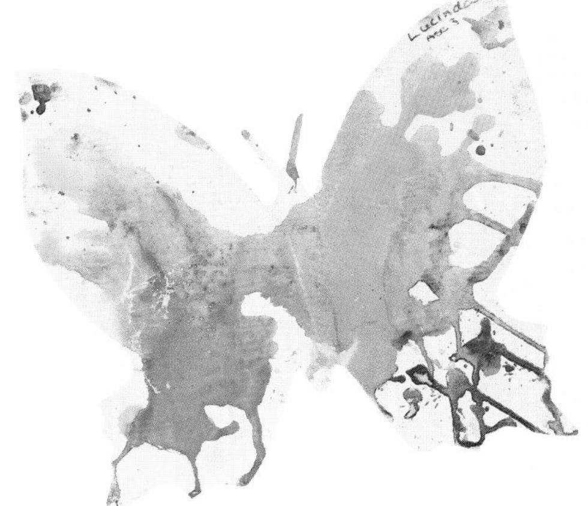

Serves 4

Ingredients:

4 TBS VEGETABLE OIL • 4 MEDIUM POTATOES, PEELED
1 COURGETTE, STALK REMOVED • 1 PEPPER, DE–SEEDED • 1 SMALL AUBERGINE • 1 LARGE ONION • 4 CLOVES GARLIC, CHOPPED
400G TIN TOMATOES, CHOPPED • 4 CARDAMOM PODS, CRUSHED
1 TSP FRESH GINGER, CHOPPED • 1 TSP CUMIN • ½ TSP GROUND CINNAMON • ½ TSP MUSTARD SEEDS • 1 TSP TURMERIC
2 TBS WINE VINEGAR • 1 TSP CHILLI POWDER • 1 TSP BROWN SUGAR • JUICE OF ONE LEMON • 4 TBS FRESH CORIANDER, CHOPPED

Method:

Cut each potato into 6, and the courgette into chunks. Dice the pepper, aubergine and onion, and chop the garlic and coriander finely. Heat the oil in a heavy saucepan until very hot and sauté the raw vegetables and potatoes until browned. Add all the other ingredients (except the coriander) and sauté for a further 5 minutes. Turn down to minimum heat and cook, covered, until the potatoes are soft. Sprinkle with fresh coriander to serve. NB: Serve with fresh tomatoes, diced, yoghurt raiita and fried bananas as well as either naan bread or rice. This is a fairly dry curry so if you prefer you can add water or vegetable stock during cooking time to create more sauce.

Vegetarian Pancake Bake

Serves 6

For the Tomato Sauce:

1 SMALL ONION • 3 CLOVES GARLIC • ½ TSP PAPRIKA
100ML TOMATO PASSATA • 2 TBS WINE VINEGAR • 1 TSP SUGAR
SEASONING • 400G TIN TOMATOES • 1 TSP DRIED THYME
• 1 BAY LEAF

For the Pancakes:

200G FLOUR • 100ML SINGLE CREAM • 450ML MILK • 2 EGGS, BEATEN • 2 TBS VEGETABLE OIL • ½ TSP SALT

For the White Sauce:

50G MARGARINE • 1 SMALL ONION • 1 LARGE TBS FLOUR
400ML MILK • 100G GRATED HARD CHEESE • SEASONING

Vegetables:

1 MEDIUM AUBERGINE • 2 MEDIUM COURGETTES • SEASONING

For the Topping:

100G GRATED CHEESE • BREADCRUMBS • A LITTLE MARGARINE

The menu of a butterfly:
Acker-senf = mustard plant
Ampfer = sorrel
Apfelbaum = apple tree

Method:

Dice the onion and finely chop the garlic. Heat the oil in a saucepan and sauté the onions and garlic until soft. Add the paprika and tomato passata and fry for a few minutes until fairly dry and starting to brown. Add the vinegar, sugar and seasoning and stir well.

Chop the tomatoes and add to the saucepan, together with the dried thyme and bay leaf. Bring to the boil and continue to cook on a fairly high heat until the sauce has reduced by one third and is creamy in consistency.

Slowly beat the cream and milk into the flour and add the eggs. Stir in the salt and oil and beat until frothy. Leave to stand for $\frac{1}{2}$ hour before using. Heat a little oil in a frying pan, wipe with a piece of kitchen towel and pour in enough mixture to cover the base of the pan. Swirl around a little if necessary. Turn after two minutes and brown on the other side. Repeat this process with the rest of the mixture, always wiping the base of the pan with a little oil in between.

Dice the onion finely. Heat the margarine and sauté the onion until soft. Take off the heat and stir in the flour. Slowly add the milk, beating constantly. Return to the heat and bring to the boil, stirring. Add the grated cheese and season. Pre–heat the oven to 180°C/Gas 4. Thinly slice the aubergine. Coarsely grate the courgettes. Place the tomato sauce in the base of an ovenproof dish. Add a layer of pancakes and cover with some white sauce. Place the slices of aubergine on top and once again cover with a layer of pancakes and white sauce. Add the courgettes and season well. Place the last of the pancakes on top and smother with the remaining white sauce. Sprinkle with the breadcrumbs and cheese and dot with some margarine. Bake in the oven for about 40 minutes until hot, and crisp on top.

Fish Dishes

Coconut Fish Indochine

Serves 4

Ingredients:

750G FILLETS OF FIRM WHITE FISH • 1 TSP HOT CHILLI SAUCE
2 TBS COCONUT MILK • 2 TBS TAMARI SAUCE OR SOY SAUCE
1 TBS SHERRY • 2 CLOVES GARLIC, CRUSHED • 5CM PIECE ROOT GINGER, PEELED AND CRUSHED • 1 TSP VEGETABLE OIL • 2 TBS FINELY SLICED SPRING ONIONS (OPTIONAL)

Method:

Marinate the fish for 15 minutes or preferably longer in the ingredients, and grill for about 4 minutes on each side or until cooked. NB: The fish may also be cooked in foil parcels with the marinade spooned over.

Mediterranean Fish in the Oven

Serves 6

Ingredients:

400G TOMATOES, SKINNED • 1 MEDIUM ONION • 4 CLOVES GARLIC
100ML OLIVE OIL • 600ML CHICKEN STOCK • ½ TBS PAPRIKA
A LITTLE CAYENNE PEPPER • PINCH OF SUGAR • SEASONING • FRESH WHOLE BASIL TO TASTE • 1.2KG FISH FILLETS

Method:

Cut the tomatoes and onion into strips. Slice the garlic. Heat half the oil and sauté the onions and garlic, add some of the stock and continue to cook for about 10 minutes. Add the paprika and cook for a further 2 minutes. Transfer to an ovenproof dish. Pre–heat the oven to 200°C/Gas 6. Add the tomatoes, season with cayenne and sprinkle with the basil. Wash the fish, salt on both sides and lay on top of the basil. Add the rest of the stock and bake in the oven for 20–25 minutes. Sprinkle with the rest of the oil.

Winter Fish Bake

Serves 4–6

Ingredients:

1KG WHITE FISH FILLETS • SALT • LEMON JUICE • 2 TBS TOMATO PASTE (PASSATA) • 2 TBS VEGETABLE OIL • 75G STREAKY BACON, DICED • 3 GHERKINS, DICED • 1 ONION, DICED • 2 TBS DIJON MUSTARD • 100G GRATED HARD CHEESE • 200ML CREAM 20G BREADCRUMBS • 30G MARGARINE

Method:

Place the fish fillets in a greased oven–proof dish and sprinkle with salt and lemon juice. Spread with the tomato paste. Heat the oil in a frying pan or wok and add the bacon and onion. Fry for a few minutes until the onion is soft and the bacon is golden. Add the gherkins and heat through. Stir in the mustard and remove from the heat. Spoon over the fish. Stir the cream into the grated cheese and spread on top of the gherkin mixture. Sprinkle with breadcrumbs and dot the margarine around. Pre–heat the oven to 180°C/Gas 4. Bake until the fish is bubbling – roughly 10–30 minutes – depending on the thickness of the fish.

Portuguese Salt Cod Bake

Serves 6

Ingredients:

$1\frac{1}{2}$ KG BACCALHAU (DRIED SALT COD) • 800G POTATOES (OPTIONAL) • 3 LEEKS, WASHED • 1 LARGE ONION • 1 TBS MARGARINE • 450G FROZEN LEAF SPINACH • 3 HARD–BOILED EGGS, PEELED AND HALVED • FRESHLY GROUND BLACK PEPPER 200ML SINGLE CREAM • 150G HARD CHEESE, GRATED 50G BREADCRUMBS

Method:

Soak the fish for 48 hours, changing the water several times. Poach the fish in boiling water for 20 minutes, leave to cool and flake, removing the bones. Part–boil the potatoes, if using. Chop the onion and leeks finely. Heat the margarine and fry until soft. Add the spinach and cook for a further 3–5 minutes. Stir in the cream and season with pepper and salt if needed. Pre–heat the oven to 180°C/Gas 4. Place one third of the spinach mixture in an oven–proof dish, slice the potatoes and place on top (if using), then cover with the fish. Spoon the remaining spinach on top and sprinkle with the breadcrumbs. Add a few knobs of margarine, place in the bottom of the oven and bake for about 10 minutes until well heated through and bubbling at the sides, and golden and crispy on top.

Fillet of Fish with Olives

Serves 4

Ingredients:

800G RED MULLET (OR OTHER WHITE FISH) • WINE VINEGAR OR LEMON JUICE • 75G OLIVES STUFFED WITH PEPPERS • 1 TBS MARGARINE • 200ML SINGLE CREAM • 150G GOUDA CHEESE, GRATED • SEASONING • 75G TOMATO PURÉE

Method:

Clean the fish and season with salt and vinegar or lemon juice. Cut into large cubes. Halve the olives and place both in a greased ovenproof dish. Pre–heat the oven to 200°C/Gas 5. Mix together the cream, grated cheese, tomato purée and season with pepper. Place on top of the fish and bake in the oven for about 20–30 minutes. Serve with boiled or creamed potatoes and fresh vegetables.

It only lives a short while in its colourful splendour, but during that time the butterfly has a taste of all the joys of life.

Prawn Curry

Serves 4

Ingredients:

1.2KG PRAWNS IN THEIR SHELLS • 1 LARGE ONION
2 GARLIC CLOVES • 1 LARGE APPLE, PEELED AND CORED
3 TBS MARGARINE • 4 TBS MILD CURRY POWDER • 3 TBS FLOUR • 1 LARGE ORANGE • 125ML WHITE WINE • 125ML RESERVED FISH STOCK • 125ML SINGLE CREAM • 100ML COCONUT MILK • SALT TO TASTE

Method:

Bring a pan of water to the boil, turn off the heat and add the prawns. Remove when the shell turns red. Reserve the stock. Dice the onion and apple and finely chop the garlic. Sauté in the margarine until soft. Add the curry powder, and sauté for a further 5 minutes. Add the flour and stir in the white wine, juice and zest of the orange and stock to form a roux. Finally pour in the cream and coconut milk. Season with salt and adjust the consistency of the liquid. Serve with rice.

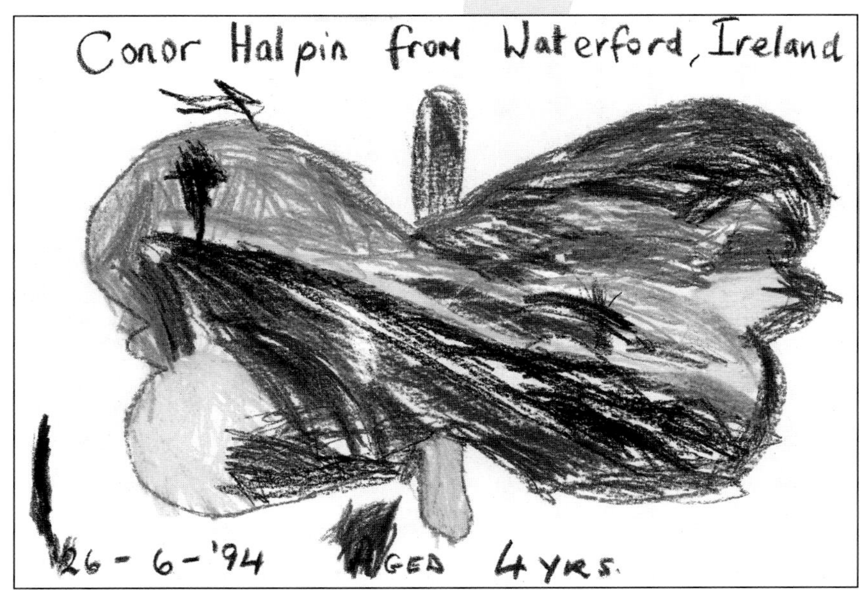

Peruvian Fried Fish with Onion Sauce

Serves 6

Ingredients:

2 RED PEPPERS, DE-SEEDED • 1 TSP PAPRIKA
1 TSP CHILLI POWDER • 500G ONIONS • 3 CLOVES GARLIC
6 TBS VEGETABLE OIL • SALT • 125ML RED WINE VINEGAR
1 TBS SUGAR • 1 TSP GROUND CARAWAY SEEDS • 1 TSP DRIED OREGANO • 850G WHITE FILLET OF FISH • PEPPER • FLOUR TO COAT • 3 TBS VEGETABLE OIL • 2 HARD-BOILED EGGS
100G BLACK OLIVES TO GARNISH

Method:

Cut the peppers into small pieces and purée together with 2 tbs of the oil. Stir in the paprika and chilli powder. Cut the onions in half and then into wedges. Chop the garlic finely. Heat the rest of the oil and sauté the onions and garlic until soft. Add the pepper purée and fry for a few minutes and add salt. Mix the vinegar with 125ml of water and add. Season with the sugar. Stir in the caraway and oregano and simmer for 10 minutes without a lid. Wash the fish and pat dry on kitchen paper. Cut fillets into strips and season with salt and pepper. Coat in flour and fry each side in hot oil for 2–3 minutes. Drain on kitchen paper and place on a serving dish. Pour over the sauce and leave to marinate for half an hour. Peel the eggs and cut into wedges. Use to garnish the fish, together with the olives. Serve with sweet potatoes.

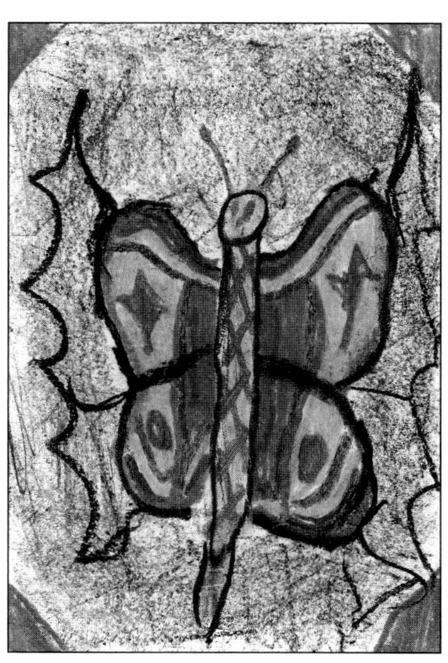

Fish Balls

Serves 4–6

Ingredients:

500G COOKED, FLAKED FISH • 1 ONION, FINELY CHOPPED
40G FRESH BREADCRUMBS • 2 EGGS, LIGHTLY BEATEN
2 TBS OLIVE OIL • 2 TBS CHOPPED PARSLEY • 1 TSP DRIED OREGANO • SEASONING • 125G FLOUR • 4–5 TBS LEMON JUICE
VEGETABLE OIL FOR FRYING

For the Sauce:

400ML FISH STOCK • SALT • 1 TBS CHOPPED FRESH PARSLEY
1 SMALL ONION, FINELY CHOPPED • 30G ROASTED AND GROUND ALMONDS

Method:

Combine the fish with the onion, breadcrumbs, eggs, olive oil, parsley, oregano and seasoning. Mix together thoroughly and form into balls about the size of a small egg. Roll the fish balls in flour, dip them in lemon juice and return to the flour. Heat the oil in a frying pan to the depth of about 5mm and fry the fish balls until golden all over. Drain on kitchen towels and place them in a shallow casserole. Add the fish stock, salt, parsley and onion, cover and simmer for about 10 minutes. Stir in the almonds and simmer, uncovered, for a further 5 minutes to thicken the sauce – longer if necessary. Serve with a green salad and rice.

Fish Stew 'Caldeirada'

Serves 4–6

Ingredients:

1KG CALDEIRADA FISH (MIXED FISH) • 4 CLOVES GARLIC
1 LARGE ONION • ½ RED PEPPER • ½ GREEN PEPPER
4 TBS VEGETABLE OIL • 400G TIN TOMATOES, CHOPPED
2 TBS LEMON JUICE • 150ML WHITE WINE • 3 SPRIGS FRESH CORIANDER • 5 SPRIGS FRESH PARSLEY • 2 BAY LEAVES
½ KG PRAWNS, DE–SHELLED (OPTIONAL) • ½ KG MUSSELS (OPTIONAL) • PLAIN YOGHURT, TO SERVE • CROUTONS

Method:

Cook the fish in salt water, making the stock. Remove the fish and reduce the stock by a quarter. De–seed the peppers. Chop, together with the onion and garlic and cook in the oil for a few minutes to soften. Add the tomatoes and stock, white wine and herbs, bring to the boil and simmer, covered, for 10 minutes. Add the de–scaled fish and prawns and mussels (if using), and cook on a very low heat for a further 10 minutes. Serve with crusty bread, some plain yoghurt and croutons.

Mistakes were made...
When we first opened
we had enough supplies
to feed half of Ethiopia –
unfortunately perishable, and no guests!
I leave the rest to your imagination...

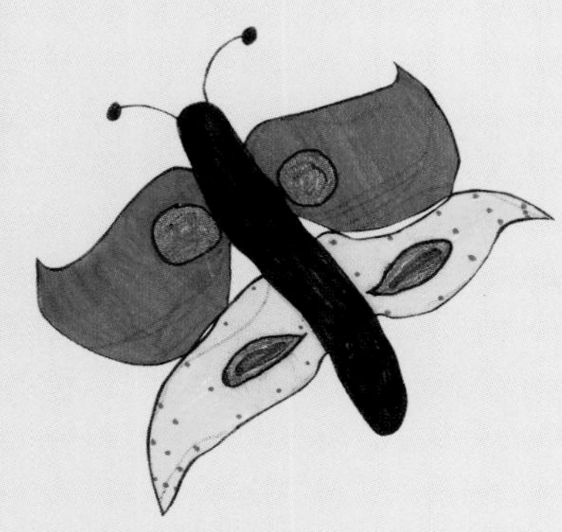

Side Dishes

German Potato Salad

Serves 6

Ingredients:

$1\frac{1}{2}$ KG POTATOES • 175ML MAYONNAISE • 125ML YOGHURT
JUICE OF $\frac{1}{2}$ LEMON • 1 LARGE ONION • 1 LARGE APPLE, PEELED AND CORED • 75G GHERKINS • PINCH SUGAR
SEASONING • MILK TO MOISTEN (IF NEEDED)

Method:

Boil the potatoes in their skins until cooked but firm. Peel as soon as they are ready to handle and cut into chunks. Finely chop the apple, onion and gherkins. In a large bowl combine the rest of the ingredients except the milk and stir in the potatoes. Leave to cool, adjust the seasoning and chill. Stir carefully before serving and add some milk if the salad is too dry. If adding milk, once again check the seasoning before serving.

NB: This goes very well with any fried or grilled meat, fish or poultry or just on its own with a fried egg on top!

German Sauerkraut

Serves 6

Ingredients:

2 TBS LARD • 2 MEDIUM ONIONS • 750G SAUERKRAUT
375ML WHITE WINE • 2 BAY LEAVES • 4–6 JUNIPER BERRIES
SEASONING • PINCH OF SUGAR • 1 RAW MEDIUM-SIZED
POTATO, GRATED

Method:

Heat the lard and sauté the onions until soft. Add the sauerkraut and fry for 5 minutes. Stir in the white wine, bay leaves and juniper berries. Bring to the boil and simmer for about 30 minutes. Season to taste, add the sugar and stir in the grated potato to thicken.

NB: This can well be made a day or two in advance, as time enhances the flavours. Goes well with creamed potatoes and a smoked rack of pork (German Kassler).

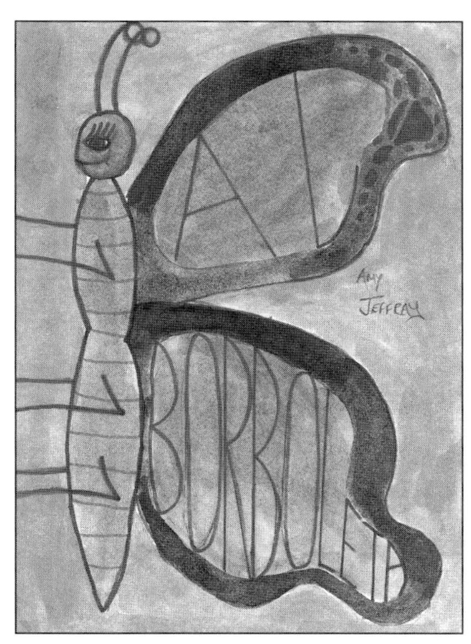

Butterflies have a better sense of smell than any other animal in the world. Their antennae receive the sexual scent of their partners as far as 10 kilometres away – so that they can then 'flutter' to their wedding.

Sesame Potatoes

Ingredients:

450G POTATOES, PEELED • SEASONING • 1 CLOVE GARLIC
1 TBS SESAME OIL • 1 LARGE EGG, BEATEN
3 TBS SESAME SEEDS

Method:

Cook the potatoes in salted boiling water. Drain thoroughly, then mash with the sesame oil. Season to taste. Allow to cool, then shape into 12 balls, about 2.5cm in diameter. Dip the balls in the beaten egg, then roll in the sesame seeds to coat. Bake in a pre–heated oven at 200°C/Gas 5 for 20 minutes, or until the seeds are golden.

'Grünkohl'

Serves 6

Ingredients:

1.5KG KALE • STOCK TO COVER • 1 LARGE ONION
• 25G MARGARINE • 250G STREAKY BACON, CHOPPED • 1 HEAPED
TBS FLOUR • SEASONING • A LITTLE BUTTER

Method:

Remove the stems from the kale. Bring some water to the boil and pour over the cabbage. Leave for 10 minutes. Remove and wash thoroughly. Return to the saucepan, cover with stock and simmer for 45 minutes. Meanwhile sauté the onion and bacon until they are golden. Drain the cabbage, stir in the flour, onion and bacon. Add the stock little by little and season. Stir in the butter and bring to the boil. Serve with any type of roast or smoked meat and boiled potatoes.

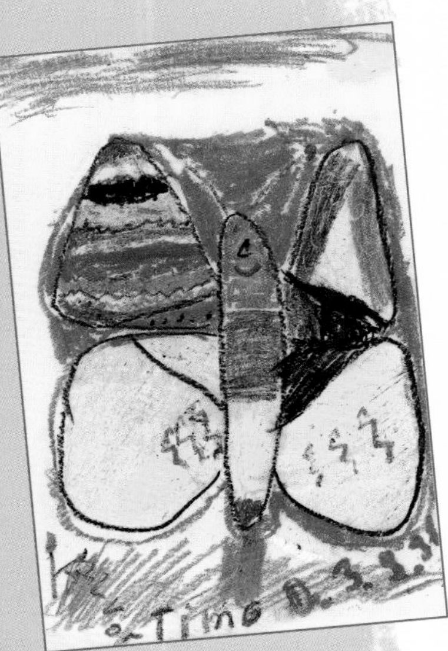

Special Red Cabbage

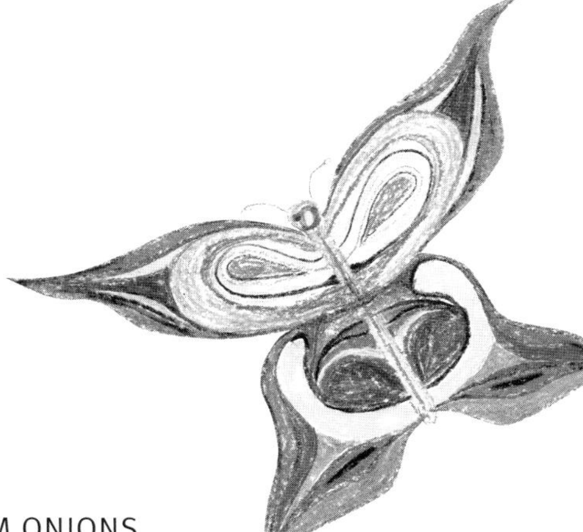

Serves 6

Ingredients:

1KG RED CABBAGE OR OUT OF A JAR OR TIN • 2 MEDIUM ONIONS
2 TBS LARD OR GOOSE FAT • 125G STREAKY BACON (OPTIONAL)
125ML RED WINE • 4 CLOVES • SEASONING • 2 APPLES, PEELED AND CORED • 1 TBS REDCURRANT JELLY OR CRANBERRY SAUCE

Method:

Cut the cabbage into quarters, remove the core and shred finely. Place in a colander and wash. The versions in tins and jars are generally just as good. Dice the onion and bacon if using. Heat the lard and sauté the onions and bacon until soft. Add the cabbage and turn in the fat for about 5 minutes until starting to soften. Add the red wine, cloves, seasoning and sliced apples. Bring to the boil. Cover and simmer for 45–60 minutes. Add the redcurrant jelly, or cranberry sauce. Alternatively, if you have neither of these, they may be substituted by 2 tbs sugar and 1–2 tbs red wine vinegar.

NB: This is delicious with roast poultry, pork or venison, and boiled potatoes.

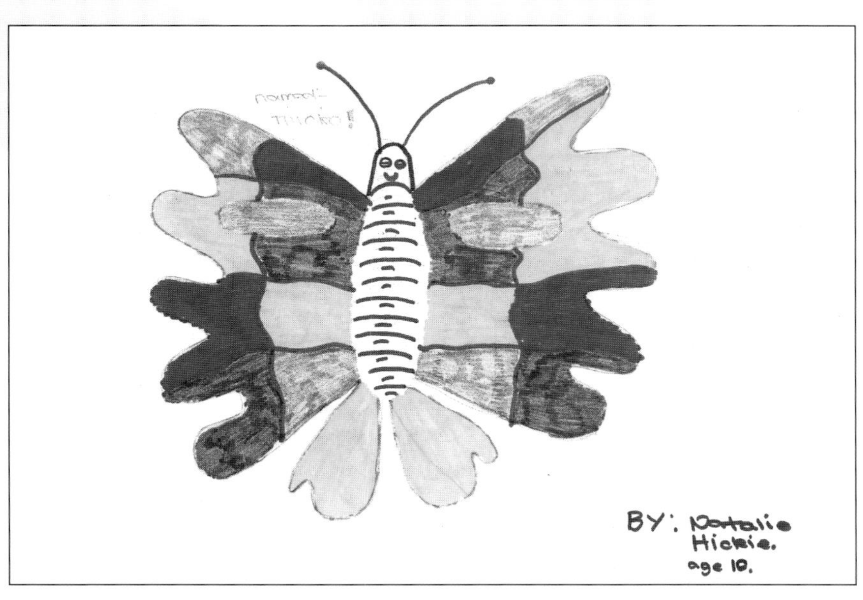

Desserts

Classic Mousse au Chocolat

Serves 6

Ingredients:

3 EGGS, SEPARATED • 110G SUGAR • 60ML MILK • 100G DARK CHOCOLATE • 10G GELATINE (ABOUT 4 SHEETS) • 200ML DOUBLE OR WHIPPING CREAM • GRAND MARNIER/RUM TO TASTE (OPTIONAL)

Method:

Beat the egg yolks and sugar until pale and fluffy. Melt the chocolate with a little milk. Add the chocolate and the rest of the milk to the egg mixture. Dissolve the gelatine and add to the mixture. Add the Grand Marnier or rum. Place in the fridge until half set (about 20 minutes to half an hour). Whisk the egg whites until they form stiff peaks. Beat cream until set. Add one at a time to the half–set chocolate mixture. Cover and chill for at least 2 hours before serving. (Guests never believed us that it is home–made – Too fluffy to be true!)

Brandied Cream Peaches

Ingredients:

4 MEDIUM PEACHES • 50G BUTTER, MELTED • 4 TBS SOFT BROWN SUGAR • 4 TBS BRANDY • CREAM TO SERVE

Method:

Halve the peaches and remove the stones. Dip the peaches in the melted butter. Put two halves onto a double thickness square of aluminium foil, sprinkle each with the sugar and 1 tbs brandy. Bring the foil up and fold together to form a parcel so the juices cannot escape. Place the four parcels on the barbecue grill for about 10 minutes or until the peaches are soft but not mushy. Serve in the parcels or open the foil and slide the peaches onto a plate. Serve with a jug of pouring cream.

Lemon Sorbet

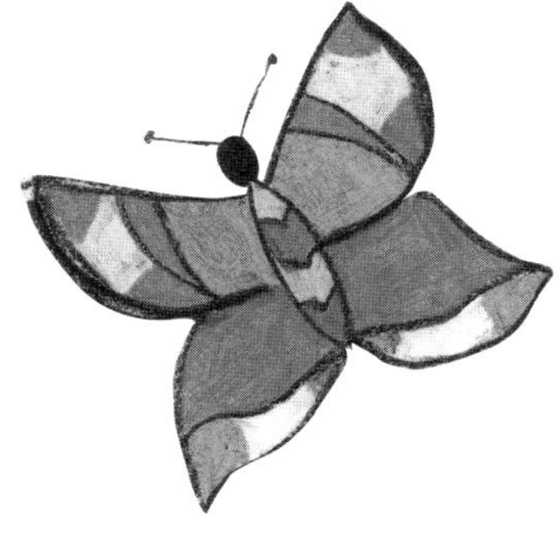

Serves 6–8

Ingredients:

400ML LEMON JUICE • ZEST OF 2 LEMONS • 100ML SODA WATER • 500ML WATER • 500G SUGAR • 3 EGG WHITES

Method:

Stir the sugar into the water, bring to the boil and simmer for 15–20 minutes. Pour into a plastic container and leave to cool. Once cold, mix with the lemon juice, zest and soda water and pour into a metal tray. Place in the freezer for several hours or overnight until well set. Remove the frozen juice 5–10 minutes before continuing. Divide the frozen juice mixture into three and beat each third with an egg white until well integrated and fluffy. Freeze until well set before serving. Serving suggestion: sprinkle with praliné (sweetened roasted almonds) and decorate with fresh mint.

NB: You can use the egg yolks to make home-made mayonnaise.

Around 165,000 butterfly species are known. Of these, 15,000 are daytime moths, the others are night-time species. In Europe alone there are 300–400 daytime moths.

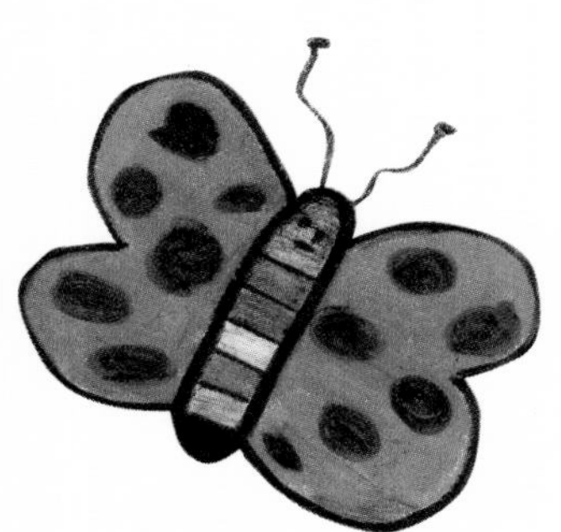

Fluffy Yoghurt Dessert with a Raspberry Sauce

For the Yoghurt Fluff:

300ML FULL–FAT YOGHURT • 350ML CRÈME FRAÎCHE
150G ICING SUGAR • 2 EGG WHITES

For the Raspberry Sauce:

600G FRESH RASPBERRIES • 80G ICING SUGAR

Method:

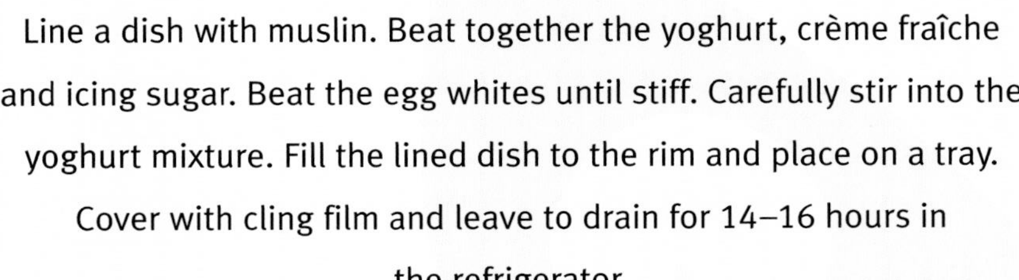

Line a dish with muslin. Beat together the yoghurt, crème fraîche and icing sugar. Beat the egg whites until stiff. Carefully stir into the yoghurt mixture. Fill the lined dish to the rim and place on a tray. Cover with cling film and leave to drain for 14–16 hours in the refrigerator.

Purée 400g of the raspberries, then put through a sieve. Stir in the icing sugar and put in the fridge until ready to use. To serve, turn out the fluff onto a serving dish, remove the gauze and pour over the sauce. Decorate with the remaining raspberries.

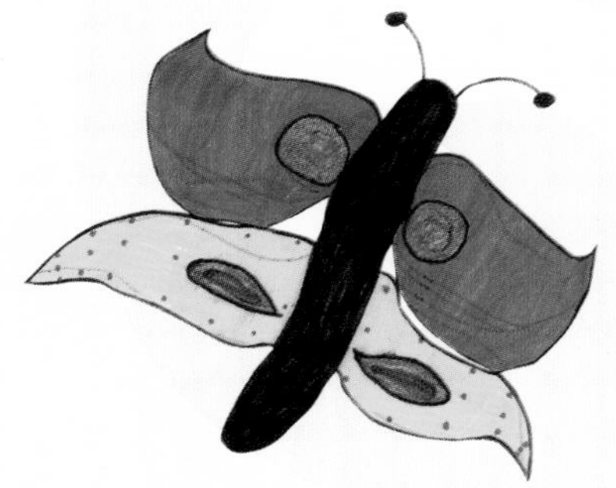

'Rote Grütze'

- the German version of Summer Pudding -

Ingredients:

600G MIXED BERRIES (RASPBERRIES, BLACKCURRANTS, STRAWBERRIES ETC) • 250G BLACK CHERRIES, WITHOUT STONES, FRESH OR TINNED • 250ML RED FRUIT JUICE 1 VANILLA POD • 60G CUSTARD POWDER • 100G SUGAR

Method:

Clean and wash the berries if using fresh ones – frozen ones are good too. Drain the cherries. Place all into a saucepan. Spoon 6 tbs of the fruit juice into a separate bowl. Pour the rest of the juice over the fruit and add the vanilla pod. Bring to the boil and continue to boil for 4 minutes.

Mix the custard powder with the remaining fruit juice and add to the fruit. Bring to the boil and add the sugar – add more sugar if desired. Remove the vanilla pod and leave to cool. Chill and serve.

NB: Only for adults: add red wine instead of fruit juice.

Certain butterfly species migrate from Africa via Italy and the Alps into Germany and further up to Iceland – 8,000 kilometres away! The fuel: nectar.

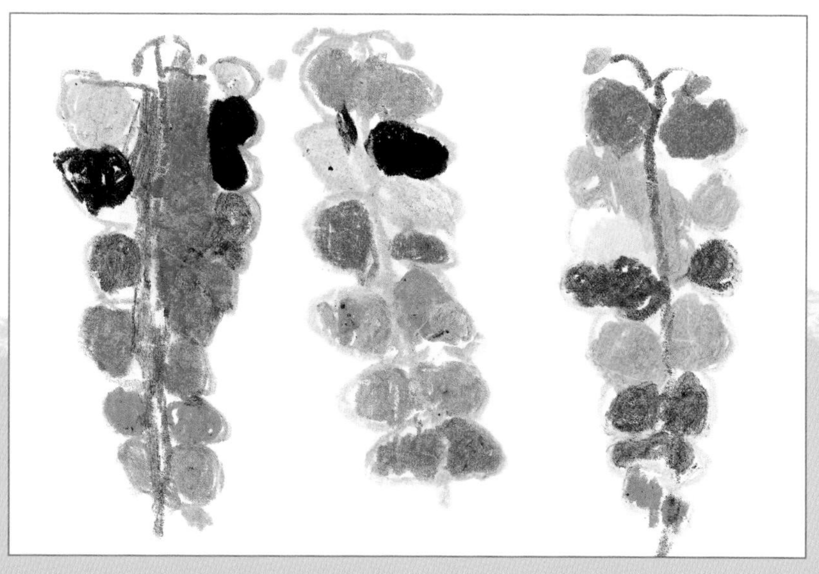

Sherry Trifle

Serves 6

Ingredients:

250G SPONGE CAKES • 6 TBS RASPBERRY JAM • 6–8 TBS MEDIUM DRY SHERRY • 400G TIN FRUIT COCKTAIL • 300ML WHIPPING CREAM • GLACÉ CHERRIES, TO DECORATE • 25G FLAKED ALMONDS

For the Custard:

600ML MILK • 3 TBS PLAIN FLOUR • 2 MEDIUM EGGS • 25G SUGAR
½ TSP VANILLA ESSENCE • 15–25G BUTTER

Method:

Cut the sponge cakes evenly in half, spread with the jam and sandwich together. Place in the base of a glass serving dish, covering the base completely. Pour the sherry evenly over the sponge cakes. Drain the tin of fruit, reserving 2–3 tbs of the juice. Arrange the fruit over the cakes and pour the juice over. The sponge cakes should be well moistened but not swimming in excess liquid. Use less if necessary. Heat the milk until warm. Meanwhile place the flour in a bowl and add the eggs and beat with a wooden spoon. Gradually stir in the warm milk and return the mixture to the pan. Heat gently until thickened, stirring constantly to prevent the custard from getting lumpy. When custard has thickened, cook for 1 minute. Remove from the heat stir in the sugar, vanilla essence and butter. Beat until the butter has melted, then pour over the sponge cakes and fruit. Leave until cool. Place in the fridge or a cool place until the custard is completely cold – this can be overnight. Whip the cream until it is stiff and standing in soft peaks. Spoon into a piping bag with a star nozzle and pipe onto the custard. Decorate with glacé cherries and flaked almonds.

NB: The sponge cakes and jam can be replaced by a jam filled Swiss roll, and the fruit cocktail by other tinned or fresh fruit.

Fig Balls

Ingredients:

400G DRIED FIGS • ZEST OF ONE ORANGE • 250G PEELED ALMONDS • 75G COOKING CHOCOLATE • 20–40ML BRANDY 100G CASTER SUGAR

Method:

Place the peeled almonds on an oven tray and roast in a hot oven until golden. Place in a food processor and mix until roughly chopped. Pour into a large mixing bowl. Put the figs, orange zest and chocolate in the food processor and whiz until quite fine. Stir into the almonds together with the brandy. Chill for at least 2 hours or overnight. Roll into balls and turn in sugar. For a more integrated and firmer mixture use the almonds while they are still hot – this will melt the chocolate. Cold almonds will leave you with pieces of chocolate and a lighter mix. Once they have been rolled in sugar the fig balls should be kept in a cool dry place but not in the fridge as this will make the sugar 'sweat'.

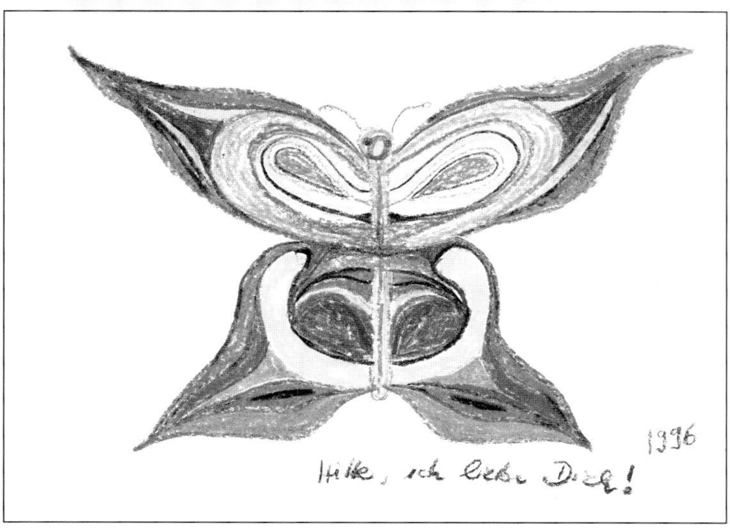

Cakes

Dr. Oetker's Cheesecake

8–12 Pieces

For the Base:

200G FLOUR • 1 LEVEL TSP BAKING POWDER • 3 HEAPED TBS CASTER SUGAR • 1 LARGE EGG • 100G MARGARINE • 1 LEVEL TSP VANILLA SUGAR

For the Cheese Mix:

40G CUSTARD POWDER • 4 EGG WHITES • 1 TBS CASTER SUGAR • 750G QUARK (GERMAN SOFT CHEESE) • 150G SUGAR 1 LEVEL TSP VANILLA SUGAR • 4 EGG YOLKS • A FEW DROPS OF LEMON EXTRACT OR LEMON JUICE TO TASTE • 250ML MILK

Method:

Mix the flour with the baking powder and sugar. Add the vanilla sugar and stir in the egg. Flake in the margarine and mix into a dough. Grease a 26–28cm spring form tin and line with the dough – the rim should be about 3cm high.

Pre–heat the oven to 175°C, Gas 2–3. Whisk the egg whites with the sugar until they form stiff peaks. Add the custard powder, quark, sugar, vanilla sugar, egg yolks, lemon extract or juice and milk. Whisk thoroughly for 1 minute with the electric whisk. Stir in the egg whites. Place on top of the pastry and level with a spoon. Bake the cake in the centre of the oven for 60–70 minutes until set and golden. If it is still slightly soft when removed, do not worry as it continues to set as it cools down. Leave to stand in the tin for 10 minutes, then cut it loose at the edges with a knife. Remove the base of the tin and place the cake on a cooling rack, replacing the rim of the tin to keep the cake in shape.

Red Wine Cake

- à la Sylvia -

12 Pieces

Ingredients:

200G CASTER SUGAR • 200G BUTTER OR MARGARINE • A FEW DROPS VANILLA ESSENCE • 4 MEDIUM EGGS • 1 TSP GROUND CINNAMON 1 TSP COCOA POWDER • 250G FLOUR • 2 TSP BAKING POWDER • 125ML RED WINE • 100G GRATED DARK CHOCOLATE 150G GROUND HAZELNUTS

Method:

Whisk the butter together with the sugar until pale and fluffy. Add the vanilla essence and the eggs, one at a time. Mix the flour with the baking powder, cinnamon and cocoa and add slowly to the mixture, stirring well. Mix in the chocolate, red wine and hazelnuts. Place in a greased loaf tin and bake in a pre–heated oven (170°C/Gas 3 1/2) for about an hour until set.

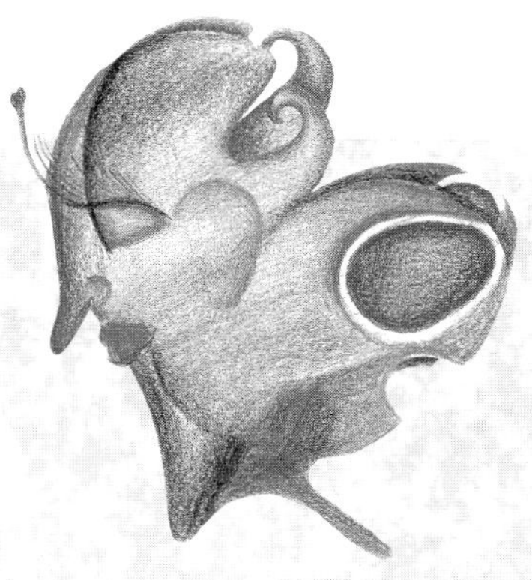

There are thousands of different species of butterflies. Each one of them needs a different plant to feed their caterpillars on.

Cakes

'Melting Moments'

12–16 Pieces

For the Apple Purée:

7 GREEN APPLES • ZEST OF 1 LEMON • 100ML WHITE WINE
125G SUGAR

For the Dough:

500G FLOUR • 375G BUTTER OR MARGARINE • 2 EGG YOLKS
2 TBS CREAM • PINCH OF SALT • 1 PACKET (11G) DRY YEAST
120G SUGAR • 2 TBS MILK

For the Icing:

250G ICING SUGAR • JUICE OF 1 LEMON • A LITTLE EGG WHITE

Method:

Peel and core the apples and cut into small pieces. Place in a saucepan with the rest of the ingredients and simmer with the lid on until the apples are very soft and have reduced to a pulp. For a smoother purée mash with a potato masher. Leave to cool. (The purée and the dough can be made the day before.) Place the flour in a large bowl. Make a dent in the centre and add the yeast, sugar and cream. Put one egg yolk, soft butter or margarine and salt on top of the flour around the edge. Form a dough and knead until pliable and shiny. Place the dough in cling film and chill for at least 6 hours.

Pre–heat the oven to 180°C/Gas 4. When ready to use, remove the dough from the film and cut into three large pieces. Knead each piece thoroughly on a floured surface, then roll into a rectangle about 40 x 15cm. Place on a lined baking tray big enough to hold all the dough. Spread the apple purée across the centre of each piece of dough, and fold up the edges. Mix the other egg yolk with the milk and spread over the edges of the dough. Bake for 40–45 minutes until golden. Leave to cool for 10–15 minutes before covering the pastry edges with the icing. Stir the lemon juice into the icing sugar and whisk with a hand whisk until smooth. Stir in the egg white.

NB: We liked to cover the apple purée with a light custard as well before baking. This is a nice alternative.

Apple Upside-Down Cake

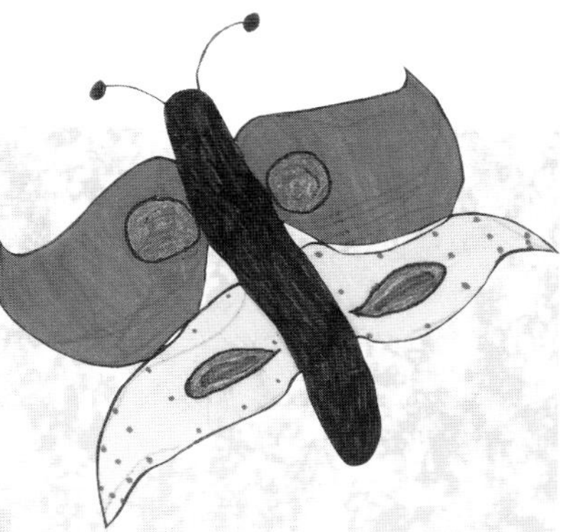

8–10 Pieces

For the Apple Base:

50G BUTTER • 120G SUGAR • 1–2 TSP GROUND CINNAMON
75G WALNUTS • 4–5 GREEN APPLES (E.G. GRANNY SMITHS)

For the Sponge:

100G MARGARINE • 200G SUGAR • 3 MEDIUM EGGS • JUICE AND ZEST OF 1 LEMON • PINCH OF SALT • 100G CORNFLOUR • 100G FLOUR • 3 TSP BAKING POWDER

Method:

Line a round loose–bottomed spring form tin with baking parchment. Melt the butter and pour into the base. Sprinkle over the sugar and walnuts. Peel and core the apples, and cut each quarter into three. Arrange the pieces of apple on top. Whisk the butter with an electric mixer until pale and fluffy. Add the sugar and continue to whisk for a few minutes. Add the eggs one at a time. Add the salt, lemon zest and juice and whisk until the sugar has dissolved. Thoroughly mix the cornflour with the flour and baking powder and sieve into the egg mixture. Spoon the sponge mixture over the apples, levelling the surface with the back of a spoon. Place in a medium (170°–180°C) pre–heated oven for 45–60 minutes, turning occasionally to ensure an even colour. Leave to cool for 10 minutes before turning out onto a dish. Carefully remove the base of the form and the baking parchment with a knife.

There are about 60 species of butterflies in Britain.

For the Base:

125G ALMONDS, PEELED AND GROUND • 125G DARK CHOCOLATE • 6 LARGE EGGS • 125G SOFT BUTTER OR MARGARINE 130G SUGAR • 2 TBS KIRSCH • PINCH OF SALT • 1 TBS VANILLA SUGAR • 125G FLOUR • 2 TSP BAKING POWDER

For the Cherry Filling:

550–650G TINNED DARK CHERRIES, STONED • 120G SUGAR 40G CORNFLOUR • 2 TBS KIRSCH

For the Chocolate Cream:

20G BITTER COCOA POWDER • 1 TBS SUGAR 250ML WHIPPING CREAM

For the Kirsch Cream:

400–500ML WHIPPING CREAM • 30G SUGAR • 3 TBS KIRSCH

For the Decoration:

200G DARK CHOCOLATE

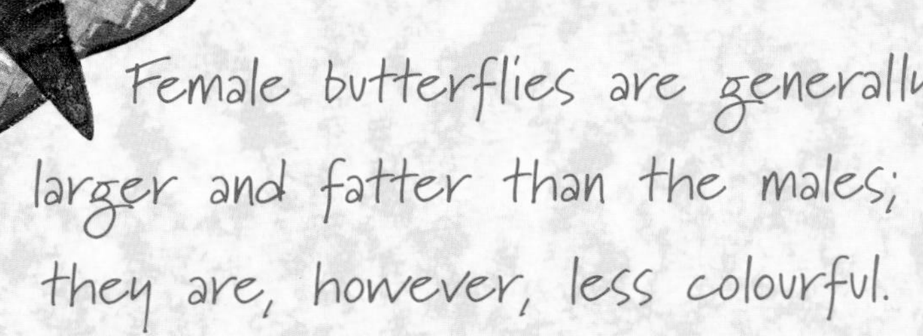

the only one that ***really*** *works*

Method:

Grate the chocolate. Separate the eggs. Whisk together the egg yolks, margarine, 65g of the sugar, Kirsch, salt and vanilla sugar and 2 tbs of water until fluffy. Mix together the almonds, chocolate, flour and baking powder. Grease and line a spring form tin. Pre–heat the oven to 175°C/ Gas 2. Whisk the egg whites with the remaining sugar until firm. Add alternative spoons of the egg white and flour mixture to the egg yolks. Spoon the mixture into the tin. Bake for 45–50 minutes until firm and golden. Place upside–down in the tin on a cooling rack and leave for at least 2 hours. Place the cherries in a sieve, and reserve the juice. Stir the cornflour into the juice. Place the cherries in a saucepan and heat. Add the liquid and sweeten according to taste. Stir in the Kirsch and leave to cool. Cut the sponge in half horizontally, and sprinkle both halves with the kirsch. Mix the cocoa powder with the sugar and 1 tbs water. Whisk the cream until firm. Stir in the cocoa mixture. Place in a piping bag with a large nozzle. Pipe circles onto the base with 1.5cm distance between them, with one large dollop in the centre. Fill the gaps with the cherry filling and place the second cake round on top, pressing down lightly. Whisk the cream and sugar until firm and add the Kirsch. Spread dome–shaped over the cake. Use a potato peeler to make rough chocolate shavings and sprinkle over the cream.

Cakes

Incredible Minute Doughnuts

Makes 12–14

Ingredients:

100G SHELLED WALNUTS • 75G SHELLED HAZELNUTS • 65G BUTTER OR MARGARINE • PINCH OF SALT • ½ TSP SUGAR • 125G FLOUR 4 LARGE EGGS • ¼ TSP BAKING POWDER • VEGETABLE OIL FOR DEEP–FRYING • 75G SUGAR • VANILLA SUGAR

Method:

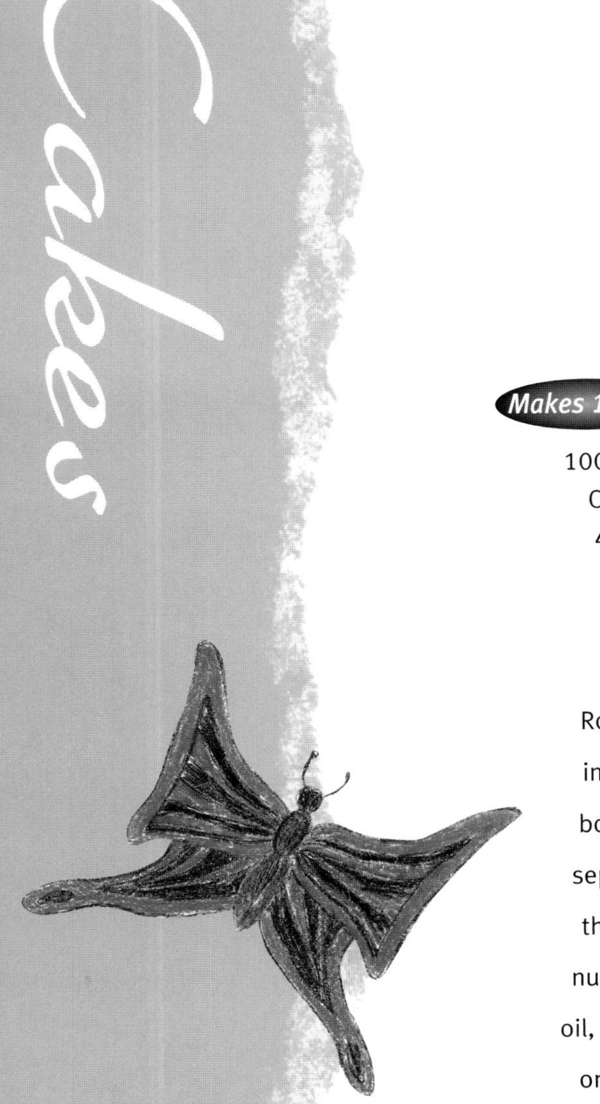

Roughly chop the walnuts and hazelnuts. Melt the butter or margarine in a saucepan, add the salt, sugar and 250ml of water and bring to the boil. Add the flour all at once and stir for 4–5 minutes until the mixture separates from the sides of the saucepan. Place in a mixing bowl. Stir in the eggs, one at a time and mix well. Then add the baking powder and nuts. Heat the oil in a deep fryer to 180°C. Dip a tablespoon into the hot oil, then place tablespoons of the mixture into it for 8–10 minutes, turning once. Mix the sugar and vanilla sugar in a bowl, remove the doughnuts with a slotted spoon, drain on kitchen paper and toss in the sugar. Serve warm.

NB: Instead of the walnuts and hazelnuts you may use almonds and raisins, and the raw mixture freezes very well.

The Irish call the butterfly deatbhan de (creature of God) the Khmers glow duw (God's shining insect).

Mississippi Mud Pie

Serves 8–10

Ingredients:

200G DIGESTIVE BISCUITS • 75G BUTTER OR MARGARINE, MELTED • 200G MARSHMALLOWS • 125ML MILK • 200G DARK CHOCOLATE • 4 TBS HOT WATER • 2 TBS INSTANT COFFEE GRANULES • 400ML WHIPPING CREAM • 75G DARK CHOCOLATE TO DECORATE

Method:

Grease and line a loose–bottomed 23cm spring form tin. Crush the biscuits and stir in the melted butter. Press into base and sides of the tin. Chill for 30 minutes. Place two–thirds of the marshmallows in a small saucepan and add the milk. Heat over a low heat, stirring constantly. Melt the chocolate and stir into the marshmallow mixture. Set aside. Dissolve the coffee granules in the hot water. Place in a small saucepan with the remaining marshmallows and heat gently, stirring constantly, until melted. Cool. Whisk the cream until firm. Stir two–thirds of it into the chocolate mix, and the remaining third into the coffee mix. Spoon the chocolate mix onto the chilled biscuit base, spread out to the edges but leave the surface uneven. Spoon the coffee mixture onto the chocolate and swirl the surface. Chill for at least 4 hours or overnight. To serve, carefully unclip the tin and remove the paper lining. Make chocolate curls with a potato peeler to decorate.

Dressings & Marinades

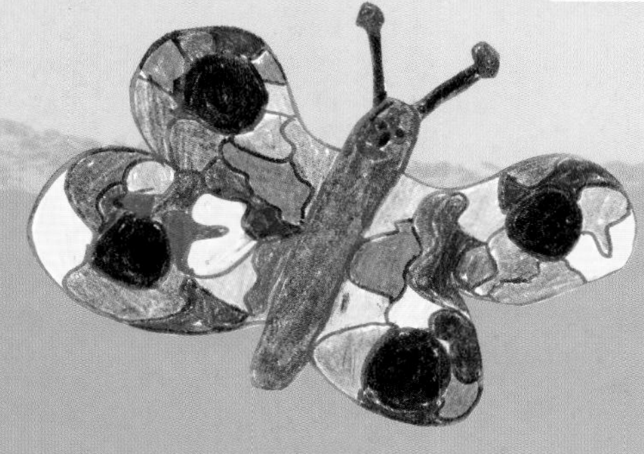

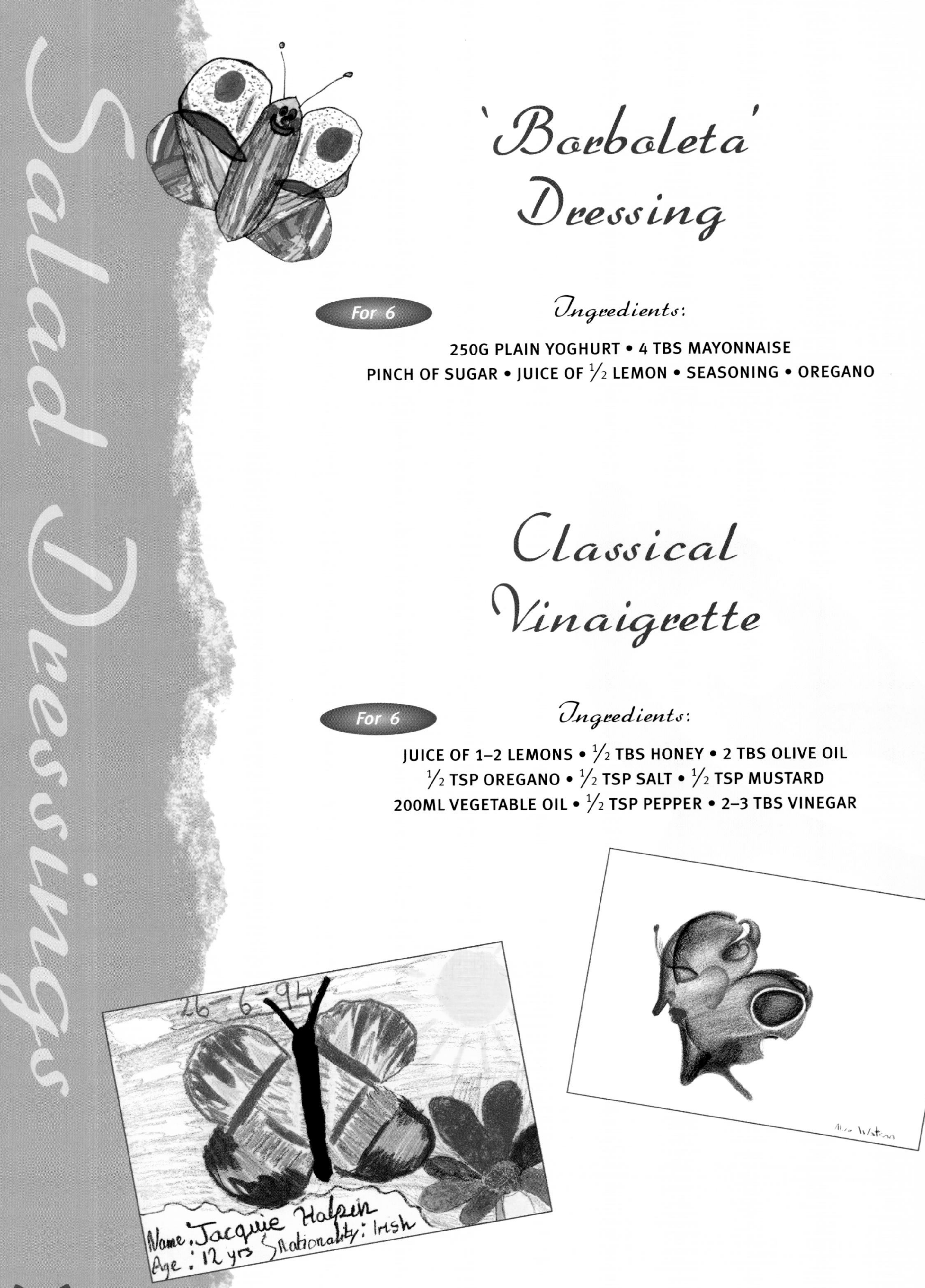

'Borboleta' Dressing

For 6

Ingredients:

250G PLAIN YOGHURT • 4 TBS MAYONNAISE
PINCH OF SUGAR • JUICE OF ½ LEMON • SEASONING • OREGANO

Classical Vinaigrette

For 6

Ingredients:

JUICE OF 1–2 LEMONS • ½ TBS HONEY • 2 TBS OLIVE OIL
½ TSP OREGANO • ½ TSP SALT • ½ TSP MUSTARD
200ML VEGETABLE OIL • ½ TSP PEPPER • 2–3 TBS VINEGAR

Horseradish Dressing

For 6

Ingredients:

6 TBS VINAIGRETTE • 1 TBS MAYONNAISE
2 TBS PLAIN YOGHURT• 1 TSP LEMON JUICE
1 TBS TOMATO KETCHUP • 1 HEAPED TSP CREAMED HORSERADISH
DROPS OF BRANDY TO TASTE • SEASONING

Caesar Salad Dressing

For 6

Ingredients:

1 HARD–BOILED EGG, CHOPPED • 2 TBS FRESH LEMON JUICE
3 ANCHOVY FILLETS, CRUSHED • 2 TSP CAPERS, FINELY CHOPPED
5 TBS OLIVE OIL • 25G GRATED PARMESAN CHEESE
2 TBS CHOPPED FRESH PARSLEY • SEASONING

India is over–rich with beautiful butterflies yet only uses the term patanga (bird) to also stand for butterfly.

Marinades for:

Meat
(Skewers)

Ingredients:

FOR 1.2 KG MEAT • 3 CLOVES GARLIC, CRUSHED • 1 HEAPED TBS BROWN SUGAR • 2 TBS LEMON JUICE • 4 TBS SOY SAUCE (TAMARI IF AVAILABLE)

Chicken Pieces
(Skewers)

Ingredients:

FOR 2 SMALL CHICKENS, JOINTED • 3 CLOVES, GARLIC, SLICED THINLY • 1 TBS PEELED AND SLICED FRESH GINGER • 2 TBS WHITE WINE • 3 TBS SOY SAUCE • 1 TBS CLEAR HONEY

Fresh Sardine Fillets
(Pickled)

Ingredients:

FOR 2KG LARGE SARDINES, FILLETED • 2 TSP SALT • 1 TSP PEPPERCORNS • 1 TBS MUSTARD SEEDS • 2 MEDIUM ONIONS, SLICED • 2 TBS SUGAR • 4 CLOVES GARLIC, PEELED AND SLICED 6 BAY LEAVES • 700ML WHITE WINE VINEGAR

Method:

Wash the fillets and leave to drain in a colander. Meanwhile bring all other ingredients to the boil and continue to simmer for 15–20 minutes until the liquid has reduced by one third. Leave until completely cold. Sterilise 2 large glass jars and layer the liquid and fish into them, starting with some liquid and ensuring that the fish is well covered at the end. Poke a fork down the sides of the glass to ensure that the liquid has reached all of the fish. Leave for 48 hours in the fridge before serving. These will keep for 2–4 weeks depending on the cooling temperature. Serve with sour cream and crackers.

Marinades for:

Monkfish
(Skewers)

Ingredients:

FOR 1KG MONKFISH • 1 TBS VINAIGRETTE • 1 TBS LEMON JUICE
1 TBS WHITE WINE • 1 TSP DRIED OREGANO • 2 BAY LEAVES
FRESHLY GROUND BLACK PEPPER

Most butterflies take one year to complete their life cycle, but some take only one or two months.

Swordfish
(Skewers)

Ingredients:

FOR 1KG SWORDFISH, ROUGHLY CUBED • 2 TBS OIL • 1 TSP PAPRIKA POWDER • 1 TBS WHITE WINE • FRESHLY GROUND BLACK PEPPER
1 TSP LEMON JUICE

Fresh Tuna
(Skewers)

Ingredients:

FOR 1 KG TUNA FILLETS, ROUGHLY CUBED • 1 TBS LEMON JUICE
2 TBS WHITE WINE • ½ TSP CRUSHED ROSEMARY • ½ TSP MIXED HERBS • 1 BAY LEAF • FRESHLY GROUND BLACK PEPPER

Olives 'Butterfly Style'

Ingredients:

FOR 1KG OLIVES • 100ML VEGETABLE OIL • 50ML WHITE WINE
4–6 CLOVES GARLIC, CRUSHED • 1 TBS COARSE SALT • 1 TBS DRIED OREGANO

Sauces-Savoury

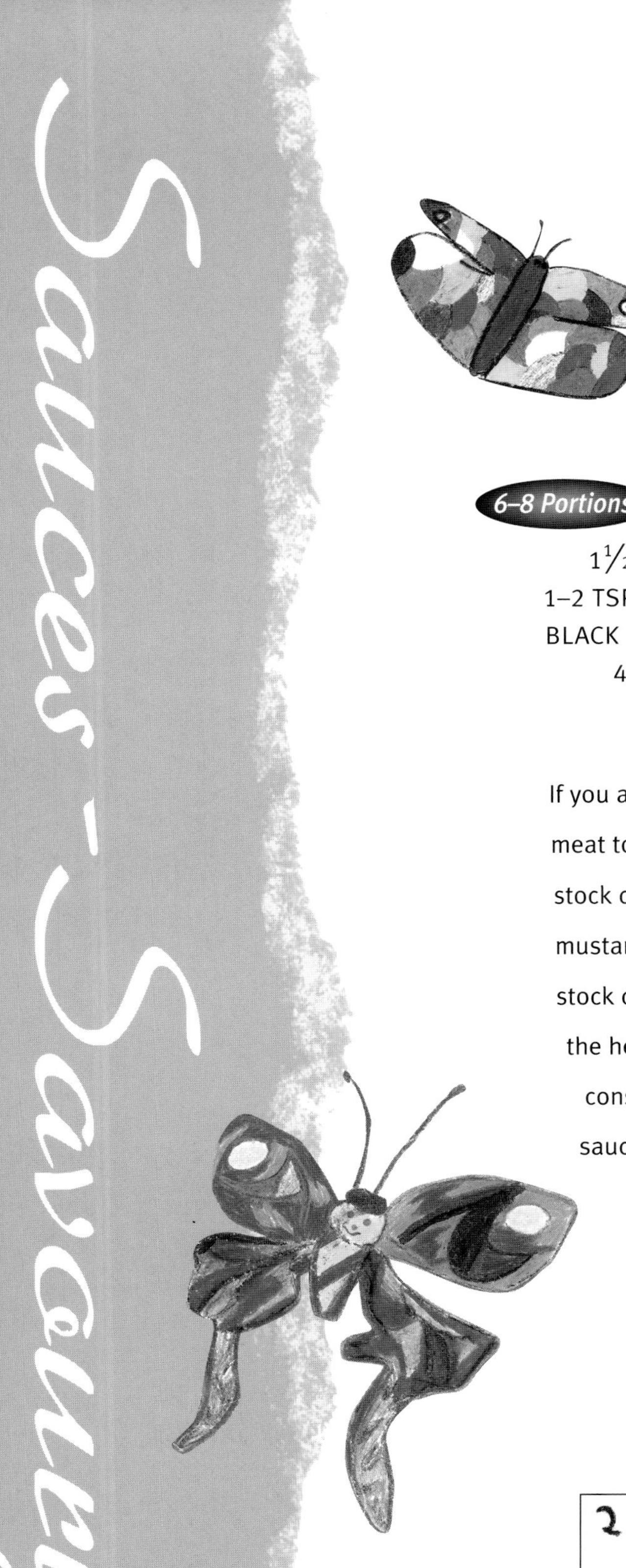

Pepper Sauce

6–8 Portions

Ingredients:

1½ TBS VEGETABLE OIL • 1 SMALL ONION, FINELY CHOPPED
1–2 TSP DIJON MUSTARD • 1 TSP TOMATO KETCHUP • 1 TBS COARSE BLACK PEPPER • 1 CHICKEN STOCK CUBE • PINCH CAYENNE PEPPER
4 TBS BRANDY • 200ML SINGLE CREAM • SALT TO TASTE

Method:

If you are using this as a steak sauce, you may have trimmings from the meat to fry in the oil first to add flavour. In this case you will not need a stock cube. Fry the onion in the same oil until golden and soft. Add the mustard, ketchup, pepper and cayenne and stir for a few minutes. Add stock cube (if using). Pour in the brandy and stir in the cream – reduce the heat to minimum and simmer without a lid until the right creamy consistency has been reached. Check the seasoning. For a milder sauce add 1 tbs flour before the cream is added and dilute further with a little milk.

Peanut Sauce

8 Portions

Ingredients:

340G JAR PEANUT BUTTER • 1 SMALL ONION • 3 GARLIC CLOVES, CRUSHED • 3/4 TSP SALT • 1 1/2 TSP CHILLI PASTE (I.E. SAMBAL) A LITTLE OIL TO SAUTÉ • 3 TBS SOY SAUCE (TAMARI IF POSSIBLE) JUICE OF 1/2 LEMON • 2 TBS BROWN SUGAR • 300–350ML WARM WATER

Method:

Heat the oil and sauté the onions for a couple of minutes. Add the garlic, salt and chilli paste and fry on a high heat until brown. Stir in the soy sauce, lemon juice and sugar and bring to the boil. Take off the heat and stir in the peanut butter. Gradually add the water until a preferred consistency has been reached. Check seasoning. Re–heat before serving.

Every butterfly goes though four very different phases in its life: egg, caterpillar, chrysalis and adult.

Garlic Mayonnaise

Ingredients:

500ML VEGETABLE OIL • 1 EGG • JUICE OF $\frac{1}{2}$ LEMON • 1 TBS FRENCH MUSTARD • 2–4 CLOVES GARLIC, CRUSHED SEASONING • FRESH PARSLEY

Method:

Place the egg, mustard, lemon juice and seasoning in a food processor. Beat until foamy. Very slowly pour in the oil with the machine constantly running. Add the garlic to taste a few drops of warm water if necessary. Adjust the seasoning and chill for a few hours before serving, sprinkled with freshly chopped parsley.

NB: This goes well with fresh raw vegetables

'I suppose you are an entomologist?' 'Not quite so ambitious as that, sir. I should like to put my eyes on the individual entitled that name. No man can be truly called an entomologist, sir; the subject is too vast for any single human intelligence to grasp.'

Oliver Wendell Holmes, The Poet at the Breakfast Table

Mr Butterfly.
Amy Esser
Age 10
1991

= 24 Agosto 1995 =

20:00 horas noite

Hoje foi um dia muito especial ... fizemos dois meses de casados, por isso escolhemos um Restaurante também especial!

Gostámos muito de TUDO, desde o atendimento (muito caloroso e cordial) à deliciosa comida. para não falar do ambiente ...!

Foi com muito agrado que aqui estivémos, esperando voltar muito em breve!

O nosso muito OBRIGADO!

Paula e Guitó

Christiane, UTE and Karl Heinrich
al Borboleta
The Worlds Greatest Restaurant
Sitis
Porto Do Lagos
Portimao
Portugal

21 Oct. 1989

The adjectives are difficult — enjoyable, nice, different, refreshing; — still not enough. Let's try warmth, fantastic food, beautiful music, special people. We always look forward to our nights here, we are never disappointed and when we leave our thoughts almost always turn to our next visit. —

Cynthia and Frank Liddy

Lovely Restaurante Lovely food lovely people
It's a pleasure to keep coming back each year
Thank you for helping to make our Portugal holiday
so pleasant.

Ann. Susans mum. Jenkins family

Give a man a fish & he eats for a day,
Teach him to fish & he eats for a life time.
A superb evening with wonderful food!
Jill & John Bathurst-Hoile. Hemingford Grey Cambridge
12.4.94.

We have found a special place when we found Al-Borboleta — all by chance on our return to Portimão.

The food — in our case, salmon & chicken, were exquisite, but the whole atmosphere — the feeling — was beautiful! We feel very much at home here, and hope you might feel the same at our home sometime!

All the best — Obrigada,

David & Barbara Waddell
123 Woodview Crescent
Ancaster, Ontario, CANADA
7 July 1996

Tuesday, 26th Sept, 1995.

We have lived on your doorstep for four years &, to our shame, have never before eaten in 'Al Borbaleta'.

We came to eat on the eve of Dirk's return to Germany & two days before Christiane's return to College in Cornwall, where she knows our 'local' & many of our friends.

The restaurant is beautiful & the ambience friendly. Especially attractive are the many drawings of butterflies done by the children of customers

Hughie really enjoyed the garlic mushrooms & the sorbet was a deliciously refreshing end to a lovely meal. The musical backing was great.

We will certainly recommend 'The Butterfly' to our friends & acquaintances & the many tourists we meet.

Lots of love & Best Wishes,

Loïs & Hughie (of the Pink Cadillacs Rock'n' Roll Showband)

10/7/95

Hope this is the 1st of many visits. – What an excellent host serving excellent food.

Bagshaw

19 + 20 June '93

As a hotelier myself, I have only one word to describe our experiences here over the past two evenings – AUSGEZEICHNET!

[signature], London.

L Mann

Poetry Focus 2020

Leaving Certificate poems and notes for **English Higher Level**

Martin Kieran & Frances Rocks

GILL EDUCATION

Gill Education
Hume Avenue
Park West
Dublin 12
www.gilleducation.ie

Gill Education is an imprint of M.H. Gill & Co.

ISBN: 978-0-7171-79886

Design: Graham Thew
Print origination: Carole Lynch

For permission to reproduce photographs, the authors and publisher gratefully acknowledge the following:

© Alamy: 21, 24, 29, 36, 52, 58, 61, 63, 64, 69, 73, 82, 85, 86, 96, 98, 142, 147, 173, 175, 177, 182, 185, 190, 193, 200, 202, 204, 218, 295, 296, 305, 336, 345, 384, 393, 400, 402, 408, 410, 412, 417, section header: Emily Dickinson, Paul Durcan, D.H Lawrence, Adrienne Rich, William Wordsworth; © Bridgeman Images: 40, 43, 102, 104, 291, 293, 320, 323, 324, 328, 396, 404, 406; © Collins Agency: 310; © E+ / Getty Premium: 106, 109, 341, 344, 360, 373, 374; © Getty Images: 5, 13, 15, 32, 54, 76, 110, 131, 158, 253, 274, 276, 279, 283, 285, 300, 303, 357; © Francine Scialom Greenblatt: 121; © iStock: 8, 19, 34, 66, 68, 79, 81, 197, 220, 224, 230, 232, 233, 237, 240, 242, 244, 246, 250, 251, 256, 257, 259, 261, 287, 290, 314, 316, 338, 349, 352, 354, 364, 369, 387, 390, 428, section header: Unseen Poetry; Courtesy of RTÉ Archives: 2, 272, section headers: Eavan Boland, Eiléan Ní Chuilleanáin; © Shutterstock: 114, 153; © Sportsfile: 137; © Topfoto: 17, 170, 209, section header: Robert Frost.

The authors and publisher have made every effort to trace all copyright holders, but if any have been inadvertently overlooked we would be pleased to make the necessary arrangement at the first opportunity.

The paper used in this book is made from the wood pulp of managed forests. For every tree felled, at least one tree is planted, thereby renewing natural resources.

Contents

*(OL) indicates poems that are also prescribed for the Ordinary Level course.

Adrienne Rich

William Wordsworth

Unseen Poem

*(OL) indicates poems that are also prescribed for the Ordinary Level course.

Introduction

Poetry Focus is a modern poetry textbook for Leaving Certificate Higher Level English. It includes all the prescribed poems for the 2020 exam as well as succinct commentaries on each one. Well-organised study notes allow students to develop their own individual responses and enhance their skills in critical literacy. There is no single 'correct' approach to answering the poetry question. Candidates are free to respond in any appropriate way that shows good knowledge of and engagement with the prescribed poems.

- **Concise poet biographies** provide context for the poems.
- **List of prescribed poems** gives a brief introduction to each poem.
- **Personal response** questions follow the text of each poem. These allow students to consider their first impressions before any in-depth study or analysis. These questions provide a good opportunity for written and/or oral exercises.
- **Critical literacy** highlights the main features of the poet's subject matter and style. These discussion notes will enhance the student's own critical appreciation through focused group work and/or written exercises. Analytical skills are developed in a coherent, practical way to give students confidence in articulating their own personal responses.
- **Analysis (writing about the poem) is provided using graded sample paragraphs** which aid students in fluently structuring and developing valid points, using fresh and varied expression. These model paragraphs also illustrate effective use of relevant quotations and reference.
- **Class/homework exercises** for each poem provide focused practice in writing personal responses to examination-style questions.
- **Summary points** provide a memorable snapshot of the key aspects to remember about each poem.
- **Full sample Leaving Certificate essays** are accompanied by marking-scheme guidelines and examiners' comments. These show the student exactly what is required to achieve a successful top grade in the Leaving Cert. The examiner's comments illustrate the use of the PCLM marking scheme and are an invaluable aid for the ambitious student.
- **Sample essay plans** on each poet's work illustrate how to interpret a question and recognise the particular nuances of key words in examination questions. Student evaluation of these essay plans increase confidence in developing and organising clear response to exam questions.
- **Sample Leaving Cert questions** on each poet are given at the end of their particular section.
- **A glossary of common literary terms** at the back of the book provides an easy reference when answering questions.
- **A critical analysis checklist** offers useful hints and tips on how to show genuine engagement with the poetry.

 **The FREE eBook contains:**

- **Investigate further** sections which contain **useful weblinks** should you want to learn more.
- **Pop-up key quotes** to encourage students to select their own individual combination of references from a poem and to write brief commentaries on specific quotations.
- Additional sample graded paragraphs called '**Developing your personal response**'.
- Audio of a selection of the poetry as read by the poets, including audio of all of Eavan Boland, Paul Durcan and Eiléan Ní Chuilleanáin poetry.

How is the Prescribed Poetry Question Marked?

Marking is done (ex. 50 marks) by reference to the PCLM criteria for assessment.

- Clarity of purpose (P): 30% of the total (15 marks)
- Coherence of delivery (C): 30% of the total (15 marks)
- Efficiency of language use (L): 30% of the total (15 marks)
- Accuracy of mechanics (M): 10% of the total (5 marks)

Each answer will be in the form of a response to a specific task requiring candidates to:

- Display a clear and purposeful engagement with the set task (P)
- Sustain the response in an appropriate manner over the entire answer (C)
- Manage and control language appropriate to the task (L)
- Display levels of accuracy in spelling and grammar appropriate to the required/chosen register (M)

General

'Students at Higher Level will be required to study a representative selection from the work of eight poets: a representative selection would seek to reflect the range of a poet's themes and interests and exhibit his/her characteristic style and viewpoint. Normally the study of at least six poems by each poet would be expected.' (DES English Syllabus, 6.3)

The marking scheme guidelines from the State Examinations Commission state that in the case of each poet, the candidates have **freedom of choice** in relation to the poems studied. In addition, there is **not a finite list of any 'poet's themes and interests'**.

Note that in responding to the question set on any given poet, the candidates must refer to the poem(s) they have studied but are not required to refer to **any specific poem(s), nor are they expected to discuss or refer to all the poems they have chosen to study**.

In each of the questions in **Prescribed Poetry**, the underlying nature of the task is the invitation to the candidates to **engage with the poems themselves**.

Exam Advice

- You are not expected to write about any **set number of poems** in the examination. You might decide to focus in detail on a small number of poems, or you could choose to write in a more general way on several poems.
- Most candidates write one or two well-developed **paragraphs** on each of the poems they have chosen for discussion. In other cases, a paragraph will focus on one specific aspect of the poet's work. When discussing recurring themes or features of style, appropriate cross-references to other poems may also be useful.

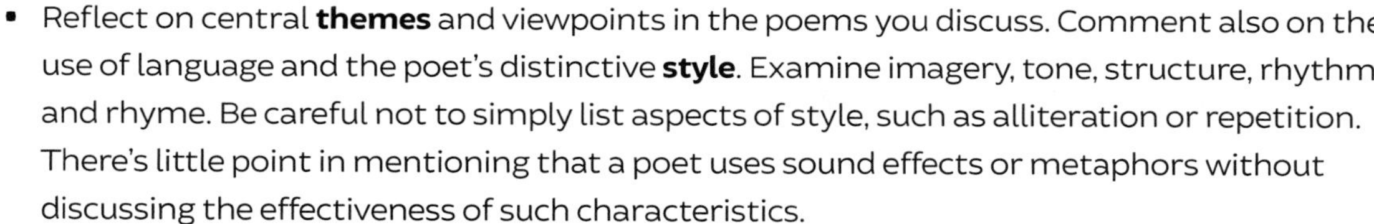

- Reflect on central **themes** and viewpoints in the poems you discuss. Comment also on the use of language and the poet's distinctive **style**. Examine imagery, tone, structure, rhythm and rhyme. Be careful not to simply list aspects of style, such as alliteration or repetition. There's little point in mentioning that a poet uses sound effects or metaphors without discussing the effectiveness of such characteristics.
- Focus on **the task** you have been given in the poetry question. Identify the key terms in the wording of the question and think of similar words for these terms. This will help you develop a relevant and coherent personal response in keeping with the PCLM marking scheme criteria.
- Always root your answers in the text of the poems. Support the points you make with **relevant reference and quotation**. Make sure your own expression is fresh and lively. Avoid awkward expressions, such as 'It says in the poem that …'. Look for alternatives: 'There is a sense of …', 'The tone seems to suggest …', 'It's evident that …', etc.
- Neat, **legible handwriting** will help to make a positive impression on examiners. Corrections should be made by simply drawing a line through the mistake. Scored-out words distract attention from the content of your work.
- Keep the emphasis on why particular poets **appeal to you**. Consider the continuing relevance or significance of a poet's work. Perhaps you have shared some of the feelings or experiences expressed in the poems. Avoid starting answers with prepared biographical sketches. Brief reference to a poet's life are better used when discussing how the poems themselves were shaped by such experiences.
- Remember that the examination encourages **individual engagement** with the prescribed poems. Poetry can make us think and feel and imagine. It opens our minds to the wonderful possibilities of language and ideas. Your interaction with the poems is what matters most. Commentary notes and critical interpretations are all there to be challenged. Read the poems carefully and have confidence in expressing your own personal response.

Eavan Boland
1944–

'Poetry begins – as all art does – where certainties end.'

Eavan Boland has been one of the most prominent voices in Irish poetry and is the author of many highly acclaimed poetry collections. Born in Dublin but raised in London, she had early experiences with anti-Irish racism that gave her a strong sense of heritage and a keen awareness of her identity. She later returned to attend school and university in Dublin, where she published a pamphlet of poetry after her graduation. Boland received her BA from Trinity College in 1966. Since then she has held numerous teaching positions and has published poetry, books of criticism and articles. She married in 1969 and has two children. Her experiences as a wife and mother have influenced her to recognise the beauty and significance of everyday living. Boland writes plainly and eloquently about her experiences as a woman, mother and exile. She has taught at several colleges in Ireland and America where she has been a professor of English at Stanford University, California. In addition to traditional Irish themes, Eavan Boland explores a wide range of interests, including incisive commentaries on contemporary subjects and intensely personal poems about history, womanhood and relationships.

Investigate Further

To find out more about Eavan Boland, or to hear readings of her poems not available in your eBook, you could do a search of some of the useful websites available such as YouTube, BBC Poetry, poetryfoundation.org and poetryarchive.org, or access additional material on this page of your eBook.

Prescribed Poems

*(OL) indicates poems that are also prescribed for the Ordinary Level course.

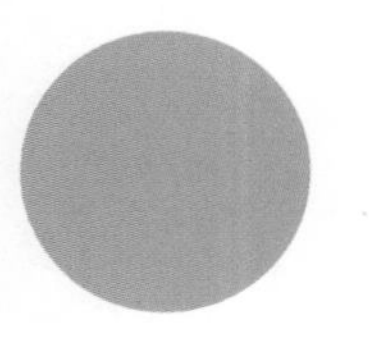

1 The War Horse

The War Horse: a powerful horse ridden in war by a knight or cavalry soldier.

This dry night, nothing unusual
About the clip, clop, casual

Iron of his shoes as he stamps death
Like a mint on the innocent coinage of earth.

I lift the window, watch the ambling feather
Of hock and fetlock, loosed from its daily tether

In the tinker camp on the Enniskerry Road,
Pass, his breath hissing, his snuffling head

Down. He is gone. No great harm is done.
Only a leaf of our laurel hedge is torn –

Of distant interest like a maimed limb,
Only a rose which now will never climb

The stone of our house, expendable, a mere
Line of defence against him, a volunteer

You might say, only a crocus its bulbous head
Blown from growth, one of the screamless dead.

But we, we are safe, our unformed fear
Of fierce commitment gone; why should we care

If a rose, a hedge, a crocus are uprooted
Like corpses, remote, crushed, mutilated?

He stumbles on like a rumour of war, huge,
Threatening; neighbours use the subterfuge

Of curtains; He stumbles down our short street
Thankfully passing us. I pause, wait,

Then to breathe relief lean on the sill
And for a second only my blood is still

With atavism. That rose he smashed frays
Ribboned across our hedge, recalling days

Of burned countryside, illicit braid:
A cause ruined before, a world betrayed.

mint: a place where money is made; a machine for making money.
coinage: collection of coins. Here it refers to imprints the horse makes on the suburban gardens.
ambling: walking at a leisurely pace.
hock: joint in the back of a horse's leg.
fetlock: tuft of hair that grows above and behind the hoof.
tether: rope for tying an animal.
tinker camp: travellers' halting-site.
snuffling: breathing noisily.

expendable: can be done without, can be sacrificed to achieve an object.

mutilated: prevented from having a limb.

subterfuge: trick used to avoid an argument or an awkward situation.

atavism: the recurrence of a trait present in distant ancestors.
frays: is strewn, ragged.
illicit braid: illegal ribbon, a reference to a 19th-century popular movement of poor Catholics in Ireland. The Ribbonmen wore a green ribbon in opposition to the Orangemen.

Personal Response

1. Boland felt that 'the daily things I did ... were not fit material for poetry'. Discuss this statement in relation to 'The War Horse'.
2. Choose one image from the poem that is particularly vivid and dramatic. Briefly explain your choice.
3. Write your own personal response to the poem, highlighting the impact it made on you.

Critical Literacy

'The War Horse' was written in 1972 by Eavan Boland after she had moved to the suburbs at the foothills of the Dublin Mountains. It was an icy winter, and the 'sounds of death from the televisions were heard almost nightly' as the news about the Northern Ireland Troubles was broadcast. In this poem, Boland questions ambivalent attitudes towards war.

This poem is based on a **real event**, **the appearance of a 'loosed' Traveller horse**, described in lines 1–9. Boland has said, 'It encompassed a real event. It entered a place in my heart and moved beyond it.' An aural description of the innocuous noise, 'nothing unusual', heralds the arrival of the animal. The horse, a menacing intruder that suggests the opposition between force and formality, wreaked havoc on the neat order of **suburban gardens**. The rigid control of the rhyming couplets mirrors the desire for order in the suburbs.

Onomatopoeia and the alliteration of the hard 'c' vividly describe the horse's walk, like something out of a young child's story: 'clip, clop, casual'. The second couplet counteracts this sense of ordinariness as it describes the damage the animal inflicts. The brutal verb 'stamps' jolts the reader as the garden, **'the innocent coinage of earth'**, is being destroyed. The simile of a mint, which puts an indelible mark on metal to make coins, is used to describe the destruction. The **consequences of war** are also permanent – people are wounded or killed ('stamps death').

The **poet is an observer**: 'I lift the window, watch'. A detailed description of the horse's leg, 'ambling feather/Of hock and fetlock', belies its capacity for

violence. There then follows an explanation of where the horse came from, the 'tinker camp on the Enniskerry Road'. The **random nature of violence** is aptly contained in the verbs 'ambling', 'loosed' and also in the long run-on line 'loosed … Road'. The sounds the animal makes are vividly conveyed using onomatopoeia: 'hissing', 'snuffling'. The moment of danger passes: 'He is gone.' We can feel the palpable relief: 'No great harm is done.' Colloquial language reduces the event to a trivial disruption.

Lines 10–16 show that the poet has adopted a **sensible approach** as she surveys the **damage**, minimising it with an emphasis on the word 'only': 'Only a leaf is torn', 'Only a crocus', 'Only a rose'. These are all 'expendable'; they can be done without. The language becomes more unsettling as violent descriptions are used to show the mangled blooms: 'like a maimed limb … which now will never climb', 'Blown from growth'. All describe a world that will never be the same again, potential that will never be realised and life that is cut short. From Boland's perspective, 'the screamless dead' can no longer command attention.

And who cares anyway? It is of 'distant interest'. This apathetic view can be taken by people as they watch atrocities in other countries. The **language of war** is prominent: 'a mere/Line of defence', 'a volunteer', the head is 'Blown'. The poet's focus has now shifted away from the horse and is concentrated on conflict, its consequences and the vulnerability of victims.

In lines 17–21, Boland realises that 'we are safe'. War calls for commitment; people must choose to take sides, to fight. This is frightening: 'our unformed fear'. It is there but not expressed, nor given substance or form. Here in this domestic incident is war in miniature, the entry of an intruder who perpetrates damage. The poet asks why the community should care about something so insignificant as a damaged rose or a crushed crocus. She is challenging people who are blasé and examining their **insularity**: 'why should we care … corpses, remote, crushed, mutilated?' Are there consequences if people do not care?

Boland criticises her own community in lines 22–30, with the neighbours described as hiding behind curtains ('subterfuge'). This 'I don't want to know' attitude reflects the **ambivalence** about the Northern Troubles in the Irish Republic during the 1970s. The tension, 'I pause, wait', is followed by release: 'breathe relief'. At the conclusion, there are two insightful views. One is the suburban woman's; the other is an Irish person's awareness of connecting with past history. There is an ancestral memory, 'atavism', which associates the smashed rose with the destruction of the Irish. The ribbon trails back to the violence of English colonialism. Boland and her neighbours chose not to confront the horse, just like the Irish did not successfully confront the invaders. The intruder (the horse, the British) destroyed something beautiful and precious (the rose, Irish culture and freedom). The mood here is one of loss and regret. Should both intruders have been challenged? How right is it to live so indifferently? The poem ends on a bleak note, a lament for **'a world betrayed'**.

Writing About the Poem

'We are collectively involved in violence which occurs in our land.' Discuss how 'The War Horse' reflects this statement. Illustrate your response with reference to the poem.

Sample Paragraph

Boland uses an ordinary, domestic incident, the arrival of a tinker's horse into a suburban Dublin garden, to explore the ambivalent attitude to wars that seem distant. The colloquial phrase 'No great harm is done' and the neighbours who use 'the subterfuge/Of curtains' both illustrate this insular approach. Everything is all right so long as 'we' are safe. The consequences of war are listed as Boland itemises them: 'maimed limb', 'now will never climb', 'expendable', 'screamless dead'. The vulnerability of the innocent victims is exposed. Can we afford to be so indifferent? The implicit statement is that we should care. She then conveys the ancestral memory of how Ireland was invaded by the British. The word 'Ribboned' recalls the Ribbonmen, a secret society that was active against the invaders for a while. We are left feeling that perhaps due to the majority of Irish people's indifference and through a lack of commitment, 'A cause' was lost. The poem ends with a lament, 'a world betrayed', with its long echoing vowel sound. I think Boland is upset at people's lack of commitment in a time of trouble.

EXAMINER'S COMMENT

This response succinctly addresses the task through a discussion on the theme and style of the poem. It ranges from the local incident to war's inevitable consequences and people's indifference. Close engagement with the text is evident in the discussion of colloquial language and sound effects. Good use is made of the rhetorical question, 'Can we afford to be so indifferent?' This well-controlled answer merits the top grade.

Class/Homework Exercises

1. Is 'The War Horse' a private poem, or does it have a wider significance? Use reference to the text in your answer.
2. Eavan Boland creates an underlying sense of threat throughout 'The War Horse'. Discuss this view using close reference to the poem.

Summary Points

- **Themes include attitudes to conflict and violence throughout Irish history.**
- **Inclusive personal pronouns and rhetorical questions used to involve readers.**
- **Use of observational details, vibrant language, striking comparisons.**
- **Contrasting atmospheres and tones – reflective, accusatory.**
- **Memorable onomatopoeic effects – assonance, alliteration, internal rhyme.**

Child of Our Time (for Aengus)

Yesterday I knew no lullaby
But you have taught me overnight to order
This song, which takes from your final cry
Its tune, from your unreasoned end its reason,
Its rhythm from the discord of your murder
Its motive from the fact you cannot listen.

We who should have known how to instruct
With rhymes for your waking, rhythms for your sleep,
Names for the animals you took to bed,
Tales to distract, legends to protect,
Later an idiom for you to keep
And living, learn, must learn from you, dead,

To make our broken images rebuild
Themselves around your limbs, your broken
Image, find for your sake whose life our idle
Talk has cost, a new language. Child
Of our time, our times have robbed your cradle.
Sleep in a world your final sleep has woken.

discord: lack of harmony among people; harsh, confused sounds; conflict.

idiom: turn of phrase; words which when used together have a different meaning from when used singly.

'our times have robbed your cradle'

Personal Response

1. Boland believes that the 'murder of the innocent' is one of the greatest obscenities. How is this explored in the poem? Write a paragraph in response.
2. Where are the two feelings, tenderness and outrage, evident in the poem? Use reference to the text in your response.
3. What is Boland implying about 'our times'? Is she satisfied or dissatisfied with what is happening? Refer closely to the text in your answer.

Critical Literacy

'Child of Our Time' was written in 1974 at the height of the Troubles in Northern Ireland. It was prompted by a harrowing newspaper picture of a fireman tenderly carrying a dead child from the rubble of a bomb explosion in Dublin. The poem is dedicated to Aengus, the infant son of the poet's friend, who had suffered cot death. This lyric is a response to the sudden and unexpected death of all young children. It also challenges adults to change their ways.

The title of this poem places the little child in a wider context than that of family and town – he is a child of 'our time'. He is our responsibility; he belongs to us. A child should be a **symbol of innocence**, growth, love, potential and the future, but this has been savagely and tragically cut short by 'our time'. Boland did not have children when she wrote this poem ('Yesterday I knew no lullaby'), but in the first stanza she describes how she has been taught to sing a lullaby which is different: 'you have taught me overnight to order/This song.'

The child's violent and tragic death demands a response, so she will form and order and 'reason' a poem from the child's 'unreasoned end'. It is a song made of harsh sounds, 'discord'. The tone moves from tender compassion ('lullaby') to indignation ('the fact you cannot listen'). There is no escaping the finality of death, yet the poet is a balanced, reasonable person trying to make **order out of disorder** in a poem that is carefully arranged in three stanzas.

The poem is also charged with both **sadness and awareness**. The compassionate voice of the poet is heard in 'rhythms for your sleep,/Names for the animals you took to bed'. However, Boland is aware of the awfulness of the event: 'final cry', 'end', 'murder'. The language is formal, as befits such a solemn occasion: 'We who should have known', 'Child/Of our time'. This poem has several elements of an elegy (a poem for the dead): it laments, praises and consoles. The poem's many half-rhymes mimic this discordant time: 'idle'/'cradle', 'order'/'murder'.

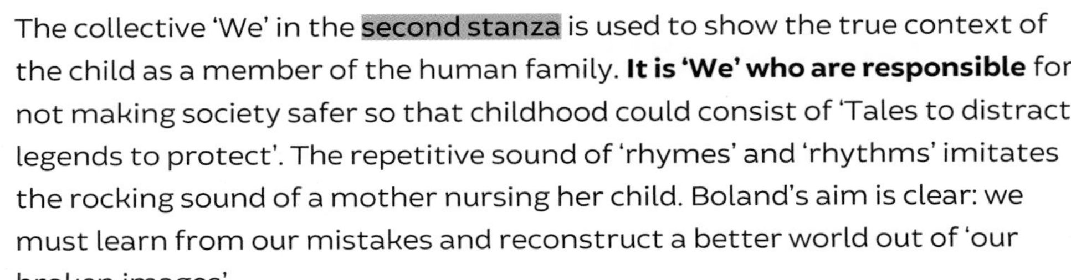

The collective 'We' in the second stanza is used to show the true context of the child as a member of the human family. **It is 'We' who are responsible** for not making society safer so that childhood could consist of 'Tales to distract, legends to protect'. The repetitive sound of 'rhymes' and 'rhythms' imitates the rocking sound of a mother nursing her child. Boland's aim is clear: we must learn from our mistakes and reconstruct a better world out of 'our broken images'.

In the third stanza, the poet is insistent that **society takes on this responsibility**, that we 'find ... a new language'. We have to engage in dialogue, not 'idle/Talk', so that we can deliver a safer world for our children. Ironically, it is the little child, who 'our time' has 'robbed' from his cradle, who will form the scaffold around which we can build a new and better society: 'rebuild/Themselves around your limbs'. The final line of the poem is a **prayer and a hope**: 'Sleep in a world your final sleep has woken.' It is a wish that the little child be at rest now and that the world may be woken to its senses by his death.

Writing About the Poem

'Eavan Boland is a "sensitive poet" who is "rarely thrown off balance by anger".' Discuss this view of the poet in relation to the poem, 'Child of Our Time'. Support your answer with reference to the text.

Sample Paragraph

'Child of Our Time' is an example of Boland's control in the face of what must be the most horrific event that humanity can witness: the brutal and senseless murder of an innocent child. The poem is carefully ordered into three that act as balanced paragraphs in an argument. The first stanza emphasises the meaningless atrocity of 'your unreasoned end'. The second places responsibility where it belongs, on the adult society that should have provided a safe environment for the young: 'We who should have known'. The third stanza urges the adults to do something now, to 'find for your sake whose life our idle/Talk has cost, a new language'. Boland's language is formal and controlled, appropriate for an elegy. When I listen to Ravel's 'Pavane for a Dead Infant', I hear the same dignified rhythm. There are just four sentences in this lyric. The child has taught the poet a lullaby with his death. The adults must learn from this tragedy – they have to learn to talk. The balance is impressive, as the poet

EXAMINER'S COMMENT

Boland's careful management of ideas is explored in this answer to advance the view that she explores the tragic event in a controlled, sensitive way. Attention is paid to the form of the poem: 'The poem is carefully ordered into three stanzas that act as balanced paragraphs in an argument.' The comment relating to music also shows good personal engagement. Clear expression and effective use of accurate quotation enhances this highly successful top-grade response.

makes order out of disorder rather than letting her anger explode. The poem lacks sentimentality or even consolation. Instead, the quiet, insistent voice states that 'we' 'must learn'. Sometimes a soft voice delivers a more powerful message. Boland sensitively deals with a tragic event with an absence of anger and with an insistence that, as a result, lessons must be learned.

Class/Homework Exercises

1. There is a 'difficult sort of comfort' in literature. Discuss this statement in relation to 'Child of Our Time'. Support the points you make with reference to the poem.
2. In 'Child of Our Time', Boland explores the universal experience of tragic violence. To what extent do you agree with this view? Support the points you make with reference to both the themes and language use in the poem.

Summary Points

- **Addresses issues surrounding the tragic death of a child.**
- **Striking images of innocence, poignant mood, repetition.**
- **Universal significance of random violence and tragedy.**
- **Solemn, didactic tone emphasised by extended uninterrupted lines.**

3 The Famine Road

During the Irish Famine of 1845–48, the British authorities organised various relief schemes. The hungry were given a small wage to buy food for participating in road building and other community projects. Many of the new roads were constructed in remote areas and served little purpose other than controlling the starving population.

'Idle as trout in light Colonel Jones,
these Irish, give them no coins at all; their bones
need toil, their characters no less.' Trevelyan's
seal blooded the deal table. The Relief
Committee deliberated: 'Might it be safe,
Colonel, to give them roads, roads to force
from nowhere, going nowhere of course?'

'one out of every ten and then
another third of those again
women – in a case like yours.'

Sick, directionless they worked; fork, stick
were iron years away; after all could
they not blood their knuckles on rock, suck
April hailstones for water and for food?
Why for that, cunning as housewives, each eyed –
as if at a corner butcher – the other's buttock.

'anything may have caused it, spores,
a childhood accident; one sees
day after day these mysteries.'

Dusk: they will work tomorrow without him.
They know it and walk clear; he has become
a typhoid pariah, his blood tainted, although
he shares it with some there. No more than snow
attends its own flakes where they settle
and melt, will they pray by his death rattle.

'You never will, never you know
but take it well woman, grow
your garden, keep house, good-bye.'

'It has gone better than we expected, Lord
Trevelyan, sedition, idleness, cured
in one; from parish to parish, field to field,
the wretches work till they are quite worn,
then fester by their work; we march the corn
to the ships in peace; this Tuesday I saw bones
out of my carriage window, your servant Jones.'

'Barren, never to know the load
of his child in you, what is your body
now if not a famine road?'

Colonel Jones: army officer and Chairman of the Board of Works.

Trevelyan: Charles Trevelyan, a senior civil servant in overall charge of famine relief.

Relief Committee: groups usually consisting of landlords, the clergy and influential people were set up to distribute food.

deliberated: considered, discussed.

spores: germs.

typhoid pariah: someone shunned because of this deadly blood disease.

death rattle: last sound of the dying.

sedition: subversion, treachery.

corn/to the ships: throughout the famine years, corn was exported from Ireland.

Personal Response

1. Describe the tone of voice in the opening stanza, using close reference to the text.
2. The poet links the abuse of famine victims with the mistreatment of women in modern society. Is this convincing? Explain your answer.
3. In your view, how chillingly pessimistic are the last three lines of the poem? Give reasons for your answer.

Critical Literacy

The poem raises interesting questions about marginalised people, a favourite theme in Boland's work. Here she makes a connection between a famine road in the 1840s and an infertile woman in modern times. Boland presents the poem as a series of dramatic moments featuring a variety of characters.

Stanza one begins with the voice of Colonel Jones, a British official, reading from a letter written by Lord Trevelyan, who had overall responsibility for famine relief. The boorish tone of the opening comments about 'these Irish' is explicitly offensive. Trevelyan's generalised insults reflect the **depth of prejudice and suspicion** felt towards an entire population, who are 'Idle as trout in light'. Such ruthless disregard is further underlined by the vivid image of the official blood-red seal. The proposed solutions – 'toil' or hard labour building roads 'going nowhere' – could hardly be more cynical and are all the more ironic coming from the 'Relief Committee'.

Stanza two (like stanzas four and six) is italicised and introduces another speaker, the authoritative voice of a consultant doctor. The unidentified voice quoting statistics to an unnamed woman is casually impersonal. The situation becomes clearer as the poem continues: the medical expert is discussing the woman's failure to have children. Boland portrays him as insensitive and patronising: 'anything may have caused it.' His tone becomes increasingly **unsympathetic as he dismisses her disappointment**: 'You never will, never you know.' He almost seems to take delight in repeating the word 'never'. The doctor's final comments are as severe as some of the remarks made by any of the British officials: 'take it well woman, grow/your garden, keep house.'

In stanza three, the poet herself imagines the terrible experiences of the famine victims. The language used to describe their struggle is

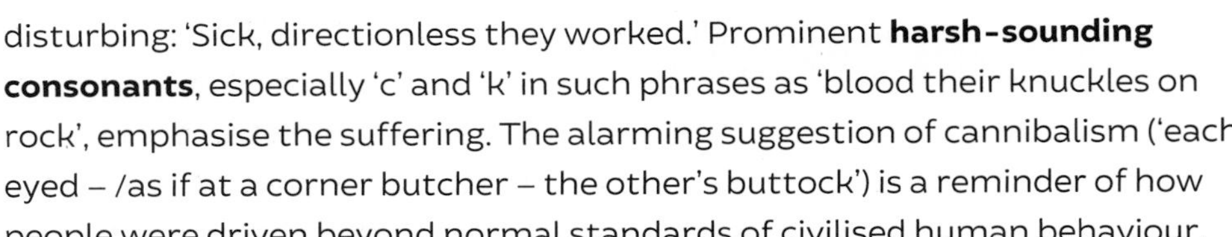

disturbing: 'Sick, directionless they worked.' Prominent **harsh-sounding consonants**, especially 'c' and 'k' in such phrases as 'blood their knuckles on rock', emphasise the suffering. The alarming suggestion of cannibalism ('each eyed – /as if at a corner butcher – the other's buttock') is a reminder of how people were driven beyond normal standards of civilised human behaviour.

Stanza five focuses on the prevalence of death throughout the long famine years. Attitudes harden as widespread disease becomes commonplace. The poet's direct description, steady rhythm and resigned tone combine to reflect the awful reality of the times: 'they will work tomorrow without him.' Boland illustrates the **breakdown of communities** with the tragic example of one 'typhoid pariah' abandoned to die without anyone to 'pray by his death rattle'.

This great human catastrophe is made all the more pathetic in stanza seven, which begins with an excerpt from Colonel Jones's response to Trevelyan: 'It has gone better than we expected.' **The offhand tone is self-satisfied** as he reports that the road-building schemes have succeeded in their real purpose of controlling the peasant population ('the wretches'). The horrifyingly detached admission – without the slightest sense of irony – of allowing the starving to 'fester' while 'we march the corn/to the ships' is almost beyond comprehension. The colonel's matter-of-fact comment about seeing 'bones/out of my carriage window' is a final reminder of the colossal gulf between the powerful and the powerless.

In the final stanza, Boland's **own feelings of revulsion** bring her back to the present when she sums up the 'Barren' reality of the childless woman 'never to know the load/of his child'. The famine road is reintroduced as a common symbol for the shared tragedies of both the victims of mass starvation and infertility. The concluding rhetorical question leaves us to consider important issues of authority and the abuse of power, whatever the circumstances.

Writing About the Poem

'Eavan Boland uses evocative symbols to address important issues.' Discuss this statement in relation to 'The Famine Road', supporting your points with suitable quotation or reference.

Sample Paragraph

The deserted famine road in Boland's poem is a haunting symbol through which we can examine aspects of power and powerlessness. The poet blends two narratives, one of a country road in the 1840s and the other of a modern-day visit to a doctor, in a series of dramatic scenes. Lord Trevelyan and the doctor abuse their power. Trevelyan's offensive

comments, 'these Irish', 'Idle as trout in light', set the tone. This ignorance is mirrored in the doctor's response to his infertile patient, 'You never will, never you know'. The harsh repetition of 'never' emphasises the awful truth to the unfortunate woman. Severe remedies are handed out to both the famine workers and the woman: the workers will 'toil' to build roads 'going nowhere', the woman will 'grow/your garden, keep house' for a non-existent family. The superior, patronising attitude of those in charge is captured in snippets of direct speech, 'It has gone better than we expected', 'but take it well woman'. Boland often focuses on the marginalised in society. None of the famine victims' voices are heard in this poem, and this omission emphasises their lack of power and their vulnerability. Instead, the 'wretches work till they are quite worn'. The alliterative 'w' stresses the futile never-ending effort. The workers cannot produce food to feed themselves, the barren woman cannot carry a child. Nothing changes. The concluding question invites us to consider the abuse of power and the raw tragedy of the victims through the image of the famine road.

EXAMINER'S COMMENT

This top-grade response traces the two interconnected narratives, focusing on the dramatic significance of these events. The similar tones of those in charge are well explored: Trevelyan's 'offensive' remarks are mirrored in 'the doctor's response to his infertile patient'. An interesting point is made about the omission of the victims' voices. Expression is controlled and confident throughout.

Class/Homework Exercises

1. To what extent does 'The Famine Road' show Eavan Boland's sympathies for the outsiders and the marginalised in society? Refer to the poem in your answer.
2. Eavan Boland makes effective use of several dramatic techniques in 'The Famine Road'. Discuss this view, supporting your points with close reference to the poem.

Summary Points

- **Dramatic recreation of famine suffering and exploitation.**
- **Updated comparison with the experience of an infertile woman.**
- **Authentic language, descriptive details, stark imagery, symbols.**
- **Sound effects echo the harsh, cynical atmosphere.**

4 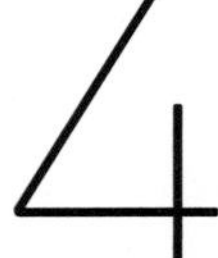 The Shadow Doll

A shadow doll was sent to the bride-to-be in Victorian times by her dressmaker. It consisted of a Victorian figurine under a dome of glass modelling the proposed wedding dress.

They stitched blooms from ivory tulle
to hem the oyster gleam of the veil.
They made hoops for the crinoline.

Now, in summary and neatly sewn –
a porcelain bride in an airless glamour –
the shadow doll survives its occasion.

Under glass, under wraps, it stays
even now, after all, discreet about
visits, fevers, quickenings and lusts

and just how, when she looked at
the shell-tone spray of seed pearls,
the bisque features, she could see herself

inside it all, holding less than real
stephanotis, rose petals, never feeling
satin rise and fall with the vows

I kept repeating on the night before –
astray among the cards and wedding gifts –
the coffee pots and the clocks and

the battered tan case full of cotton
lace and tissue-paper, pressing down, then
pressing down again. And then, locks.

tulle: fine net fabric.

oyster: off-white colour.

crinoline: hooped petticoat.

discreet: careful to avoid embarrassment by keeping confidences secret; unobtrusive.

quickenings: sensations; a woman's awareness of the first movements of the child in the womb.

bisque: unglazed white porcelain.

stephanotis: scented white flowers used for displays at both weddings and funerals.

Personal Response

1. What style of language is used to describe the doll? Do you consider it beautiful or stifling, or both? Illustrate your response with reference to the poem.
2. Choose two phrases from the poem that you found particularly interesting. Explain the reasons for your choice.
3. Do you think marriage has changed for the modern bride? Refer to the last two stanzas in your answer.

Critical Literacy

'The Shadow Doll' is taken from the 1990 collection of poems, *Outside History*. The shadow doll wore a model of the wedding dress for the bride-to-be. Boland uses the doll as a symbol to explore the submission and silence surrounding women and women's issues by placing the late-twentieth century and Victorian times side by side.

The first two stanzas describe the doll vividly, with her 'ivory tulle' and 'oyster gleam'. The 'porcelain doll' is a **beautiful, fragile object**, but the 'ivory' and 'oyster' colours are lifeless. Passivity and restriction are being shown in the phrase 'neatly sewn'. The pronoun 'it' is used – the woman is seen as an object, not a real flesh-and-blood human being. The community is described in the preparations: 'They stitched', 'They made'. Are they colluding in the constraint? The phrase 'airless glamour' conveys an allure that has been deprived of life-giving oxygen. The occasion of the marriage is long gone, but the doll remains as a reminder, a shadow of what was.

The **language of containment** and imprisonment is continued in stanza three: 'Under glass, under wraps.' The doll is silent and 'discreet'; it knows but does not tell. The bride would have kept the doll throughout her life, so the doll would have been present at all major events such as marriage, childbirth, sickness and intimate moments, 'visits, fevers, quickenings and lusts'. These experiences are not explored in poetry, which is why women and their issues are 'outside history'. They are neither recorded nor commented on.

Stanza four sees the **pronoun change to 'she'** as the poet imagines the Victorian bride considering her own wedding: 'she could see herself/inside it all.' It is as if she becomes like the doll, assuming a mask of 'bisque features' and unable to feel real life: 'holding less than

'a porcelain bride'

real/stephanotis', 'never feeling/satin rise and fall with the vows'. The only remnant of her life is the silent doll. Stanza five ends with the word 'vows', and this is the link into the next stanza, which is a view from the twentieth-century bride where the narrative voice becomes 'I'.

The poet is 'repeating' the same vows as the Victorian bride. Are these entrapping and imprisoning women? Like the Victorian bride, the modern bride is surrounded by things ('cards and wedding gifts'), yet she is 'astray' (stanza six), with the same **sense of disorientation** coming over her. Is she feeling this because she is losing her individual identity as she agrees to become part of a couple?

Stanza seven increases the **feelings of restriction** when the suitcase is described as 'battered', and there is the added emphatic repetition of 'pressing down'. Finally, the single monosyllable 'locks' clicks the poem to an end. The onomatopoeic sound echoes through the years as Boland voices the silence in the depressing ending. For some women, little has changed since Victorian times.

Writing About the Poem

'Boland's poems often end on a bleak note.' Discuss how 'The Shadow Doll' reflects this statement. Illustrate your response with reference to the text.

Sample Paragraph

The onomatopoeia of the monosyllabic word 'locks' echoes with frightening intensity at the end of 'The Shadow Doll'. It suggests to me the clang of a prison door as the prisoner is denied freedom. This poem explores the nature and meaning of marriage for women. It starts with the description of the Victorian doll with its wedding dress, which seems to become a stifling mask fitted on a living, breathing woman, 'airless glamour', 'Under glass', 'under wraps'. The modern bride is 'astray'. Marriage is shown as confining and silencing, 'discreet'. The repetition of the phrase 'pressing down' has an almost nightmarish sense of claustrophobia. Both the Victorian bride and the modern bride are surrounded by objects, 'seed pearls', 'stephanotis', 'the cards and wedding gifts'. I find it strange that there is no mention of the groom, or friends or families. Instead there is a growing sense of isolation and intimidation culminating in the echoing phrase 'And then, locks'. What or who is locked in? What or who is locked out?

EXAMINER'S COMMENT

This short response carefully considers the effect of the poem's ending and Boland's exploration of the theme of marriage as a repressive and restricting force in women's lives. The paragraph also touches on interesting questions about the narrow views expressed in the poem. A real sense of individual engagement is evident, particularly in the comment about the final two rhetorical questions. Top-grade standard.

Class/Homework Exercises

1. 'In her poetry, Boland uses concrete images to explore themes.' In your opinion, how valid is this statement? Use reference to 'The Shadow Doll' in your answer.
2. In 'The Shadow Doll', Boland succeeds in highlighting the experience of women in patriarchal societies. Discuss this view using close reference to the poem.

Summary Points

- **Themes include the changing nature of marriage and the oppression of women.**
- **Effective concrete details, symbolism, confinement imagery, repetition.**
- **Dreamlike sense of disorientation.**
- **Varying tones – reflective, sympathetic, critical and hopeful.**

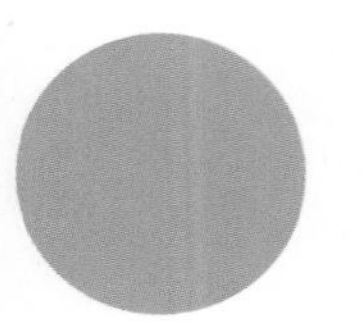

5 White Hawthorn in the West of Ireland

Hawthorn is a flowering tree that blossoms in springtime. It is associated with fairy tales and superstitions in Irish folklore. People believed that it was unlucky to cut hawthorn or to keep it indoors.

I drove West
in the season between seasons.
I left behind suburban gardens.
Lawnmowers. Small talk.

Under low skies, past splashes of coltsfoot,
I assumed
the hard shyness of Atlantic light
and the superstitious aura of hawthorn.

All I wanted then was to fill my arms with
sharp flowers,
to seem, from a distance, to be part of
that ivory, downhill rush. But I knew,

I had always known
the custom was
not to touch hawthorn.
Not to bring it indoors for the sake of

the luck
such constraint would forfeit –
a child might die, perhaps, or an unexplained
fever speckle heifers. So I left it

stirring on those hills
with a fluency
only water has. And, like water, able
to re-define land. And free to seem to be –

for anglers,
and for travellers astray in
the unmarked lights of a May dusk –
the only language spoken in those parts.

the season: between spring and summer.

coltsfoot: wild plant with yellow flowers.
assumed: became part of.
Atlantic light: unsettled weather causes the light to vary.
superstitious aura: disquiet associated with hawthorn stories.

forfeit: lose, risk.

heifers: cows which have not yet had calves.

Personal Response

1. Describe the poet's changing mood as she travels from her suburban home to the West. Refer to the text in your answer.
2. There are many beautiful images in the poem. Choose two that you find interesting and briefly explain their appeal.
3. What is the significance of the white hawthorn? What might it symbolise? Refer closely to the poem in your answer.

Critical Literacy

In this poem, the folklore associated with hawthorn in rural Ireland is seen as symbolic of an ancient 'language' that has almost disappeared. Boland structures her themes around the image of a journey into the West. It seems as though she is hoping to return to her roots in the traditional landscape of the West of Ireland.

The poem opens on a conversational note. Boland's clear intention is to leave the city behind: 'I drove West/in the season between seasons'. Her tone is determined, dismissing the **artificial life of suburbia** ('Lawnmowers. Small talk.') in favour of the freedom awaiting her. Stanza one emphasises the poet's strong desire to get away from her cultivated suburban confines, which seem colourless and overly regulated. The broken rhythm of line 4 adds to the abrupt sense of rigidity.

'the superstitious aura'

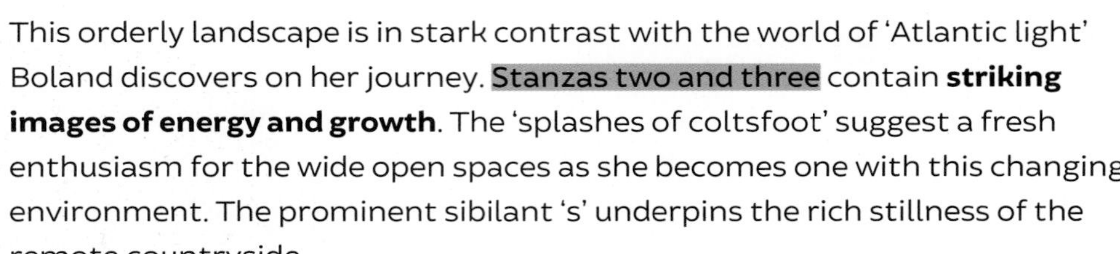

This orderly landscape is in stark contrast with the world of 'Atlantic light' Boland discovers on her journey. Stanzas two and three contain **striking images of energy and growth**. The 'splashes of coltsfoot' suggest a fresh enthusiasm for the wide open spaces as she becomes one with this changing environment. The prominent sibilant 's' underpins the rich stillness of the remote countryside.

She seems both fearful and fascinated by the hawthorn's 'superstitious aura'. The experience is similar to an artist becoming increasingly absorbed in the joy of painting. Run-on lines and the frequent use of the pronoun 'I' accentuate our appreciation of the **poet's own delight** in 'that ivory, downhill rush'.

Stanzas four and five focus on the mystery and superstition associated with hawthorn in Irish folk tradition. Boland's awareness of the **possible dangers** check her eagerness as she considers the stories that have been handed down: 'a child might die, perhaps.' The poet is momentarily caught between a desire to fill her arms with these wild flowers and her own disquieting belief in the superstitions. Eventually, she decides to follow her intuition and respect the customs of the West:
'So I left it.'

The personification ('stirring') of the hawthorn in stanza six reinforces Boland's regard for this unfamiliar landscape as a **living place**. The poet's imagination has also been stirred by her journey. In comparing the hawthorn to water, she suggests its elemental power. Both share a natural 'fluency' which can shape and 're-define land'.

The poet links the twin forces of superstition and landscape even more forcibly in stanza seven. They both defy time and transcend recorded history. The hawthorn trees give the poet a **glimpse of Ireland's ancient culture**. Although nature remains elusive, Boland believes that for outsiders like herself – visiting 'anglers' and tourists – it is 'the only language spoken in these parts'. Her final tone is one of resignation as she accepts that she can never fully understand Ireland's unique landscape or the past.

Writing About the Poem

'Boland uses a variety of poetic techniques to create poems which allow readers to contemplate the beauty and mystery of nature.' Discuss this statement, with particular reference to 'White Hawthorn in the West of Ireland'.

Sample Paragraph

Eavan Boland creates vivid word pictures of two contrasting landscapes, the ordered urban and the wild rural. She decisively sets off on her journey, 'I left behind suburban gardens'. Suddenly the view opens out to the big western skyline, full of variable weather, 'the hard shyness of Atlantic light'. The magic of the countryside is encapsulated in the 'superstitious aura of hawthorn'. The lush assonance of this line's broad vowels contrasts abruptly with the sharp sounds of the town's descriptive details. The short lines of the first stanza are replaced by long run-on lines mirroring the energy of nature, 'that ivory downhill rush', and the poet's delight, 'All I wanted then was to fill my arms/with sharp flowers'. But there is another aspect to nature foreshadowed in the adjective, 'sharp'. Cutting the hawthorn is considered bad luck in the countryside and Boland respects the local tradition, 'So I left it'. She, like the other tourists, may enjoy, but not fully understand the wild beauty of nature, 'the only language spoken in those parts'. Because of Boland's remarkable poetic skills, readers are left puzzling over nature's beauty, 'astray in/the unmarked lights of a May dusk'.

EXAMINER'S COMMENT

This answer focuses on how aspects of Boland's style contribute to communicating her message that nature may be appreciated but never entirely understood. A developed discussion encompasses the poet's use of varying tones and sound effects: 'The lush assonance of this line's broad vowels contrast sharply with the sharp sounds of the town's descriptive details.' Accurate quotation supports the discussion throughout. A confident top-grade standard.

Class/Homework Exercises

1. What do you think Eavan Boland has learned from her journey to the West of Ireland? Refer to the poem, 'White Hawthorn in the West of Ireland', in your answer.
2. Boland makes effective use of both visual and aural imagery to celebrate the Irish landscape in this poem. Discuss this statement, using close reference to the text.

Summary Points

- **Beauty of the native landscape and Irish traditions are central themes.**
- **Contrast between urban and rural landscapes.**
- **Reflective tone reveals the poet's personal feelings and attitudes.**
- **Vivid visual imagery, free rhythm, striking onomatopoeia and sibilant effects.**

6 Outside History

There are outsiders, always. These stars –
these iron inklings of an Irish January,
whose light happened

thousands of years before
our pain did: they are, they have always been
outside history.

They keep their distance. Under them remains
a place where you found
you were human, and

a landscape in which you know you are mortal.
And a time to choose between them.
I have chosen:

out of myth into history I move to be
part of that ordeal
whose darkness is

only now reaching me from those fields,
those rivers, those roads clotted as
firmaments with the dead.

How slowly they die
as we kneel beside them, whisper in their ear.
And we are too late. We are always too late.

inklings: slight idea or suspicion; clues.

history: record or account of past events and developments; the study of these.

mortal: destined to die.

myth: tale with supernatural characters; untrue idea or explanation; imaginary person; story with a germ of truth in it.
ordeal: painful experience.

clotted as: clogged up.

firmaments: sky or heavens.

Personal Response

1. How are the stars 'outsiders'? Do you think they are an effective symbol for those who are marginalised and regarded as of no importance? Discuss, using reference from the poem.
2. In your opinion, what does Boland mean by the final line of the poem?
3. Write a short personal response to 'Outside History', highlighting the impact the poem made on you.

Critical Literacy

'Outside History' was written in 1990 as part of a collection of poems that were arranged to reflect the changing seasons. This poem is set in January. Boland believes that it is important to remember the experiences of those who have not been recorded in history. These are the outsiders, 'the lost, the voiceless, the silent' to whom she gives a hauntingly beautiful voice.

Lines 1–6. The poem opens with an **impersonal statement**: 'There are outsiders, always'. The poet is referring to those who have not been recorded in history. The stars are also outsiders, standing outside and above human history. At their great distance, they are shown as cold and distant ('iron', 'Irish January'). They have a permanence and longevity that are in contrast to human life: 'whose light happened/thousands of years before/our pain did.' The run-on line suggests the light that travels thousands of years to reach us. The phrase 'outside history' is placed on its own to emphasise how the stars do not belong to human history.

Lines 7–10. The poet stresses **the remoteness of the stars**: 'They keep their distance'. They don't want to be involved. Now she turns to 'you', a member of the human race, and places 'you' in context with the words 'place' and 'landscape'. This is where 'you found/you were human' and 'mortal'. Unlike the stars; 'you' are a suffering member of the human race who is subject to ageing and death. The line 'And a time to choose between them' could refer to choosing between the perspective of the stars, i.e. remaining at an uninvolved distance, or the perspective of a member of the human race, i.e. involved and anguished.

Lines 11–18. The phrase 'I have chosen' marks a **turning point** in the poem. Boland has made a deliberate decision, moving away from 'myth' and tradition. She felt that myth obscures history. She regarded figures like Caitlín Ní Houlihán and Dark Rosaleen, female symbols for Ireland, as 'passive', 'simplified' and 'decorative' emblems in male poems. For the poet, history was laced with myths, which, in her opinion, were as unreal, cold and distant as the stars are from reality. She regarded these mythic emblems as false and limiting, 'a corruption'. Boland is trying to achieve a sense of

belonging and wholeness by unwinding the myth and the stereotype. She wanted reality rather than the glittering image of the stars: 'out of myth into history I move to be/part of that ordeal.'

Just as the stars' light travelled vast distances to reach us, so the darkness of unwritten history is travelling to reach her 'only now'. The run-on stanza again suggests great distances that had to be covered for the poet to connect with the past. There follows a description that recalls the **Irish famine**: 'those fields', 'those rivers', 'those roads' which were covered with 'the dead'. The paradoxical phrase 'clotted as/firmaments' uses the language of the stars to describe the numberless bodies strewn everywhere as a result of the famine. This condensed image evokes a poignant sense of the soft mounds of victims lying as numberless as the stars.

Lines 19–21. The concluding stanza changes to the collective 'we'. Is this referring to the Irish people accepting responsibility for **honouring the dead** and being part of history? The rite of contrition is being said: 'As we kneel beside them, whisper in their ear.' It was believed that the person's soul would go to rest in heaven as he or she had made their peace with God, but the repetition of the last line stresses that the words of comfort have come 'too late'. The people don't know they are being honoured by the poet. Nevertheless, the poem stands as a testament to them and their unrecorded history. Has Boland changed her attitude from the beginning of the poem: 'There are outsiders, always'? Has she brought them in from the cold sidelines, including them into history? Or has she (and we) left it too late?

Writing About the Poem

'Eavan Boland's poetry gives a haunting voice to the marginalised and dispossessed in society.' Discuss this statement, with particular reference to 'Outside History'.

Sample Paragraph

In our modern affluent world, there are many marginalised people. A stark statement opens the poem, 'There are outsiders, always', reminiscent of Christ's statement that the poor are always with us. I found the symbol of the stars effective because they represented the cold distance the outsiders must feel as they look in, but don't belong, 'they have always been/outside history'. The sympathetic tone and the alliterative phrase, 'iron inklings of an Irish January' evocatively capture the predicament facing marginalised people. The stars show no human empathy with the dispossessed, 'They keep their distance'. But Boland has 'chosen' to embrace her humane side. She will be 'part of that ordeal'

in order to give a voice to those forgotten, 'whose darkness is/only now reaching me'. The run-on stanza indicates how long it has taken. She gives them an unforgettable voice, recalling their tragic story, 'those roads clotted as/ firmaments with the dead'. The blunt verb 'clotted' resounds with the obscenity of what happened to the unknown victims, evoking anonymous mounds of earth where they lay. The poem ends with the melancholy realisation, 'And we are too late'. They won't know that they are being remembered. The dispossessed may not, but Boland has given them a voice – both to present and future generations.

EXAMINER'S COMMENT

As part of a full essay this perceptive reading of Boland's poem addresses the task directly in a series of accurately referenced arguments. Excellent use of quotation throughout supports the thoughtful discussion points. Expression is also clear and impressive, 'But Boland has chosen to embrace her humane side'. An informed exploration of the poet's language also ensures the top-grade standard.

Class/Homework Exercises

1. Does 'Outside History' make a compelling case on behalf of voiceless and marginalised people? Support your answer with close reference to the text of the poem.
2. In your opinion, what does the dominant tone throughout the poem reveal about Eavan Boland as a person? Support your answer with close reference to the text.

Summary Points

- **Key themes – exclusion of the marginalised.**
- **Boland's distrust of myth, history and stereotypes.**
- **Varying tones – reflective, regretful, didactic.**
- **Effective use of repetition, striking imagery.**

7 The Black Lace Fan My Mother Gave Me

It was the first gift he ever gave her,
buying it for five francs in the Galeries
in pre-war Paris. It was stifling.
A starless drought made the nights stormy.

Galeries: Paris store.

They stayed in the city for the summer.
They met in cafés. She was always early.
He was late. That evening he was later.
They wrapped the fan. He looked at his watch.

She looked down the Boulevard des Capucines.
She ordered more coffee. She stood up.
The streets were emptying. The heat was killing.
She thought the distance smelled of rain and lightning.

These are wild roses, appliquéd on silk by hand,
darkly picked, stitched boldly, quickly.
The rest is tortoiseshell and has the reticent,
clear patience of its element. It is

appliquéd: trimming.
tortoiseshell: clear decorative material.
reticent: reserved, restrained.

a worn-out, underwater bullion and it keeps,
even now, an inference of its violation.
The lace is overcast as if the weather
it opened for and offset had entered it.

bullion: treasure.

The past is an empty café terrace.
An airless dusk before thunder. A man running.
And no way now to know what happened then –
none at all – unless, of course, you improvise:

improvise: make up, imagine.

The blackbird on this first sultry morning,
in summer, finding buds, worms, fruit,
feels the heat. Suddenly she puts out her wing –
the whole, full, flirtatious span of it.

flirtatious: enticing, playful.
span: extent, measure.

Personal Response

1. The setting is important in this poem. Briefly explain what it contributes to the atmosphere, referring to the text in your answer.
2. Comment on the effect of the short sentences and irregular rhythms in the first three stanzas.
3. Did you like this poem? Give reasons for your response, referring to the text of the poem in your answer.

Critical Literacy

Set in pre-war Paris in the 1930s, the incident that occurs is the giving of a gift, a black lace fan that the poet's father gave to her mother. A fan was usually seen as a sign of romantic love and desire. However, its significance here is never entirely explained to us. Maybe this is in recognition of our inability to fully understand other people's relationships or to recall the past and the effect it has on us. Boland's poem is one of those attempts.

Stanza one begins on a narrative note as the poet recreates a pivotal moment in her parents' lives back in the 1930s. **The fan was a special symbol of young love** and was important because it was 'the first gift' from her father to her mother. Other details of the precise cost and the 'stifling' weather add to the importance of the occasion. Although the Parisian

'And no way now to know what happened then'

setting is romantic, the mood is tense. Their courtship is framed in a series of captured moments, as though Boland is flicking through an old photo album.

In stanzas two and three, short sentences and the growing unevenness of the rhythm add to this cinematic quality: 'They met in cafés. She was always early.' The hesitant relationship between the lovers is conveyed repeatedly through their nervous gestures: 'He looked at his watch', 'She stood up'. Boland builds up the tension through references to the heat wave: 'the distance smelled of rain and lightning.' The image might also suggest the **stormy nature of what lay ahead** for the couple.

Stanzas four and five focus on the elegant lace fan in **vivid detail**. Boland notes its decorative qualities, carefully embroidered with the most romantic 'wild roses' and fine 'tortoiseshell'. She seems fascinated by the painstaking craft ('stitched boldly') involved in creating this beautiful token of love. But the poet's appreciation of the fan becomes diminished with guilt. The tortoiseshell has suffered 'violation' at the expense of the gift. In Boland's mind, the delicate colours decorating the fan came from 'a worn-out, underwater bullion'. The tone is suddenly downbeat as the thought throws a shadow ('The lace is overcast') on her parents' relationship.

In stanza six, the poet returns to the romantic Parisian drama of the 'empty café terrace', but admits that she can never know what really happened that fateful evening in the 'airless dusk before thunder'. Instead, she must 'improvise' it. But at least the romantic moment is preserved in her imagination. Not for the first time, however, there is an underlying suggestion of the reality of relationships over time, and the balance of joy and disappointment that is likely. For Boland, the fan is only a small part of her parents' story. Perhaps she realises that **the past can never be completely understood**.

The striking image of a blackbird dominates the final stanza. The poet returns to the present as she observes the bird 'in summer, finding buds'. The movement of the blackbird's wing is an unexpected link with the black lace fan all those years ago. While the souvenir is old, its significance as a symbol of youthful romance can still be found elsewhere. For the first time, **Boland now seems to understand the beauty of her parents' love** for each other. The last lines are daring and appear to describe both the blackbird and her mother as a young girl holding her new gift: 'Suddenly she puts out her wing –/the whole, full, flirtatious span of it.' The energetic pace of the lines combine with the alliterative sounds and sibilant music to produce a lively sense of celebration at the end.

Writing About the Poem

'Eavan Boland takes a balanced, unsentimental view of relationships.' To what extent is this true of 'The Black Lace Fan My Mother Gave Me'? Support your answer with reference to the poem.

Sample Paragraph

This poem is not a typical love poem. It is out of the ordinary in ways. The poet does not try to glorify the relationship when they first met. Indeed, they seem unsure of each other. The poet tries to work out the story behind their relationship by looking at the lace fan. She imagines the intense heat of Paris: 'It was stifling.' References to the weather hint at an uncomfortable relationship: 'The heat was killing.' Boland might be referring indirectly to the future problems in the couple's marriage over the years. The fact that the Second World War was about to break out is also a bad sign. Having said that, the gift of the fan is a symbol of the attraction the couple felt. It is a traditional image of true romance. The poet shows the reality of the relationship by noting the unsentimental details: 'He was late', 'She stood up.' There was nervousness and excitement when they were first infatuated with each other, but their love was to change over time. She also compares the fan to a blackbird's wing which excites the poet. This gives us a final impression that Boland is happy to imagine the youthful love between her parents back in the 1930s. In a way, the poem is as much about the love Boland herself feels for her parents as about their love.

EXAMINER'S COMMENT

This paragraph focuses well on the way love is presented throughout the poem. The answer would have been improved by a less note-like commentary at the beginning. Good use is made of suitable quotations and this high-grade response is well-rounded off with an effective point about the poet's own enduring love for her parents.

Class/Homework Exercises

1. Comment on Eavan Boland's use of symbolism in 'The Black Lace Fan My Mother Gave Me', referring to the text in your answer.
2. What does Boland's poem reveal about her parents' relationship? Support the points you make with reference to both the subject matter and language use in the poem.

Summary Points

- **Themes include romantic love and changing family relationships.**
- **Striking language – central symbol of the fan, dramatic image of the blackbird.**
- **Evocative atmosphere of 1930s Paris.**
- **Vivid detail; varying tones – reflective, nostalgic, realistic.**

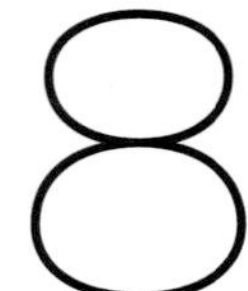

8 This Moment

A neighbourhood.
At dusk.

Things are getting ready
to happen
out of sight.

Stars and moths.
And rinds slanting around fruit.

But not yet.

One tree is black.
One window is yellow as butter.

A woman leans down to catch a child
who has run into her arms
this moment.

Stars rise.
Moths flutter.
Apples sweeten in the dark.

rinds: peels.

Personal Response

1. Choose either one visual or one aural image from the poem, and briefly comment on its effectiveness. Support your answer by referring to the text.
2. Comment on how Boland manages to create drama within the poem.
3. What do you think is the central theme in the poem? Refer closely to the text in your answer.

Critical Literacy

In this short lyric poem, Eavan Boland captures the experience of a passing moment in time. It is clear that she is moved by the ordinariness of suburban life, where she glimpses the immeasurable beauty of nature and human nature. The occasion is another reminder of the mystery and wonder of all creation, as expressed by the American poet Walt Whitman, who wrote, 'I know of nothing else but miracles'.

The poem's opening lines introduce a suburban area in any part of the world. Boland pares the scene down to its essentials. All we learn is that it is dusk, a time of transition. The atmosphere is one of quiet intensity. Full stops break the rhythm and force us to evaluate what is happening. Although we are presented with an **anonymous setting**, it seems strangely familiar. The late evening – especially as darkness falls – can be a time for reflecting about the natural world.

The stillness and dramatic anticipation intensify further in lines 3–8. Something important is about to happen 'out of sight'. Boland then considers some of nature's wonders: 'Stars and moths.' In the twilight, everything seems mysterious, even 'rinds slanting around fruit'. The poet's eye for detail is like that of an artist. The rich, sensory image of the cut fruit is exact and tactile. She uses simple language precisely to create a **mood of natural calmness** that is delayed for a split second ('But not yet').

There is time for two more **vivid images** in lines 9–10. The startling colour contrast between the 'black' tree and the window that is 'yellow as butter' has a cinematic effect. The simile is homely, in keeping with the domestic setting. Repetition of 'One' focuses our attention as the build-up continues. Again, Boland presents the sequence of events in a series of brief glimpses. It is as if she is marking time, preparing us for the key moment of revelation.

This occurs in lines 11–13. The central image of the mother and child intuitively reaching out for each other is a powerful symbol of unconditional love. It is every bit as wonderful as any of life's greatest mysteries. The three lines become progressively condensed as the child reaches her mother. The syntax suggests their eagerness to show their love for each other. Boland's decision to generalise ('A woman' and 'a child') emphasises the **universal significance** of 'this moment'. The crucial importance of people's feelings transcends time and place.

There is a slight tone of anti-climax about the last three lines. However, Boland rounds off her description of the moment by placing it within a wider context. The constant expression of family love is in harmony with everything else that is beautiful in nature. This feeling is suggested by the recurring sibilant 's' sounds and the carefully chosen verbs ('rise', 'flutter' and 'sweeten'), all of which celebrate the excitement and **joy of everyday human relationships**.

Writing About the Poem

'Eavan Boland's poetry deals effectively with important contemporary issues.' Discuss this statement, with particular reference to her poem, 'This Moment'.

Sample Paragraph

Eavan Boland places her poem in a contemporary setting, a Dublin suburb at dusk. The short, pithy lines, 'A neighbourhood./At dusk', set a modern, minimalist tone for this anonymous, yet familiar scene which is played out across countless estates worldwide. The mystery of this transition time between day and night is caught in the economical run-on lines, 'Things are getting ready/to happen/out of sight'. In this 'not yet' moment, the mysterious powers and actions of nature are observed, 'And rinds slanting around fruit'. Yet, I also feel there is a slight tinge of danger, reminding me of the serpent in the Garden of Eden waiting to pounce. Boland's famous painterly eye precisely captures this moment at dusk, the silhouetted tree, the window lit by its electric lamp, 'One tree is black./One window is yellow as butter'. Suddenly a child runs into a waiting mother's arms, 'A woman leans down to catch a child'. The general terms used emphasise the universal significance of this experience of a child returning to the security of a loving mother's arms. The tension of the moment is relaxed as if nature exhales, all is now in its rightful place. A series of gentle verbs: 'rise', 'flutter' and 'sweeten' chart its peaceful movement. Boland's poem describes a common social issue – how in this uncertain modern world, every parent heaves a sigh of relief when a child returns safely home.

EXAMINER'S COMMENT

This competent response addresses both the theme and style of the poem. A developed discussion deals with Boland's use of free verse and economical language. An interesting personal reading of the poem is given in the line, 'I also feel there is a slight tinge of danger ...'. This well-written, successful answer engages closely with the text of the poem. Top-grade standard.

Class/Homework Exercises

1. Comment on the poet's tone in 'This Moment'. Refer to the text in your discussion.
2. A sense of intense mystery is often found in Boland's poetry. To what extent is this true of 'This Moment'? Support your answer with close reference to the poem.

Summary Points

- **Themes include the mystery of nature and the beauty of loving relationships.**
- **Effective use of simple language and succinct dramatic style.**
- **Vivid, sensuous imagery; sibilant and assonant effects.**
- **Varying moods – subdued, reflective, celebratory.**

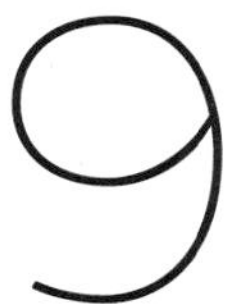

The Pomegranate

The pomegranate (from a French word meaning an apple with many seeds) is a pulpy oriental fruit.

The only legend I have ever loved is
the story of a daughter lost in hell.
And found and rescued there.
Love and blackmail are the gist of it.
Ceres and Persephone the names.
And the best thing about the legend is
I can enter it anywhere. And have.
As a child in exile in
a city of fogs and strange consonants,
I read it first and at first I was
an exiled child in the crackling dusk of
the underworld, the stars blighted. Later
I walked out in a summer twilight
searching for my daughter at bed-time.
When she came running I was ready
to make any bargain to keep her.
I carried her back past whitebeams
and wasps and honey-scented buddleias.
But I was Ceres then and I knew
winter was in store for every leaf
on every tree on that road.
Was inescapable for each one we passed.
And for me.
                    It is winter
and the stars are hidden.
I climb the stairs and stand where I can see
my child asleep beside her teen magazines,
her can of Coke, her plate of uncut fruit.
The pomegranate! How did I forget it?
She could have come home and been safe
and ended the story and all
our heart-broken searching but she reached
out a hand and plucked a pomegranate.
She put out her hand and pulled down
the French sound for apple and
the noise of stone and the proof
that even in the place of death,
at the heart of legend, in the midst
of rocks full of unshed tears
ready to be diamonds by the time

Ceres and Persephone: mythological figures. Ceres was the goddess of earth and motherhood. Persephone was her beautiful daughter who was forced by Pluto to become his wife and was imprisoned in Hades, the underworld. Ceres was determined to find Persephone and threatened to prevent anything from growing on the earth until she was allowed to rescue her daughter. But because Persephone had eaten sacred pomegranate seeds in Hades, she was condemned forever to spend part of every year there.
city of fogs: London, where the poet once lived.

buddleias: ornamental bushes with small purple flowers.

the story was told, a child can be
hungry. I could warn her. There is still a chance.
The rain is cold. The road is flint-coloured.
The suburb has cars and cable television.
The veiled stars are above ground.
It is another world. But what else
can a mother give her daughter but such
beautiful rifts in time?
If I defer the grief I will diminish the gift.
The legend will be hers as well as mine.
She will enter it. As I have.
She will wake up. She will hold
the papery flushed skin in her hand.
And to her lips. I will say nothing.

rifts: gaps, cracks.
defer: delay.

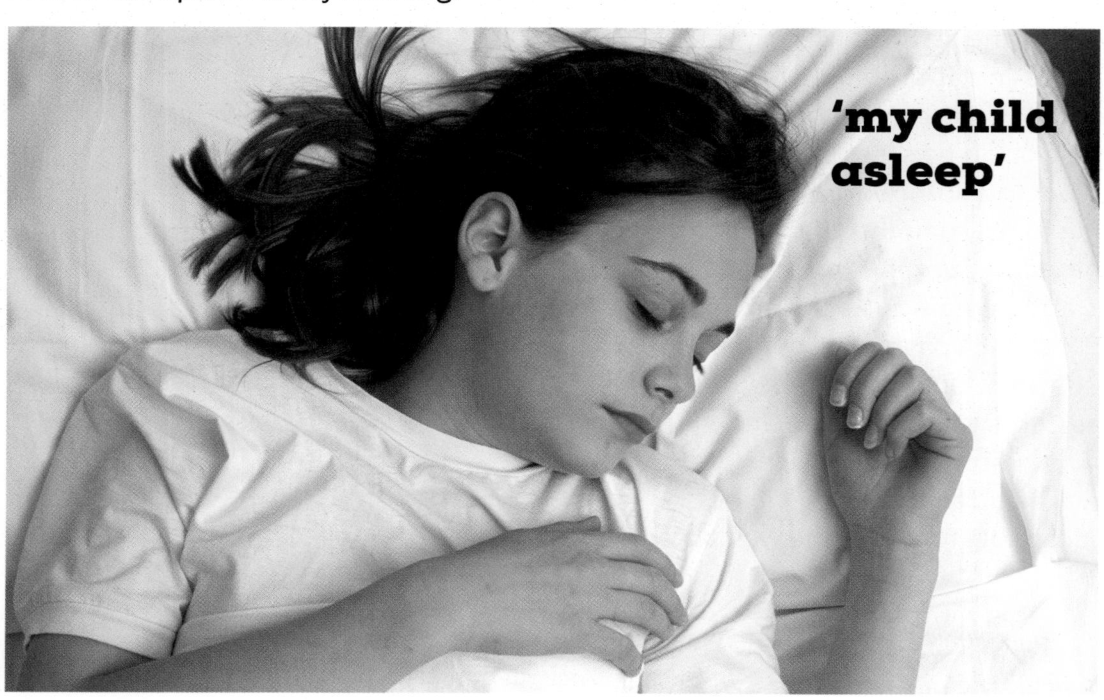

Personal Response

1. Boland conveys a sense of the city of London in this poem. How does she succeed in doing this? Refer closely to the text in your answer.
2. From your reading of this poem, what do you learn about the relationship between the poet and her daughter? Refer to the text in your answer.
3. Comment on the poet's mood in the last five lines of the poem.

Critical Literacy

In the poem, narrated as one unrhymed stanza, Boland explores the theme of parental loss by comparing her own experiences as a mother and daughter with the myth of Ceres and Persephone. Although it is a personal poem, it has a much wider relevance for families everywhere.

Boland presents this exploration of the mother–child relationship as a dramatic narrative. In the opening lines, the poet tells us that she has always related to 'the story of a daughter lost in hell'. This goes back to her early experience as 'a child in exile' living in London. Her **sense of displacement** is evident in the detailed description of that 'city of fogs and strange consonants'. Like Persephone trapped in Hades, Boland yearned for home. But the myth has a broader relevance to the poet's life – she 'can enter it anywhere'. Years later, she recalls a time when, as a mother, she could also identify with Ceres, 'searching for my daughter'.

Lines 13–18 express the intensity of Boland's feelings for her child: she was quite prepared 'to make any bargain to keep her'. The **anxious tone** reflects the poet's awareness of the importance of appreciating the closeness between herself and her teenage daughter while time allows. She expresses her maternal feelings through rich natural images: 'I carried her back past whitebeams.' But she is also increasingly aware that both she and her daughter are getting older. This is particularly evident in line 20, as she anticipates an 'inescapable' change in their relationship: 'winter was in store for every leaf.'

Line 24 marks a defining moment ('It is winter') for them both. Observing her daughter asleep in her bedroom, Boland now sees herself as Ceres and the 'plate of uncut fruit' as the pomegranate. This marks the realisation that **her child has become an adult**. The poet imagines how different it might have been had Persephone not eaten the fruit – 'She could have come home' and ended all the 'heart-broken searching'. But Persephone deliberately made her choice, a decision that is emphasised by the repeated mention of her gesture ('she reached/out a hand', 'She put out her hand'). Significantly, Boland is sympathetic: 'a child can be/hungry.'

In line 42, the poet considers alerting her daughter ('I could warn her') about the dangers and disappointments that lie ahead. **Harsh imagery** suggests the difficulties of modern life: 'The rain is cold. The road is flint-coloured.' Boland wonders if 'beautiful rifts in time' are the most a mother can offer. Such delaying tactics may only postpone natural development into adulthood.

In the end, she decides to 'say nothing'. There is a clear sense of resignation in the final lines. The poet accepts the reality of change. Boland's daughter will experience the same stages of childhood and motherhood as the poet herself: 'The legend will be hers as well as mine.' This truth is underlined by the recurring use of 'She will', a recognition that her daughter's destiny is in her own hands. The **poem ends on a quietly reflective note** as Boland respectfully acknowledges the right of her daughter to mature naturally and make her own way in life.

Writing About the Poem

'Eavan Boland's use of mythical references vividly illuminates her own personal experiences.' Discuss this statement, with particular reference to Boland's poem, 'The Pomegranate'.

Sample Paragraph

Eavan Boland has been very successful in blending her own life as a child and mother with Persephone and Ceres. The fact that she uses an ancient legend adds a touch of mystery to the theme of mother–daughter relationships. This gives the poem a universal quality. First, she compares herself to Persephone, the exiled child in London where the stars were 'blighted'. This links the grimy city life to the underworld of Hades. But Boland is more concerned with the present and her fears of losing her own daughter who is growing up fast. By describing her fears through the old story of Ceres, she increases our understanding of how anxious she was feeling. Both parents were 'searching' desperately. Together, the legend and the true life story of the poet and her reluctance to come to terms with her daughter growing up really show how parents have to let go of their children and give them the freedom to make their own mistakes and learn for themselves. Most parents find it hard to give their children freedom. Overall, the mythical references emphasise the universality of Boland's natural feelings for her daughter. I thought they were very effective in conveying the poem's central theme.

EXAMINER'S COMMENT

There are some very good points here in response to a challenging question. Although the answer shows personal engagement, it could be rooted more thoroughly in the text through a more extensive use of quotation. Some sentences are overlong and the expression is repetitive at times (with overuse of the words 'fears' and 'freedom'). Points would need to be more developed to achieve the top grade.

Class/Homework Exercises

1. What image of Eavan Boland herself emerges from 'The Pomegranate'? Refer closely to the text in your answer.
2. Boland manages to create a series of powerfully evocative moods throughout this poem. Discuss this statement, supporting your answer with close reference to the text.

Summary Points

- **Boland considers the complexity of mother-daughter relationships.**
- **Striking images – nature, family and the difficulties of modern life.**
- **Mythical references reflect a timeless, universal sense of loss.**
- **Tones vary – empathetic, anxious, resigned.**

10 Love

Dark falls on this mid-western town
where we once lived when myths collided.
Dusk has hidden the bridge in the river
which slides and deepens
to become the water
the hero crossed on his way to hell.

Not far from here is our old apartment.
We had a kitchen and an Amish table.
We had a view. And we discovered there
love had the feather and muscle of wings
and had come to live with us,
a brother of fire and air.

We had two infant children one of whom
was touched by death in this town
and spared: and when the hero
was hailed by his comrades in hell
their mouths opened and their voices failed and
there is no knowing what they would have asked
about a life they had shared and lost.

I am your wife.
It was years ago.
Our child was healed. We love each other still.
Across our day-to-day and ordinary distances
we speak plainly. We hear each other clearly.

And yet I want to return to you
on the bridge of the Iowa river as you were,
with snow on the shoulders of your coat
and a car passing with its headlights on:

I see you as a hero in a text –
the image blazing and the edges gilded –
and I long to cry out the epic question
my dear companion:

mid-western town: In 1979, Boland lived in the United States and attended the prestigious Iowa Writers' Workshop.
myths: fictitious tales with supernatural characters and events.

hero: Aeneas was a hero in the Aeneid. He visited the underworld by crossing the River Styx where he saw his dead companions, but they could not communicate with him.
Amish: strict American religious sect that makes functional, practical furniture without decoration.

epic: great, ambitious.

Will we ever live so intensely again?
Will love come to us again and be
so formidable at rest it offered us ascension
even to look at him?

But the words are shadows and you cannot hear me.
You walk away and I cannot follow.

formidable: very impressive.

'comrades in hell'

Personal Response

1. This poem is an open and honest meditation on the nature of love. Write your own personal response to it, referring to the text in your answer.
2. Choose one image from the poem that you think is particularly effective. Briefly explain your choice.
3. Explain the significance of the last section of the poem: 'But the words are shadows and you cannot hear me./You walk away and I cannot follow'. In your opinion, is this a positive or negative ending?

Critical Literacy

'Love' is part of a sequence of poems called 'Legends' in which Boland explores parallels between myths and modern life. She records her personal experience of family life in Iowa at a time when her youngest daughter was seriously ill and came close to death. This is interwoven with the myth of Aeneas returning to the underworld. The narrative poem explores the nature of human relationships and how they change over time. It also shows the unchanging nature of human experience down through the ages.

Lines 1–6. The poem opens in darkness, **remembering the past**. Boland's personal experience was in 'this mid-western town' in Iowa, and she connects this with the myth of Aeneas visiting the underworld. Aeneas crosses the bridge on the River Styx to reach Hades, the land of the Shades ('the hero crossed on his way to hell'). Boland and her husband were also experiencing their own hell as they visited their very sick little girl in hospital.

Lines 7–12. These lines give us a **clear, detailed picture of their domestic life**: 'a kitchen', 'an Amish table', 'a view'. The poem is written in loose, non-rhyming stanzas, which suits reminiscences. The couple's internal emotional life is shown in the **striking metaphor** 'love had the feather and muscle of wings'. Love was beating, alive, vibrant. The word 'feather' suggests it could soar to great heights, while 'muscle' signifies that it was extraordinarily powerful. This natural, graceful love was palpable, substantial, elemental, 'a brother of fire and air'.

Lines 13–19. The **personal drama** of the sick daughter who 'was touched by death' is recalled. But Boland did not lose her child. The verb 'spared' links us with the myth again. Aeneas is in the underworld, but because his comrades are shadows, they cannot ask the questions they are longing to ask about the life they once shared. This mythical reference reflects the couple's inability to express their intense feelings at such a critical time. The moment of communication is lost: 'there is no knowing what they would have asked.'

Lines 20–36. The poet goes on to consider the **changing nature of love**. The 'we' becomes 'I'– 'I am your wife'. Do they, as husband and wife, communicate as deeply as they did before? Her tone is matter-of-fact, almost businesslike. She wants to recapture the intensity of their love and shared times, when she saw her husband as 'a hero in a text'. In her memory of him, he is outlined by the cars' lights as they pass on the bridge. Described as 'blazing' and 'gilded', he is contrasted to the darkness of the night, as Aeneas is contrasted with the darkness of the underworld. Boland longs to experience that special time, that transcendence, again.

The closing lines are dominated by rhetorical questions: 'Will we ever live so intensely again?' The inference is no. She can imagine asking these questions

about the life they shared, but she cannot actually articulate them. This is **similar to Aeneas' dilemma** – his comrades wished to ask questions about the life they shared with him, but 'their voices failed'. Neither Boland nor the 'comrades' could express their feelings. The words of the questions remain unformed, unspoken, 'shadows'.

Lines 37–38. The poem ends with a two-line stanza in which the poet accepts that the **gap cannot be bridged**: 'You walk away and I cannot follow'. There is a real sense of loss and resignation in Boland's final tone.

Writing About the Poem

Memory is one of the central themes in Boland's poem, 'Love'. In your opinion, does the poet convey this theme effectively? Refer to the text in your answer.

Sample Paragraph

By blending myth and personal experience, Boland gives her poems a true sense of universality. But she also blends timelines, the past and the present tenses to give a quality of timelessness. In 'Love', the immediacy and freshness of a potent memory is captured by her use of the present tense: 'Dark falls', 'here is our old apartment'. The recent past is shown in the past tense as she recalls what they had: 'We had a kitchen and an Amish table./We had a view', 'love … had come to live with us', 'We had two infant children'. In the past they had a life together which was lived very intensely. Are they missing any of this now? The tense then changes to the present as Boland states her identity: 'I am your wife.' Here she honestly and openly explores her concerns about the changing nature of love. Their moment of crisis is over: 'Our child was healed.' Realistically she appraises the current situation and notes 'words are shadows', 'you cannot hear me'. The intense personal nature of their love has changed. Like Aeneas' comrades, she cannot express her question ('voices failed'), and her husband, like Aeneas, cannot hear. The changing tenses add a compelling timeless quality to the experience of memory, as time shared is recalled. The poem ends with the never-changing realisation that time cannot be relived.

EXAMINER'S COMMENT

An unusual approach is taken as the response focuses on the use of tenses as a stylistic feature to communicate theme: 'The changing tenses add a compelling timeless quality to the experience of memory.' There is evidence of close reading of the poem and effective use of quotation throughout. Expression is varied and fluent. This assured response, e.g. 'The poem ends with the never-changing realisation that time cannot be relived', deserves a high grade.

Class/Homework Exercises

1. The poem, 'Love', illustrates Boland's subtle skill in conveying significant universal truths through her exploration of personal relationships. Discuss this view, supporting your points with close reference to the text.
2. 'When myths collided.' Do you consider Boland's use of myths in her work effective in exploring her themes? Discuss, referring closely to the poem, 'Love'.

Summary Points

- **The changing nature of romantic love is a central theme.**
- **References to Greek mythology used to explore parallels with modern life.**
- **Use of detailed description, striking metaphors, rhetorical questions.**
- **Contrasting tones of relief, nostalgia, reflection and resignation.**

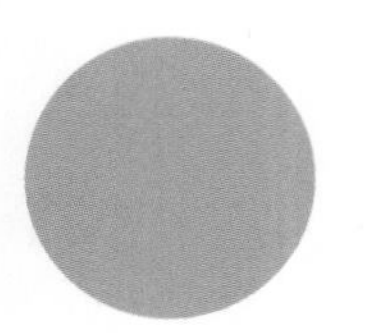

Leaving Cert Sample Essay

'Boland's reflective insights offer fresh perspectives on a variety of universal themes.' To what extent do you agree or disagree with this statement? Support your answer with reference to both the subject matter and language use in the poetry of Eavan Boland on your course.

Sample Essay
(Boland's reflections offer fresh perspectives)

1. Eavan Boland is a distinctive Irish poet whose work ranges widely over basic themes and issues which relate to the lives of very many people. She writes movingly about love, family relationships, conflict and the experience of being marginalised. Her poems are often thought-provoking – particularly when she explores the treatment of women in society. For me, Boland's observations have provided new outlooks on many important issues.

2. Several poems, including 'The Shadow Doll' and 'The Famine Road', contrast past and present eras to examine how women have been expected to behave in a predominantly patriarchal world. In 'The Shadow Doll', Boland focuses on an object associated with Victorian weddings – a small porcelain doll in an enclosed glass case. The precise descriptive details of a 'porcelain bride in an airless glamour' suggest Boland's understanding of how young women were once viewed in marriage. She emphasises the idea of oppression and even suffocation. The poet's language highlights a sense of imprisonment – 'stitched blooms', 'hoops', 'neatly sewn'. The hesitant rhythm and repetition of 'Under glass, under wraps' adds to the notion of helplessness. In some ways, the symbolism seems a little too obvious for modern readers who are more aware of sexist attitudes, but I believe that there are still great pressures on girls to look and act in particular ways. The final lines are almost surreal as Boland recalls that on the night before her own wedding, she herself felt strangely objectified, 'astray among the cards and wedding gifts'.

3. Boland often challenges society's patriarchal attitudes, reminding readers that women are expected to conform. Although 'The Famine Road' is primarily concerned with the callous treatment of Ireland's starving people during the mid-19th century, the poet also links their suffering to the lives of infertile women in today's world. Interlinked with the 19th-century voices, Boland introduces the modern voice of an insensitive doctor who curtly dismisses the infertile patient he is treating: 'take it well woman.' The stark experience of famine victims and the disappointment of being unable to have a child are effectively illustrated

by the shared image of the famine road. The realities of suffering and loss are universal and timeless.

4. As Eavan Boland lived in Ireland during the Troubles of the 1970s, it is not surprising that she writes about the tragic violence of that period. For a young person nowadays, that whole era seems distant and unreal. However, in 'Child of our Time', the poet presents a startling reminder of the tragic reality of conflict by commemorating a baby killed in the 1974 Dublin bombing. Boland dedicates the poem to a friend's baby who had died in infancy. What I found of greatest interest is the way the entire poem celebrates the precious quality of every child's life. The tone varies from tender sympathy to bitter anger, emphasising the responsibility adults have to protect innocent children.

5. The early lines demand that the older generation should create 'order' out of the 'discord' resulting from the unfortunate child's 'murder'. Boland's voice is measured, laying the blame on society at large – 'We who should have known'. The inclusive pronoun involves the reader directly. Soft, gentle sound effects, such as 'rhymes for your waking, rhythms for your sleep', reflect the simple world of childhood. However, the poem's increasingly reverential tone builds to a prayerful conclusion hoping that the child's short life will affect future generations, so that people find 'a new language'. In one way, Boland is giving readers a lead here by speaking out clearly against those who have lost respect for human life. This short dramatic poem challenges us to value every individual.

6. 'This Moment' and 'White Hawthorn in the West of Ireland' are both reflective poems which encourage readers to consider the beauty and mystery of nature. In the short lyric, 'This Moment', the poet focuses on the wonder of time itself when 'Things are getting ready/to happen'. The setting – 'a neighbourhood' – could be anywhere. Vivid details of the natural world, such as 'Stars and moths', create a mood of heightened anticipation – the shock of each moment of being alive. The final image – 'A woman leans down to catch a child' – is a simple but powerful symbol of universal love, highlighting perhaps the single most important aspect of human life. Such an insight is typical of Eavan Boland who also captures the strange beauty of the Irish landscape in 'White Hawthorn in the West of Ireland'. Describing a journey from Dublin to the West, she is able to link the wild natural vegetation – 'sharp flowers' – with traditional Irish superstitions. The hawthorn is part of the native landscape and culture – a reminder that our identity is defined by many different forces.

INDICATIVE MATERIAL

- Explorations of the changing aspects of love and relationships.
- Refreshing celebration of natural beauty and tradition.
- Intense engagement with the marginalised and dispossessed.
- Subversive attitude to women's experience in a patriarchal world.
- Challenging views on Irishness, conflict, myth and history.
- Striking imagery emphasises thoughts and emotions.
- Varying moods/tones convey renewed understanding and empathy.

7. I have always found a quietly graceful quality in Boland's writing. Her measured observational poems often make a dramatic impact. Her short narratives have an unsettling intensity which makes the reader think more deeply about important aspects of life. In particular, she writes with great honesty and insight about Irish identity and the female experience.

(approx. 840 words)
(45–50 minutes)

EXAMINER'S COMMENT

A very well-structured top-grade essay which addresses the question confidently. Points are developed effectively and illustrated by apt quotations and references. Expression is also highly impressive and well controlled: 'The hesitant rhythm and repetition of "Under glass, under wraps" add to the notion of helplessness.' Some examples of the varying tones would have highlighted the discussion in paragraph 4. Good use is made of cross references in paragraph 6. The close analysis of the poet's language is to be commended – particularly in Paragraphs 2 and 5.

GRADE: H1
P = 15/15
C = 15/15
L = 15/15
M = 5/5
Total = 50/50

Sample Leaving Cert Questions on Boland's Poetry

1. **'Eavan Boland addresses contemporary modern-day issues through effective comparisons from history and mythology.' Discuss this statement, supporting your answer with reference to the poems by Boland on your course.**
2. **'Boland deals with issues which are both private and personal, but which also have a universal appeal.' Discuss this view, supporting your answer with reference to the poetry of Eavan Boland on your course.**
3. **'Boland communicates profound insights into human relationships through language that is both lyrical and expressive.' Discuss this statement, supporting your answer with reference to the poetry of Eavan Boland on your course.**

First Sample Essay Plan (Q2)

'Eavan Boland deals with issues which are both private and personal, but which also have a universal appeal.' Discuss this statement, supporting your answer with reference to the poetry of Eavan Boland on your course.

Intro: A personal response is required referring to both subject matter and style. Both tasks, the private and personal and the universal dimensions of her poetry, should be explored.

Point 1: 'Child of Our Time' – personal response to newspaper picture of fireman carrying dead child after bomb given widespread resonance by saying all of us need to find 'a new language'. Personal tone both compassionate and admonishing. Use of formal language suited to elegy and prayer.

Point 2: 'The Pomegranate' – deals with the relationship between mother and daughter, particularly the wrenching moment of separation despite the mother's worry of no longer being able to protect her child. This personal situation is directly linked to the myth of Persephone and Ceres, giving it a timeless, universal dimension.

Point 3: 'Love' also uses a myth, Aeneas and the underworld, to portray a personal experience which has universal appeal. The changing nature of love and family crises are both common human experiences.

Point 4: 'The War Horse' – metaphorical poem about attitudes to war. Rigid, controlled couplets show the suburban desire for order. The epic title broadens the appeal of the poem. The blending of past and present blurs the boundaries of time.

Point 5: 'This Moment' – a moment in suburbia, at dusk, recollected with painterly precision. The collective experience is shown through the use of general terms and details enabling a universal significance to the private event.

Conclusion: Boland refers to specific personal moments or events and gives them a widespread interest by linking them with mythology, by changing tones and by her vivid visual descriptions. Her poetry often transcends the particular to become general.

NOTE

As you may not be familiar with some of the poems referred to in the sample plans below, substitute poems that you have studied closely.

Exam candidates usually discuss three or four poems in their answers. However, there is no set number of poems or formulaic approach expected.

Key points about a particular poem can be developed over more than one paragraph.

Paragraphs may also include cross-referencing and discussion of more than one poem.

Remember that there is no single 'correct' answer to poetry questions, so always be confident in expressing your own considered response.

MARKING SCHEME GUIDELINES

Candidates are free to agree and/or disagree with the statement, but they should engage with how the poet's reflections offer 'fresh perspectives on a variety of universal themes'. Reward responses that include clear analysis of both themes and language use (though not necessarily equally) in Boland's poetry.

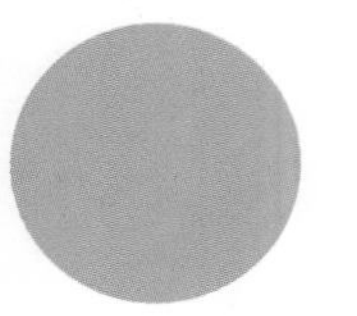

Sample Essay Plan (Q2)

Develop **one** of the points on the previous page into a paragraph.

Sample Paragraph: Point 3

By interweaving myth with a personal story, Boland creates poetry that becomes universally appealing. She uses this technique in the poem 'Love'. Here the story of Aeneas, who goes to the underworld where his dead comrades are, is interwoven with an actual story of Boland's, when her daughter was seriously ill. In each there is a hero, Aeneas and Boland's husband. Each has their own trauma to deal with. Aeneas cannot hear what 'his comrades in hell' want to ask, as their 'voices failed'. The questions they wanted to ask 'about a life they had loved and shared' will never be known. Similarly, Boland is unable to ask about a life she and her husband had known as she feels unable to voice the question, 'Will we ever live so intensely again?' They had lived in this way when one of their children was 'touched by death in this town and spared'. Often in times of tragedy, people are capable of great things. To Boland, her husband was 'a hero in a text'. Although their feelings for each other are unchanged ('We love each other still'), she longs for the love they once shared. It was an almost spiritual experience. But, just as Aeneas is never asked questions by his comrades, so her husband is never asked her question. Instead the 'words are shadows'. Once again, a domestic event is transformed into a wider arena by entangling it with a myth.

EXAMINER'S COMMENT

As part of a full essay answer, this is a highly impressive top-grade paragraph that gives a personal response firmly rooted in the text. The paragraph focuses on the use of myth by Boland to explore the wider dimensions of domestic situations. Impressive vocabulary makes this a very successful effort, 'a domestic event is transformed into a wider arena by entangling it with a myth.'

Second Sample Essay Plan (Q3)

'Boland communicates profound insights into human relationships through language that is both lyrical and expressive.' Discuss this statement, supporting your answer with reference to the poetry of Eavan Boland on your course.

Intro: Boland – a compassionate and honest observer, develops new perspectives into the complex relationships humans form, using emotive, musical language and diverse, rich imagery.

Point 1:: 'The War Horse' – uneasy relationship between the intrusive Traveller horse and the reticent suburban poet is recreated through evocative alliteration and onomatopoeia ('clip, clop, casual') and shocking

imagery ('a crocus, its bulbous head/Blown from growth'). Personal pronouns ('You', 'we') draw the reader into the small domestic drama.

Point 2: 'The Black Lace Fan My Mother Gave Me' – poem is built around the central symbol of romance. Boland imagines her parents as young lovers in Paris. Their edgy excitement is suggested by the 'stifling' atmosphere and vivid images of nervous anticipation as they 'met in cafes'. Lyrical description and evocative tones convey the timelessness of youthful love.

Point 3: 'White Hawthorn in the West of Ireland' – contrast between the two different relationships the poet has with the suburban and rural landscape. The urban environment is caught in short, clipped, pedantic sentences ('I left suburban gardens./Lawnmowers. Small talk'). Flowing lines and dynamic images of growth evoke the abundance of the countryside ('to be part of/that ivory downhill rush'). Disquieting rural superstitions are also referenced ('a child might die').

Point 4: 'Outside History' – Boland wishes to place the dispossessed, with whom she empathises, in prime place, contrasting with the focus on the powerful in 'The Famine Road'. Condensed imagery suggests the reality of the victims of history ('roads clotted as/firmaments with the dead'). Despite the elegiac repetition of the conclusion ('too late ... too late'), the poem stands as a memorial to the forgotten due to the poet's choosing to enter into a relationship with those 'whose darkness is/only reaching me from those fields'.

Conclusion: Boland explores the complex relationships humans form with one another, with objects and with their environment. She makes the personal political, decoding the hidden fragmentary messages from the past. This sympathetic blending of past and present provides an interesting experience for the reader, resulting in timeless poetry.

Sample Essay Plan (Q3)

Develop **one** of the above points into a practice paragraph of your own. (You may wish to use a different poem that you have studied rather than the one illustrated above.)

Sample Paragraph: Point 2

Boland's poem, 'The Black Lace Fan My Mother Gave Me', uses the fan as a symbol of the enduring, if sometimes difficult, nature of her parents' relationship in a series of evocative moments. Boland dares to describe the ordinariness of love. An unsettled listless mood pervades the 1930s

pre-war Parisian setting suggested through the sibilant alliteration, 'stifling', 'starless', 'stormy'. The difficulty of achieving harmony between two separate individuals is reflected in the short sharp sentences and the uneven rhythm, 'She was always early./He was late'. Yet the promise of the couple's blossoming love is vividly depicted in the 'wild roses, appliquéd on silk by hand' on the fan. But the reality of how relationships become inevitably tarnished is also relayed, 'overcast', 'empty', 'airless'. The unexpected link between the sudden arrival of the lively blackbird and the fan concludes the poem on an optimistic note. The vivid image of the little bird opening its wing, 'the whole, full, flirtatious span of it', reminds the poet of how her mother as a young girl could have opened her precious love token. Boland provides a fresh insight into the dynamics of romantic love by carefully balancing the joy and disappointment experienced.

EXAMINER'S COMMENT

As part of a full essay answer to Q3, this is an informed and focused high-grade response that shows genuine engagement with the poem. References to the dramatic interaction between the poet's parents effectively illustrate the couple's youthful nervousness. The detailed analysis of Boland's style (mood, rhythm, imagery, etc.) is also impressive.

Class/Homework Exercise

1. **Write one or two paragraphs in response to the question: 'Boland communicates profound insights into human relationships through language that is both lyrical and expressive.' Discuss this statement, supporting your answer with reference to the poetry of Eavan Boland on your course.**

 Revision Overview

'The War Horse'
Themes of violence, warfare, death, suburban domestic incident, memory.

'Child of Our Time'
Elegy, response to theme of random tragedy unleashed by lack of communication.

'The Famine Road'
Two parallel narratives explore themes of oppression and victimisation, the famine and the infertile woman.

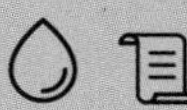

'The Shadow Doll'
Theme of women's oppression, emotions and sexuality suppressed.

'White Hawthorn in the West of Ireland'
Journey into West becomes reflection on thematic contrast between orderly suburbia and wild, mystical beauty of Irish landscape.

'Outside History'
Compelling examination of theme of the marginalised.

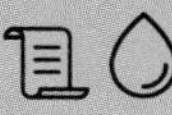

'The Black Lace Fan My Mother Gave Me'
Challenging alternative account of the theme of relationship between men and women.

'This Moment'
Reflection on theme of traditional role of women as mothers.

'The Pomegranate'
Reflective examination of themes of complex mother-daughter relationship and ageing process.

'Love'
Two narratives address theme of changes in relationships, personal story of young love and Aeneas' return to the underworld.

Last Words

'Eavan Boland's work continues to deepen in both humanity and complexity.'
Fiona Sampson

'Memory, change, loss, the irrecoverable past – such are the shared conditions of humankind, with which she scrupulously engages.'
Anne Stevenson

'Poets are those who ransack their perishing mind and find pattern and form.'
Eavan Boland

CONFICT

DEATH

SUFFERING

HISTORY/ MEMORY

RELATIONSHIPS

TRAVEL/ JOURNEYS

NATURE

TIME

LOVE

Emily Dickinson 1830–86

'Forever is composed of nows.'

Emily Dickinson was born on 10 December 1830 in Amherst, Massachusetts. Widely regarded as one of America's greatest poets, she is also known for her unusual life of self-imposed social seclusion. An enigmatic figure with a fondness for the macabre, Dickinson never married. She was a prolific letter-writer and private poet, though fewer than a dozen of her poems were published during her lifetime. It was only after her death in 1886 that her work was discovered. It is estimated that she wrote about 1,770 poems, many of which explored the nature of immortality and death, with an almost mantric quality at times. Ultimately, however, she is remembered for her distinctive style, which was unique for the era in which she wrote. Her poems contain short lines, typically lack titles and often ignore the rules of grammar, syntax and punctuation, yet she expressed far-reaching ideas within compact phrases. Amidst paradox and uncertainty, her poetry has an undeniable capacity to move and provoke.

Investigate Further

To find out more about Emily Dickinson, or to hear readings of her poems, you could do a search of some of the useful websites available such as YouTube, BBC Poetry, poetryfoundation.org and poetryarchive.org, or access additional material on this page of your eBook.

Prescribed Poems

○ **1 '"Hope" is the thing with feathers'**
In this upbeat poem, Dickinson addresses the experience of hope and imagines it as having some of the characteristics of a small bird. **Page 54**

○ **2 'There's a certain Slant of light'**
A particular beam of winter light puts the poet into a depressed mood in which she reflects on human mortality and our relationship with God. **Page 58**

○ **3 'I felt a Funeral, in my Brain' (OL)**
Dickinson imagines the experience of death from the perspective of a person who is about to be buried. **Page 62**

○ **4 'A Bird came down the Walk'**
The poet observes a bird and tries to establish contact with it, revealing both the beauty and danger of nature. **Page 66**

○ **5 'I heard a Fly buzz– when I died' (OL)**
Another illustration of Dickinson's obsession with the transition of the soul from life into eternity. **Page 69**

○ **6 'The Soul has Bandaged moments'**
This intricate poem explores the soul's changing moods, from terrified depression to delirious joy. **Page 72**

○ **7 'I could bring You Jewels– had I a mind to'**
In this short love poem, Dickinson celebrates nature's simple delights and contrasts the beauty of an everyday flower with more exotic precious gifts. **Page 76**

○ **8 'A narrow Fellow in the Grass'**
Using a male perspective, the poet details the fascination and terror experienced in confronting a snake. **Page 79**

○ **9 'I taste a liquor never brewed'**
Dickinson uses an extended metaphor of intoxication in this exuberant celebration of nature in summertime. **Page 82**

○ **10 'After great pain, a formal feeling comes'**
A disturbing examination of the after-effects of suffering and anguish on the individual. **Page 86**

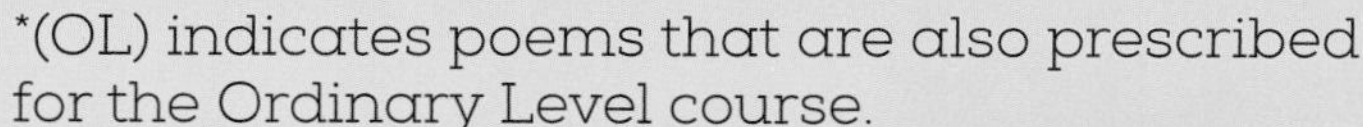
*(OL) indicates poems that are also prescribed for the Ordinary Level course.

1 'Hope' is the thing with feathers

'Hope' is the thing with feathers–
That perches in the soul–
And sings the tune without the words–
And never stops–at all–

And sweetest–in the Gale–is heard–
And sore must be the storm–
That could abash the little Bird
That kept so many warm–

I've heard it in the chillest land–
And on the strangest Sea–
Yet, never, in Extremity,
It asked a crumb–of Me.

And sweetest–in the Gale–is heard: hope is most comforting in times of trouble.
abash: embarrass; defeat.

in Extremity: in terrible times.

'And sweetest–in the Gale–is heard–'

Personal Response

1. What are the main characteristics of the bird admired by Dickinson?
2. Would you consider Dickinson to be an optimist or a pessimist? How does the poem contribute to your view?
3. In your view, what is the purpose of the poem – to instruct, to explain, to express a feeling? Support your response by reference to the text.

Critical Literacy

Few of Emily Dickinson's poems were published during her lifetime and it was not until 1955, 69 years after her death, that an accurate edition of her poems was published, with the original punctuation and words. This didactic poem explores the abstraction, hope. It is one of her 'definition' poems, wherein she likens hope to a little bird, offering comfort to all.

The dictionary definition of hope is an expectation of something desired. The Bible refers to hope, saying, 'Hope deferred maketh the heart sick', while the poet Alexander Pope (1688–1744) declares that 'Hope springs eternal in the human breast'. In stanza one, Dickinson explores hope by using the **metaphor of a little bird** whose qualities are similar to those of hope: non-threatening, calm and powerful. Just like the bird, hope can rise above the earth with all its troubles and desperate times. Raised in the Puritan tradition, Dickinson, although rejecting formal religion, would have been aware of the religious symbolism of the dove and its connection with divine inspiration and the Spirit or Holy Ghost, as well as the reference to doves in the story of Noah's Ark and the Flood. Hope appears against all odds and 'perches in the soul'. But this hope is not easily defined, so she refers to it as 'the thing', an inanimate object.

This silent presence is able to **communicate** beyond reason and logic and far **beyond the limitations of language**: 'sings the tune without the words'. Hope's permanence is highlighted by the unusual use of dashes in the punctuation: 'never stops—at all—.' This effective use of punctuation suggests the ongoing process of hope.

Stanza two focuses on the tangible qualities of hope (sweetness and warmth) and shows the spiritual, emotional and psychological **comfort found in hope**. The 'Gale' could refer to the inner state of confusion felt in the agony of despair. The little bird that comforts and shelters its young offers protection to 'so many'. The vigour of the word 'abash' suggests the buffeting wind of the storm against which the little bird survives. The last two lines, which run on, convey the welcoming, protective circle of the little bird's wing.

A **personal experience of hope in times of anguish** ('I've heard') is referred to in stanza three. Extreme circumstances are deftly sketched in the phrases 'chillest land' and 'strangest Sea'. This reclusive poet, who spent most of her life indoors in her father's house, deftly catches an alien, foreign element. She then explains that hope is not demanding in bad times; it is generous, giving rather than taking: 'Yet, never, in Extremity,/It asked a crumb—of Me.' The central paradox of hope is expressed in the metaphor of the bird, delicate and fragile, yet strong and indomitable. The tiny bird is an effective image for the first stirring of hope in a time of despair. In the solemn ending, the poet gives hope the dignified celebration it deserves.

Dickinson is a unique and original talent. She used the metre of hymns. She also uses their form of the four-line verse. Yet this is not conventional poetry, due to Dickinson's use of the dash to slow the line and make the reader pause and consider. Ordinary words like 'at all' and 'is heard' assume a tremendous importance and their position is to be considered and savoured. **Her unusual punctuation has the same effect, as it highlights the dangers ('Gale', 'Sea').** The alliteration of 's' in 'strangest Sea' and the run-on line to suggest the circling comfort of the little bird all add to the curious music of Dickinson's poems. The buoyant, self-confident tone of the poem is in direct contrast to the strict Puritanical tradition of a severe, righteous God, with which she would have been familiar in her youth and which she rejected, preferring to keep her Sabbath 'staying at home'.

Writing About the Poem

'Emily Dickinson's poetry contains an intense awareness of the private, inner self.' Discuss this view with particular reference to '"Hope" is the thing with feathers'.

Sample Paragraph

Everyone has experienced moments of depression when it seems that nothing is ever going to go right again. Dickinson, with her simple image of the bird singing, provides an optimistic response to this dark state of mind. She then develops this metaphor throughout the poem, comforting us with the thought that the bird (symbolising hope) can communicate with us without the need for the restrictions of language, 'sings the tune without words'. There is no end to hope. It 'never stops at all'. Dickinson understands the darkness of despair, 'in the Gale', 'the strangest Sea'. The use of capital letters seems to emphasise the deep terror of the individual. But the bird of hope provides comfort and warmth ('sweetest'). The poet uses enjambment effectively in the lines 'That could abash the little Bird/That kept so many warm'. The run-on rhythm suggests the protection of hope encircling us, just as the wing of

the bird protects her young in the nest. This is an upbeat introspective poem in which Dickinson is instructing the reader that one should never give up. The phrase 'perches in the soul' suggests to me that the poet regards hope as coming of its own choice. Hope is generous, always giving, 'Yet, never, in Extremity,/It asked a crumb—of Me'. I think the use of the capital for 'Me' shows the heightened concern of someone when faced with despair.

EXAMINER'S COMMENT

This coherent and focused response shows a good understanding of the poem and a clear awareness of Dickinson's reflective tone. Effective use made of accurate quotations. The commentary on enjambment and movement ('run-on rhythm suggests the protection of hope encircling us') is impressive. A solid top-grade answer.

Class/Homework Exercises

1. 'Dickinson is a wholly new and original poetic genius.' Do you agree or disagree with this statement? Support your response with reference to '"Hope" is the thing with feathers'.
2. 'Emily Dickinson often uses concrete language to communicate abstract ideas in her unusual poems.' Discuss this view, with reference to '"Hope" is the thing with feathers'.

Summary Points

- **The poem explores the concept of hope and its impact on human life.**
- **Effective use of the extended metaphor of 'the little bird'.**
- **Symbols represent the challenges people face in life.**
- **Variety of tones – assured, personal, reflective, optimistic, etc.**

2 There's a certain Slant of light

There's a certain Slant of light,
Winter Afternoons—
That oppresses, like the Heft
Of Cathedral Tunes—

Heavenly Hurt, it gives us—
We can find no scar,
But internal difference,
Where the Meanings, are—

None may teach it—Any—
'Tis the Seal Despair—
An imperial affliction
Sent us of the Air—

When it comes, the Landscape listens—
Shadows—hold their breath—
When it goes, 'tis like the Distance
On the look of Death—

Slant: incline; fall; interpretation.

oppresses: feels heavy; overwhelms.
Heft: strength; weight.

Any: anything.

Seal Despair: sign or symbol of hopelessness.
imperial affliction: God's will for mortal human beings.

'Heavenly Hurt, it gives us—'

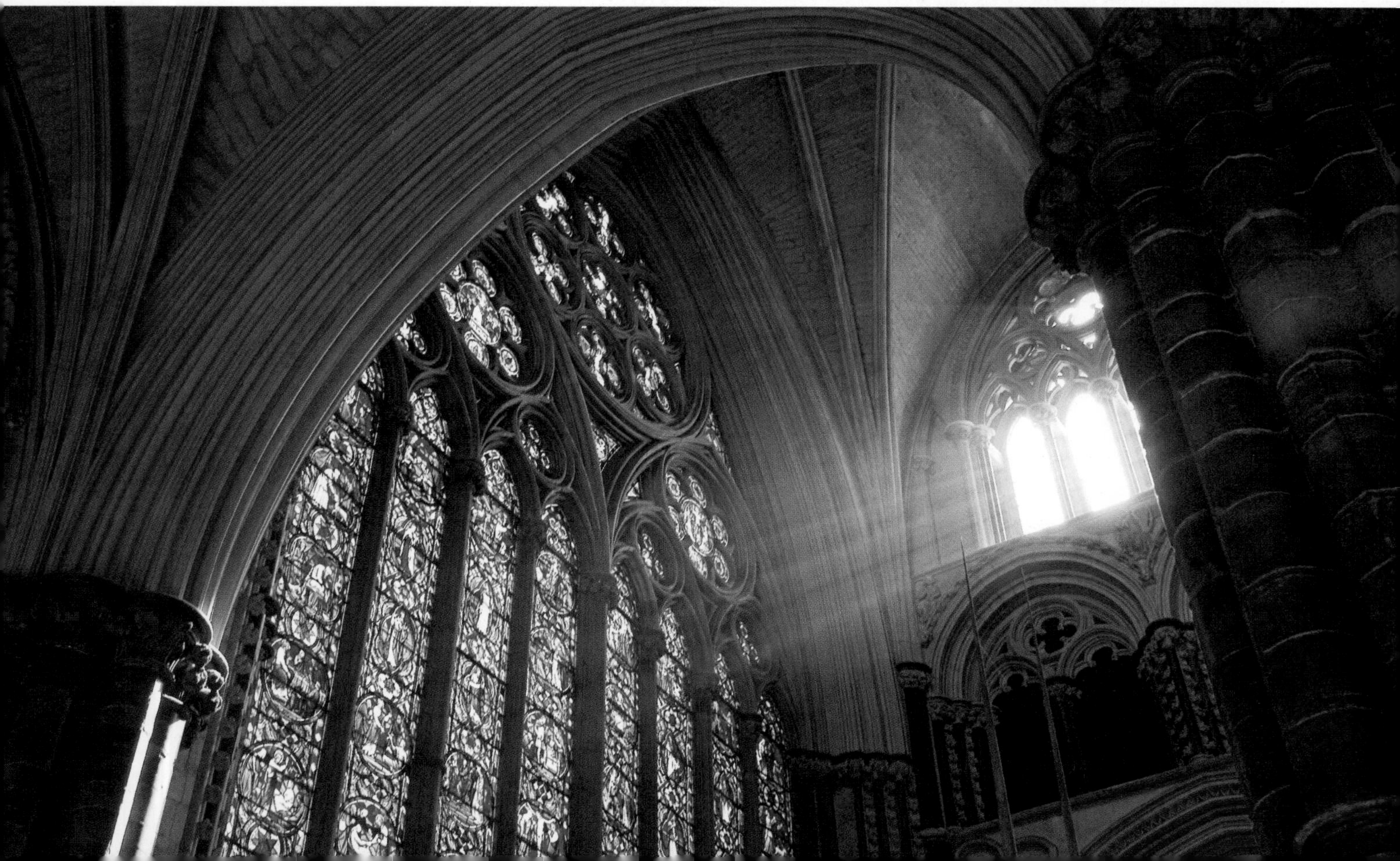

Personal Response

1. Describe the mood and atmosphere created by the poet in the opening stanza.
2. Comment on Dickinson's use of personification within the poem.
3. Write your own personal response to the poem, supporting your views with reference or quotation.

Critical Literacy

Dickinson was a keen observer of her environment, often dramatising her observations in poems. In this case, a particular beam of winter light puts the poet into a mood of depression as the slanting sunlight communicates a sense of despair. The poem typifies her creeping fascination with mortality. But although the poet's subject matter is intricate and disturbing, her own views are more difficult to determine. Ironically, this exploration of light and its effects seems to suggest a great deal about Dickinson's own dark consciousness.

From the outset, Dickinson creates an uneasy atmosphere. The setting ('Winter Afternoons') is dreary and desultory. Throughout stanza one, there is an underlying sense of time weighing heavily, especially when the light is compared to solemn cathedral music ('Cathedral Tunes'). We usually expect church music to be inspirational and uplifting, but in this case, its 'Heft' has a burdensome effect which simply 'oppresses' and adds to the **downcast mood**.

In stanza two, the poet considers the significance of the sunlight. For her, its effects are negative, causing pain to the world: 'Heavenly Hurt, it gives us.' The paradoxical language appears to reflect Dickinson's ironic attitude that **human beings live in great fear of God's power**. Is there a sense that deep down in their souls ('Where the Meanings, are'), people struggle under the weight of God's will, fearing death and judgement?

This feeling of humanity's helplessness is highlighted in stanza three: 'None may teach it' sums up the predicament of our limitations. Life and death can never be fully understood. Perhaps this is our tragic fate – our 'Seal Despair'. Dickinson presents **God as an all-powerful royal figure** associated with suffering and punishment ('An imperial affliction'). Is the poet's tone critical and accusatory? Or is she simply expressing the reality of human experience?

Stanza four is highly dramatic. **Dickinson personifies a terrified world** where 'the Landscape listens'. The earlier sombre light is now replaced by 'Shadows' that 'hold their breath' in the silence. The poet imagines the shocking moment of death and the mystery of time ('the Distance'). While the poem's ending is open to speculation, it seems clear that Dickinson is exploring the transition from life into eternity, a subject that is central to her writing. The

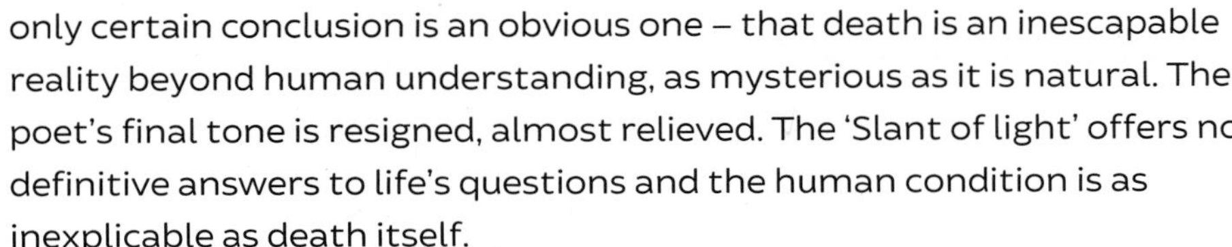

only certain conclusion is an obvious one – that death is an inescapable reality beyond human understanding, as mysterious as it is natural. The poet's final tone is resigned, almost relieved. The 'Slant of light' offers no definitive answers to life's questions and the human condition is as inexplicable as death itself.

Throughout the poem, Dickinson's fragmented style is characterised by her **erratic punctuation and repeated use of capital letters**. She uses the dash at every opportunity to create suspense and drama. For the poet, the winter light is seen as an important sign from God, disturbing the inner 'Landscape' of her soul. In the end, the light (a likely metaphor for truth) causes Dickinson to experience an inner sadness and a deep sense of spiritual longing.

Writing About the Poem

In your view, what is the central theme in this poem? Support the points you make with suitable reference to the text.

Sample Paragraph

I think that death is the main theme in all of Emily Dickinson's poems, including this one. The poem is very atmospheric, but the light coming through the church window can be interpreted as a symbol of God, hope for the world. However, Dickinson's language is quite negative and it could be argued that our human lives are under pressure and that fear of eternal damnation is also part of life. The phrases 'Heavenly Hurt' and 'imperial affliction' suggest that we are God's subjects, trying to avoid sin in this life in order to find salvation after death. One of the central points in the poem is the fear of dying people have. All humans can do is 'hold their breath'. I believe that the central message is that death comes to us all and we must accept it. The mood throughout the poem is oppressive, just like the sunlight coming in through the church window and the depressing 'Cathedral Tunes'. The poet's distinctive punctuation, using dashes and abrupt stops and starts, is part of the tense mood of the poem. Dickinson's theme is quite distressing and the broken rhythms and disturbing images such as 'Seal Despair' and 'Shadows' add to the uneasiness of the theme that death is unavoidable.

EXAMINER'S COMMENT

Well-written, top-grade response that shows good engagement with both the poem and the question. References and succinct quotations used effectively to illustrate the poet's startling consideration of death. Confident and varied discussion of the poet's style throughout.

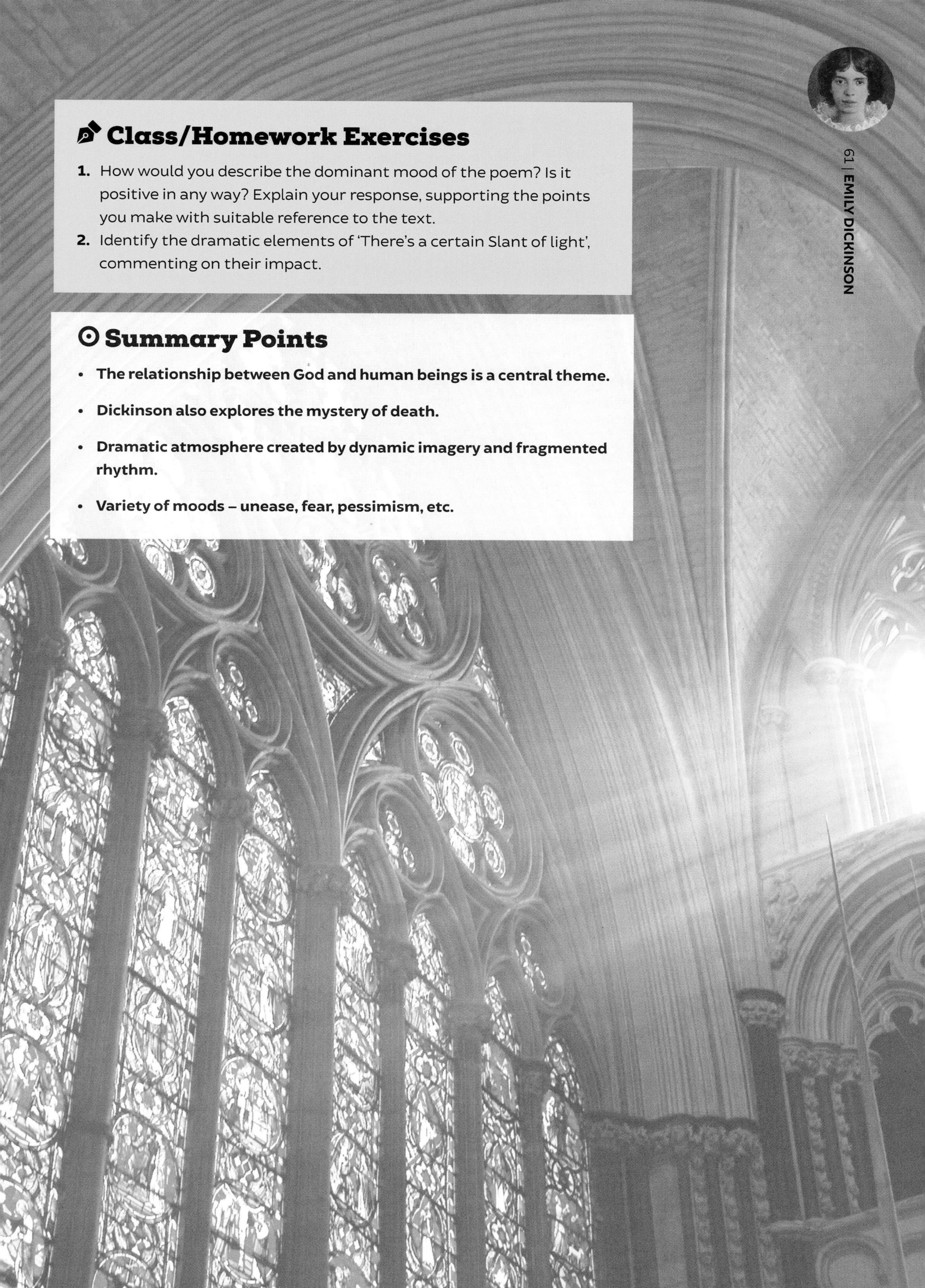

Class/Homework Exercises

1. How would you describe the dominant mood of the poem? Is it positive in any way? Explain your response, supporting the points you make with suitable reference to the text.
2. Identify the dramatic elements of 'There's a certain Slant of light', commenting on their impact.

Summary Points

- **The relationship between God and human beings is a central theme.**
- **Dickinson also explores the mystery of death.**
- **Dramatic atmosphere created by dynamic imagery and fragmented rhythm.**
- **Variety of moods – unease, fear, pessimism, etc.**

3 I felt a Funeral, in my Brain

I felt a Funeral, in my Brain,
And Mourners to and fro
Kept treading—treading—till it seemed
That Sense was breaking through—

And when they all were seated,
A Service, like a Drum—
Kept beating—beating—till I thought
My Mind was going numb—

And then I heard them lift a Box
And creak across my Soul
With those same Boots of Lead, again,
Then Space—began to toll,

As all the Heavens were a Bell,
And Being, but an Ear,
And I, and Silence, some strange Race
Wrecked, solitary, here—

And then a Plank in Reason, broke,
And I dropped down, and down—
And hit a World, at every plunge,
And Finished knowing—then—

treading: crush by walking on.
Sense: faculty of perception; the senses (seeing, hearing, touching, tasting, smelling); sound, practical judgement.

toll: ring slowly and steadily, especially to announce a death.

As all: as if all.

And Being, but an Ear: all senses, except hearing, are now useless.

'And then a Plank in Reason, broke'

Personal Response

1. Do you find the images in this poem frightening, macabre or coldly realistic? Give reasons for your answer, supported by textual reference.
2. Where is the climax of the poem, in your opinion? Refer to the text in your answer.
3. Write a short personal response to the poem, highlighting the impact it made on you.

Critical Literacy

This poem is thought to have been written in 1861, at a time of turbulence in Dickinson's life. She was having religious and artistic doubts and had experienced an unhappy time in a personal relationship. This interior landscape paints a dark picture of something falling apart. It is for the reader to decide whether it is a fainting spell, a mental breakdown or a funeral. That is the enigma of Dickinson.

The startling perspective of this poem in stanza one can be seen as the view experienced by a person in a coffin, if the poem is read as an **account of the poet imagining her death**. Alternatively, it could refer to the suffocating feeling of the breakdown of consciousness, either through fainting or a mental breakdown. Perhaps it is the death of artistic activity. Whichever reading is chosen, and maybe all co-exist, the **interior landscape of awareness is being explored**. The use of the personal pronoun 'I' shows that this is a unique experience, although it has relevance for all. The relentless pounding of the mourners walking is reminiscent of a blinding migraine headache. The repetition of the hard-sounding 't' in the verb 'treading—treading' evocatively describes this terrible experience. The 'I' is undergoing an intense trauma beyond understanding: 'Sense was breaking through.' This repetition and disorientation are synonymous with psychological breakdown.

Stanza two gives a **first-person account of a funeral**. The mourners are seated and the service has begun. Hearing ('an Ear') is the only sense able to perceive. All the verbs refer to sound: 'tread', 'beat', 'heard', 'creak', 'toll'. The passive 'I' receives the experience, hearing, not listening, which is an active process. The experience is so overwhelming that 'I' thought the 'Mind was going numb', unable to endure any more. The use of the past tense reminds the reader that the experience is over, so is the first-person narrative told from beyond the grave? Is this the voice of someone who has died? Or is it the voice of someone in the throes of a desperate personal experience? The reader must decide.

The reference to 'Soul' in stanza three suggests a **spiritual dimension** to the experience. The 'I' has started to become disoriented as the line dividing an external experience and an internal one is breaking. The mourners 'creak across my Soul'. The oppressive, almost suffocating experience is captured in the onomatopoeic phrase 'Boots of Lead' and space becomes filled with the tolling bell. Existence in stanza four is reduced totally to hearing. The fearful transitory experience of crossing from awareness to unconsciousness, from life to death, is being imagined. The 'I' in stanza four is now stranded, 'Wrecked', cut off from life. The person is in a comatose state, able to comprehend but unable to communicate: 'solitary, here.' The word 'here' makes the reader feel present at this awful drama.

Finally, in stanza five, a new sensation takes over, **the sense of falling uncontrollably**. The 'I' has finished knowing and is now no longer aware of surroundings. Is this the descent into the hell of the angels in Paradise Lost? Is it the descent of the coffin into the grave? Or is it the descent into madness or oblivion? The 'I' has learned something, but it is not revealed. The repetition of 'And' advances the movement of the poem in an almost uncontrollable way, mimicking the final descent. The 'I' is powerless under the repetitive verbs and the incessant rhythm punctuated by the ever-present dash. This poem is extraordinary, because before the study of psychology had defined it, it is a step-by-step description of mental collapse. Here is 'the drama of process'.

Writing About the Poem

'"I felt a Funeral, in my Brain" is a detailed and intense exploration of the experience of death.' Discuss this statement, using references from the text to support your views.

Sample Paragraph

When I first read Emily Dickinson's poem 'I felt a Funeral, in my Brain', I was reminded of the surreal paintings of Salvador Dali, where everything was vivid, but not quite right. Dickinson's imagined funeral suggests the losing of the grip on life by the individual 'I'. The incessant noise ('treading', 'beating') induces an almost trance-like state as the brain cannot function anymore, and so becomes numb. The poet suggests that awareness is dramatically reduced to a single sense – hearing – 'an Ear'. I also find the perspective of the poem chilling. The idea that this is the view of someone lying in the coffin observing their own funeral is macabre. But the most compelling line in the poem is 'And then a Plank in Reason, broke'. This graphically conveys the snap of reason as the 'I' loses finally a grip on consciousness and slips away, hurtling away uncontrollably into another dimension. Even the punctuation, with the use of commas, conveys this divided reality. But the most unnerving word is yet to come – 'then'. Does the poet suddenly understand? What exactly does the poet know? Is it about the existence or non-existence of an afterlife? As always, Dickinson leaves us with unanswered questions.

EXAMINER'S COMMENT

A sustained personal response which attempts to stay focused throughout. The intensity within the poem is conveyed through a variety of expressions ('incessant noise', 'dramatically', 'compelling', 'unnerving') and there is some worthwhile discussion on how features of the poet's style advance the theme of death. A solid high-grade answer.

Class/Homework Exercises

1. 'She seems as close to touching bottom here as she ever got.' Discuss this view of Emily Dickinson with reference to the poem 'I felt a Funeral, in my Brain'.
2. Comment on the conclusion of the poem. Did you think it is satisfactory? Or does it leave unanswered questions?

Summary Points

- **Themes include the imagined experience of loss of control and death.**
- **Vivid imagery depicts funeral scene.**
- **Introspective tones of uncertainty, shock and terror.**
- **Insistent rhythms, anguished tone, abrupt syntax all create dramatic impact.**
- **Striking use of onomatopoeia – assonance, repetition, etc.**

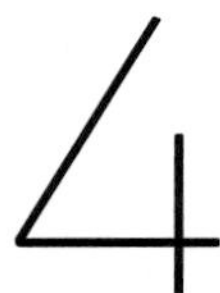

4 A Bird came down the Walk

A Bird came down the Walk—
He did not know I saw—
He bit an Angleworm in halves
And ate the fellow, raw,

And then he drank a Dew
From a convenient Grass—
And then hopped sidewise to the Wall
To let a Beetle pass—

He glanced with rapid eyes
That hurried all around—
They looked like frightened Beads, I thought—
He stirred his Velvet Head

Like one in danger, Cautious,
I offered him a Crumb
And he unrolled his feathers
And rowed him softer home—

Than Oars divide the Ocean,
Too silver for a seam—
Or Butterflies, off Banks of Noon
Leap, plashless as they swim.

Angleworm: small worm used as fish bait by anglers.

the Ocean: Dickinson compares the blue sky to the sea.
silver: the sea's surface looks like solid silver.
a seam: opening; division.
plashless: splashless; undisturbed.

Personal Response

1. In your view, what does the poem suggest about the relationship between human beings and nature?
2. What is the effect of Dickinson's use of humour in the poem? Does it let you see nature in a different way? Support the points you make with reference to the text.
3. From your reading of the poem, what impression of Emily Dickinson herself is conveyed? Refer to the text in your answer.

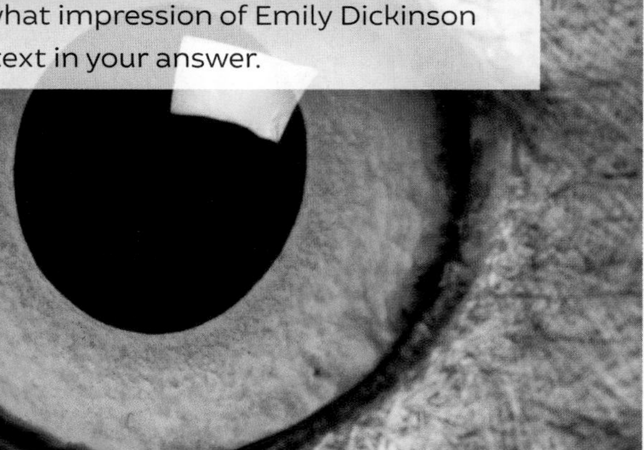

'He glanced with rapid eyes'

Critical Literacy

In this short descriptive poem, Dickinson celebrates the beauty and wonder of animals. While the bird is seen as a wild creature at times, other details present its behaviour and appearance in human terms. The poem also illustrates Dickinson's quirky sense of humour as well as offering interesting insights into nature and the exclusion of human beings from that world.

The poem begins with an everyday scene. Because the bird is unaware of the poet's presence, it behaves naturally. Stanza one demonstrates the **competition and danger of nature**: 'He bit an Angleworm in halves.' Although Dickinson imagines the bird within a human context, casually coming 'down the Walk' and suddenly eating 'the fellow, raw', she is amused by the uncivilised reality of the animal kingdom. The word 'raw' echoes her self-deprecating sense of shock. Despite its initial elegance, the predatory bird could hardly have been expected to cook the worm.

The poet's comic portrayal continues in stanza two. She gives the bird certain social qualities, drinking from a 'Grass' and politely allowing a hurrying beetle to pass. The tone is relaxed and playful. The slender vowel sounds ('convenient') and soft sibilance ('sidewise', 'pass') add to the seemingly refined atmosphere. However, the mood changes in stanza three, reflecting the bird's cautious fear. Dickinson observes the rapid eye movement, 'like frightened Beads'. Such **precise detail increases the drama of the moment**. The details of the bird's prim movement and beautiful texture are wonderfully accurate: 'He stirred his Velvet Head.' The simile is highly effective, suggesting the animal's natural grace.

The danger becomes more explicit in stanza four. Both the spectator and the observed bird are 'Cautious'. The crumb offered to the bird by the poet is rejected, highlighting the **gulf between their two separate worlds**. The description of the bird taking flight evokes the delicacy and fluidity of its movement: 'And he unrolled his feathers/And rowed him softer home.' The confident rhythm and emphatic alliteration enrich our understanding of the harmony between the creature and its natural environment. The sensual imagery captures the magnificence of the bird, compared to a rower moving with ease across placid water.

Stanza five develops the metaphorical description further, conveying the bird's poise and mystery: 'Too silver for a seam.' Not only was its flying seamless, it was smoother than that of butterflies leaping 'off Banks of Noon' and splashlessly swimming through the sky. The **breathtaking image and onomatopoeic language** remind us of Dickinson's admiration for nature in all its impressive beauty and is one of the most memorable descriptions in Dickinson's writing.

 Writing About the Poem

In your view, does Dickinson have a sense of empathy with the bird? Support your response with reference to the poem.

Sample Paragraph

It is clear from the start of the poem that Emily Dickinson is both fascinated and amused by the appearance of a small bird in her garden. She seems surprised and almost honoured that out of nowhere 'A Bird came down the Walk'. When it suddenly swallows a worm 'raw', she becomes even more interested. The fact that she admits 'He did not know I saw' tells me that she really has empathy for the bird. Her tone suggests that she feels privileged to watch and she certainly doesn't want to disturb it in its own world. The poet also finds the bird's antics funny. Although it devours the snail, it still behaves very mannerly towards the beetle. Near the end, Dickinson shows her feelings for the bird when it becomes frightened and she notices its 'rapid eyes'. She sees that it is 'in danger'. The fact that she offered it a crumb also shows her empathy. At the very end, she shows her admiration for the beauty and agility of the bird as it flies off to freedom – to its 'softer home'. The descriptions of it like a rower or a butterfly also suggest that she admires its grace.

EXAMINER'S COMMENT

Apt references and short quotations are effectively used to illustrate the poet's regard for the bird. The answer ranges well over much of the poem and considers various tones (including fascination, amusement, reverence, concern and admiration). A confident high-grade response.

Class/Homework Exercises

1. Comment on Dickinson's use of imagery in 'A Bird came down the Walk'. Support the points you make with the aid of suitable reference.
2. In your opinion, what does the poem suggest about the differences (or similarities) between animals and humans? Support your response with reference to the text.

Summary Points

- **Exploration of the wonder of nature.**
- **Interesting use of personification gives the bird social graces.**
- **Impact of sensuous imagery, metaphorical language, sibilant effects.**
- **Contrasting tones – bemused, concerned, surprised, upbeat, etc.**

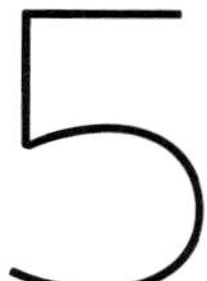

5 I heard a Fly buzz—when I died

I heard a Fly buzz—when I died—
The Stillness in the Room
Was like the Stillness in the Air—
Between the Heaves of Storm—

The Eyes around—had wrung them dry—
And Breaths were gathering firm
For that last Onset—when the King
Be witnessed—in the Room—

I willed my Keepsakes—Signed away
What portion of me be
Assignable—and then it was
There interposed a Fly—

With Blue—uncertain stumbling Buzz—
Between the light—and me—
And then the Windows failed—and then
I could not see to see—

Heaves: lift with effort.

Onset: beginning.
the King: God.

Keepsakes: gifts treasured for the sake of the giver.

interposed: inserted between or among things.

'Heavenly Hurt, it gives us—'

Personal Response

1. How would you describe the atmosphere in the poem? Pick out two phrases which, in your opinion, are especially descriptive and explain why you chose them.
2. Do you think Dickinson uses contrast effectively in this poem? Discuss one contrast you found particularly striking.
3. Write a brief personal response to the poem, highlighting its impact on you.

Critical Literacy

Dickinson was fascinated by death. This poem examines the moment between life and death. At that time, it was common for family and friends to be present at deathbed vigils. It was thought that the way a person behaved or looked at the moment of death gave an indication of the soul's fate.

The last moment of a person's life is a solemn and often sad occasion. The perspective of the poem is that of the person dying and this significant moment is dominated by the buzzing of a fly in the room in the **first stanza**. This is **absurdly comic and strangely distorts** this moment into something grotesque. Surely the person dying should be concerned with more important matters than an insignificant fly: 'I heard a Fly buzz—when I died.' The room is still and expectant as the last breaths are drawn, a stillness like the moments before a storm. All are braced for what is to come. The word 'Heaves' suggests the force of the storm that is about to break.

The **second stanza** shows us that the mourners had now stopped crying and were holding their breath as they awaited the coming of the 'King' (God) into the room at the moment of death. The phrase 'Be witnessed' refers to the dying person and the mourners who are witnessing their faith, and it conjures up all the solemnity of a court. The word 'firm' also suggests these people's steadfast religious beliefs. The **third stanza** is concerned with putting matters right. The dying person has made a will – 'What portion of me be/Assignable' – and what is not assignable belongs to God. The person is awaiting the coming of his/her Maker, 'and then it was/There interposed a Fly' – the symbol of decay and corruption appeared. Human affairs cannot be managed; real life intervenes. The **fly comes between ('interposed') the dying person and the moment of death, which trivialises** the event.

The fractured syntax of the **last stanza** shows the **breakdown of the senses** at the moment of death: 'Between the light—and me.' Sight and sound are blurring. The presence of the fly is completely inappropriate, like a drunken person at a solemn ceremony, disturbing and embarrassing and interrupting proceedings. The fly is now between the dying person and the source of light. Does this suggest that the person has lost concentration on higher things, distracted by the buzzing fly? The sense of sight then fails: 'And then the Windows failed.' The moment of death had come and gone, dominated by the noisy fly. Has the fly prevented the person from reaching another dimension? Is death emptiness, just human decay, as signified by the presence of the fly, or is there something more? Do we need comic relief at overwhelming occasions? Is the poet signalling her own lack of belief in an afterlife with God? Dickinson, as usual, intrigues, **leaving the reader with more questions than answers**, so that the reader, like the dying person, is struggling to 'see to see'.

Writing About the Poem

'Dickinson's poems on mortality often lead to uncertainty or despair.' Discuss this statement with particular reference to 'I heard a Fly buzz—when I died'.

Sample Paragraph

The view of this deathbed scene is from the dying person's perspective. The problem is that everyone is distracted by the inappropriate arrival of a noisy fly! Dickinson seems to be saying that life and death are random and disorganised – and this goes against the human desire for order and control, 'Signed away/What portion of me be/Assignable'. I feel that the poet may be suggesting that the dying person, distracted by the fly is, therefore, cheated in some way. The momentous occasion has passed, dominated by a buzzing fly. Are we being told that we often lose concentration at important moments, for absurd reasons, and so lose valuable insight? Dickinson's voice is far from reassuring. Instead, she dispassionately draws a deathbed scene and lets us 'see to see'. Are we – like the dying person – distracted and unable to achieve greater wisdom? The divided voice, that of the person dying and that of the person after death leaves us with mysteries – is death just the final absurd stage in the meaningless cycle of life? In the end, this poem leaves me with bleak uncertainties about the human condition and its ability to exercise control.

EXAMINER'S COMMENT

This solid, high-grade response includes interesting and thought-provoking ideas on a challenging question. Comments show some good personal engagement with the poem and the issues raised by Dickinson. Expression is impressive and apt quotations are used effectively throughout the answer. References to the dramatic style and tone would have improved the standard.

Class/Homework Exercises

1. Comment on how Dickinson's style contributes to the theme or message in this poem. Refer closely to the text in your response.
2. Is there any suggestion that the speaker in this poem believes in a spiritual afterlife? Give a reason for your response, supporting your views with reference to the text.

Summary Points

- **Dickinson raises questions about death and the possibility of an afterlife.**
- **Surreal sense of the absurd throughout.**
- **Dramatic elements – the deathbed scene, still atmosphere, observers, noises, etc.**
- **Contrasting tones include disbelief, confusion, resignation and helplessness.**
- **Effective use of contrast and symbols (light, the fly) and repetition.**

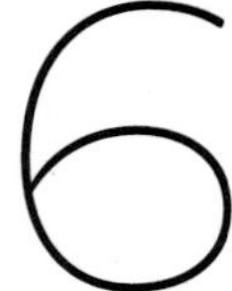

The Soul has Bandaged moments

The Soul has Bandaged moments—
When too appalled to stir—
She feels some ghastly Fright come up
And stop to look at her—

Salute her—with long fingers—
Caress her freezing hair—
Sip, Goblin, from the very lips
The Lover—hovered—o'er—
Unworthy, that a thought so mean
Accost a Theme—so—fair—

The soul has moments of Escape—
When bursting all the doors—
She dances like a Bomb, abroad,
And swings upon the Hours,

As do the Bee—delirious borne—
Long Dungeoned from his Rose—
Touch Liberty—then know no more,
But Noon, and Paradise—

The Soul's retaken moments—
When, Felon led along,
With shackles on the plumed feet,
And staples, in the Song,

The Horror welcomes her, again,
These, are not brayed of Tongue—

Bandaged moments: painful experiences.
appalled: shocked, horrified.
stir: act; retaliate.

Accost: address.

Escape: freedom.

like a Bomb: dramatically.
abroad: in unusual directions.

Dungeoned: imprisoned in the hive.

Felon: criminal.

shackles: chains, ropes.
plumed: decorated.
staples: fastenings.

brayed: inarticulate.

Personal Response

1. What details in the poem evoke the feelings of 'ghastly Fright' experienced by the soul? Support your answer with quotation or reference.
2. Choose one comparison from the poem that you find particularly effective. Explain your choice.
3. Comment on Dickinson's use of dashes in this poem, briefly explaining their effectiveness.

Critical Literacy

Throughout much of her poetry, Dickinson focuses on the nature of consciousness and the experience of being alive. She was constantly searching for meaning, particularly of transient moments or changing moods. This search is central to 'The Soul has Bandaged moments', where the poet takes us through a series of dramatic images contrasting the extremes of the spirit and the conscious self.

Stanza one introduces the soul as being fearful and vulnerable, personified as a terrified female who 'feels some ghastly Fright', with the poem's stark

'As do the Bee—delirious borne—'

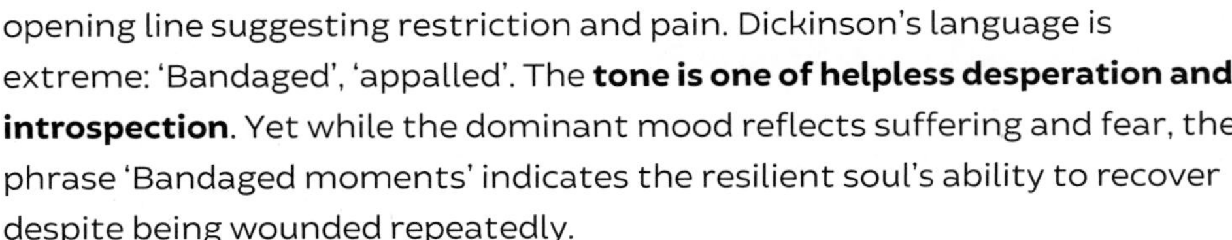

opening line suggesting restriction and pain. Dickinson's language is extreme: 'Bandaged', 'appalled'. The **tone is one of helpless desperation and introspection**. Yet while the dominant mood reflects suffering and fear, the phrase 'Bandaged moments' indicates the resilient soul's ability to recover despite being wounded repeatedly.

Stanza two is unnervingly dramatic. The poet creates a mock-romantic scene between the victimised soul and the 'ghastly Fright' figure, now portrayed as a hideous goblin and her would-be lover, their encounter depicted in terms of gothic horror. The soul experiences terrifying fantasies as the **surreal sequence becomes increasingly menacing** and the goblin's long fingers 'Caress her freezing hair'. The appearance of an unidentified shadowy 'Lover' is unexpected. There is a sense of the indecisive soul being caught between two states, represented by the malevolent goblin and the deserving lover. It is unclear whether Dickinson is writing about the choices involved in romantic love or the relationship between herself and God.

The stanza ends inconclusively, juxtaposing two opposites: the 'Unworthy' or undeserving 'thought' and the 'fair' (worthy) 'Theme'. The latter might well refer to the ideal of romantic love. If so, it is confronted by erotic desire (the 'thought'). Dickinson's disjointed style, especially her frequent use of dashes within stanzas, isolates key words and intensifies the overwhelmingly **nightmarish atmosphere**.

The feeling of confused terror is replaced with ecstatic 'moments of Escape' in stanzas three and four. The soul recovers in triumph, 'bursting all the doors'. This **explosion of energy** ('She dances like a Bomb') evokes a rising mood of riotous freedom. Explosive verbs ('bursting', 'dances', 'swings') and robust rhythms add to the sense of uncontrollable excitement. Dickinson compares the soul to a 'Bee—delirious borne'. After being 'Long Dungeoned' in its hive, this bee can now enjoy the sensuous delights of 'his Rose'.

The mood is short-lived, however, and in stanzas five and six, 'The Horror' returns. The soul becomes depressed again, feeling bound and shackled, like a 'Felon led along'. **Dickinson develops this criminal metaphor** – 'With shackles on the plumed feet' – leaving us with an ultimate sense of loss as 'The Horror welcomes her, again'. Is this the soul's inevitable fate? The final line is unsettling. Whatever horrible experiences confront the soul, they are simply unspeakable: 'not brayed of Tongue.'

As always, Dickinson's poem is open to many interpretations. Critics have suggested that the poet is dramatising the turmoil of dealing with the loss of creativity. Some view the poem's central conflict as the tension between romantic love and sexual desire. Others believe that the poet was exploring the theme of depression and mental instability. In the end, readers must find their own meaning and decide for themselves.

Writing About the Poem

Comment on the dramatic elements that are present in the poem, supporting the points you make with reference to the text.

Sample Paragraph

'The Soul has Bandaged moments' is built around a central conflict between two opposing forces, the 'Soul', or spirit, and its great enemy, 'Fright'. Dickinson sets the dramatic scene with the Soul still recovering – presumably from the last battle. It is 'Bandaged' after the fight with its arch enemy. The descriptions of the soul's opponent are startling. Fright is 'ghastly', a 'Horror' and a sleazy 'Goblin' who is trying to seduce the innocent soul. Some of Dickinson's images add to the dramatic tension. In the seduction scene, the goblin is described as having 'long fingers'. His intended victim is seen as helpless, petrified with fear. The goblin uses its bony claws to 'Caress her freezing hair'. Both characters seem to have come out of an old black-and-white horror movie. The drama continues right to the end. The soul is compared to a 'Felon' who has just been recaptured and is being led away in 'shackles'. Such images have a distressing impact in explaining the pressures on the soul to be free. Finally, Dickinson's stop-and-start style is also unsettling. Broken rhythms and her condensed use of language increase the edgy atmosphere throughout this highly dramatic poem.

EXAMINER'S COMMENT

An assured and focused top-grade response, showing a clear understanding of the poem's dramatic features. The answer addressed both subject matter and style, using back-up illustration and integrated quotes successfully. Expression throughout was also excellent.

Class/Homework Exercises

1. How would you describe the dominant tone of 'The Soul has Bandaged moments'? Use reference to the text to show how the tone is effectively conveyed.
2. Identify the poem's surreal aspects and comment on their impact.

Summary Points

- **An intense exploration on the nature of spiritual awareness.**
- **Dickinson focuses on a series of traumatic experiences.**
- **Effective use of dramatic verbs and vivid imagery.**
- **The soul is personified to convey various states – fear, joy, terror, etc.**

7 I could bring You Jewels—had I a mind to

I could bring You Jewels—had I a mind to—
But You have enough—of those—
I could bring You Odors from St. Domingo—
Colors—from Vera Cruz—

Berries of the Bahamas—have I—
But this little Blaze
Flickering to itself—in the Meadow—
Suits Me—more than those—

Never a Fellow matched this Topaz—
And his Emerald Swing—
Dower itself—for Bobadilo—
Better—Could I bring?

Odors: fragrances, perfumes.
St. Domingo: Santo Domingo in the Caribbean.
Vera Cruz: city on the east coast of Mexico.

Bahamas: group of islands south-east of Florida.
Blaze: strong fire or flame; very bright light.

Dower: part of her husband's estate allotted to a widow by law.
Bobadilo: braggart; someone who speaks arrogantly or boastfully.

'Never a Fellow matched this Topaz–'

Personal Response

1. Does the poet value exotic or homely gifts? Briefly explain your answer.
2. Write your own personal response to the poem, highlighting its impact on you.
3. What is the tone in this poem: arrogant, humble, gentle, strident, confident? Quote in support of your opinion.

Critical Literacy

Although described as a recluse, Dickinson had a wide circle of friends. She wrote letter-poems to them, often representing them as flowers, 'things of nature which had come with no practice at all'. This poem is one without shadows, celebratory and happy, focusing out rather than in as she concentrates on a relationship.

In the first stanza, the poem opens with the speaker **considering the gift she will give** her beloved, 'You'. The 'You' is very much admired, and is wealthy ('You have enough'), so the gift of jewels is dismissed. The phrase 'had I a mind to' playfully suggests that maybe the 'I' doesn't necessarily wish to present anything. There is a certain coquettish air evident here. A world of privilege and plenty is shown as, one after another, expensively exotic gifts are considered and dismissed. These include perfumes and vibrant colours from faraway locations, conjuring up images of romance and adventure: 'Odors from St. Domingo.'

The second stanza continues the list, with 'Berries of the Bahamas' being considered as an option for this special gift, but they are not quite right either. The tense changes to 'have I' and the laconic listing and dismissing stops. A small wildflower 'in the Meadow', 'this little Blaze', is chosen instead. This 'Suits Me'. Notice that it is not that this suits the other person. **This gift is a reflection of her own unshowy personality**. The long lines of considering exotic gifts have now given way to shorter, more decisive lines.

In the third stanza, the speaker has a definite note of conviction, as she confidently states that 'Never a Fellow matched' this shining gift of hers. No alluring, foreign gemstone, be it a brilliant topaz or emerald, shines as this 'little Blaze' in the meadow. The gift glows with colour; it is natural, inexpensive and accessible. The reference to a dower might suggest a gift given by a woman to a prospective husband. This **gift is suitable** for a Spanish adventurer, a 'Bobadilo'. The assured tone is clear in the word 'Never' and the jaunty rhyme 'Swing' and 'bring'. The final rhetorical question suggests that this is the best gift she could give. The poem shows that **the true value of a present cannot be measured in a material way**.

Writing About the Poem

'Dickinson is fascinated by moments of change.' Discuss this statement with reference to 'I could bring You Jewels—had I a mind to'.

Sample Paragraph

In this lively poem, the speaker considers what present would be most suitable to give to her arrogant lover. The first instant of change occurs when this confident woman dismisses expensive, exotic gifts, 'But You have enough' and chooses something which is natural and simple – and, more importantly – which is to her liking: 'Suits Me.' The simple flower she offers is unexpectedly beautiful – this 'little Blaze/ Flickering to itself' suggests the hidden passion of the woman herself. The unpretentious meadow flower is free and easily picked, but how it shines! The changing breathless tone reflects the love she feels. The little flower is brighter than any precious stone of 'Topaz' or 'Emerald'. Now short, crisp lines ring out with the self-belief of a woman who knows best. Even the rhyme changes from the slant rhyme, where she is considering her options ('those'/'Cruz') in the first stanza, to the more definite jaunty full rhyme of 'Swing' and 'bring' in the final stanza. I really enjoyed how Dickinson explored the very feminine trait of considering everything, and then finally deciding, after humorous hesitation. Dickinson is certainly fascinated by the spontaneity of life.

EXAMINER'S COMMENT

A confident top-grade response to the question, backed up with a convincing use of quotation. Good discussion about changes in thought and tone. The point about the change in line length was particularly interesting. Assured, varied vocabulary is controlled throughout and the paragraph is rounded off impressively.

Class/Homework Exercises

1. 'Dickinson disrupts and transforms our accepted view of things.' What is your opinion of this statement? Refer to 'I could bring You Jewels—had I a mind to' in support of your response.
2. Comment on the impact of Dickinson's use of sound effects in the poem.

Summary Points

- **Central themes include the wonder and beauty of nature.**
- **Celebratory mood conveyed by powerful visual imagery and lively rhythm.**
- **Simplicity of the wildflower contrasted with extravagant glamour.**
- **Confident, optimistic tone contrasts with the poet's downbeat poems.**

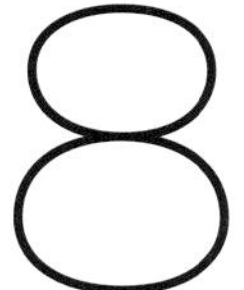

A narrow Fellow in the Grass

A narrow Fellow in the Grass
Occasionally rides—
You may have met Him—did you not
His notice sudden is—

The Grass divides as with a Comb—
A spotted shaft is seen—
And then it closes at your feet
And opens further on—

He likes a Boggy Acre
A Floor too cool for Corn—
Yet when a Boy, and Barefoot—
I more than once at Noon
Have passed, I thought, a Whip lash
Unbraiding in the Sun
When stooping to secure it
It wrinkled, and was gone—

Several of Nature's People
I know, and they know me—
I feel for them a transport
Of cordiality—

But never met this Fellow
Attended, or alone
Without a tighter breathing
And Zero at the Bone—

a spotted shaft: patterned skin of the darting snake.

Whip lash: sudden, violent movement.
Unbraiding: straightening out, uncoiling.

transport: heightened emotion.

cordiality: civility, welcome.

Zero at the Bone: cold terror.

Personal Response

1. Select two images from the poem that suggest evil or menace. Comment briefly on the effectiveness of each.
2. How successful is the poet in conveying the snake's erratic sense of movement? Refer to the text in your answer.
3. Outline your own feelings in response to the poem.

'His notice sudden is—'

Critical Literacy

In this poem, one of the few published during her lifetime, Dickinson adopts a male persona remembering an incident from his boyhood. Snakes have traditionally been seen as symbols of evil. We still use the expression 'snake in the grass' to describe someone who cannot be trusted. Central to this poem is Dickinson's own portrayal of nature – beautiful, brutal and lyrical. She seems fascinated by the endless mystery, danger and unpredictability of the natural world.

The opening lines of stanza one casually introduce a 'Fellow in the Grass'. (Dickinson never refers explicitly to the snake.) The **conversational tone immediately involves readers** who may already 'have met Him'. However, there is more than a hint of warning in the postscript: 'His notice sudden is.' This underlying wariness now appears foreshadowed by the menacing adjective 'narrow' and by the disjointed rhythm and slightly awkward word order.

Dickinson focuses on the volatile snake's dramatic movements in stanza two. The verbs 'divide', 'closes' and 'opens' emphasise its dynamic energy. The snake suddenly emerges like a 'spotted shaft'. The poet's **comparisons are particularly effective**, suggesting a lightning bolt or a camouflaged weapon. Run-on lines, a forceful rhythm and the repetition of 'And' contribute to the vivid image of the snake as a powerful presence to be treated with caution.

Stanza three reveals even more about the snake's natural habitat: 'He likes a Boggy Acre.' It also divulges the speaker's identity – an adult male remembering his failed boyhood efforts to capture snakes. The memory conveys something of the intensity of childhood experiences, especially of dangerous encounters with nature. The boy's innocence and vulnerability ('Barefoot') contrasts with the 'Whip lash' violence of the wild snake. **Dickinson's attitude to nature is open to interpretation**. Does the threat come from the animal or the boy? Did the adult speaker regard the snake differently when he was young? The poet herself clearly appreciates the complexities found within the natural world and her precisely observed descriptions ('Unbraiding', 'It wrinkled') provide ample evidence of her interest.

From the speaker's viewpoint in stanza four, nature is generally benign. This positive image is conveyed by the affectionate tribute to 'Nature's People'. The familiar personification and personal tone underline the mutual 'cordiality' that exists between nature and human nature. Despite this, **divisions between the two worlds cannot be ignored**. Indeed, the focus in stanza five is on the sheer horror people experience when confronted by 'this Fellow'. The poet's sparse and chilling descriptions – 'tighter breathing', 'Zero at the Bone' – are startling expressions of stunned terror.

As in other poems, Dickinson attributes human characteristics to nature – the snake 'Occasionally rides', 'The Grass divides' and the bogland has a 'Floor'. One effect of this is to highlight the **variety and mystery of the**

natural environment, which can only ever be glimpsed within limited human terms. The snake remains unknowable to the end, dependent on a chance encounter, a fleeting glance or a trick of light.

Writing About the Poem

Comment on the effectiveness of Dickinson's use of the male persona voice in 'A narrow Fellow in the Grass'. Support the points you make with reference to the poem.

Sample Paragraph

In some of her poems, Emily Dickinson chose to substitute her own voice with that of a persona, a fictional narrator. This is the case in 'A narrow Fellow in the Grass', where she uses a country boy to tell the story of his experiences trying to catch snakes when he was young. It is obvious that he has a great love for nature, but neither is he blind to the cold fear he felt when he came face to face with the 'spotted shaft'. Dickinson's use of language emphasises his youthful terror. She lets him remember his encounter exactly as it happened. The images are powerful and disturbing: 'a tighter breathing.' The boy remembers shuddering with uncontrollable fright, 'Zero at the Bone'. The description is dramatic and I found I could relate to the boy's sense of horror. The poem is all the more effective for being centred around one terrified character, the young boy. I can visualise the child in his bare feet trying to catch a frightened snake in the grass. It is only later that he realises the great danger he was in and this has taught him a lifelong lesson about nature. By using another speaker's persona, Dickinson explores the excitement and danger of nature in a wider way that allows readers to imagine it more clearly.

EXAMINER'S COMMENT

A well-written and sustained response that includes some good personal engagement and a great deal of insightful discussion – particularly regarding the conflict between the boy and the snake. References and quotations are well used throughout the answer to provide a very interesting high-grade standard.

Class/Homework Exercises

1. In your opinion, how does Dickinson portray nature in 'A narrow Fellow in the Grass'? Support your points with reference to the poem.
2. Identify the dramatic moments in this poem and comment on their impact.

Summary Points

- **Dickinson explores contrasting aspects of the natural world.**
- **Effective use of everyday conversational language.**
- **The poet adopts the persona of a young boy who encounters a snake.**
- **Dramatic atmosphere concludes on a note of terror.**

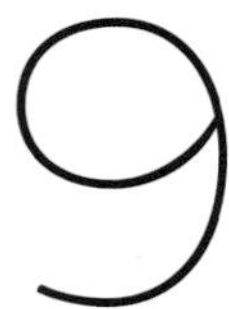

9 I taste a liquor never brewed

I taste a liquor never brewed—
From Tankards scooped in Pearl—
Not all the Vats upon the Rhine
Yield such an Alcohol!

Inebriate of Air—am I—
And Debauchee of Dew—
Reeling—thro endless summer days—
From inns of Molten Blue—

When 'Landlords' turn the drunken Bee
Out of the Foxglove's door—
When Butterflies—renounce their 'drams'—
I shall but drink the more!

Till Seraphs swing their snowy Hats—
And Saints—to windows run—
To see the little Tippler
Leaning against the—Sun—

Tankards: one-handled mugs, usually made of pewter, used for drinking beer.
Vats: large vessels used for making alcohol.

Debauchee: someone who has overindulged and neglected duty.

Seraphs: angels who are of the highest spiritual level.

Tippler: a person who drinks often, but does not get drunk.

'Not all the Vats upon the Rhine/ Yield such an Alcohol!'

Personal Response

1. What is the mood in this poem? Does it intensify or change? Use references from the text in your response.
2. Which stanza appeals to you most? Discuss both the poet's style and content in your answer.
3. Write a brief personal response to the poem, highlighting its impact on you.

Critical Literacy

This 'rapturous poem about summer' uses the metaphor of intoxication to capture the essence of this wonderful season. Dickinson's family were strict Calvinists, a religion that emphasised damnation as the consequence of sin. Her father supported the Temperance League, an organisation that warned against the dangers of drink.

This poem is written as a **joyful appreciation of this wonderful life**. The tone is playful and exaggerated from the beginning, as the poet declares this drink was never 'brewed'. The reference to 'scooped in Pearl' could refer to the great, white frothing heads of beer in the 'Tankards'. The poet certainly conveys the merriment of intoxication, as the poem reels along its happy way. The explanation for all this drunkenness is that the poet is drunk on life ('Inebriate', 'Debauchee'). The pubs are the inns of 'Molten Blue', i.e. the sky (stanza two). It is like a cartoon, with little drunken bees being shown the door by the pub owners as they lurch about in delirious ecstasy. The drinkers of the natural world are the bees and butterflies, but she can drink more than these: 'I shall but drink the more!' This roots the poem in reality, as drunken people always feel they can manage more.

But this has caused uproar in the heavens, as the angels and saints run to look out at this little drunk, 'the little Tippler'. She stands drunkenly leaning against the 'Sun', a celestial lamppost. The final dash suggests the crooked stance of the little drunken one. **There is no heavy moral at the end of this poem. In fact, there seems to be a slight note of envy for the freedom and happiness being experienced by the intoxicated poet**. Are the angels swinging their hats to cheer her on in her drunken rebellion? Is this poem celebrating the reckless indulgence of excess? Or is the final metaphor of the sun referring to Christ or to the poet's own arrival in heaven after she indulgently enjoys the beauty of the natural world?

Nature is seen as the spur for high jinks and good humour. The riddle of the first line starts it off: how was the alcohol 'never brewed'? The exaggerated imagery, such as the metaphor of the flower as a pub and the bee as the drunk, all add to the fantasy land atmosphere. The words 'Inebriate', 'Debauchee' and 'renounce' are reminiscent of the language which those

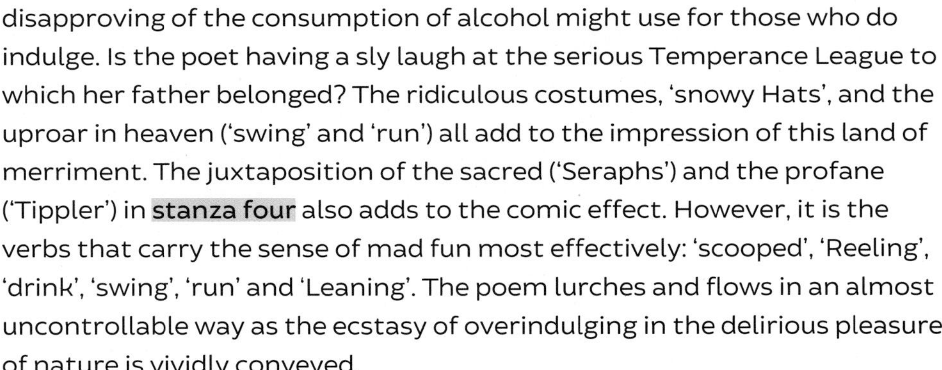

disapproving of the consumption of alcohol might use for those who do indulge. Is the poet having a sly laugh at the serious Temperance League to which her father belonged? The ridiculous costumes, 'snowy Hats', and the uproar in heaven ('swing' and 'run') all add to the impression of this land of merriment. The juxtaposition of the sacred ('Seraphs') and the profane ('Tippler') in stanza four also adds to the comic effect. However, it is the verbs that carry the sense of mad fun most effectively: 'scooped', 'Reeling', 'drink', 'swing', 'run' and 'Leaning'. The poem lurches and flows in an almost uncontrollable way as the ecstasy of overindulging in the delirious pleasure of nature is vividly conveyed.

There are two different types of humour present in this irrepressible poem – the broad humour of farce and the more **subversive humour of irony**. She even uses the steady metre of a hymn, with eight syllables in lines one and three and six syllables in lines two and four. Dickinson seems to be standing at a distance, smiling wryly, as she gently deflates.

Writing About the Poem

'Dickinson was always careful to avoid expressing excessive emotion, even of joy.' Discuss this statement with reference to 'I taste a liquor never brewed'.

Sample Paragraph

I don't agree about the question. This is a very funny poem and the poet is actually enjoying herself. She is clearly drunk on nature and it is humourous when the angels are waving their little white caps, egging her on. I think this is really a very happy go lucky poem, filled with joy, unlike most of Emily Dickenson's disturbing poems we studied about death, funerals and souls. It goes to show that she also writes happier poetry when she wants to. Dickenson is an excentric writer who hardly ever uses normal punctuation or grammar. Her poems are hard to make out as they don't have normal sentences but use a lot of dashes and capital letters for the important words. There is a good comparison for drinking all through this poem to describe being drunk on nature. The poem is definately full of joy, eg the story about the bee. The lines describing the little tippler leaning against the paling post are also really joyful. I think everyone should be able to enjoy Emily's brilliant poem as it has many happy images such as the drinking bee and the little tippler.

EXAMINER'S COMMENT

This note-like answer shows limited engagement with the poem. While there is a recognition of the poem's joyful tone and some supportive reference, the lack of substantial analysis is noticeable. Language use is repetitive, expression is flawed and there are several mechanical mistakes. The over-enthusiastic ending is not convincing. Closer study of the poem and greater care in writing the response would raise the standard from a basic grade.

Class/Homework Exercises

1. 'Hypersensitivity to natural beauty produced Dickinson's poetry.' Do you agree or disagree with this statement? Refer to the poem 'I taste a liquor never brewed' in your response.
2. Identify the childlike elements of the poem and comment on their impact.

Summary Points

- **The poem highlights Dickinson's close relationship with nature.**
- **Exuberant mood conveyed by sibilant sounds, vivid images, lively rhythm, etc.**
- **Extended metaphor of intoxication used effectively throughout.**
- **Dominant sense of delight, celebration and good humour.**

10 After great pain, a formal feeling comes

After great pain, a formal feeling comes—
The Nerves sit ceremonious, like Tombs—
The stiff Heart questions was it He, that bore,
And Yesterday, or Centuries before?

The Feet, mechanical, go round—
Of Ground, or Air, or Ought—
A Wooden way
Regardless grown,
A Quartz contentment, like a stone—

This is the Hour of Lead—
Remembered, if outlived,
As Freezing persons, recollect the Snow—
First—Chill—then Stupor—then the letting go—

formal: serious; exact.

ceremonious: on show.

He: the stiff Heart, or possibly Christ.

bore: endure; intrude.

Ought: anything.

Quartz: basic rock mineral.

Hour of Lead: traumatic experience.

Stupor: numbness; disorientation.

Personal Response

1. Comment on the poet's use of personification in the opening stanza.
2. How does the language used in the second stanza convey the condition of the victim in pain?
3. Write your own short personal response to the poem.

'First—Chill—then Stupor'

Critical Literacy

Dickinson wrote 'After great pain' in 1862, at a time when she was thought to have been experiencing severe psychological difficulties. The poet addresses the effects of isolation and anguish on the individual. Ironically, the absence of the personal pronoun 'I' gives the poem a universal significance. The 'great pain' itself is never fully explained and the final lines are ambiguous. Like so much of Dickinson's work, this dramatic poem raises many questions for consideration.

From the outset, Dickinson is concerned with the emotional numbness ('a formal feeling') that follows the experience of 'great pain'. The poet's authoritative tone in stanza one reflects a first-hand knowledge of trauma, with the adjective 'formal' suggesting self-conscious recovery from some earlier distress. Dickinson personifies the physical response as order returns to body and mind: 'The Nerves sit ceremonious, like Tombs.' The severe pain has also shocked the 'stiff Heart', which has become confused by the experience. Is the poet also drawing a parallel with the life and death of Jesus Christ (the Sacred Heart), crucified 'Centuries before'? The images certainly suggest timeless suffering and endurance. This **sombre sense of loss** is further enhanced by the broad vowel assonance of the opening lines.

The feeling of stunned inertia continues into stanza two. In reacting to intense pain, 'The Feet, mechanical, go round'. It is as if the response is unfocused and indifferent, lacking any real purpose. Dickinson uses two **analogies to emphasise the sense of pointless alienation**. The reference to the 'Wooden way' might be interpreted as a fragile bridge between reason and insanity, or this metaphor could be associated with Christ's suffering as he carried his cross to Calvary. The level of consciousness at such times is described as 'Regardless grown', or beyond caring. Dickinson's second comparison is equally innovative: 'A Quartz contentment' underpins the feeling of complete apathy that makes the victims of pain behave 'like a stone'. Is she being ironic by suggesting that the post-traumatic state is an escape, a 'contentment' of sorts?

There is a disturbing sense of resignation at the start of stanza three: 'This is the Hour of Lead'. The dull weight of depression is reinforced by the insistent monosyllables and solemn rhythm, but the devastating experience is not 'outlived' by everyone. Dickinson outlines the aftermath of suffering by using one final comparison: 'As Freezing persons.' This shocking simile evokes the unimaginable hopelessness of the victim stranded in a vast wasteland of snow. The poem's last line traces the tragic stages leading to oblivion: 'First—Chill—then Stupor—then the letting go—.' The inclusion of the dash at the end might indicate a possibility of relief, though whether it is through rescue or death is not revealed. In either case, **readers are left with an acute awareness of an extremely distraught voice**.

Writing About the Poem

One of Dickinson's great achievements is her ability to explore the experience of deep depression. To what extent is this true of her poem 'After great pain, a formal feeling comes'? Refer closely to the text in your answer.

Sample Paragraph

'After great pain' is a very good example of Emily Dickinson's skill in addressing controversial and distressing subjects, such as mental breakdown. Although she never really explains what she means by the 'pain' referred to in the first line, she deals with the after-effects of suffering throughout the poem. What Dickinson does very well is to explain how depression can lead to people becoming numb, beyond all emotion. I believe this is what she means by 'a formal feeling'. She uses an interesting image of a sufferer's nerves sitting quietly in a church at a funeral service. They 'sit ceremonious'. This same idea is used to describe the mourners following the hearse – 'Feet mechanical'. I get the impression that grief and mourning can destroy people's confidence and make them numb. Dickinson's images are compelling and suggest the coldness experienced by patients who have suffered depression. They are 'like a stone'. The best description is at the end, when she compares sufferers to being lost in the snow. They will slowly fade into a 'stupor' or death wish. I think Dickinson is very good at using images and moods to explore depression. She is very good at suggesting shock in this poem.

EXAMINER'S COMMENT

Although the expression is slightly awkward in places, there are a number of interesting points in the response – particularly the discussion of 'a formal feeling' and the exploration of key images in the poem. Expression is controlled throughout and supportive references are used effectively. A solid high-grade standard.

Class/Homework Exercises

1. In your opinion, what is the dominant mood in 'After great pain, a formal feeling comes'? Is it one of depression, sadness or acceptance? Refer closely to the text in your answer.
2. In your view, which metaphor in the poem best conveys a sense of deep depression? Briefly explain your choice.

Summary Points

- **Intense exploration of depression and psychological suffering.**
- **Effective use of vivid imagery, personification and serious tone.**
- **Disturbing mood throughout is solemn and sombre.**
- **Ambiguous open-ended conclusion.**

Leaving Cert Sample Essay

'Emily Dickinson's distinctive style of poetry reflects a wide range of powerful emotions.' Discuss this view, supporting the points you make with suitable reference to the poems by Dickinson on your course.

Sample Essay (Dickinson's distinctive style of poetry reflects a wide range of powerful emotions)

1. Emily Dickinson is probably best known for her unique use of language. She is usually associated with short phrases, broken rhythms, capital letters and the constant use of dashes in place of ordinary punctuation. Many of her condensed poems are like puzzles where the reader is forced to seek through odd sentences in order to find the poet's true meaning. I found Dickinson's poetry intriguing because of this. However, her poems about nature were quirky and even humorous at times. On other occasions, she seemed edgy, obsessed with death and depression.

2. The oddness of Dickinson's poetry would, I feel, appeal to many young people of my age group. She is an original writer – and her eccentric style seems strangely modern. In the dramatic poem 'Slant of Light', Dickinson takes an unlikely approach. When one thinks of light, one normally imagines brightness and joy. But the winter light in this poem is coldly oppressive, suggesting Dickinson's deep despair. A sense of finality is present throughout – particularly in the chill setting. It is the end of the year – 'Winter afternoons' so the light is fading. Dickinson immediately expresses religious doubts. The 'Cathedral Tunes' offer no comfort – instead, the church music is harsh. The poet's fearful fascination with death is clearly evident in her portrayal of a merciless, vengeful God subjecting humans to 'Heavenly Hurt, it gives us'.

3. This sense of terror is a recurring emotion in Dickinson's poetry. 'I felt a Funeral, in my Brain' is especially harrowing. Using nightmarish imagery, she imagines the experience of her own burial, with 'Mourners to and fro'. Her helplessness and isolation is powerfully conveyed through the repeated references to sounds 'threading—threading'. The funeral drum haunts her – 'beating—beating'. This awful alienation is forcefully expressed by a pounding rhythm which echoes the funeral march and reminds us of the poet's panic. The stark image of a coffin being lowered into a grave is suggested in the final stanza – 'And I dropped down, and down'. Dickinson's fragmented syntax reinforces the powerlessness of the 'solitary' speaker who is being lowered into her final resting place. There is something surreal about the graveyard scene which Dickinson creates, but she manages to communicate some of the trauma surrounding the disturbing subject of death.

MARKING SCHEME GUIDELINES

Candidates are free to agree and/or disagree with the given statement. However, they should show clear evidence of personal engagement with Dickinson's poetry. The key terms ('distinctive style' and 'wide range of powerful emotions') should be addressed either implicitly or explicitly. Allow for a wide range of approaches in the answering.

INDICTIVE MATERIAL

- Startling treatment of recurring themes: consciousness, death, nature.
- Dramatic moments of crucial experiences.
- Widely varying moods/atmospheres of anguish/celebration.
- Unconventional punctuation and syntax highlight emotions.
- Realistic/pessimistic attitudes, etc.

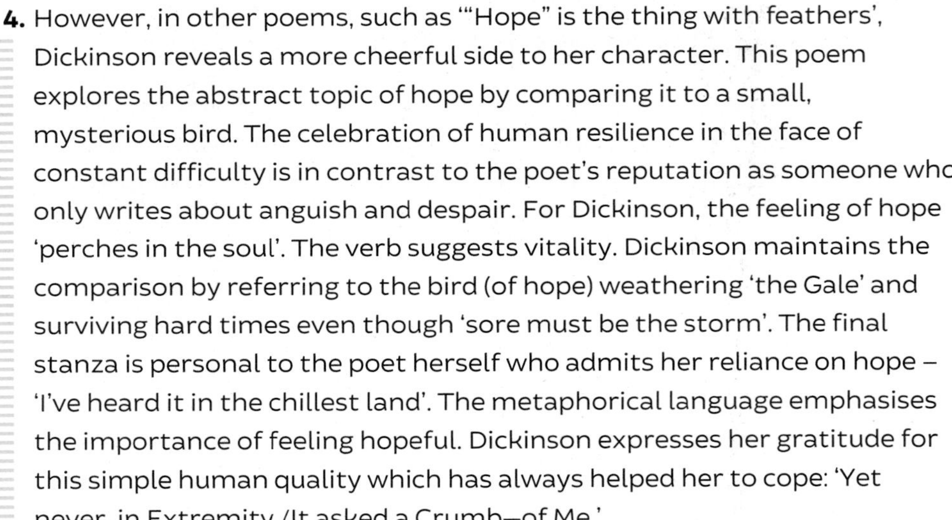

4. However, in other poems, such as '"Hope" is the thing with feathers', Dickinson reveals a more cheerful side to her character. This poem explores the abstract topic of hope by comparing it to a small, mysterious bird. The celebration of human resilience in the face of constant difficulty is in contrast to the poet's reputation as someone who only writes about anguish and despair. For Dickinson, the feeling of hope 'perches in the soul'. The verb suggests vitality. Dickinson maintains the comparison by referring to the bird (of hope) weathering 'the Gale' and surviving hard times even though 'sore must be the storm'. The final stanza is personal to the poet herself who admits her reliance on hope – 'I've heard it in the chillest land'. The metaphorical language emphasises the importance of feeling hopeful. Dickinson expresses her gratitude for this simple human quality which has always helped her to cope: 'Yet never, in Extremity,/It asked a Crumb—of Me.'

5. Emily Dickinson's individual style of writing is seen in another poem, 'A narrow Fellow in the Grass'. In this seemingly ordinary domestic drama, Dickinson takes a young boy's perspective to express the excitement and shock of seeing a snake that frightened him – 'His notice sudden is'. The snake is personified and unpredictable – a 'spotted shaft'. I thought the poet was expressing feelings of surprise when confronted with the unexpected. Everyone experiences shock at some time in their lives. Dickinson ranges over a variety of emotional responses throughout this narrative poem, firstly accepting the snake as another part of the natural world, but later reacting with complete terror – feeling 'Zero at the Bone'. She is horrified by it but is still intrigued by the possibility of what the deadly snake might do.

6. Dickinson's poems covered a great many emotions. She even sees the natural world in a comic way – particularly in 'A Bird came down the Walk'. The oddness of her poems really enticed me, the more I read them. She is a highly imaginative poet who can see animals in human terms. The bird 'drank a dew/From a convenient grass'. But the same bird soon reminds the poet that nature can be dangerous and should be treated with caution – 'He bit an Angleworm in halves/And ate the fellow, raw'. I liked the way Dickinson switches moods and expresses contrasting feelings. For me, she is a really fresh and original poetic voice who is always realistic about life.

(approx. 780 words)
(45–50 minutes)

EXAMINER'S COMMENT

This is a top-grade personal response that tries hard to remain focused on the question. While some of the points are slightly forced (e.g. in paragraph 5), there is close engagement with both the content and style of poems used for discussion. Intelligent use of quotations throughout. Overall, the expression is varied, fluent and well managed.

GRADE: H1
P = 14/15
C = 13/15
L = 14/15
M = 5/5
Total = 46/50

Sample Leaving Cert Questions on Dickinson's Poetry

1. **'Emily Dickinson's unique poetic style is perfectly suited to the extraordinary experiences which she explores in her poems.' Do you agree with this assessment of Dickinson's poetry? Support your answer with suitable reference to the poems by Dickinson on your course.**
2. **'A dark, eccentric vision is at the heart of Emily Dickinson's most dramatic poems.' Discuss this view, supporting the points you make with reference to the poems by Dickinson on your course.**
3. **'Dickinson's exploration of profound life experiences is effectively conveyed through her innovative style.' Discuss this statement, supporting your answer with reference to the poetry of Emily Dickinson on your course.**

NOTE

As you may not be familiar with some of the poems referred to in the sample plans below, substitute poems that you have studied closely.

Exam candidates usually discuss three or four poems in their answers. However, there is no set number of poems or formulaic approach expected.

Key points about a particular poem can be developed over more than one paragraph.

Paragraphs may also include cross-referencing and discussion of more than one poem.

Remember that there is no single 'correct' answer to poetry questions, so always be confident in expressing your own considered response.

First Sample Essay Plan (Q1)

'Emily Dickinson's unique poetic style is perfectly suited to the extraordinary experiences which she explores in her poems.' Do you agree with this assessment of Dickinson's poetry? Support your answer with suitable reference to the poems by Dickinson on your course.

Intro: Dickinson is an original voice who addresses abstract subject matter, such as states of consciousness, hope, death and the relationship between nature and human nature. Her energetic style is in keeping with the intensity of her experiences.

Point 1: '"Hope" is the thing with feathers' – metaphorical language reflects the small bird's presence to illustrate and highlight various aspects of hope and human resilience.

Point 2: Dramatic atmospheres in 'I felt a Funeral, in my Brain' and 'I Heard a Fly buzz—when I died'. Surreal imagery, haunting aural effects and fragmented rhythms effectively convey disorientation and powerlessness.

Point 3: The poet's strangely realistic view of nature evident in 'A Bird came down the Walk'. Use of odd, precise details, onomatopoeic language and comic moments enhance the reader's understanding of Dickinson's attitude.

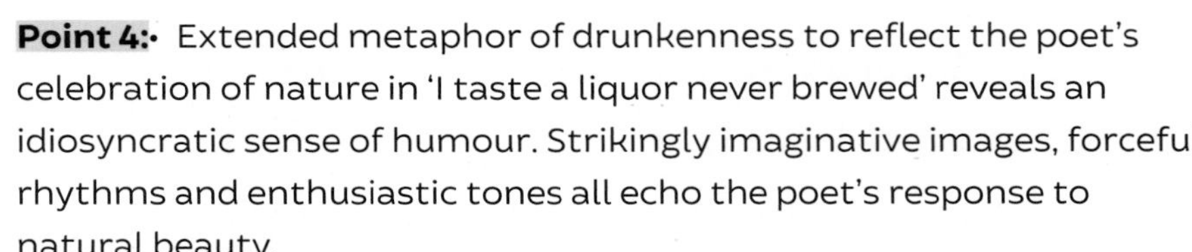

Point 4: • Extended metaphor of drunkenness to reflect the poet's celebration of nature in 'I taste a liquor never brewed' reveals an idiosyncratic sense of humour. Strikingly imaginative images, forceful rhythms and enthusiastic tones all echo the poet's response to natural beauty.

Conclusion: Condensed poetic forms, compressed syntax and daring language use is entirely appropriate to Dickinson's insightful reflections and dramatisations. Readers can engage more immediately with the intensity of the poet's heightened experiences.

Sample Essay Plan (Q1)

Develop **one** of the above points into a paragraph.

Sample Paragraph: Point 2

In both 'I felt a Funeral, in my Brain' and 'I heard a Fly buzz—when I died', Emily Dickinson creates a disturbing account of the sensation of dying. The two poems are dramatic, with a central speaker experiencing death through terrifying images. I thought the poet's style is perfectly in keeping with this alarming subject in 'I felt a Funeral', especially her presentation of the 'Mourners' who keep 'treading' as the coffin is lowered – ' I dropped down, and down'. Repetition – the unreal drum 'beating—beating' – and short, broken phrasing emphasised the feeling of sheer dread and helplessness. Dickinson's vivid imagery and sounds add to the feeling of being overpowered. There is a more absurd atmosphere in 'I heard a Fly buzz—when I died'. The whole exaggerated scene seems distorted, particularly when the insignificant insect became the centre of attention, an 'uncertain stumbling Buzz'. The typically broken sentences also conveyed the confusion of the scene. From the dying person's perspective, there are 'Eyes around', 'Stillness in the Air' and thoughts about the afterlife, 'that last Onset'. The ending stops abruptly, 'I could not see to see', a line suggesting the dreadful frustration and struggle, a desperation for clarity. I find that Dickinson's dramatic language conveys the reality of such troubling experiences very effectively.

EXAMINER'S COMMENT

As part of a full examination essay, this is a clear personal response that addresses the question directly. The sustained focus on Dickinson's language use is aptly supported with very effective use of quotation. Both poems were treated succinctly and included some thoughtful discussion. Well-controlled expression added to the quality of the response. Grade H1.

Sample Essay Plan (Q3)

'Dickinson's exploration of profound life experiences is effectively conveyed through her innovative style.' Discuss this statement, supporting your answer with reference to the poetry of Emily Dickinson on your course.

Intro: Dickinson – looks to understand death, mental anguish and intensely vivid moments of joy. Through her inventive approach to language, she invites readers to join with her as she tells 'the truth, but tells it slant'.

Point 1: 'After great pain, a formal feeling comes' – surreal sequence, alliteration, unusual syntax and monosyllabic words create a vivid exploration of disorientation.

Point 2: 'I could bring You Jewels—had I a mind to' – unusual appreciation of nature's simple joys. Chooses a simple, modest meadow flower ('But this little Blaze/Flickering to itself'). Alliteration, onomatopoeia, a run-on line and the monosyllabic broad vowel sound describe the strong impact of the flower. The dynamic verb 'Flickering' suggests its lively movement. Teasing dismissal of rich, exotic gifts: 'Topaz', 'Emerald'.

Point 3: 'I taste a liquor never brewed' – another poem delighting in the natural world's everyday delights. Startling extended metaphor of stages of intoxication irrepressibly conveys the delirious pleasures of nature, ('When landlords turn the drunken Bee/out of the Foxglove's door'). Unconventional use of capital letters evokes a fantastical landscape. Subversive use of a hymn metre in a poem extolling the pleasures of drink is sardonic.

Point 4: 'A narrow Fellow in the Grass' – contrasting description of the brutal, unpredictable aspects of nature. Personification increases the surreal unnerving quality, 'the Grass divides', the bogland has a 'Floor'. The snake's sudden movements mirrored in descriptive verbs, 'Unbraiding', 'wrinkled'. The discomforting experience and extreme fright are conveyed in the cryptic phrase, 'Zero at the Bone', alarming readers.

Conclusion: Dickinson's disconcerting use of humour, unconventional punctuation, dramatic use of personification coupled with unusual imagery disrupt the reader's conventional awareness of life experiences.

Second Sample Essay Plan (Q3)

Develop **one** of the points on the previous page into a practice paragraph of your own.

Sample Paragraph: Point 1

Dickinson's startling poem, 'After great pain, a formal feeling comes', uses a surreal menacing sequence to examine how emotional numbness, 'a formal feeling', often follows a difficult experience, 'great pain'. Emphatic alliteration ('formal feeling') underlines the constrictive paralysis of emotion into which a person sinks after trauma. There is a disturbing sense of losing control as the 'Feet, mechanical, go round'. The line suggests a complete lack of purpose or direction in the body's movements. Unusual syntax mimics the awkward, artificial movement of an inanimate puppet figure. The bridge between sanity and insanity, 'A Wooden way', is breaking, leaving the helpless individual incapable of rational thought – 'regardless grown'. Monosyllables describe this nightmarish experience of sinking into total inertia, 'First—Chill'. The poet creates a vivid sense of the descent into despair ('then the letting go—). The final dash marks the disorientating awareness of the swirling 'Snow'. By this stage, all sense of direction has been lost. Dickinson is challenging us to become aware of the numbing aftermath of tragedy.

EXAMINER'S COMMENT

As part of a full essay answer to Q3, this is an impressive top-grade standard that shows close engagement with Dickinson's poetry. Incisive discussion of the poet's curious style (sound effects, syntax, punctuation, etc.) is also commendable. Excellent use of quotations and the expression is exceptionally good throughout (e.g. 'the constrictive paralysis of emotion', 'disorientating awareness').

Class/Homework Exercise

1. **Write one or two paragraphs in response to the question, 'Dickinson's exploration of profound life experience is effectively conveyed through her innovative style.' Discuss this statement, supporting your answer with reference to a poem of Emily Dickinson's that you have studied closely.**

 Revision Overview

'"Hope" is the thing with feathers'
Theme of hope, extended metaphor, unusual punctuation, reflective, optimistic tones.

'There's a certain Slant of light'
Reflection on human mortality and our relationship with God, personification, fragmented rhythm and style add to unease and pessimism.

'I felt a Funeral, in my Brain'
Shocking introspection on loss and death, first person perspective, onomatopoeia and repetition.

'A Bird came down the Walk'
Bemused observation of nature, personification, rich imagery and sound effects.

'I heard a Fly buzz–when I died'
Dramatic exploration of death and the afterlife, surreal, use of contrast and symbols add to feeling of helplessness.

'The Soul has Bandaged moments'
Unsettling examination of nature of consciousness, central conflict, changing moods.

'I could bring You Jewels–had I a mind to'
Treatment of relationship, celebration of nature, vivid imagery, optimistic tone.

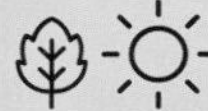

'A narrow Fellow in the Grass'
Danger and beauty in nature, use of persona, colloquial language, concluding tone of terror.

'I taste a liquor never brewed'
Joyful celebration of nature, extended metaphor, subversive humour.

'After great pain, a formal feeling comes'
Disturbing examination of depression, rich imagery, sombre tone, ambiguous ending.

Last Words

'The Dickinson dashes are an integral part of her method and style ... and cannot be translated ... without deadening the wonderful naked voltage of the poems.'
Ted Hughes

(On her determination to hide secrets) 'The price she paid was that of appearing to posterity as perpetually unfinished and wilfully eccentric.'
Philip Larkin

'The Brain–is wider than the Sky–
The Brain is deeper than the sea–'
Emily Dickinson

JOY/HOPE

NATURE

RELIGION/ SPIRITUALITY

SUFFERING

DEATH

MEANING OF LIFE

Paul Durcan
1944–

'That's what poetry is about: getting out of your miserable self and opening your eyes.'

Paul Durcan is one of modern Ireland's foremost and most prolific poets. He is known for his controversial, comic and deeply moving poems. An outspoken critic of his native country, he has traced its emergence from the repressions of the 1950s to the contradictions of the present day.

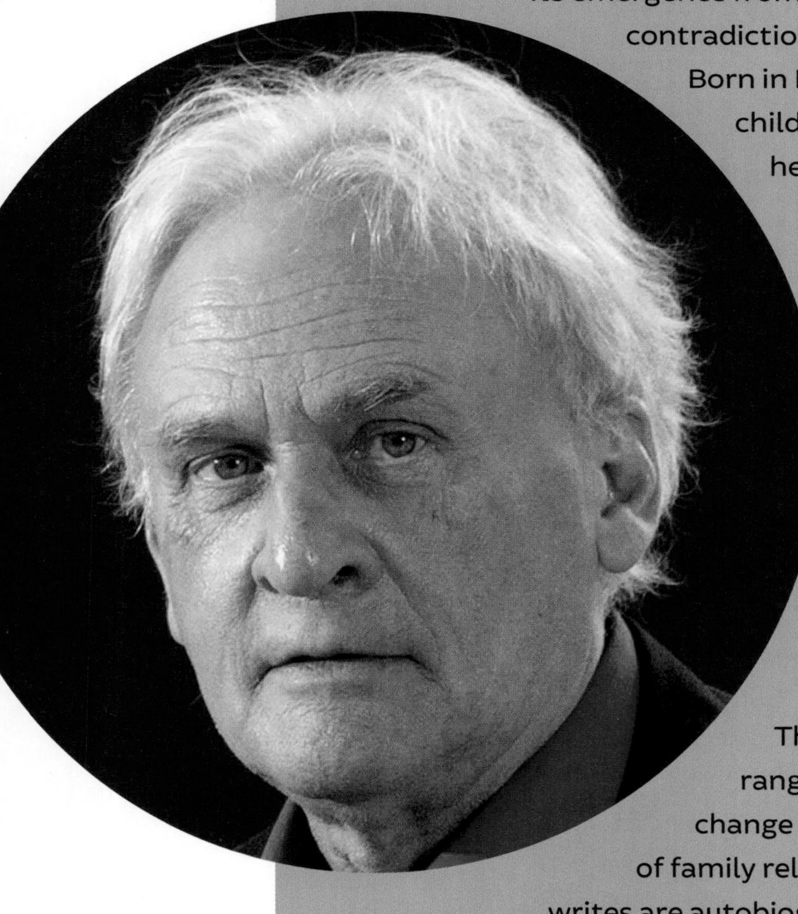

Born in Dublin in 1944, Durcan spent much of his childhood with relatives in County Mayo. In 1967, he met Nessa O'Neill. The couple later married and had two daughters. The marriage ended in 1984.

Among Durcan's many poetic influences are Eliot, Hopkins and Kavanagh. A variety of voices can be heard throughout Durcan's distinctive work, by turns hilarious, humane and heartbreaking. He uses many different forms, including dramatic monologues, ballads, mock news reports, songs and even prayers. His poetry can be surreal, mystical, passionate and ironic.

The subject matter of Paul Durcan's poems ranges widely, from explorations of cultural change in contemporary Ireland to intimate studies of family relationships. Many of the narrative poems he writes are autobiographical, often filled with black humour and satirical jibes. They seem to be carefully designed for oral appreciation.

Investigate Further

To find out more about Paul Durcan, or to hear readings of his poems not available in your eBook, you could do a search of some of the useful websites available such as YouTube, BBC Poetry, poetryfoundation.org and poetryarchive.org, or access additional material on this page of your eBook.

Prescribed Poems

1 'Nessa'
This deeply personal poem is centred around swimming, an extended metaphor conveying both the delights and dangers of falling in love. **Page 98**

2 'The Girl with the Keys to Pearse's Cottage'
This poem addresses aspects of Irish identity, belonging and the instability of place. **Page 102**

3 'The Difficulty that is Marriage'
In this short, introspective reflection, Durcan suggests that while true love is not free of problems, it can still endure despite all the obstacles. **Page 106**

4 'Wife Who Smashed Television Gets Jail' (OL)
Durcan sometimes uses a mock journalistic style, particularly in his humorous critiques of Irish society. **Page 110**

5 'Parents' (OL)
This poem raises interesting questions about parent-child communication, a recurring theme in Paul Durcan's work. **Page 114**

6 '"Windfall", 8 Parnell Hill, Cork'
This long poem recounts both the happiness of family love and domesticity, and the bitter consequences of a marriage. **Page 118**

7 'Six Nuns Die in Convent Inferno'
In this lengthy narrative poem about a fire that destroyed a Dublin convent in 1986, Durcan characteristically transforms the details of the tragedy into an extended exercise in spiritual reflection. **Page 127**

8 'Sport' (OL)
Another painfully autobiographical poem in which Durcan recalls a football match from his youth and explores the troubled relationship he had with his father. **Page 136**

9 'Father's Day, 21 June 1992'
On a crucial train journey from Dublin to Cork, the poet confronts the erosive effects of time on his role as a husband and father. **Page 141**

10 'The Arnolfini Marriage'
This dramatic monologue was inspired by the famous Jan Van Eyck oil painting, which is believed to represent a rich Italian merchant and his wife. **Page 146**

11 'Rosie Joyce'
Durcan has often used travel as a metaphor for reflection or soul-searching. In this upbeat poem celebrating the birth of his granddaughter, he remembers a car journey he took in May 2001 from Mayo to Dublin: **Page 151**

12 'The MacBride Dynasty'
This poem relates the time Durcan's mother made a personal journey back to her hometown to introduce her young son, 'the latest addition' to the family dynasty, to her uncle's famous wife, Maud Gonne. **Page 157**

13 Three Short Poems: 'En Famille, 1979', 'Madman', 'Ireland 2002' Page 162

*(OL) indicates poems that are also prescribed for the Ordinary Level course.

1 Nessa

I met her on the first of August
In the Shangri-La Hotel,
She took me by the index finger
And dropped me in her well.
And that was a whirlpool, that was a whirlpool,
And I very nearly drowned.

Take off your pants, she said to me,
And I very nearly didn't;
Would you care to swim? she said to me,
And I hopped into the Irish Sea.
And that was a whirlpool, that was a whirlpool,
And I very nearly drowned.

On the way back I fell in the field
And she fell down beside me,
I'd have lain in the grass with her all my life
With Nessa:
She was a whirlpool, she was a whirlpool,
And I very nearly drowned.

O Nessa my dear, Nessa my dear,
Will you stay with me on the rocks?
Will you come for me into the Irish Sea
And for me let your red hair down?
And then we will ride into Dublin City
In a taxi-cab wrapped up in dust.
Oh you are a whirlpool, you are a whirlpool,
And I am very nearly drowned.

Shangri-La: legendary location often used in a similar context to the Garden of Eden to represent a hidden paradise. The Shangri-La Hotel was located in Dalkey, Co. Dublin.
index finger: forefinger, pointer finger, trigger finger; often used to make a warning gesture.
whirlpool: swirling body of water produced by the meeting of opposing currents.

on the rocks: a phrase describing a drink served with ice cubes; also refers to a disaster at sea.

'And that was a whirlpool'

Personal Response

1. What impression of Nessa do you get from reading the poem? Refer to the text in your answer.
2. Comment on the effectiveness of the poet's use of the whirlpool image.
3. Write your own personal response to the poem, highlighting the impact it made on you.

Critical Literacy

This well-known love poem comes from Paul Durcan's second collection, *O Westport in the Light of Asia Minor* (1975). The poet has said that he first met Nessa O'Neill in the bar of the Shangri-La Hotel in Dalkey when he was at a wedding reception there in August 1967. Soon afterwards, the couple moved to London and married. 'Nessa' includes elements of the aisling (dream vision) poetry tradition, which dates from late 17th-century Gaelic literature, when Ireland was often represented by an enchanting female figure. Durcan's poem is centred around swimming, an extended metaphor conveying both the delights and dangers of falling in love.

The poem's title and dramatic opening lines emphasise the significance of meeting Nessa 'on the first of August'. This date also marks the traditional Celtic harvest festival, a time for celebrations and arranging marriages. The Irish term *Lughnasa* even echoes Nessa's own name. From the outset, Durcan's first-person presentation associates the woman who was to be his soulmate with mythology. Their introduction 'In the Shangri-La Hotel' seems a suitably exotic setting, suggesting the close spiritual union the couple would share. However, line 3 foreshadows the uncertainty of romance as the poet recalls being led 'by the index finger'. Durcan uses the poem's central **metaphor of swimming to express exhilaration and risk-taking**. The lovers' intimacy is evoked in the erotic image of the wishing well, 'a whirlpool' in which he 'very nearly drowned'. The repetition and insistent rhythm of line 5 reflects the continuing fascination of this unforgettable turning point in the poet's life.

The tone is a mixture of colloquial intimacy and self-mocking incantation. From the outset, Durcan highlights Nessa's power to enchant. His **wry humour** is apparent in the self-deprecating comments about his initial nervousness: 'take off your pants, she said to me,/And I very nearly didn't'. The breathless enthusiasm of their first encounter is evident in lively phrasing: 'I hopped into the Irish Sea' (line 10). The poet's signature use of refrain forces the reader to appreciate the personal upheaval caused by his relationship with Nessa.

Line 13 marks a noticeable change of mood. Durcan focuses on the aftermath ('the way back') of that first swim when Nessa 'fell down beside me'. The **enduring remorse of knowing and losing love** is clear in the regretful line 'I'd have lain in the grass with her all my life'. The contrasting brevity and precise lyrical simplicity of line 16 ('With Nessa') is almost immediately undermined by the stark realisation of the whirlpool symbol as the poet faces the reality of love's impermanence. The poem's **richly textured final section** is particularly tender: 'O Nessa my dear, Nessa my dear' (line 19). Durcan delicately repeats his wife's name. Ironically, his plaintive desire for her to 'stay with me on the rocks' reveals a yearning for a marriage that was inevitably doomed. The poet's powerful vision of Nessa encompasses elements of both dreams and nightmares. Imagining her as an idealised heroic creature ('for me let your red hair down'), he wonders if she can still be with him in the sea. The heart-rending fantasy is abruptly replaced by a darker image of the couple journeying through Dublin 'In a taxi-cab wrapped up in dust' (line 24). An unmistakable sense of death – coupled with the acceptance of lost love – is tinged with the notion that their kindred spirits are united forever.

The hypnotic rhythm of the last two lines brings the poet's reflection of that special day when he met his beloved Nessa up to date. Using the present tense verb in the refrain, Durcan emphasises the ongoing and relentless hurt of the relationship breakdown: 'I am very nearly drowned.' Such **an honest expression of emotion and personal vulnerability** is characteristic of the poet. It has been said that the tragedy at the heart of Paul Durcan's writing is that he cannot accept tragedy. This is undoubtedly the case in 'Nessa', leaving readers with the lasting impression of a man who is still profoundly shocked by the enduring power of romantic love.

Writing About the Poem

'What often defines Paul Durcan's poetry is an underlying sense of failure in personal relationships.' Do you agree with this view? Give reasons for your response, referring to Durcan's poem 'Nessa'.

Sample Paragraph

While Paul Durcan's poem, 'Nessa', is primarily a loving tribute to his ex-wife, it is also a warning that love doesn't always last. The suggestion of a relationship failing is suggested in the first stanza when Durcan describes their 'whirlpool' romance. This dramatic image indicates the wildness of their feelings and that they were taking a chance marrying. A whirlpool is exciting, but also precarious. Durcan uses the refrain at the end of each stanza to reinforce the idea of being unsuccessful in love. Looking back on their marriage, he seems to be really reprimanding

himself for his own carelessness. As though he took love for granted when he 'hopped into the Irish Sea'. I think he blames the failure of the relationship on himself, as suggested by the phrase 'I fell'. Durcan's tone of longing – 'Will you stay with me on the rocks?' – is very well expressed in this tragic poetic metaphor. Nessa is pictured as a beautiful and mysterious woman whose 'red hair' mesmerised the poet. The end really brings out the tragic disappointment of the couple's separation as Durcan makes it clear that the distress still exists – 'you are a whirlpool'. His tone at the end is of anguish and disillusionment. The loss of true love of each other will remain with him forever.

EXAMINER'S COMMENT

A focused personal response that addresses the question directly and traces the progress of thought in the poem. The critical discussion touches on several interesting aspects relating to the predominant sense of failure. Supportive quotes are integrated effectively into the answer. Impressive expression, overall, ensures that this is a top-grade response.

Class/Homework Exercises

1. 'Durcan's inventive poetry is filled with dramatic tension.' Discuss this statement in relation to 'Nessa'.
2. Paul Durcan's personal relationships have often been described as power struggles. Discuss this view with particular reference to the poem 'Nessa'.

Summary Points

- **Personal exploration of the intense experience of romantic love.**
- **Effective use of extended swimming/whirlpool metaphor.**
- **Dramatic atmosphere; varying tones – nostalgic, regretful.**
- **Hypnotic rhythm; emphatic refrain, memorable visual/cinematic effects.**

2 The Girl with the Keys to Pearse's Cottage

to John and Judith Meagher

When I was sixteen I met a dark girl;
Her dark hair was darker because her smile was so bright;
She was the girl with the keys to Pearse's Cottage;
And her name was Cáit Killann.

The cottage was built into the side of a hill;
I recall two windows and cosmic peace
Of bare brown rooms and on whitewashed walls
Photographs of the passionate and pale Pearse.

I recall wet thatch and peeling jambs
And how all was best seen from below in the field;
I used sit in the rushes with ledger-book and pencil
Compiling poems of passion for Cáit Killann.

Often she used linger on the sill of a window;
Hands by her side and brown legs akimbo;
In sun-red skirt and moon-black blazer;
Looking toward our strange world wide-eyed.

Our world was strange because it had no future;
She was America-bound at summer's end.
She had no choice but to leave her home –
The girl with the keys to Pearse's Cottage.

O Cáit Killann, O Cáit Killann,
You have gone with your keys from your own native place.
Yet here in this dark – El Greco eyes blaze back
From your Connemara postman's daughter's proudly mortal face.

Pearse's Cottage: Pádraic Pearse, Irish teacher and political activist who was one of the leaders of the 1916 Easter Rising, owned a small cottage in Rosmuc, Connemara. Pearse believed that the key to national identity and independence was knowledge of the language.
cosmic: endless, universal.

jambs: wooden doorframes.

rushes: marsh plants.
ledger-book: book used to keep records.

akimbo: standing confidently.

El Greco: Spanish Renaissance painter famous for his fantastical portraits.

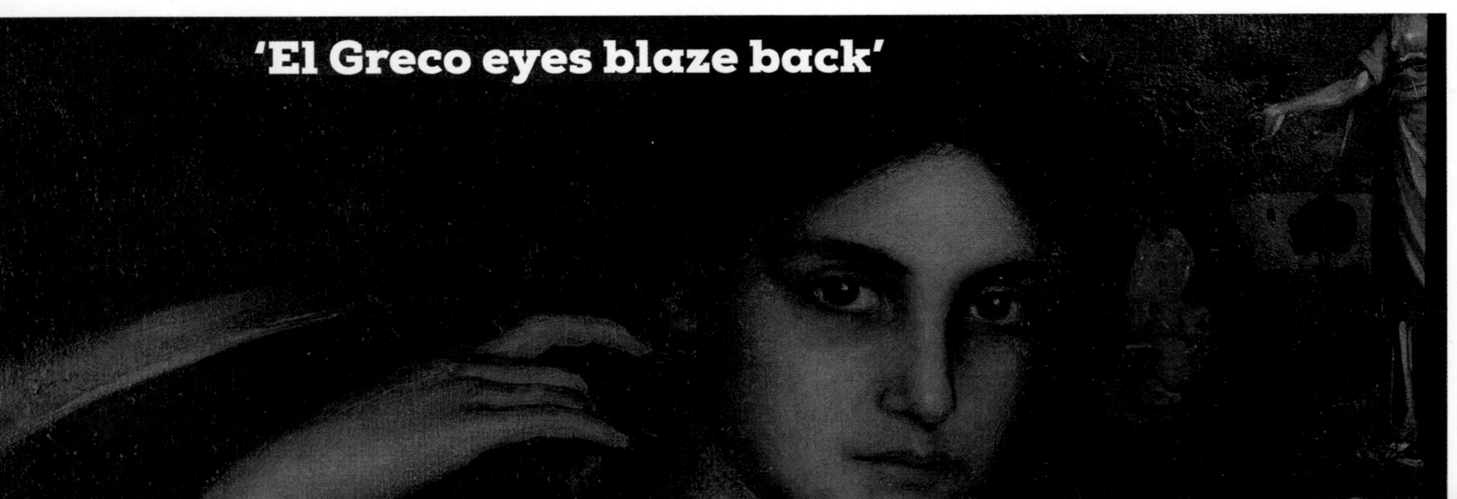

'El Greco eyes blaze back'

Personal Response

1. Describe the atmosphere of country life that the poet creates in lines 5–10.
2. Select one image from the poem that you find particularly interesting. Briefly explain your choice.
3. Write a brief personal response to the poem, highlighting its impact on you.

Critical Literacy

'The Girl with the Keys to Pearse's Cottage' was published in Paul Durcan's first poetry collection, *O Westport in the Light of Asia Minor*, in 1975. Themes of identity, belonging and the instability of place are frequently addressed in Durcan's work. The concept of home is a recurring concern. In this case, the poet narrates a poem of love and loss which includes some elements of the traditional Irish ballad. The poetic voice incorporates both the experiences of the poet's 16-year-old self and his mature adult attitude to the painful legacy of emigration.

The poem's opening lines immediately bring the reader back to a bittersweet moment in Durcan's life: 'When I was sixteen I met a dark girl.' The **strong visual awareness and effective use of repetition** ('dark', 'dark hair', 'darker') suggest the native Irish colouring of the young girl. Her dazzling smile is captured in the long line that culminates with the monosyllabic adjective 'bright', perhaps mirroring sudden sunshine bursting from the clouds over the West of Ireland. We learn that the young woman held the 'keys to Pearse's Cottage'. Had she the means to unlock the secret of his house as well as enabling visitors to enter there? Reverently, the narrator reveals the identity of his lost love: 'And her name was Cáit Killann.'

The second stanza describes Pearse's cottage in remarkable detail: 'built into the side of a hill.' Durcan draws the reader into a romanticised place of 'cosmic peace'. He makes effective use of alliteration to emphasise the **simplicity and lack of ostentation** of the two-bedroomed house, with its 'bare brown rooms' and 'whitewashed walls'. In stark contrast to this are the photographs of the fiery nationalist politician himself, 'the passionate and pale Pearse'.

Stanza three delves further into the poet's memory ('I recall wet thatch and peeling jambs') as the ordinary scene opens up its secrets under the poet's observant gaze. This is a place that is past its best days, tired and weary. Is this how the people of the countryside regarded their environment? The **personal autobiographical detail** is conveyed in the picture of the young poet who sits 'in the rushes with ledger-book and pencil'. Instead of creating accounts, he compiles 'poems of passion' for the girl he loves. Again, alliteration suggests the copious number of poems the infatuated young poet wrote. The naive awkwardness of expressing his feelings in a book dedicated to dry statistics reflects the engaging sincerity of youth.

In stanza four, Durcan lyrically recalls Cáit Killann's languid grace: 'she used linger on the sill of a window.' The slender vowel 'i' delineates her confident, sensuous movements. Suddenly, the pen portrait erupts into colour – 'brown

legs', 'sun-red skirt', 'moon-black blazer'. These compound words indicate both her extraordinary effect on the poet and also **her effortless harmony with the native environment**. The beautiful Cáit belongs here. She gazes 'wide-eyed' and innocent 'toward our strange world'. Readers are left to wonder what she is about to discover.

The adult poet's answer in the penultimate stanza is that 'Our world was strange because it had no future'. His tone is suddenly bitter in response to the bleak realisation that emigration engulfs this crumbling place. 'She was America-bound at summer's end', almost as if she were a migratory bird. The stark political reality becomes a personal experience: 'she had no choice but to leave her home.' **Durcan has always addressed public issues** and he leaves us in no doubt of his own deep awareness that Irish life is lived in transit. Our young migrants become the diaspora scattered around the globe.

The final stanza is defined by a grief-stricken poetic voice lamenting the departure of someone who is loved. The poet repeats Cáit's name tenderly. **Plaintive assonant sounds** echo the traditional mourning or keening that was once found in the West of Ireland: 'O Cáit Killann, O Cáit Killann.' Now that she has left her 'own native place', it is as though a young plant was roughly torn from the Irish soil and transplanted elsewhere to bloom. The poet clearly regards Ireland as a 'dark' country, yet the memory of Cáit's vivid 'El Greco eyes' remains and illuminates. In celebrating the alluring looks of the 'postman's daughter', Durcan has coloured the ordinariness of Connemara with the exotic fascination of international artistic beauty. El Greco, the Spanish painter, dared to view the world his way, sometimes representing it through exquisite portraits of intriguing women with shining eyes.

For Durcan, Cáit Killann also carried her own extraordinary light. The intensity of her gaze is conveyed in the explosive alliterative phrase 'blaze back' from her 'proudly mortal face'. Just like the poet, we mourn her loss. Through his use of metaphor, Durcan has transformed this native Irish girl into a striking icon. In addition, he has brought the reader to a different vantage point from which to view **the tragedy of emigration**, which is such an intrinsically Irish experience. Is this realistic viewpoint similar to the perspective from which Pearse's cottage might be perceived: 'all was best seen from below in the field'? Does something have to be viewed from a distance in order to understand it? Have we been brought to a moment of epiphany as we contemplate the sombre reality of exile? At any rate, Cáit Killann remains a powerfully sad and realistic symbol of Irish emigration, an ironic reminder of what has become of Pearse's idealistic dreams.

Writing About the Poem

'In the poetry of Paul Durcan, reality is frequently shaped by the imagination.' Discuss this statement in relation to the poem, 'The Girl with the Keys to Pearse's Cottage'. Support your views with close reference to the text.

Sample Paragraph

Durcan's keen observation of mundane detail, 'wet thatch', 'bare brown rooms', 'whitewashed walls', etc., all root the poem firmly in the reality of rain-soaked Connemara. All is calm, 'cosmic peace', on the surface. Yet bubbling beneath this seeming ordinariness, strong feelings flow, portrayed vividly in the photographs of the 'passionate and pale Pearse' who once inhabited this place. The longing of a sixteen-year-old boy for the beautiful 'postman's daughter' can be sensed as he sat 'in the rushes' while 'Compiling poems of passion' for her. The girl of the 'sun-red skirt' is brought into another world through Durcan's inspired reference to her 'El Greco eyes'. The ordinary is opened up by his inventive metaphor. The Spanish painter, El Greco, saw things in a unique way – exactly like Cáit, 'Looking toward our strange world wide-eyed'. She seems surprised or perplexed at what she sees, perhaps because she is being forced to leave her native land, 'America-bound at summer's end'. Despite the sacrifice of the 1916 Rising, of which Pearse was a leader, this country is still unable to support its own people. But is the girl truly gone? I believe that she exists only in the poet's memory. Suddenly the reality of this little place in the West of Ireland has been formed by the imagination of the poet to represent the tragedy of emigration.

EXAMINER'S COMMENT

A good personal response which engages well with the poem. Carefully considered terms, such as 'inventive' and 'inspired', indicate a sustained focus on addressing the question directly. Overall, the expression is very well managed, particularly the first sentence. Accurate quotations are effectively integrated into the critical discussion. A highly successful top-grade response.

Class/Homework Exercises

1. 'Paul Durcan's poetry is often concerned with the world of the Irish countryside that has now disappeared.' Discuss this statement in relation to 'The Girl with the Keys to Pearse's Cottage'. Support the points you make with reference to the text.
2. Durcan's poems address both personal and public themes. To what extent is this true of 'The Girl with the Keys to Pearse's Cottage'? Support your answer with reference to the text.

Summary Points

- **Prominent themes include idealism, national identity, home, exile, love and loss.**
- **Evocative images of Irish rural life and female beauty.**
- **Variety of tones – nostalgic, angry, sad.**
- **Effective use of autobiographical detail, symbolism, irony, repetition.**

The Difficulty that is Marriage

Difficulty: challenge, complication, problem.
Marriage: formal union of a couple; a close blend or mixture of two things.

We disagree to disagree, we divide, we differ;
Yet each night as I lie in bed beside you
And you are faraway curled up in sleep
I array the moonlit ceiling with a mosaic of question marks;
How was it I was so lucky to have ever met you?
I am no brave pagan proud of my mortality
Yet gladly on this changeling earth I should live for ever
If it were with you, my sleeping friend.
I have my troubles and I shall always have them
But I should rather live with you for ever
Than exchange my troubles for a changeless kingdom.
But I do not put you on a pedestal or throne;
You must have your faults but I do not see them.
If it were with you, I should live for ever.

array: adorn, arrange in an impressive way.
mosaic: pattern, montage.

pagan: unbeliever, atheist.
mortality: humanity, transience, death.
changeling: transient, secretly exchanged.

troubles: afflictions, difficulties.

exchange: swap, substitute.

pedestal: raised platform, exalted position.
faults: failings, weaknesses.

'a mosaic of question marks'

Personal Response

1. Why, in your opinion, would Paul Durcan regard marriage as a difficulty? Refer to the poem to support your response.
2. Choose one image from the poem that you thought was particularly effective and explain your choice.
3. Write a brief personal response to the poem, highlighting its impact on you.

Critical Literacy

Paul Durcan published 'The Difficulty that is Marriage' in his collection *Teresa's Bar* (1976). In considering his relationship with his wife, the poet's lyrical voice clearly reflects his intense personal romanticism. He observes and explores a small everyday event, a married couple sharing a bed together, but who are estranged from each other. Reflecting on his upbringing, Durcan once said, 'We were educated to believe that women were, on the one hand, untouchable and pure and on the other hand, that they were the source of all evil ... women represent and embody freedom ... living in much closer harmony with their true selves.' The title of this very personal poem suggests that while true love is not immune from problems, it will endure despite such obstacles.

The opening line of this dramatic monologue is broken into abrupt staccato sections by its frequent punctuation marks and the deadening alliterative letter 'd': 'We disagree to disagree, we divide, we differ.' Durcan cleverly pinpoints the destructive conflict in a marriage as two individuals try to live as a couple. In this case, they cannot even agree that they can disagree. After this turmoil of daily married life, three run-on lines smoothly convey, in unforced conversational tones, the stillness of the marriage bed: 'each night as I lie in bed beside you.' But while the couple are physically present in the one space, mentally and emotionally they are worlds apart. She is 'faraway curled up in sleep', content and at peace with herself. In contrast, the poet is lying awake, thinking, questioning. **Durcan's strong visual sensibility is evident** in the descriptive 'I array the moonlit ceiling with a mosaic of question marks'. The image has the immediacy of a snapshot coupled with surrealism as the reader views the ceiling patterned with the question marks of uncertainties: 'How was it I was so lucky to have ever met you?' Is the relationship broken into countless pieces by constant soul-searching and argument? Is the poet trying to reassemble the fragments into an ideal shape?

Durcan has always portrayed himself as an admirer of women, and on numerous occasions has cast his wife, Nessa, in her heroic role as someone to be admired, the one person who provides stability in his insecure life. In line 6, he expresses the male pain of never doing well enough, criticising his

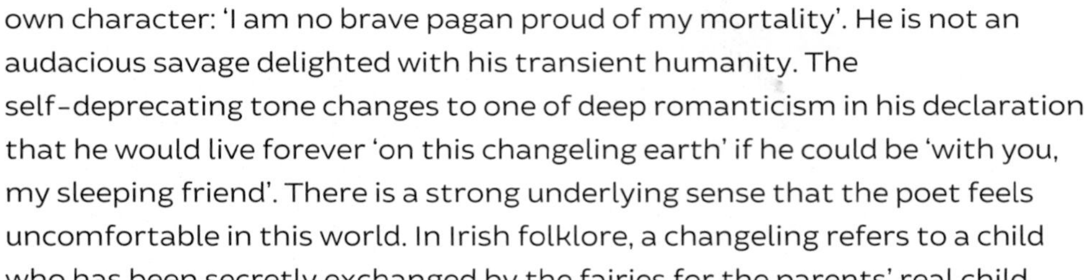

own character: 'I am no brave pagan proud of my mortality'. He is not an audacious savage delighted with his transient humanity. The self-deprecating tone changes to one of deep romanticism in his declaration that he would live forever 'on this changeling earth' if he could be 'with you, my sleeping friend'. There is a strong underlying sense that the poet feels uncomfortable in this world. In Irish folklore, a changeling refers to a child who has been secretly exchanged by the fairies for the parents' real child.

Line 9 reveals the dark side of Durcan's personality, 'I have my troubles', which is a common Irish euphemism for serious problems. Durcan has spoken of being committed by his family, against his will, to a range of psychiatric treatments, including electric convulsive therapy. He subsequently suffered from depression and has admitted, 'I think I came out of it with a kind of melancholia'. **Is the poet casting himself here in the role of sacrificial victim?** His father, with whom he had a difficult relationship, predicted that he would never be free of misfortune: 'Nemesis will follow you all the days of your life.' Is this why Durcan sees this earth as a 'changeling' place? Three words resonate: 'changeling', 'exchange' and 'changeless'. Is he willing to swap his longing for peace if he can always be with his beloved? 'But I should rather live with you for ever/Than exchange my troubles for a changeless kingdom.'

Paradoxically, while the poet denies that he exaggerates his feelings for his wife by exalting her 'on a pedestal or throne' (line 12) as if she were a saint or queen, at the same time he appears to worship her. He declares that 'You must have your faults', yet disarmingly admits, 'but I do not see them'. This short, introspective poem concludes with a statement of heightened romanticism: 'If it were with you, I should live for ever.' The **reverential tone** suggests a strong sense of the spiritual fulfilment he receives from their relationship. Yet although this poem shows such high regard for his wife, Durcan remains the leading man throughout, demanding to be noticed despite all his charming self-criticism. Alternatively, it is possible to read the poem more generously in the light of another of the poet's statements: 'Heaven is other people: a house where there are no women and children is a very empty house.'

Writing About the Poem

'Paul Durcan has the gift of being able to make something out of nothing.' Discuss this statement with reference to his poem 'The Difficulty that is Marriage'. Support the points you make with reference to the text.

Sample Paragraph

'The Difficulty that is Marriage' explores the deep gulf between couples and the challenges they face. This is a universal theme that very many people can relate to. The obstacles to a successful relationship are vividly conveyed in the alliterative, broken opening line, 'We disagree to disagree, we divide, we differ'. The woman's ability to be content with herself is evident in the simple phrase, 'faraway curled up in sleep'. In contrast, the man's anxiety is revealed in the cleverly constructed imaginative line, 'I array the moonlit ceiling with a mosaic of question marks'. Ironically, this married couple appear close, but really inhabit different universes. Durcan addresses a crucial issue, the reality of complicated human relationships. Using the direct language of genuine emotion, the husband longs to be 'with you for ever'. We are left wondering if, instead of outlining differences, did the poet convey these feelings to his partner? I wonder did he ever tell her 'How was it I was so lucky to have ever met you'? Or did he just paint patterns on the ceiling? Perhaps this is the real difficulty of marriage, no one really knows for certain what the other is thinking or feeling. Durcan skilfully presents an ordinary occurrence, a married couple at night, one awake, one asleep, and creates a very important something out of a very mundane nothing.

EXAMINER'S COMMENT

This is a competent response to a challenging question. There is a good personal approach throughout which shows engagement with the poem: 'We are left wondering if, instead of outlining differences, did the poet convey these feelings to his partner?' Among several interesting points is the focus on the complexity of relationships: 'no one really knows for certain what the other is thinking or feeling.' Effective use is made of accurate quotation. Expression is also clear and well controlled. A highly successful answer.

Class/Homework Exercises

1. 'Poetry has to be fundamentally cinematic, painterly and musical.' Discuss this view in relation to Durcan's poem 'The Difficulty that is Marriage'. Refer closely to the text in your answer.
2. In your opinion, what does Paul Durcan's poem reveal about his married relationship? Support the points you make with close reference to the text.

Summary Points

- **Explores the trials and triumphs of married relationships.**
- **Characteristically candid and emotional poetic voice.**
- **Tones vary – detached, personal, reflective, sardonic, reverential, loving.**
- **Dramatic monologue, contrast, exaggerated visual images.**

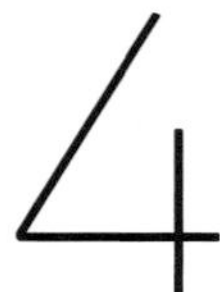

4 Wife Who Smashed Television Gets Jail

'She came home, my Lord, and smashed in the television;
Me and the kids were peaceably watching *Kojak*
When she marched into the living room and declared
That if I didn't turn off the television immediately
She'd put her boot through the screen;
I didn't turn it off, so instead she turned it off –
I remember the moment exactly because Kojak
After shooting a dame with the same name as my wife
Snarled at the corpse – Goodnight, Queen Maeve –
And then she took off her boots and smashed in the television;
I had to bring the kids round to my mother's place;
We got there just before the finish of *Kojak*;
(My mother has a fondness for *Kojak*, my Lord);
When I returned home my wife had deposited
What was left of the television into the dustbin,
Saying – I didn't get married to a television
And I don't see why my kids or anybody else's kids
Should have a television for a father or mother,
We'd be much better off all down in the pub talking
Or playing bar-billiards –
Whereupon she disappeared off back down again to the pub.'
Justice O'Brádaigh said wives who preferred bar-billiards to family television
Were a threat to the family which was the basic unit of society
As indeed the television itself could be said to be a basic unit of the family
And when as in this case wives expressed their preference in forms of violence
Jail was the only place for them. Leave to appeal was refused.

my Lord: official form of address to a judge in court.
Kojak: American TV crime drama starring Telly Savalas. The series was popular in Ireland during the mid-1970s.

Queen Maeve: legendary Irish queen with a colourful reputation.

bar-billiards: group table game in which short cues are used.

appeal: review to challenge a court sentence.

'peaceably watching *Kojak*'

Personal Response

1. In your opinion, what is the main point or message of this poem? Refer to the text in your response.
2. Comment on Durcan's use of irony throughout the poem, supporting the points you make with reference to the text.
3. Write a paragraph outlining your own feelings in response to this poem. Refer to the text in your answer.

Critical Literacy

In his hard-hitting critiques of Irish society, one of Paul Durcan's signatures is the poem written as pseudo-reportage, where an unlikely event is depicted in a seemingly journalistic style. Humour has always been an essential component of the distinctive Durcan style. This poem is divided into two sections: the first 21 lines in the voice of the husband and the final five-line report of the judge's opinion and verdict. The poet's father was a circuit court judge.

The news headline title and matter-of-fact simplicity of the opening lines increase their dramatic impact. There is an instantaneous quality to the initial evidence presented by the aggrieved husband who acts as a witness in the matter of his wife's prosecution, protesting that at the moment the act of violence occurred, 'Me and the kids were peaceably watching *Kojak*'. Unable to see the irony of viewing a violent TV drama, the man is immediately **ridiculed and mocked** by Durcan. His assertive wife is identified as 'Queen Maeve' solely because the husband describes Kojak as 'shooting a dame with the same name' (line 8). This instantly associates her with one of the great legendary symbols of female power – a queen of Connaught in the Ulster Cycle of Irish myths. However, in the real patriarchal world of Durcan's Ireland, the modern Maeve is merely seen as a deranged troublemaker.

The husband proceeds to condemn himself further by boasting that instead of taking his wife seriously, he has still not come to terms with the interruption to one of his favourite TV programmes. It is unsurprising to learn that he rushes off to seek comfort from his mother, who shares his 'fondness for *Kojak*' (line 13). However, aggressive as his wife's actions may be, it soon becomes clear that it is **her words and attitudes that serve to justify her condemnation**. As the story unfolds, Durcan slips effortlessly from the real to the surreal, often to inspired comic effect. When the distressed husband returns home, he discovers that his wife has dumped 'What was left of the television into the dustbin' (line 15).

In direct opposition to her uncommunicative husband and children, she boldly states: 'I don't see why my kids or anybody else's kids/Should have a

television for a father or mother' (lines 17–18). **Durcan's bizarre humour is laced with unsmiling undertones.** For him, TV violence and escapism compete with the less glamorous facts of real life. As a result, any interference with the illusions that television creates can now be treated as serious crimes. The reader's sympathy for the eponymous wife is further generated by exposing the dramatic delusions of the male judge.

In the poem's final lines, the satire becomes much more intense. Durcan undermines the astounding moral certainty in the arrogant speech delivered by 'Justice O'Brádaigh', who declares that 'the television itself could be said to be a basic unit of the family' (line 24). The unashamed verdict promotes the idea that **virtual violence has a rightful place at the heart of family life**, a reason for the judge to state that 'Jail was the only place' for transgressors such as Maeve, who will not be allowed to challenge her sentence since 'Leave to appeal was refused'. The snarling tone of such a dismissive ruling is in keeping with Justice O'Brádaigh's prevailing mindset of disdainful self-delusion.

What sustains the tragicomic structure of this poem is Durcan's skilful depiction of the contrasting characters who are party to the scene: the precious husband, his frustrated wife and the condescending judge. Significantly, the wife herself is never directly heard**. Durcan is uncompromising in exposing negative attitudes towards voiceless women** – especially women who dare to resist the bounds of rigid expectations. His disapproval of the conventional pieties of Ireland's conspiratorial, male-dominated society is characteristic of his poetry. However, a close reading of 'Wife Who Smashed Television Gets Jail' reveals that it is not the medium of television, but its abuse, that Durcan calls into question. As usual, in addressing such cultural issues, the poet entertains and gives pause for thought.

Writing About the Poem

'Paul Durcan's deep sense of outrage is often evident in his poetry.' Discuss this view in relation to 'Wife Who Smashed Television Gets Jail', using references from the poem to support your answer.

Sample Paragraph

Paul Durcan has a reputation for producing what appear to be light-hearted poems, but his anger is never far from the surface. This is true of 'Wife Who Smashed Television Gets Jail' where he confronts society's ignorance and hypocrisy. The idea of a wife being taken to court by a man who gives more attention to his TV seems ridiculous, but the real point is that women have very little power. I could easily imagine

Durcan's anger at the man's superior tone – 'Me and the kids were peaceably watching *Kojak*'. Even his comment about the detective 'shooting a dame' is a reminder that it's a man's world. Durcan barely conceals his rage that men – the husband, the TV hero and the influential judge – all represent a macho world. I thought the last line – 'Leave to appeal was refused' – summed up the poet's appreciation of how women in Irish society are marginalised. The poet seems to be saying that it is nearly impossible not to be part of the patriarchal culture that prevents many women from expressing the view that emotions and communication are more important than escapist TV violence. The outrage was present throughout the poem especially during the comic scenes.

EXAMINER'S COMMENT

This is a clearly focused personal response showing good engagement with the poem. The focus on the dominance of male characters provided worthwhile support. Valuable use was also made of suitable references – particularly the Kojak quotation which was very effective. Expression was well controlled throughout. In-depth analysis secures a high grade.

Class/Homework Exercises

1. 'Humour and surrealism are Durcan's most powerful satirical weapons.' Discuss this statement with reference to the poem 'Wife Who Smashed Television Gets Jail'.
2. Durcan has been described as a 'feminist writer'. Based on your reading of this poem, do you agree or disagree with this view? Support your answer with reference to the text.

Summary Points

- **Durcan criticises aspects of Irish patriarchal society.**
- **Effective use of irony, surreal humour.**
- **Satirical exaggeration, comic journalistic writing style.**
- **Varying tones – ridicule, sympathy, outrage.**

Parents

A child's face is a drowned face:
Her parents stare down at her asleep
Estranged from her by a sea:
She is under the sea
And they are above the sea:
If she looked up she would see them
As if locked out of their own home,
Their mouths open,
Their foreheads furrowed –
Pursed-up orifices of fearful fish –
Their big ears are fins behind glass
And in her sleep she is calling out to them
    Father, Father
    Mother, Mother
But they cannot hear her:
She is inside the sea
And they are outside the sea.
Through the night, stranded, they stare
At the drowned, drowned face of their child.

Estranged: separated.

furrowed: wrinkled.

Pursed-up orifices: open-shaped mouths.

stranded: abandoned.

'And in her sleep she is calling out to them'

Personal Response

1. Write a paragraph giving your own immediate reaction to reading 'Parents'. Refer to the text in your answer.
2. Select one image from the poem that you find particularly unsettling and briefly explain your choice.
3. Using reference to the text, comment on the poem's dramatic features.

Critical Literacy

'Parents' was published in Paul Durcan's 1978 collection, *Sam's Cross*. The poem raises interesting questions about parent–child communication, a recurring theme in Durcan's work. Characteristically, some of the poet's perceptions have a disturbing quality which convey shock as well as intensity.

The poem's opening metaphor – 'A child's face is a drowned face' – has a startling effect. The devastating image represents every parent's greatest fear and introduces an **overwhelmingly anxious mood** that will dominate the entire poem. Durcan develops the sea metaphor in lines 2–3, creating a desperate scene of helplessness, as the parents can only stare down at their precious child, 'Estranged from her by a sea'. The lack of intimate communication – symbolised by the impenetrable ocean – is a central theme. There is something unsettling about the parents' realisation that they are already detached from their newborn child and that they can never know her as much as they would wish.

Lines 4–5 reflect their sense of shock at the unfathomable gulf that exists between them and the child: 'She is under the sea/And they are above the sea.' The separate lines and contrasting prepositions emphasise the obstacle. Repetition and a deliberate rhythm further underline Durcan's sombre tone. For the first time in the poem, the child's perspective is presented when she imagines her parents being 'locked out of their own home' (line 7). Just as she is no longer within the security of the womb, they are also leading independent lives. Her growing understanding of the world is described in a series of increasingly distorted images. The 'furrowed' looks on her parents' foreheads are unnerving. The **surreal underwater sequence** becomes even more grotesque when Durcan compares the concerned adult expressions to 'Pursed-up orifices of fearful fish'. To the confused and frightened infant, the parents' ears are 'fins behind glass'.

Through lines 12–14, the developing drama of the parent–child exchange becomes all the more poignant. Durcan's dark vision of the child's distressed cry for attention ('Father, Father/Mother, Mother') transcends the moment and highlights the trauma of unfulfilled relationships between parents and children, lasting perhaps throughout entire lifetimes. For the poet, however, there is no denying the harsh fact of disconnection revealed in line 15: 'But

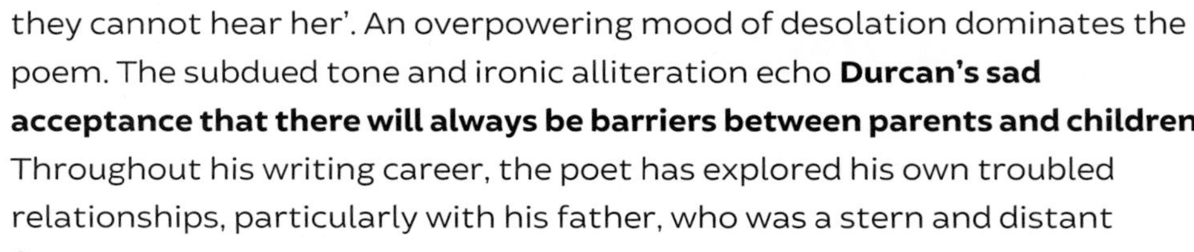

they cannot hear her'. An overpowering mood of desolation dominates the poem. The subdued tone and ironic alliteration echo **Durcan's sad acceptance that there will always be barriers between parents and children**. Throughout his writing career, the poet has explored his own troubled relationships, particularly with his father, who was a stern and distant figure.

There is a restrained **sense of resignation** in lines 16–19. Durcan repeats the stark truth about separation between individuals, contrasting the child 'inside the sea' with her parents, who are 'outside'. The final elegiac mood is achieved by the exaggerated illustration of the ever-watchful parents, who are left 'stranded', faced with the challenge of coming to terms with the 'drowned, drowned face of their child'. The repetition of 'drowned' in the long final line leaves readers thinking of the many questions raised in this short poem. As always, Durcan has addressed important issues, not just about how individual human beings interact, but about the mystery of life itself.

Writing About the Poem

'Paul Durcan writes well about detachment and isolation.' Discuss this view, with particular reference to 'Parents'. Refer closely to the text in your response.

Sample Paragraph

Durcan addresses interesting aspects of human experience in his poetry, and this is certainly the case in 'Parents'. The poem focuses on one set of unnamed parents and their young child, but takes a very negative view of the relationship. From the start, the parents are disconnected from their baby daughter, imagining that her sleeping face is 'a drowned face'. Their imagined fear of her death immediately suggests that her life is outside of their control. Durcan uses shocking sea images to show the lack of close contact with the child who appears to be 'under the sea'. This gap exists between them and they can never know her completely. Their panic is conveyed very effectively in nightmarish terms. The child sees them as alien, almost intimidating, like 'fearful fish'. She calls to them but 'they cannot hear her'. I felt this was a really heartbreaking moment, especially as the poet repeated her frantic words, 'Father, Father/Mother, Mother'. The separation they feel in never fully communicating is seen at the end of the poem where the parents are 'stranded' – another sea image

EXAMINER'S COMMENT

A successful response which tackles the question directly. Suitable references and quotations sustain the focused discussion of Durcan's treatment of isolation. There is some good personal engagement, particularly in the final sentence. The answer traces the development of thought in the poem very effectively, using the poet's succession of shocking images. Expression is varied and assured throughout, guaranteeing a top grade.

– 'Through the night'. This tragic insight into the distances between people is reinforced in the last line by the repetition of 'drowned' – a final reminder of detachment and alienation.

Class/Homework Exercises

1. 'Durcan's most compelling poems often raise significant questions about the complexity of human relationships.' To what extent is this true of 'Parents'? Support your answer with reference to the poem.
2. Durcan's poetic voice has been noted for its insistent, hypnotic rhythms. To what extent is this the case in 'Parents'? Support your answer with close reference to the text.

Summary Points

- **Durcan raises penetrating questions about parent–child relationships.**
- **Contrasting moods/tones – anxious, serious, intense, poignant, resigned.**
- **Striking and sustained visual imagery of the sea – distorted, unnerving.**
- **Effective use of powerful language and free rhythm.**

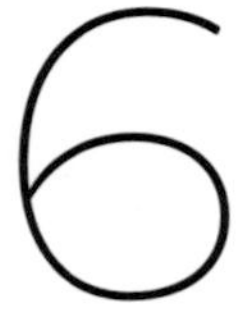

'Windfall', 8 Parnell Hill, Cork

But, then, at the end of day I could always say –
Well, now, I am going home.
I felt elected, steeped, sovereign to be able to say –
I am going home.
When I was at home I liked to stay at home;
At home I stayed at home for weeks;
At home I used sit in a winged chair by the window
Overlooking the river and the factory chimneys,
The electricity power station and the car assembly works,
The fleets of trawlers and the pilot tugs,
Dreaming that life is a dream which is real,
The river a reflection of itself in its own waters,
Goya sketching Goya among the smoky mirrors.
The industrial vista was my Mont Sainte-Victoire.
While my children sat on my knees watching TV
Their mother, my wife, reclined on the couch
Knitting a bright-coloured scarf, drinking a cup of black coffee,
Smoking a cigarette – one of her own roll-ups.
I closed my eyes and breathed in and breathed out.

It is ecstasy to breathe if you are at home in the world.
What a windfall! A home of our own!
Our neighbours' houses had names like 'Con Amore',
'Sans Souci', 'Pacelli', 'Montini', 'Homesville'.
But we called our home 'Windfall'.
'Windfall', 8 Parnell Hill, Cork.
In the gut of my head coursed the leaf of tranquillity
Which I dreamed was known only to Buddhist Monks
In lotus monasteries high up in the Hindu Kush.
Down here in the dark depths of Ireland,
Below sea level in the city of Cork,
In a city as intimate and homicidal as a Little Marseilles,
In a country where all the children of the nation
Are not cherished equally
And where the best go homeless, while the worst
Erect block-house palaces – self-regardingly ugly –
Having a home of your own can give to a family
A chance in a lifetime to transcend death.

Windfall: something good received unexpectedly; something the wind has blown down.

elected, steeped, sovereign: slang terms for being very lucky.

winged: high-backed chair; capable of flight.

life is a dream: play by the Spanish playwright Calderon, which deals with the problems of distinguishing between illusion and reality.

Goya: Spanish romantic painter whose works contain a subversive imaginative element.

smoky mirrors: a reference to a painting by Goya of a Spanish king with his family containing an image of Goya himself in a dark mirror looking out at the viewer. The message is one of underlying corruption and decay.

Mont Sainte-Victoire: beautiful French mountain often painted by Paul Cézanne.

Buddhist Monks: monks who live a simple meditative life. They believe that married couples should respect each other's beliefs and privacy.

lotus: sacred. The lotus refers to an exotic water lily and to a fruit that causes dreamy forgetfulness.

Hindu Kush: mountain range stretching from Afghanistan to Pakistan, meaning 'Kills the Hindu', a reference to the many Indian slaves who perished there from harsh weather conditions.

Marseilles: oldest city in France, a Mediterranean port that suffered many sieges and where 'La Marseillaise', the French national anthem, came from. It had a colony of famous artists and is now a gateway for immigrants from the African continent.

block-house palaces: a disparaging reference to new high-rise buildings that sprang up in modern Ireland.

At the high window, shipping from all over the world
Being borne up and down the busy, yet contemplative, river;
Skylines drifting in and out of skylines in the cloudy valley;
Firelight at dusk, and city lights;
Beyond them the control tower of the airport on the hill –
A lighthouse in the sky flashing green to white to green;
Our black-and-white cat snoozing in the corner of a chair;
Pastels and etchings on the four walls, and over the mantelpiece
'Van Gogh's Grave' and 'Lovers in Water';
A room wallpapered in books and family photograph albums
Chronicling the adventures and metamorphoses of family life:
In swaddling clothes in Mammy's arms on baptism day;
Being a baby of nine months and not remembering it;
Face-down in a pram, incarcerated in a high chair;
Everybody, including strangers, wearing shop-window smiles;
With Granny in Felixstowe, with Granny in Ballymaloe;
In a group photo in First Infants, on a bike at thirteen;
In the back garden in London, in the back garden in Cork;
Performing a headstand after First Holy Communion;
Getting a kiss from the Bishop on Confirmation Day;
Straw hats in the Bois de Boulougne, wearing wings at the seaside;

Mammy and Daddy holding hands on the Normandy Beaches;
Mammy and Daddy at the wedding of Jeremiah and Margot;
Mammy and Daddy queuing up for *Last Tango in Paris*;
Boating on the Shannon, climbing mountains in Kerry;
Building sandcastles in Killala, camping in Barley Cove;
Picnicking in Moone, hide-and-go-seek in Clonmacnoise;
Riding horses, cantering, jumping fences;
Pushing out toy yachts in the pond in the Tuileries;
The Irish College revisited in the Rue des Irlandais;
Sipping an *orange pressé* through a straw on the roof of the Beaubourg;
Dancing in Père Lachaise, weeping at Auvers.
Year in, year out, I pored over these albums accumulating,
My children looking over my shoulder, exhilarated as I was,
Their mother presiding at our ritual from a distance –
The far side of the hearthrug, diffidently, proudly.
Schoolbooks on the floor and pyjamas on the couch –
Whose turn is it tonight to put the children to bed?

Our children swam about our home
As if it was their private sea,
Their own unique, symbiotic fluid
Of which their parents also partook.
Such is home – a sea of your own –
In which you hang upside down from the ceiling

'Van Gogh's Grave': Vincent van Gogh (1853–90) was a famous Dutch post-Impressionist painter who suffered, like Durcan, from depression. He was a tortured soul who lived for his art.
'Lovers in Water': a reference to a painting by modern artist Francine Scialom Greenblatt that refers to a private place made public.
swaddling: strips of cloth wrapped around a newborn child to calm it; also a reference to how the infant Jesus is described in the gospel account.

***Last Tango in Paris*:** romantic movie (1972) about a love affair that ends in tragedy.

Beaubourg: small, stylish hotel in Paris.
Père Lachaise: largest cemetery in Paris, containing the graves of many famous people.
Auvers: village where Van Gogh lived.

symbiotic: safe, secure; similar to the natural pre-birth environment.

With equanimity, while postcards from Thailand on the mantelpiece
Are raising their eyebrow markings benignly:
Your hands dangling their prayers to the floorboards of your home,
Sifting the sands underneath the surfaces of conversations,
The marine insect life of the family psyche.
A home of your own – or a sea of your own –
In which climbing the walls is as natural
As making love on the stairs;
In which when the telephone rings
Husband and wife are metamorphosed into smiling accomplices,
Both declining to answer it;
Initiating, instead, a yet more subversive kiss –
A kiss they have perhaps never attempted before –
And might never have dreamed of attempting
Were it not for the telephone belling.
Through the bannisters or along the bannister rails
The pyjama-clad children solemnly watching
Their parents at play, jumping up and down in support,
Race back to bed, gesticulating wordlessly:
The most subversive unit in society is the human family.

We're almost home, pet, almost home ...
Our home is at ...
I'll be home ...
I have to go home now ...
I want to go home now ...
Are you feeling homesick?
Are you anxious to get home? ...
I can't wait to get home ...
Let's stay at home tonight and ...
What time will you be coming home at? ...
If I'm not home by six at the latest, I'll phone ...
We're nearly home, don't worry, we're nearly home ...

But then with good reason
I was put out of my home:
By a keen wind felled.
I find myself now without a home
Having to live homeless in the alien, foreign city of Dublin.
It is an eerie enough feeling to be homesick
Yet knowing you will be going home next week;
It is an eerie feeling beyond all ornithological analysis
To be homesick knowing that there is no home to go home to:
Day by day, creeping, crawling,
Moonlighting, escaping,
Bed-and-breakfast to bed-and-breakfast;
Hostels, centres, one-night hotels.

equanimity: composure, calmness.
benignly: compassionately, favourably.
psyche: consciousness; soul.
metamorphosed: changed.
accomplices: partners – usually in crime.
subversive: unsettling, rebellious.
gesticulating: gesturing dramatically.
keen: sharp, biting.
alien: unfamiliar, strange.
eerie: scary, unnatural.
ornithological: scientific study of birds.

Homeless in Dublin,
Blown about the suburban streets at evening,
Peering in the windows of other people's homes,
Wondering what it must feel like
To be sitting around a fire –
Apache or Cherokee or Bourgeoisie –
Beholding the firelit faces of your family,
Beholding their starry or their TV gaze:
Windfall to Windfall – can you hear me?
Windfall to Windfall …
We're almost home, pet, don't worry anymore, we're almost home.

Apache: Native American tribe from Arizona.
Cherokee: Native American tribe from the southern United States.
Bourgeoisie: conservative middle class, chiefly concerned with wealth.

'Lovers in Water'

Personal Response

1. In your opinion, what is Durcan's central theme or point in this poem? Briefly explain your response.
2. The poet uses conversational language throughout the poem. What effect do you think this has on the reader?
3. Comment on the tone of the concluding line, 'We're almost home, pet, don't worry anymore, we're almost home'. Does the poet really believe this or is there a darker meaning?

Critical Literacy

'"Windfall", 8 Parnell Hill, Cork' was published in Paul Durcan's collection *The Berlin Wall Café* (1985). It chronicles not only the happy domesticity Durcan enjoyed in his marriage with his wife, Nessa, and their two daughters, but also the bitter consequences of the break-up of that marriage for the poet. The intensity of the pain of separation is searing as the ex-husband unflinchingly discloses the disintegration of his relationship. Paul Durcan has commented, 'Hardly a day goes by that I don't think about our marriage ... I put the breakdown of our marriage down to my stupidity'.

The opening line is written in the conditional tense and expresses a possibility for the future. The poet used to be able to say, 'Well, now, I am going home', as if all the ills of the world could be left outside when he retreated to his one safe place of contentment. Durcan explains how good he felt that he could make that statement: 'I felt elected, steeped, sovereign.' He felt chosen, 'steeped' in luck, free and dominant. But there is a note of regret here, clearly suggesting that he can no longer return home. The importance of **home is emphasised** by continual repetition: 'When I was at home I liked to stay at home;/At home I stayed at home for weeks'. From his privileged position in his 'winged chair', the poet could survey the familiar sights of the city port, 'the river and the factory chimneys'. He meditates, 'Dreaming that life is a dream which is real'. For Durcan, however, reality becomes uncertain, unfocused, 'The river a reflection of itself in its own waters'.

His mind turns to a painting by Goya where the painter has depicted himself in a 'smoky' mirror behind a group of people peering out at the viewer. The industrial vista of Cork seems every bit as important for the poet as Mont Sainte-Victoire was for another artist, Paul Cézanne. **A happy picture of domesticity** soon replaces the fluid, unsettling river images. We see Durcan and his family forming a secure, close-knit group: 'my children sat on my knees watching TV.' It is a picture of indolence. Their mother is described separately, as if not quite belonging to this unit. In contrast to the poet, she is much more engaged, 'Knitting', 'drinking', 'Smoking'. But Durcan is oblivious and blissfully happy in his comfortable habitat: 'I closed my eyes and breathed in and breathed out.'

Section two (line 20) conveys the heights of emotion, 'ecstasy', felt when an individual is at ease in the right place, 'at home in the world'. The poet describes this as a 'windfall', something good that has been received unexpectedly. The tone is complacent – almost cynical – when he recalls the names of his neighbours' homes: 'Con Amore' (with love), 'Sans Souci' (without worries), 'Homesville'. Some other houses are called after popes, suggesting the controlling religious influence on the local community. Durcan points out that he and his wife were above all that – 'But we called our home "Windfall"', as though nature itself had provided this haven for his family. Already there is an underlying suggestion that he took too much for granted. He **still feels a sense of deep serenity** in the depths of his being, 'the leaf of tranquillity', known only to the ascetic monks who lived in Asia's remote mountain ranges.

The exotic image of 'lotus monasteries' evokes the **idealised state of wistful forgetfulness** enjoyed both by the monks and the poet himself. But this restful dreamscape is rudely torn apart by the shocking reality of bourgeois Ireland's 'dark depths'. Cork city is 'intimate', private and personal, but also 'homicidal', murderous, just like the subversive city of Marseilles, where the French Revolution started. Characteristically, Durcan makes a bitter reference to the Irish Constitution, which had not fulfilled its promises and instead produced 'a country where all the children of the nation/Are not cherished equally'. He ridicules the greed of the rising moneyed classes and their 'block-house palaces'. This section concludes (lines 36–37) that 'Having a home of your own' allows a family to 'transcend death'. Some of the poet's ancestors had once been evicted from their holding in County Mayo. Durcan has said that in his own family, 'there was only one value and that was money'.

The dreamy sight of changing skies opens the poem's third section (line 38). Tall ships are 'drifting in and out of skylines in the cloudy valley'. **Family harmony appears to reign**: 'Our black-and-white cat snoozing in the corner of a chair.' The living room is filled with pictures and old photo albums that record in detail the changes in family life over two generations. But another disturbing note is struck as the poet describes early pictures of himself 'Face-down in a pram, incarcerated in a high chair'. Durcan was once regarded by his own relations as the black sheep of the family and at one time he was even confined to a psychiatric hospital. As he studies the albums, he feels betrayed by the false expressions: 'shop-window smiles.' The seemingly random collection of memories ranges widely over significant times and various places at home, at school and on holiday. The young Durcan is seen behaving wildly, 'Performing a headstand after First Holy Communion'. Yet he seems more forlorn than bitter. Is the concluding image, 'wearing wings at the seaside', a reference to his innocence or his wish to escape?

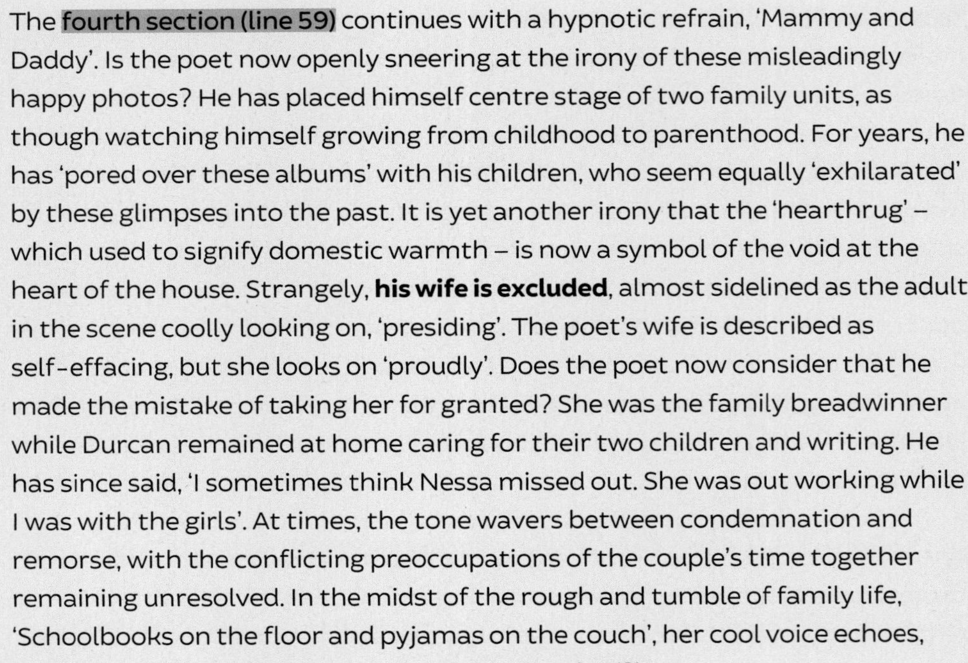

The fourth section (line 59) continues with a hypnotic refrain, 'Mammy and Daddy'. Is the poet now openly sneering at the irony of these misleadingly happy photos? He has placed himself centre stage of two family units, as though watching himself growing from childhood to parenthood. For years, he has 'pored over these albums' with his children, who seem equally 'exhilarated' by these glimpses into the past. It is yet another irony that the 'hearthrug' – which used to signify domestic warmth – is now a symbol of the void at the heart of the house. Strangely, **his wife is excluded**, almost sidelined as the adult in the scene coolly looking on, 'presiding'. The poet's wife is described as self-effacing, but she looks on 'proudly'. Does the poet now consider that he made the mistake of taking her for granted? She was the family breadwinner while Durcan remained at home caring for their two children and writing. He has since said, 'I sometimes think Nessa missed out. She was out working while I was with the girls'. At times, the tone wavers between condemnation and remorse, with the conflicting preoccupations of the couple's time together remaining unresolved. In the midst of the rough and tumble of family life, 'Schoolbooks on the floor and pyjamas on the couch', her cool voice echoes, 'Whose turn is it tonight to put the children to bed?'

An allegorical **dream scene** reveals the spiritual and emotional aspects of ordinary family life in section five (line 76): 'Our children swam about our home/As if it was their private sea'. Their idyllic, unrestrained happiness is caught in the image of the 'symbiotic fluid' of which everyone 'partook'. Durcan believed that home was a place where one could be at liberty without consequences, even hanging 'upside down from the ceiling/With equanimity'. However, the sibilant line 'Sifting the sands underneath the surfaces of conversations' sounds a warning note. Is someone scrutinising, negatively reviewing? The couple are happy when they are partners in crime, 'smiling accomplices', preferring to continue kissing rather than answer the phone. There are signs that the poet could only relate to his wife when she was not behaving as a responsible adult. Meanwhile, the children watch their 'parents at play' sharing another 'subversive kiss' before running 'wordlessly' to bed. But from his intense study of the 'family psyche', Durcan has learned that **the challenges of an intimate relationship can be destructive**. His ringing assertion that 'The most subversive unit in society is the human family' abruptly contradicts any nostalgic homesickness he may have been experiencing.

In the sixth section (line 102), a reassuring parental voice is heard: 'We're almost home, pet, almost home'. The poet follows up with a litany of everyday phrases, some hanging unfinished, and all containing the word 'home'. It is as if this ubiquitous term – the crucial concept of 'home' and belonging – highlights **the overwhelming sense of security and safety he associates with family life**: 'If I'm not home by six at the latest, I'll phone...' The comforting tone concludes this short section as if Durcan himself and his family have almost made it 'home'. As always, the immediacy of his poetic voice resonates with readers,

reinforcing the universal importance of close family relationships. Inevitably, however, all the celebration of domesticity – whether real or imagined – is shattered in the penultimate section (line 114): 'But then with good reason/I was put out of my home.' The poet no longer refers to 'our home', as in the previous section, but to 'my home'. Does he think he has an absolute right to be there? Durcan frankly admits that he was expelled 'with good reason'. But what was this reason – depression, alcoholism, a refusal to mature? Is he assuming the manipulative posture of the bad boy, disarmingly admitting his faults so that he will be immediately forgiven? There is more than a hint of **self-pity** in the claim that he was finally brought down 'By a keen wind'. Is this sharp, biting force really his wife? Typically self-absorbed, the poet goes on to describe his experience of being without a home. He now has to live in the 'alien, foreign city of Dublin', a frightening, disorienting experience. He has discovered how strange it is to be 'homesick' and regards it as totally unnatural, 'beyond all ornithological analysis' if 'there is no home to go home to'. **Short lines effectively convey the aimless wanderings of a homeless man.** 'Day by day' he spends his time 'creeping, crawling,/Moonlighting, escaping'. What a contrast to his previous idyllic existence, when he was in control of his home in his 'winged chair', surveying his own 'Mont Sainte-Victoire' with his happy children on his knees. Now he moves restlessly from 'Bed-and-breakfast to bed-and breakfast;/Hostels, centres, one-night hotels'.

The poem's bittersweet final section (line 127) refers again to a 'Windfall', but now the word is said with **bitter irony**. It no longer refers to his comfortable home, but to himself as a rootless object 'Blown about the suburban streets at evening'. Longingly, he peers 'in the windows of other people's homes,/ Wondering what it must feel like/To be sitting around a fire'. This basic experience is enjoyed by all races and societies, 'Apache or Cherokee' or the middle-class 'Bourgeoisie'. They all have the privilege of looking at their families' faces illuminated by firelight, whether they gaze at the stars or the TV screen. The poet now resembles a distressed vessel that had been cast adrift. He is calling frantically for assistance: 'can you hear me?' At this point, the calming tones of a parent return, tenderly reassuring a distracted child: 'We're almost home, pet, don't worry anymore, we're almost home.' Is this longing so deeply ingrained in Durcan that he takes refuge in convincing himself that it is still a possibility? Or is the reality the awful truth that he can never again go back to '"Windfall", 8 Parnell Hill, Cork'?

Writing About the Poem

'Paul Durcan charms readers with his self-critical revelations while concealing his own self-centredness.' Discuss this statement in relation to the poem '"Windfall", 8 Parnell Hill, Cork'. Refer closely to the text in your response.

Sample Paragraph

In this poem, Durcan charms us by presenting memorable images of cosy family living, 'my children sat on my knees watching TV', 'Our children swam about our home'. I did feel sympathy for him when I heard his graphic account of homelessness, 'creeping, crawling' as though he was unwanted, going from one anonymous place to another, 'Hostels, centres, one-night hotels'. He appears rootless, a windfall, belonging nowhere, 'Blown about the suburban streets at evening'. But his admission of being 'put out' of his home 'with good reason' seems as if he is condemning himself just to get pity. His wife is busily 'Knitting'. She is 'presiding' while the poet and his children look at old pictures of him 'dancing'. She is the breadwinner and the adult in the relationship, 'Whose turn is it tonight to put the children to bed?' I believe that his wife was becoming frustrated, 'Sifting the sands underneath the surfaces of conversations'. She finally refused to accept her husband's selfish behaviour. In my opinion, this poem is not really about Durcan's home, but about himself. He does attempt to hide his self-centred character. At the same time, I still feel sorry for him. He ends up as a lonely man who has lost all, reduced to the pitiful state of peering into other people's homes and who can never say 'Well, now, I am going home'.

EXAMINER'S COMMENT

The paragraph touches on interesting aspects of how the poet appears to readers and there is a good attempt at addressing the crucial relationship between Durcan and his wife. Points are well illustrated with accurate quotation. There is some direct personal engagement: 'At the same time, I still feel sorry for him.' However, note-like commentary weakens the response: 'He ends up as a lonely man who has lost all.' Although the task is addressed, the quality of expression lowers the mark to a good middle grade.

Class/Homework Exercises

1. 'In many of his poems, Paul Durcan relishes conflict and exhibitionism.' Discuss this statement in relation to '"Windfall", 8 Parnell Hill, Cork'. Support the points you make with suitable reference.
2. Based on your reading of this poem, describe Durcan's views on Irish family life. Support your answer with close reference to the text.

Summary Points

- **Key themes – domestic family happiness and the pain of broken relationships.**
- **Autobiographical/personal details; intense rhythms.**
- **Varying tones – reflective, ironic, celebratory, wistful, regretful, self-critical.**
- **Effective use of repetition, vivid images/metaphors.**

Six Nuns Die in Convent Inferno

Inferno: uncontrollable fire, conflagration.

To the
happy memory of six Loreto nuns
who died
between midnight and morning of
2 June 1986

I

We resided in a Loreto convent in the centre of Dublin city
On the east side of a public gardens, St Stephen's Green.
Grafton Street – the *paseo*
Where everybody *paseo*'d, including even ourselves –
Debouched on the north side, and at the top of Grafton Street,
Or round the base of the great patriotic pebble of O'Donovan Rossa,
Knelt tableaus of punk girls and punk boys.
When I used pass them – scurrying as I went –
Often as not to catch a mass in Clarendon Street,
The Carmelite Church in Clarendon Street
(Myself, I never used the Clarendon Street entrance,
I always slipped in by way of Johnson's Court,
Opposite the side entrance to Bewley's Oriental Café),
I could not help but smile, as I sucked on a Fox's mint,
That for all the half-shaven heads and the martial garb
And the dyed hair-dos and the nappy pins
They looked so conventional, really, and vulnerable,
Clinging to warpaint and to uniforms and to one another.
I knew it was myself who was the ultimate drop-out,
The delinquent, the recidivist, the vagabond,
The wild woman, the subversive, the original punk.
Yet, although I confess I was smiling, I was also afraid,
Appalled by my own nerve, my own fervour,
My apocalyptic enthusiasm, my other-worldly hubris:
To opt out of the world and to
Choose such exotic loneliness,
Such terrestrial abandonment,
A lifetime of bicycle lamps and bicycle pumps,
A lifetime of galoshes stowed under the stairs,
A lifetime of umbrellas drying out in the kitchens.

I was an old nun – an agèd beadswoman –
But I was no daw.
I knew what a weird bird I was, I knew that when we

paseo: pedestrian area where people can take a leisurely stroll.

Debouched: emerged into the open.

O'Donovan Rossa: Jeremiah O'Donovan Rossa (1831–1915) was a prominent Irish Republican. Durcan refers to his large stone memorial as a 'pebble'.

tableaus: groups posing as though in a theatrical freeze.

martial garb: military-style clothes.

warpaint: heavy make-up.

recidivist: undesirable character.

apocalyptic: ruinous.

hubris: excessive pride or arrogance.

daw: jackdaw, noisy crow.

Went to bed we were as eerie an aviary as you'd find
In all the blown-off rooftops of the city:
Scuttling about our dorm, wheezing, shrieking, croaking,
In our yellowy corsets, wonky suspenders, strung-out garters,
A bony crew in the gods of the sleeping city.
Many's the night I lay awake in bed
Dreaming what would befall us if there were a fire:
No fire-escapes outside, no fire-extinguishers inside;
To coin a Dublin saying,
We'd not stand a snowball's chance in hell. Fancy that!
It seemed too good to be true:
Happy death vouchsafed only to the few.
Sleeping up there was like sleeping at the top of the mast
Of a nineteenth-century schooner, and in the daytime
We old nuns were the ones who crawled out on the yardarms
To stitch and sew the rigging and the canvas.
To be sure we were weird birds, oddballs, Christniks,
For we had done the weirdest thing a woman can do –
Surrendered the marvellous passions of girlhood,
The innocent dreams of childhood,
Not for a night or a weekend or even a Lent or a season,
But for a lifetime.
Never to know the love of a man or a woman;
Never to have children of our own;
Never to have a home of our own;
All for why and for what?
To follow a young man – would you believe it –
Who lived two thousand years ago in Palestine
And who died a common criminal strung up on a tree.

As we stood there in the disintegrating dormitory
Burning to death in the arms of Christ –
O Christ, Christ, come quickly, quickly –
Fluttering about in our tight, gold bodices,
Beating our wings in vain,
It reminded me of the snaps one of the sisters took
When we took a seaside holiday in 1956
(The year Cardinal Mindszenty went into hiding
In the US legation in Budapest.
He was a great hero of ours, Cardinal Mindszenty,
Any of us would have given our right arm
To have been his nun – darning his socks, cooking his meals,
Making his bed, doing his washing and ironing.)
Somebody – an affluent buddy of the bishop's repenting his affluence –
Loaned Mother Superior a secluded beach in Co. Waterford –
Ardmore, along the coast from Tramore –

aviary: enclosure or large cage for birds.

schooner: fast sailing ship.
yardarms: parts of a mast from which sails are hung.
rigging: ropes and other supports for sails.
Christniks: fans of Jesus; a pun on the word 'Beatniks'.

Lent: six-week period of penance leading up to Easter in Christian liturgy.

young man: a reference to Jesus.

snaps: photographs.

Cardinal Mindszenty: József Mindszenty (1892–1975), leader of the Catholic Church in Hungary. He was jailed for opposing communism.

affluence: wealth, privileged circumstances.

A cove with palm trees, no less, well off the main road.
There we were, fluttering up and down the beach,
Scampering hither and thither in our starched bathing-costumes.
Tonight, expiring in the fire, was quite much like that,
Only instead of scampering into the waves of the sea,
Now we were scampering into the flames of the fire.

That was one of the gayest days of my life,
The day the sisters went swimming.
Often in the silent darkness of the chapel after Benediction,
During the Exposition of the Blessed Sacrament,
I glimpsed the sea again as it was that day.
Praying – daydreaming really –
I became aware that Christ is the ocean
Forever rising and falling on the world's shore.
Now tonight in the convent Christ is the fire in whose waves
We are doomed but delighted to drown.
And, darting in and out of the flames of the dormitory,
Gabriel, with that extraordinary message of his on his boyish lips,
Frenetically pedalling his skybike.
He whispers into my ear what I must do
And I do it – and die.
Each of us in our own tiny, frail, furtive way
Was a Mother of God, mothering forth illegitimate Christs
In the street life of Dublin city.
God have mercy on our whirring souls –
Wild women were we all –
And on the misfortunate, poor fire-brigade men
Whose task it will be to shovel up our ashes and shovel
What is left of us into black plastic refuse sacks.
Fire-brigade men are the salt of the earth.

Isn't it a marvellous thing how your hour comes
When you least expect it? When you lose a thing,
Not to know about it until it actually happens?
How, in so many ways, losing things is such a refreshing experience,
Giving you a sense of freedom you've not often experienced?
How lucky I was to lose – I say, lose – lose my life.
It was a Sunday night, and after vespers
I skipped bathroom so that I could hop straight into bed
And get in a bit of a read before lights out:
Conor Cruise O'Brien's new book *The Siege*,
All about Israel and superlatively insightful
For a man who they say is reputedly an agnostic –
I got a loan of it from the brother-in-law's married niece –
But I was tired out and I fell asleep with the book open

Benediction: Catholic religious service of blessing.
Exposition of the Blessed Sacrament: prayerful part of Catholic devotion to the Blessed Sacrament (the consecrated bread and wine believed to be the real presence of Jesus Christ).

Gabriel: angel who served as God's messenger.
Frenetically: frantically, wildly.

Conor Cruise O'Brien: prominent Irish politician, writer and academic (1917–2008).
agnostic: religious sceptic.

Face down across my breast and I woke
To the racket of bellowing flame and snarling glass.
The first thing I thought was that the brother-in-law's married niece
Would never again get her Conor Cruise O'Brien back
And I had seen on the price-tag that it cost £23.00:
Small wonder that the custom of snipping off the price
As an exercise in social deportment has simply died out;
Indeed a book today is almost worth buying for its price,
Its price frequently being more remarkable than its contents.

The strange Eucharist of my death –
To be eaten alive by fire and smoke.
I clasped the dragon to my breast
And stroked his red-hot ears.
Strange! There we were, all sleeping molecules,
Suddenly all giving birth to our deaths,
All frantically in labour.
Doctors and midwives weaved in and out
In gowns of smoke and gloves of fire.
Christ, like an Orthodox patriarch in his dressing-gown,
Flew up and down the dormitory, splashing water on our souls:
Sister Eucharia; Sister Seraphia; Sister Rosario;
Sister Gonzaga; Sister Margaret; Sister Edith.
If you will remember us – six nuns burnt to death –
Remember us for the frisky girls that we were,
Now more than ever kittens in the sun.

Eucharist: Thanksgiving; refers to the Mass and Holy Communion (the consecrated bread and wine).
dragon: mythical creature representing fire.
molecules: body particles.

Orthodox patriarch: leader of the Eastern Orthodox Church, the second largest Christian Church in the world.

II

When Jesus heard these words at the top of Grafton Street
Uttered by a small, agèd, emaciated, female punk
Clad all in mourning black, and grieving like an alley cat,
He was annulled with astonishment, and turning round
He declared to the gangs of teenagers and dicemen following him:
'I tell you, not even in New York City
Have I found faith like this.'

emaciated: skinny, skeletal.

dicemen: street performers, mime artists.

That night in St Stephen's Green,
After the keepers had locked the gates,
And the courting couples had found cinemas themselves to die in,
The six nuns who had died in the convent inferno,
From the bandstand they'd been hiding under, crept out
And knelt together by the Fountain of the Three Fates,
Reciting the Agnus Dei: reciting it as if it were the torch song
Of all aid – Live Aid, Self Aid, AIDS, and All Aid –
Lord, I am not worthy
That thou should'st enter under my roof;
Say but the word and my soul shall be healed.

Fountain of the Three Fates: St Stephen's Green statue of the Three Fates or Graces controlling human destiny.
Agnus Dei: Lamb of God (Latin), referring to Christ, a contemplative prayer.
Live Aid, Self Aid: popular charities.
AIDS: acquired immune deficiency syndrome, a syndrome caused by human immunodeficiency virus (HIV).

Personal Response

1. Based on your reading of the poem, what is your impression of convent life in Ireland? Refer to the text in your answer.
2. Briefly describe Durcan's attitude to the nuns and their way of life. Is he always sympathetic to them? Explain your response.
3. Choose one short section of the poem that you consider particularly dramatic. Discuss the poet's language use, commenting on its effectiveness.

'six nuns burnt to death'

Critical Literacy

Paul Durcan has a reputation for being an incisive social commentator. His journalistic approach ranges widely over contemporary events, defining him as a poet of the present moment. But the poet is never content with mere reportage. This long narrative poem about a fire that destroyed a Dublin convent in 1986 characteristically transforms the details of the tragedy into an extended exercise in spiritual reflection. He focuses on one elderly nun who narrates the story of this disaster and reveals the personal choices she had made and her memories of happier times.

Durcan's poems are predominantly narrative in form, but they often combine incidents, impressions and flights of fancy. In this case, the title juxtaposes the dramatic newspaper heading, 'Six Nuns Die in Convent Inferno', with the poignant memorial celebrating the women who dedicated their lives to Christ. What is most evident in the opening lines of Part I is the spirited voice of the nun who provides a short history of the Loreto convent where she 'resided'. The **gentle, self-deprecating humour** of the sisters joining the Grafton Street crowds and 'scurrying' past punks who 'Knelt' indicates a lively sense of irony.

The narrator is particularly amused by the displays of youthful rebelliousness she notices: 'the half-shaven heads' and 'dyed hair-dos' (lines 15–16). She is also convinced that **her 'subversive' choice of vocation** makes her 'the ultimate drop-out'. In retrospect, she is still shocked by her decision to 'opt out of the world' and follow the religious life in all its 'exotic loneliness'. But despite the long 'lifetime' of 'bicycle pumps' and 'umbrellas drying out', she always understood the significance of her alternative calling as a nun: 'I knew what a weird bird I was' (line 33). From her 'agèd beadswoman' perspective, stooped and dressed in black, she is able to imagine how she must appear to outsiders, who might compare her eccentric appearance in full religious habit to 'a daw' – not that any criticism dampens her enthusiasm. Durcan develops the bird metaphor – 'we were as eerie an aviary as you'd find', suggesting the enclosed convent environment.

The speaker's **reflections become increasingly surreal** when she recalls occasional fears ('what would befall us if there were a fire') and the accompanying prospect of a 'Happy death'. Durcan uses a dramatic sailing image to bring to mind the thought of being accidentally killed while 'sleeping at the top of the mast/Of a nineteenth-century schooner'. His attitude to the nuns, encompassing both admiration and astonishment, shows how closely he himself identifies with these unusual women who have 'Surrendered the marvellous passions of girlhood'. He also acknowledges the contribution made by the Loreto nuns in Ireland to providing spiritual guidance and education. Their essential work is compared to the sailors who 'stitch and sew the rigging and the canvas'. The poet's trademark repetition

emphasises their sacrifice and isolation: 'Never to have children ... Never to have a home of our own' (lines 57–58).

Many of Durcan's more loosely structured poems are composed by 'cutting' and 'reassembling' various narrative scenes. In line 63, the speaker remembers the 'disintegrating dormitory' and the terrifying ecstasy of 'Burning to death in the arms of Christ'. Amid the chaos – accentuated by exclamatory language – there is **the unsettling sense of souls desperate to emerge as angels**: 'Beating our wings in vain.' In another sudden change of space and time, the narrator associates this crucial moment with an earlier experience when the nuns 'took a seaside holiday in 1956'. The nostalgia for a simpler, old-fashioned era is apparent in the innocent hero-worship of Cardinal Mindszenty and the youthful pleasures of carefree times, 'scampering into the waves'. However, the fond memory is short-lived and the secluded beach abruptly becomes the raging fire that consumed the sisters: 'Now we were scampering into the flames.'

Nevertheless, the elation experienced by the speaker during moments of devout prayer is expressed in terms of the 'day the sisters went swimming'. Durcan uses the nun's elegiac recollection to emphasise the central importance of unconditional Christian faith. Her **visionary account** equates Christ with all of the natural world, including 'the fire in whose waves/We are doomed but delighted to drown' (lines 93–94). A touch of black humour is added to her portrait when she imagines the 'boyish' angel Gabriel, 'Frenetically pedalling his skybike'. Her childlike sincerity is also obvious when she worries about the 'poor fire-brigade men' and the loss of a book she borrowed from her niece – 'it cost £23.00'.

Throughout the poem, Durcan promotes the radical Christian values of charity, piety and the achievement of sanctity through suffering, all virtues epitomised in Christ's own life on earth. The nun who narrates this tragic story readily accepts her fate as God's will: 'The strange Eucharist of my death' (line 132). In trying to make sense of the horrific event, the poet interweaves an ingenious series of random insights ('all sleeping molecules') and nightmarish images ('I clasped the dragon to my breast'). The inferno itself is personified, dramatising this central moment of Christian renewal – the paradoxical transition into the spiritual afterlife from earthly existence, 'giving birth to our deaths'. But we are never allowed to forget that at the heart of this sacrifice is the reality of human loss: 'six nuns burnt to death.' As the individual names are recorded precisely, readers can share **Durcan's tender and sad compassion**. The narrator's modest request – to be remembered as 'the frisky girls that we were' (line 146) – is particularly moving. Characteristically playful to the end, she chooses a universal image of childhood innocence to describe her vision of eternal happiness: 'Now more than ever kittens in the sun.'

The 18 lines that make up Part II of the poem are told as third person narrative. The didactic tone echoes countless gospel stories. Durcan imagines the aftermath of the tragedy, with Jesus relocated to Grafton Street, where he is humbled by the story of the grieving nun, now in the persona of 'a small, agèd, emaciated, female punk' (line 149). His shocked reaction ('annulled with astonishment') reflects the poet's well-documented objections to current Catholic teaching on aspects of marriage breakdown. Within this framework, linking the six nuns' deaths to the vulnerability of some women today, **Durcan achieves a bizarre satirical effect**. But while he mocks Ireland's conservative Catholic lawmakers, he shows the highest regard for the unshakable faith of individuals, such as the victims of the convent fire.

The poem ends as it began, back in St Stephen's Green, where a final dramatic scenario is played out under cover of darkness. Trancelike, the dead nuns kneel 'by the Fountain of the Three Fates' happily chanting the Agnus Dei (line 161) 'as if it were the torch song' at an outdoor music festival. **The words of this Communion prayer are spoken in preparation for the Divine encounter** – sentiments that are entirely in keeping with the faith of the six Loreto sisters. Durcan's tone of conviction and use of italics reflect the significance of recognising human unworthiness and the acceptance of divine healing love.

From the outset, the poet has venerated the nuns who lost their lives, articulating their religious impulses in particular. The poem's surreal and theatrical elements broaden our understanding of Durcan's subject matter, increasing the clarity of **his imaginative vision**. In blending psychological and physical impressions, he has managed to translate the sensational newspaper story of the inferno into an incisive exploration of individual religious experience.

Writing About the Poem

'Durcan's unique poetic voice is particularly evident in his elegies for victims.' Discuss this view based on your reading of 'Six Nuns Die in Convent Inferno', supporting the points you make with reference to the poem.

Sample Paragraph

Paul Durcan's poetry is always accessible and his distinctive voice is evident in 'Six Nuns Die in Convent Inferno'. This elegy shows his great sympathy for the victims of the 1986 fire, but also shows their deaths in the true religious sense. The nuns are now with God. The rambling anecdotal style is typical of Durcan. His narrator is one of the nuns who

died, a jolly person, still childish and mischievous. She sees herself as a comic character and refers to the O'Donovan Rossa memorial as 'the patriotic pebble'. She saw death – even the terrible inferno – as a 'very strange Eucharist', a release. The poem wandered in and out of times in her life, mixing the fire scene with her everyday walks around Stephen's Green and vivid memories of a holiday in Tramore. Durcan always uses names to create a sense of place. His respect for the nuns was obvious in his use of prayers. The whole poem paid tribute to the nuns' deep faith, suggesting that they are obsessed with religion. Durcan's conclusion was dreamlike, showing the spirits of the six nuns celebrating their entry to Heaven through a vibrant image of dancing in the dark. I thought the tribute was sincere without being sentimental, another typical feature of Durcan's poems.

EXAMINER'S COMMENT

This fresh response shows clear personal engagement with the poem: 'I liked the way her character was gradually revealed.' The answer touches on several interesting points – focusing particularly well on characteristics of Durcan's style, for example his anecdotal approach and use of place names. The expression is satisfactory, but more use could be made of supportive quotations (and some are slightly inaccurate). Falls just below the top grade.

Class/Homework Exercises

1. 'Durcan makes good use of surrealistic effects in addressing religious themes.' Discuss this statement based on your reading of 'Six Nuns Die in Convent Inferno'. Support the points you make with reference to the poem.
2. 'Vivid imagery is often a feature of Paul Durcan's most compelling poems.' To what extent is this the case in 'Six Nuns Die in Convent Inferno'? Support your answer with reference to the text.

Summary Points

- **Narrative of the fire tragedy becomes an extended spiritual reflection.**
- **Key themes include personal choices, sacrifice, faith, the religious life.**
- **Fragmented, theatrical structure; striking images – realistic, surreal.**
- **Varying tones – ironic, compassionate, satirical, critical.**

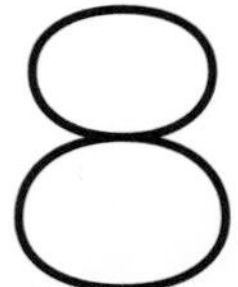

8 Sport

Sport: an activity involving effort and skill in which an individual or team compete; also refers to a person who behaves in a good way in response to teasing or defeat.

There were not many fields
In which you had hopes for me
But sport was one of them.
On my twenty-first birthday
I was selected to play
For Grangegorman Mental Hospital
In an away game
Against Mullingar Mental Hospital.
I was a patient
In B Wing.
You drove all the way down,
Fifty miles,
To Mullingar to stand
On the sidelines and observe me.

I was fearful I would let down
Not only my team but you.
It was Gaelic football.
I was selected as goalkeeper.
There were big country men
On the Mullingar Mental Hospital team,
Men with gapped teeth, red faces,
Oily, frizzy hair, bushy eyebrows.
Their full forward line
Were over six foot tall
Fifteen stone in weight.
All three of them, I was informed,
Cases of schizophrenia.

There was a rumour
That their centre-half forward
Was an alcoholic solicitor
Who, in a lounge bar misunderstanding,
Had castrated his best friend
But that he had no memory of it.
He had meant well – it was said.
His best friend had had to emigrate
To Nigeria.

fields: pitches, areas, disciplines.

away game: played at an opponent's place, seen as an advantage to the opposing team.

observe: examine, consider, scrutinise.

schizophrenia: long-term mental disorder with symptoms including emotional instability, detachment from reality and withdrawal into self.

castrated: removed testicles; deprived of power, made docile.

To my surprise,
I did not flinch in the goals.
I made three or four spectacular saves,
Diving full stretch to turn
A certain goal around the corner,
Leaping high to tip another certain goal
Over the bar for a point.
It was my knowing
That you were standing on the sideline
That gave me the necessary motivation –
That will to die
That is as essential to sportsmen as to artists.
More than anybody it was you
I wanted to mesmerise, and after the game –
Grangegorman Mental Hospital
Having defeated Mullingar Mental Hospital
By 14 goals and 38 points to 3 goals and 10 points –
Sniffing your approval, you shook hands with me.
'Well played, son.'

I may not have been mesmeric
But I had not been mediocre.
In your eyes I had achieved something at last.
On my twenty-first birthday I had played on a winning team
The Grangegorman Mental Hospital team.
Seldom if ever again in your eyes
Was I to rise to these heights.

flinch: cower, dodge, shy away.

motivation: reasons to act and be enthusiastic.

mesmerise: fascinate, captivate.

Sniffing: snorting, showing contempt for.

mesmeric: brilliant, hypnotic.
mediocre: only average, amateurish; ordinary.

'I had achieved something'

Personal Response

1. Based on an initial reading of the poem, what is your impression of Paul Durcan's father? Refer closely to the text in your response.
2. Trace the changing tones of voice as the poem progresses. Support your answer with appropriate reference.
3. Are you sympathetic or not to the character of Durcan himself that emerges from the poem? Refer to the text to support the points you make.

Critical Literacy

'Sport' is from Paul Durcan's collection *Daddy, Daddy*, for which he was awarded the Whitbread Prize (1990). This poem is painfully autobiographical, as he not only recalls a difficult time in his youth, but also explores the troubled relationship he had with his father. Durcan has remarked: 'My father would say, "Paul is a sissy. Come on, be a man." I was aware of his deep disappointment.'

The poet's father was a judge in the circuit court. He was an introverted man, apparently ill-suited to the legal profession. Nevertheless, Durcan shared 'many rich moments' with him in early childhood. But in the mid-1950s, 'the picture darkened' when the young Durcan was about 10. Paul began to receive beatings and there was pressure about exam performance. He contracted a serious bone disease at 13, which ended his athletic career. Because of difficulties with his behaviour in his late teens, members of his wider family had him committed to a psychiatric hospital.

The poem opens candidly, with Durcan addressing his father directly. He immediately registers an acute awareness of his father's disappointment with him in many areas: 'there were not many fields/In which you had hopes for me/But sport was one of them.' Sometimes, when men find it hard to communicate, they can relate through sport. They can express their emotions as they discuss the winning or losing of a match without being considered odd. The Gaelic football game Durcan recalls was played on his 21st birthday, the day he becomes a man. In line 6, **the chilling context of this occasion** is revealed. It was an 'away game' between the inmates of 'Grangegorman Mental Hospital' and 'Mullingar Mental Hospital'. Durcan is 'a patient/In B Wing', a vulnerable individual. He acknowledges his father's efforts to attend the match, driving 'Fifty miles,/To Mullingar to stand/On the sidelines'. The inference is that the father was never really involved in the poet's life. Durcan also suggests his father's judgemental character when he is described as coming to 'observe me'. It is almost as if his son was a laboratory specimen. The curt tone clearly indicates that **his father's attendance was far from supportive**.

Nevertheless, there is no denying the son's extreme anxiety to impress: 'I was fearful I would let down/Not only my team but you' (lines 15–16). The young man was obviously keen to please his father in this unlikely Gaelic match, where he had been 'selected as goalkeeper'. Durcan's fondness for dark humour is evident in his exaggerated description of the opposition players. The Mullingar team had 'gapped teeth, red faces,/Oily, frizzy hair, bushy eyebrows'. They scarcely seemed human. **Odd details reflect the poet's visual alertness.** The opposing team consisted of 'big country men' whose 'full forward line/Were over six foot tall/Fifteen stone in weight'. These three suffered from schizophrenia, a withdrawal from reality into fantasy. As if the situation was not surreal enough already, Durcan recounts the 'rumour' (line 28) about another member of the Mullingar team, 'an alcoholic solicitor' who

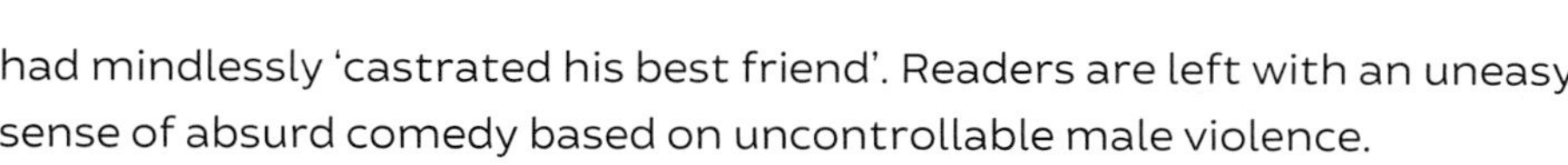

had mindlessly 'castrated his best friend'. Readers are left with an uneasy sense of absurd comedy based on uncontrollable male violence.

As for the game itself, the poet is amazed by his own performance: 'To my surprise,/I did not flinch in the goals.' The dramatic jargon of sports writing is used, perhaps self-mockingly, to describe his exploits on the field of play, making 'spectacular saves' that were at 'full stretch'. Action-packed verbs convey his tremendous agility – 'Diving', 'Leaping' – and all for the approval of his father, 'knowing/That you were standing on the sideline'. Durcan makes a revealing comment in line 47 that **both artists, such as himself, and sportsmen must have absolute motivation** – 'That will to die'. They will give their all and risk everything in their desire to succeed.

The young man's need to make an impact on his father accelerates: 'it was you/I wanted to mesmerise.' Characteristically, the overwhelmingly decisive triumph of Durcan's team is recorded with **mock-heroic pride**: '14 goals and 38 points to 3 goals and 10 points.' Despite this great triumph, however, the father's minimal response, his monosyllabic ruling, is less than enthusiastic: 'Well played, son.' There is no embrace. Instead, a formal handshake takes place. The disappointment of the young man contrasts with the emotionally stilted father 'Sniffing ... approval'. Is he suggesting that his son is merely satisfactory, damning him with faint praise? Of course, we see everything from the son's perspective. During the early 1960s, a father's function in Irish society was to fund and guide his family. Overt displays of affection were not common between parents and children, especially sons. Is Durcan's forensic examination of the father–son relationship almost as unhealthy as his father's scrutiny of him? Are both tragically locked into damaging behavioural attitudes?

In the poem's concluding section, Durcan ruefully admits, 'I may not have been mesmeric' (line 56). Yet he also asserts 'But I had not been mediocre' and had indeed 'achieved something at last'. The phrase 'at last' forcefully expresses how intensely aware the poet is of his father's lack of confidence in him. After all, he had accomplished something, playing on a 'winning team'. It was, however, a mental hospital patients' team. Does this matter greatly to the father – and to the son? **The poem ends on a poignant note**: 'seldom if ever again in your eyes/Was I to rise to these heights.' Dark shadows of family relationships were cast by the father's continuing disappointment. The son is still devastated about what it means to be a man and always to feel not quite good enough. As the poet himself has stated elsewhere, even though the father 'loved books', it was always clear that 'the more it looked like I was going to be a writer, the more he was against it'.

Writing About the Poem

'Durcan's poetry is not just revealing, it also has a shockingly frank quality.' Discuss this statement in relation to the poem 'Sport'. Refer closely to the text in your answer.

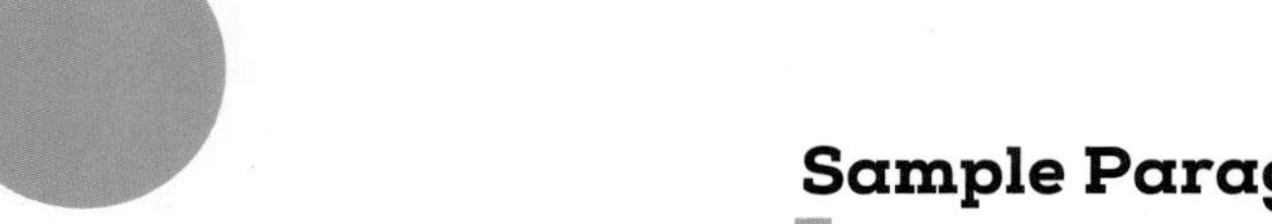

Sample Paragraph

The highly personal poem 'Sport' comes from Durcan's collection *Daddy, Daddy*, whose title is a reference to the American poet Sylvia Plath's cry to her father, 'Daddy, daddy, you bastard, I'm through'. I think the lines in 'Sport' are almost as shocking. They convey, in a frank manner, the longing of the son for his father's approval. Durcan reveals his lack of confidence in lines such as, 'I was fearful I would let down/Not only my team but you'. Like most young men, he desperately wanted to 'mesmerise' his uncommunicative father. The urgent tone seems to suggest the spellbinding effect he wishes to make on him. I thought the father's lukewarm response was hurtful, especially when he uttered the cold words 'Well played, son'. The poet does not shy away from disclosing that just as his father stood on 'the sidelines' to 'observe' him, he now appears obsessed with studying his father and is still trying to understand him after so many years. I believe he feels just as let down by his father's behaviour as his father is by his: 'But I had not been mediocre.' His continuing disappointment mirrors his father's feelings towards him as he notes in the concluding lines, 'Seldom if ever again in your eyes/Was I to rise to these heights'. Durcan is actually quite brave to detail the awkward relationship he had with his father with such devastating honesty.

EXAMINER'S COMMENT

A well-written paragraph that uses suitable reference to outline the poet's central theme, the difficult father-son relationship. The use of pertinent descriptive terms, such as 'uncommunicative', 'lukewarm' and 'devastating', helps to define their strained relationship. There is clear evidence throughout of close engagement with the poem: 'I believe he feels just as let down by his father's behaviour as his father is by his.' A highly successful response which merits the top grade.

Class/Homework Exercises

1. 'Paul Durcan blends fact, fiction and fantasy to create a realistic view of the world.' Discuss this viewpoint in relation to the poem, 'Sport'. Support your opinions with close reference to the text.
2. In your opinion, what kind of relationship did the poet have with his father? Support your answer with close reference to the poem, 'Sport'.

Summary Points

- **Characteristically personal exploration of a complex father–son relationship.**
- **Effective use of tragicomedy, mock-heroism and irony.**
- **Tone varies – casual, sad, comic, self-mocking.**
- **Revealing narrative/descriptive details, lively verbs.**

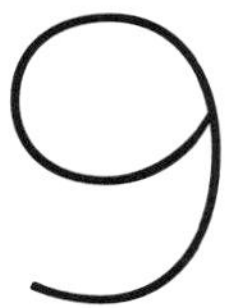

9 Father's Day, 21 June 1992

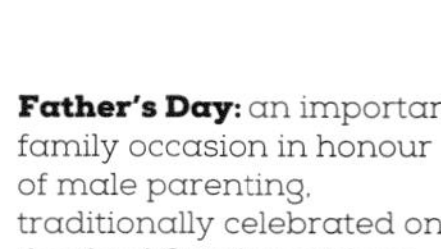

Father's Day: an important family occasion in honour of male parenting, traditionally celebrated on the third Sunday of June.

Just as I was dashing to catch the Dublin–Cork train,
Dashing up and down the stairs, searching my pockets,
She told me that her sister in Cork wanted a loan of the axe;
It was late June and
The buddleia tree in the backyard
Had grown out of control.
The taxi was ticking over outside in the street,
All the neighbours noticing it.
'You mean that you want me to bring her down the axe?'
'Yes, if you wouldn't mind, that is –'
'A simple saw would do the job, surely to God
She could borrow a simple saw.'
'she said that she'd like the axe.'
'OK. There is a Blue Cabs taxi ticking over outside
And the whole world inspecting it,
I'll bring her down the axe.'
The axe – all four-and-a-half feet of it –
Was leaning up against the wall behind the settee –
The fold-up settee that doubles as a bed.
She handed the axe to me just as it was,
As neat as a newborn babe,
All in the bare buff.
You'd think she'd have swaddled it up
In something – if not a blanket, an old newspaper,
But no, not even a token hanky
Tied in a bow round its head.
I decided not to argue the toss. I kissed her goodbye.

The whole long way down to Cork
I felt uneasy. Guilt feelings.
It's a killer, this guilt.
I always feel bad leaving her
But this time it was the worst.
I could see that she was glad
To see me go away for a while,
Glad at the prospect of being
Two weeks on her own,
Two weeks of having the bed to herself,
Two weeks of not having to be pestered
By my coarse advances,

buddleia tree: colourful flowering shrub; butterfly bush.

swaddled: wrapped.

token: symbolic, nominal.

argue the toss: dispute the issue.

prospect: expectation.

pestered: bothered.

coarse advances: unrefined sexual demands.

Two weeks of not having to look up from her plate
And behold me eating spaghetti with a knife and fork.
Our daughters are all grown up and gone away.
Once when she was sitting pregnant on the settee
It snapped shut with herself inside it,
But not a bother on her. I nearly died.

As the train slowed down approaching Portarlington
I overheard myself say to the passenger sitting opposite me:
'I am feeling guilty because she does not love me
As much as she used to, can you explain that?'
The passenger's eyes were on the axe on the seat beside me.
'Her sister wants a loan of the axe ...'
As the train threaded itself into Portarlington
I nodded to the passenger 'Cúl an tSúdaire!'
The passenger stood up, lifted down a case from the rack,
Walked out of the coach, but did not get off the train.
For the remainder of the journey, we sat alone,
The axe and I,
All the green fields running away from us,
All our daughters grown up and gone away.

Cúl an tSúdaire: Irish name for Portarlington (literally 'back of the tanner', referring to the tannery once located there). Durcan might well be making a snide comment about the town's humble origins.

'the train threaded itself into Portarlington'

Personal Response

1. In your opinion, what does the poem's first stanza reveal about the relationship between the poet and his wife? Refer closely to the text in your answer.
2. Select one image (or line) that has a surreal or bizarre impact in the poem. Briefly explain your choice.
3. Comment on the significance of the poem's final line: 'All our daughters grown up and gone away.'

Critical Literacy

Because so much of his poetry has been autobiographical, Durcan's insecure relationships are already widely known. 'Father's Day, 21 June 1992' is taken from *A Snail in my Prime* (1993) and recounts a crucial train journey when the poet confronts the adverse effects of time on his role as a husband and father. Typically, the poem alternates between tragicomedy, surreal scenes and devastating self-awareness. The abrupt changes of tone and mood are likely to be disconcerting for readers, who can never be completely sure about the poet's true feelings.

In the anecdotal opening lines, Durcan assumes the persona of a slightly befuddled figure 'dashing' about the house. From the outset, there are suggestions of marriage difficulties, particularly in his petulant account of his wife's attitude towards him: 'She told me that her sister in Cork wanted a loan of the axe.' Everyone involved in this uneasy family drama seems slightly eccentric. **Durcan often finds grim humour in the most unexpected circumstances.** Is he suggesting that his sister-in-law is dangerously deranged? The poet's mention of the garden shrub that is now 'out of control' adds to the unstable atmosphere. Could this be a reference to his officious wife and her sister? Or is the marriage itself veering close to crisis? Meanwhile, the waiting taxi is 'ticking over', another possible symbol of the explosive domestic situation.

The strained exchange between the couple (lines 9–16) illustrates their barely concealed frustration with each other. Although the poet is reluctant to bring an axe on public transport, his wife is politely insistent: 'if you wouldn't mind.' She seems to be a strangely disembodied presence, reflecting the considerable lack of communication in the marriage. In choosing to do as he is asked on this occasion – 'I decided not to argue the toss' – Durcan indicates a history of marital disagreements. Almost as a defence mechanism to block out the truth about a relationship under threat, **Durcan's description of the scene becomes increasingly trancelike**. He exaggerates the importance of the axe – 'all-four-and-a-half feet of it' – comparing it to 'a newborn babe' (line 21). The simile has a poignant association with happier times, when his infant children represented what

was truly meaningful about Father's Day. In a blurred state of distorted memories and nostalgic self-pity, the poet personifies the axe and wonders why it could not have been 'swaddled' or at least gift-wrapped with 'a bow round its head'.

Durcan's small domestic narrative develops in the poem's second stanza. On the train journey from Dublin to Cork, his tone is much more reflective as he laments his guilty mood: 'I always feel bad leaving her.' Acknowledging that his wife is 'glad' to be alone, he indulges in mock-serious self-recrimination. Not only will she will welcome a fortnight's break from his 'coarse advances', but she will no longer have to endure his irritating table manners, 'eating spaghetti with a knife and fork' (line 41). Whether such overstated self-accusation is totally sincere is, of course, open to question. At any rate, whatever humour that exists is soon replaced with **the stark reality of loss** that is at the heart of the poet's unhappiness: 'Our daughters are all grown up.' This heartbreaking admission, enhanced by broad assonant effects, provides a momentary explanation for the couple's failing marriage. However, in a sudden change in tone, the poet recalls another comic occasion when his wife was pregnant and almost got trapped in the fold-up settee. Ironically, the memory does not lessen his deep sense of disappointment.

The third stanza is set at Portarlington Station, where Durcan seems overwhelmed by profound feelings of sorrow. However, the normality of his situation quickly turns into an anarchic event. In a dreamlike sequence, the poet imagines confiding in another passenger about his guilt 'because she does not love me/As much as she used to'. **The surreal sense of disorientation grows** when the encounter is viewed from the perspective of the stranger, whose 'eyes were on the axe on the seat beside me'. Needless to say, when Durcan calls out the station name in Irish, 'Cúl an tSúdaire', the frightened passenger leaves the coach as quickly as possible. Again, the farcical episode is underpinned with underlying heartbreak.

In the final lines, we see a broken human abandoned in a bizarre world of utter isolation: 'we sat alone,/The axe and I.' The ending is particularly lyrical, evoking the sadness of innocent times gone forever: 'All the green fields running away from us.' Durcan often uses the metaphor of travel to express significant changes in his life. The train journey to Cork is a remarkably sombre one, depicting a forlorn man still struggling to come to terms with the effects of time and the devastating fact that 'All our daughters' are 'grown up and gone away'. The concluding mood is one of estrangement and desolation. Durcan is only too aware that he no longer has a reason to celebrate Father's Day.

Writing About the Poem

'Father's Day, 21 June 1992' is one of Paul Durcan's most personal and revealing poems. What aspects of the poem affected you most?

Sample Paragraph

After studying 'Father's Day, 21 June 1992', I had mixed feelings. In some ways, the poem is a desperately sad memory of the time when Durcan realised his marriage was ending. The couple seemed like strangers – 'I decided not to argue the toss'. The mood in the family home is awkward. The discussion about bringing an axe on the train seems ludicrous, but it's difficult not to have sympathy for both the poet and his wife. There is a distance between them, evident in the ironic comment, 'I kissed her goodbye'. For me, the most moving part of the poem is Durcan's acknowledgement 'Our daughters are all grown up and gone away'. The serious tone and slow rhythm of this long thoughtful line, filled with mournful assonance, emphasises the poet's essential depression. He now accepts that there is nothing to keep his marriage alive and the poem's concluding lines left me genuinely sympathetic. Father's Day has lost all meaning for Durcan. The image of 'All our green fields running away from us' is very appropriate. As he looks out of the train window, the beauty of the Irish countryside is out of reach for the ageing poet. I thought this was a very moving symbol of his empty life – and I felt it was in keeping with the elegiac mood.

EXAMINER'S COMMENT

A very good personal response, showing true engagement with the poem: 'the poem's concluding lines left me genuinely sympathetic.' The focus throughout is on the emotional interaction with the poet's experience of failure and loss. Effective use was made of supportive quotes. Expression is also clear and varied: 'The serious tone and the slow rhythm of this long thoughtful line, filled with mournful assonance, emphasises the poet's essential depression.' In-depth analysis merits the top grade.

Class/Homework Exercises

1. 'The use of humour in Paul Durcan's poems provides revealing insights into his complex personal relationships.' Discuss this view, with particular reference to 'Father's Day, 21 June 1992'.
2. Trace the changing tones in the poem, 'Father's Day, 21 June 1992'. Support your answer with close reference to the text.

Summary Points

- **Durcan considers the destructive impact of time on his role as husband and father.**
- **Dislocated dreamlike atmosphere, heightened drama, edgy dialogue.**
- **Effective use of travel metaphor, irony, surreal scenes.**
- **Contrasting tones of discomfort, dark humour, reflection and resignation.**

10 The Arnolfini Marriage

after Jan Van Eyck

We are the Arnolfinis.
Do not think you may invade
Our privacy because you may not.

We are standing to our portrait,
The most erotic portrait ever made,
Because we have faith in the artist

To do justice to the plurality,
Fertility, domesticity, barefootedness
Of a man and a woman saying 'we':

To do justice to our bed
As being our most necessary furniture;
To do justice to our life as a reflection.

Our brains spill out upon the floor
And the terrier at our feet sniffs
The minutiae of our magnitude.

The most relaxing word in our vocabulary is 'we'.
Imagine being able to say 'we'.
Most people are in no position to say 'we'.

Are you? Who eat alone? Sleep alone?
And at dawn cycle to work
With an Alsatian shepherd dog tied to your handlebars?

We will pause now for the Angelus.
Here you have it:
The two halves of the coconut.

The Arnolfini Marriage: Painted by the Dutch artist Jan Van Eyck in 1434 and regarded as a masterpiece, it has become a well-known symbol of marriage yet it retains its mystery.

Arnolfinis: Generally believed to represent the Italian merchant Giovanni and his wife Constanza, possibly in their home in the Flemish city of Bruges, perhaps undertaking a civil marriage ceremony. It was commissioned a year after Constanza died.
invade: infringe, violate, intrude on.
privacy: undisturbed time, secrecy.
erotic: sensual, suggestive.
faith: complete trust.

To do justice: to be fair and reasonable.
plurality: range, various meanings, truth.
barefootedness: In 15th-century Flanders, it was traditional to remove shoes for a wedding ceremony. This emphasised the marriage rite's blessedness and inviolability.

reflection: light thrown back from a surface; image formed by a reflection; a serious thought.

minutiae: small, precise details.
magnitude: greatness, importance.

Angelus: Christian devotional prayers commemorating the announcement to Mary that she was going to give birth to Jesus, the son of God.
coconut: fruit of the coconut palm, consisting of a hard fibrous husk and white inner core.

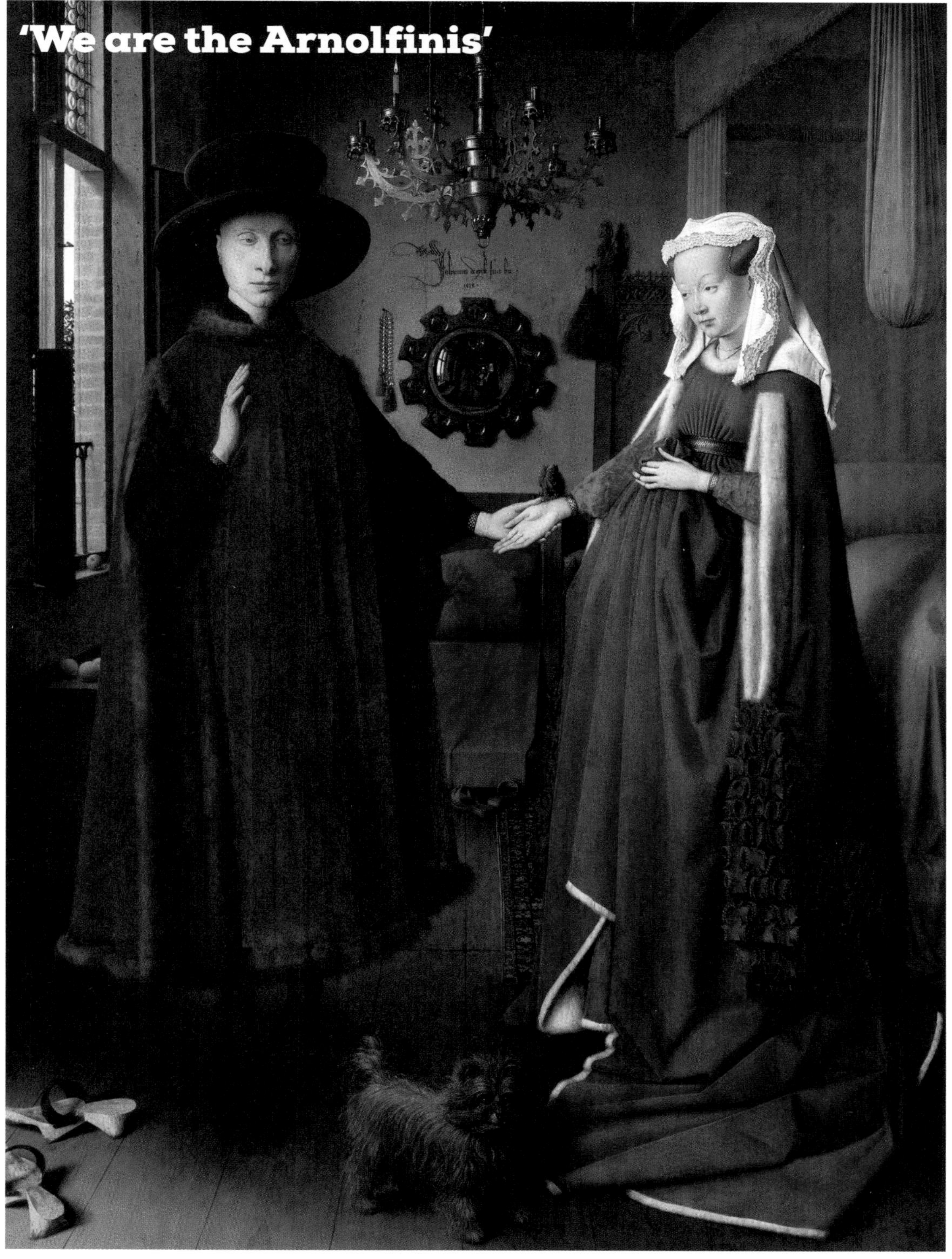

Personal Response

1. Based on your reading of the poem, do you think that the speakers are trying to shock or discomfort the reader? Briefly explain your views.
2. What, in your opinion, is Durcan's attitude towards the Arnolfinis? Refer to the poem in your answer.
3. Select one image from the poem that you found particularly interesting. Comment on its effectiveness.

Critical Literacy

Paul Durcan's collection *Give Me Your Hand* (1994) was inspired by paintings in London's National Gallery. He has taken some of the most famous paintings in the world and interpreted them with his own distinctive poetic voice. We see the artwork 'through the prism of his imagination' as he projects himself into the famous characters of the paintings, slipping in and out of the pictures and 'sending us on flights of our own'. 'The Arnolfini Marriage' was inspired by the Jan Van Eyck oil painting, which is believed to represent a rich Italian merchant and his wife. It was painted in Bruges in 1434, 'in its own way new and revolutionary ... For the first time in history, the artist became the perfect eye-witness'.

The opening line of this dramatic monologue simply states, 'We are the Arnolfinis', a confident declaration by an assured, well-to-do couple. Durcan assumes their persona. The regular form of the poem – eight three-line stanzas – mirrors the orderly composition of the portrait. The speakers issue a stern warning to the reader: 'Do not think you may invade/Our privacy because you may not'. The formal tone contains more than a suggestion that Durcan is casting a satirical eye on the prim couple. Although this painting has become a famous symbol of marriage, representing the Arnolfinis in the intimate environment of their home, it conceals as much as it reveals. It is, however, an utterly convincing picture of a room as well as the people who inhabit it. Argument rages over the original painting, but the most recent view suggests that the couple are Giovanni and Constanza Arnolfini. Some critics maintain that the woman is simply holding up her full-skirted dress in the contemporary fashion. Although the wife looks pregnant, there are no recorded children for this couple. In the painting, the man's hand is raised as if taking an oath. Is it a record of a marriage contract in the form of a painting? **Durcan is clearly fascinated – both by the questions raised and by the answers we will never know**, since we cannot 'invade' the couple's 'privacy'.

The announcement at the start of the second stanza is also intriguing: 'We are standing to our portrait'. It is as if they are taking up position in readiness for military action. Is the poet suggesting that marriage can also have its share of conflict? Nonetheless, the speakers describe the painting as the 'most erotic portrait ever made'. It is certainly a sensual, stimulating picture celebrating the couple's sexual relationship as well as the sanctity of marriage. Throughout stanza three, Durcan emphasises the faith the Arnolfinis have in the artist's ability 'to do justice to the plurality' of their married lives. **There are many aspects to a man and woman saying 'we'.** A chance of having children, 'Fertility', is now possible. The challenge of living together as man and wife, 'domesticity', must now be faced. The removal of shoes, 'barefootedness', could suggest the vulnerability of laying bare one's soul to another in an intimate relationship. Going barefoot also means landing on the forefoot, the centre of gravity. This guarantees optimum balance and increased stability – but is this true for every marriage?

In stanza four, the Arnolfinis assert that they want the artist to 'do justice' and be objective in his depiction of their 'bed/As being our most necessary furniture'. It is central to their marriage. They hope the artist will execute a work of integrity, 'to our life as a reflection'. They want a true likeness. **Durcan's fondness for the surreal** becomes evident in the fifth stanza with the introduction of a more disturbing image: 'Our brains spill out upon the floor.' Does this suggest the suppressed aggression within the relationship? Meanwhile, the little dog, usually a symbol of loyalty, is sniffing 'the minutiae of our magnitude', the small details that reveal the couple's sense of their importance. In the sixth stanza, the repetition of 'we' shows the complacency of the couple now that they are man and wife: 'The most relaxing word in our vocabulary is "we".' They luxuriate in their ability to say it: 'imagine being able to say "we".' Then they realise that most people are not so fortunate – 'are in no position to say "we".' Durcan has used the process of repetition to develop this thought. But is he also thinking about his own marriage and that he never expected it to fail?

The tone of the seventh stanza sharply challenges us with the uncomfortable question: 'Are you?' The solitary state of the reader is highlighted by the emphatic 'Who eat alone? Sleep alone?' Durcan sketches some of the mundane routines of modern life for people who 'at dawn cycle to work'. **What a contrast to the opulence of the Arnolfinis.** He uses another surreal image ('an Alsatian shepherd dog tied to your handlebars') to perhaps exaggerate the insecurity of our contemporary world.

In the last stanza, the couple 'pause now for the Angelus'. This Christian act of devotion commemorates the occasion when the angel Gabriel declared to Mary that she was to conceive the son of God: 'blessed is the fruit of thy womb, Jesus.' Here is the good news, the possibility of redemption. A final dreamlike image is presented when the two figures in the portrait are seen as 'The two halves of the coconut'. Is Durcan laughing at the Arnolfinis? Or does this naive metaphor refer to the Hindu custom of breaking a coconut at a wedding to ensure the blessing of the gods? In some other societies, the coconut is regarded as the tree that provides all the necessities of life. As always, the poem (like the Van Eyck painting) shows and conceals equally. Once again, **boundaries are blurred** as the reader is challenged to view the accepted norms relating to married life in a different way.

Writing About the Poem

'Durcan's poetry celebrates plurality of perspective.' Discuss this statement in relation to the poem 'The Arnolfini Marriage'. Refer closely to the text in your response.

Sample Paragraph

In 'The Arnolfini Marriage', Paul Durcan clearly demonstrates the important role the artist adopts in showing how necessary it is to hold more than one view on things, 'we have faith in the artist/To do justice to the plurality'. Durcan wants us to consider this portrait of the Arnolfinis as a symbol of marriage and all it entails. Is it a battlefield, 'We are standing to our portrait'? Is it a contented, cosy state, 'The most relaxing word in our vocabulary is "we"'? This poem reminds me of the cult of celebrity in our times. We see someone's image and we feel we know this person intimately. Durcan warns us of this, one-sided view, 'Do not think you may invade/Our privacy'. Although we see these people in the most intimate of settings, beside a bed, we do not know the real purpose of the painting. The poet recognises a number of meanings in the picture: a record of a civil marriage, a wish for a fertile marriage or a memorial to a dead wife. A surreal image concludes the poem, 'two halves of the coconut'. Is it a reference to a blessing of a wedding? As usual, the nonconformist Durcan has succeeded in showing us that there are many ways to view someone or something. He has challenged our fixed notions of the way things are. After all, who goes to work with 'an Alsatian shepherd dog tied' to a bicycle? The puzzles in the poem show the complexity of humanity.

EXAMINER'S COMMENT

Overall, a well-focused response that addresses a demanding question. There is effective use of quotation throughout and some good personal engagement with the poem. Apart from an over-reliance on questions, the paragraph offers several interesting discussion points about Durcan's perspective. The focus on addressing the task ('He has challenged our fixed notions of the way things are.') in the question merits the top grade.

Class/Homework Exercises

1. 'Durcan does verbally what painting does visually.' Discuss this view, using suitable reference to the poem 'The Arnolfini Marriage'.
2. Some of Durcan's poems are known for their strange, dreamlike quality. To what extent is this true of 'The Arnolfini Marriage'? Support your response with close reference to the text.

Summary Points

- **Dramatic monologue where Durcan assumes the personas of the rich married couple.**
- **Effective use of repetition, questions, suggestion.**
- **Characteristic fondness for distorted/surreal description.**
- **Contrasting tones – formal, reflective, challenging.**

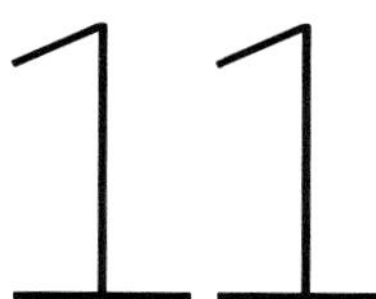

Rosie Joyce

I

That was that Sunday afternoon in May
When a hot sun pushed through the clouds
And you were born!

I was driving the two hundred miles from west to east,
The sky blue-and-white china in the fields
In impromptu picnics of tartan rugs;

When neither words nor I
Could have known that you had been named already
And that your name was Rosie –

Rosie Joyce! May you some day in May
Fifty-six years from today be as lucky
As I was when you were born that Sunday:

To drive such side-roads, such main roads, such ramps, such roundabouts,
To cross such bridges, to by-pass such villages, such towns
As I did on your Incarnation Day.

By-passing Swinford – Croagh Patrick in my rear-view mirror –
My mobile phone rang and, stopping on the hard edge of P. Flynn's highway,
I heard Mark your father say:

'A baby girl was born at 3.33 p.m.
Weighing 7 and a 1/2 lbs in Holles Street.
Tough work, all well.'

II

That Sunday in May before daybreak
Night had pushed up through the slopes of Achill
Yellow forefingers of Arum Lily – the first of the year;

Down at the Sound the first rhododendrons
Purpling the golden camps of whins;
The first hawthorns powdering white the mainland;

impromptu: spontaneous, spur-of-the-moment.

Incarnation Day: Rosie's day of birth, seen by Durcan as blessed.
Croagh Patrick: Co. Mayo mountain and place of religious pilgrimage.
P. Flynn's highway: satirical reference to an impressive new road in the constituency of a former government minister, Padraig Flynn.

Holles Street: Dublin maternity hospital.

Arum Lily: colourful flower.

the Sound: the small village of Achill Sound on Achill Island.
rhododendrons: vivid shrubs that flower in springtime.
whins: gorse; wild bushes with yellow flowers.
hawthorns: thorny hedgerow bushes that usually have white flowers.

The first yellow irises flagging roadside streams;
Quills of bog-cotton skimming the bogs;
Burrishoole cemetery shin-deep in forget-me-nots;

The first sea pinks speckling the seashore;
Cliffs of London Pride, groves of bluebell,
First fuchsia, Queen Anne's Lace, primrose.

I drove the Old Turlough Road, past Walter Durcan's Farm,
Umbrella'd in the joined handwriting of its ash trees;
I drove Tulsk, Kilmainham, the Grand Canal.

Never before had I felt so fortunate
To be driving back into Dublin city;
Each canal bridge an old pewter brooch.

I rode the waters and the roads of Ireland,
Rosie, to be with you, seashell at my ear!
How I laughed when I cradled you in my hand.

Only at Tarmonbarry did I slow down,
As in my father's Ford Anglia half a century ago
He slowed down also, as across the River Shannon

We crashed, rattled, bounced on a Bailey bridge;
Daddy relishing his role as Moses,
Enunciating the name of the Great Divide

Between the East and the West!
We are the people of the West,
Our fate to go East.

No such thing, Rosie, as a Uniform Ireland
And please God there never will be;
There is only the River Shannon and all her sister rivers

And all her brother mountains and their family prospects.
There are higher powers than politics
And these we call wildflowers or, geologically, people.

Rosie Joyce – that Sunday in May
Not alone did you make my day, my week, my year
To the prescription of Jonathan Philbin Bowman –

Quills of bog-cotton: stems of sedge plants with flower heads resembling tufts of cotton.

sea pinks: grass-like stalks with pink flowers.
London Pride: long-stemmed evergreen plant that flowers in pale pink clusters.
fuchsia: widely cultivated bush with brilliant deep purplish-reddish colours.
Queen Anne's Lace: tall plant with fern leaves and bright white flowers.

pewter: dark grey-coloured metal.

Ford Anglia: brand of family car.

Bailey bridge: small temporary bridge.
relishing: delighting in, appreciating.
Moses: Biblical figure and religious prophet chosen by God to lead the Jewish people out of slavery.

geologically: geographically, in natural history.

Jonathan Philbin Bowman: journalist and broadcaster.

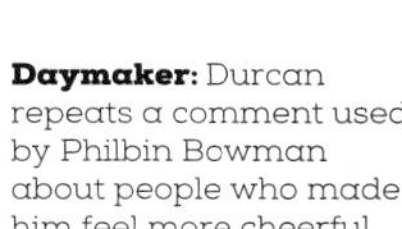

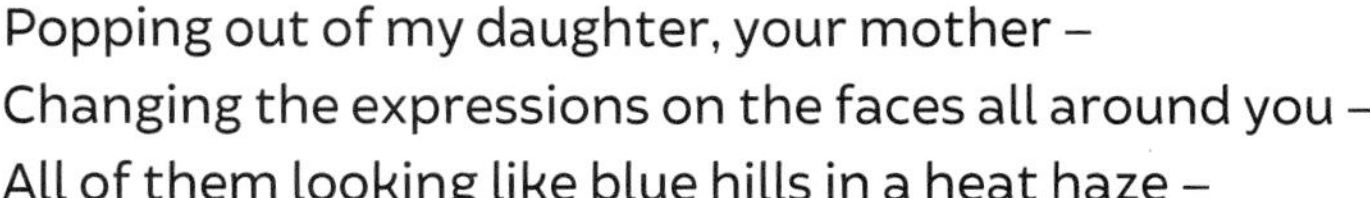

Daymaker!
Daymaker!
Daymaker!

Popping out of my daughter, your mother –
Changing the expressions on the faces all around you –
All of them looking like blue hills in a heat haze –

But you saved my life. For three years
I had been subsisting in the slums of despair,
Unable to distinguish one day from the next.

III

On the return journey from Dublin to Mayo
In Charlestown on Main Street
I meet John Normanly, organic farmer from Curry.

He is driving home to his wife Caroline
From a Mountbellew meeting of the Western Development Commission
Of Dillon House in Ballaghadereen.

He crouches in his car, I waver in the street,
As we exchange lullabies of expectancy;
We wet our foreheads in John Moriarty's autobiography.

The following Sunday is the Feast of the Ascension
Of Our Lord into Heaven:
Thank You, O Lord, for the Descent of Rosie onto Earth.

Daymaker: Durcan repeats a comment used by Philbin Bowman about people who made him feel more cheerful.

subsisting: struggling to live.

wet our foreheads: colloquial expression for having a celebratory drink (based on baptising a newborn child).
John Moriarty: Irish philosopher and mystic.
Feast of the Ascension: important Christian day commemorating the bodily ascension of Jesus into heaven.

'There is only the River Shannon'

Personal Response

1. Based on your reading of Section I of the poem, describe Paul Durcan's mood as he drives to Dublin. Support your answer with reference to the text.
2. What does Durcan reveal about his attitude to Ireland in Section II? In your response, use suitable reference to the poem.
3. Vivid imagery is a recurring feature of this poem. Select one image that you consider particularly striking and comment briefly on your choice.

Critical Literacy

'Rosie Joyce' (taken from Paul Durcan's 2004 collection, *The Art of Life*) celebrates the birth of the poet's granddaughter. Her arrival into the world represents a wonderful new beginning in the poet's life. He has frequently used the motif of travel to signify self-renewal, opportunities to reflect on change and emotional development. In this case, Durcan recalls a car journey he took in May 2001 from County Mayo to Dublin. Along the way, images of landscape and movement reveal his newfound sense of optimism.

The casual, narrative opening of Section I is typical of so many of Durcan's autobiographical poems. There is a nostalgic quality to the description of that golden Sunday afternoon: 'a hot sun pushed through the clouds' (line 2). Rosie's birth is immediately symbolised through images drawn from the world of nature. **The idyllic setting reflects Durcan's euphoric tone** perfectly. Breathless exclamatory phrasing ('And you were born!') and the repetition of the child's name convey the poet's immense joy. Run-on lines underpin the insistent rhythm. It is Rosie's 'Incarnation Day' (line 15), a special occasion on which the poet feels truly blessed.

Driving 'two hundred miles from west to east', Durcan is intensely aware of the newness of nature that is reflected all around him. Seeing the world through a child's eyes, he takes great delight in listing everything he notices: 'such side-roads, such main roads, such ramps, such roundabouts.' His deeply satisfying sense of freedom to travel through the country at large is palpable. By persistently naming local places ('By-passing Swinford – Croagh Patrick in my rear-view mirror'), **Durcan acknowledges their equally distinctive importance**. He recounts the crucial details of the telephone message alerting him of Rosie's birth. The simple facts recording the baby's weight and time of birth – 'A baby girl was born at 3.33 p.m.' (line 19) – contrast sharply with Durcan's highly emotional response.

Section II focuses on the Irish landscape in summertime. Durcan highlights the colourful diversity and energy of an island in bloom: 'Yellow forefingers of Arum Lily – the first of the year' (line 24). **The sense of regeneration is everywhere**: 'the first rhododendrons', 'first hawthorns', ' first yellow irises'. Repetition suggests the widespread growth and the careful choice of

forceful verbs ('powdering', 'skimming', 'speckling') adds to our understanding of the vivid power of nature at its height. Everywhere he looks, Durcan sees the shrubs and flowers celebrating Rosie's birth – even the graveyard at Burrishoole is 'shin-deep in forget-me-nots' (line 30). The poet mentions more of the place-names on his cross-country route: 'the Old Turlough Road, past Walter Durcan's Farm.' The intimacies of setting and the poet's enthusiastic voice carry into reflections of his excitement: 'Never before had I felt so fortunate' (line 37). Indeed, his great desire to be with Rosie seems almost biblical: 'I rode the waters and the roads of Ireland.'

The poet's careful observation of rural villages reminds him of a journey he once took 'half a century ago'. During that earlier drive, he remembers his father 'relishing his role as Moses' as he named the River Shannon as 'the Great Divide/Between the East and the West' (lines 48–49). Durcan takes the opportunity of his granddaughter's birth to present his own view: 'No such thing, Rosie, as a Uniform Ireland.' The poet develops his plea for tolerance and acceptance by emphasising the diversity of the country's geography: 'There is only the River Shannon and all her sister rivers/And all her brother mountains.' With simple clarity ('There are higher powers than politics'), **the poet dismisses the boundaries of class, religion and gender that have often divided Irish people**. After emphatically expressing devotion to his '*Daymaker*' granddaughter, Durcan names Rosie as his personal saviour in a tone that is manifestly reverential: 'you saved my life. For three years/I had been subsisting in the slums of despair' (lines 67–68).

In Section III, the mood is much more subdued as the poet recounts details of his 'return journey from Dublin to Mayo'. The daily social routines that mark small communities are illustrated by the chance meeting in Charlestown between Durcan and an old friend, an 'organic farmer from Curry'. Somewhat typically of Irish people's behaviour, their encounter is not without its awkward nuances: 'He crouches in his car, I waver in the street' (line 76). Before long, however, the two men share a drink in honour of the new baby. They discuss the life of Co. Kerry poet and philosopher, John Moriarty. This seemingly mundane moment represents what is best about Ireland's cultural and communal identity. **Rosie Joyce has now been accepted into her new natural and spiritual environment.** The cycle of life and death continues. In the poem's final lines, Durcan returns to his earlier religious mood with a formal offering of thanksgiving for his granddaughter's life. The motif becomes deliberately whimsical and prayer-like, building to a high point: 'Thank you, O Lord, for the Descent of Rosie onto Earth.'

Writing About the Poem

'Paul Durcan frequently uses journeys as a metaphor for reflection or soul-searching.' Discuss this statement with particular reference to 'Rosie Joyce'.

Sample Paragraph

Durcan's love of travel is evident in 'Rosie Joyce'. Journeys are often metaphors for new insights into life. His car journey from Mayo to visit his infant granddaughter in Dublin gives him the perfect opportunity. He begins to think deeply about what it means to be Irish. Everything on the route fills him with joy – and his upbeat tone is emphatic as he drives past 'such villages, such towns'. He is particularly excited by the colourful vegetation – 'Purpling the golden camps of whins'. The variety and energy of nature thrills him. But the journey also reminds him of his youth when his father would tell him how the River Shannon was the 'Great Divide/Between the East and the West'. However, Durcan no longer agrees and his message to his granddaughter is a resounding one: 'No such thing, Rosie, as a Uniform Ireland.' The trip has given the poet a chance to clarify his views on the diverse Ireland that Rosie will know. I thought Durcan's description of the island as a place of great scenic variety was central to the poem – 'There is only the River Shannon and all her sister rivers'. He is welcoming the child into a pluralist Ireland – where he accepts cultural diversity. He sees people as being equal, above politics and other such labels. For Durcan, the physical and spiritual journey – one of great happiness and discovery – is a glimpse of how the first Christians felt when they celebrated the birth of Jesus.

EXAMINER'S COMMENT

This clearly written response focuses effectively on the significance of the poet's journey – both on a personal and cultural level. Useful quotations support key discussion points and the expression is generally well handled (although dashes are overused). There is also some good engagement with the poem, especially when discussing Durcan's varied tones, e.g. 'his upbeat tone is emphatic'. A top-grade response.

Class/Homework Exercises

1. 'Durcan's poems can be challenging at times, but they provide a singularly refreshing view of Ireland.' Discuss this view with particular reference to 'Rosie Joyce'. Support the points you make with reference to the poem.
2. Paul Durcan's poems have been described as diary entries which reveal the poet's private life. Discuss this view with particular reference to the poem, 'Rosie Joyce'.

Summary Points

- **Characteristically introspective exploration of regeneration.**
- **Effective use of the extended travel metaphor.**
- **Detailed description, recurring images of movement, landscape, birth.**
- **Contrasting moods and tones of delight, reflection and resignation.**

12 The MacBride Dynasty

What young mother is not a vengeful goddess
Spitting dynastic as well as motherly pride?
In 1949 in the black Ford Anglia,
Now that I had become a walking, talking little boy,
Mummy drove me out to visit my grand-aunt Maud Gonne
In Roebuck House in the countryside near Dublin,
To show off to the servant of the Queen
The latest addition to the extended family.
Although the eighty-year-old Cathleen Ni Houlihan had taken to her bed
She was keen as ever to receive admirers,
Especially the children of the family.
Only the previous week the actor MacLiammóir
Had been kneeling at her bedside reciting Yeats to her,
His hand on his heart, clutching a red rose.
Cousin Séan and his wife Kid led the way up the stairs,
Séan opening the door and announcing my mother.
Mummy lifted me up in her arms as she approached the bed
And Maud leaned forward, sticking out her claws
To embrace me, her lizards of eyes darting about
In the rubble of the ruins of her beautiful face.
Terrified, I recoiled from her embrace
And, fleeing her bedroom, ran down the stairs
Out onto the wrought-iron balcony
Until Séan caught up with me and quieted me
And took me for a walk in the walled orchard.
Mummy was a little but not totally mortified:
She had never liked Maud Gonne because of Maud's
Betrayal of her husband, Mummy's Uncle John,
Major John, most ordinary of men, most
Humorous, courageous of soldiers,
The pride of our family,
Whose memory always brought laughter
To my grandmother Eileen's lips. 'John,'
She used cry, 'John was such a gay man.'
Mummy set great store by loyalty; loyalty
In Mummy's eyes was the cardinal virtue.
Maud Gonne was a disloyal wife
And, therefore, not worthy of Mummy's love.
For dynastic reasons we would tolerate Maud,
But we would always see through her.

vengeful: vindictive.
goddess: deity, powerful creature.
Spitting: hissing.
dynastic: old established family superiority.

Maud Gonne: English-born Irish revolutionary who had a stormy relationship with W. B. Yeats. She married Major John MacBride, with whom she had one son.

Cathleen Ni Houlihan: Cathleen is an old woman of Ireland who mourns the loss of her four provinces, which have been taken by the English. Maud Gonne played her in Yeats's famous play.
MacLiammóir: Micheál MacLiammóir, a flamboyant English-born Irish actor.
Yeats: famous Irish poet who celebrated Maud Gonne in his poetry throughout his life.
Cousin Séan: Séan MacBride was Maud and Major John's only son. He went on to win a Nobel Peace Prize.
lizards: reptiles with rough, prickly skin.
recoiled: jumped back, flinched.

wrought-iron: tough form of iron fashioned into swirling shapes.
mortified: embarrassed, uncomfortable.

Uncle John: Major John MacBride was the uncle of Paul Durcan's mother. He was executed by the British for his part in the 1916 Rising.

cardinal: greatest, essential.
disloyal: treacherous, unfaithful.

tolerate: endure, accept.
see through: see the reality, realise the truth about.

'the ruins of her beautiful face'

Personal Response

1. From your reading of the poem, briefly describe Durcan's attitude to Maud Gonne when he was taken to meet her.
2. Surreal imagery is a feature of Paul Durcan's poetry. Choose one surreal image from the poem that made an impact on you and discuss its effectiveness.
3. Comment on Durcan's use of repetition in this poem. Support your answer with reference to the text.

Critical Literacy

'The MacBride Dynasty' was published in Paul Durcan's 2007 collection, *The Laughter of Mothers*. These poignant poems commemorate his mother, Sheila MacBride Durcan. They contrast sharply with the many withering poems about his father, Judge John Durcan. The poet's mother was the niece of one of the renowned martyrs of 1916, Major John MacBride, the husband of Maud Gonne. This poem relates the time Durcan's mother made a personal journey back to her hometown to introduce her young son ('the latest addition' to the family dynasty), to her uncle's famous wife.

The opening lines dramatically pose an intriguing question with mock solemnity: 'What young mother is not a vengeful goddess/Spitting dynastic as well as motherly pride?' The epic reference suggests the angry response to a slur on the family name. **The MacBrides regarded themselves as a family of significance** in the Mayo region, as can be seen from the poem's title. They were a dynasty, a prominent and powerful family who retained their power and influence through several generations. If an injustice is perceived to have been done to one of the family, the other members close ranks against the outsider. The onomatopoeic verb 'Spitting' graphically depicts the mythical outrage of the young mother. Precise details root the visit to 'grand-aunt Maud' firmly in reality: 'In 1949 in the black Ford Anglia.' At that time, most people in Ireland could not afford to own a car. Broad-vowelled assonance ('walking, talking') mimics the babbling of the five-year-old Durcan as the proud mother drives to Roebuck House to show off her young son to Maud. A sly reference is made to Gonne's autobiography, *A Servant of the Queen*, which refers to a vision she had of the Irish queen of old, Cathleen Ni Houlihan. The reference is also ironic since Gonne was an Irish nationalist who rejected the British queen.

The lengthy run-on line 9 describes how the 80-year-old Maud had 'taken to her bed'. Is there a suggestion that she is a self-indulgent woman? She is referred to as the mythical character she played in Yeats's drama. In this personal narrative, **Durcan seems to be slowly dismantling the popular image of Maud Gonne** as a beautiful young woman, the feminist Irish activist loved by Yeats. Her vanity is obvious: 'She was keen as ever to receive admirers.' The rarefied, overly dramatic world she existed in is cleverly demonstrated by the intimate anecdote showing the famous Irish actor MacLiammóir on his knees at her bedside, 'clutching a red rose' while reciting the poetry of Yeats to her. Is the tone slightly disapproving? The formal, almost regal atmosphere of the house is captured in the description of how 'Cousin Séan and his wife Kid led the way up the stairs' as the door was opened and the arrival of Durcan's mother was announced. But the young Durcan is no MacLiammóir. He does not pay court, but runs away, terrified at this monster 'sticking out her claws' and whose 'lizards of eyes' flitted quickly about. With this bizarre image, the leading lady of

nationalistic politics is reduced to a crumbling wreck as the devastation of her beauty by the cruel hand of time is laid bare: 'In the rubble of the ruins of her beautiful face' (line 20). The alliteration stresses the poignancy of this devastating portrait.

Maud Gonne's relationship with the MacBrides was intricate. She had turned down Yeats's offers of marriage and had married Major John in Paris in 1903. When the marriage ended, she made allegations of domestic violence. She raised her son in Paris until MacBride's execution and then returned to Ireland. The run-on lines (lines 21–25) convey the alarm of a little boy terrified out of his wits until his cousin calms him down with a 'walk in the walled orchard'. The long vowel 'a' and the gentle 'w' alliteration produce a soothing effect. Line 26 carefully records his mother's subtle reaction to his behaviour: 'a little but not totally mortified.' **Was she secretly glad that her little son had not behaved well to a woman she did not respect?** The poet candidly reveals the source of his mother's distaste for Gonne: her 'Betrayal of her husband'. In contrast, a much more favourable picture is painted of Major John, not only through the poet's voice, but also his mother's. He is the 'pride of our family'. His light-heartedness is also noted: he 'always brought laughter/To my grandmother Eileen's lips'.

Durcan's ability to capture Irish speech is shown in line 35: 'Mummy set great store by loyalty.' The admirable characteristic is repeated: 'loyalty/In Mummy's eyes was the cardinal virtue.' But Maud had committed the cardinal sin of being 'a disloyal wife', for which there is no forgiveness. The repetition of the word 'Mummy' – delivered in a highly sarcastic tone – shows how the poet is influenced by his mother's judgement that Maud was 'not worthy of Mummy's love'. **Is Durcan also critical of his intolerant mother**, who adopts a superior attitude to the infamous Maud? Once again, the underlying MacBride tensions are exposed. The family ('we') would accept her grudgingly, but only 'For dynastic reasons'. The chilling qualification is in the final line: 'But we would always see through her.' History might well be fooled by Maud's mythical status, but the family knew what she truly was. Has Durcan succeeded in debunking another official state myth? No person or thing is immune to criticism or satirical comment. As a challenging poetic voice, he has always 'seen through' falseness. He believes language in Ireland has been abused 'by poets as much as by gunmen and churchmen'. Is he also criticising Yeats?

Writing About the Poem

'Durcan's confessional poetry often blends private and public aspects of family life.' Discuss this statement with reference to 'The MacBride Dynasty'.

Sample Paragraph

From the title of the poem to the slyly humorous last line, Durcan captures what others miss. He does not shy away from questioning popular, widely accepted beliefs. In this poem, he exposes not only the power struggles within a self-important family, the 'MacBride Dynasty', but also he reveals the real Maud Gonne as she is in the ill-health and arrogance of her later years, 'She was keen as ever to receive admirers'. The poet publicly deals with private matters and personally comments on some famous Irish public figures. The one-sided stance adopted by the MacBride family is clear for all to see in the flattering portrait of 'Uncle John'. His mother's critical attitude to the 'disloyal' Maud is revealed. She would 'tolerate' this woman, but only for 'dynastic reasons'. The poet reveals the elderly Maud Gonne to the public gaze, 'In the rubble of the ruins of her beautiful face'. Her power to influence has disappeared. In a way, she is a pathetic figure. She is now seen as a reptile with 'claws' and 'lizards of eyes darting about'. The absurdity between reality and image is being exposed through this fantasy. She is no longer the woman Yeats worshipped. A great myth has been exposed to the public. Now, not only Durcan but we too can 'see through' and are not fooled by the deceptive appearance of 'a red rose'.

EXAMINER'S COMMENT

This is a very good attempt at addressing a challenging question. There is close engagement with the poem: 'The absurdity between reality and image is being exposed through this fantasy', and a clear thematic response. Overall, points are effectively supported by useful reference and quotation. Ideas are expressed fluently throughout: 'The poet deals publicly with private matters.' A very high standard which deserves the top grade.

Class/Homework Exercises

1. 'Poetry is a form of entertainment, but it is not cheap.' Discuss this statement made by Durcan in relation to the poem 'The MacBride Dynasty'. Support your views with suitable reference to the text.
2. Durcan's poetic voice often goes beyond critical comment and can even become cruel on occasion. Discuss this view, supporting your answer with particular reference to 'The MacBride Dynasty'.

Summary Points

- **Autobiographical/anecdotal poem commemorating the poet's family.**
- **Dramatic opening, bizarre scenes, dark humour.**
- **Effective use of authentic speech patterns.**
- **Use of photographic imagery, run-on lines, assonance, repetition.**
- **Contrasting tones – critical, sardonic, reflective, sarcastic.**

13 Three Short Poems

Paul Durcan's enigmatic two-line poems are sharp and epigrammatic. They are also characteristic of his richly textured work in accommodating his contradictory responses to Ireland and to personal relationships.

En Famille, 1979

Bring me back to the dark school – to the dark school of childhood:
To where tiny is tiny, and massive is massive.

'En Famille, 1979' almost appears to be a cry for help, as though the poet has never come to terms with the traumatic effects of his earliest experiences. The 'dark school' presents **a disturbing metaphor of his boyhood** and the force of his most intimate hopes and fears. Repetition and the exaggerated extremes of 'tiny' and 'massive' suggest childhood innocence. Durcan's use of the French title phrase (meaning 'with one's family' or 'at home') is heartbreakingly poignant.

Madman

Every child has a madman on their street:
The only trouble about *our* madman is that he's our father.

'Madman' offers further evidence that Paul Durcan's **poetry can encompass nightmares as well as dreams**. Despite this poem's humorous whimsy and surface levity, there is something harrowing about the admission. Terms such as 'madman' are often used casually. Within the immediate family context, however, the word takes on a much greater personal significance.

Ireland 2002

Do you ever take a holiday abroad?
No, we always go to America.

'Ireland 2002' is typical of those small 'nutshell poems' that aim to encapsulate a given period of recent history or define Irish contemporary life. The piece is usually read as a **trenchantly satirical criticism of the country's moneyed classes**, for whom America isn't considered 'abroad'. It could also refer to Ireland's history of emigration to the United States and that our diaspora no longer seems foreign. The poem is a reminder of how Ireland has become so culturally influenced by US fashions and attitudes over recent times. Durcan's glib tone echoes the self-absorbed nature of complacent Celtic Tiger Ireland at its height.

Leaving Cert Sample Essay

'Paul Durcan's poetry dares to explore the hidden areas of life in a confidential yet authoritative manner.' Discuss this view, supporting your response with suitable reference to the poems by Durcan on your course.

MARKING SCHEME GUIDELINES

Candidates are free to agree and/ or disagree with the statement. The key terms ('dares to explore the hidden areas of life' and 'confidential yet authoritative manner') should be addressed either explicitly or implicitly. Evidence of genuine engagement with the poems should be rewarded. Allow for a wide range of approaches in the answering.

Sample Essay
(Durcan's poetry dares to explore the hidden areas of life)

1. Paul Durcan probes dark, bitter themes of contemporary Irish life, emigration and strained relationships. His meditations and monologues challenge the accepted views on Irish life as he keenly observes and elusively slides into surreal images to examine this odd world of ours. Like one of his favourite poets, Kavanagh, he sees the extraordinary in the ordinary and he enables readers to view life, as his character Cáit does, 'Looking toward our strange world wide-eyed'.

2. The poet addresses the sombre reality of emigration in 'The Girl with the Keys to Pearse's Cottage'. The young Irish girl's future was 'America-bound at summer's end'. This was no fun-filled adventure, no world-exploring gap year. 'She had no choice but to leave her home.' She was so much part of her landscape with her 'sun-red skirt and moon-black blazer', yet she is torn from her native environment. Her intriguing character is caught in the surprising alliterative image, 'El Greco eyes blaze back'. The piercing eyes, so similar to the exotic Spanish painter's portraits, illuminate the darkness felt by the poet at his personal loss. Durcan bitterly laments his loss with the repetitive phrase, 'O Cáit Killann, O Cáit Killann'. I was convinced by his obvious frustration in his account of the hidden tragedy of emigration which pulls people from their homes and shatters families.

3. Durcan is not afraid to expose intimate family relationships in all their complexities. 'Sport' explores the troubled relationship he had with his father. The devastation he experienced as a young man desperately attempting to impress his father is evident in the bleak phrases 'I was fearful I would let you down', 'Seldom if ever again in your eyes/Was I to rise to these heights'. Durcan had just played a game of football on the side of Grangegorman Mental Hospital to which he had been committed. The poet's efforts in this game are described in the typically heightened language of sports writing, 'I did not flinch', 'spectacular saves', 'Diving at full stretch'. However, he was met by his father 'Sniffing' his 'approval' as he coldly 'shook hands' with his son. I felt the aching longing of the poet to be regarded and praised, 'I may not have been mesmeric/But I had not

been mediocre'. Durcan made me realise the hurt that is caused by the lack of close communication between family members.

4. Marriage is successfully scrutinised in several of Durcan's poems, including 'The Arnolfini Marriage', after the famous Dutch painting of a self-assured couple. He uses the language of military combat, 'We are standing to our portrait' to suggest that marriage can be a battle of wills. The vulnerability of this intimate relationship is conveyed by the detail of the couple's bare feet, 'barefootedness'. Durcan shows the complacent contentment of the married couple basking in the embrace of their togetherness, 'the most relaxing word in our vocabulary is "we"'. A series of sharp staccato questions blast out as the poet questions 'Who eat alone? Sleep alone?' – contrasting the individual life of the reader with the cosy intimacy of the two Arnolfinis. In presenting different views on married life, the poet challenged me to look again at the accepted norms of marriage.

5. Characteristically, Durcan spares neither himself nor the reader when he exposes the shocking consequences of a marriage break-up. 'Nessa' examines his personal relationship with his wife through the extended metaphor of a whirlpool, which is at once exciting and dangerous. Nessa is described as if she were an enchantress in an old Irish aisling leading the hopelessly devoted lover away, 'She took me by the index finger'. Her intoxicating attraction is echoed in the poet's hypnotic phrase, 'She was a whirlpool, she was a whirlpool'. The poem's central metaphor is a powerful literary device for reflecting on the contradictions of married life. Once again, Durcan is showing us contrasting views of romantic love. There is the thrill and exhilaration of Nessa seducing him, 'for me let your red hair down'. But there is also the destruction of the individual self, 'And I very nearly drowned'. The poem ends with a series of poignant questions reflecting Durcan's deep sense of loss – 'Will you stay with me on the rocks', 'Will you come for me into the Irish Sea'. This honest expression of emotion and admission of personal vulnerability act as a reminder that serious relationships can be overwhelming.

INDICATIVE MATERIAL

- Provocative treatment of key themes, such as history, love, family.
- Convincing treatment of compelling personal disclosures.
- Addresses revealing aspects of intimate relationships and identity.
- Confident plurality of perspectives challenge views of readers.
- Repetition as a powerful process for epiphany and self-discovery.
- Sense of place and community adds authenticity.
- Effective use of surreal imagery, symbolism, colloquial language, etc.

EXAMINER'S COMMENT

A solid top-grade answer showing some clear personal interaction with Durcan's poetry. Well written and focused on addressing the question. Most main points are dealt with effectively and there is good use of apt quotation. Some of the poems discussed, such as 'Sport', would have benefitted from a more thorough treatment of the striking techniques (e.g. varying tones and irony) that are used to expose the poet's preoccupations.

GRADE: H1
P = 14/15
C = 13/15
L = 13/15
M = 5/5
Total = 45/50

6. Paul Durcan, with audacious authority, has stirred up accepted views by peering under the stones of society's accepted norms on such universal themes as emigration and relationships. He has allowed me to see the familiar world in a new light which enabled me to question and challenge. His 'bittersweet clowning' has produced intimate poems which truly reveal the essential oddness at the heart of the everyday secret areas of life.

(approx. 815 words)
(45–50 minutes)

Sample Leaving Cert Questions on Durcan's Poetry

1. 'Paul Durcan's poetry reflects a broad range of powerful feelings communicated through thought-provoking imagery.' Do you agree with this assessment of his poetry? Your answer should focus on the poet's themes and the way he expresses them. Support the points you make with suitable reference to the poems by Durcan on your course.

2. 'Durcan's vision of life is conveyed in poems that are both satirical and self-critical.' Discuss this statement, supporting your answer with suitable reference to the poetry of Durcan on your course.

3. 'Durcan explores the complexity of human experience in a candid and appealing manner.' Discuss this statement, supporting your answer with reference to the poetry of Paul Durcan on your course.

First Sample Essay Plan (Q1)

'Paul Durcan's poetry reflects a broad range of powerful feelings communicated through thought-provoking imagery.' Do you agree with this assessment of his poetry? Your answer should focus on the poet's themes and the way he expresses them. Support the points you make with suitable reference to the poems by Durcan on your course.

Intro: Identify the elements of the question to be addressed ('broad range of powerful feelings', 'thought-provoking imagery'). Introduce Durcan as a searingly honest poet who lays himself bare in the exploration of strong emotions arising from personal experiences. Communicates different aspects of the situations through precise and surreal imagery delivered in a variety of tones.

NOTE

If you are not familiar with some poems referred to in the sample plans below, substitute poems that you have studied closely when writing practice responses.

Exam candidates usually discuss three or four poems in their answers. However, there is no set number of poems or formulaic approach expected.

Key points about a particular poem can be developed over more than one paragraph.

Paragraphs may also include cross-referencing and comparative discussions of poems.

Remember that there is no single 'correct' answer to Leaving Cert poetry questions, so always be confident in expressing your own considered response.

Point 1: Despair and frustration at the common Irish experience of emigration, 'The Girl with the Keys to Pearse's Cottage'. Arresting image 'El Greco eyes blaze back' captures the essence of the girl and highlights the poet's deep yearning.

Point 2: : Fear of change is emphasised in '"Windfall", 8 Parnell Hill, Cork'. Different aspects of home are examined in similes such as 'a city as intimate and homicidal as a Little Marseilles'.

Point 3: The challenge of being oneself when in a troubled relationship is shown in his deep disappointment at the cold response of his father in 'Sport'. An image of precise detail conveys the moment 'Sniffing your approval'.

Point 4: : Durcan is joyful as he is deeply moved by the lasting power of love in 'Nessa'. The image of a whirlpool expresses the excitement and danger of a close romantic relationship.

Point 5: Bizarre imagery and a variety of tones allow Durcan to explore icons and myths in 'The MacBride Dynasty'.

Conclusion: The sensitive poet, Durcan, illuminates our complex world, challenging us to view and reconsider its multifaceted aspects.

Sample Essay Plan (Q1)

Develop **one** of the above points into a paragraph.

Sample Paragraph: Point 5

The disapproving feeling of Paul Durcan's mother towards her relative, Maud Gonne, and her pride in her own family is provocatively conveyed in the poem 'The MacBride Dynasty'. Maud Gonne was a revered figure in early 20th-century Irish history, beloved of the poet W. B. Yeats and wife of Major John MacBride, a patriot of the 1916 Rising. She was greatly admired and the 'actor MacLiammóir/Had been kneeling at her bedside reciting Yeats to her'. Through two intimate perspectives, Durcan's mother's and his five-year-old self, a different picture of this symbolic woman emerges. The young Durcan's terror of this iconic woman is revealed through surreal imagery. He cruelly paints a devastating portrait of the once-beautiful Maud, 'sticking out her claws/To embrace me, her lizards of eyes darting about'. Through this monstrous

EXAMINER'S COMMENT

As part of a full essay, this solid response is very well-rooted in the text. Quotes are integrated effectively and expression is both varied and assured throughout: 'Durcan's terror of this iconic woman is revealed through surreal imagery', 'the cutting tone of this line slashes through the veneer of Maud's greatness'. Lively expression and a clear focus on the task guarantee a top grade.

imagery, Durcan challenges the accepted view of this famous woman. A similarly negative portrait of Maud is shown through the dismissive comment delivered at the conclusion of the poem, 'But we would always see through her'. She had been viewed and judged by the family as unworthy because of her behaviour towards her husband, the relative of Durcan's mother who 'set great store by loyalty' and Maud had not matched up. The cutting tone of this line slashes through the veneer of Maud's greatness.

Second Sample Essay Plan (Q3)

'Durcan explores the complexity of human experience in a candid and appealing manner.' Discuss this statement, supporting your answer with reference to the poetry of Paul Durcan on your course.

Intro: Durcan – through conversational, colloquial language and striking imagery, an intimate portrayal of a complex man emerges. Allows intimate and honest access to aspects of his personal experiences.

Point 1: 'The Difficulty that is Marriage' – honest exploration of the complexities and contradictions of married life. Poet's mixed feelings echoed in onomatopoeia – harsh opening line contrasts with gentle conclusion. Appeal of varying tones – reflective, self-critical, humorous, romantic. Idealistic conclusion is engaging.

Point 2: 'Wife Who Smashed TV Gets Jail' – entertaining, satirical poem examines tensions and difficulties (love, control) within modern Irish family. Use of direct dialogue, colloquial language, familiar cultural references ('Me and the kids were peaceably watching *Kojak*'), symbols from everyday life ('playing bar-billiards'), bizarre humour add to poem's appeal.

Point 3: 'Parents' – disturbing autobiographical poem offers rich insights into parent–child communication. Surreal underwater sequence ('Pursed-up orifices of fearful fish') underline the separate lives experienced within the family unit. Tone of tragic resignation emphasised through repetition ('they stare/At the drowned, drowned face of their child').

Point 4: 'Rosie Joyce' – metaphor of journey communicates joyous observation of personal life experience – welcoming new family member. Run-on lines in keeping with euphoric tone. Widens into reflection, glorifying a diverse Ireland, beautiful as 'wildflowers'.

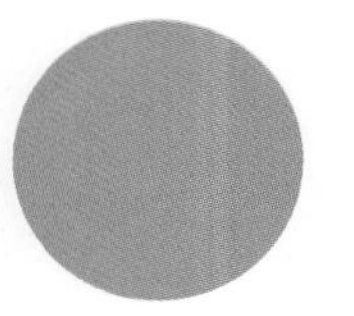

Conclusion: Durcan stirs up accepted views, peers beneath society's norms regarding universal theme of family – difficulty in sustaining relationships, awareness of difference between individual, joy of grandchildren and pluralism. 'I'm trying to record, in verse, a moment – like a photograph – things that happened.'

Sample Essay Plan (Q3)

Develop **one** of the points on the previous page into a practice paragraph of your own.

Sample Paragraph: Point 1

An honest expression of personal vulnerability is characteristic of Durcan. His tone in his poem, 'The Difficulty that is Marriage', is one of intense romanticism despite the abrupt staccato sections in the opening line, 'We agree to disagree, we divide, we differ'. The deadening alliterative letter 'd' pinpoints the destructive conflict in a marriage as two separate individuals attempt to live as a harmonious unit. Although physically present in the one space, 'in bed beside you', the couple are worlds apart, mentally and emotionally. The content wife is 'faraway curled up in sleep' while the poet tosses and turns, questioning. A beautiful, surreal image depicts his anxiety, 'I array the moonlit ceiling with a mosaic of question marks'. Although he worships his wife, placing her 'on a pedestal or throne', he keeps himself at the centre of the poem, 'I have my troubles, and I shall always have them'. The repetition of the first person pronoun shows his self-obsession, despite the surface of charming self-deprecation.

EXAMINER'S COMMENT

As part of a full essay answer to Q3, this is an impressive top-rate response that shows close engagement with both the poem and the question. Insightful, higher-order comments are supported aptly by accurate quotation and reference. Expression throughout is controlled and the paragraph is rounded off excellently.

Class/Homework Exercise

1. **Write one or two paragraphs in response to the question: 'Durcan explores the complexity of human experience in a candid and appealing manner.' Discuss this statement, supporting your answer with reference to a poem of Paul Durcan's that you have studied closely.**

 Revision Overview

'Nessa'
Dramatic anecdotal presentation of theme of romantic adventure, giddy experience of falling in love.

'The Girl with the Keys to Pearse's Cottage'
Narrative exploration of themes of teenage infatuation, loss, identity.

'The Difficulty that is Marriage'
Critical dramatic monologue probes themes of marital fragility and conflict.

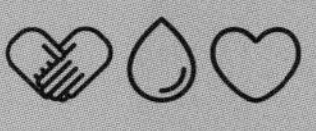

'Wife Who Smashed Television Gets Jail'
Humorous mock journalistic report on theme of modern family life.

'Parents'
Unsettling dramatic study of themes of death and the afterlife, surreal moments, use of contrast and symbols add to feeling of helplessness.

'"Windfall", 8 Parnell Hill, Cork'
Intimate chronicle of themes of personal domestic bliss and bitter consequences of the break-up of a relationship.

'Six Nuns Die in Convent Inferno'
Reflective analysis of nuns' religious philosophy through first-person narrative of elderly nun.

'Sport'
Candid investigation of troubled relationship between father and son.

'Father's Day, 21 June 1992'
Train journey becomes occasion for reflection on adverse effect of time on poet's role as husband and father.

'The Arnolfini Marriage'
Challenging dramatic monologue scrutinising marriage and good fortune.

'Rosie Joyce'
Newfound enthusiastic celebration of birth of poet's granddaughter.

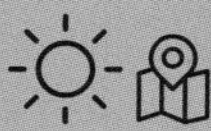

'The MacBride Dynasty'
Anecdotal family journey. Thematic questioning of accepted beliefs of the self-important. Exposure of distance between reality and fantasy.

Last Words

'His songs celebrate our small mercies and tender decencies in a world that favours the corrupt.'
Paula Meehan

'He makes particularly engaging poems out of passing conversations – "You're looking great – are you going to a wedding?"/"Oh God no – I'm coming back from a wake"'.
Deirdre Collins

'Like all first-class comedians, he is deadly serious.'
Terry Eagleton

LOVE

RELATIONSHIPS

SUFFERING

HISTORY/ MEMORY

TRAVEL/ JOURNEYS

RELIGION/ SPIRITUALITY

TIME

JOY/HOPE

Robert Frost
1874–1963

'A poem begins in delight and ends in wisdom.'

One of the great 20th-century poets, Robert Frost is highly regarded for his realistic depictions of rural life and his command of American colloquial speech. His work frequently explores themes from early 1900s country life in New England, often using the setting to examine complex social and philosophical ideas. Nature is central to his writing. While his poems seem simple at first, they often transcend the boundaries of time and place with metaphysical significance and a deeper appreciation of human nature in all its beauty and contradictions. Despite many personal tragedies, Frost had a very successful public life. It is ironic that such a calm, stoical voice emerged from his difficult background. At times bittersweet, sometimes ironic, or often marvelling at his surroundings, Robert Frost continues to be a popular and often-quoted poet. He was honoured frequently during his lifetime, receiving four Pulitzer Prizes.

Investigate Further

To find out more about Robert Frost, or to hear readings of his poems, you could do a search of some of the useful websites available such as YouTube, BBC Poetry, poetryfoundation.org and poetryarchive.org, or access additional material on this page of your eBook.

 Revision Overview

'Nessa'
Dramatic anecdotal presentation of theme of romantic adventure, giddy experience of falling in love.

'The Girl with the Keys to Pearse's Cottage'
Narrative exploration of themes of teenage infatuation, loss, identity.

'The Difficulty that is Marriage'
Critical dramatic monologue probes themes of marital fragility and conflict.

'Wife Who Smashed Television Gets Jail'
Humorous mock journalistic report on theme of modern family life.

'Parents'
Unsettling dramatic study of themes of death and the afterlife, surreal moments, use of contrast and symbols add to feeling of helplessness.

'"Windfall", 8 Parnell Hill, Cork'
Intimate chronicle of themes of personal domestic bliss and bitter consequences of the break-up of a relationship.

'Six Nuns Die in Convent Inferno'
Reflective analysis of nuns' religious philosophy through first-person narrative of elderly nun.

'Sport'
Candid investigation of troubled relationship between father and son.

'Father's Day, 21 June 1992'
Train journey becomes occasion for reflection on adverse effect of time on poet's role as husband and father.

'The Arnolfini Marriage'
Challenging dramatic monologue scrutinising marriage and good fortune.

'Rosie Joyce'
Newfound enthusiastic celebration of birth of poet's granddaughter.

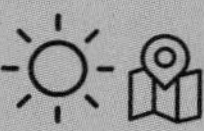

'The MacBride Dynasty'
Anecdotal family journey. Thematic questioning of accepted beliefs of the self-important. Exposure of distance between reality and fantasy.

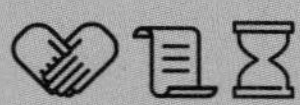

Last Words

'His songs celebrate our small mercies and tender decencies in a world that favours the corrupt.'
Paula Meehan

'He makes particularly engaging poems out of passing conversations – "You're looking great – are you going to a wedding?"/"Oh God no – I'm coming back from a wake"'.
Deirdre Collins

'Like all first-class comedians, he is deadly serious.'
Terry Eagleton

Robert Frost
1874–1963

'A poem begins in delight and ends in wisdom.'

One of the great 20th-century poets, Robert Frost is highly regarded for his realistic depictions of rural life and his command of American colloquial speech. His work frequently explores themes from early 1900s country life in New England, often using the setting to examine complex social and philosophical ideas. Nature is central to his writing. While his poems seem simple at first, they often transcend the boundaries of time and place with metaphysical significance and a deeper appreciation of human nature in all its beauty and contradictions. Despite many personal tragedies, Frost had a very successful public life. It is ironic that such a calm, stoical voice emerged from his difficult background. At times bittersweet, sometimes ironic, or often marvelling at his surroundings, Robert Frost continues to be a popular and often-quoted poet. He was honoured frequently during his lifetime, receiving four Pulitzer Prizes.

Investigate Further

To find out more about Robert Frost, or to hear readings of his poems, you could do a search of some of the useful websites available such as YouTube, BBC Poetry, poetryfoundation.org and poetryarchive.org, or access additional material on this page of your eBook.

Prescribed Poems

Note that Frost uses American spellings in his work.

○ **1 'The Tuft of Flowers' (OL)**
One of Frost's best-loved works, this poem describes how a simple clump of wild flowers succeeds in uniting two separate people.
Page 172

○ **2 'Mending Wall' (OL)**
Repairing a damaged wall between his neighbour and himself, Frost considers the theme of community and fellowship, and wonders if 'Good fences make good neighbors'. **Page 176**

○ **3 'After Apple-Picking'**
Set on his New England farm at the end of the apple harvest, Frost meditates on the nature of work, creativity and of what makes a fulfilled life. **Page 181**

○ **4 'The Road Not Taken'**
Another of Frost's most popular poems. Using the symbol of a remote country crossroads, the poet dramatises the decisions people face in life – and the consequences of their choices.
Page 185

○ **5 'Birches'**
The sight of some forest birches excites Frost's imagination to associate childhood games of swinging on the trees with the process of writing poetry.
Page 189

○ **6 'Out, Out–' (OL)**
This affecting poem is based on an actual story of a serious chainsaw accident. Despite the tragedy, Frost leaves readers in no doubt of life's grim reality: 'It goes on'. **Page 193**

○ **7 'Spring Pools'**
In this captivating lyric poem, the fragile beauty and transience of the pools give Frost an acute awareness of the natural cycle of growth, decay and renewal.
Page 197

○ **8 'Acquainted with the Night'**
This short lyric depicts the dark, alienating side of urban life.
Page 200

○ **9 'Design'**
Frost's sonnet, depicting nature as volatile and terrifying, addresses the possibility of an underlying plan or design for the universe.
Page 204

○ **10 'Provide, Provide'**
Another poem that deals with some of Frost's favourite themes – time, old age and independence.
Page 207

*(OL) indicates poems that are also prescribed for the Ordinary Level course.

1 The Tuft of Flowers

Tuft: cluster, bunch.

I went to turn the grass once after one
Who mowed it in the dew before the sun.

The dew was gone that made his blade so keen
Before I came to view the levelled scene.

I looked for him behind an isle of trees;
I listened for his whetstone on the breeze.

But he had gone his way, the grass all mown,
And I must be, as he had been – alone,

'As all must be,' I said within my heart,
'Whether they work together or apart.'

But as I said it, swift there passed me by
On noiseless wing a bewildered butterfly,

Seeking with memories grown dim o'er night
Some resting flower of yesterday's delight.

And once I marked his flight go round and round,
As where some flower lay withering on the ground.

And then he flew as far as eye could see,
And then on tremulous wing came back to me.

I thought of questions that have no reply,
And would have turned to toss the grass to dry;

But he turned first, and led my eye to look
At a tall tuft of flowers beside a brook,

A leaping tongue of bloom the scythe had spared
Beside a reedy brook the scythe had bared.

The mower in the dew had loved them thus,
By leaving them to flourish, not for us,

Nor yet to draw one thought of ours to him,
But from sheer morning gladness at the brim.

turn: upturn; toss grass to dry it out.

keen: sharp; effective.

whetstone: stone used for sharpening scythes.

tremulous: trembling or nervous.

brook: stream.

scythe: implement used for cutting grass or hay.

The butterfly and I had lit upon,
Nevertheless, a message from the dawn,

That made me hear the wakening birds around,
And hear his long scythe whispering to the ground,

And feel a spirit kindred to my own;
So that henceforth I worked no more alone;

But glad with him, I worked as with his aid,
And weary, sought at noon with him the shade;

And dreaming, as it were, held brotherly speech
With one whose thought I had not hoped to reach.

'Men work together,' I told him from the heart,
'Whether they work together or apart.'

lit upon: discovered.

kindred: closely related to.

'A leaping tongue of bloom'

Personal Response

1. Describe the dominant mood in lines 1–10 of the poem.
2. Choose two images from the poem that you found particularly interesting and effective. Briefly explain your choice in both cases.
3. Would you describe the poem as uplifting? Give reasons for your answer.

Critical Literacy

The poem describes how a simple, uncut clump of wild flowers can unite two separate people. It is one of Frost's best-loved works and typifies his technique of bringing readers through an everyday rustic experience to reveal a universal truth – in this case about alienation, friendship and communication. The poem consists of 20 rhymed couplets written in strict verse. Frost once remarked that 'writing without structure is like playing tennis without a net'.

The narrative voice in the opening section of the poem is relaxed, in keeping with the unhurried rhythm. Frost's initial tone is low-key and noncommittal. The speaker has gone out to turn the grass so that it can dry. Someone else had mowed it earlier 'in the dew before the sun'. Lines 5–6 reveal the speaker's sense of solitude and isolation; the unnamed mower has 'gone his way'. This leads him to consider **the loneliness of the scene and of human experience**. The introspective mood becomes more depressed as the poet searches for his fellow worker. Figurative descriptions of the 'levelled scene' and 'an isle of trees' add to the atmosphere of pessimism as the speaker implies that he must also be 'alone'. For Frost, this is the essential human experience for all, 'Whether they work together or apart'.

The poem's middle section is marked by the sudden appearance of a 'bewildered butterfly'. After fluttering 'round and round' looking for the 'resting flower' that gave it such delight the day before, it then flies close to the speaker: 'on tremulous wing came back to me.' The adjective 'tremulous' suggests fragility and a **new sense of excited anticipation in the air**. The butterfly seems to reflect the speaker's 'questions that have no reply'. Perhaps they have both enjoyed great happiness in the past. The butterfly eventually turns and leads the speaker to a 'tall tuft of flowers beside a brook' that have escaped the mower's scythe – not by accident, but because 'he had loved them' and left them to flourish out of 'sheer morning gladness'.

The significance of the meadow flowers and the brook cannot be overlooked, because here the **mood suddenly changes to optimism**. The presence of the mysterious butterfly establishes communication between the early morning mower and the narrator. Frost suggests this connection with his vivid description of the spared flowers as 'A leaping tongue of bloom'. In the final section, the speaker and the butterfly 'lit upon,/ Nevertheless, a message from the dawn'. With images such as the 'wakening birds around' and a 'spirit kindred to my own', we might assume that this 'message' could indeed be one of human friendship and communal love.

The ending is paradoxical: 'Men work together ... Whether they work together or apart'. However, **Frost believed in spiritual presence and was inspired by an overwhelming sense of fellowship**. Although apart, the speaker and the absent mower are working with a shared appreciation of nature's beauty and a common commitment to a better world. The poem could also be interpreted biographically, since Frost had lost several of his loved ones and may well have written it as an emotional outlet. Even though his family

members were deceased, he remains close to them in spirit. Whatever the poet's intention, readers can draw their own conclusions from the poem.

Writing About the Poem

In your view, is 'The Tuft of Flowers' a dramatic poem? Refer closely to the text in your answer.

Sample Paragraph

'The Tuft of Flowers' has been described as a lyrical soliloquy. The narrative element is there from the start. The first mower seems a mysterious character. The central character (poet) is obviously close to nature as he goes about his work turning the grass. His inner drama interests me most, as his attitude changes from loneliness at the beginning to happiness and companionship. The two moods contrast dramatically. First, the sadness of 'I listened for his whetstone' and 'brotherly speech' and then the more sociable 'Men work together'. The vivid imagery is also dramatic, especially the butterfly's flight – 'On noiseless wing' – and the description of the small outcrop of flowers – 'A leaping tongue of bloom'. Frost sets his poems in the secluded New England landscape and this provides a beautiful location for what are deep meditations about the important questions in life – 'questions that have no reply'. The rhythm or movement of the poem quickens in the final lines as the poet expresses his positive view of life – 'Men work together'. I thought this was the ideal way to round off this quietly dramatic poem.

EXAMINER'S COMMENT

A very well controlled answer focusing on some key dramatic elements, such as the use of the character's 'inner drama' and 'lyrical soliloquy'. Good personal interaction and commentary. References were handled effectively and points were clearly presented: 'The rhythm or movement of the poem quickens in the final lines as the poet expresses his positive view of life – "Men work together".' A highly successful top-grade response.

Class/Homework Exercises

1. In your opinion, what is Frost's main theme or message in 'The Tuft of Flowers'? Refer closely to the text of the poem in your answer.
2. 'The poetry of Robert Frost is known for its simple, everyday language.' To what extent is this evident in 'The Tuft of Flowers'? Support your answer with reference to the poem.

Summary Points

- **Typically narrative style – from the poet's own personal experience.**
- **Human fellowship and how humans can learn from nature are central themes.**
- **Contrasting moods – pessimism changes to optimism.**
- **Rhyming couplets create unity and help in expressing the poet's ideas.**
- **Effective use of onomatopoeia, rich imagery and symbolism.**

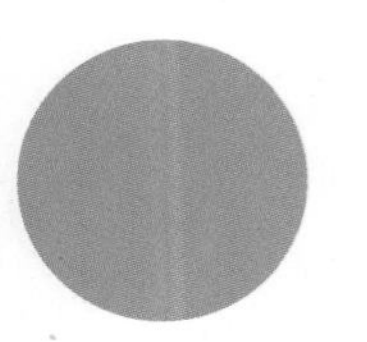

2 Mending Wall

Something there is that doesn't love a wall,
That sends the frozen-ground-swell under it,
And spills the upper boulders in the sun;
And makes gaps even two can pass abreast.
The work of hunters is another thing:
I have come after them and made repair
Where they have left not one stone on a stone,
But they would have the rabbit out of hiding,
To please the yelping dogs. The gaps I mean,
No one has seen them made or heard them made,
But at spring mending-time we find them there.
I let my neighbor know beyond the hill;
And on a day we meet to walk the line
And set the wall between us once again.
We keep the wall between us as we go.
To each the boulders that have fallen to each.
And some are loaves and some so nearly balls
We have to use a spell to make them balance:
'Stay where you are until our backs are turned!'
We wear our fingers rough with handling them.
Oh, just another kind of out-door game,
One on a side. It comes to little more:
There where it is we do not need the wall:
He is all pine and I am apple orchard.
My apple trees will never get across
And eat the cones under his pines, I tell him.
He only says, 'Good fences make good neighbors.'
Spring is the mischief in me, and I wonder
If I could put a notion in his head:
'Why do they make good neighbors? Isn't it
Where there are cows? But here there are no cows.
Before I built a wall I'd ask to know
What I was walling in or walling out,
And to whom I was like to give offense.
Something there is that doesn't love a wall,
That wants it down.' I could say 'Elves' to him,
But it's not elves exactly, and I'd rather
He said it for himself. I see him there
Bringing a stone grasped firmly by the top
In each hand, like an old-stone savage armed.

Something there is that doesn't love a wall: ice and frost often erode walls.

abreast: side by side.

Good fences make good neighbors: one reading is that a strong fence protects by keeping people apart.

Elves: small supernatural beings, often malevolent.

He moves in darkness as it seems to me,
Not of woods only and the shade of trees.
He will not go behind his father's saying,
And he likes having thought of it so well
He says again, 'Good fences make good neighbors.'

'No one has seen them made'

Personal Response

1. In your opinion, who or what is it that doesn't love a wall? Support your answer with reference to the poem.
2. There are two speakers in the poem. Which one is the wiser, in your view? Refer to the text in your answer.
3. Point out two examples of humour in the poem and comment on how effective they are in adding to the message of 'Mending Wall'.

Critical Literacy

This popular poem of Robert Frost's was written in 1913 and appears first in his second collection, *North of Boston.* When the land was being cleared for agriculture, the stones gathered were made into walls. Robert Frost once said this poem 'contrasts two types of people'. President John F. Kennedy asked Frost to read this poem to Khrushchev, Russia's leader at the time of the Cuban Missile Crisis, when there was a possibility of another world war.

'Mending Wall' was responsible for building a picture of Frost as an ordinary New England farmer who wrote about normal events and recognisable settings in simple language. Line 1 is mysterious: 'Something there is that doesn't love a wall.' **A force is at work to pull down the barriers** people insist on erecting. The speaker repairs the holes in the wall left by hunters: 'I have come after them and made repair.' But there are other holes in the wall, though 'No one has seen them made or heard them made'. In a yearly ritual, 'at spring mending-time', the poet and his neighbour meet to carry out repairs. Each looks after his own property as they walk along: 'To each the boulders that have fallen to each.' But a tone of coldness creeps into the poem amid this neighbourly task, with the repetition of how the wall has separated them at all times: 'set the wall between us', 'keep the wall between us'.

It is a difficult task, as the stones fall off as quickly as they are placed: 'Stay where you are until our backs are turned!' The **good-humoured banter** of the workers comes alive in the humorous remark, and readers feel as if they are there in New England watching the wall being repaired. The light-hearted mood is continued in line 21 when the poet describes the activity as an 'out-door game'. Then he comments that they don't even really need the wall where it is: 'He is all pine and I am apple orchard.' The poet jokes that his apple trees cannot go over and eat his neighbour's pine cones. His neighbour then speaks: 'Good fences make good neighbors.' He comes across as a serious type, quoting old sayings, in **contrast** to the mischievous poet: 'Spring is the mischief in me.' Frost is associating himself with the turbulent force that is pushing through the land, creating growth and pulling down walls. The neighbour is shown as one who has accepted what has been said without question, one who upholds the status quo.

In line 30, the poet poses questions to himself and wishes he could say to his neighbour, 'Why do they make good neighbours?' **He begins to consider what a wall is keeping in and keeping out**. He also wonders what is pulling down the wall. He mockingly suggests 'Elves', then discounts that. Frost depicts his rather uncommunicative neighbour in a series of unflattering images: 'an old-stone savage armed', 'He moves in darkness'. Is the poet saying that we must question received wisdom and not blindly follow what we are told? The neighbour, who accepts, is presented as a figure of repression who 'moves in darkness'. He just repeats 'Good fences make good neighbors' like a mantra. Is the poet suggesting that there are some people who derive comfort from just remaining the same, who do not welcome change ('He will not go behind his father's saying')?

The tone of the poem changes as the easy, neighbourly sociability of a shared task is replaced by a **feeling of tension**, first in the effort to keep the tumbling wall upright, and then in the opposite attitudes of the two neighbours – the mischievous, questioning poet and the taciturn, unquestioning neighbour. The desire for human co-operation is often stopped, not by outside circumstances, but by a lack of desire on the part of the people involved. This is the poet commenting on human dilemmas. The easy-going, almost ruminative tone of someone musing to himself is written in blank verse, unrhymed iambic pentameter. The colloquial conversational phrases are all tightly controlled throughout this thought-provoking poem.

Writing About the Poem

'Frost's deceptively simple poems explore profound truths about life.' Discuss this statement in relation to the poem 'Mending Wall'.

Sample Paragraph

Frost has very successfully given us a picture of two opposite personalities in this poem. The moody neighbour who doggedly walks on his side of the wall, 'We keep the wall between us both as we go', is vividly described. Here is a person who accepts what was told to him without question 'Good fences make good neighbors'. It is as if he is reciting the two-times tables. This is fact. He is comfortable in his traditional mindset. 'He will not go behind his father's saying.' The poet describes him in unflattering terms, referring to him as 'an old stone-armed savage'. He also states that he was one who moved 'in darkness'. Frost does not agree with this unquestioning attitude. It is not only a wall which divides these two, there is a completely different mindset. The poet has a lively personality, 'Stay where you are until our backs have turned', regarding the work as a game. However, he asks the fundamental question about any boundary, 'I'd ask to know/What I was walling in or out'. He also asks the sensitive question about who he was likely to give offence to, with his wall. This apparently simple poem sticks in the reader's mind long after the reading. We are left wondering, are walls natural or necessary? Must we break down barriers to live as good neighbours? What if we are over-run?

A solid response exploring the distance between contrasting personalities, a traditionalist and a maverick. Points are well developed through a fluent use of language, 'It is as if he is reciting the two-times tables. This is fact'. The questions towards the end show a lively engagement with the poem. However, the response is slightly marred by inaccurate quoting: 'an old stone-armed savage', 'walling in or out'. This prevents the answer achieving the highest grade.

Class/Homework Exercises

1. Comment on Frost's use of imagery in 'Mending Wall'. Do you find it effective? Refer closely to the text in your answer.
2. 'Frost's poems often have a universal significance and raise interesting questions about human relations.' To what extent do you agree or disagree with this view? Support your answer with reference to 'Mending Wall'.

Summary Points

- **Key themes include community, fellowship, boundaries and borders.**
- **Characteristic use of accessible, everyday language and humorous touches.**
- **Effective use of symbolism, slow-moving rhythm and unrhymed blank verse.**
- **Variety of tones: narrative, relaxed, interrogative, apprehensive and reflective.**

3

After Apple-Picking

My long two-pointed ladder's sticking through a tree
Toward heaven still,
And there's a barrel that I didn't fill
Beside it, and there may be two or three
Apples I didn't pick upon some bough.
But I am done with apple-picking now.
Essence of winter sleep is on the night,
The scent of apples: I am drowsing off.
I cannot rub the strangeness from my sight
I got from looking through a pane of glass
I skimmed this morning from the drinking trough
And held against the world of hoary grass.
It melted, and I let it fall and break.
But I was well
Upon my way to sleep before it fell,
And I could tell
What form my dreaming was about to take.
Magnified apples appear and disappear,
Stem end and blossom end,
And every fleck of russet showing clear.
My instep arch not only keeps the ache,
It keeps the pressure of a ladder-round.
I feel the ladder sway as the boughs bend.
And I keep hearing from the cellar bin
The rumbling sound
Of load on load of apples coming in.
For I have had too much
Of apple-picking: I am overtired
Of the great harvest I myself desired.
There were ten thousand thousand fruit to touch,
Cherish in hand, lift down, and not let fall.
For all
That struck the earth,
No matter if not bruised or spiked with stubble,
Went surely to the cider-apple heap
As of no worth.
One can see what will trouble
This sleep of mine, whatever sleep it is.
Were he not gone,
The woodchuck could say whether it's like his
Long sleep, as I describe its coming on,
Or just some human sleep.

Essence: scent.

glass: ice.

hoary: covered in frost.

russet: reddish-brown.

ladder-round: a rung or support on a ladder.

stubble: remnant stalks left after harvesting.

woodchuck: groundhog, a native American burrowing animal.

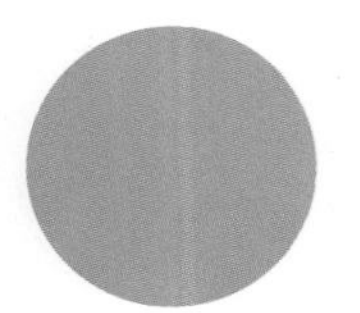

Personal Response

1. Select one image that evokes the hard, physical work of apple-picking. Comment on its effectiveness.
2. What do you understand lines 27–29 to mean?
3. Write a short personal response to this poem.

Critical Literacy

The poem is a lyrical evocation of apple harvesting in New England. Frost takes an ordinary experience and transforms it into a meditative moment. Harvesting fruit soon becomes a consideration of how life has been experienced fully but with some regrets and mistakes. Frost chose not to experiment but to use a traditional writing style, or as he said, he preferred 'the old-fashioned way to be new'. 'After Apple-Picking' is not free verse, but it is among Frost's least formal works, containing 42 lines varying in length, a rhyme scheme that is also highly irregular and no stanza breaks.

'Toward heaven still'

The speaker in the poem (either Frost himself or the farmer persona he often adopted) feels himself drifting off to sleep with the scent of apples in the air. He thinks of the ladder he has left in the orchard still pointing to 'heaven'. Is the poet suggesting that his work has brought him closer to God? The slow-moving rhythm and broad vowel sounds ('two-pointed', 'bough', 'drowsing') in the opening lines reflect his **lethargic mood**. Although he seems close to exhaustion, he is pleased that the harvest is complete: 'But I am done with apple-picking now.' Ironically, his mind is filled with random thoughts about the day's work. The drowsy atmosphere is effectively communicated by the poet's mesmerising description: 'Essence of winter sleep is on the night.'

This dream-like state releases Frost's imagination and he remembers the odd sensation he felt while looking through a sheet of ice he had removed earlier from a drinking trough. While the memory is rooted in reality, it appears that he has experienced the world differently: 'I cannot rub the strangeness from my sight.' As he is falling asleep, he is conscious that his dreaming will be associated with **exaggerated images of harvesting**: 'Magnified apples appear and disappear' (line 18). The poet emphasises the sensuousness of what is happening. The vivid apples display 'every fleck of russet' and he can feel the pressure of the 'ladder-round' against his foot. He hears the 'rumbling sound' of the fruit being unloaded. The images suggest abundance: 'load on load of apples', 'ten thousand thousand'. Frost's use of repetition, both of evocative sounds and key words, is a prominent feature of the poem that enhances our appreciation of his intense dream.

Physically and mentally tired, the poet also relives the anxiety he had felt about the need to save the crop from being 'bruised or spiked with stubble', and not to lose them to 'the cider-apple heap'. In the poem's closing lines, which seem deliberately vague and distorted, Frost wonders again about the nature of consciousness: 'This sleep of mine, whatever sleep it is.' Like so many of his statements, the line is rich in possible interpretations. For some critics, the poem appears to be exploring the art and craft of writing. Others take a broader view, seeing it as **a metaphor for how human beings live their lives**. The poet's own final thoughts are of the woodchuck's winter retreat, before he eventually surrenders to his own mysterious 'sleep'.

'After Apple-Picking' is typical of Frost's work. Despite the apparent cheerfulness of much of the writing, it has **undertones of a more sober vision of life**. As always, there is a thoughtful quality to the poem. The reference to the approach of winter hints at the constant presence of mortality. Frost's question about what kind of sleep to anticipate suggests untroubled oblivion or possibly some kind of renewal, just as the woodchuck reawakens in the springtime after its long hibernation.

Writing About the Poem

'Frost's work has a surface cheerfulness which conceals a more serious vision of life.' Discuss this statement in relation to the poem, 'After Apple-Picking'. Support your answer with reference to the poem.

Sample Paragraph

In 'After Apple-Picking', Robert Frost creates a mood of otherworldliness. At the start, his accurate description of the orchard is realistic. But some of the poem seems symbolic – such as the mention of the ladder pointing to heaven which might suggest Frost's religious feelings. The setting is calm and the poet feels tired but satisfied after his demanding physical work – 'there's a barrel that I didn't fill'. But his tiredness soon makes his mood more dreamy – 'Essence of winter sleep is on the night'. The sibilance and slender vowels add to this languid atmosphere. I could trace a growing surreal quality to the poem as Frost drifts in and out of consciousness, remembering flashes of his work – 'The scent of apples: I am drowsing off'. He mentions 'sleep' repeatedly, reflecting his deep weariness. The rhythm is slow and irregular, just like his confused thoughts. By the end of the poem, he is in a dream-like state, equally obsessed with apple-picking and his own need for sleep. He even wonders about 'whatever sleep it is'. As he drifts off, he thinks of the animals that sleep through the winter and compares himself to the woodchuck. The whimsical mood reflects his deep interest in nature and is a characteristic of this great American poet.

EXAMINER'S COMMENT

This is a very well written and accomplished answer that ranges widely and shows some close personal engagement: 'I could trace a growing surreal quality to the poem as Frost drifts in and out of consciousness, remembering flashes of his work.' There is an assured sense of the central mood and this is supported with apt quotations. Interesting references to Frost's style ensure the highest grade.

Class/Homework Exercises

1. Comment on the effectiveness of the poem's imagery in appealing to the senses. Refer closely to the text in your answer.
2. 'Many of Frost's poems appear simple, but often have layers of underlying meanings.' Discuss this view, with particular reference to 'After Apple-Picking'.

Summary Points

- **Subject matter considers creativity, human achievement and the cycle of life.**
- **Dreamlike atmosphere and contrasting tones – peaceful, nostalgic, regretful.**
- **Rich sensory imagery and symbolism convey underlying themes.**
- **Effective use of repetition, sibilance and assonance throughout.**

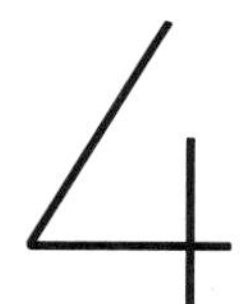

The Road Not Taken

Two roads diverged in a yellow wood,
And sorry I could not travel both
And be one traveler, long I stood
And looked down one as far as I could
To where it bent in the undergrowth;

Then took the other, as just as fair,
And having perhaps the better claim,
Because it was grassy and wanted wear;
Though as for that, the passing there
Had worn them really about the same,

And both that morning equally lay
In leaves no step had trodden black.
Oh, I kept the first for another day!
Yet knowing how way leads on to way,
I doubted if I should ever come back.

I shall be telling this with a sigh
Somewhere ages and ages hence:
Two roads diverged in a wood, and I—
I took the one less traveled by,
And that has made all the difference.

diverged: separate and go in different directions.

undergrowth: small trees and bushes growing beneath larger trees in a wood.

claim: attraction, entitlement.

'where it bent in the undergrowth'

Personal Response

1. In your opinion, is this a simple poem or does it have a more profound meaning? Outline your views, supporting them with relevant quotation.
2. Select one image from the poem that you consider particularly effective or interesting. Briefly justify your choice.
3. Frost has been described as someone who 'broods and comments on familiar country things ... catching a truth in it'. In your view, what is the tone of this poem? Does it change or remain the same?

Critical Literacy

One of Frost's most popular poems, it was the first published in the collection *Mountain Interval* (1916). It was inspired by his friend, the poet Edward Thomas. Frost told Thomas, 'No matter which road you take, you'll always sigh, and wish you'd taken another'. Frost also said he was influenced by an event which happened to him at a crossroads after a winter snowstorm in 1912. He met a figure, 'my own image', who passed silently by him. Frost wondered at 'this other self'. The poem dramatises the choices we make in life and their consequences.

Huge themes are summarised in this simple narrative. In the first stanza, the speaker stands in a wood where two roads run off in different directions. He has to make a decision – which one will he take? The roads are 'about the same', so the emphasis is not on the decision, but on the **process of decision-making and its consequences**. The speaker decides that he cannot see where the first road is leading ('it bent in the undergrowth'), so he chooses the other one, though it is unclear why. The reference to the 'yellow wood' suggests that the poet is mature enough to realise the consequences of his decision. He won't have this opportunity again: 'I doubted if I should ever come back.' The beautiful image of the 'yellow wood' conjures up a picture of the autumn in New England, but it also has a deeper meaning and is tinged with regret. A person can't do everything in life; choice is part of the human condition.

Frost has said, 'I'm not a nature poet. There's always something else in my poetry'. Here, in this simple act, he **explores what it means to be human** and dramatises the decision-making process. There is the human desire to avoid making a decision ('sorry I could not travel both') and the consideration of the possible choices ('long I stood/And looked down one as far as I could'). The regular rhyme scheme mirrors the poet looking this way and that as he tries to decide which to choose *(abaab, cdccd, efeef, ghggh).* This unusual rhyme also underlines the unusual choice made. Frost felt that 'the most important thing about a poem ... is how wilfully, gracefully, naturally entertainingly and beautifully its rhymes are'.

In stanza two, **he makes the decision**: he 'took the other one'. Why? Was it because it 'was grassy and wanted wear'? Is this someone who is individualistic and likes to do something different to the crowd? Does this suggest a desire for adventure? Then the poet becomes increasingly mischievous. After pointing out the difference between the two roads, he now declares that they were not so different: 'the passing there/Had worn them really about the same.'

In the third stanza, he continues to **point out the similarity of the two roads**, which 'equally lay'. So is the idea that if you choose the less conventional route in life, you may not end up having adventures? The reader is now as confused as the poet was when trying to decide what to do. A second great truth is then revealed: no matter what we get, we always want what we don't have. The regret is palpable in the emphatic 'Oh, I kept the first for another day!' But, of course, there won't be another day, because time marches on and we cannot return to the past; we can only go on, as 'way leads on to way'.

At the start of stanza four, the poet realises in **hindsight** that he will tell of this day in the future, 'ages and ages hence', but it will be 'with a sigh'? Has his choice resulted in suffering? Frost's own personal life was littered with tragedy. Does the repetition of 'I' and the inclusion of the dash suggest that the poet is asserting his maverick individuality as he resolutely declares: 'I took the one less traveled by,/And that has made all the difference'? Do you think he feels he made the right choice for himself?

This common experience of choice and decision-making is caught succinctly in Frost's simple narrative. It sounds like a person thinking aloud; the language seems ordinary. Yet upon closer examination, we become aware of the **musical sound effects**. The repeated 'e', coupled with the sibilant 's' sounds ('it was grassy') and alliteration ('wanted wear') convey a calm, deliberating voice. This poem is inclusive rather than exclusive, as it invites the reader to share in the poet's decision-making.

Writing About the Poem

'Frost uses traditional form not in an experimental way, but adapted to his purpose.' Discuss this statement with reference to 'The Road Not Taken'. Refer to the poem in your answer.

Sample Paragraph

Frost forms his poems not in an experimental way, but in a deliberate way which suits his purpose. He uses iambic pentameter, a traditional metre used by Shakespeare and it is an ironic, sceptical voice, 'yet knowing how way leads on to way', which resonates in 'The Road Not Taken'. The structure of the poem mirrors the deliberating process, as first the speaker tries to avoid making a choice, then considers the alternatives, 'long I stood'. The decision is made and almost immediately there is a sense of regret: 'Oh, I kept the first for another day.' The rhyme scheme of the first stanza is *abaab*. This mirrors the unusual choice the poet made. Frost believed in the 'sound of sense', as he tells us that we can know what is going on even through a closed door by the sound, not necessarily the meaning of words. This is illustrated in the line, 'Because it was grassy and wanted wear'. The alliteration and sibilance suggest an almost idyllic wilderness. So Frost structures the form of his poems for a purpose. In this poem the rhyme scheme mimics the glancing this way and that as the speaker tries to decide what route to take. These are some of the ways Frost uses form for a purpose, rather than experimenting just for its own sake.

EXAMINER'S COMMENT

This thoroughly developed answer shows a deep sense of engagement, particularly the discussion on the poetic voice: 'an ironic, sceptical voice, "Yet knowing how way leads on to way".' Points on style range widely and clearly demonstrate an understanding of Frost's skill in using structure, rhyme and sound effects. Expression is also excellent throughout. The well-sustained focus and integrated quoting ensure that the standard reached the highest grade.

Class/Homework Exercises

1. Frost's ambition was to 'write a few poems it will be hard to get rid of'. To what extent is this true of 'The Road Not Taken'?
2. 'The ending of "The Road Not Taken" has often been described as ambiguous and inconclusive.' Discuss this view, with particular reference to the poem.

Summary Points

- **Key themes – the natural world and the consequences of making choices in life.**
- **The autumnal setting provides a suitable context for this simple narrative.**
- **Reflective tone and characteristically simple language throughout.**
- **Effective use of emphatic rhyme and appealing musical sibilant effects.**

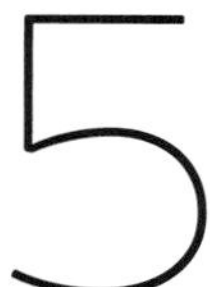

Birches

When I see birches bend to left and right
Across the lines of straighter darker trees,
I like to think some boy's been swinging them.
But swinging doesn't bend them down to stay.
Ice-storms do that. Often you must have seen them
Loaded with ice a sunny winter morning
After a rain. They click upon themselves
As the breeze rises, and turn many-colored
As the stir cracks and crazes their enamel.
Soon the sun's warmth makes them shed crystal shells
Shattering and avalanching on the snow-crust—
Such heaps of broken glass to sweep away
You'd think the inner dome of heaven had fallen.
They are dragged to the withered bracken by the load,
And they seem not to break; though once they are bowed
So low for long, they never right themselves:
You may see their trunks arching in the woods
Years afterwards, trailing their leaves on the ground
Like girls on hands and knees that throw their hair
Before them over their heads to dry in the sun.
But I was going to say when Truth broke in
With all her matter-of-fact about the ice-storm
I should prefer to have some boy bend them
As he went out and in to fetch the cows—
Some boy too far from town to learn baseball,
Whose only play was what he found himself,
Summer or winter, and could play alone.
One by one he subdued his father's trees
By riding them down over and over again
Until he took the stiffness out of them,
And not one but hung limp, not one was left
For him to conquer. He learned all there was
To learn about not launching out too soon
And so not carrying the tree away
Clear to the ground. He always kept his poise
To the top branches, climbing carefully
With the same pains you use to fill a cup
Up to the brim, and even above the brim.

birches: deciduous trees with smooth, white bark.

click: tapping sound made by the branches when they touch.

crazes their enamel: cracks the ice on the trees.
crystal shells: drops of melting ice on branches.
avalanching: collapsing.

bracken: fern leaves.

limp: loose; wilted.

Then he flung outward, feet first, with a swish,
Kicking his way down through the air to the ground.
So was I once myself a swinger of birches.
And so I dream of going back to be.
It's when I'm weary of considerations,
And life is too much like a pathless wood
Where your face burns and tickles with the cobwebs
Broken across it, and one eye is weeping
From a twig's having lashed across it open.
I'd like to get away from earth awhile
And then come back to it and begin over.
May no fate willfully misunderstand me
And half grant what I wish and snatch me away
Not to return. Earth's the right place for love:
I don't know where it's likely to go better.
I'd like to go by climbing a birch tree,
And climb black branches up a snow-white trunk
Toward heaven, till the tree could bear no more,
But dipped its top and set me down again.
That would be good both going and coming back.
One could do worse than be a swinger of birches.

swish: whoosh.

willfully: deliberately.

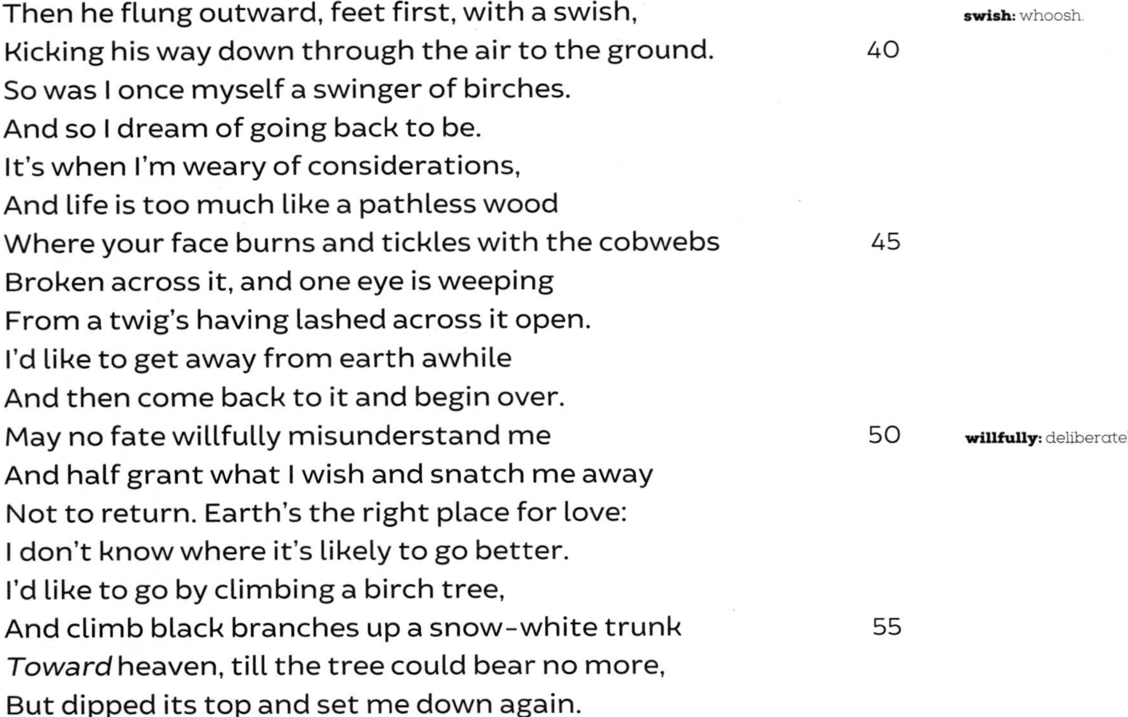

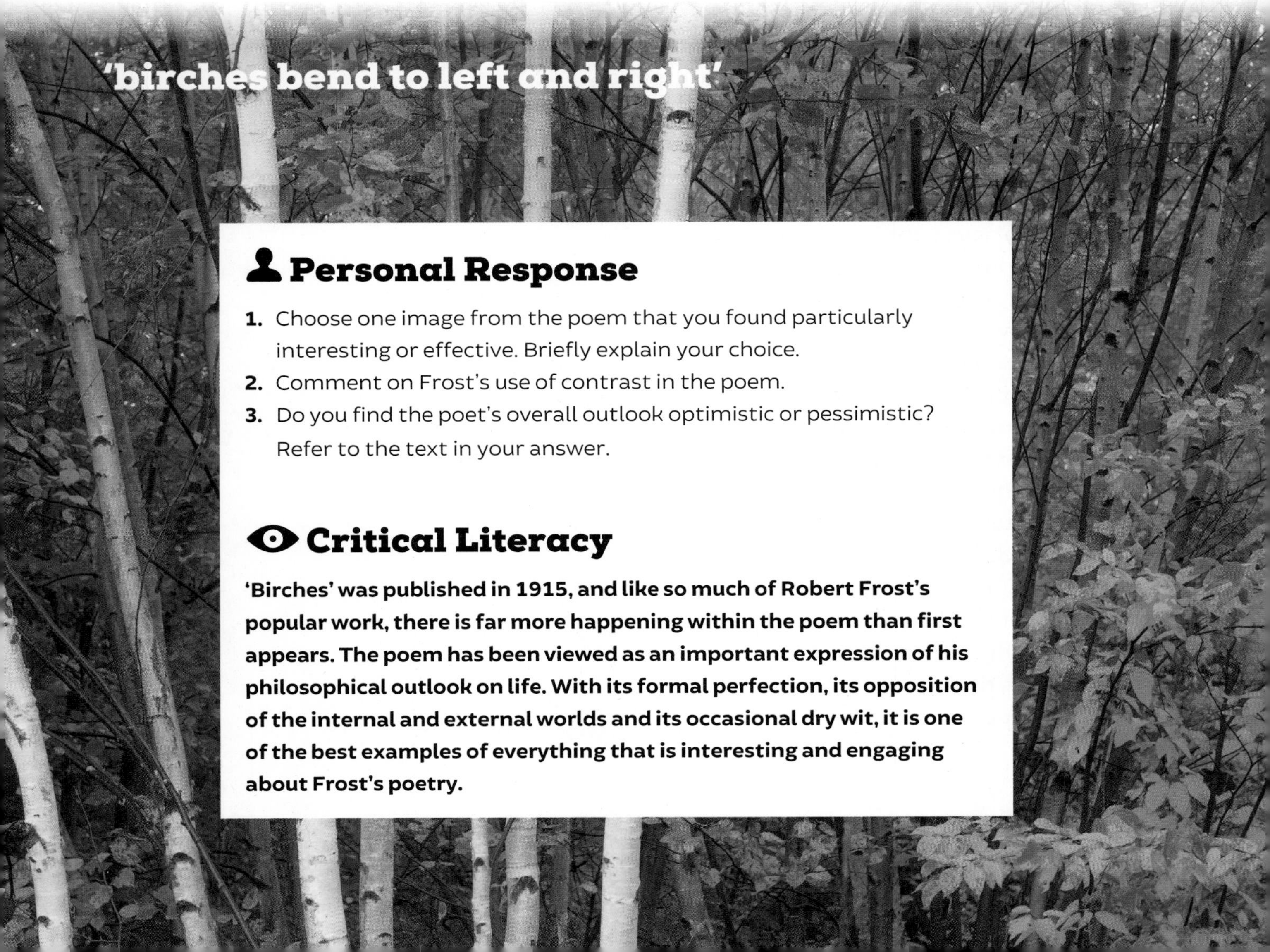

Personal Response

1. Choose one image from the poem that you found particularly interesting or effective. Briefly explain your choice.
2. Comment on Frost's use of contrast in the poem.
3. Do you find the poet's overall outlook optimistic or pessimistic? Refer to the text in your answer.

Critical Literacy

'Birches' was published in 1915, and like so much of Robert Frost's popular work, there is far more happening within the poem than first appears. The poem has been viewed as an important expression of his philosophical outlook on life. With its formal perfection, its opposition of the internal and external worlds and its occasional dry wit, it is one of the best examples of everything that is interesting and engaging about Frost's poetry.

The opening description of the leaning birches is interesting, as Frost compares them to the 'straighter darker trees'. The scene immediately brings him back to his childhood and he likes to think that 'some boy's been swinging them'. This tension between what has actually happened and what the poet would like to have happened – between the real world and the world of the imagination – runs through much of the poem. Throughout lines 1–20, he wonders why the birches are bent 'to left and right'. He accepts that the true reason is because of the ice weighing them down. The poet's **precise, onomatopoeic language** – particularly the sharp 'c' effect in 'cracks and crazes their enamel' – echoes the tapping sound of the frozen branches. Vivid, sensual imagery brings the wintry scene to life: 'crystal shells', 'snow crust', 'withered bracken'. Frost's conversational tone is engaging: 'You'd think the inner dome of heaven had fallen.' Characteristically, he adds a beautiful simile, comparing the bent branches 'trailing their leaves on the ground' to girls who are drying their cascading hair in the sunshine.

In the poem's second section (lines 21–40), Frost resists the accurate explanation ('Truth') for the bent trees, preferring to interpret the scene imaginatively. He visualises a lonely boy ('too far from town to learn baseball') who has learned to amuse himself among the forest birches. In simple, factual terms, the poet describes the boy as he 'subdued his father's trees'. We are given a sense of his youthful determination to 'conquer' them all until 'not one was left'. His persistence teaches him valuable lessons for later life. Swinging skilfully on the trees, the boy learns 'about not launching out too soon'. Readers are left in no doubt about the rich **metaphorical significance of the birches**. In highlighting the importance of 'poise' and 'climbing carefully', Frost reveals his belief in discipline and artistry as the important elements of a successful life ('to fill a cup/Up to the brim'). Such symbolism is a common feature of his poetry.

Lines 41–59 are more nostalgic in tone. Frost recalls that he himself was once 'a swinger of birches' and extends the metaphor of retreating into the world of imagination and poetry. The similarities between climbing birches and writing poems become more explicit: 'I'd like to get away from earth.' However, he stresses that he does not wish for a permanent escape because 'Earth's the right place for love'. Is this what poets do when they withdraw into their imaginations and reflect on reality in an attempt to explore the beauty and mystery of life? They are dreamers, idealists. The birch trees are similarly grounded, but they also reach '*Toward* heaven'. The emphatic image (the italics are Frost's) suggests his continuing aspiration for **spiritual fulfilment through the poetic imagination**: 'That would be good both going and coming back.' Frost ends his poem by stating his satisfaction with overcoming challenges and benefiting from the desire to achieve by writing: 'One could do worse than be a swinger of birches.'

Writing About the Poem

'Frost's search for spiritual fulfilment is effectively captured through detailed description.' Discuss this statement in relation to the poem, 'Birches'. Support your answer with reference to the text.

Sample Paragraph

Frost's simple images create a natural connection between the poet and his readers. I very much liked the closely observed descriptions of the ice-covered branches: 'the sun's warmth makes them shed crystal shells.' The sibilance here adds to the beauty of the language. Using onomatopoeia, Frost captures the subtle sounds of the forest in the bitter weather. The trees 'click upon themselves'. The poet obviously loved nature and had a keen eye for its beauty. I also liked his comparison of the trail of leaves to the 'girls on hands and knees that throw their hair'. It was dramatic, fresh and unusual. The boy's movement playing on the trees is dynamic: 'Then he flung outward, feet first, with a swish.' Near the end of the poem, Frost describes a harsher side of the forest when 'your face burns and tickles with the cobwebs'. As someone who spent my childhood in the country, I could relate to this tactile image. Frost is a wonderful writer whose poems give a clear sense of the New England landscape. 'Birches' is a very successful piece of description, mainly due to the poet's precise choice of words and the vivid imagery.

EXAMINER'S COMMENT

This paragraph showed a good knowledge of the text and a clear personal appreciation of Frost's writing skills: 'The sibilance here adds to the beauty of the language.' However, the response does not fully address the task and there is no reference to the 'search for spiritual fulfilment'. This weakens the answer, which deserves a middle grade.

Class/Homework Exercises

1. In your opinion, what is the central theme or message in 'Birches'? Support your answer with reference to the text.
2. 'While Frost's poetry contains elements of suffering, there are also moments of comfort and joy in his work.' To what extent is this true of 'Birches'? Support your answer with reference to the poem.

Summary Points

- **Central themes include childhood, creativity, imagination and escapism.**
- **Motion of swinging can be seen as a metaphor for transcending harsh realities.**
- **Recurring contrasts: light/darkness, love/pain, life/death, Heaven/Earth.**
- **Effective use of descriptive details, striking images, sibilance and assonance.**
- **Tones vary: reflective, nostalgic, philosophical.**

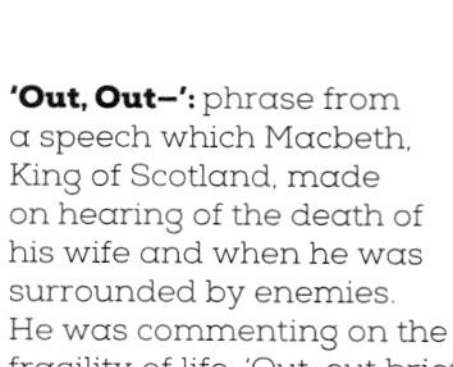

'Out, Out—'

The buzz-saw snarled and rattled in the yard
And made dust and dropped stove-length sticks of wood,
Sweet-scented stuff when the breeze drew across it.
And from there those that lifted eyes could count
Five mountain ranges one behind the other
Under the sunset far into Vermont.
And the saw snarled and rattled, snarled and rattled,
As it ran light, or had to bear a load.
And nothing happened: day was all but done.
Call it a day, I wish they might have said
To please the boy by giving him the half hour
That a boy counts so much when saved from work.
His sister stood beside them in her apron
To tell them 'Supper.' At the word, the saw,
As if to prove saws knew what supper meant,
Leaped out at the boy's hand, or seemed to leap—
He must have given the hand. However it was,
Neither refused the meeting. But the hand!
The boy's first outcry was a rueful laugh,
As he swung toward them holding up the hand
Half in appeal, but half as if to keep
The life from spilling. Then the boy saw all—
Since he was old enough to know, big boy
Doing a man's work, though a child at heart—
He saw all spoiled. 'Don't let him cut my hand off—
The doctor, when he comes. Don't let him, sister!'
So. But the hand was gone already.
The doctor put him in the dark of ether.
He lay and puffed his lips out with his breath.
And then—the watcher at his pulse took fright.
No one believed. They listened at his heart.
Little—less—nothing!—and that ended it.
No more to build on there. And they, since they
Were not the one dead, turned to their affairs.

'Out, Out—': phrase from a speech which Macbeth, King of Scotland, made on hearing of the death of his wife and when he was surrounded by enemies. He was commenting on the fragility of life: 'Out, out brief candle. Life's but a walking shadow' (Shakespeare).

lifted eyes: reference to Psalm 21 – 'I will lift up mine eyes unto the hills' – but the people here don't. The sunset is ignored.

Vermont: a state in New England, America.

ether: form of anaesthetic.

Personal Response

1. What kind of world is shown in the poem? Consider the roles of adults and children. Refer to the text in your response.
2. Choose one image from the poem that you find particularly vivid and dramatic. Briefly explain your choice.
3. In your opinion, what is the central theme or message of 'Out, Out—'? Refer closely to the poem in your response.

Critical Literacy

Based on an actual event that occurred in 1910, the poem refers to a tragic accident when the son of a neighbour of Frost's was killed on his father's farm. By chance, he had hit the loose pulley of the sawing machine and his hand was badly cut. He died from heart failure due to shock. The event was reported in a local paper.

This **horrifying subject matter**, the early violent death of a young boy, was, in Frost's opinion, 'too cruel' to include in his poetry readings. The title, which is a reference to a speech from Shakespeare's *Macbeth*, is a telling comment on how tenuous our hold on life is. The scene is set in a busy timber yard: a world of actual hard, rattling, buzz saw, snarling action. In line 1, Frost's rasping onomatopoeic sounds give a vivid sound picture of the noisy, dangerous yard. The **long, flowing, descriptive lines** paint a picture of a place full of menace where work has to be done. But there is beauty in the midst of this raw power: 'Sweet-scented stuff when the breeze drew across it.' The soft sibilant 's', the assonance of the long 'e' and the compound word 'Sweet-scented' all go to show the surprising beauty to be found in the midst of the practical 'stove-length sticks of wood'.

The **surroundings are also beautiful**, if only the people would look up. But they, unlike the poet, are unaware of 'Five mountain ranges one behind the other/Under the sunset far into Vermont', as their focus is on the work. The repetition of the verbs 'snarled and rattled' mimics the action of the repeated sawing. The detail 'As it ran light, or had to bear a load' shows how the saw pushed through the wood, then lightly ran back through the cut. Line 9 tells us that the day was 'all but done'. A foreshadowing of the impending tragedy is given in 'I wish they might have said'. This is the only time in the whole poem when the personal pronoun 'I' is used. The poet's compassionate understanding for the young boy is evident as he explains how much it matters to a boy to be given precious time off from such hard work: 'That a boy counts so much.' The colloquial language in line 10, 'Call it a day', brings the reader right into this rural scene, rooting the poem in ordinary day-to-day life. The tragic irony is embedded in the line, for soon there will be no more days for the boy.

A domestic detail adds to the reality of this scene as the boy's sister appears 'in her apron/To tell them "Supper"'. In this central episode in line 14, the saw suddenly becomes personified, as if it too 'knew what supper meant'. The fragmented language, 'Leaped out at the boy's hand, or seemed to leap—', reminds us of the fragmented teeth of the saw as it seeks its prey. The mystifying accident is referenced in 'seemed to'. How could it have happened? The helplessness of the victim, the boy, is shown: 'Neither refused the meeting.' We are reminded of someone almost paralysed into inaction at the split second of a horrific accident. Was this destiny? Is the poet adversely commenting on the mechanisation of farming, or on the practice of getting a boy to do a man's job? **All the attention is now focused on the shocking injury**: 'But the hand!' The pity of the event is palpable in this climactic phrase.

The boy's reaction is chilling and poignant. He holds up the hand, 'spilling' its life blood. He pathetically asks for help, begging his sister not to let the doctor amputate his hand: 'Don't let him.' Now the poet interjects: 'So.' What more is to be said? It is like a drawn-out breath after the tension of the awful accident. The harsh reality is there for all to see: 'the hand was gone already.' The boy realised this when he 'saw all'. Without the use of his hands, there would be no man's work for him any more: 'He saw all spoiled.'

The closing section in lines 28–31 shows the details of the medical help: the 'dark of ether', the boy's breath 'puffed'. Now the lines break up into fragments as the terrible final act of the tragedy unfolds: 'No one believed.' The heartbeats ebbed away: 'Little—less—nothing!' The **sober reality hits home**: 'and that ended it.' There is now no future for the boy: 'No more to build on.' Frost has said that the reality of life is that 'it goes on'. And so the people there, because they were not the one dead, 'turned to their affairs'. No matter what horror happens in life, a new day comes. Neither the people nor the poet are being callous and unfeeling. Seamus Heaney refers to this as the 'grim accuracy' of the poem's conclusion. The long line length also signals the return to normality.

The tone in this narrative poem shades from the anger and menace of the saw, to the calm of the beautiful rural countryside, to the wistful reflections of the poet and on to the fear and horror of the accident. In the end, Frost's ironic tone gives way to the cold fear of the finality of death, when all is changed forever.

Writing About the Poem

In writing about Frost, Seamus Heaney commented, 'Here was a poet who touched things as they are, somehow'. Discuss this statement with reference to the poem, 'Out, Out—'.

Sample Paragraph

'Out, Out–' is one of Frost's most unsettling poems. The tragic story of a young boy who suffers a terrible accident while working in a saw-mill is a shocking reminder of how fragile life can be. I think it was very brave of the poet to just say things as they are, rather than pretending that life is not dark sometimes. I also felt as if I were actually in the timber yard as the saw 'snarled and rattled' in Vermont. The detail of sound and smell, 'Sweet-scented stuff', brought me there. It reminded me of Kavanagh, our Irish poet, who could see beauty in the most ordinary places. Frost, it seems to me, is also commenting negatively on the practice of having a young boy perform a man's job. The wistful 'I wish they might have said' condemns those who insisted on getting the job finished at the expense of the boy. It was too much to ask of a 'big boy', a 'child at heart'. The reality of the boy's life fading away was vividly captured by the poet in the line 'Little—less—nothing!' The punctuation adds to the effect of the heartbeat becoming weaker and finally stopping. Frost dared to say what life is like. He 'touched things as they are'. He achieved this by his craftsmanship as a poet, and his compassionate eye as a human being.

EXAMINER'S COMMENT

A thoughtful, personal exploration of the poem, using quotations that are carefully integrated into the answer, all of which results in a well-deserved top grade. Contemporary references illustrate the continuing relevance of Frost as a realistic voice. The point regarding Frost's skilful use of punctuation is well developed: 'The punctuation adds to the effect of the heartbeat becoming weaker and finally stopping.'

Class/Homework Exercises

1. It has been said that Frost's poems are 'little voyages of discovery'. Write a personal response to this poem, using quotations from the poem to support your answer.
2. 'Frost's poems are filled with disturbing reminders of life's harsh realities.' Discuss this view, with particular reference to 'Out, Out–'.

Summary Points

- **Key themes – life's unfairness and unpredictability of human existence.**
- **Highly dramatic poem, with characters facing a crisis in a particular setting.**
- **Powerful onomatopoeic effects: alliteration and assonance.**
- **Contrasting images – beautiful landscape, dangerous sawmill.**

Spring Pools

These pools that, though in forests, still reflect
The total sky almost without defect,
And like the flowers beside them, chill and shiver,
Will like the flowers beside them soon be gone,
And yet not out by any brook or river,
But up by roots to bring dark foliage on.

The trees that have it in their pent-up buds
To darken nature and be summer woods—
Let them think twice before they use their powers
To blot out and drink up and sweep away
These flowery waters and these watery flowers
From snow that melted only yesterday.

defect: blemish; flaw.

brook: small stream.

foliage: plants; undergrowth.

'darken nature'

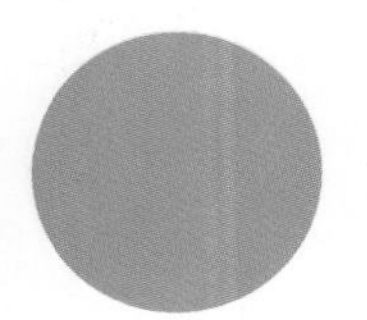

Personal Response

1. What aspects of the spring pools are conveyed in the first stanza? Refer to the text in your answer.
2. Choose one image from the poem that you found particularly striking. Briefly explain your choice.
3. Write your own personal response to the poem.

Critical Literacy

'Spring Pools' captures a moment at the end of winter during which the poet reflects on the natural cycle of growth, decay and renewal. Rain falls from the sky, settles in pools and is then drawn up into the trees. In recalling the origins of this beautiful lyric poem, Frost commented, 'One night I sat alone by my open fireplace and wrote "Spring Pools". It was a very pleasant experience, and I remember it clearly, although I don't remember the writing of many of my other poems.'

The poem's title seems to celebrate new growth and regeneration. Ironically, stanza one focuses mainly on the fragility of nature. As always, Frost's **close observation of the natural world is evident** from the start. The clear pool water mirrors the overhead sky 'almost without defect'. While the simple images of the forest and flowers are peaceful, there is no escaping the underlying severity of 'chill and shiver'. The entire stanza of six lines is one long sentence. Its slow-moving pace, repetition and assonant vowels ('pools', 'brook', 'roots') enhance the sombre mood. Pool water will be absorbed by the tree roots to enrich the leaves and create 'dark foliage'. Then water and flowers will all 'soon be gone'. Frost pays most attention to the interdependence within the natural world and the transience of the beauty around him.

In stanza two, the poet addresses the trees directly, warning them to 'think twice before they use their powers'. He personifies them as an intimidating presence, associating them with dark destructiveness and 'pent-up' energy to 'blot out and drink up and sweep away'. Such forceful language combines with a resurgent rhythm to emphasise the power of the trees. The tone **becomes increasingly regretful** in the final lines. We are left with another evocative image of how nature's beauty is subject to constant change: 'snow that melted only yesterday.'

Frost's **poem is typically thought-provoking**, touching on familiar themes regarding the mysteries of nature and the passing of time. Some critics interpret 'Spring Pools' as a metaphor for the creative process – water has long been a symbol of inspiration. Frost's own writing is wonderfully controlled, in keeping with the sense of order within the natural world that he describes. Both stanzas mirror each other perfectly and the *aabcbc* rhyme scheme completes the fluency of the lines.

Writing About the Poem

'Reflective consideration of nature is central in Frost's thought-provoking poetry.' Discuss this statement in relation to the poem, 'Spring Pools'. Refer closely to the text in your response.

Sample Paragraph

There is a sense of loss going through much of Frost's poem 'Spring Pools'. It struck me first in the negative language of the opening stanza. Frost refers to the perfect sky 'without defect', implying that something might soon destroy the perfection. The peaceful setting of the winter flowers is also spoiled when the poet points out that they 'chill and shiver'. The mood is downbeat – everything will end inevitably and 'soon be gone'. The image of the trees ('dark foliage') adds to my sense of this depressing feeling. In the second part of the poem, Frost points out the irony of springtime as a season of decay just as much as of growth. To some degree, I think this is a realistic view, but it does take away from the joy of spring. The mood deteriorates as the poem continues. The trees are seen as destructive, drying up the water and removing the flowers. They 'darken nature' – a dramatic way of summing up the overall mood of this poem.

EXAMINER'S COMMENT

This focused paragraph uses quotations effectively to communicate the central mood of the poem, 'Frost refers to the perfect sky "without defect", implying that something might soon destroy the perfection'. Some further discussion of style, particularly tone and rhythm, would have added to the answer which just fails to achieve the top grade.

Class/Homework Exercises

1. In your view, what is the central theme or message of 'Spring Pools'? Refer closely to the poem in your answer.
2. 'One of Frost's great skills is the craftsmanship he displays in using sounds to convey meaning.' Discuss this statement, with particular reference to 'Spring Pools'.

Summary Points

- **Central themes include time itself and the cycle of life, death and renewal.**
- **Contrasting moods – serious, sombre, pensive and regretful.**
- **Rich, musical effects: assonance, sibilance and emphatic end-rhyme.**
- **Characteristic use of simple, accessible language and sensuous imagery.**

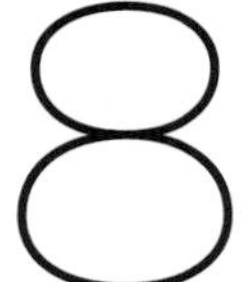

8 Acquainted with the Night

I have been one acquainted with the night.
I have walked out in rain—and back in rain.
I have outwalked the furthest city light.

I have looked down the saddest city lane.
I have passed by the watchman on his beat
And dropped my eyes, unwilling to explain.

I have stood still and stopped the sound of feet
When far away an interrupted cry
Came over houses from another street,

But not to call me back or say good-bye;
And further still at an unearthly height,
One luminary clock against the sky

Proclaimed the time was neither wrong nor right.
I have been one acquainted with the night.

luminary clock: moon; a real clock shining with reflected light; simply passing time.
Proclaimed: announced.

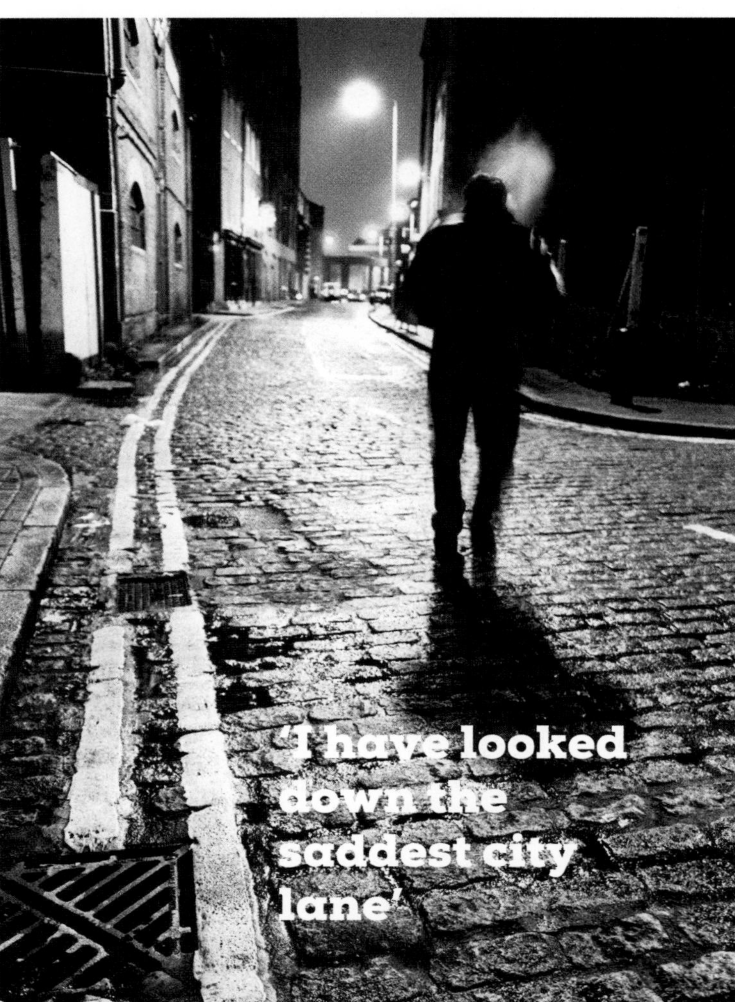

Personal Response

1. In your opinion, what is the central theme or message of this poem? Refer to the text in your answer.
2. Is there a sense of drama in this poem? Refer to the text in your answer.
3. Write your own personal response to the poem.

Critical Literacy

'Acquainted with the Night' is a sonnet from Robert Frost's collection, *West-Ring Brook* (1928). Unusually, it is set in a bleak city rather than the countryside. This is one of Frost's darkest poems and portrays an isolated figure filled with despair. It is reminiscent of the Modernist poets, such as T. S. Eliot, or the American artist Edward Hopper, whose paintings frequently showed solitary individuals.

The 20th century was a time of huge social upheaval and warfare, and was primarily focused on material progress rather than spiritual awareness. It was the century of the individual, rather than the community. Many people became alienated, lonely and confused. The certainty that institutions bring was lost, moral codes were abandoned and the traditional comforts of extended family and community began to disappear. Frost's poem begins with a declaration: 'I have been one acquainted with the night.' It is a frank statement, rather like the admissions made at an AA meeting. It is also reminiscent of the Old Testament reference to **one who was despised and rejected by men**, a man of sorrows 'acquainted with grief'. The second line in this first stanza shows the direction that the poem will take. There are two journeys: the body travels outwards towards the edge of the city ('I have walked out in rain') while the mind travels inwards to the edge of the psyche ('and back in rain').

This **alienation is echoed in the form of the poem**, which is not a conventional 14-line sonnet (either three quatrains and a rhyming couplet, or an octet and sestet); here there is a terza rima format. The poet uses a three-line rhyming stanza, concluding with a rhyming couplet (aba, bcb, cdc, ded, ff). The terza rima was used by the great Italian poet Dante in his famous poem 'The Divine Comedy' to describe the descent into hell. Is Frost using this structure in his poem because he is describing his descent into his own private hell? (His life had included many family tragedies.) This is a highly personal poem, as it uses 'I' at the beginning of seven of its fourteen lines. The rhythm imitates a slow walking movement: 'I have outwalked the furthest city light.' The poet has now gone beyond the last visible sign of civilisation. The use of iambic pentameter is the metre closest to the speaking voice in English, and the measured flow underlines the poet's melancholy mood.

The **solemn, sombre mood** of overwhelming anxiety is shown in the long vowel sounds of the second stanza: 'I have looked down the saddest city lane.' The broad vowels 'a' and 'o' lengthen the line and show the world-weariness of one who has seen and experienced too much. Although it is set at night, the traditional time for romance and lovers, we are presented with never-ending rain and gloom. A listless mood is created by the repetition of 'I have'. The run-on line suggests the relentless trudging of this weary man who is too caught up in his own dark thoughts to even bother communicating with the 'watchman'. He is 'unwilling to explain' and is jealously guarding his privacy. Is this walk symptomatic of his inner state? Can nothing penetrate this extreme loneliness?

The run-on line continues in the third stanza. Frost comes to an abrupt stop on his journey as an 'interrupted cry' rings out across the **desolate urban landscape**. Who cried? Why? And why was the cry 'interrupted'? Is something awful happening to someone? Can anything be done about it? It seems not. The poet merely remarks in the next stanza that it has nothing to do with him, 'not to call me back or say good-bye'. This is the chilling aspect of living in a big city: the sense of just being another person nobody cares about. These others have no substance, being reduced to the 'sound of feet' or a 'cry'.

In the fourth stanza, the poet speaks of a 'luminary clock'. This could be the moon or a real clock that is reflecting light. Is it symbolic of time passing incessantly? Why is it at an 'unearthly height'? Is it because time rules the human world and nothing can change this? The final couplet proclaims that the 'time was neither wrong nor right'. We are left wondering what the time was neither right nor wrong for – what was supposed to happen? There is a real **sense of confusion** here, and echoes of Hamlet's declaration that 'the time is out of joint'. The poem ends as it begins: 'I have been one acquainted with the night'. We have come full circle, though **nothing has been achieved**. We have experienced the darkness with the poet. There is no sense of comfort or guidance, only the realisation of spiritual emptiness and a hostile world.

Writing About the Poem

'Robert Frost writes dramatic lyrics of homelessness.' Discuss this statement in relation to the poem 'Acquainted with the Night'. Refer closely to the text in your response.

Sample Paragraph

The sense of homelessness is palpable in this unconventional sonnet. The individual in the poem seems to be always on his own, not connected either with family, friend or acquaintance, a loner in a big anonymous city. The form of the poem mirrors this individualism. There is no network to comfort this man, no community to offer help and encouragement. The hero does not want to engage, 'And dropped my eyes'. The poem is like a mini drama as the main character plays out his exterior action: 'I have walked out in rain', and his interior journey, 'unwilling to explain'. The setting is vividly realised as the bleak urban landscape is drawn with its endless rain and strange noises. So there is character, action, setting and mood. The music of this lyrical poem is the rhythm of a slow walk as the steady iambic pentameter tempo steps out a hypnotic beat: 'I have outwalked the furthest city light.' The broad vowels add to this sombre music as the poem grinds on relentlessly: 'I have looked down the saddest city lane.' This is indeed dark mood music, as the drawn-out vowel sounds 'lane', 'explain', 'beat' and 'feet' tap out the despair of this lonely man.

EXAMINER'S COMMENT

This paragraph addresses the three elements of the question ('homelessness', 'dramatic' and 'lyric'). The response shows a real appreciation of poetic technique, as the terms are not only explained, but are examined well in relation to the poem: 'The music of this lyrical poem is the rhythm of a slow walk as the steady iambic pentameter tempo steps out a hypnotic beat.' Assured expression throughout. A highly successful top-grade answer.

Class/Homework Exercises

1. Seamus Heaney describes this poem as 'dark'. What type of darkness is there? Is it literal or metaphorical or both? Refer to the text in your answer.
2. 'The personal narrative voice in Frost's poems can give readers an added sense of realism.' Discuss this view, with particular reference to 'Acquainted with the Night'.

Summary Points

- **Time, loneliness and the breakdown of communication are key themes.**
- **Powerful evocation of the anonymous urban atmosphere.**
- **The darkness symbolises a pervading sense of spiritual emptiness.**
- **Effective use of simple language, repetition, assonance and end-rhyme.**

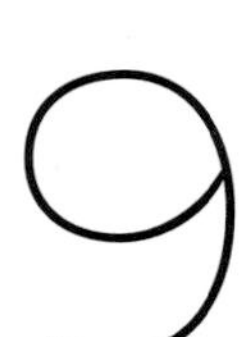

Design

The poem's title refers to the argument that the natural design of the universe is proof of God's existence.

I found a dimpled spider, fat and white,
On a white heal-all, holding up a moth
Like a white piece of rigid satin cloth—
Assorted characters of death and blight
Mixed ready to begin the morning right,
Like the ingredients of a witches' broth—
A snow-drop spider, a flower like froth,
And dead wings carried like a paper kite.

What had that flower to do with being white,
The wayside blue and innocent heal-all?
What brought the kindred spider to that height,
Then steered the white moth thither in the night?
What but design of darkness to appall?—
If design govern in a thing so small.

dimpled: indented.

heal-all: plant (once used as a medicine).

blight: disease in plants; evil influence.

witches' broth: revolting recipes used to cast spells.

thither: to there, to that place.

appall: horrify (to make pale, literally).

'a dimpled spider, fat and white'

Personal Response

1. How important a part does the colour white play in this poem? Refer to the text in your answer.
2. Select one comparison from the poem that you consider particularly effective. Briefly explain your choice.
3. Write a short personal response to the poem, highlighting the impact it made on you.

Critical Literacy

'Design' explores our attempts to see order in the universe – and our failure to recognise the order that is present in nature. Frost's sonnet raises several profound questions. Is there a design to life? Is there an explanation for the evil in the world? The poet was fascinated by nature from a philosophical point of view. His choice of the traditional sonnet form allows him to address such an important theme in a controlled way.

In the opening line, Frost describes how he finds a 'dimpled spider, fat and white' on a flower, 'holding up a moth' it has captured. The adjective 'dimpled' usually has harmless connotations far removed from the world of arachnids, but in this context, and combined with the word 'fat', it suggests an unattractive image of venomous engorgement. The colour white (used four more times in this short poem) also tends to have positive overtones of innocence and goodness. But most spiders are brown or black, and purity here quickly gives way to pale ghastliness. Indeed, the **tone becomes increasingly menacing** as the octave proceeds. The unwary moth has been lured to its grizzly death on the 'white heal-all' flower, which makes the situation even more deceitful.

Frost's chilling similes reflect the deathly atmosphere. The hapless moth is held 'Like a white piece of rigid satin cloth'. The 'characters of death' in this grim drama are compared to the 'ingredients of a witches' broth'. Lines 7–8 are particularly ironic. Frost then revises his view of the grotesque scene, seeing the **tragic coincidence** involving the 'snow-drop spider' and 'a flower like a froth'. While the images appear attractive, there is a lingering suggestion of gloom and ferocity.

The focus changes in the sestet as the tone grows passionately angry. Frost uses a series of **rhetorical questions demanding an explanation** for what he has witnessed: 'What had that flower to do with being white'? Is this implying that nature isn't so innocent after all? He reruns the sequence of events and wonders what 'steered the white moth thither in the night'. The possibility that such a catastrophic event might be part of a great 'design of darkness' appalls the poet. However, the poem's final line ('If design govern in a thing so small') is the most intriguing of all. The word 'if' leaves the possibility that there is no grand plan for the universe, that it is all accidental. Whether predestination or chance is the more terrifying reality is left for readers to consider.

Writing About the Poem

'Frost presents contrasting views on nature in his thought-provoking poetry.' Discuss this statement in relation to the poem, 'Design'. Refer closely to the text in your answer.

Sample Paragraph

In 'Design', Frost takes an ironic approach to nature. Unlike other poems (e.g. 'The Tuft of Flowers'), where he ends up being reassured by the beauty of his natural environment, 'Design' is disquieting. The first few lines describe a repulsive side of nature's basic law – kill or be killed. I found the image of the bloated spider quite revolting: 'fat and white.' The poet conveys a strong sense of the violence that takes place when nature begins 'the morning right'. Dead moths are routine – often in beautiful settings. Nature is full of such contradictions. The image of the moth like a 'white piece of rigid satin cloth' suggested the lining of a coffin and reminded me that we see signs of mortality all around us. At the same time, Frost seems to be realistic about nature. Even in violent situations, there are beautiful creatures. The 'dead wings' are compared to a graceful 'paper kite'. Overall, the poet probably shows a less attractive side to nature in the poem, but it is not altogether bleak. I liked the way he managed simple language to raise deep and disturbing questions about our natural world.

EXAMINER'S COMMENT

A balanced response, demonstrating a good understanding of the poem. References and quotations were carefully chosen and used effectively. Genuine engagement, e.g. 'The image of the moth like a "white piece of rigid satin cloth" suggested the lining of a coffin and reminded me that we see signs of our own mortality all around us'. Varied, confident expression underpins the top-grade standard.

Class/Homework Exercises

1. Sonnets frequently move from description to reflection ('sight to insight'). To what extent is this true of 'Design'? Refer closely to the poem in your answer.
2. 'Robert Frost often expresses complex ideas by using starkly contrasting images.' Discuss this statement, with particular reference to Frost's poem, 'Design'.

Summary Points

- **Sonnet form used to explore the dark unpredictability of nature.**
- **The poet challenges the belief of a divine design for the world.**
- **Variety of tones – ironic, disturbing, confrontational.**
- **Effective use of vivid imagery, startling contrasts and descriptive details.**

Provide, Provide

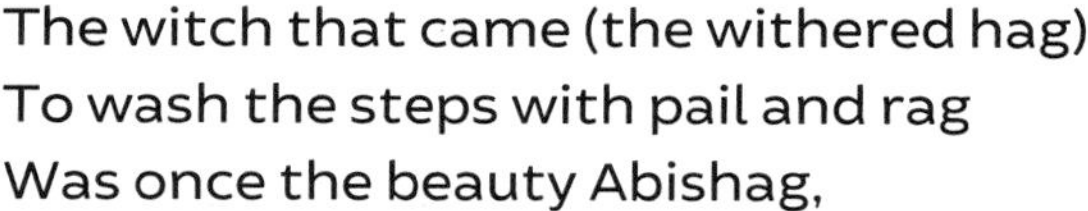

The witch that came (the withered hag)
To wash the steps with pail and rag
Was once the beauty Abishag,

The picture pride of Hollywood.
Too many fall from great and good
For you to doubt the likelihood.

Die early and avoid the fate.
Or if predestined to die late,
Make up your mind to die in state.

Make the whole stock exchange your own!
If need be occupy a throne,
Where nobody can call *you* crone.

Some have relied on what they knew;
Others on being simply true.
What worked for them might work for you.

No memory of having starred
Atones for later disregard,
Or keeps the end from being hard.

Better to go down dignified
With boughten friendship at your side
Than none at all. Provide, provide!

Abishag: beautiful young woman who comforted King David in his old age.

crone: witchlike; old, withered woman.

Atones: makes amends (for sin or wrongdoing).

boughten: bought.

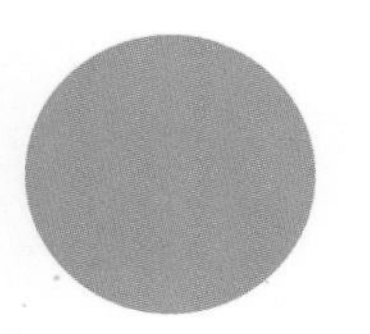

Personal Response

1. Is the advice given in the poem to be taken seriously or humorously, or a mixture of both? Discuss, using reference from the poem to support your answer.
2. What elements in the poem resemble a fairy tale or fable? Are they upbeat and reassuring or dark and disturbing? Briefly explain your answer.
3. What conclusion, if any, does the poem come to? Refer to the text to support your view.

Critical Literacy

'Provide, Provide' was written at the height of Frost's fame, in a collection entitled *A Further Rage* (1936). It was based on a real woman he had seen cleaning steps. The poem contrasts with most of Frost's work, as the tone is bitter and the emphasis is on material success. The Great Depression, a time of mass unemployment in America, was taking place. Is Frost suggesting that self-sufficiency is the answer?

The first stanza advises us to **plan for the future**. Why? A cold, bleak scene of a withered old woman doing a menial job of washing steps is given as a salutary picture of not providing. This is what happened to Abishag. The reference to the biblical character adds a timeless element – this is a truth for all generations. In this poem, old age equals diminishing beauty and success.

In stanza two, the destructive element of time is stressed as the poem comes to the present, 'Hollywood'. Even in the dream factory, beauty does not last. The tone of the poem is one of **addressing a public audience**, as if at an evangelical rally: 'For you to doubt the likelihood.' Fortune is fickle, as most people know.

The poem now offers **mock advice: the only solution is to die young** ('Die early'). Images of icons hover in our minds of tragic, famous deaths of the young and beautiful, such as James Dean and Marilyn Monroe. In the third stanza, **the only other solution is to become wealthy** and 'die in state'. An imperative verb, 'Make', in the fourth stanza encourages us to grab material success: 'Make the whole stock exchange your own!' The exclamation mark captures the mood of exhortation that pervades this unusual poem. The quaint image of the throne adds to the timeless element, as it is a universal symbol of power and wealth. Only political power, privilege and riches provide protection against the harsh reality of ageing. If 'you' don't want the same fate as Abishag, 'you' must be alert. Stanza five reminds us that there are always choices in life. Some people succeed on knowledge and ability, others on being honest and genuine.

Independence was very important to Frost. Now, in stanza six, the poem cautions us that even if our early lives were wonderful, 'having starred', that memory is not a safeguard against the misfortune that might happen later in life. Black humour in the final stanza suggests, with wry, unsentimental honesty, that it is better to **buy friendship** ('boughten') than suffer loneliness at the end of life. Is this cynical view that bought friends are better than none realistic? The poem concludes with great urgency: 'Provide, provide!' Frost did not believe in a benevolent God ruling the universe, but rather takes the view that there is an indifferent God and we are subject to random darkness. This is by no means an affirmative poem.

Frost favoured **traditional poetic structures**, declaring that he was 'one of the notable craftsmen of this time'. Here the full rhyme of *aaa, bbb, ccc, ddd,* etc. does not seem strained. We hardly notice it in such a carefully crafted poem of seven triplets. The rhythmic pattern of blank verse, set against colloquial speech, gives this poem its energy. The use of the imperative verbs, especially 'Provide, provide', demands that the reader take the poet's message on board. Frost presents **painful ideas** – in this instance a cynical view of fame and success – **in a controlled form**. He has said, 'The poems I make are little bits of order.'

Writing About the Poem

'Poetry is a momentary stay against confusion.' Discuss this statement in relation to the poem, 'Provide, Provide'. Use references from the text to support your views.

Sample Paragraph

The bleak situation painted by Frost is very different from his other poems where a quiet, sensible speaking voice alerts us to the beauties of nature. In 'Provide, Provide', the focus is on 'look out for your old age, as no one is going to want you'. I wonder if Frost was uncomfortable about being famous. Did he find the whole fame business tacky and shallow? The poem is stating that change is the only certainty and encourages us to get ourselves in order if we don't want to have a miserable time when looks and youth are gone. I like the mock serious tone in which this message is delivered: 'If need be occupy a throne,/Where nobody can call you crone.' I think this dry, cynical tone appeals especially to today's reader who is saturated with this 'fame' issue. I also think that humour is very effective in delivering a message, particularly one as unappealing as this. The airbrushed perfection of the groomed Hollywood stars is captured perfectly in the alliterative phrase: 'The picture pride of Hollywood.' But the poet knew that this is not how it is – 'the end' is 'hard'. Frost said, 'If you suffer any sense of confusion in life, the best thing you can do is make little poems'.

EXAMINER'S COMMENT

This lively, personal approach to a very challenging question effectively explores Frost's own personal circumstances, his views on poetry and life. In-depth discussion of Frost's style is satisfying – 'The airbrushed perfection of the groomed Hollywood stars is captured perfectly in the alliterative phrase: "the picture pride of Hollywood".' Impressive vocabulary and confident expression throughout. A top-grade answer.

Class/Homework Exercises

1. 'A poem begins in delight and ends in wisdom.' Is this a valid statement in relation to the poem 'Provide, Provide'? Use quotation from the poem in your explorations.
2. 'In many of his poems, Robert Frost reveals himself as neither an optimist nor a pessimist, but as a realist.' To what extent is this true of 'Provide, Provide'? Support your answer with reference to the poem.

Summary Points

- **Central themes – time's erosive power, transience and endurance.**
- **Characteristically simple, accessible language and colloquial speech.**
- **Range of tones: serious, light-hearted, mocking, ironic, cynical.**
- **Effective use of contrasting images, repetition.**

Leaving Cert Sample Essay

'Frost makes effective use of language and imagery to provide rich insights into human experience.' Discuss this view, supporting your answer with reference to the poetry of Robert Frost on your course.

MARKING SCHEME GUIDELINES

Candidates are free to agree and/or disagree with the statement. However, the key terms ('effective use of language and imagery', 'rich insights into human experience') should be addressed. Reward evidence of genuine engagement with the prescribed poems of Robert Frost.

INDICATIVE MATERIAL

- Explores universal human condition – possibilities/ inevitabilities/ tragedies/simple pleasures.
- Accessibility of conversational language, plainness of expression, narrative approach.
- Evocative imagery, sensuous details, rich symbolism add appeal.
- Profound ideas – transience, fellowship, alienation – expressed in homely/rural style, etc.

Sample Essay
(Effective use of language and imagery provide rich insights into human experience)

1. Frost has a reputation for simple subject matter – mending a wall, choosing a road, saving for old age – but he also explores complex issues. His sensible speaking voice reflects on change, isolation, human suffering, choice, regret and our relations with other people and the world of nature. Simple, conversational language makes him an accessible poet. He adopted the persona of the New England farmer inspired by nature. He was also a rebel who took the road 'less traveled by'. Frost chose not to follow the fashion of writing in free verse. Instead he preferred the forms and patterns of traditional poetry.

2. His reflective poem, 'Mending Wall', refers to an annual ritual when two neighbours would inspect and mend their boundary wall. This communal activity not only connects, it also reveals gaps in understanding between two men. The speaker in the poem delights in the wayward and the wild, 'Spring is the mischief in me'. On the other hand, his neighbour is a figure of repression who 'walks in darkness' because he receives wisdom from previous generations without questioning it. Instead, he chants the mantra, 'Good walls make good neighbors'. A powerful simile, 'like an old-stone savage', reveals a man who does not welcome change. Frost is asking us to consider whether it is necessary to break down barriers in order to live as good neighbours. Colloquial phrases gently draw us into this thought-provoking poem which reveals how co-operation between people is prevented by a lack of desire rather than outside circumstances. A slow-moving rhythm, 'something there is that doesn't love a wall' mirrors the unhurried movement of the two farmers at their steady painstaking work.

3. Nature also provides the starting point for another intricate insight in Frost's dramatic poem, 'The Road Not Taken'. Here he examines the process of decision-making and its consequences. The metaphor of the road guides readers through the different stages of making choices. There is the common human desire to avoid deciding, 'sorry I could not travel both'. The inventive rhyme scheme mimics the speaker glancing right and left while trying to decide. He then makes his choice – he 'took

the other one' and immediately regrets it. Frost is reminding us that no matter what humans have, they always desire what they don't possess, 'Oh, I kept the first for another day!' The poet is also pointing out that no one can return to the past, 'way leads on to way'. He calmly accepts, 'two roads diverged in a wood and I—/I took the one less traveled by'.

4. A very different dark and bitter tone is found in 'Provide, Provide'. Another truth is revealed, the sad reality of what happens to a person if no provision is made for the future. Neither youth, beauty nor fame last forever. Change is the only certainty. The reference to the biblical character, 'the beauty Abishag', and the symbol of the 'throne' adds to the universal significance of the poem. Frost's cynical advice, 'Die early and avoid the fate', reveals the poet's belief in an indifferent God and the ominous random forces which govern the universe. Strong imperative verbs add further energy to the poem, 'Make up your mind', 'Better go down', 'Provide, provide!'.

5. This harsh view of reality is also presented in the poet's characteristic colloquial language, 'wash the steps with pail and rag'. A striking contrast to this bleak view is the polished fantasy of Hollywood glamour, 'The picture pride'. The alliteration underlines the crafted illusion. In response to this dark vision, Frost created a poem to stand as a little bit of 'order'. Seven three-line stanzas, carefully rhymed, present his sobering idea that fame and success don't last. The poet emphasises the universal truth about the inevitability of ruin and decay. Nothing is forever.

6. Frost was a keen observer of nature's mystery. Many of his poems touch on the harmony of the natural world. He seems to always suggest that people should look to nature for meaning and fulfilment – whether in the trees or pools or in the changing seasons. But while he did not deny the harshness of life, Frost brings people in touch with its sometimes sad beauty and its simple pleasures through carefully controlled colloquial language and rich insights into the human experience.

(approx. 710 words)
(45–50 minutes)

EXAMINER'S COMMENT

An assured response, addressing the question in a focused way and showing close engagement with some of Frost's poems. The excellent introductory paragraph provided a broad overview that was followed up with very good analysis of several key poems, illustrating how the poet's distinctive style delivered interesting insights into nature and human nature. While some of the ideas mentioned in the final paragraph might have been developed more, the impressive expression and perceptive critical commentary guarantee the essay's top-grade standard.

GRADE: H1
P = 14/15
C = 13/15
L = 14/15
M = 5/5
Total = 46/50

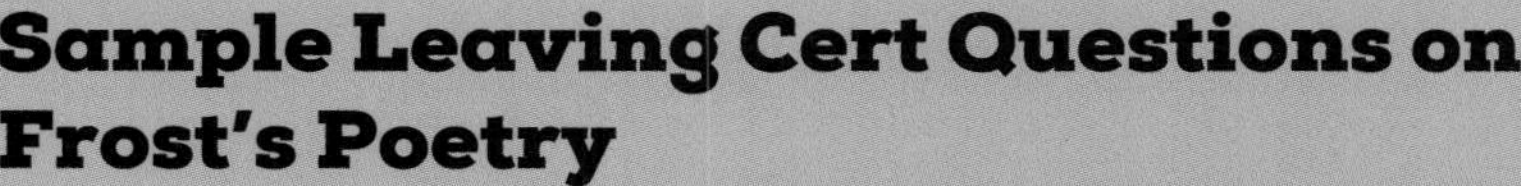

Sample Leaving Cert Questions on Frost's Poetry

1. **'Robert Frost's poetry has a contemporary feel, yet he uses traditional poetic techniques.' Discuss this statement, supporting your answer with reference to both the subject matter and style of the Frost poems on your course.**
2. **'Frost's poetry makes a powerful impact on the reader both through his outlook and use of language and imagery.' To what extent do you agree or disagree with this view? Support your answer with suitable reference to the poetry by Frost on your course.**
3. **'Robert Frost creates complex and interesting poetry from seemingly ordinary subjects.' Discuss this statement, supporting your answer with reference to the poetry of Robert Frost on your course.**

First Sample Essay Plan (Q2)

'Frost's poetry makes a powerful impact on the reader both through his outlook and use of language and imagery.' To what extent do you agree or disagree with this view? Support your answer with suitable reference to the poetry by Frost on your course.

NOTE

As you may not be familiar with some of the poems referred to in the sample plans below, substitute poems that you have studied closely.

Exam candidates usually discuss three or four poems in their answers. However, there is no set number of poems or formulaic approach expected.

Key points about a particular poem can be developed over more than one paragraph.

Paragraphs may also include cross-referencing and discussion of more than one poem.

Remember that there is no single 'correct' answer to poetry questions, so always be confident in expressing your own considered response.

Intro: Interesting themes, individualistic style. His fascination with nature and human nature. Favourite poem – 'The Road Not Taken'.

Point 1: Family – background tragic, yet it is the still, calm voice which sounds from the poem. He explores man's relationship with nature.

Point 2: 'Sound of sense' – 'Writing with your ear to the voice'. Use of first person in 'Out, Out—'. Powerful, dramatic poem highlighting the random events of life and human resilience.

Point 3: Formal rhyme – traditionalist, good craftsman, – exploration of alienation and spiritual emptiness in the modern world; striking images, repetition, disturbing urban atmosphere. 'Acquainted with the Night.'

Point 4: Metaphors – Doesn't force, allows the metaphors to speak for themselves, e.g. road is a metaphor for a life choice in 'The Road Not Taken'. Wall – symbol of human and political divisions in 'Mending Wall'.

Point 5: Other themes – natural world, endurance, ordinary life, etc. 'Spring Pools' – offers insights into the natural cycle; evocative atmosphere, sensual imagery.

Conclusion: Wrote about ordinary people living ordinary lives. View of nature bleak. Aware of time and effect on human beings.

Sample Essay Plan (Q2)

Develop **one** of the points on the previous page into a paragraph.

Sample Paragraph: Point 2

The subject matter of Frost's poetry is rooted in the natural world. But it was nature which was thought-provoking, a stimulus for the poet, leading to insight and revelation: 'A poem begins in delight and ends in wisdom.' Frost was and is accessible. He was influenced by current events and was inspired by a newspaper article to write the chilling poem of injured innocence, 'Out, Out—'. Frost believed in endurance: 'In three words I can sum up everything I've learned about life – it goes on.' The young boy's tragic accident is outlined in a series of graphic images that I found genuinely shocking. The timber yard saw 'Leaped out at the boy's hand'. In a traumatic state, he then 'lay and puffed his lips out with his breath'. In the aftermath of his death, the quiet response of all the other workers was almost as shocking. Frost's matter-of-fact account – told largely in a factual unemotional way – effectively highlighted the reality of such routine events. Darkness erupts in a random manner with tragic consequences, as in 'Out, Out—'.

EXAMINER'S COMMENT

As part of a full essay answer, this exploration shows a close knowledge of Frost's aims, his appreciation of nature and understanding of the human condition. Expressive language throughout, e.g. 'Darkness erupts in a random manner with tragic consequences' raises the answer to the top grade.

Sample Essay Plan (Q3)

'Robert Frost creates complex and interesting poetry from seemingly ordinary subjects.' Discuss this statement, supporting your answer with reference to the poetry of Robert Frost on your course.

Intro: Frost – an oft-quoted poet, achieved his wish to 'write a few poems it will be hard to get rid of'. His calm, stoical voice examines nature and human nature, exposing the metaphysical significance of a simple tuft of flowers, farm work, woodland pools and nature.

Point 1: 'Birches' – simple childhood memory poem teaches a thought-provoking lesson about how people live. Poet considers the power of his redemptive imagination. He likes the freedom of escaping but also feels the need to stay in touch with reality.

Point 2: 'After Apple-Picking' – ordinary experience of farm work transformed into subtle reflection on the disappointment of human accomplishment, writing and cycle of life. Lyrical monologue creates lethargic mood through broad vowels and sibilance ('I cannot rub the strangeness from my sight'). Poem's dreamlike atmosphere vividly evoked through repetition ('load on load of apples').

Point 3:: 'Spring Pools' – fascinating lyric poem addresses philosophical subjects - the cycle of life and the creative process. Dark mood created through slender assonance ('chill and shiver') and slow-paced broad vowels ('pools', 'brook', 'roots'). Intricate sounds convey meaning. Structure of reflecting stanzas mimics the image of the sky in the pool.

Point 4: 'Design' – traditional sonnet form similarly controls the response to the exploration of good and evil. Gross adjectives in octet ('dimpled', 'fat', 'white') create a deceitful and menacing world. Reflective sestet contains a list of terrifying challenging questions about the random or divine nature of the design of our world ('What but design of darkness to appall?').

Conclusion: Frost's deceptively simple poems offer profound truths (about human fellowship, the cycle of life, creativity, the nature of the design of our world) through vivid imagery, sound effects, structure and repetition.

Sample Essay Plan (Q3)

Develop **one** of the above points into a practice paragraph of your own. (You may wish to use a different poem that you have studied rather than the one illustrated above.)

Sample Paragraph: Point 1

Frost's charming reminiscent poem, 'Birches', teaches us an intricate life lesson on the power of a person's imaginative life. Using a developed metaphor, the poet compares human experience to a popular pastime from his boyhood, swinging on branches. A series of thoughts (from memory and fantasy) express the poet's philosophical outlook on life. He believed in discipline, beautifully expressed in the alliterative phrase, 'climbing carefully'. He also promotes persistence, 'He learned all there was/To learn'. The struggles and burdens of adulthood, 'weary of considerations', are evoked in the description of the ice-laden branches as cracked glazes on pottery. The ice is personified as a potter which, 'cracks and crazes their enamel'. Against this destruction, the poet

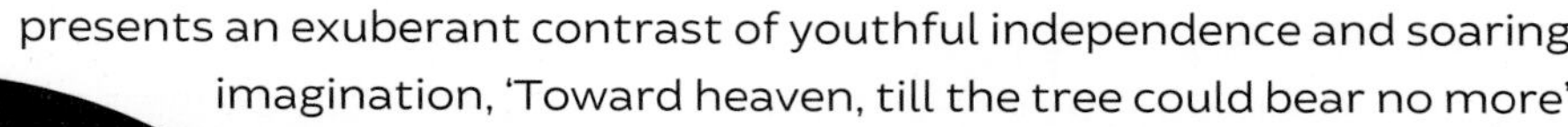

presents an exuberant contrast of youthful independence and soaring imagination, 'Toward heaven, till the tree could bear no more'. The poem does not have a rigid rhyme scheme. Instead, the commentary is written in blank verse. This mirrors the freedom of youth and the flow of imagination. Yet while boys swing on the branches, the trees are only bent momentarily and every tree is still connected to the earth. The poem's final lines are a reconciliation of human aspiration and reality, 'going and coming back'. He wants to return to earth and begin life anew.

EXAMINER'S COMMENT

As part of a full essay answer to Q3, this is a top-rate response to a challenging question. Clearly focused discussion points show a close understanding of the subtle development of thought within the poem. Very good expression of higher order ideas throughout (e.g. 'final lines are a reconciliation of human aspiration and reality'). The answer also benefits greatly from accurate and well-integrated quotations.

Class/Homework Exercise

1. **Write one or two paragraphs in response to the question: 'Robert Frost creates complex and interesting poetry from seemingly ordinary subjects.' Discuss this statement, supporting your answer with reference to the poetry of Robert Frost on your course.**

 Revision Overview

'The Tuft of Flowers'
Lyrical soliloquy meditating on themes of loneliness and methods of communication.

'Mending Wall'
Dramatic monologue addresses two contrasting perspectives (narrator/ neighbour).

'After Apple-Picking'
Thought-provoking monologue inspired by rustic activity leads to contemplation of creative process.

'The Road Not Taken'
Simple narrative exploring themes of individualism, personal choice and the consequences of making decisions.

'Birches'
Detailed descriptive nature poem reveals poet's philosophy on life.

'Out, Out–'
Dramatic narrative poem of shocking fatal accident, widening to meditation on the brevity of human existence and nature's indifference.

'Spring Pools'
Lyrical poem presents nature's destructive capabilities – blight, darkness, death. The natural world can renew itself, yet time dominates creation.

'Acquainted with the Night'
Dark meditative sonnet. Lyrical exploration of isolation and difficulties of communication through dramatic presentation of lonely figure in alien urban landscape.

'Design'
Stimulating sonnet challenges accepted belief in ordered universe and benign creator.

'Provide, Provide'
Wry illustration of time's ravages and consequences. Contrasting images of youth/age, beauty/ugliness, wealth/ poverty.

Last Words

'Like a piece of ice on a hot stove, the poem must ride on its own melting.'
Robert Frost

'Robert Frost: the icon of the Yankee values, the smell of wood smoke, the sparkle of dew, the reality of farm-house dung, the jocular honesty of an uncle.'
Derek Walcott

'I'll say that again, in case you missed it first time round.'
Robert Frost

RELATIONSHIPS

NATURE

MEANING OF LIFE

TIME

TRAVEL/ JOURNEYS

SUFFERING

D. H. Lawrence
1855–1930

'Ours is an excessively conscious age. We know so much, we feel so little.'

David Herbert Lawrence was born in Nottinghamshire, England, on 11 September 1885. A miner's son, he was to become a rebellious and polemical writer with radical views. Though better known as a novelist (*The Rainbow, Women in Love, Lady Chatterley's Lover*), Lawrence was also a prolific poet.

His collected writings represent an extended reflection on the dehumanising effects of modernity and industrialisation. In them, Lawrence confronts issues relating to emotional health and happiness, spontaneity, human sexuality and instinct.

Some of his best-loved poems address the physical and inner life of plants and animals; others are bitterly satirical and express outrage at the hypocrisy of conventional society. In much of his later poetry, he attempted to capture emotion through free verse.

D. H. Lawrence travelled extensively and spent many years in Italy. A lifelong sufferer from tuberculosis, he died on 2 March 1930 in the South of France. He is now widely regarded as one of the most influential writers of the 20th century.

Investigate Further

To find out more about D. H. Lawrence, or to hear readings of his poems, you could search some useful websites such as YouTube, BBC Poetry, poetryfoundation.org and poetryarchive.org, or access additional material on this page of your eBook.

Prescribed Poems

○ **1 'Call into Death'**
Written the year his mother died of cancer, Lawrence's poem addresses one of the great taboos of society – the reality that death comes to all. **Page 220**

○ **2 'Piano'**
One of D. H. Lawrence's best-known lyrics in which the poet reminisces about an idyllic moment from childhood and his conflicted desire to return to its warmth and security. **Page 224**

○ **3 'The Mosquito'**
This dramatic poem is presented in the form of an imagined one-sided dialogue during a confrontation between man and insect. **Page 228**

○ **4 'Snake'**
In this famous poem, Lawrence examines the conflict between education (and accepted social attitudes) and the desires people often hold. **Page 235**

○ **5 'Humming-Bird' (OL)**
Lawrence re-interprets the geological past and restores it to its own special sense of excitement. **Page 242**

○ **6 'Intimates'**
This short, witty poem dramatises the negative aspects of love and challenges appearances in relationships. **Page 246**

○ **7 'Delight of Being Alone'**
One of D. H. Lawrence's most conventional and beautiful poems, it expresses the poet's romantic attitudes about the pleasures of being alone and reflects his closeness to nature. **Page 250**

○ **8 'Absolute Reverence'**
Although Lawrence insists that he feels 'absolute reverence to nobody and to nothing human', this short poem expresses his pantheistic, mystical reverence towards a universal life force. **Page 251**

○ **9 'What Have They Done to You?'**
This fiercely persuasive condemnation of modernity describes Lawrence's aversion to machines and the industrial age. **Page 252**

○ **10 'Baby-Movements II: "Trailing Clouds"' (OL)**
This early Lawrence poem is part of a two-poem sequence ('Baby-Movements'), apparently based on a description of his landlady's baby daughter. **Page 256**

○ **11 'Bavarian Gentians'**
Lawrence explores his own journey towards death as portrayed through a variety of moods, including awareness, anger, terror and eventual acceptance. **Page 259**

*(OL) indicates poems that are also prescribed for the Ordinary Level course.

1 Call into Death

Since I lost you, my darling, the sky has come near,
And I am of it, the small sharp stars are quite near,
The white moon going among them like a white bird among snow-berries,
And the sound of her gently rustling in heaven like a bird I hear.

And I am willing to come to you now, my dear,
As a pigeon lets itself off from a cathedral dome
To be lost in the haze of the sky; I would like to come
And be lost out of sight with you, like a melting foam.

For I am tired, my dear, and if I could lift my feet,
My tenacious feet, from off the dome of the earth
To fall like a breath within the breathing wind
Where you are lost, what rest, my love, what rest!

snow-berries: round white berries eaten by birds, but poisonous to humans.

dome: round roof.

haze: mist, cloud.

tenacious: clinging, firmly held.

'among snow-berries'

Personal Response

1. Lawrence's poems explore difficult subject matter. In your opinion, what is the main theme or message of 'Call into Death'? Support your answer with reference to the text.
2. Lawrence uses several similes in this poem. Choose one that appeals to you and comment briefly on its effectiveness.
3. Write your own personal response to the poem, highlighting the impact it made on you.

Critical Literacy

'Call into Death' is part of D. H. Lawrence's two-volume *Collected Poems* (1928). He divided the collection into 'Rhyming Poems' and 'UnRhyming Poems' (to which this particular poem belongs). Lawrence wrote this poem in 1910, the year his mother died of cancer, confessing 'in that year, for me, everything collapsed, save the mystery of death, and the haunting of death in life. I was twenty-five and from the death of my mother, the world began to dissolve around me, beautiful, iridescent, but passing away substanceless. Till I almost dissolved away myself and was very ill ...'

This tender 12-line elegy has the poet crying out in the direction of death like a mystic in the desert, attempting to get attention. Lawrence's relationship with his mother was close, 'so sensitive to each other that we never needed words'. The poet had also suffered several relationship break-ups in the year prior to his mother's death. Genuine emotion is caught in the plain, honest conversational expression: 'Since I lost you, my darling' (line 1). Lawrence turns his back on traditional poetry that elaborated and decorated poetic verse for effect, not feeling. He believes that the experiences of loss have given him a **new insight into life**, the oneness of the ordered universe, 'the sky has come near'. He feels part of it now: 'I am of it.' The sibilant alliteration, 'small, sharp stars', accentuates the pinpoint light radiating from these planets.

Lawrence's vivid **observational skill** is displayed in the beautiful simile of the moon moving like 'a white bird among snow-berries' (line 3). A haunting sense of the unity of all creation is conveyed in the imagery pattern. The long irregular line length mirrors the moon's majestic journey through the heavens, while insistent rhyme ('near', 'hear') adapts to the idea of the oneness of the universe and man. Onomatopoeia ('rustling') conveys the soft sound of the mother bird searching for food. Lawrence fully acknowledges the natural inclusion of death in life, just as the 'white moon' shines in the dark sky – though it is not always visible to the human eye – and the 'white bird' is camouflaged among the white berries.

The second verse opens with a warm term of endearment, 'my dear', as the poet wishes to immediately and voluntarily join his loved one, 'I am willing to come to you now'. Using another simile, Lawrence expresses his wish to launch himself into oblivion, 'As a pigeon lets itself off from a cathedral dome/To be lost in the haze of the sky' (lines 6–7). The bird disappears from view of the human world, lost in the mist and clouds, yet it still lives. **Death and life are not separate events**, but part of the whole human experience. Like the bird, Lawrence needs to become invisible to the human eye and join his beloved, 'like a melting foam'. Irregular rhyme ('dome', 'come', 'foam') adds a subtle quality to the harmonious mood. The repetition of the suffix 'ing' in the first and last lines of the two verses knits them closely together ('darling'/'rustling', 'willing'/'melting').

The **lethargic mood** in the third verse is in contrast to the previous two. Lawrence admits the reason for his wish to leave this world, 'For I am tired'. But his feet cling stubbornly to the earth, 'tenacious'. The repetition of 'feet' suggests the sheer physical effort the poet is making in his attempt to escape, not like the bird from the dome of a cathedral, but from the 'dome of the earth' (line 10). However, there is a final sense of resurgence as he imagines the effortless flight into the realm of his loved one. Lawrence sees himself easing into death with the grace of a breath joining the wind. The gentle repetition and affectionate tone of 'what rest, my love, what rest' brings the poem to a serene conclusion.

The poet has succeeded in **confronting one of the great taboos** of society, the terrifying reality that death comes to all. He has even emphasised its advantages. Characteristically, his honest poetry confronts one of life's bitterest experiences, death and loss. In the final poignant verse, Lawrence changes his linking mechanism, joining the verb 'lift' in line 9 with 'lost' in its concluding line, and unlike the previous two verses, there is no rhyme. His wish is not granted. He cannot yet escape the earth.

Writing About the Poem

'D. H. Lawrence's poetry addresses complex ideas in fresh, vivid yet controlled language.' Discuss this statement in relation to 'Call into Death'.

Sample Paragraph

The complex concept of death in the midst of life is explored successfully by Lawrence in 'Call into Death'. One of his beliefs was that death is not an end, but is part of the cycle of life. If something is not seen by humans, that does not mean it is not there. It is still there. The human eye may not always be able to see the moon or a high flying bird, but they are still

there. Using precisely observed details from the natural world, Lawrence puts forward his intricate view of life and death. Repetition and the comparison of 'a white bird among snow-berries' illustrates the difficulty of seeing what is actually there. The ease of the descent into oblivion is vividly captured by another simile, 'a pigeon lifts itself off from a cathedral dome'. Bodily substance disappears into another simile, 'melting foam'. But the wish and the reality conflict. Hard 't' sounds show the strong pull of the earth on the living, 'tired', 'lift', 'feet', 'tenacious'. Yet the poem ends with the wish of entering another level of consciousness, spontaneously falling into easeful death, as naturally as 'a breath' joins 'the breathing wind'. Life is not final any more than the dead are totally disconnected from the living; they exist in our memory.

EXAMINER'S COMMENT

Shows close engagement with the poem. Overall, a high-grade standard that focuses well on the two elements of the question – ideas and style. Despite some slight awkwardness of expression, there are some supported discussion points that effectively explore Lawrence's beliefs in the natural life cycle and his innovative use of sound effects.

Class/Homework Exercises

1. 'Lawrence's poems are spontaneous and fresh, but they often investigate dark and disturbing subjects.' Discuss this view with reference to the poem 'Call into Death'.
2. 'Lawrence's personal poetry engages readers through carefully composed language and imagery.' To what extent is this true of 'Call into Death'? Support your answer with reference to the poem.

Summary Points

- **Central themes include death, loss, longing, grief, escape, peace.**
- **Poetic techniques – irregular line length, rhyme and linking devices, sound effects.**
- **Effective use of imagery drawn from the natural world.**
- **Varied tones – affection, sorrow, longing, tiredness, sense of achievement, etc.**

2 Piano

Softly, in the dusk, a woman is singing to me;
Taking me back down the vista of years, till I see
A child sitting under the piano, in the boom of the tingling strings
And pressing the small, poised feet of a mother who smiles as she sings.

In spite of myself, the insidious mastery of song
Betrays me back, till the heart of me weeps to belong
To the old Sunday evenings at home, with winter outside
And hymns in the cosy parlour, the tinkling piano our guide.

So now it is vain for the singer to burst into clamour
With the great black piano appassionato. The glamour
Of childish days is upon me, my manhood is cast
Down in the flood of remembrance, I weep like a child for the past.

vista: scenic view, panorama.

poised: perched, composed.

insidious: subtle, deceptive.
Betrays: tricks, compels.

clamour: loud noise, racket.
appassionato: impassionate performance.
glamour: charm, mystique.

'great black piano appassionato'

Personal Response

1. Based on your reading of the poem, do you agree that memory can be both fascinating and troubling? Support your answer with reference to the text.
2. Choose one aural image from the poem that appeals to you and comment briefly on its effectiveness.
3. Write your own personal response to the poem, highlighting the impact it made on you.

Critical Literacy

'Piano' is one of D. H. Lawrence's earliest and best-known lyrical poems. It was published in 1918 when he was 33 years old. In this candid record of controlled emotion, Lawrence reminisces about his happy childhood and his conflicted desire to return to its warmth and security. He believed in the 'rich, piercing rhythm of recollection, the perfected past'.

Lyrical poetry expresses strong emotion, typically from a first-person point of view. Lawrence's title has multiple aspects. While 'Piano' refers to the concert that the adult poet is attending in the present, it is also a reference to Lawrence's childhood memory of listening to his mother playing. Interestingly, the word 'piano' itself is the Italian musical direction to play softly.

Aptly, the poem begins with the adverb, 'Softly'. Immediately, a **gentle mood** is being created, 'in the dusk', just between evening and night-time. The atmosphere is entirely appropriate for a poem exploring connections and disconnections between past and present. Lawrence describes a somewhat anonymous event: 'a woman is singing', the atmospheric 's' sounds similar to that of a whisper. The absence of detail initially suggests a lack of engagement on his part but it also releases him to travel down the 'vista of years'. This metaphor of such a panoramic view evokes the wide expanse of the past which poet and reader alike must journey through to reach childhood again. Each has to travel 'back down' from the heights of maturity and adulthood.

The recollections of the past are sharp and detailed, in contrast to the bland opening scene in the present. The **descriptive flashback** reveals a tender image of a young child sitting 'under the piano', pressing his mother's feet while she plays and sings. In line 3, the viewpoint suddenly changes to the third person ('A child') as the poet realises that he is no longer that little boy. The use of tactile imagery and the present tense ('sitting', 'pressing') conjures up a vivid sensual memory. Indeed, the scene is one of familiar comfort and childlike innocence, of intimacy and security.

Lawrence makes full use of **aural techniques**, particularly assonance ('boom', 'tingling strings') to convey the contrasting deep and high piano notes. The mother's grace and skill are highlighted in the detail 'small, poised feet'. Simple language has established a nostalgic, happy serenity throughout the first stanza. Sibilant 's' and slender vowel sounds ('smiles', 'sings') evoke an ideal picture of a relaxed family scene.

In the more sombre second quatrain, the poet indulges in self-analysis. The focus on how the flashback makes him feel brings the outlook back to the first person. Lawrence recalls his childhood days with reluctance ('In spite of myself'). Knowing that he is being sentimentally nostalgic, he is unwilling to return to the past – as many people are – because sometimes it is simply too sad to remember happy times and to realise that they are gone for good. A run-on line features the subtle, **treacherous allure of earlier times**, 'the insidious mastery of song/Betrays me back'. The explosive 'b' in the alliterative phrase delivers the message that he feels he has been cheated. As an adult, Lawrence is now aware of the gap between his idealised childhood perceptions and the reality of loss.

Yet he has been inveigled into the past by the singing and he is overwhelmed ('the heart of me weeps'). The disjointed syntax reflects his obvious distress. Lawrence desperately **longs for his old identity** back in the comforting family home. His romantic feelings flow, unstoppable for 'the old Sunday evenings at home', 'And hymns in the cosy parlour'. The cold 'winter outside' provides a fitting contrast to this warm sanctuary. Ironically, the 'tinkling piano' still acts as a moral compass. In childhood, it represented the close connection ('our

guide') between mother and child. Now it counsels the poet about the gulf between childhood and adulthood.

The third stanza opens with the conjunction, 'So', indicating the effects of revisiting the past. Lawrence is now no longer interested in the present. He feels it is both useless and arrogant ('vain') of the musician at the concert to display vocal artistry. His wry dismissal is expressed in the negative phrase, 'burst into clamour'. The heavily stressed 'great black piano appassionato' contrasts starkly with the appealing 'tinkling piano' and its broad vowels mimic the melodramatic artistic display of emotion. The **poet admits that he has been seduced** by 'The glamour/Of childish days'. Even the unusual juxtaposition of the more adult noun 'glamour' alongside 'childish' suggests the superficial deception of memory. Lawrence accepts that he is looking at the past through rose-tinted glasses.

In the end, the **power of remembrance breaks him**, 'my manhood is cast/Down'. He has been led from the beginning ('Taking me back', 'Betrays me back') although he is fighting what he sees as a sentimental response. Placing the adverb 'Down' at the beginning of the line emphasises the conflict Lawrence is experiencing by being lured back in time. He reverts to behaving in the frank, open manner of a child, publicly displaying his feelings, 'I weep like a child'. The gentle sounds of his mother on a Sunday evening have surpassed the sophisticated dramatic performance of the singer in the present. More than anything, he now wants 'the past'.

Although the poem explores the floodgates unleashed by random memories, its **form is tightly controlled**. Three quatrains (four-line stanzas) trace the progress of thought in the poem, alternating present and past with inner and outer feelings. The couplet rhyme scheme *(aa-bb-cc-dd-ee-ff)* is reminiscent of a simple hymn or nursery rhyme. The sprung rhythm (irregular metrical stress on key words) reflects ordinary speech ('Softly', 'Taking', 'Betrays', 'Down'). However, the long, irregular line lengths at the conclusion of each stanza and the frequent use of enjambment suggest the uncontrolled 'flood of remembrance' that can sweep away restraint.

Throughout this beautiful and haunting poem, Lawrence is writing from the perspective of a middle-aged man. But in his subconscious mind, his childhood and adulthood are almost one, as he weeps 'like a child for the past'. In this there is a duality and a contrast. As in so much of his poetry, he portrays the complex workings and dealings of the human heart in a characteristically refined and elegant manner.

Writing About the Poem

'D. H. Lawrence's poems often explore the devastating consequences of memory in carefully composed lines.' Discuss this view, with particular reference to 'Piano'.

Sample Paragraph

Lawrence carefully crafts his lyric poem, 'Piano', into three quatrains which move seamlessly from present to past and back again. Using rhyming couplets ('me'/'see', 'strings'/'sings', 'song'/'belong'), the poet seeks to control the overpowering 'flood of remembrance' activated by the spark, 'in the dusk, a woman is singing to me'. The secretive, underhand way memory works soon overcomes him emotionally. The adult Lawrence is 'cast /Down', broken and weeping for what can never be, a return to the happy security of childhood days. The poem itself works just as 'insidiously' on the readers, pulling them back through the rhythms and rhymes reminiscent of simple childhood songs. Lawrence's memories will not be contained neatly into the three quatrains, but break through in frequent enjambment ('The glamour/Of childish days') and irregular line lengths, particularly in the last two lines of the first stanza when he describes his memory of sitting as a child under the piano. The poet's careful juxtaposition of the appealing 'glamour' of childhood with the discordant 'clamour' of the singer clearly shows how memory has conquered him. The poem concludes with the realisation of his paradoxical position, openly expressing his distress and nostalgia for the past while still feeling guilty at his betrayal of the present.

EXAMINER'S COMMENT

A well-written response that focuses effectively on the poet's use of language techniques in treating the theme of memory. Informed discussion points on structure, rhyme, enjambment and contrast are aptly illustrated. Assured expression (using varied sentence length and impressive vocabulary) throughout contributes greatly to the top-grade standard.

Class/Homework Exercises

1. 'Lawrence's poetry often struggles to record immature experience faithfully and yet at the same time escape from it.' In your opinion, how true is this of 'Piano'? Support your answer with reference to the poem.
2. 'D. H. Lawrence explores the country of the heart in intricate, sensual poetry.' To what extent is this evident in 'Piano'? Support your answer with reference to the poem.

Summary Points

- **Central themes include recollection, loneliness, self-awareness.**
- **The opening stanza juxtaposes the present with childhood recollections.**
- **Aural effects – repetition, assonance and onomatopoeia – vividly recreate the past.**
- **The poem's structure reflects the poet's struggle with memory.**
- **Conflicting moods of nostalgia, regret, longing and pragmatism vie in this lyric.**

The Mosquito

When did you start your tricks,
Monsieur?

What do you stand on such high legs for?
Why this length of shredded shank,
You exaltation?

Is it so that you shall lift your centre of gravity upwards
And weigh no more than air as you alight upon me,
Stand upon me weightless, you phantom?

I heard a woman call you the Winged Victory
In sluggish Venice.
You turn your head towards your tail, and smile.

How can you put so much devilry
Into that translucent phantom shred
Of a frail corpus?

Queer, with your thin wings and your streaming legs,
How you sail like a heron, or a dull clot of air,
A nothingness.

Yet what an aura surrounds you;
Your evil little aura, prowling, and casting a numbness on my mind.

That is your trick, your bit of filthy magic:
Invisibility, and the anaesthetic power
To deaden my attention in your direction.

But I know your game now, streaky sorcerer.
Queer, how you stalk and prowl the air
In circles and evasions, enveloping me,
Ghoul on wings
Winged Victory.

Settle, and stand on long thin shanks
Eyeing me sideways, and cunningly conscious that I am aware,
You speck.

Mosquito: Spanish word meaning 'little fly'. This small midge-like insect feeds on blood and is a transmitter of harmful diseases.

tricks: mischievous, deceitful actions.
Monsieur: formal address to a Frenchman ('sir').

shredded shank: ragged lower legs.
exaltation: joy.

Winged Victory: statue of Nike, Greek Goddess of Victory.
sluggish: listless, slow-moving.

translucent: glowing, radiant.
phantom: ghost, spirit.
corpus: body, mass.

heron: long-legged fish-eating bird.
clot: lump.

aura: force, glow.

anaesthetic: deadening, numbing.

sorcerer: magician, wizard.

evasions: avoidances, equivocations.
Ghoul: ghost, spirit.

speck: spot, scrap.

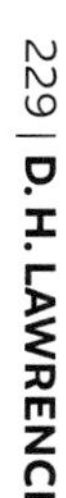

I hate the way you lurch off sideways into air
Having read my thoughts against you.

Come then, let us play at unawares,
And see who wins in this sly game of bluff.
Man or mosquito.

You don't know that I exist, and I don't know that you exist.
Now then!

It is your trump,
It is your hateful little trump,
You pointed fiend,
Which shakes my sudden blood to hatred of you:
It is your small, high, hateful bugle in my ear.

Why do you do it?
Surely it is bad policy.

They say you can't help it.

If that is so, then I believe a little in Providence protecting the innocent.
But it sounds so amazingly like a slogan
A yell of triumph as you snatch my scalp.

Blood, red blood
Super-magical
Forbidden liquor.

I behold you stand
For a second enspasmed in oblivion,
Obscenely ecstasied
Sucking live blood,
My blood.

Such silence, such suspended transport,
Such gorging,
Such obscenity of trespass.

You stagger
As well as you may.
Only your accursed hairy frailty,
Your own imponderable weightlessness
Saves you, wafts you away on the very draught my anger makes in its snatching.

lurch: stagger, sway.

game of bluff: contest, scam.

trump: winner, decider.

fiend: villain, devil.

Providence: destiny, wisdom.

enspasmed: suddenly caught.
oblivion: unconsciousness, nothingness.

obscenity: indecency.
trespass: invasion.

imponderable: unknown.
wafts: blows.
draught: breeze.

Away with a paean of derision,
You winged blood-drop.

Can I not overtake you?
Are you one too many for me,
Winged Victory?
Am I not mosquito enough to out-mosquito you?

Queer, what a big stain my sucked blood makes
Beside the infinitesimal faint smear of you!
Queer, what a dim dark smudge you have disappeared into!

Siracusa

paean: rapturous expression.
derision: contempt, mockery.

infinitesimal: tiny, insignificant.
smear: mark, splodge.
smudge: spot, scrap.

'I know your game now, streaky sorcerer'

Personal Response

1. Based on your reading of the poem, describe the encounter between man and creature. In your opinion, is it fascinating or disturbing, or both? Support your answer with reference to the text.
2. Choose one example of repetition used in the poem that appeals to you and comment briefly on its effectiveness.
3. Write your own personal response to the poem, highlighting the impact it made on you.

Critical Literacy

D. H. Lawrence's 1923 poetry collection, *Birds, Beasts and Flowers*, was named after a Victorian hymn and included 'The Mosquito'. Lawrence reflects on the 'otherness' of the non-human world in this visualisation of the animal kingdom. He wrote 'The Mosquito' on 17 May 1920 while staying at the Grand Hotel in Syracuse, Sicily. In his memoirs, Lawrence recalls it as 'a rather dreary hotel – and many bloodstains of squashed mosquitos on the bedroom walls'. He exclaimed, 'Ah, vile mosquitos!' This inspired his confident, witty poem.

'The Mosquito' is an odd, contradictory poem in the form of an imagined **one-sided dialogue** on the occasion when man confronts insect. The narrative voice is presented in verse paragraphs and the spaces between are occupied by the presence of the mosquito whose internal responses are interpreted by the poet.

The mosquito is a small midge-like fly that lives by piercing human skin and sucking blood. This can cause a nasty rash. The insect, while not dangerous itself, can be the carrier of diseases, such as malaria and the Zika virus.

At first, the speaker is slightly condescending, **adopting a superior attitude to the little mosquito** by addressing it sarcastically with extravagant titles ('Monsieur', 'You exaltation') and wondering about its deceptive 'tricks' (line 1). The poet poses a series of questions: 'What do you stand on such high legs for?' Alliteration suggests the insect's threadlike thinness, 'shredded shank' (line 4). Yet, while physically insignificant, the creature has the ability to defy the forces of nature – and is able to 'lift your centre of gravity upwards' – unlike human beings. Its flimsy buoyancy fools the poet who can barely feel it, 'Stand upon me weightless'. Lawrence remains focused on the insect's insubstantiality – like a spirit or 'phantom' (line 8). It reminds him of how a woman he once knew described the mosquito as 'the Winged Victory', a famous statue in the Louvre Museum honouring Nike, the Greek goddess of Victory. Both insect and statue inhabit moments where action and stillness meet. The ominous irony is that the malaria-transmitting mosquito, winged itself, can boast its own past conquests of mankind. The poet notes that the creature's flowing movement and action of alighting contrasts sharply with the stagnant canals of Venice.

In line 11, Lawrence describes the mosquito's threatening action in the alliterative phrase, 'You turn your head towards your tail'. It is almost as if **the creature is aware of its own power**. He even imagines it beginning to 'smile', turning the tables on him and gaining control. In response, Lawrence's own attitude also changes. He no longer regards the insect with patronising amusement, but becomes puzzled and afraid. The poet recognises the insect's slightness ('translucent phantom shred/Of a frail corpus') as bizarre, 'Queer' (line 15). He attempts to rationalise the flimsiness of what he sees, 'thin wings and streaming legs' by using the simile, 'like a heron', the long-legged wading bird. Yet the mosquito still has a forceful quality. Lawrence becomes fascinated by its 'evil little aura'. He sees it as a 'prowling' predator stalking its prey. It has assumed the position of authority and the poet is reduced to the paralysis of a victim, 'casting a numbness on my mind'. The extended line winds slowly – just like the encircling insect.

By line 20, Lawrence finally has the answer to the question he initially posed regarding the mosquito's 'tricks'. He accepts that it can cast a spell ('filthy magic') – the undetected creature has the power to sedate or freeze its prey. He even suggests the hypnotic effect of the insect through internal half-rhymes ('attention', 'direction'). However, in line 23 the poet suddenly becomes hyper-aware, 'I know your game now'. **The battle between nature and human nature is on**. The striated insect's mesmerising quality is conveyed in the soft sibilant description, 'streaky sorcerer'. Lawrence regards its ability to inhabit the air as unsettling and eerie. Broad vowels capture the lazy circling of the hunter-insect ('stalk', 'prowl') while the poet continues to feel increasingly trapped. In frustration, he resorts to name-calling, 'Ghoul on wings', but then he remembers the statue to Victory. Is the insect about to get its victory by alighting on the poet? The tension rises.

Once again, **the insect out-manoeuvres the man**. Not only does the mosquito use its ace card, but it also sounds its 'high, hateful bugle' in the poet's ear. He analyses the mosquito's behaviour, using formal business language to criticise its tactics, 'Surely it is bad policy'. But the creature does not operate in this way, surviving instead on instinct. A single, stand-alone line announces, 'They say you can't help it'. For a moment, Lawrence relaxes because he believes that 'Providence' is protecting the blameless, 'the innocent'. But he becomes aware of the insect's mantra ('slogan') and the climax of the poem is reached in line 48 when the mosquito finally strikes ('snatch my scalp'). Sinister sibilance underlines the the insect's deceit.

A striking incantatory passage draws attention to **the goal of the mosquito**, 'Blood, red blood'. Its sole quest was always for something 'Super-magical/ Forbidden liquor'. The creature is consumed into total ecstasy as it gorges on the poet's blood, 'enspasmed in oblivion'. Lawrence is outraged because it has invaded his blood-being, ('My blood') and has grossly violated their

separateness by crossing a forbidden frontier, 'Such obscenity of trespass' (line 59). The exaggerated effect of the mosquito's action on the poet is conveyed in the repetition of 'Such'.

Lawrence is satisfied at witnessing the insect 'stagger', commenting wryly, 'As well as you may'. He now treats it as one who has become intoxicated. But once more, it is the mosquito's weightlessness that lifts it out of harm and past the poet's exhaling breath. The **insect's escape is caricatured** by the very long line, 'Saves you, wafts you away on the very draught my anger makes in its snatching'. We can sense Lawrence's extreme frustration in his futile attempts to catch the annoying creature.

Not for the first time, the **mosquito reigns supreme**, emitting a 'paean of derision', a joyful expression of disdain. And once again, Lawrence is reduced to impotent abuse: 'You winged blood-drop' (line 66). Three rapid quick-fire questions simulate the poet's breathless dash as he rushes around the room attempting to catch the tiny creature, culminating in the pathetic, convoluted 'Am I not mosquito enough to out-mosquito you?' The poet is now less important than his enemy. He has fallen very far from his opening position of the condescending man patronising the little insect. The mosquito is 'Winged Victory'. Yet, while Lawrence reluctantly admits to some admiration for its cleverness and strategy, it is not enough to prevent him from swatting it, reducing the creature to a 'dim dark smudge'.

So **the man eventually kills**. Is this how humans react when confronted by something beyond their understanding? Lawrence comments on how remarkably big the 'stain' of his own blood is in contrast to the tiny 'infinitesimal faint smear' (line 72) of the insect. Is he attempting to reassert his earlier dominance? We are left to consider whether man has really won by this act of annihilation. Or has the insect actually reduced man to the animal status, persuading him to follow the law of the jungle, kill or be killed?

As in so much of his narrative poetry, Lawrence writes in **free verse**. Certain repeated words ('Queer', 'Such', 'Winged Victory'), spacing between the verse paragraphs, and the internal pattern of sounds ('shredded shank', 'attention', 'direction') all create rhythm and structure. The carefully chosen vocabulary ('devil', 'evil', 'filthy', 'evasions', 'sideways', 'cunningly', 'fiend', 'obscenity of trespass', 'accursed') adds to the association of the insect with wickedness in the poet's mind.

Lawrence believed that free verse was appropriate for poetry of the 'immediate present'. Through this form, he involves the reader in his account of a random clash between man and nature. The poem follows the rhythm of **a hostile exchange**, tracing the outraged thoughts and almost manic tussle of wills between human and creature from the opening threat and ensuing contest to bloodshed and closing death.

Writing About the Poem

'D. H. Lawrence's poems capture the raw physical world with intensity and vigour.' Discuss this view, with particular reference to 'The Mosquito'.

Sample Paragraph

'The Mosquito' opens with a direct address from the patronising speaker who is quick to mock the mosquito – 'When did you start your tricks, Monsieur?' Lawrence immediately creates the vividly individualised presence of the insect with its 'shredded shanks' as it confronts the human. Through the poet's skill, we nervously follow the angry human as he observes the increasingly annoying insect. His growing irritation is conveyed in vindictive references to the insect's perceived personality, 'pointed fiend'. The mosquito never stops moving, it preys, it will 'stalk and prowl the air'; and manoeuvre in 'circles and evasions'. The creature is gradually challenging the human's supremacy by its 'anaesthetic power'. The man's helplessness is graphically conveyed through forceful language, 'deaden my attention in your direction'. The predator succeeds in 'enveloping', sealing the man. But it is the act of sucking blood from the outraged victim that is most intensely and vigorously highlighted. Short, abrupt lines conjure up the power of the mosquito as it gorges on 'Blood, red blood', 'My blood'. Its intense action is emphasised through repetition ('Such gorging'), which almost leaves it helpless, 'You stagger'. Reading the poem, I get a strong sense of how the insect is only following the rules of the natural world, obeying its instinct for survival.

EXAMINER'S COMMENT

Very good confident response that focuses on the raw physicality of nature. Discussion points are suitably supported with suitable references. Expression is impressive, with a strong, varied vocabulary ('individualised presence', 'perceived personality', 'manoeuvre', 'mystical transcedence'). Overall, a top-grade response, well rounded off with the concluding sentence.

Class/Homework Exercises

1. 'D. H. Lawrence strips away sentimentality and consolation through his free verse poems.' In your opinion, how true is this of 'The Mosquito'? Support your answer with reference to the poem.
2. 'Conflict and drama are recurring features in Lawrence's poems.' Discuss this statement, with particular reference to 'The Mosquito'.

Summary Points

- **Man's relationship with nature and the animal world is a central theme.**
- **Powerful aural effects – repetition, alliteration, sibilant 's'.**
- **Satanic and magical terms, unusual similes and metaphors.**
- **Long sweeping lines interspersed with short one-/two-word lines.**
- **Range of attitudes, e.g. arrogance, uneasiness, derision, frustration, fulfilment, aggression, etc.**

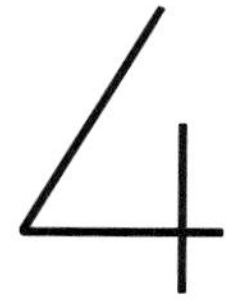

Snake

A snake came to my water-trough
On a hot, hot day, and I in pyjamas for the heat,
To drink there.

In the deep, strange-scented shade of the great dark carob-tree
I came down the steps with my pitcher
And must wait, must stand and wait, for there he was at the trough before me.

He reached down from a fissure in the earth-wall in the gloom
And trailed his yellow-brown slackness soft-bellied down, over the edge of the stone trough
And rested his throat upon the stone bottom,
And where the water had dripped from the tap, in a small clearness,
He sipped with his straight mouth,
Softly drank through his straight gums, into his slack long body,
Silently.

Someone was before me at my water-trough,
And I, like a second-comer, waiting.

He lifted his head from his drinking, as cattle do,
And looked at me vaguely, as drinking cattle do,
And flickered his two-forked tongue from his lips, and mused a moment,
And stooped and drank a little more,
Being earth-brown, earth-golden from the burning bowels of the earth
On the day of Sicilian July, with Etna smoking.

The voice of my education said to me
He must be killed,
For in Sicily the black, black snakes are innocent, the gold are venomous.

And voices in me said, If you were a man
You would take a stick and break him now, and finish him off.

But must I confess how I liked him,
How glad I was he had come like a guest in quiet, to drink at my water-trough
And depart peaceful, pacified, and thankless,
Into the burning bowels of this earth?

snake: limbless reptile; some are poisonous.
trough: container.

carob-tree: Mediterranean red-flowered tree.
pitcher: container, small bucket.

fissure: crevice, opening.

slackness: looseness, sagging.

second-comer: late arrival.

mused: reflected, wondered.

bowels: depths, underground.
Etna: Mount Etna, an active volcano in Sicily.

venomous: poisonous, deadly.

Was it cowardice, that I dared not kill him?
Was it perversity, that I longed to talk to him?
Was it humility, to feel so honoured?
I felt so honoured.

perversity: obstinacy, contrariness.

And yet those voices:
If you were not afraid, you would kill him!

And truly I was afraid, I was most afraid,
But even so, honoured still more
That he should seek my hospitality
From out the dark door of the secret earth.

He drank enough
And lifted his head, dreamily, as one who has drunken,
And flickered his tongue like a forked night on the air, so black,
Seeming to lick his lips,
And looked around like a god, unseeing, into the air,
And slowly turned his head,
And slowly, very slowly, as if thrice adream,
Proceeded to draw his slow length curving round
And climb again the broken bank of my wall-face.

thrice adream: in deep unconsciousness.

And as he put his head into that dreadful hole,
And as he slowly drew up, snake-easing his shoulders, and entered farther,
A sort of horror, a sort of protest against his withdrawing into that horrid black hole,
Deliberately going into the blackness, and slowly drawing himself after,
Overcame me now his back was turned.

I looked round, I put down my pitcher,
I picked up a clumsy log
And threw it at the water-trough with a clatter.

clatter: crashing sound.

I think it did not hit him,
But suddenly that part of him that was left behind convulsed in undignified haste.
Writhed like lightning, and was gone
Into the black hole, the earth-lipped fissure in the wall-front,
At which, in the intense still noon, I stared with fascination.

convulsed: shuddered, collapsed.

Writhed: thrashed, struggled.

And immediately I regretted it.
I thought how paltry, how vulgar, what a mean act!
I despised myself and the voices of my accursed human education.

paltry: low, contemptible.

And I thought of the albatross,
And I wished he would come back, my snake.

For he seemed to me again like a king,
Like a king in exile, uncrowned in the underworld,
Now due to be crowned again.

And so, I missed my chance with one of the lords
Of life.
And I have something to expiate;
A pettiness.

Taormina

albatross: white ocean bird; a metaphor for worry or guilt. In Coleridge's poem, 'The Rime of the Ancient Mariner', an albatross was the bird that a sailor repented killing.

expiate: correct, redress.

pettiness: spitefulness, small-mindedness.

Personal Response

1. In your own words, describe the mood and atmosphere that Lawrence creates in lines 1–13.
2. Choose two vivid images from the poem and comment briefly on the effectiveness of each.
3. In your view, what is the central theme or message of 'Snake'? Support your answer with reference to the poem.

Critical Literacy

'Snake' was written when D. H. Lawrence was living in Taormina, a hilltop town on the east coast of Sicily, in 1920–21, and is probably his best-known poem. It dramatises a confrontation between the refined human mind and the native forces of the earth, embodied by a snake that appears one morning at the narrator's water-trough. The experience is transformed by Lawrence and invested with mythical grandeur. The poem can be examined not only as a prime example of Lawrence's free verse technique, but as one in which the 'immediate present' comes to life on the page and in the mind of the reader.

The poem's opening lines establish the sweltering Mediterranean setting. 'On a hot, hot day', Lawrence's narrator takes his pitcher to the water-trough. Repetition – a prominent feature of this free verse poem – initiates the **hypnotic rhythm**. Lawrence's style is simple, the diction colloquial, and the word order that of common speech. But the effect is reserved and dignified. Domestic and exotic images are combined as the pyjama-clad human observes the snake 'In the deep, strange-scented shade of the great dark carob-tree'. At first, the presumptuous narrator views the snake as an intruder forcing him to 'stand and wait'.

Light and dark are contrasted in the snake's vivid golden colour and the surrounding gloom. Lawrence conveys the creature's physicality with emphasis on his 'straight mouth', 'slack long body' and flickering 'two-forked tongue'. Run-through lines and emphatic sibilant sounds suggest the snake's **slow, subtle movement**. The poet stretches his sentences, using multiple adjectives in lines such as 'yellow-brown slackness' and 'soft-bellied down' (line 8). Many phrases such as these use hyphenation, so that several words are elongated. Lawrence also hooks his sentence-long stanzas together by beginning lines with conjunctions: 'And must wait', 'And trailed'. When we trace the visual structure of the lines on the page, it seems almost as if the snake has swallowed the poem's form.

Lines 7–13 provide a **sensual description** of the animal's precise behaviour. Unlike the human observer, it acts entirely on instinct. Yet Lawrence personifies the reptile: 'He reached down', 'sipped with his straight mouth'.

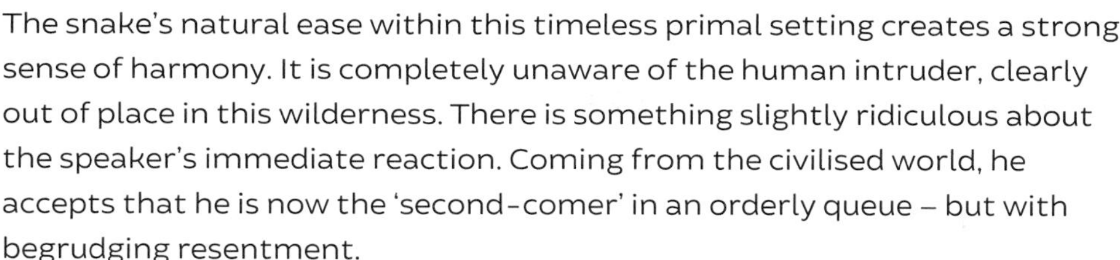

The snake's natural ease within this timeless primal setting creates a strong sense of harmony. It is completely unaware of the human intruder, clearly out of place in this wilderness. There is something slightly ridiculous about the speaker's immediate reaction. Coming from the civilised world, he accepts that he is now the 'second-comer' in an orderly queue – but with begrudging resentment.

The tense stand-off between the human and natural worlds continues through lines 16–26. Compelled by an inherent reverence, the narrator watches closely as the snake drinks. He focuses on its graceful movements, comparing it to domesticated farm animals, 'drinking cattle'. Slow, deliberate rhythms suggest the intense heat and languor of the **sultry Mediterranean atmosphere**. But this is where the snake is in its true element: 'earth-golden from the burning bowels of the earth.' Meanwhile, distant volcanic smoke from Mount Etna testifies to the inner earth's hidden powers.

Both fear and fascination are evident in the speaker's **internal struggle** between rational and natural feelings. His 'education' has always warned him that the snake is dangerous: 'in Sicily the black, black snakes are innocent, the gold are venomous.'

Although he has been taught to destroy these creatures, he cannot bring himself to harm the snake because he 'liked him' and was glad 'he had come like a guest in quiet' (line 28). This tense scene can also be interpreted on a symbolic level. Associated with evil, the snake assumes a more ominous meaning. Emerging from the 'burning bowels of this earth', it is particularly suggestive of the biblical serpent.

The narrator continues to struggle with the two conflicting 'voices' he hears: one insists that the snake should be killed while the other maintains that it deserves respect and must therefore be spared. In his **conflicted, deepening consciousness**, the speaker moves from casual description to insightful confession. An urgent series of rhetorical questions reflects this intense inner debate: 'Was it cowardice, that I dared not kill him?' Increasingly conscious that he does not belong in the underworld of the snake, he wavers between an uncomfortable sense of 'perversity' and feeling 'honoured' (line 32). But the expectations of his masculine conditioning persist: 'If you were a man', '*If you were not afraid, you would kill him!*'

The powerfully crafted syntax and unbroken rhythm of lines 41–49 work together to produce a **mesmerising effect**. Repeated references to the snake's dreamlike and unhurried presence add to the wistful tone. The narrator envisions this majestic creature as a mythical lord of the underworld ('like a god, unseeing'), an embodiment of all those mysterious forces of nature that man fears and neglects. Lawrence's detailed imagery is characteristically compelling. The snake's black tongue flickers 'like a forked night on the air', the dramatic simile suggesting a lightning flash plunging the noon-day scene into momentary night. It seems as though dark powers inhabit the 'door of the secret earth': Mount Etna might erupt, the deadly snake might strike. Suddenly the tone becomes harsh and ugly as the speaker reverts to the conditioned reflex of a rationalistic culture.

Faced with the snake's withdrawal into a fissure ('the blackness'), the narrator's **fearful imagination takes over** and he almost becomes incoherent. His disgust expresses itself in hysterical terms – 'dreadful', 'horrid'. He is overcome by 'a sort of protest' that causes him to act: 'I picked up a clumsy log/And threw it at the water-trough' (line 56). This cowardly action has an instant effect; the snake loses its former dignity and becomes 'convulsed', an obscene writhing thing, a reptile of the mind.

It's interesting that the narrator expresses neither triumph nor relief, but **deep revulsion** and self-disgust at causing such pointless violence: 'immediately I regretted it' (line 63). He regards his behaviour as 'mean' and 'vulgar', likening himself to the fictional Ancient Mariner who killed the albatross and was then compelled to acknowledge his offence. The speaker's 'paltry' action leads him to reverse the usual hierarchy. It is his 'human education' that is 'accursed', while in its majestic naturalness, the snake remains 'one of the lords /Of life' (line 71). The snake has recoiled into the underground and now appears to be like 'a king in exile', whereas in the open air it was a powerful sovereign. The ending fades away on a note of self-loathing as the narrator comes to terms with the 'pettiness' of what he has done.

Lawrence's 'Snake' is a typically resonant discourse between the teachings of reason and natural intuition. The poet presents us with a triumph of style and idiom, a highly memorable example of free verse where perception is embodied in rhythms that are an essential part of the poem's meaning. Religious terminology – of atoning for sin – would indicate that Lawrence is using the snake as a symbol of the battle between good and evil. Perhaps its real significance lies in the wider questions it raises about how human beings face up to the moral challenges of the natural world.

Writing About the Poem

'Drama and tension are recurring features of Lawrence's poems.' Discuss this statement, with particular reference to 'Snake'.

Sample Paragraph

D. H. Lawrence's poem 'Snake' has many dramatic elements, particularly conflict. The poet sets the scene on a 'hot day' in Sicily where the central character is in his pyjamas beside a water-trough. The atmosphere is edgy with intense heat. He is immediately challenged by the 'yellow-brown' snake seeking water and a stalemate occurs. In the background, a volcanic mountain adds to the tension – 'Etna smoking'. I thought that the real conflict was taking place within the man's mind, saying 'take a stick and break him now'. This internal debate is agonising. Several rhetorical questions show how conflicted the man is – 'Was it cowardice?' His upbringing and 'education' tell him to kill but he feels 'so honoured' that the snake is seeking 'hospitality'. This drama continues throughout the poem. Lawrence also uses striking, dramatic images of darkness and light to illustrate the conflict between good and evil. The snake has come from 'the dark door of the secret earth'. When the drama reaches a climax and the man throws the stick at the snake, it retreats back into the 'horrid black hole'. In a way, the conflict has been resolved and the man is left with his guilt – an anti-climax.

EXAMINER'S COMMENT

Informed discussion focusing well on aspects of drama (setting, conflict, tension, climax, contrasting images). Ranges over a variety of points, e.g. 'internal debate is agonising'. Supporting quotations are integrated successfully into the commentary. Expression is clear, but slightly pedestrian, e.g. the second-last sentence. Overall, a good, solid response that just falls short of the top grade.

Class/Homework Exercises

1. 'D. H. Lawrence makes effective use of rhythm and repetition to convey meaning in his poems.' To what extent is this true of 'Snake'? Support your answer with reference to the poem.
2. 'Lawrence's poetry often addresses themes that have a universal significance.' To what extent do you agree with this view? Support your answer with reference to 'Snake'.

Summary Points

- **Key themes include the natural world, human culture, nature, sin and guilt.**
- **Conflicting 'voices' within him represent natural instinct and cultural conditioning.**
- **Dramatic tension created by the confrontation between man and nature.**
- **Effective use of precise description, vivid imagery, contrasting tones and moods.**
- **The rhythm of the loose verse often suggests the snake's movement.**

Humming-Bird

There are over 300 species of humming-birds. All are small and brilliantly coloured. They get their name from the humming sound created by their rapidly beating wings. They are the only group of birds able to fly backwards.

I can imagine, in some otherworld
Primeval-dumb, far back
In that most awful stillness, that only gasped and hummed,
Humming-birds raced down the avenues.

Before anything had a soul,
While life was a heave of Matter, half inanimate,
This little bit chipped off in brilliance
And went whizzing through the slow, vast, succulent stems.

I believe there were no flowers then,
In the world where the humming-bird flashed ahead of creation.
I believe he pierced the slow vegetable veins with his long beak.

Probably he was big
As mosses, and little lizards, they say, were once big.
Probably he was a jabbing, terrifying monster.

We look at him through the wrong end of the long telescope of Time,
Luckily for us.

Española

Primeval-dumb: pre-historic, elemental, primordial.

Matter: substance.
inanimate: lifeless.

succulent stems: luscious stalks.

'ahead of creation'

Personal Response

1. From your reading of lines 1–4, what image do you get of the prehistoric world? Support your answer with reference to the text.
2. Choose two aural images from the poem that appeal to you and comment briefly on their effectiveness.
3. In your opinion, what point is Lawrence making in line 15: 'We look at him through the wrong end of the long telescope of Time'?

Critical Literacy

Like so many of the poems in Lawrence's *Birds, Beasts and Flowers* collection (published in 1923), 'Humming-Bird' has a fresh, modern feel and spontaneity. It is thought that Lawrence wrote this short poem after reading several vivid descriptions of humming-birds, so it is probably not a record of immediate experience. Instead, the poet reinterprets the geological past and restores it to its own special sense of excitement. Through his poetic imagination, he creates a timeless image of the humming-bird whose life force evokes the hidden power of its evolution.

The poem travels 'far back' in geological time to the origin and predominance of the humming-bird. Lawrence sets the chilling scene: 'some otherworld/Primeval-dumb.' He imagines the 'most awful stillness' of a strange pre-historic setting. When the humming-bird appears, it flashes through the poem: 'raced down the avenues.' The ecstatic opening four lines include playful internal rhyme ('dumb', 'some') and sibilant effects ('stillness', 'gasped') that suggest the **unexpected presence** of these primal creatures.

Dynamic verbs ('chipped off', 'whizzing') capture the life force and energy of the humming-bird, highlighting the 'awful stillness' of the surrounding 'half inanimate' natural environment where sprawling plants leave only 'avenues' between them. **Lawrence controls the pace of the poem** beautifully – contrasting the lumbering 'heave of Matter' with the agility and darting pace of the humming-bird, which is 'a little bit chipped off in brilliance' (line 7). In this unfamilar primeval location, these small birds provide an unexpected striking flash of colour.

The poet is filled with enthusiasm and a childlike sense of wonder about pre-human times, 'Before anything had a soul'. He sees the humming-bird as the first independent entity to evolve from undifferentiated matter – the original isolated soul. Lawrence is also **a master of free verse and informal language**. Throughout 'Humming-Bird', the pace alternates between the shorter curt lines and the longer free-winging descriptions associated with the bird in flight: 'And went whizzing through the slow, vast succulent stems' (line 8). Throughout the poem, this jaunty lilt to the rhythm mirrors the bird's swift movement.

In imagining the long distant past, Lawrence considers how the earliest birds would have survived in a flowerless environment by living off the sap of plants ('pierced the slow vegetable veins'). A range of song-like **auditory techniques** – the onomatopoeic verb, slender vowels and the alliterative 'v' effect – echoes the determined efforts to survive within the prehistoric habitat.

Reiteration and recapitulation are features of Lawrence's train of thought, which is propelled forward and held together by such repeated phrasing as 'in some otherworld', 'In that most awful stillness' and 'I believe', 'I believe'. Such repetition continues into the poem's final lines where the poet speculates on the likely size of the first humming-bird: 'Probably he was big' and 'Probably he was a jabbing, terrifying monster' (line 14). The emphasis on the humming-bird's antecedents is disturbingly realistic. But although this is a somewhat bizarre vision, Lawrence clearly rejoices at the nightmare image he has created.

He concludes on **an ironic note**, personifying the bird and showing it appropriate respect. The thought that the prehistoric creature was 'once big' – and indeed monstrous – should make us revise our attitude to his smaller, contemporary counterpart 'through the long telescope of Time'. The poet might well be reminding readers that humans were not always masters of creation. Is he warning us against complacency and that there will also be something new to displace the old?

The 'long telescope of Time' – the image magnified by the capitalised 'T' – occupies an extended line, whereas the succinct line 16 startles us with the implication of **human limitation**. Today's humming-birds are small and – as the telescope metaphor indicates – we see them in inappropriate scale. The colloquial final line, 'Luckily for us', half-humorously leaves the reader to decide how a proper perspective might challenge our own human status and exaggerated sense of self-importance.

Lawrence's **witty poem quivers with energy**, mirroring the alternating order and chaos inherent in creation. It typifies many of the poet's hallmarks – the lightness of touch, the immediacy of the voice and quicksilver language – all of which are the perfect embodiment of the wondrous humming-bird.

Writing About the Poem

'D. H. Lawrence's most memorable poems have a spontaneity and sense of drama that make an immediate impact on readers.'

Sample Paragraph

'Humming-Bird' is an exotic, highly imaginative poem in which the poet imagines the bird in a primeval-dumb world, in an 'awful stillness' before 'anything had a soul,/While life was a heave of Matter'. Lawrence begins with the words 'I imagine' and then takes us on a dreamlike journey to when life was starting to evolve on Earth. It's a very dramatic scene. Then suddenly out of the great void, the humming-bird is seen as flashing 'ahead of creation', piercing 'the slow vegetable veins with his long beak'. The images of nature are vivid and cinematic. The sense of immediacy is evident in the conversational language and everyday speech rhythms used by the poet – 'This little bit chipped off in brilliance' for example, referring to how the colourful bird accidentally evolved into life. Some of the expressions are youthful – 'Probably he was big' and 'Luckily for us'. The poet's tone is always one of excitement and wonder. I liked Lawrence's personal enthusiasm and his fascination with these tiny birds. The poem was both thoughtful and playful – almost like a song in its lively rhythm – the kind of spontaneous poetry that I enjoy.

EXAMINER'S COMMENT

A good personal response to the question. The focus on spontaneity is sustained throughout and includes interesting points on Lawrence's dreamlike poetic vision and informal language use. There is also some impressive discussion on key aspects of dramatic style (imagery, rhythm and tone). Overall, a confident high-grade standard.

Class/Homework Exercises

1. 'Lawrence often makes imaginative use of evocative sound effects to convey meaning in his poetry.' Discuss this statement with particular reference to 'Humming-Bird'.
2. 'Throughout much of his poetry, D. H. Lawrence is primarily interested in making discoveries.' Discuss this view, with particular reference to 'Humming-Bird'.

Summary Points

- **Free verse achieves greater emotional intensity than simple fragmented prose.**
- **Lawrence articulates the essence of the humming-bird.**
- **He also challenges us to re-evaluate our views on evolution.**
- **Effective use of varying line lengths and informal tone.**
- **Wide-ranging aural effects – repetition, sibilance, assonance and alliteration.**

Intimates

Intimates: close friends (n.), implies (v.).

Don't you care for my love? she said bitterly.

I handed her the mirror, and said:
Please address these questions to the proper person!
Please make all requests to head-quarters!
In all matters of emotional importance
please approach the supreme authority direct!
So I handed her the mirror.

And she would have broken it over my head,
but she caught sight of her own reflection
and that held her spellbound for two seconds
while I fled.

Personal Response

1. Based on your reading of the poem, describe the relationship between the speaker and his female companion. Support your answer with reference to the text.
2. Lawrence uses several poetic techniques in the poem, including direct speech, repetition, alliteration and run-on lines. Choose one technique that particularly appeals to you and comment briefly on its effectiveness.
3. Write your own personal response to the poem, highlighting the impact it made on you.

Critical Literacy

'Intimates' is a short, witty poem from Lawrence's collection, *More Pansies*, published in 1932 after his death from tuberculosis. In his introduction, the poet wrote: 'This little bunch of fragments is offered as a bunch of pensées ... handful of thoughts.' They were based on 'Pensées' by the French philosopher Blaise Pascal, fragments of thoughts and theology, such as, 'Do you believe people to wish good of you? Don't speak'. Lawrence also refers to the French word 'panser', to dress or bandage a wound. He regarded these verses as medicinal, administering them to the emotional wounds we suffer in modern civilisation. He regarded 'Each little piece' as a thought which comes from the heart, 'with its own blood and instinct running in it ... if you hold my pansies properly to the light, they may show a running vein of fire'.

The title, 'Intimates', if used as a noun suggests a loving relationship, but if as a verb, it can mean 'insinuates' or 'hints'. Lawrence sets up the expectation that this couple really understand each other. However, the poem begins with jolting directness and readers are placed, without warning, in the middle of a **spiteful argument** between the couple. A woman's acerbic question plaintively intones, 'Don't you care for my love?' (line 1). She is complaining about a lack of concern for her happiness and the welfare of their relationship. The use of the verb 'said' indicates that this is more a statement than a plea. Her tone is harsh: 'bitterly.' The implication is clearly that the man is not particularly interested.

But he is stung into action and hands her 'the mirror'. The definite article suggests that she used this mirror frequently. In a clipped detached tone, he issues a list of formal requests. The repeated use of the word 'Please', usually found in polite conversation, seems not only absurd but sardonic and cold. The alliteration of the hard 'p' sound ('Please', 'proper person') conveys an anger barely concealed. The adjective 'proper' (line 3) not only refers to the correct person to whom the questions should be addressed, but also indicates a prudish one. Meanwhile, he continues to reprimand her, 'Please make all requests to head-quarters'. The **sarcastic inference** of this odd remark suggests that the fraught relationship is being controlled by a third party or some other outside influence.

The speaker feels increasingly **frustrated**, as it appears that the woman is not even listening to him. Paradoxically, in stilted language that is anything but sensitive, he directs that 'all matters of emotional importance', should be with the person who has the unnamed official power that can enforce obedience, 'please approach the supreme authority direct' (line 6). He then concludes his terse argument with the conjunction 'So'. It is left to the reader to decide whether the section concludes as 'and then' he handed her the mirror or 'therefore' he handed her the mirror. If the latter is the case, it would signify that he thinks he has won the argument. Lawrence places a creative pause at this stage to allow us to imagine the woman's feelings of anger rising.

Line 8 discloses that the speaker knew precisely what he was doing all along and is also able to predict the outcome of his actions. He has given his companion the mirror to look at her reflection because, in his opinion, she feels that she is the 'the proper person', the 'head-quarters', 'the supreme authority'. This implies a certain smugness in the woman's attitude; she is always right. We are left with the impression that **this is not the first hurtful exchange** between the couple. These 'intimates' know each other very well and so can deliver cruel blows in a quarrel. The conditional 'she would have broken it over my head' infers that their rows often descend into physical violence.

However, the mood changes on the conjunction 'but'. Wryly, the speaker recounts how the woman sees herself in the mirror and becomes mesmerised by 'her own reflection'. The use of the pronoun 'own' and the emphatic verb 'spellbound' paint a picture of an extremely **self-interested person**. Run-on lines capture the 'two seconds' she spends gazing at herself. They hint at the vanity of the fairy tale Wicked Queen who asks 'Mirror, mirror on the wall, who is the fairest of them all?' Line 11 heralds the man's last evasive action, 'while I fled'. Fearing the worst, he makes a hasty escape while his companion is preoccupied. The monosyllabic verb 'fled' has a finality that suggests a victory of sorts in this particular skirmish. The man has escaped the stifling constraints of the woman's demands – for the moment.

While the female character in this poem has been exposed as domineering and self-obsessed, the man's behaviour throughout has not exactly been admirable. Is the poet suggesting that while the couple know each other well, they are by no means 'Intimates'? The only victim of their feud is the relationship itself. This unsettling poem challenges readers. The poet has **presented this small domestic drama through quoted conversation and actions**, but has refrained from commenting directly. Is the poem simply holding up a reflective surface allowing the reader to look at personal relationships and the lack of successful communication? Lawrence believed that poetry makes us more aware of ourselves. 'Intimates' provides an opportunity to examine the conflict between frustration and fulfilment in relationships and in ourselves.

Writing About the Poem

'D. H. Lawrence believed that all poems should be personal sentiments with a sense of spontaneity.' Discuss this statement in relation to the poem 'Intimates'.

Sample Paragraph

In this elegant, bitter poem, Lawrence parachutes unsuspecting readers into the midst of the swirling emotions of a squabbling couple. 'Intimates' opens on the jarring note of a complaining woman, 'Don't you care for my love?' The spontaneous combustion of frustration and lack of fulfilment is conveyed through reported conversations and the behaviour of the woman and her partner. I felt as though I was actually eaves-dropping on a private moment. The man's spontaneous action in handing the mirror to the self-obsessed woman and his list of deeply wounding orders suggests a dysfunctional couple. Genuine personal sentiments are disclosed – the woman does not feel appreciated while he feels harangued by 'the supreme authority'. At the same time, the reader's sympathy sways towards the rather vain woman who is subjected to such derision. She also has to contend with a man who runs away – another unexpected development. He, however, feels stifled by her superiority, 'the proper person'. An insistent rhyme adds to the man's growing feeling of claustrophobia, 'said', 'head', 'fled'. Through capturing the spontaneity of the fight, Lawrence reveals the truth to all couples, the irony that scoring points in an argument is not genuine contact and only succeeds in destroying the relationship.

EXAMINER'S COMMENT

Good, intelligent high-grade response that engages closely with the poem. The idea of spontaneity is addressed effectively through specific expressions (such as 'parachutes', 'spontaneous', 'unexpected' and 'growing'). Apt quotations are successfully integrated into the discussion and assured vocabulary ('derision', 'harangued by', 'contend with', 'feeling of claustrophobia', etc.) is impressive.

Class/Homework Exercises

1. 'Lawrence's poetry often uses particular everyday scenes to explore issues that have much wider universal significance.' Discuss this view with reference to the poem, 'Intimates'.
2. 'D. H. Lawrence's carefully crafted poetry frequently challenges social constraints.' To what extent is this true of 'Intimates'? Support your answer with reference to the poem.

Summary Points

- **Central themes include conflict, lack of communication, vanity, deception.**
- **Poetic techniques – direct speech, contrast between personal and formal language, alliteration, repetition, run-on lines, creative pause, paradox.**
- **Varied tones – disappointment, hurt, anger, sarcasm, mockery, etc.**

7 Delight of Being Alone

I know no greater delight than the sheer delight of being alone.
It makes me realise the delicious pleasure of the moon
that she has in travelling by herself: throughout time,
or the splendid growing of an ash-tree
alone, on a hill-side in the north, humming in the wind.

Critical Literacy

This is one of Lawrence's most conventional and beautiful poems. It was published after his death in *Last Poems* (1932).

The simple directness and sincerity of the opening line shows Lawrence's enthusiasm for 'the sheer delight of being alone'. His emphasis on 'delight' establishes the mood of deep satisfaction. The poet's acknowledgment of the 'delicious pleasure of the moon' is enhanced by the use of **richly sibilant sounds**. As always, Lawrence's appreciation of nature is beyond doubt. The moon has long been a traditional symbol of solitude and self-sufficiency – and the poet now senses its mysterious power 'throughout time'.

To some extent, line 2 reads like an excerpt from the diary of a man who is seriously ill and close to death. This would explain Lawrence's desire to take up a form outside of his human body, that of the night-wandering moon. He is also drawn to the 'splendid growing of an ash-tree ... humming in the wind', described with characteristically precise eloquence. The poem takes on a **mystical quality** with the final suggestion that Lawrence's soul may return to become part of the greater spirit of the timeless natural world. Lawrence's attraction to the moon and the lonely tree on a hillside is the refuge of his poetic imagination – the last refuge.

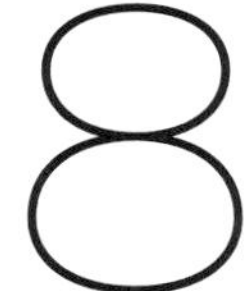

Absolute Reverence

I feel absolute reverence to nobody and to nothing human,
neither to persons nor things nor ideas, ideals nor religions nor institutions,
to these things I feel only respect, and a tinge of reverence
when I see the fluttering of pure life in them.

But to something unseen, unknown, creative
from which I feel I am a derivative
I feel absolute reverence. Say no more!

reverence: devotion, worship.
ideals: dreams, principles.
institutions: organisations, establishments.
tinge: touch, hint.

derivative: product, result.

Critical Literacy

D. H. Lawrence always maintained that he was 'a profoundly religious man'. His religion was certainly real enough, but unorthodox and informal. For Lawrence, it was essentially mystical, similar to other visionary poets, such as Shelley and Yeats.

The poem's emphatic opening establishes Lawrence's belief that all of reality is identical with divinity. His passionate tone ('I feel absolute reverence to nobody and to nothing human') can be understood positively as the view that nothing exists outside of God. He goes on to clarify his deeply felt opposition to conventional doctrines and organised religions.

The poet's sympathies lie entirely with what he calls 'the fluttering of pure life', an image that immediately evokes the vitality and beauty of nature. His God is the transcendent reality of which the material universe and human beings are mere manifestations.

D. H. Lawrence's poetry is a long and rich exploration of reverence towards the mystery of embodied life: 'something unseen unknown, creative/from which I feel I am derivative.' There is no logic in such lines, but they sum up Lawrence's pantheistic, mystical, unswerving and wholly sincere worship of life and the life force that lies at the root of all his thinking.

'fluttering of pure life'

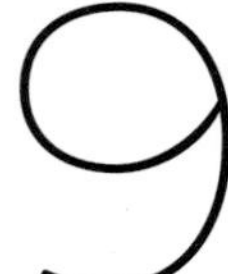

What Have They Done to You?

What have they done to you, men of the masses, creeping back
and forth to work?

What have they done to you, the saviours of the people, oh what have
they saved you from while they pocketed the money?

Alas, they have saved you from yourself, from your own frail dangers
and devoured you from the machine, the vast maw of iron.

They saved you from your squalid cottages and poverty of hand to
mouth
and embedded you in workmen's dwellings, where your wage is the
dole of work, and the dole is your wage of nullity.

They took away, oh they took away your man's native instincts and
intuitions
and gave you a board-school education, newspapers, and the cinema.

They stole your body from you, and left you an animated carcass
to work with, and nothing else:
unless goggling eyes, to goggle at the film
and a board-school brain, stuffed up with the ha'penny press.

Your instincts gone, your intuitions gone, your passions dead
Oh carcass with a board-school mind and a ha'penny newspaper
intelligence,
what have they done to you, what have they done to you, Oh what
have they done to you?

Oh look at my fellow-men, oh look at them
the masses! Oh, what has been done to them?

the masses: the working classes.

saviours: redeemers, protectors.

Personal Response

1. In your opinion, what is the dominant tone of this poem? Is it angry, powerful, ironic, sentimental, uncontrolled, etc.? Support your answer with reference to the text.
2. Choose one memorable image (visual or aural) from the poem and comment on its effectiveness.
3. Based on your reading of the poem, what impression do you get of the poet, D. H. Lawrence? Support your answer with reference to the text.

Critical Literacy

D. H. Lawrence did not profess to be a socialist, but there can be no doubt that he possessed strong ideas about what he believed was wrong with the money-wages-profit system and what sort of society would be best for humans to live in. Lawrence describes his aversion to modernity in 'What Have They Done To You?'. The poem is thought to have been written during the poet's visits to Majorca and Tuscany in 1929.

Throughout his literary work and poetry, D. H. Lawrence expressed his criticism of modernisation as reflected in urban poverty, steel mills and factory work. The poem opens with an **impassioned rhetorical question** that directly challenges uncontrolled materialism: 'What have they done to you, men of the masses, creeping back and forth to work?' The alliterative 'm' sound suggests the countless numbers of industrialised employees who are diminished by their adverse working conditions. Lawrence's choice of the emotive verb, 'creeping', emphasises the notion of suppression and dependency.

The impassioned rhetorical tone and emotive language, which will dominate the entire poem, continues in line 2 as the poet mocks the so-called 'saviours of the people'. In accusing the wealthy employers of exploitation ('they pocketed the money'), Lawrence points out the obvious irony that this was the only saving involved. But the poet's anger is moderated with expressions of **regretful frustration** ('Alas'). However, his compassion for the poor and their 'frail dangers' is quickly replaced by fury at what he sees as their victimisation. The new industrial age has: 'devoured you with the machine, the vast maw of iron.' Lawrence's choice of violent metaphorical language symbolises the monstrous dehumanising effect of mass mechanisation.

Lines 5–6 focus on the wretched 'hand to mouth' living conditions of working-class people who are expected to be grateful for any kind of employment. Repulsive imagery ('squalid cottages') and broad vowel

'the vast maw of iron'

assonance ('mouth', 'dole', 'nullity') add to our understanding of the pathos Lawrence associates with such widespread hardship. The extended line lengths and turgid rhythms also suggest their relentless struggle for survival.

A significant change of emphasis occurs in line 7, however, when **the poet broadens his scathing criticism**. Up until this point, the 'they' targeted by Lawrence referred to the powerful factory owners and captains of industry. Now he turns his attention to the **wider establishment forces** in politics and education: 'board-school education, newspapers, and the cinema.' From his point of view, ordinary people are not just oppressed by poverty, but are also controlled through the conservative school system. In addition, their lives are further diminished by cheap journalism and popular entertainment.

The tone becomes increasingly melodramatic as Lawrence rages against the ruling class – those who misuse power to stifle creativity and reduce the common worker to a passive 'animated carcass' (line 9). In a series of exasperated outbursts, he again attacks the country's press and media, and castigates the film industry – presumably for producing undemanding escapism designed for 'goggling eyes'. The 'ha'penny press' is further accused of keeping readers' minds 'stuffed up' with useless information.

The poet's central argument that most ordinary citizens are systematically diverted from improving their lives builds to a climax in the final lines. Questions now begin with the exclamatory 'Oh', highlighting the anguish he feels. The plaintive repetition of 'what have they done to you?' is all but an **admission of utter despair**. In contrast to the protracted oratorical style throughout the poem, the ending is terse and to the point. Lawrence's reference to his 'fellow-men' (line 16) has particular significance both with and without irony. While he is aiming a final cynical blow at those who have no respect for humanity, there is no denying the poet's own tender feeling for other people. Indeed, the entire poem is primarily a persuasive expression of Lawrence's aversion to modernity – articulated through repetitive language describing the monotonous, menial tasks of factories and the enslavement of his fellow Britons. In strongly denouncing the dehumanising effects of industrialisation, the poet raises interesting questions about modern society and community, about freedom and constraint. It is left to readers to decide whether Lawrence's use of hyperbole and excessive rhetoric enriches or devalues his sentiments.

Writing About the Poem

'D. H. Lawrence writes dramatic poems that often combine polemical commentary with heartfelt compassion.' Discuss this view, with particular reference to 'What Have They Done to You?'.

Sample Paragraph

When we first studied 'What Have They Done to You?', it actually seemed much more like a political speech rather than a poem. Lawrence held very strong views and believed that the traditional English way of life had changed for the worst. In his opinion, factory towns and sweatshops had turned workers into slaves. The poem has a dramatic opening, with an oratorical tone: 'What have they done to you, men of the masses?' The poem is filled with persuasive techniques, especially repetition. Lawrence uses negative images of 'squalid' houses and assembly-line workers being 'devoured' by the 'vast maw of iron'. He views modern-day life as totally unnatural. Although the language suggests savagery, there is always a sense that the poet's main concern is with the vulnerable workers and their poverty-stricken families. Expressive verbs such as 'took away' and 'stole' express his compassionate concern for these unfortunate people. The 'animated carcass' comparison combines Lawrence's anger at their mistreatment with his sympathy for such people. This dual tone goes through the poem. He ends with the expression, 'Oh look at my fellow-men' – which, for me, perfectly sums up his heartfelt attitude.

EXAMINER'S COMMENT

A high-grade response. The introductory comments showed engagement with Lawrence's strongly held views. Points were developed and aptly illustrated with accurate quotation. Some impressive discussion regarding the poet's persuasive style and use of negative language was balanced by illustrations of his sympathetic tone.

Class/Homework Exercises

1. 'Lawrence is severely critical of what he views as "a state of suppression" in which individuals are tormented and made inhuman by the processes of industrialisation.' Discuss this statement with reference to 'What Have They Done to You?'.
2. In your opinion, how relevant is 'What Have They Done to You?' to modern times? Support your answer with reference to the poem.

Summary Points

- **Key themes: the suppression of natural human individuality by industrialisation.**
- **Contrasting tones: anger, frustration, sympathy, irony, anguish, dejection.**
- **Effective use of metaphorical language, onomatopoeia and vivid imagery.**
- **Rhetorical style – repetition, questions, speech rhythms, emotive language, etc.**

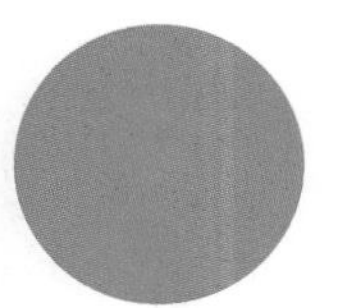

10 Baby-Movements II: 'Trailing Clouds'

As a drenched, drowned bee
Hangs numb and heavy from the bending flower,
So clings to me,
My baby, her brown hair brushed with wet tears
And laid laughterless on her cheek,
Her soft white legs hanging heavily over my arm
Swinging to my lullaby.
My sleeping baby hangs upon my life
As a silent bee at the end of a shower
Draws down the burdened flower.
She who has always seemed so light
Sways on my arm like sorrowful, storm-heavy boughs,
Even her floating hair sinks like storm-bruised young leaves
Reaching downwards:
As the wings of a drenched, drowned bee
Are a heaviness, and a weariness.

numb: dazed, deadened.

clings: attaches.

burdened: laden, weighed down.

boughs: small branches.

'the burdened flower'

Personal Response

1. Why, in your opinion, does Lawrence compare the sleeping child to 'a drenched, drowned bee'? Support your answer with reference to the text.
2. Lawrence makes use of sound throughout the poem. Choose one aural image from the poem and briefly comment on its effectiveness.
3. Write your own personal response to the poem, highlighting the impact it made on you.

Critical Literacy

'Trailing Clouds' is part of a two-poem sequence called 'Baby-Movements', one of D. H. Lawrence's earliest works. It was first published in 1909, apparently based on a description of his landlady's baby daughter. The poem was later renamed 'A Baby Asleep After Pain'. Lawrence's original title had been taken from a poem by William Wordsworth ('trailing clouds of glory do we come/From God, who is our home'). Wordsworth believed in the eternal spiritual nature of life.

Lawrence's opening lines are dominated by the striking image of a 'drenched, drowned bee'. The speaker – most likely the voice of the baby's mother – compares the clinging infant to the dying insect on the 'bending flower'. The poet is fond of images drawn from the natural world, such as the **bee and flower motif**. His rhythms are apparently casual, yet carefully controlled. The alliterative 'd' sound suggests a laden inertia. Broad vowel assonance ('Hangs numb and heavy') adds to the pain the bee feels.

Lines 4–7 focus closely on the mother's natural sense of connection with her child ('My baby') and their close physical interaction. There is a hypnotic, dreamlike quality to the description. The combined force of **multiple sound effects** – alliteration, assonance and sibilance – is remarkable for the lucidity, lightness and vivid precision that Lawrence achieves. The infant's hair is 'brushed with wet tears/And laid laughterless on her cheek'. The poet does not treat his images as abstract or merely visual. They are dynamic and changeable – 'legs hanging heavily', 'Swinging'. Tactile images suggest the contact between bodies. The baby appears to be almost an extension of her mother's body ('over my arm'). Such clarity of diction and use of luminous details are characteristic of Lawrence. The mother's attentive rocking movement is matched by instinctive tenderness echoed in the gentle sound of the 'lullaby'.

The poem's central simile is repeated in lines 8–10. This fragile, helpless child is utterly reliant on her mother: 'My sleeping baby hangs upon my life.' Is there a hint that the strain is nearly too much to bear? The **lethargic mood** continues, expressed mostly through onomatopoeic effects: 'Draws down the burdened flower.' While Lawrence cannot resist the impulse to rhyme ('shower', 'flower'), the restraint in the ebb and flow of the language is mesmerising.

Imagistic in its loosened rhythms, the poem repeatedly focuses on the similarity between the dazed, heavy bee and the infant in her mother's arms. But the **tone changes** towards the end as the reality of the baby's dependency becomes evident. The child is no longer 'so light'; indeed, her mother's arms now seem 'like sorrowful, storm-heavy boughs' (line 12). Once again, the powerful assonance adds to the poignancy. There is a disquieting awareness of being weighed down – both physically and emotionally. Is this a natural reaction to parental responsibility? Or a deeper realisation about the cycle of life and death?

Over the course of this short poem, Lawrence has interwoven a lyrical scene with a disturbing dramatic situation. The final lines are infused with a deep sense of despondency. In a nightmarish sequence, the child's 'floating hair' is now sinking 'like storm-bruised young leaves'. We are left with a distressing image of a person struggling helplessly, being **overwhelmed by a greater natural power** just like the 'drenched, drowned bee'. D. H. Lawrence's poetry often shows a concern with the pressures of life and culture. His oblique approach is open to various interpretations about the experience of motherhood, but there is no denying the concluding mood of complete surrender to an inevitable 'weariness'.

Writing About the Poem

'D. H. Lawrence's poems can offer revealing insights into disturbing themes.' Discuss this view, with reference to 'Trailing Clouds'.

Sample Paragraph

The title seemed ambiguous. Nature is beautiful, but can quickly become stormy. In comparing the tiny baby to a drowned bee, the poet appeared to be already mourning the child's life. The baby 'clings' to its parent for dear life. To me, the verb suggested desperation – as though life is a struggle that ends in death for everyone. The child has been crying and its wet hair lies 'laughterless'. The mood is negative throughout. There are so many downbeat references to the baby, 'legs hanging heavily'. Nature grows even more ominous with the mention of 'storm-heavy boughs' and a truly stark image of the baby drowning like the bee. The ending is surreal, a feeling of being out of control, 'Reaching downwards'. Lawrence seems to be exploring the idea of human life being determined by time and fate. As in the natural world, humans are subject to unknown forces outside their power. The final lines comparing the bee's wings to 'a weariness' are the most disturbing of all and emphasises Lawrence's pessimistic outlook on life.

EXAMINER'S COMMENT

A solid high-grade response that explored interesting aspects of the poem and included some well-focused discussion about Lawrence's 'negative outlook'. Incisive points on imagery and mood were effectively illustrated. Expression was impressive throughout, with some good use of vocabulary ('ambiguous', 'ominous', 'surreal'). Overall, a good personal answer.

Class/Homework Exercises

1. Identify and comment on Lawrence's portrait of the sleeping child in the poem, '"Trailing Clouds"'. In your opinion, is it realistic or sentimental? Support your answer with reference to the text.
2. 'Lawrence often makes use of carefully organised imagery to create thought-provoking moments of drama and tension.' To what extent is this true of '"Trailing Clouds"'? Support your answer with reference to the poem.

Summary Points

- **Imagistic style – effective use of repetition, rhyme, visual and aural imagery.**
- **Poem is structured around the extended bee and flower simile.**
- **Lawrence explores aspects of life's transience and touches on spiritual themes.**
- **Contrasting moods and atmospheres – tender, reflective, oppressive, fearful, etc.**

11 Bavarian Gentians

Not every man has gentians in his house
In soft September, at slow, sad Michaelmas.
Bavarian gentians, tall and dark, but dark
darkening the daytime torch-like with the smoking blueness of Pluto's gloom,
ribbed hellish flowers erect, with their blaze of darkness spread blue,
blown flat into points, by the heavy white draught of the day.

Torch-flower of the blue-smoking darkness, Pluto's dark-blue blaze
black lamps from the halls of Dis, smoking dark blue
giving off darkness, blue darkness, upon Demeter's yellow-pale day
whom have you come for, here in the white-cast day?

Reach me a gentian, give me a torch!
let me guide myself with the blue, forked torch of a flower
down the darker and darker stairs, where blue is darkened on blueness
down the way Persephone goes, just now, in first-frosted September,
to the sightless realm where darkness is married to dark
and Persephone herself is but a voice, as a bride,
a gloom invisible enfolded in the deeper dark
of the arms of Pluto as he ravishes her once again
and pierces her once more with his passion of the utter dark
among the splendour of black-blue torches, shedding fathomless darkness
    on the nuptials.

Give me a flower on a tall stem, and three dark flames,
for I will go to the wedding, and be wedding-guest
at the marriage of the living dark.

Bavarian Gentians: small trumpet-shaped blue flower.

Michaelmas: feast of St Michael the Archangel, 29 September, protector against the dark of night.

Pluto: ruler of the underworld (Hades), god of death and earth's fertility.

Dis: Roman god of the underworld where souls go after death.

Demeter: goddess of the harvest and agriculture; mother of Persephone.

Persephone: abducted bride of Pluto.

nuptials: wedding ceremony.

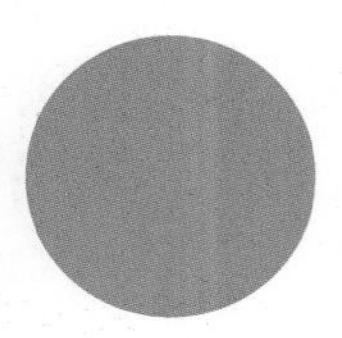

Personal Response

1. Based on your reading of the poem, outline Lawrence's attitude to death. Support your answer with reference to the text.
2. Choose one aural image from the poem that appeals to you and comment briefly on its effectiveness.
3. Write your own personal response to the poem, highlighting the impact it made on you.

Critical Literacy

'Bavarian Gentians' is one of D. H. Lawrence's final poems, published posthumously in 1932. He wrote the poem in September 1929 when he was suffering from tuberculosis, a disease of the lungs, from which he would soon die. Lawrence's early life had been spent in the English coal mining town of Eastwood. Later on, he wrote of remembering 'a sort of inner darkness, like the gloss of coal in which we moved and had our being'.

The first stanza opens with a modest, off-hand observation: 'Not every man has gentians in his house/In soft September, at slow, sad Michaelmas.' The sensual evocation of autumn is conveyed in the slow, reflective pace of the two run-on lines where sibilant 's' sounds establish a soporific (sleep-inducing) mood. The September setting is significant – the month facing into winter, the season of decay. Michaelmas (line 2) is the Christian feast of St Michael, known as the 'protector against the devil, especially at the time of death'. For Lawrence, the gentians signify the shadow of death. The depressive person often obsesses over a particular object or event and Lawrence is fascinated by the intense blue of the flowers. The colour blue has long been associated with sadness; people in a downbeat mood are said to be suffering from 'the blues'. The tone is **dejected and dreamy**, seducing the reader with its slow rhythm. However, the momentum builds through slightly modified repetition, 'tall and dark', 'dark/darkening'.

The flowers seem to throw no light at all on the day. Then, suddenly, they change into magical tokens, becoming 'torch-like' (line 4). In the poet's imagination, their deep colour reminds him of the blue-black of the fires of Hell, 'smoking blueness of Pluto's gloom'. The reader is persuaded by Lawrence's **obsessive preoccupation** to closely observe every detail of the 'ribbed hellish flowers erect'. Their majestic 'blaze of darkness' (line 5) is again linked to the flash of fire. Their posture ('blown flat into points' by 'the heavy white draught' of wind) is carefully noted. The bright white of the day is a stark contrast to the darkness of both the flowers and Pluto's wretched underworld. All through this section, the languor is similar to falling into a trance brought on by the contemplation of these beautiful blue flowers.

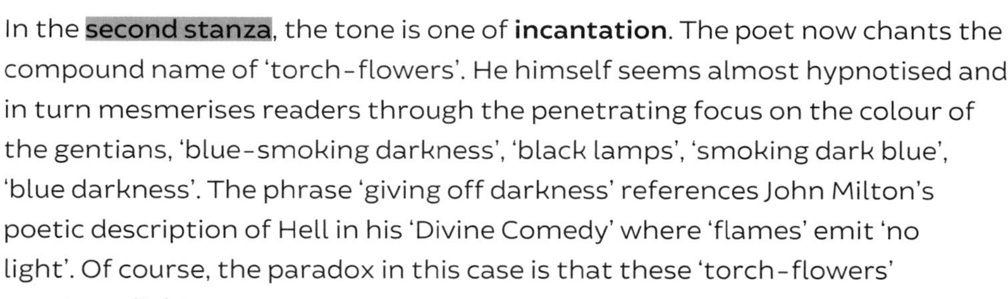

In the second stanza, the tone is one of **incantation**. The poet now chants the compound name of 'torch-flowers'. He himself seems almost hypnotised and in turn mesmerises readers through the penetrating focus on the colour of the gentians, 'blue-smoking darkness', 'black lamps', 'smoking dark blue', 'blue darkness'. The phrase 'giving off darkness' references John Milton's poetic description of Hell in his 'Divine Comedy' where 'flames' emit 'no light'. Of course, the paradox in this case is that these 'torch-flowers' create no light.

The infernal darkness of the gentians not only alludes to Lawrence's gloomy mood, but also to the darkness of the underworld where Pluto reigns supreme 'in the halls of Dis'. Image after image of darkness permeate these lines just as Lawrence's infected lungs became flooded with tuberculosis when he was faced imminent death. The poet is all too aware of the answer to his question (line 10), 'whom have you come for here in the white-cast day?' The combined force of irregular metre and sonorous sound effects add to the **unsettling atmosphere**.

Throughout the poem, Lawrence alludes to **Greek myth**. Pluto, the ruler of the underworld, abducts Persephone, the daughter of the goddess of fertility, Demeter. Although Pluto makes Persephone his queen, Demeter secures a compromise: Persephone can return every April to her mother for six months, after which (in 'first-frosted September') she must go back to her husband and the underworld. During the time Persephone is away from her mother, Demeter mourns her absence and the countryside becomes barren. When

Persephone returns in springtime, the earth becomes fertile once again. In the third stanza, the mood changes dramatically. The tone turns imperative, electrified into action through energetic verbs, 'Reach me', give me'. Lawrence now intends to use the gentians as a torch to lead him into death. **No longer a helpless victim** (in stark contrast to the abducted Persephone), he is determined to act independently: 'let me guide myself.' Long run-on lines spiral into a vortex while the poet descends 'down the darker and darker stairs'. Emphatic use of the heavy alliterative 'd' sound suggests the dismal atmosphere of the underworld where 'blue is darkened on blueness'. The colour of the flowers is becoming extinguished by the enveloping desolation.

It is a vision of unrelenting gloom: 'the sightless realm where darkness is married to dark.' The cadence of the line falls on the last monosyllabic word, imitating Persephone's (and the poet's) descent into Hades. She now loses her body – becoming 'but a voice' – and is cloaked in 'the arms of Pluto' who claims his bride in a macabre fantasy 'among the splendour of black-blue torches'. Pluto's desire for Persephone ('his passion of the utter dark;') is reflected in the strong sexual imagery. Throughout this **surreal Gothic scene**, the gentians shine in the incomprehensible atmosphere of an extraordinary wedding, not with light but 'shedding fathomless darkness on the nuptials'.

In the concluding three lines, the tone changes once more. There is a sense of **dignified acceptance** in the poet's formal request, 'Give me a flower', contrasting with the earlier desperate grasp ('Reach'). Calmly and courageously, Lawrence accepts the inevitable invitation of death: 'I will go to the wedding.' Paradoxically, he describes the place where Pluto and Persephone have their marriage ceremony as 'the living dark'. This refers to the ability of the dark earth to receive the dead flower's seed in autumn and to bring it back to life the following spring. Nature buries and regenerates. The compelling drama concludes with the poet preparing to enter this dark realm forever. Does he hope for an afterlife in death?

'Bavarian Gentians' is sustained by a combination of repetitive rhythm, monotonous melody and the obsessive litanies expressing the poet's deepest thoughts and fears. In the end, Lawrence succeeds in uniting the natural beauty of the blue flowers with an overflowing description of their colour, leading to an erotically and morbidly charged descent into the mythical underworld. He is a poet without a mask.

Writing About the Poem

'D. H. Lawrence's last poems study death with precise, reverential fascination.' Discuss this view, with particular reference to 'Bavarian Gentians'.

Sample Paragraph

'Bavarian Gentians' explores the fall towards oblivion through a keen description of its seductive powers. Hypnotically, the poet weaves the 'blue-smoking darkness' of the flowers through the poem so that they become both the guide to death as well as a symbol of it. Strict observation not only of the flower's colour but also its texture ('ribbed') and shape ('blown flat into points') causes this beautiful flower to become a focal point, enabling both the poet and reader to pass from acute awareness to a trance-like state of meditation. The terror of the descent into nothingness is conveyed in the spine-chilling alliterative phrase 'down the darker and darker stairs'. Soft sweeping syllables swirl as Lawrence relates the classic myth of Pluto and Persephone's nuptials ('splendour', 'shedding fathomless darkness'). He presents us with the threshold between life and death as the earth buries and nurtures. Pluto embraces his bride just as death claims the poet. The poem ends on a dignified note. Respectfully, Lawrence accepts the invitation in the slow-moving line, 'for I will go to the wedding, and be wedding guest'. The struggle with death now loses importance as the poet quietly approaches 'the living dark'. This entrancing poem reveals death through awed, detailed absorption.

EXAMINER'S COMMENT

A mature and thoughtful response to the question. Informed discussion points focus throughout on the poet's precise style and reverential tone. Excellent use of accurate quotations and support reference. Expression is also impressive: varied sentence length, wide-ranging vocabulary and good control of syntax. Top-grade standard.

Class/Homework Exercises

1. 'Lawrence's sensual language and vivid imagination convey his intense vision of life.' In your opinion, how true is this of 'Bavarian Gentians'? Support your answer with reference to the poem.
2. 'D. H. Lawrence's dark themes are explored through honest free verse.' To what extent is this evident in 'Bavarian Gentians'? Support your answer with reference to the poem.

Summary Points

- **Direct, immediate exploration of death, oblivion, self-awareness.**
- **Rolling, dreamlike style, irregular line length and metre.**
- **Repetition and other aural effects create spell-binding fantasy.**
- **Use of Greek mythology enriches the poem's universal appeal.**
- **Dramatic impact of colour imagery patterns.**
- **Poet's own journey towards death portrayed through moods of awareness, anger, terror and acceptance.**

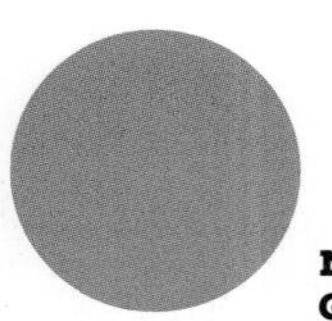

MARKING SCHEME GUIDELINES

Responses to the question should contain clear evidence of engagement with the poetry by Lawrence on the course. Expect a wide variety of approaches in the candidates' answering, but they should focus on the poet's distinctive language use in exploring provocative themes and issues.

INDICATIVE MATERIAL

- Unusual viewpoint and perspective, often challenging and confrontational.
- Personal approach to love, memory, death, nature, modernity, cosmic harmony.
- Experimental style, free verse, range of tones, striking description.
- Startling imagery, contrasting moods, irregular rhyme, rhythm and line length.

Leaving Cert Sample Essay

'D. H. Lawrence's poetry is notable for both its provocative subject matter and distinctive language use.' Discuss this view, supporting your answer with suitable reference to the poems by Lawrence on your course.

Sample Essay
(Lawrence's provocative subject matter and distinctive language use)

1. D. H. Lawrence, rebel and mystic, believed 'when genuine passion moves you, say what you've got to say'. Exploring disturbing, challenging, sensual and vexing themes, Lawrence employed free verse and precise diction to create deep, resonant, unforgettable poetry. As readers, we are challenged and consoled in diverse poems such as 'Piano', 'The Mosquito', 'Snake' and 'Blue Gentians', which investigate relationships, memory, loss, nature and death.

2. A gentle, conversational remark opens Lawrence's paradoxical memory poem, 'Piano'. 'Softly in the dusk, a woman is singing to me.' This catapults reader and poet down the 'vista' of the past where exact details and the use of the present tense brings to life the tender scene of a little child 'sitting under the piano', 'pressing the small, poised feet of a mother'. Both reader and poet vividly experience the recollection through Lawrence's skilful use of onomatopoeia ('boom', 'tinkling') and assonance ('tingling strings'). The past is being brought into the present. However, Lawrence avoids sentimental clichés. Instead, he honestly confronts the uncomfortable reality that none of us can ever go back to the security of a simpler past, 'with winter outside'. The adult poet who cannot become a child again weeps inconsolably 'Down the flood of remembrance'. Long, irregular run-on lines capture the non-stop flow of memories, 'the insidious mastery of song/Betrays me back'. The effect is bound to provoke readers who can usually relate to nostalgic feelings.

3. In the poems 'The Mosquito' and 'Snake', Lawrence creates brilliant evocations of the natural world, catching its physical presence with vigour. The poet showcases nature's creatures, which are all instinct and immediacy without the human's restrictions. A confrontation between the refined, civilised human mind and the subterranean forces of the earth is dramatised in 'Snake'. Through an inventive use of syntax, the poet describes a creature that does not rationalise but acts on natural intuition – he 'flickered his two-forked tongue from his lips'. When describing the logical human narrator, the poet uses much more

complex expression – 'The voice of my education said to me/He must be killed,/For in Sicily ... the gold are venomous'. As in the poem 'Piano', the narrator wants to relive the past, 'I wished he could come back', but no amount of wishing will change what has been done. Lawrence confronts the reader with yet another uncomfortable truth.

4. However, in 'The Mosquito', this conflict between man and creature has a different outcome. Lawrence is furious that this little insect has dared to cross the boundaries of 'otherness' and attacked him. Unlike the narrator in 'Snake', who is filled with guilt for attacking the snake, the insect glories in his attack on the man, entering into a state of ecstasy, 'enspasmed in oblivion'. This time, the poet uses repetition to effectively describe the aftermath of the encounter, 'Such silence', 'Such gorging', 'Such obscenity'. There is no guilt, the insect is at one with the natural world, a mosquito has followed its natural instinct. In these poems, Lawrence clearly shows the beautiful diversity of nature, the snake's 'yellow-brown slackness soft-bellied', an insect's 'shredded shank' and 'streaming legs'. He is demonstrating how humans have lost a sense of oneness with the universe.

5. Lawrence also makes inventive use of animals as images in 'Call into Death' and 'Trailing Clouds'. The bird images, 'white bird among snow-berries'; 'gently rustling in heaven like a/bird' in 'Call into Death' shows how life continues, even if unseen, and this can be an image for what happens in death. The life force continues in a different form to that of the mortal human. The disturbing image of a 'drenched drowned bee' in 'Trailing Clouds' suggests Lawrence's desire for oblivion.

6. In 'Bavarian Gentians', the subject of death is again addressed. Similar to 'Piano', the poem opens with a simple observation, 'Not every man has gentians in his house'. Through the hypnotic repetition of 'blue-smoking darkness', the poet then confronts the terrifying reality of death – 'darkness is married to dark'. He uses the beautiful Greek myth of Persephone and Pluto to show how life continues even after death, although in a different form. Lawrence is going towards death voluntarily, 'let me guide myself', lit by the dark blue gentians, 'Torch-flowers of the blue-smoking darkness'. The poet accepts death in the image of a 'wedding guest' about to take his place in the 'living dark'. Lawrence rebels against the 'normal approach' to dying. Through his compelling rhythms and interweaving lines, he invites the reader to take part in this magnificent final journey.

7. I found Lawrence to be an extraordinary poetic voice through poems that grow naturally from intense emotion, with their irregular line-length, rhyme and rhythm. Clear-cut, accurate descriptions, repetition, sound-effects and clever contrasts all add to these disturbing, challenging poems which cause the modern reader to stop and consider some of life's great questions.

(approx. 825 words)

(45–50 minutes)

EXAMINER'S COMMENT

An accomplished top-grade response showing very good engagement with Lawrence's poetry. The opening gives a useful overview, mentioning the poems that will be discussed. Focus is maintained on the poet's unusual approach in challenging conventional views. Cross-referencing works very well, reflecting a broad appreciation of themes and style – and excellent use is made of supportive reference and quotation. Paragraph 5 is slight, however, and points lack development. Otherwise, expression is impressive throughout and the essay is rounded off confidently.

GRADE: H1
P = 15/15
C = 13/15
L = 13/15
M = 5/5
Total = 46/50

N.B. Access your eBook for additional sample paragraphs and a list of useful quotes with commentary.

Sample Leaving Cert Questions on Lawrence's Poetry

1. **'D. H. Lawrence's stark, innovative poetry celebrates sensuality in an over-intellectualised world.' Discuss this view, supporting your answer with reference to the poems by Lawrence on your course.**
2. **'Lawrence's intensely confessional poetry contains a richness of wide-ranging imagery.' Discuss this statement, supporting your answer with reference to the poetry of Lawrence on your course.**
3. **'D. H. Lawrence, the rebel poet, is passionately in love with language.' To what extent do you agree with this view? Support the points you make with reference to the poems by Lawrence on your course.**

First Sample Essay Plan (Q1)

'D. H. Lawrence's stark, innovative poetry celebrates sensuality in an over-intellectualised world.' Discuss this view, supporting your answer with reference to the poems by Lawrence on your course.

Intro: Lawrence – master craftsman, profound thinker – creator of raw, honest poetry glorying in nature's creative beauty, critical of modern society. Unique and intense poetic voice – free verse, precise description, experimental structures, startling imagery patterns.

Point 1: 'Delight of Being Alone' and 'Absolute Reverence' champion Lawrence's belief in living through the senses – 'It makes me realise the delicious pleasure of the moon/that she has in travelling by herself' (emphatic sibilance and line length). Worships divine in nature – 'But to something unseen, unknown ... I feel absolute reverence'. Curt dismissal of modern analytical approach, 'Say no more!'

Point 2: 'What Have They Done to You?' – extended reflection on dehumanising effects of industrialisation. Use of contrasting verbs to showcase the difference between oppressed work force, joyless and passive ('creeping') and capitalist employers. Repetition of refrain 'What have they done to you?' mimics monotonous factory work.

Point 3: 'Humming-Bird' – visualising creature's physicality. Assonance highlights natural beauty of bird, 'This little bit chipped off in brilliance'. Dynamic verbs used to celebrate this beautiful bird ('flashed', 'whizzing', 'pierced'). Similarly, in 'Snake', the conflict focuses on the relationship between nature and human nature.

Point 4: 'Intimates' – honest exploration of deadening effect of modern relationships. In this domestic drama, the couple communicate through words rather than senses. Contrasting language and varying tones throughout.

Conclusion: Poetry defined by two elements: Lawrence's glorification of the natural world and his condemnation of modern civilisation. Recurring tensions between heart and head. Unique style dominated by careful observation, searing honesty, varied structure and innovative language use.

NOTE

If you are not familiar with some poems referred to in the sample plans below, substitute poems that you have studied closely when writing practice responses.

Exam candidates usually discuss three or four poems in their answers. However, there is no set number of poems or formulaic approach expected.

Key points about a particular poem can be developed over more than one paragraph.

Paragraphs may also include cross-referencing and comparative discussions of poems.

Remember that there is no single 'correct' answer to Leaving Cert poetry questions, so always be confident in expressing your own considered response.

Sample Essay Plan (Q1)

Develop **one** of the above points into a paragraph.

Sample Paragraph: Point 4

The difficulty the modern world has in forming successful relationships is explored in the ironically titled 'Intimates'. Lawrence focuses on a bitter marital row. The couple's knowledge of each other does not add warmth and intimacy, but is used to bombard each other with hurtful weapons. The opening question, 'Don't you care for my love?' suggests an unhappy

woman who craves attention and affection. The man's startling reaction, 'I handed her the mirror', signals his spiteful attack. The poet juxtaposes the polite, formal request 'please', which is transformed into sharp sarcasm as part of a withering list of directions aimed at his partner. Their relationship is defined by the words they say. His fury at the woman's assumed superiority is conveyed in the references to the 'proper person', 'head-quarters', 'supreme authority'. Now the woman is invited to see herself as she really is, the source of power, not a helpless victim. The contrasting line lengths at the conclusion highlight the woman's 'spellbound' inspection of herself. The relationship is cold, lacking sensuality or feeling. The man's final comment, 'while I fled', imitates his frantic dash for freedom from the stifling verbal arguments. This relationship is doomed because it is based on harsh intellectualising.

EXAMINER'S COMMENT

As part of a full essay, this is an informed response that illustrates Lawrence's interest in the tension between emotion and rationality. Key sentences address the essay wording, e.g. 'Their relationship is defined by the words they say'. The paragraph traces the progress of thought within the poem, using apt references along the way to illustrate discussion points. Syntax is well controlled and there is no awkwardness in the expression. Expressive adjectives such as 'startling' and 'stifling' maintain the focus on an important element of the question ('innovative'). A confident, top-grade answer.

N.B. Access your eBook for additional sample paragraphs and a list of useful quotes with commentary.

Second Sample Essay Plan (Q3)

D.H. Lawrence, the rebel poet, is passionately in love with language.' To what extent do you agree with this view? Support the points you make with reference to the poems by Lawrence on your course.

Intro: Lawrence – rebellious outsider from working class background. Believed 'man had lost the art of living'. Hard, radical views – dares to address society's taboos (death and men's expression of emotion), also challenges man's exploitative use of power to dominate nature and fellow men. Great creature poems confront modern man's distance from nature.

Point 1: 'Call into Death' – last of society's taboos, death comes to all. Controlled 12-line elegy contains the raw emotion of a son at his mother's death. Plain, conversational language expresses loss, 'Since I lost you, my darling'. Death is seen as part of natural cycle of life – not seen but still present. Uses fresh simile from natural world ('like a white bird among snow-berries'). Onomatopoeia ('rustling') shows life force continues. Become one with universe ('melting foam', 'breathing wind').

Point 2: 'Piano' – another relationship poem. Again, tightly controlled form (3 quatrains, couplet rhyming scheme) contain floodgates of unmanly emotive memories. Vivid flashback to childhood. Aural effects conjure the music – onomatopoeia for the low notes ('boom') and assonance for the high notes ('tingling strings'). Tactile sensual memory ('sitting', 'pressing'). Sibilant 's' creates serenely happy scene ('small', 'smiles', 'sings').

Point 3: 'The Mosquito' – challenges man's destruction of what he does not understand through examination of man's combative relationship with nature's creatures. Startling use of satanic and supernatural imagery shows man's contempt for creature ('evil little aura', 'filthy magic', 'streaky sorcerer', 'Ghoul on wings'). Sickening vampire-like image of mosquito sucking 'Blood, red blood'. Onomatopoeia emphasises the obscenity of 'Gorging' on 'My blood'.

Point 4: 'What Have They Done to You?' - poet challenges man's exploitative use of power to dominate nature. Intense poetic voice and rhetorical language depict the oppressive industrial age that dehumanised ('devoured') the 'masses'. Raging tone: 'They stole your body from you, and left you an animated carcass.'

Conclusion: Lawrence – we should be 'true' to our 'animal instincts'. Fresh, controlled language and imagery show how to understand that death is part of the cycle of life, how to express emotion, how to respect the harmony of living systems.

Sample Essay Plan (Q3)

Develop **one** of the above points into a practice paragraph of your own.

Sample Paragraph: Point 4

Lawrence's poem, 'What Have They Done to You?' attacks man's inhumanity to his fellow man – particularly those who exploit the working class. This scathing assault on industrialisation is contained in a list of rhetorical questions. The human being's individuality has been suppressed to the state of a drone insect. The workers are 'creeping', thoughtlessly going 'back and forth' to monotonous jobs, their motion similar to the mindless movement of the great machines in their factories. Lawrence strikes at the greedy industrialists, the so-called 'saviours of the people', charging them with theft ('took away', 'stole'). His love of vibrant imagery is evident in personifying the factory as a mechanical monster which 'devoured' the working man in its 'vast maw'.

EXAMINER'S COMMENT

As part of a full essay answer to Q3, this is a confident top-grade response that remains focused on Lawrence's love of language. Well-supported discussion points highlight a range of the poet's stylistic features – including rhetorical questions, graphic imagery and sound effects. Impressive expression (e.g. 'scathing assault', 'demeaned to its physical essence') and assured language control throughout.

Broad assonance underlines the horrific dehumanisation. The poet's aversion to what is happening is vividly shown in the alliterative 'men of the masses'. All individuality is squashed in to one indistinguishable amount. Ugly repetition shows his repugnance, 'goggling eyes, to goggle at the film'. The poem is filled with energetic language. Man is demeaned to its physical essence, 'carcass'. All through the poem, long, irregular run-on lines express his anger. A curt ending sharply contrasts with a heartfelt expression of pity, 'Oh, what has been done to them?'

Class/Homework Exercise

1. **Write one or two paragraphs in response to the question: 'D.H. Lawrence, the rebel poet, is passionately in love with language.' To what extent do you agree with this view? Support the points you make with reference to the poems by Lawrence on your course.**

 Revision Overview

'Call into Death'
Plaintive elegy addresses complex subjects, including themes of loss and death.

'Piano'
First-person reminiscence of past domestic scene, juxtaposed with present. Themes of childhood, memory and identity.

'The Mosquito'
Detailed exploration of one of the poet's recurring themes, man versus nature, dramatised through his encounter with the mosquito.

'Snake'
Addresses man's position in the natural world. Simple narrative account with snake, using internal conversation.

'Humming-Bird'
Dramatic and challenging imaginary account of evolution of bird. Free verse structure reflects random aspect of nature.

'Intimates'
Witty account of problems of communication. Dialogue and actions of bitter row between two lovers.

'Delight of Being Alone'
Beautiful autobiographical poem addresses positive and adverse aspects of isolation.

'Absolute Reverence'
Reveals the poet's mystical view of life. Reverence only for creative force in contrast to all that he does not revere.

'What Have They Done to You?'
Scathing critique of contemporary British society.

'Baby-Movements II: "Trailing Clouds"'
Formal imagistic ode addresses transience and loss of innocence.

'Bavarian Gentians'
Personal study of poet's journey towards self-awareness and death.

Last Words

'Lawrence was in a direct line of descent from such earlier poets as Blake, Coleridge and Whitman, for whom imagination was everything.'
Keith Sagar

'The accuracy of Lawrence's observations haunts the mind permanently.'
Kenneth Roxroth

'These are my tender administrations to the mental and emotional wounds we suffer from.'
D. H. Lawrence

DEATH

CHILDHOOD

HISTORY/ MEMORY

NATURE

CONFICT

TIME

RELATIONSHIPS

RELIGION/ SPIRITUALITY

Eiléan Ní Chuilleanáin

1942–

'I chose poetry because it was different.'

Eiléan Ní Chuilleanáin is regarded by many as one of the most important contemporary Irish women poets. Her subject matter ranges from social commentary and considerations of religious issues to quiet, introspective poems about human nature. Ní Chuilleanáin is noted for being mysterious and complex; her poems usually have subtle messages that unfold only through multiple readings. She is well read in history, and a strong sense of connection between past and present characterises her work, in which she often draws interesting parallels between historical events and modern situations. Many of her poems highlight the contrast between fluidity and stillness, life and death, and of the undeniable passing of time and humanity's attempts to stop change. She herself has frequently referred to the importance of secrecy in her poetry. Most critics agree that Ní Chuilleanáin's poems resist easy explanations and variously show her interest in explorations of transition, the sacred, women's experience and history.

Investigate Further

To find out more about Eiléan Ní Chuilleanáin, or to hear readings of her poems not available in your eBook, you could search some useful websites such as YouTube, BBC Poetry, poetryfoundation.org and poetryarchive.org, or access additional material on this page of your eBook.

Prescribed Poems

○ **1 'Lucina Schynning in Silence of the Nicht'**
While this strangely compelling poem touches on fascinating aspects of Irish history, it is much more than a meditation on past events. **Page 274**

○ **2 'The Second Voyage'**
Transitions are central to Ní Chuilleanáin's poems. Here, she explores the relationship between past and present through the story of Odysseus, who is frustrated by his ocean journeys and decides that his next voyage will be on land. **Page 278**

○ **3 'Deaths and Engines'**
The poet contextualises her experience of death within the setting of another 'burnt-out' ruin, the abandoned wreckage of an aircraft engine. **Page 283**

○ **4 'Street' (OL)**
This typically elusive drama includes various references to Mary Magdalene and the experience of women throughout history. **Page 287**

○ **5 'Fireman's Lift'**
Following her mother's death, the poet used the scene depicted in the painter Correggio's masterpiece, *Assumption of the Virgin*, as the setting for this extraordinary poem.
Page 291

○ **6 'All for You'**
This multi-layered narrative offers glimpses of salvation and hope.
Page 295

○ **7 'Following'**
A vividly realised journey by a young girl through a busy Irish fair day invites readers into this mysterious story. **Page 299**

○ **8 'Kilcash'**
This version of the old Irish elegy, *Caoine Cill Chais*, mourns the death of Margaret Butler, Viscountess Iveagh. **Page 304**

○ **9 'Translation'**
Ní Chuilleanáin's poem was read at the reburial ceremony to commemorate Magdalene laundry women from all over Ireland.
Page 309

○ **10 'The Bend in the Road'**
The poet recalls a journey when a child was suffering from car sickness. For her, the roadside location marks the realisation of time passing. **Page 314**

○ **11 'On Lacking the Killer Instinct'**
The poem intrigues and unsettles from its vivid opening description of a stationary hare – engrossed and 'absorbed'. **Page 319**

○ **12 'To Niall Woods and Xenya Ostrovskaia, Married in Dublin on 9 September 2009' (OL)**
This epithalamium (celebrating the wedding of Eiléan Ní Chuilleanáin's son Niall and his bride, Xenya) is the introductory dedication in her poetry collection *The Sun-fish*. **Page 324**

*(OL) indicates poems that are also prescribed for the Ordinary Level course.

1 Lucina Schynning in Silence of the Nicht

Moon shining in silence of the night
The heaven being all full of stars
I was reading my book in a ruin
By a sour candle, without roast meat or music
Strong drink or a shield from the air
Blowing in the crazed window, and I felt
Moonlight on my head, clear after three days' rain.

I washed in cold water; it was orange, channelled down bogs
Dipped between cresses.
The bats flew through my room where I slept safely.
Sheep stared at me when I woke.

Behind me the waves of darkness lay, the plague
Of mice, plague of beetles
Crawling out of the spines of books,
Plague shadowing pale faces with clay
The disease of the moon gone astray.

In the desert I relaxed, amazed
As the mosaic beasts on the chapel floor
When Cromwell had departed and they saw
The sky growing through the hole in the roof.

Sheepdogs embraced me; the grasshopper
Returned with lark and bee.
I looked down between hedges of high thorn and saw
The hare, absorbed, sitting still
In the middle of the track; I heard
Again the chirp of the stream running.

Title: Lucina is another name for Diana, the moon goddess. In Roman mythology, Lucina was the goddess of childbirth. Ní Chuilleanáin's title comes from the opening line of 'The Antichrist', a satirical poem by the Scottish poet William Dunbar (c. 1460–1517).

cresses: small strongly flavoured leaves.

plague: curse, diseased group.

spines: inner parts, backs.

astray: off course.

mosaic: mixed, assorted.

Cromwell: Oliver Cromwell (1599–1658), controversial English military and political leader who led an army of invasion in 1649–50, which conquered most of Ireland. Cromwell is still regarded largely as a figure of hatred in the Irish Republic, his name being associated with massacre, religious persecution and mass dispossession of the Catholic community.

chirp: lively sound, twitter.

'shining in silence of the night'

Personal Response

1. How would you describe the atmosphere in the poem's opening stanza? Refer to the text in your answer.
2. Choose one image taken from the natural world that you found particularly interesting. Comment briefly on its effectiveness.
3. Based on your reading of this poem, do you think Ní Chuilleanáin presents a realistic view of Irish history? Give reasons for your response.

Critical Literacy

Eiléan Ní Chuilleanáin takes her title from a Middle Scots poem by William Dunbar. 'Lucina Schynning in Silence of the Nicht' is set in a ruin somewhere in Ireland, after Oliver Cromwell had devastated the country in 1649. However, Ní Chuilleanáin's beautiful and haunting poem is much more than a meditation on an historical event. The poet achieves immediacy by means of a dramatic monologue that recreates the whisperings of desolation in the aftermath of Cromwell's march through Ireland.

As in so many of her poems, Ní Chuilleanáin invites readers into a **strangely compelling setting**. The poet personifies the moon, creating an uneasy atmosphere. Silence enhances the dramatic effect: 'The heaven being all full of stars.' This eerie scene is described in a series of random details. The language – with its archaic Scottish dialect – is note-like and seemingly timeless. There is a notable absence of punctuation and a stilted rhythm as the unknown speaker's voice is introduced: 'I was reading my book in a ruin' (line 3). The series of fragmentary images – 'a sour candle', 'the crazed window' – are immediately unsettling, drawing us back to a darker age in Ireland's troubled history.

Characteristically, Ní Chuilleanáin leaves readers to unravel the poem's veiled meanings and the identity of the dispossessed narrator is never made known. Instead, this forlorn figure 'without roast meat or music' is associated with material and cultural deprivation – **a likely symbol of an oppressed Ireland**? Does the absence of 'Strong drink or a shield' add to the notion of a defeated people? Despite the obvious indications of almost incomprehensible suffering, some respite can still be found: 'I felt/Moonlight on my head, clear after three days' rain' (line 7). This simple image of nature – illuminating and refreshing – suggests comforting signs of recovery.

Ní Chuilleanáin's startling drama moves into the wild Irish landscape: 'I washed in cold water; it was orange.' The sense of native Irish resistance against foreign invasion is clearly evident in the reference to Dutch-born Protestant William of Orange, who defeated the army of Catholic James II at the Battle of the Boyne in 1690. But the poet focuses on the speaker's experience of displacement, illustrating the **alienation which existed within nationalist Ireland**. The narrator, surrounded by animal life and the open sky, becomes an extension of animate and inanimate nature: 'The bats flew through my room ... Sheep stared at me' (line 10).

In an increasingly surreal atmosphere, the mood becomes much more disturbed. The poet's apocalyptic dream-vision highlights the 'waves of darkness' in an uninterrupted nightmarish sequence of repulsive images: 'plague/Of mice, plague of beetles/Crawling'. The **emphatic repetition of 'plague' resonates with images of widespread misery, disease and famine**. Nor does the poet ignore the distorted history of Ireland that has resulted from prejudice, propaganda and vested interest 'Crawling out of the spines of books' (line 14). What stands out, however, is Ní Chuilleanáin's ability to suggest distressing glimpses of our island's dark past, poignantly depicted in her heart-rending language describing innocent death: 'Plague shadowing pale faces with clay/The disease of the moon gone astray.'

There is a distinctive change of mood in lines 17–20 as the speaker reflects on the aching aftermath in the period after 'Cromwell had departed'. References to Christian retreat and renewal indicate the **consolation provided by religious faith**: 'In the desert I relaxed, amazed/As the mosaic beasts on the chapel floor'. This sense of wonder through the possibility of spiritual fulfilment is developed in the metaphorical image of 'The sky growing through the hole in the roof'. As always, landscape and nature are features of Ní Chuilleanáin's poem, allowing readers access to her subtle thinking.

In sharp contrast to the earlier trauma, the final tone is remarkably composed and harmonious. The language – which has been somewhat archaic throughout much of the poem – is noticeably biblical: 'Sheepdogs embraced me; the grasshopper/Returned with lark and bee.' **There is an unmistakable sense of survival and newfound confidence** in line 23: 'I looked down between hedges of high thorn.' Ní Chuilleanáin's recognition of 'The hare, absorbed, sitting still' (a cross-reference to her poem 'On Lacking the Killer Instinct') reinforces the feeling of quiet resignation. Is she alluding to the maturity and relative peace of the present Irish state? At any rate, the poem ends on a hopeful note of vigorous resilience, with one of nature's liveliest sounds, 'the chirp of the stream running'.

Throughout this elusive poem, Ní Chuilleanáin has explored fascinating aspects of Irish history – a story that has been often lost in the 'silence of the night'. So much of Ireland's past is marked by exploitation and resistance. The poem has deep undercurrents of countless conflicts springing from both without and within. The moon has long been associated with love, beauty, loneliness, lunacy and death. Some critics have suggested that Ní Chuilleanáin's poem uses the moon to symbolise the struggle of women through the centuries. As usual, readers are free to judge for themselves. However, there is little doubt that 'Lucina Schynning in Silence of the Nicht' presents us with **an intense, self-enclosed world** – but one where the tensions and aspirations of Ireland's complex story are imaginatively encapsulated.

Writing About the Poem

'Eiléan Ní Chuilleanáin's poems offer rich rewards to the perceptive reader.' Discuss this view, with particular reference to 'Lucina Schynning in Silence of the Nicht'.

Sample Paragraph

While I first found Ní Chuilleanáin's poetry obscure and quite difficult, I really enjoyed reading 'Lucina Schynning'. The strange title and eerie atmosphere under the moonlight is typical of a poet who makes us, the reader, imagine the 'world' of the poem. I found it all very dramatic. The narrative voice seemed very traumatised and was convincing as it represented Ireland's troubled history – 'I washed myself in cold water', 'Behind me, waves of darkness'. What I really liked about the poet was that she suggested, rather than explained. The description of Irish people starving and dying was very moving – especially because of the word 'plague'. Ní Chuilleanáin's images of suffering were balanced by the positive ending. The character in the poem was at one with nature – 'sheep embraced me'. The poem asked many questions about how people today look at the past. I thought the final lines were really encouraging. The poet used many simple nature images such as the hare 'sitting still' and the 'chirp of the stream' to show a present-day Ireland where there is peace and contentment – unlike the war-torn past of the history books. Overall, I did enjoy 'Lucina Schynning' as it reminded me that there is still meaning in the beauty of nature.

EXAMINER'S COMMENT

This sensitive reaction to Ní Chuilleanáin's poem reflected on both the subject matter and style of the text using accurate quotations to support the discussion points. The poem's narrative was disclosed by drawing together its significant details. Very impressive vocabulary throughout: 'The narrative voice seemed very traumatised and was convincing as it represented Ireland's troubled history.' A solid high-grade response.

N.B. Access your eBook for additional sample paragraphs and a list of useful quotes with commentary.

Class/Homework Exercises

1. 'Ní Chuilleanáin's distinctive poetry is filled with subtle messages.' Discuss this statement, with particular reference to 'Lucina Schynning in Silence of the Nicht'.
2. 'Eiléan Ní Chuilleanáin's "Lucina Schynning in Silence of the Nicht" is a highly atmospheric poem that has an elusive dreamlike quality.' To what extent do you agree or disagree with this statement? Support your answer with reference to the poem.

Summary Points

- **Evocative mid-17th-century Irish setting.**
- **Dramatic monologue form recreates Irish alienation after Cromwell's invasion.**
- **Themes include suffering, loss, human resilience and the celebration of nature.**
- **Effective use of startling imagery, repetition, sibilance and alliteration.**

2 The Second Voyage

Odysseus rested on his oar and saw
The ruffled foreheads of the waves
Crocodiling and mincing past: he rammed
The oar between their jaws and looked down
In the simmering sea where scribbles of weed defined
Uncertain depth, and the slim fishes progressed
In fatal formation, and thought
If there was a single
Streak of decency in these waves now, they'd be ridged
Pocked and dented with the battering they've had,
And we could name them as Adam named the beasts,
Saluting a new one with dismay, or a notorious one
With admiration; they'd notice us passing
And rejoice at our shipwreck, but these
Have less character than sheep and need more patience.

I know what I'll do he said;
I'll park my ship in the crook of a long pier
(And I'll take you with me he said to the oar)
I'll face the rising ground and walk away
From tidal waters, up riverbeds
Where herons parcel out the miles of stream,
Over gaps in the hills, through warm
Silent valleys, and when I meet a farmer
Bold enough to look me in the eye
With 'where are you off to with that long
Winnowing fan over your shoulder?'
There I will stand still
And I'll plant you for a gatepost or a hitching-post
And leave you as a tidemark. I can go back
And organise my house then.
But the profound
Unfenced valleys of the ocean still held him;
He had only the oar to make them keep their distance;
The sea was still frying under the ship's side.
He considered the water-lilies, and thought about fountains
Spraying as wide as willows in empty squares,

Odysseus: Greek mythic king and warrior. He is also the literary hero of Homer's epic tale, *The Odyssey*, which tells of Odysseus's 10-year struggle to return home from the Trojan War.
ruffled: wrinkled, tangled.
Crocodiling: gliding.
mincing: moving daintily.
Pocked: disfigured.
notorious: infamous.
herons: long-necked wading birds.
parcel: mark, measure.
Winnowing: probing.

The sugarstick of water clattering into the kettle,
The flat lakes bisecting the rushes. He remembered spiders and frogs
Housekeeping at the roadside in brown trickles floored with mud,
Horsetroughs, the black canal, pale swans at dark:
His face grew damp with tears that tasted
Like his own sweat or the insults of the sea.

bisecting: cutting through.

'the simmering sea'

Personal Response

1. From your reading of the first stanza (lines 1–15), describe Odysseus's relationship with the sea. Refer to the text in your response.
2. Select two interesting images from the poem and comment on the effectiveness of each.
3. Write your own personal response to 'The Second Voyage', supporting the points you make with reference to the text.

Critical Literacy

The relationship between past and present is one of Eiléan Ní Chuilleanáin's recurring themes. In addressing the present within the context of history, she often explores contrasts, such as life and death, motion and stillness, and the inevitable tension between time passing and people's desire to resist change. 'The Second Voyage' refers to the Greek hero Odysseus, whose first epic journey was a relentless battle with the treacherous ocean. But growing frustrated by the endless struggle against nature, he decides that his next voyage will be on land and therefore less demanding.

From the outset, Odysseus is presented as a slightly bemused and ridiculous figure. There is a cartoon-like quality to the exaggerated ocean setting as Ní Chuilleanáin immediately portrays this legendary hero resting on his oar and watching the 'ruffled foreheads of the waves/Crocodiling and mincing past' (line 3). The poet expands this metaphor, describing the waves as great beasts to be challenged: 'he rammed/The oar between their jaws.' **Ní Chuilleanáin's derisive humour mocks the great wanderer's inflated sense of his own masculinity.** But there is no denying that Odysseus is still excited by the 'Uncertain depth' beneath him. For him, anything is possible at sea, where he is truly in his element. The personification is childlike, suggesting his peevish annoyance at being unable to conquer the ocean waves, which don't possess 'a single/Streak of decency' (line 9).

Ní Chuilleanáin's tone is playfully critical. As always, the poet's skill lies in her vigorous images, such as the 'slim fishes' beneath 'scribbles of weeds'. Odysseus's powerful physicality is contrasted with the seemingly pretty waves, which somehow resist the 'battering they've had'. Lording over this surreal scene and filled with disappointment, the egotistical Greek warrior thinks about the Garden of Eden. He is soon envying Adam, who was given God-given control over all living things and had 'named the beasts' of the earth. Completely unaware of the irony of his excessive pride, Odysseus is overwhelmed by self-pity and resorts to ridiculing these foolish waves, which fail to 'rejoice at our shipwreck' (line 14).

Ní Chuilleanáin develops the whimsical drama by letting us hear Odysseus's petulant voice as he prepares to seek recognition onshore. Armed with renewed confidence and his trusty oar – ('I'll take you with me he said to the oar') – he sets out to 'face the rising ground' and seek affirmation far away 'From tidal waters'. But despite the purposeful rhythm and self-assured tone, there is a strong underlying sense that he is deluding himself. The landscape might be serenely beautiful, but it is confined. Unlike the boundless sea, birds define it: 'herons parcel out the miles of stream' (line 21). Yet the brave warrior is eager to boast of his exploits in the outside world and hopes to tell his story to the first farmer he meets who is 'Bold enough to look me in the eye'. **Odysseus even tries to convince himself that it is time to put down roots**, to plant his oar as 'a gatepost or a

hitching-post'. Then he will be ready to return home and 'organise my house'. However, the laboured rhythm and imposing multi-syllabic language convey his half-heartedness about settling down.

Indeed, there are already signs that Odysseus will never surrender the freedom and adventure of dangerous ocean voyages. The powerful oar, which once signified dynamism and exhilaration, is now seen as a decorative symbol of stillness, a 'Winnowing fan'. Unable to deny his true destiny any longer, **he accepts that he cannot ignore his urge to control the sea**: the 'Unfenced valleys of the ocean still held him' (line 32). But his ironic situation remains; while the freedom he yearns for is unattainable on land, he is still unable to conquer the seemingly infinite sea.

The poem's final section is sympathetic to Odysseus's dilemma. Ní Chuilleanáin replaces the pompous first-person pronouns with her own measured narrative account: 'He considered the water-lilies, and thought about fountains' (line 35). The poet makes extensive use of **contrasting water images to highlight land and sea**. Unlike the water 'frying under the ship's side', settled life appears controlled, but unattractive ('Horsetroughs, the black canal'). His uneasy memories of home ('water clattering', 'pale swans at dark') are ominous. For Odysseus, his second excursion into landlocked civilisation offers so little fulfilment that 'His face grew damp with tears'. The hero is forever drawn to that first epic voyage and the wonderful experience of ocean living, with which he is inextricably bound: 'Like his own sweat or the insults of the sea.'

The fluctuating water images – another familiar feature of Eiléan Ní Chuilleanáin's writing – reflect the complex narrative threads throughout the poem. Transitions of various kinds are central to her work. The poet has also been very involved in translating texts, and believes that because of the limits imposed by the translator, the process can never be completely true to the original language. Some literary critics see 'The Second Voyage' as an **extended metaphor exploring how language and culture resist translation**, but like so many of Ní Chuilleanáin's enigmatic poems, the ultimate interpretation is left to individual readers themselves.

Writing About the Poem

'Ní Chuilleanáin's poetry makes effective use of contrasts to illuminate her themes.' Discuss this view, with particular reference to 'The Second Voyage'.

Sample Paragraph

Contrasting themes, such as life and death, permanence and transience, and motion and stillness are all prominent within Ní Chuilleanáin's 'The Second Voyage'. Such contrasts make it easier to understand her poetic world. The description of arrogant Odysseus who 'rammed' his oar against the waves shows a macho larger-than-life character whose extrovert behaviour could not be more unlike the silent sea with its 'Uncertain depth' which he will never tame. Momentarily, the irritated hero makes up his mind to undertake a new 'voyage' by seeking glory on land. But the reality of settled life disappoints him. Revealing images of fixed landmarks – 'a gatepost', 'hitching-post', 'tidemark' – all convey the sense of motionless disinterest. Odysseus is immediately aware of the contrasting dynamic qualities of the sea's 'Unfenced valleys'. Throughout the last stanza, Odysseus debates the relative attractions of land and sea. I found it interesting that the man-made images were all water-based – 'fountains', 'brown trickles', 'the black canal' – and all lacking the danger of the open sea which Odysseus longs for. The ending of the poem rounds off the choices facing Odysseus. Once again, Ní Chuilleanáin succeeds in juxtaposing his love-hate obsession with the mysterious ocean as his tears taste 'Like his own sweat or the insults of the sea'.

EXAMINER'S COMMENT

The introductory overview established a very good basis for exploring interesting contrasts within the poem. There is some well-focused personal engagement with the text: 'I found it interesting that the man-made images were all water-based.' Suitable quotations provide valuable support. Diction and expression – in the final sentence, for example – are also excellent. This confident response fully merits the top grade.

N.B. Access your eBook for additional sample paragraphs and a list of useful quotes with commentary.

Class/Homework Exercises

1. 'Eiléan Ní Chuilleanáin presents readers with unsettling scenes, both real and otherworldly.' Discuss this statement, with particular reference to 'The Second Voyage'. Refer to the text in your answer.
2. 'In "The Second Voyage", Ní Chuilleanáin addresses the idea of transition and the difficulties associated with change.' Discuss this view, supporting your answer with reference to the poem.

Summary Points

- **Imaginative use of mythic tale of Greek hero.**
- **Sardonic humour evident in vivid personification of the sea.**
- **Unsettling scenes, both real and otherworldly.**
- **Contrasting themes (transience, masculinity, freedom, etc.).**
- **Vibrant water imagery is a powerful motif.**
- **Alliteration and sibilance create dynamic sound effects.**
- **Direct dialogue adds immediacy.**

Deaths and Engines

We came down above the houses
In a stiff curve, and
At the edge of Paris airport
Saw an empty tunnel
– The back half of a plane, black
On the snow, nobody near it,
Tubular, burnt-out and frozen.

Tubular: cylindrical, tube shaped.

When we faced again
The snow-white runways in the dark
No sound came over
The loudspeakers, except the sighs
Of the lonely pilot.

The cold of metal wings is contagious:
Soon you will need wings of your own,
Cornered in the angle where
Time and life like a knife and fork
Cross, and the lifeline in your palm
Breaks, and the curve of an aeroplane's track
Meets the straight skyline.

contagious: catching.

The images of relief:
Hospital pyjamas, screens round a bed
A man with a bloody face
Sitting up in bed, conversing cheerfully
Through cut lips:
These will fail you some time.

conversing: chatting.

You will find yourself alone
Accelerating down a blind
Alley, too late to stop
And know how light your death is;

Accelerating: speeding.

You will be scattered like wreckage,
The pieces every one a different shape
Will spin and lodge in the hearts
Of all who love you.

lodge: settle.

'snow-white runways'

Personal Response

1. Describe the atmosphere at the airport in lines 1–12. Refer to the text in your response.
2. Based on your reading of lines 13–25, choose one image that you found particularly memorable and comment on its effectiveness.
3. Write your personal response to 'Deaths and Engines', referring closely to the poem in your answer.

Critical Literacy

'Deaths and Engines' contextualises Eiléan Ní Chuilleanáin's experience of death – and particularly her father's death – within the setting of another 'burnt-out' ruin: the abandoned wreckage of an aircraft engine. Characteristically, the poet's metaphorical sense is so complete that at times it dominates the poem, constantly inviting readers to tease out meaningful connections within the language.

As with so many of her poems, Ní Chuilleanáin begins mid-narrative – as dreams often do – with an aeroplane coming in to land in Paris. The sense of danger as the plane descends in 'a stiff curve' is typical of the edgy imagery found in stanza one. **The memory immediately suggests a moment of insight – of coming down to earth**: 'We came down above the houses/In a stiff curve.' Details are stark – particularly the absorbing description of the 'empty tunnel' and the peculiar sight of the 'back half of a plane' that has been 'burnt-out and frozen' against the wintry landscape. The contrast of the deserted 'black' wreckage 'On the snow' accentuates the visual effect, adding drama to the memory.

Stanza two emphasises the surreal nature of the hushed 'snow-white runways in the dark'. The poet continues to construct a dreamlike sense of uneasy silence and chilling alienation. The only sounds coming over the loudspeakers are the unsettling 'sighs/Of the lonely pilot'. There is an underlying suggestion of a weary individual – perhaps facing death. This is given a wider relevance by the unnerving opening of stanza three: 'The cold of metal wings is contagious.' For the poet, this insightful moment marks a changing perspective: 'Soon you will need wings of your own.' The 'you' might refer to Ní Chuilleanáin's dying father or the poet herself or possibly the reader. From this point onwards, the metaphor of the wrecked aircraft is central to the fragmentary memories of her father's illness and death. **The poet interweaves two narratives**: the trajectory of the plane as it 'Meets the straight skyline' and the mark of her father's natural life span ('the lifeline in your palm'). Ní Chuilleanáin uses the memorable image of the crossed knife and fork to suggest the inescapable destiny that confronts the dying.

The poet's familiar preoccupations of tension and mystery are even more obvious in stanza four. Disjointed scenes of 'Hospital pyjamas, screens round

a bed' are introduced as 'images of relief'– at least temporarily. **But the prevailing mood is of inevitable death** – 'These will fail you some time'. The poet expresses the final reality of every human being in stanza five: 'You will find yourself alone.' Ní Chuilleanáin conveys the nightmarish realisation of irreversible death through recognisable images of losing control: 'Accelerating down a blind/Alley, too late to stop.' Run-on lines and a persistent rhythm add to the sense of powerlessness. Once again, there are echoes of the 'empty tunnel' and the 'burnt-out' plane. Nevertheless, in imagining her father's final moments, the poet can relate to his experience of dying as a release, so that they both understood 'how light your death is'.

The resigned tone of stanza six reflects Ní Chuilleanáin's deeper understanding of mortality. In celebrating her father's life within a context of enduring love, the poet is able to simultaneously dismantle and preserve the relationship she has had with her father. She returns to the image of the wrecked aeroplane, accepting that in death, 'You will be scattered like wreckage'. However, far from feeling sadness for her father's loss, **Ní Chuilleanáin takes comfort in knowing that he will live 'in the hearts Of all who love you'**. The sentiment is subdued and poignant, and all the more powerful since it comes from a poet who rarely expresses her feelings directly.

To a great extent, the poem is about families and how they process their personal tragedies. As always, Ní Chuilleanáin's oblique approach is open to many interpretations. But she seems to be suggesting that it takes the sudden shock of death to acknowledge the closeness of relationships in our lives. Typically, in dealing with such emotional subjects as separation, grief and the death of a loved one, **the poet never lapses into sentimentality**. 'Deaths and Engines' was written during the escalation of violence in Northern Ireland, and some critics have understood the poem as a commentary on the human cost of conflict. In the end, readers are left to make up their own minds.

Writing About the Poem

'Ní Chuilleanáin's poems of separation and estrangement transcend the limits of personal experience.' Discuss this view, with particular reference to 'Deaths and Engines'.

Sample Paragraph

One of the most interesting aspects of Ní Chuilleanáin's poetry is her focus on the natural life cycle. Even though she deals with the distressing subject of her father's death in 'Deaths and Engines', I found the poem to be more uplifting than depressing. In closely comparing his death to the wrecked plane she saw in Paris, 'Tubular, burnt-out and frozen', she

eventually realises that all the 'pieces' of the wreckage 'Will spin and lodge in the hearts/Of all who love you'. Just because death has separated her from her father physically does not mean the end of their love. The poem also shows Ní Chuilleanáin empathising with her father and stressing the individual experience of death for every human being: 'You will find yourself alone/Accelerating down a blind/Alley, too late to stop.' Her message is simple – every individual must face death unaccompanied. In her poems, Ní Chuilleanáin can really accept the natural cycle – and this has meaning for every reader. In 'Fireman's Lift', for example, she also came to terms with a close family death – that of her mother – by comparing her passing to the glorious Assumption of the Virgin Mary. I believe that such poems transcend the individual and emphasise the naturalness of separation and loss.

EXAMINER'S COMMENT

This is a well-focused response to the question and shows a close understanding of the poem, particularly in the cross-reference to 'Fireman's Lift'. Accurate quotations are used effectively to support key points. Expression is fluent, varied and clear, with some good personal engagement, such as in the final sentence. A very assured performance securing the highest grade.

N.B. Access your eBook for additional sample paragraphs and a list of useful quotes with commentary.

Class/Homework Exercises

1. 'What defines Eiléan Ní Chuilleanáin's poetry is its imaginative power and precision of language.' Discuss this statement, with particular reference to 'Deaths and Engines'.
2. 'In "Deaths and Engines", Ní Chuilleanáin explores aspects of suffering and death by effectively using the metaphor of an aeroplane coming in to land.' Discuss this view, with reference to the poem.

Summary Points

- **Key themes – memory, family bonds and coming to terms with death.**
- **An underlying sense of tension pervades the poem.**
- **Effective use of metaphor, contrast and repetition throughout.**
- **Positive conclusion: love can transcend death.**

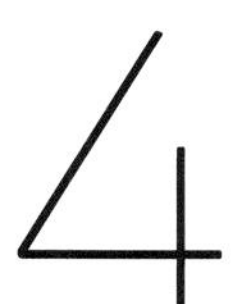

Street

He fell in love with the butcher's daughter
When he saw her passing by in her white trousers
Dangling a knife on a ring at her belt.
He stared at the dark shining drops on the paving-stones.

One day he followed her
Down the slanting lane at the back of the shambles.
A door stood half-open
And the stairs were brushed and clean,
Her shoes paired on the bottom step,
Each tread marked with the red crescent
Her bare heels left, fading to faintest at the top.

Dangling: hanging freely, displaying.

shambles: untidy market scene; place of slaughter.

tread: undersole of a shoe; top surface of a step in a staircase.
crescent: half-moon; sickle shape.
fading: dwindling, perishing.
faintest: weakest, exhausted.

'And the stairs were brushed and clean'

Personal Response

1. Why do you think Ní Chuilleanáin chose to name her poem 'Street' and yet gives the street no name? Give reasons for your response.
2. Which image did you find most intriguing in the poem? Refer closely to the text in your answer.
3. Were you satisfied by the poem's conclusion? Briefly explain your response.

Critical Literacy

'Street' is a short lyric poem from Ní Chuilleanáin's collection *The Magdalene Sermon* (1989). Mary Magdalene was the first person to witness the Resurrection of Christ and these poems reflect on women's religious experiences. The poems also depict edges, borders and crossings between different kinds of worlds as though passing through thresholds and intersections from one realm of experience to another, just as Christ rose from the dead. Characteristically, the poet reveals and conceals women and their strange responsibilities in a graceful, luminous voice.

Ní Chuilleanáin believed in the importance of the ordinary and the domestic as new metaphors for human experience. In the first section of the poem, she quietly tells a somewhat unusual tale, giving readers a memorable glimpse into another reality. It is the story of a man falling in love with a woman, 'the butcher's daughter'. Flowing run-on lines depict the rising emotions of the man as he catches sight of her 'in her white trousers'. This colour is often associated with purity and innocence, but it is also the traditional colour butchers wear in their work. **A close-up shot captures a disturbing detail**. 'Dangling' describes the careless movement of the knife as it sways from the 'ring at her belt'. The verb is carefully positioned at the beginning of the line, as it tantalises and entices like a piece of shining jewellery; yet this knife has a deadly purpose. The man is captivated: 'He stared at the dark shining drops on the paving-stones.' Has this knife recently been used? Has blood just been spilled? Is he, as if in a fairy tale, suddenly enthralled by the glittering yet lethal trade of the slaughterer?

In the second section, the narrative continues, becoming increasingly menacing: 'One day he followed her.' The assonant 'ow' sound disquietly enhances his journey. Ní Chuilleanáin specialises in the 'poetic of descriptive places'. The man's journey takes him 'Down the slanting lane at the back of the shambles'. **Varying line lengths add to the growing tension**. The adjective 'slanting' suggests a sinister backstreet where everything is oblique, tilted, half-concealed. The 'shambles' is a rough market where meat is carved and animals are slaughtered. To the outside world, it is a place of violence and mayhem. Is Ní Chuilleanáin making a hidden reference to the slaughter of Christ on the cross? 'A door stood half-open'. Does the door

admit or shut out? Is this a symbol of the threshold between life and death which Christ breached? As always, the poet invites the reader to make sense of the clues. A secret is being half-revealed, a mystery is being highlighted. Where does the door lead?

Eiléan Ní Chuilleanáin often peoples her poems with women who studiously attend to their chores. (Mary Magdalene attended to Jesus, washing his feet with her tears and drying them with her hair.) Here 'the stairs were brushed and clean'. Are they awaiting a visit or is this the attention to hygiene which is normal in the butchering trade? This poet's population of silent figures disclose little information. The 'butcher's daughter' had left 'shoes paired on the bottom step'. Yet even this tangible detail reveals only mystery. The full narrative is missing. Is there a suggestion that the man and woman will soon be a pair as well? An inviting flight of stairs leads to all sorts of possibilities. **Ní Chuilleanáin has created a typically ambivalent scenario** filled with underlying danger and excitement. This dreamlike encounter is imbued with an unforgettable atmosphere of edgy anticipation as profound silence echoes.

The poem concludes with a defined image. The girl's 'bare heels' have left traces which become more indistinct as they ascend the stairs. This is emphasised by the alliterative phrase 'fading to faintest'. These are 'marked with the red crescent', like a secret sign beckoning through the enjambed lines. **The mystery resonates**. What really is marked with the bow shapes? The stairs? Her shoes? The heels? Readers are kept wondering. What does the future hold for this couple? Detailed close-ups have been presented, yet there are tantalising gaps in the narrative as we are left like the man who was enticed by the 'Dangling' knife, lured into this ominous atmosphere. As in so many of her elusive dramas, disrupting patterns of communication allows the poet to draw attention to the problem of communication itself. Is this the rounded insight to be glimpsed in the poem?

Writing About the Poem

'Poems of waiting, dramatic and incident rich, are told quietly by Ní Chuilleanáin.' Discuss this statement in relation to the poem 'Street'.

Sample Paragraph

I felt that the poem 'Street' invited me into its dreamlike, surreal yet tangible world rather like the man is lured by the 'butcher's daughter'. I was caught as if in a dream, that state of consciousness between sleep and wakefulness, where details are clearly recognisable, 'the dark shining drops', 'the red crescent/her bare heels left', yet their meaning is shrouded in mystery. Just as the 'half-open' door both invites and repels, this poem reveals and conceals. Will the encounter take place between

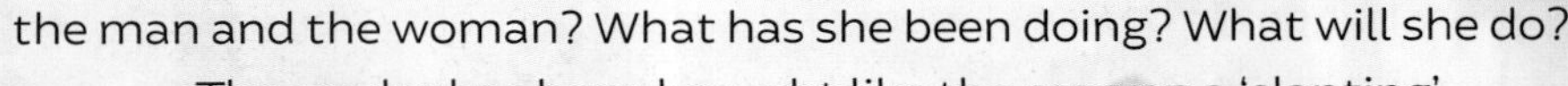

the man and the woman? What has she been doing? What will she do? The reader has been brought like the man on a 'slanting' journey. The full view of the lane was obscured from him, the full story is hidden by the obliqueness of the poem. Yet just like a dream the atmosphere is unforgettable, the waiting is palpably ominous. The poem disappears at its conclusion as the 'red crescent' marks flow 'fading to faintest at the top'. Suspense and tension reverberate. As in life nobody knows what will happen next. This tale is told calmly as the poet leaves us to complete the story for ourselves. The reader is led like the man, by well-realised signs, 'drops', a 'lane', a 'door', 'stairs' and footprints as if following a trail in a fairy tale. Yet the poet does not release the dramatic tensions at the poem's conclusion leaving it to resonate in the reader's consciousness.

EXAMINER'S COMMENT

This response shows a remarkably close reading of the poem, using suitable reference and quotation to address the task in the question throughout. Discussion is coherent and the analysis incisive, especially the point about the dreamlike atmosphere. Expression is also impressive – fluent, varied and well controlled: 'the full story is hidden from the reader by the obliqueness of the poem.' Deserves the top grade.

N.B. Access your eBook for additional sample paragraphs and a list of useful quotes with commentary.

Class/Homework Exercises

1. 'Ní Chuilleanáin's poetry is oblique, yet concrete.' Discuss this statement in relation to 'Street'.
2. 'Ní Chuilleanáin creates an unnerving nightmarish atmosphere in her poem, "Street".' To what extent do you agree with this view? Support your answer with reference to the text.

Summary Points

- **Highly dramatic poem filled with suspense and intrigue.**
- **Close-up details create interest.**
- **Run-through lines add a sense of urgency.**
- **Sense of mystery resonates at the end.**

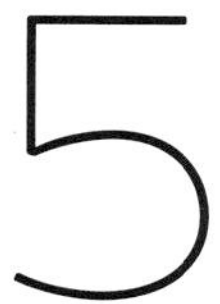

Fireman's Lift

Fireman's Lift: The term refers to a technique commonly used by emergency service workers to carry someone to safety by placing the carried person across the shoulders of the carrier.

I was standing beside you looking up
Through the big tree of the cupola
Where the church splits wide open to admit
Celestial choirs, the fall-out of brightness.

The Virgin was spiralling to heaven,
Hauled up in stages. Past mist and shining,
Teams of angelic arms were heaving,
Supporting, crowding her, and we stepped

Back, as the painter longed to
While his arm swept in the large strokes.
We saw the work entire, and how the light

Melted and faded bodies so that
Loose feet and elbows and staring eyes
Floated in the wide stone petticoat
Clear and free as weeds.

This is what love sees, that angle:
The crick in the branch loaded with fruit,
A jaw defining itself, a shoulder yoked,

The back making itself a roof
The legs a bridge, the hands
A crane and a cradle.

Their heads bowed over to reflect on her
Fair face and hair so like their own
As she passed through their hands. We saw them
Lifting her, the pillars of their arms

(Her face a capital leaning into an arch)
As the muscles clung and shifted
For a final purchase together
Under her weight as she came to the edge of the cloud.

Parma 1963 – Dublin 1994

cupola: dome-shaped roof.

Celestial: heavenly, divine.

spiralling: whirling, twisting.

crick: arch, strain.

yoked: forced, strained.

capital: upper section of a column supporting a ceiling or arch.

The Assumption of the Virgin: Roman Catholic Church teaching states that the Virgin Mary, having completed the course of her earthly life, was assumed (or elevated) body and soul into heavenly glory. Antonio Allegri da Correggio (1489–1534), usually known as Correggio, was the foremost painter of the Parma school of the Italian Renaissance. One of his best-known works, The *Assumption of the Virgin*, is a fresco which decorates the dome of the Duomo (Cathedral) of Parma, in northern Italy.

'spiralling to heaven'

Personal Response

1. Based on your reading of the poem, comment on the appropriateness of the title, 'Fireman's Lift'.
2. Choose one visual image from the poem which you consider particularly effective. Briefly explain your choice.
3. Write your own short personal response to the poem.

Critical Literacy

This extraordinary poem describes the scene depicted in the painter Correggio's masterpiece, *Assumption of the Virgin*. In 1963 Eiléan Ní Chuilleanáin and her mother had visited Parma Cathedral. Following her mother's death in 1994, the poet used the visit as the setting for 'Fireman's Lift', describing it as a 'cheering-up poem, when my mother was dying because I absolutely knew that she would want me to write a poem about her dying ...'

The poem begins with Ní Chuilleanáin's vivid memory of the moment when she and her mother were looking up at Correggio's celebrated ceiling mural. In the opening stanza, she invites readers into the Italian setting: 'I was standing beside you looking up/Through the big tree of the cupola.' There is **an immediate dreamlike sense of intimacy and closeness between mother and daughter**, as though they were both aware that something significant was happening. From the outset, the focus is on the majestic painting's mystery and symbolism, reaching heavenwards to imagined 'Celestial choirs'.

Stanza two emphasises the struggle of the angels to lift Mary into the heavens, and the awkwardness and wonder of being pushed in such a similar manner to birth. We are encouraged to become part of the dynamic scene within the reality of this great spectacle. The dynamic verbs 'spiralling' and 'heaving' suggest **the physical effort involved in raising the Virgin from her earthly life**. Line breaks and frequent commas are used to create a sluggish pace. Ní Chuilleanáin is drawn to the collective energy which becomes a fireman's lift of 'Teams of angelic arms', and the effort to raise Mary 'Past mist and shining' is relentless.

Ní Chuilleanáin then considers the overwhelming effect of Correggio's 'work entire', designed to give the illusion of real and simulated architecture within the painted fresco. This awe-inspiring achievement is reflected in the pulsating run-through rhythms and hushed tones of stanzas three and four. **Dramatic images of the angelic figures and saints assisting Mary's Assumption give expression to the artist's powerful vision**: 'Melted and faded bodies' are intermingled with 'elbows and staring eyes'. Within the dome/petticoat image, Ní Chuilleanáin describes Correggio's Virgin passing into another glorious life. All the time, this vortex of bodies and faces around

her are fully engaged in assisting Mary to reach the waiting Christ. Stanza five defines an important turning point for the poet, who can now make sense of her mother's death through a fresh understanding of Correggio's perspective: 'This is what love sees, that angle.' **The assured tone marks a coming-to-terms with deep personal loss**. Ní Chuilleanáin's renewed appreciation of the painting enables her to accept the burden of letting the dead go. Her resignation is evident in the poignant image of a 'branch loaded with fruit', an obvious symbol of the natural cycle.

Stanzas six and seven return to **Correggio's mesmerising skill in his interaction of art and architecture** within the cathedral dome. This intricate collusion is seen in sharper focus, providing a context for Ní Chuilleanáin to reassert her changing relationship with her mother. The restless limbs of the painted angels are in perfect harmony with the great Duomo ceiling: 'The back making itself a roof/The legs a bridge.' This intriguingly harmonious composition merging paint and plaster adds to the urgency of ensuring that the dying soul achieves its ultimate ascension to heaven.

The final stanzas observe the figures attending on Mary, 'heads bowed over to reflect on her/Fair face'. Their tenderness is evident in both sound and tone. The poet has said that, on one level, 'Fireman's Lift' is about the nurses who looked after her mother when she was dying. Typically, the poet broadens our understanding of suffering, showing people caring and concerned. The concluding lines, however, acknowledge **the strength of spirit which Ní Chuilleanáin singles out as the hallmark of her mother's life and death**. This is reflected in the purposeful expression on the Virgin's face: 'As the muscles clung and shifted/For a final purchase.' Tactile 'u' sounds ('usc', 'ung', 'urch', etc.) and the drawn-out rhythms emphasise that body goes with soul in the movement across this threshold: 'to the edge of the cloud.'

Death and rebirth are recurring themes in Ní Chuilleanáin's work. But in honouring her mother's life and associating her passing with the Assumption of the Virgin, the poet has brought together Italian art, religion and a deep sense of sorrow. Essentially, however, **'Fireman's Lift' is a moving expression of the poet's enduring love** for her mother. It is not unusual for readers of Ní Chuilleanáin's poetry to encounter beautiful images which leave them searching. Nevertheless, this poem has a universal significance. It is infused with an astounding sense of love, loss and triumph as the ascending figure disappears into the clouds. Poised on the edge of this unknowable boundary, the rest is mystery.

Writing About the Poem

'For Eiléan Ní Chuilleanáin, boundaries and transitions are central concerns.' Discuss this view with particular reference to 'Fireman's Lift'.

Sample Paragraph

I found 'Fireman's Lift' both puzzling and interesting. Ní Chuilleanáin managed to link her mother's death with the famous painting by Antonio Correggio, *Assumption of the Virgin*. In describing her memory of a holiday visit to Parma Cathedral, the poet seemed to enter the reality of the mural and see her own relationship with her mother in a new way – almost like one of the angels who desperately tries to raise Mary to heaven, 'Teams of angelic arms were heaving'. The transition is shown in terms of brute strength – the Virgin is 'Hauled up in stages'. But the poet also reflects the transition between this life and the next in the optical illusions painted on the dome's structure. Everything appears to be integrated – for example, the hands of angels act as a 'crane and a cradle' supporting Mary. She leans on the 'pillars of their arms'. This metaphor blurs the distinction between stonework and painted figures. The poet sees no difference between her own prayers for her mother's soul and the work of the saints who raise the Virgin. To me, Ní Chuilleanáin is absorbed in the art work. I found this typical of her poetry in that she wanders beyond borders and margins, just as Correggio did within his celebrated painting.

EXAMINER'S COMMENT

An incisive response which addresses this challenging question directly. There is good personal interaction: 'To me, Ní Chuilleanáin is absorbed in the art work', and effective use of supportive references. Clearly made points explore the poet's emphasis on the blurred lines within the Correggio painting, and between it and Ní Chuilleanáin's own involvement. Such in-depth analysis merits the top grade.

N.B. Access your eBook for additional sample paragraphs and a list of useful quotes with commentary.

Class/Homework Exercises

1. 'Eiléan Ní Chuilleanáin's poems explore the persistence of memory in a highly distinctive style.' Discuss this statement with particular reference to 'Fireman's Lift'.
2. '"Fireman's Lift" is typical of Ní Chuilleanáin's poems in that it is layered with hidden meaning.' To what extent do you agree with this view? Support your answer with reference to the text.

Summary Points

- **Characteristic narrative opening recalling a significant memory.**
- **Effective use of run-on lines, symbolism, dramatic images of art and architecture.**
- **Vivid details and powerful verbs suggest physical effort.**
- **Key themes – death, rebirth, family relationships and enduring love.**

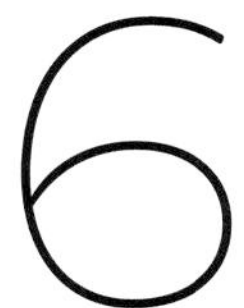

All for You

Once beyond the gate of the strange stableyard, we dismount.
The donkey walks on, straight in at a wide door
And sticks his head in a manger.

The great staircase of the hall slouches back,
Sprawling between warm wings. It is for you.
As the steps wind and warp
Among the vaults, their thick ribs part; the doors
Of guardroom, chapel, storeroom
Swing wide and the breath of ovens
Flows out, the rage of brushwood,
The roots torn and butchered.

It is for you, the dry fragrance of tea-chests
The tins shining in ranks, the ten-pound jars
Rich with shrivelled fruit. Where better to lie down
And sleep, along the labelled shelves,
With the key still in your pocket?

wind: curve, meander.
warp: bend, buckle.
vaults: large rooms often used for storage; chambers beneath a church.
ribs: curved structures that support a vault.
brushwood: undergrowth, small twigs and branches.

Personal Response

1. Would you agree that there is a dramatic trance-like atmosphere in this poem? Support your answer with reference to the text.
2. Choose one particularly vivid image from the poem and briefly explain its effectiveness.
3. Write your own individual response to the poem, referring closely to the text in your answer.

Critical Literacy

'All for You' comes from Eiléan Ní Chuilleanáin's *The Brazen Serpent* (1994). The book's title refers to the biblical story of Moses and the Israelites in the desert. God had become angry with his people, as they had spoken against their leader, Moses, and He let fierce snakes crawl among them and bite them. Moses prayed for the people and God instructed Moses to make a bronze serpent and place it upon a pole in public view. Anyone who was bitten could then look on the brazen snake and they would be cured. This

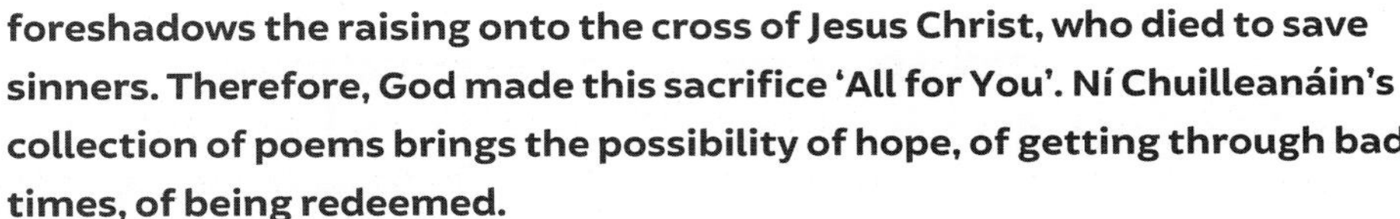

foreshadows the raising onto the cross of Jesus Christ, who died to save sinners. Therefore, God made this sacrifice 'All for You'. Ní Chuilleanáin's collection of poems brings the possibility of hope, of getting through bad times, of being redeemed.

Ní Chuilleanáin **collapses time and distinctions betweeen places** in 'All for You'. Line by line, the reader is drawn into deeper water until the bottom can no longer be touched, a recurring feature of this poet's complex work. The first three lines describe a scene that resonates with detail from the Bible story of the birth of Jesus: 'the strange stableyard', 'The donkey', the 'manger'. Why is the stableyard 'strange'? In the biblical account, Joseph and Mary had to leave their home town and travel to Bethlehem to be listed for a tax census. As is often the case with Ní Chuilleanáin's dramatic presentations, the reader must piece together a bare minimum of narrative sense. However, there is a sense of inevitability about the journey being described.

In lines 4–11, a noticeably different time and space is realised. What follows is **a series of evocative images and metaphors relating to a transitional experience**. Personification brings a staircase vividly to life as it 'slouches back', lolling and slumping – 'Sprawling' almost like a reclining animal as it sits between the 'warm wings' of the hall. Is it ominous or welcoming? It is waiting, as the bronze serpent awaited the Israelites, like a gift 'for you'. Ní Chuilleanáin does not determine the identity of 'you', instead leaving it open to speculation so that 'you' could have a universal application and refer to anyone. Is this gift for all? The poet's descriptive talent engages the reader as the grand staircase is depicted with great clarity, yet its full significance is never defined. Alliteration ('wind and warp') conveys the stairs' sinuous movement, curling like an uncoiling animal through the 'thick ribs' of the intimidating vaults.

The architectural metaphor is a strong element in Ní Chuilleanáin's poetry, which is full of mysterious crannies and alcoves. Could this imposing building be a convent waiting to welcome a young woman as its doors open, revealing the imposing interior of 'guardroom, chapel' and 'storeroom'? The poet's three aunts were nuns and she has commented, 'One is constantly made aware of the fact that the past does not go away, that it is walking around the place causing trouble at every moment.' Is this reference therefore autobiographical or does it encompass a wider significance? Could the staircase lead to salvation and heaven?

A rush of heat from the nearby ovens is suddenly palpable – again conveyed through the poet's effective working of personification: 'the breath of ovens/Flows out.' Ní Chuilleanáin uses a violent image to describe the fierce temperature: 'the rage of brushwood.' This is continued

in the savagery with which the kindling has been collected: 'roots torn out and butchered.' Is there an echo of the biblical tale of the burning bush from the **Book of Exodus**, where God directed Moses to the Promised Land? This story teaches that we should be able to obey God whenever he calls us. Is the poet also referencing the story of Christ, 'butchered' on the cross for the sins of the world? The forceful rhythm of these dramatic lines creates an intensity, a climax of dread, almost like an ecstatic spiritual experience.

There is a marked **change of tone** in the last five lines. All the tension eases within the ordered space of the building's provisions store. Readers are now immersed in the moment, smelling the 'dry fragrance of tea-chests', observing 'tins shining in ranks, the ten-pound jars'. Repetition of the rich 'r' sound suggests the store's abundance of goods. Yet there is also an unease secreted in this image of confined order. The fruit is 'shrivelled', the fragrance is 'dry'. Is there a life withering, unable to reproduce? Is this another central dimension of religious life? The poem concludes with a rhetorical question intimating that there is nowhere better to take rest, just as Joseph and Mary did long ago in that 'strange stable yard', than here 'along the labelled shelves'. The body's surrender and submission to God's will enables it to act.

Another biblical reference is suggested in the final detail of the 'key still in your pocket'. In Isaiah 33:6, faith is the key to salvation: 'He will be the sure foundation of your times, a rich store of salvation and wisdom and knowledge; the fear of the Lord is the key to this treasure.' Ní Chuilleanáin's poem focuses on the experience of Christian faith as imagined through the imposing challenge and triumph of religious vocations. The 'key' image is typically contradictory – symbolising both confinement and freedom. Is the poet presenting the central paradox of Christian belief? Can the soul's redemption only be achieved through submission to God's will? Characteristically, Ní Chuilleanáin's multi-layered narrative has been subtly woven, offering a glimpse, perhaps, of salvation and hope.

Writing About the Poem

'Eiléan Ní Chuilleanáin's poetry is an unshaped fire demanding to be organised into a sequence of words and images.' Discuss this statement in relation to 'All for You'.

Sample Paragraph

'All for You' is an unsettling poem which seems to emerge from the subconscious like an unformed fire. The poem springs from the idea of a gift which is 'All for You'. Like an 'unshaped fire', the poem's religious theme 'Flows out' like the heat from the ovens. Yet it is carefully layered.

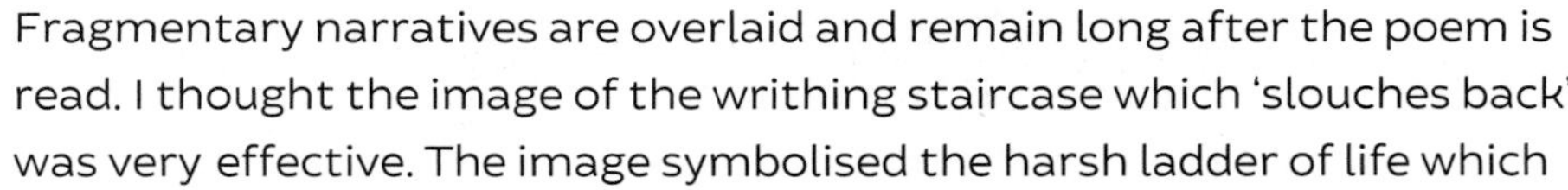

Fragmentary narratives are overlaid and remain long after the poem is read. I thought the image of the writhing staircase which 'slouches back' was very effective. The image symbolised the harsh ladder of life which Christians must climb to reach salvation. Ní Chuilleanáin's use of alliteration, 'wind and warp', emphasised the twisting turns life takes and also called to mind the uncoiling serpent – the devil, perhaps. I got the sense of being in a strange building with old-fashioned rooms and vaults. The storeroom imagery reflected the enclosed religious world, with 'the dry fragrance of tea-chests' and 'shrivelled fruit'. The sense of routine and order was also present: 'The tins shining in ranks.' Ironically, this strict religious life of submission represented the 'key' to salvation. The repetition of 'It is for you' suggests a generous God wishing to give a precious gift and what gift could be more important than the gift of hope? All the poet's ideas are expressed in patterns of visionary and spiritual language which can be seen as a powerful 'unshaped fire'.

EXAMINER'S COMMENT

A clear personal response to a challenging question. Key discussion points are very well developed and effectively illustrated. This shows a good understanding of this complex poem – and particularly the poet's use of dense symbols and overlapping images. Expression throughout is confident, fluent and well controlled. An excellent response that merits the highest grade.

N.B. Access your eBook for additional sample paragraphs and a list of useful quotes with commentary.

Class/Homework Exercises

1. 'Ní Chuilleanáin's language is subtle and acute enough to undertake its most difficult subject: how we perceive and understand the world.' Discuss this statement in relation to the prescribed work of the poet on your course.
2. '"All for You" illustrates Ní Chuilleanáin's deep interest in the mysteries of Christianity.' To what extent do you agree with this view? Support your answer with reference to the poem.

Summary Points

- **The poem explores various aspects of choosing the Christian life.**
- **Personification and architectural imagery create a sense of mystery.**
- **Effective use of biblical and religious references.**
- **Descriptive details and provocative images add drama.**

Following

Following: coming after in time or sequence, people about to be mentioned or listed; those who admire or support somebody.

So she follows the trail of her father's coat through the fair
Shouldering past beasts packed solid as books,
And the dealing men nearly as slow to give way –
A block of a belly, a back like a mountain,
A shifting elbow like a plumber's bend –
When she catches a glimpse of a shirt-cuff, a handkerchief,
Then the hard brim of his hat, skimming along,

Until she is tracing light footsteps
Across the shivering bog by starlight,
The dead corpse risen from the wakehouse
Gliding before her in a white habit.
The ground is forested with gesturing trunks,
Hands of women dragging needles,
Half-choked heads in the water of cuttings,
Mouths that roar like the noise of the fair day.

She comes to where he is seated
With whiskey poured out in two glasses
In a library where the light is clean,
His clothes all finely laundered,
Ironed facings and linings.
The smooth foxed leaf has been hidden
In a forest of fine shufflings,
The square of white linen
That held three drops
Of her heart's blood is shelved
Between the gatherings
That go to make a book –
The crushed flowers among the pages crack
The spine open, push the bindings apart.

beasts: animals at an Irish mart.
dealing men: dealers, men who bargain as they buy and sell animals at an Irish fair.
plumber's bend: length of 18 inches from the bend of the elbow to the tip of the middle finger.
brim: edge.

wakehouse: house, particularly in Ireland, where a dead person is laid out; people come to console the grieving relatives and to pay their respects to the deceased.

cuttings: small pieces of plants.

facings: strengthening linings; collar, cuffs and trimmings on a uniform coat.
linings: layers of material used to cover and protect.
foxed: soiled; marked with fox-like reddish spots and stains, often found on old books and documents.
leaf: single sheet of paper.
shufflings: walking slowly and awkwardly.

spine: vertical back of book to which pages are attached.
bindings: material which holds pages together.

Personal Response

1. Based on your reading of the poem, show how Ní Chuilleanáin conjures up the atmosphere of an Irish fair day. Refer closely to the text in your response.
2. In your opinion, how many settings are there in this poem? Which one did you prefer? Give reasons for your choice, quoting to support your answer.
3. Choose one vivid image from the third stanza of the poem and briefly explain its effectiveness.

Critical Literacy

Eiléan Ní Chuilleanáin often assumes a storytelling role in her poems as she relates memories from the past. She readjusts the perspective of readers by taking us into the lives of ordinary people who literally and physically made history. In her collection *The Brazen Serpent*, Ní Chuilleanáin highlights family and women as makers of history. She hints at the untold through her use of characters, silences and secrets. These confidential witnesses, like the poet herself, reconstruct subtle revelations of family unease and discontentment. Female imagery expresses what is silenced. The poet frequently explores religious themes as well as death and rebirth. Quietly and precisely, she offers us the comfort that the past does not go away.

In the opening section, the poet begins her story in her usual oblique, non-confessional style, yet deeply engages the reader despite her seeming

detachment. A vividly realised journey by a girl through the hurly-burly of an Irish fair day catapults the reader into the story. She is trying to follow her father through the dense crowds: 'the trail of her father's coat through the fair.' Long run-on lines and broad vowels convey the difficulty of negotiating the route as she attempts to push past 'beasts packed as solid as books'. This unusual simile illustrates the tightly packed rows of animals. Nor could she easily make her way through the dealers, men caught up in the very serious business of buying and selling, making a deal. Their thick-set bodies, bulky like their animals, are described through a tumbling list of similes and metaphors to highlight their immobile weight: 'A block of a belly, a back like a mountain.' A 'shifting elbow' is like the measure used in plumbing. All these images reinforce the **tough, masculine world of the fair**. Ní Chuilleanáin has pushed the reader, through her unwavering gaze, into the poem's self-enclosed world.

Suddenly, in line 6, the girl catches a glimpse of her father. This is shown by a list of his clothing: 'a shirt-cuff, a handkerchief,/Then the hard brim of his hat.' His progress is swift and effortless. He moves as swiftly as the punctuation (a series of fast-moving commas) accelerates the motion of the line. Sharp contrast in the verbs used to describe the progress of the girl and her father **highlight their different rates of success in moving through the fair**. The girl is struggling, 'Shouldering past', while the father moves with ease, 'skimming along'. Is Ní Chuilleanáin suggesting that a woman finds it difficult to negotiate a man's world? The poet has hypnotically caught the excitement as well as the danger of the fair day.

Distance and time blur in the second section. Ní Chuilleanáin shifts the scene and time frame from the noise and physical bulk of the fair to the **'shivering bog'**. Personification and slender vowels effectively convey the cold 'starlight' scene she is revisiting, 'tracing light footsteps', mapping faint prints. **A surreal, nightmarish world is presented**, as 'The dead corpse risen from the wakehouse' appears 'before her in a white habit'. Whose corpse is this? The effortless sense of 'Gliding' suggests the agile movement of the father. Momentarily, the packed animals of the fair have given way to the ground 'forested with gesturing trunks'. Now the heavy trees are highlighting her way, she will ultimately follow her father into death. Thin waving rushes are evocatively described as 'Hands of women dragging needles'. Their slow cumbersome movement is presented in visionary terms. Is this a reference to the story from the Bible when the Pharaoh of Egypt decreed that because of the increasing numbers of Israelites, all first-born boys were to be drowned in the River Nile? Are these the half-choked heads? Is this the wail of Israelite women and children as they cry and 'roar' like the beasts in the fair, aware of their fate? Or is it a reference to the subordination of women as they work?

In the poem's concluding section, the girl meets her father in a much more hospitable setting with 'whiskey poured in two glasses', 'His clothes all finely

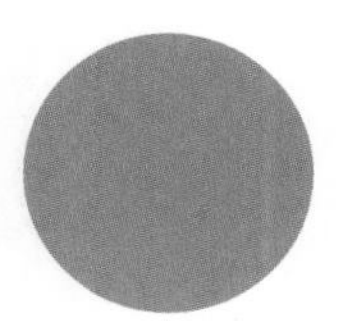

laundered'. Within these domestic interiors of the poet's imagination lies the remote **possibility of utopia**. The 'square of white linen', redolent of the survivor's suffering, shrunk and stained by the body's signifiers of hurt, becomes a relic of love and loss. Ní Chuilleanáin has commented, 'A relic is something you enclose, and then you enclose the reliquary in something else. In the *The Book of Kells* exhibition, the book satchel is in leather, which is meant to protect, and there is a shrine which in turn is meant to protect the book.' A relic is associated with people seeking comfort in difficult times. The past is beautifully evoked in the phrase 'The smooth foxed leaf has been hidden', with its haunting image of time-stained pages. Inside the book are 'crushed flowers', reminders that love was violated, yet something of it remains.

These memories have tremendous power; they 'crack' and push apart as if being reborn. Living and dead touch each other through such memories. The dust and noise of the cattle market, the cold starry bog have all evaporated to be replaced by this interior where the 'light is clean', making it easy to see. Comfort and hope are being offered as the poem suggests that the past is not dead.

Writing About the Poem

'Ní Chuilleanáin's poems explore how the most basic legends – family stories – fragment and alter in each individual's memory.' Discuss this statement with particular reference to the poem 'Following'.

Sample Paragraph

Ní Chuilleanáin's poem, 'Following', dredges up fragments of uniquely Irish family stories (the fair day, a wake, women sewing) and rearranges them, as cards are moved in 'shufflings'. This reconstructs and transforms the past so that we can see and understand from a new perspective. We are brought as followers, just like the girl in the fair, on a journey to discover that the past is not dead, but resonates through the present by means of relics, 'The square of white linen', and so gives hope and comfort to those left behind. The title suggests that we are all following one another through life, but at different paces, like the girl and the father in the fair. In the masculine world of the fair, 'beasts packed solid as books' the girl found it hard to negotiate her way. The poet has identified the difficult role women have in life, 'dragging needles', employed in domestic drudgery. These women are unable to express their concerns, 'Half-choked'. The legends become 'crushed flowers' yet the poet suggests that they are so potent that they can 'crack' open the book in which they are enclosed. I felt that she was communicating the message of hope that the past does not stay in the past but reverberates

through the present. Our memories do not remain 'shelved' but live again in the present through the power of relics.

N.B. Access your eBook for additional sample paragraphs and a list of useful quotes with commentary.

EXAMINER'S COMMENT

This is a very impressive response which deserves the highest grade. The focus throughout is firmly placed on addressing the various parts of the question. Quotations are integrated effectively and the answer ranges widely from the title to the individual stories and the imagery used in conveying the narratives. Language is carefully controlled to express points clearly, e.g. 'This reconstructs and transforms the past so that we can see and understand from a new perspective'.

Class/Homework Exercises

1. 'The mysterious writing style of Ní Chuilleanáin allows the reader to explore the poems on many levels, each tracking a different aspect of the cycle of life.' Discuss this statement in relation to the prescribed poems of this poet on your course.
2. 'Ní Chuilleanáin's unsettling poetic voice can often seem deceptively simple.' Discuss this statement with particular reference to the poem 'Following'. Support your answer with reference to the text.

Summary Points

- **The poet assumes a familiar story-telling role in this mystery tale.**
- **Themes include Irish identity and the power of memory.**
- **Effective use of commas, dashes and run-on lines.**
- **Prominent sound effects (alliteration and assonance) add emphasis.**

8 Kilcash

Title: Eiléan Ní Chuilleanáin's translation of the early 19th-century ballad *Caoine Cill Chais* (The Lament for Kilcash), an anonymous lament that the castle of Cill Chais stood empty, its woods cut down and all its old grandeur disappeared. Kilcash was one of the great houses of a branch of the Butler family near Clonmel, Co. Tipperary, until well into the 18th century. Ní Chuilleanáin's poem encompasses several generations of the Butler family, but the presiding spirit is that of Margaret Butler, Viscountess Iveagh (who died in 1744).

From the Irish, c. 1800

What will we do now for timber
With the last of the woods laid low –
No word of Kilcash nor its household,
Their bell is silenced now,
Where the lady lived with such honour,
No woman so heaped with praise,
Earls came across oceans to see her
And heard the sweet words of Mass.

the last of the woods: a reference to the mass clearance of native Irish forests by plantation settlers to create agricultural land and to fuel the colonial economy. The woodland belonging to the Butlers of Kilcash were sold in 1797 and 1801.
the lady: Margaret Butler, Viscountess Iveagh, a staunch Catholic (d. 1744).

It's the cause of my long affliction
To see your neat gates knocked down,
The long walks affording no shade now
And the avenue overgrown,
The fine house that kept out the weather,
Its people depressed and tamed;
And their names with the faithful departed,
The Bishop and Lady Iveagh!

The Bishop: Catholic clergy – including Lady Iveagh's brother-in-law – were often given shelter in Kilcash.
commotion: noise, clamour.

The geese and the ducks' commotion,
The eagle's shout, are no more,
The roar of the bees gone silent,
Their wax and their honey store
Deserted. Now at evening
The musical birds are stilled
And the cuckoo is dumb in the treetops
That sang lullaby to the world.

lullaby: soothing song.

Even the deer and the hunters
That follow the mountain way
Look down upon us with pity,
The house that was famed in its day;
The smooth wide lawn is all broken,
No shelter from wind and rain;
The paddock has turned to a dairy
Where the fine creatures grazed.

paddock: enclosure.

Mist hangs low on the branches
No sunlight can sweep aside,
Darkness falls among daylight
And the streams are all run dry;
No hazel, no holly or berry,
Bare naked rocks and cold;
The forest park is leafless
And all the game gone wild.

And now the worst of our troubles:
She has followed the prince of the Gaels –
He has borne off the gentle maiden,
Summoned to France and to Spain.
Her company laments her
That she fed with silver and gold:
One who never preyed on the people
But was the poor souls' friend.

My prayer to Mary and Jesus
She may come safe home to us here
To dancing and rejoicing
To fiddling and bonfire
That our ancestors' house will rise up,
Kilcash built up anew
And from now to the end of the story
May it never again be laid low.

prince of the Gaels: probably a reference to the 18th Earl of Ormonde.
the gentle maiden: Countess, wife of the 18th Earl.

preyed: harmed, took advantage of.

'affording no shade now'

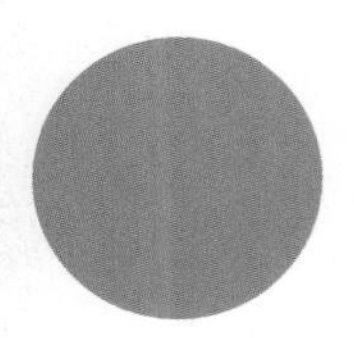

Personal Response

1. From your reading of the poem, what is your impression of Lady Iveagh? Refer to the text in your answer.
2. Choose one interesting image from 'Kilcash' that you consider particularly effective. Give reasons to explain why this image appealed to you.
3. Write your own individual response to the poem, referring closely to the text in your answer.

Critical Literacy

'Kilcash' comes from Eiléan Ní Chuilleanáin's *The Girl Who Married the Reindeer* (2001). Many of the poems in this collection deal with outsiders and the dispossessed. Kilcash was the great house of one of the branches of the Butler family near Clonmel, Co. Tipperary, until the 18th century. The Butlers were Catholic landed gentry who had come to Ireland as part of an Anglo-Norman invasion during the 12th century and had taken over vast amounts of land. Over time, the family became absorbed into Irish ways. Ní Chuilleanáin's version of the traditional Irish elegy, *Caoine Cill Chais*, mourns the death of Margaret Butler, Viscountess Iveagh.

Stanza one opens with a plaintive voice lamenting 'What will we do now for timber'. The ballad was originally composed in the early 1800s following the demise of the Butlers of Kilcash and the eventual clearing of the family's extensive woodlands, which had supplied timber for local people. **The early tone typifies the entire poem's sense of hopelessness now that the woods are 'laid low'.** The systematic felling of trees is symbolic of the decline of this aristocratic Catholic family. Following colonisation, the Irish were consigned to nature as a symbol of their barbarity. In some British circles, they were referred to as the 'natural wild Irish' because the country's remote boglands and forests offered shelter to Irish rebels. The poem emphasises the uneasy silence around Kilcash and the speaker pays extravagant tribute to 'the lady' of the house, who is immediately associated with Ireland's Catholic resistance: 'Earls came across oceans to see her.'

As always, Ní Chuilleanáin's approach is layered, recognising the genuine feelings of loss while suggesting a misplaced dependence on all those who exploited the native population. For the most part, however, the poem's anonymous narrator appears to express the desolation ('long affliction') felt by the impoverished and leaderless Irish of the time. There is no shortage of evidence to illustrate what has happened to the 'fine house'. Throughout stanzas two and three, broad assonant sounds add to the maudlin sentiments. The **'neat gates knocked down' and the 'avenue overgrown' reflect the dramatic turnaround in fortunes**. But is Ní Chuilleanáin's translation of the old song also unearthing an underlying sense of delight in the sudden fall of the mighty? There is 'no shade now' for the once powerful gentry as well as the impoverished community. Many of the references to

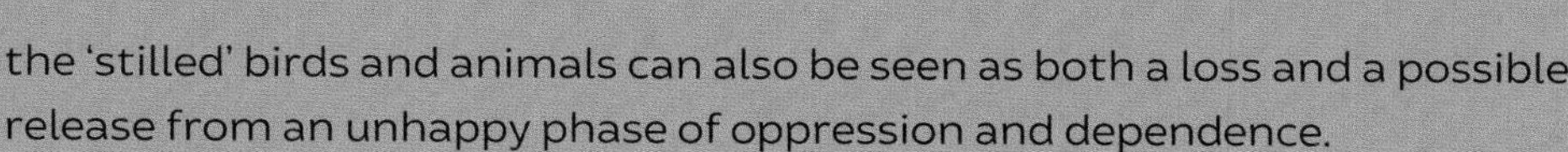

the 'stilled' birds and animals can also be seen as both a loss and a possible release from an unhappy phase of oppression and dependence.

Images of hardship taken from nature dominate stanzas four and five. The abandoned peasants are depicted as pitiable. The atmosphere becomes increasingly disturbing as the natural world order is transformed: 'Darkness falls among daylight/And the streams are all run dry.' **As in so many other Irish legends, the landscape reflects the terms of the Butlers' exile: 'The forest park is leafless.'** Negative language patterns – 'No sunlight', 'No hazel, no holly' – highlight the sense of mordant despondency resulting from abandonment. Relentlessly, the regular lines and ponderous rhythm work together to create a monotonous trance-like effect. The extravagant praise for 'the gentle maiden' (a likely reference to the wife of the 18th Earl) dominates stanza six. As a representative of the Butler dynasty, her absence is seen as 'the worst of our troubles' and she is glorified as someone 'who never preyed on the people' despite her privileged lifestyle.

The prayer-like tone of the final stanza is in keeping with the deep yearning for a return to the old ways in Kilcash. The Catholic allusion also reinforces the central importance of religion in expressing political and cultural identity. In wishing to restore the former Gaelic order, the speaker imagines lively scenes of communal celebration: 'fiddling and bonfire.' **The aspiration that the castle will be 'built up anew' offers a clear symbol of recovery.** This rallying call is in keeping with traditional laments and is characteristic of the poet's sympathies for the oppressed. Ní Chuilleanáin has retained the rhetorical style of Gaelic poetry throughout, revealing the experience of isolated communities through numerous images of restless desolation and uncomfortable silences.

'Kilcash' marks a significant transition in Irish history. As the old native aristocracy suffered military and political defeat and, in many cases, exile, the world order that had supported the bardic poets disappeared. In these circumstances, it is hardly surprising that much Irish poetry of this period laments these changes and the poet's plight. However, **Ní Chuilleanáin's translation of the old ballad differs from other versions in being more ambivalent towards Viscountess Iveagh and what she represented**. Is the poem a poignant expression of loss and a genuine tribute to those landlords who were seen as humane? Does the poet satirise the subservient native Irish who had been conditioned to accept some convenient generosity from the Catholic gentry? To what extent did the original lament present a romantic distortion of Ireland's history? Readers are left to decide for themselves.

Writing About the Poem

'Eiléan Ní Chuilleanáin's poems retain the power to connect past and present in ways that never cease to fascinate.' Discuss this statement, with particular reference to 'Kilcash'.

Sample Paragraph

On a first reading, I thought that 'Kilcash' was a simple adaptation of the old Gaelic ballad, *Caoine Cill Chais*. After studying the poem, however, I feel that Ní Chuilleanáin has raised many interesting questions about Irish history. The opening lament of the deprived peasants seems self-pitying – 'What will we do now for timber'. The compliments paid to Lady Iveagh (Margaret Butler) are lavish and focus on her Catholic faith and support for the old Gaelic culture – 'Earls came across oceans to see her'. As a young person looking back on this period of upheaval, I could appreciate the way dispossessed Irish people had become dependent on the Catholic gentry as symbols of freedom. The poem repeatedly places 'the lady' as the epitome of hope – 'the poor souls' friend'. It was interesting to see how the flight of the Butlers reduced people to complete dependence, so that all they could do was pray for a miraculous reversal of history 'that our ancestors' house will rise up'. The main insight I gained from the poem was that colonisation – whether by Catholic or Protestant landlords – had broken the Irish spirit. Ní Chuilleanáin manages to link past and present very subtly, broadening our view of the complex relationships between powerful interests and a conquered population.

EXAMINER'S COMMENT

An assured personal response, focused throughout and very well illustrated with suitable quotations. The paragraph carefully highlights Ní Chuilleanáin's exploration of the plight of the native Irish community in various ways: 'the original bard's view of the 18th-century Butler line is buried beneath Ní Chuilleanáin's'. Points are clearly expressed throughout in this excellent, top-grade answer.

N.B. Access your eBook for additional sample paragraphs and a list of useful quotes with commentary.

Class/Homework Exercises

1. 'Ní Chuilleanáin's distinctive poetic world provides an accessible platform for marginalised voices.' Discuss this view, with particular reference to 'Kilcash'.
2. 'While Eiléan Ní Chuilleanáin's poems often deal with complex themes, they have an enigmatic quality that engages readers.' To what extent is this true of 'Kilcash'? Support your answer with close reference to the poem.

Summary Points

- **Traditional lament for Catholic aristocracy raises questions about Ireland's past.**
- **Desolate landscape and negative language reflect the mood of hopelessness.**
- **Regular rhythm, the prayer-like tone and stark images emphasise the atmosphere.**
- **Ambivalent ending intrigues readers about the poet's own viewpoint.**

9 Translation

for the reburial of the Magdalenes

The soil frayed and sifted evens the score –
There are women here from every county,
Just as there were in the laundry.

White light blinded and bleached out
The high relief of a glance, where steam danced
Around stone drains and giggled and slipped across water.

Assist them now, ridges under the veil, shifting,
Searching for their parents, their names,
The edges of words grinding against nature,

As if, when water sank between the rotten teeth
Of soap, and every grasp seemed melted, one voice
Had begun, rising above the shuffle and hum

Until every pocket in her skull blared with the note –
Allow us now to hear it, sharp as an infant's cry
While the grass takes root, while the steam rises:

Washed clean of idiom · the baked crust
Of words that made my temporary name ·
A parasite that grew in me · that spell
Lifted · I lie in earth sifted to dust ·
Let the bunched keys I bore slacken and fall ·
I rise and forget · a cloud over my time.

Subtitle: The Magdalenes refers to Irish women, particularly unmarried mothers, who were separated from their children and forced to work in convent laundries. Inmates were required to undertake hard physical labour, including washing and needlework. They also endured a daily regime that included long periods of prayer and enforced silence. In Ireland, such institutions were known as Magdalene laundries. It has been estimated that up to 30,000 women passed through such laundries in Ireland, the last one of which (in Waterford) closed on 25 September 1996.
frayed: ragged.
sifted: sorted, examined.
the laundry: clothes washing area.

blared: rang out, resounded.

idiom: language, misinterpretation.

parasite: bloodsucker.

Personal Response

1. Comment on the effectiveness of the poem's title, 'Translation', in relation to the themes that Ní Chuilleanáin addresses in the poem.
2. Choose one image from the poem that you found particularly interesting. Briefly explain your choice.
3. How does the poem make you feel? Give reasons for your response, supporting the points you make with reference to the text.

'Washed clean of idiom'

Critical Literacy

During the early 1990s, the remains of more than 150 women were discovered at several Dublin religious institutions as the properties were being excavated. The bones, from women buried over a very long period, were cremated and reburied in Glasnevin Cemetery. Eiléan Ní Chuilleanáin's poem was read at the reburial ceremony to commemorate Magdalene laundry women from all over Ireland. 'Translation' links the writer's work with the belated acknowledgement, in the late 20th century, of the stolen lives and hidden deaths of generations of Irishwomen incarcerated in Magdalene convents.

The poem begins with a macabre description of the Glasnevin grave where the reburial is taking place: 'The soil frayed and sifted evens the score.' Ní Chuilleanáin expresses the feelings of the mourners ('here from every county') who are **united by a shared sense of injustice**. This dramatic ceremony represents a formal acknowledgement of a dark period in Ireland's social history. Line 4 takes readers back in time behind convent walls and imagines the grim laundry rooms in which the Magdelene women worked: 'White light blinded and bleached out/The high relief of a glance.'

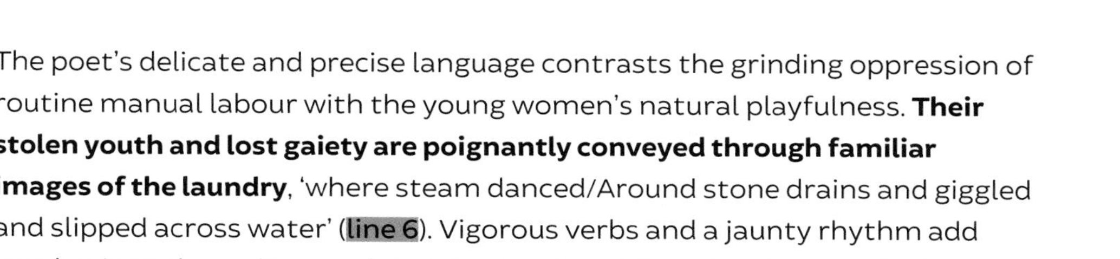

The poet's delicate and precise language contrasts the grinding oppression of routine manual labour with the young women's natural playfulness. **Their stolen youth and lost gaiety are poignantly conveyed through familiar images of the laundry**, 'where steam danced/Around stone drains and giggled and slipped across water' (line 6). Vigorous verbs and a jaunty rhythm add emphasis to the sad irony of their broken lives. The relentless scrubbing was intended to wash away the women's sins. However, no matter how much the women washed, they were considered dirty and sinful throughout their lives.

All through the poem, Ní Chuilleanáin focuses on the importance of words and naming as though she herself is aiming to make sense of the shocking Magdalene story. But how is she to respond to the women who have come to the graveyard, 'Searching for their parents, their names'? Typically, the language is dense and multi-layered. In death, these former laundry workers are mere 'ridges under the veil' of the anonymous earth. The metaphor in line 7 also evokes images of the stern Magdalene nuns. **Ní Chuilleanáin sees all these women as victims of less enlightened times**, ironically recalled in the prayer-like note of invocation: 'Assist them now.'

The poem's title becomes clear as we recognise **Ní Chuilleanáin's intention to communicate ('translate') decades of silence into meaningful expression on behalf of the Magdalene laundry inmates**. Their relentless efforts to eventually become a 'voice' is compared to the almost impossible challenge of 'rising above the shuffle and hum' within the noisy laundry itself. In line 9, Ní Chuilleanáin visualises the women setting 'The edges of words grinding against nature' until their misrepresentation is overcome as it is turned to dust along with their bodies.

From line 13, much of the **focus is placed on exploring the experience of one of the nuns who managed the laundries**. As the true history emerges, she is also being cleansed of 'the baked crust/Of words that made my temporary name'. The 'temporary name' is her name in religion, that is, the saint's name she chose upon entering strict convent life, which, as Ní Chuilleanáin notes, involved relinquishing her previous identity as an individual. She too has been exploited and the poet's generous tone reflects an understanding of this woman, who is caught between conflicting influences of duty, care, indoctrination and doubt, 'Until every pocket in her skull blared'. The evocative reference to the 'infant's cry' echoes the enduring sense of loss felt by young mothers who were forced to give up their babies shortly after birth.

In the poem's final lines, we hear the voice of a convent reverend mother, whose role is defined by 'the bunched keys I bore'. The reburial ceremony has also cleansed her from 'that spell' which maintained the cruel system she once served. Almost overwhelmed, she now recognises the 'parasite' power 'that grew in me' and only now can the keys she carries, an obvious symbol of her role as gaoler, 'slacken and fall'. **Bleak, disturbing images and broken**

rhythms have an unnerving, timeless effect. This woman's punitive authority over others has haunted her beyond the grave.

In the end, Ní Chuilleanáin's measured and balanced approach shows genuine compassion for all institutionalised victims, drawing together the countless young women and those in charge in their common confinement. In addition to their time spent in convents, they are now reunited, sifting the earth that they have all become. **The tragic legacy of these institutions involves women at many levels.** Nevertheless, the poem itself is a faithful translation, as these victims have been raised from their graves by the poet's response to their collective dead voice. Ní Chuilleanáin relates their compelling story to 'Allow us now to hear it'. She also tenderly acknowledges the complete silencing of the Irish Magdalenes as they did their enforced and, in some cases, lifelong penance.

Although Eiléan Ní Chuilleanáin's mournful 'translation' reveals glimpses of their true history, **none of these Magdalene women can ever be given back the lives they had before they entered the laundries**. The poem stops short of pretending to even the score in terms of power between those in authority and the totally subservient and permanently disgraced women under their control. At best, their small voices rise up together like 'steam' and form a 'cloud over my time' (line 21). This metaphor of the cloud can be construed as a shadow of shame over Irish society, but it can also be seen as a warning that the cycle of abuse is likely to be repeated.

Writing About the Poem

'Ní Chuilleanáin's poems address important aspects of women's experiences in an insightful fashion.' Discuss this view, with particular reference to 'Translations'.

Sample Paragraph

I would agree that 'Translations' deals with an issue which is important to Irish women. The scandal of what happened to the unfortunate girls who were locked up in Magdalene convents deserves to be publicised. Ní Chuilleanáin's poem certainly gave me a deeper understanding of their story. The dramatic description of the reburial service was attended by relatives 'from every county', suggesting the scale of the mistreatment. The details of the cold laundries – where 'White light blinded' seemed a subtle way of symbolising the misguided actions of those religious orders who punished young girls. I admired the poet's fair treatment of those nuns who are also presented as being imprisoned, even replacing their own natural identities with 'temporary' saints' names. The last stanza was revealing as it envisaged one of the severe nuns who was still

confused by her part in the cruelty. She only recognises the 'parasite' of heartless authority within her when it is too late. The poet makes it clear that she was a product of an oppressive Catholic Ireland. In my opinion, 'Translation' succeeds in explaining the true story of the Magdalene women. It is all the more powerful because Ní Chuilleanáin avoids being over-emotional. Her quiet tone conveys sensitivity and sadness for this dreadful period which still lingers like 'a cloud over my time'.

EXAMINER'S COMMENT

This top-grade response shows a clear understanding of Ní Chuilleanáin's considered approach to her theme, empathising with both those imprisoned and those in charge. Short quotations are well integrated while discussion points are clear and coherent, ranging over much of the poem. There is also some very good personal interaction, including the final sentence. An excellent standard.

N.B. Access your eBook for additional sample paragraphs and a list of useful quotes with commentary.

Class/Homework Exercises

1. 'Eiléan Ní Chuilleanáin's poetry offers a variety of interesting perspectives that vividly convey themes of universal relevance.' Discuss this statement with particular reference to 'Translation'.
2. 'In her poem, "Translation", Ní Chuilleanáin's poetic voice is both critical and compassionate.' Discuss this statement with particular reference to the text.

Summary Points

- **The poet addresses aspects of the Magdalene laundries scandal.**
- **Several changes and translations are explored in the poem.**
- **Sensuous imagery evokes the harsh atmosphere in the laundry.**
- **Effective use of sound, contrast, mood and viewpoint throughout.**

The Bend in the Road

This is the place where the child
Felt sick in the car and they pulled over
And waited in the shadow of a house.
A tall tree like a cat's tail waited too.
They opened the windows and breathed
Easily, while nothing moved. Then he was better.

Over twelve years it has become the place
Where you were sick one day on the way to the lake.
You are taller now than us.
The tree is taller, the house is quite covered in
With green creeper, and the bend
In the road is as silent as ever it was on that day.

Piled high, wrapped lightly, like the one cumulus cloud
In a perfect sky, softly packed like the air,
Is all that went on in those years, the absences,
The faces never long absent from thought,
The bodies alive then and the airy space they took up
When we saw them wrapped and sealed by sickness
Guessing the piled weight of sleep
We knew they could not carry for long;
This is the place of their presence: in the tree, in the air.

creeper: climbing plant.

cumulus: rounded, fluffy.

Personal Response

1. 'The importance of memory is a key theme in many of Ní Chuilleanáin's poems.' To what extent is this true of 'The Bend in the Road'? Briefly explain your answer.
2. Choose one image from 'The Bend in the Road' that you consider effective. Give reasons why this image appealed to you.
3. How would you describe the poem's conclusion? Is it mysterious? Hopeful? Comforting? Bitter? Briefly explain your response.

Critical Literacy

'The Bend in the Road' is part of Eiléan Ní Chuilleanáin's poetry collection *The Girl Who Married the Reindeer*. In many of these poems, the autobiographical becomes transformed as Ní Chuilleanáin takes a moment in time and fills it with arresting images, exact description, stillness and secrecy, linking together selected memories from various times and places. This poem's title suggests that the road will go on even though it is not visible at the moment.

Stanza one opens with Ní Chuilleanáin pointing to the exact place where 'the child/Felt sick in the car and they pulled over'. The memory of such a familiar occurrence is given significance by the use of the demonstrative pronoun, 'This'. Run-on lines catch the flurry of activity as concerned adults attend to the sick child. Everything is still as they 'waited' for the sickness to pass. This suspended moment resonates as they linger 'in the shadow of a house'. **For a split second, an ominous – almost surreal – atmosphere begins to develop.** The poet introduces a slightly sinister simile, 'A tall tree like a cat's tail', peeking in from the world of fairy tale. Then the tree is personified: it 'waited too' as people and landscape merge in the moment of hush. Suddenly, a simple action ('They opened the windows') relieves the tension and everyone 'breathed/Easily'. The position of the adverb at the beginning of the line captures the relief at the recovery of the child. Yet the stationary atmosphere remained: 'while nothing moved.' However, the routine narrative of everyday life quickly resumes: 'Then he was better.'

In the second stanza, this roadside location takes on the shared resonance of memory: 'Over twelve years.' Readers are left imagining how the adults and child, when passing 'the place', would point it out as 'Where you were sick one day on the way to the lake'. The length of the line mirrors the long car journey. There is a sense of time being concentrated. Ní Chuilleanáin marvels at how the child has grown to adulthood: 'You are taller now than us.' The place has also changed – and even the tree is 'taller'. Assonance pinpoints how the nearby house is becoming yet more mysterious, 'quite covered in/With green creeper'. The insidious 'ee' sound mimics the silent takeover of the house by nature, as it recedes more and more into the shadows. Nature is alive. Creepings and rustlings stir, dispersing solidity and sureness. The poet cleverly places the line as if on a bend at the turn of a line: 'the bend/In the road is as silent as ever it was on that day.' Everything seems focused on the serenity of the place. **A bend in a road prevents seeing what is coming next. Is this an obvious symbol of the human experience?** No one knows what lies ahead. The tone of this reflective stanza is introspective as Ní Chuilleanáin considers the undeniable passing of time and the human condition.

In the final stanza, memory and place interplay with other recollections. The poet's attention turns towards the sky, which she imagines 'Piled high' with past experiences. A lifetime's memories now tower 'like the one cumulus cloud/In a perfect sky'. The alliteration of the hard 'c' successfully captures the billowing cloud as it sails through the sky. **Similarly, the recollections of 'all that went on in those years' heave and surge as they drift through the poet's consciousness.** Naturally, they flow from the exact description of 'the bend/In the road'. They are now visible as feelings of loss expand into the present: 'The faces never long absent from thought.' Ní Chuilleanáin had lost not only her father and mother, but also her sister. But she remembers them **similarly** as they were, 'bodies alive then and the airy space they took up', just as the cloud in the sky. Poignantly, the poet also recalls them in their final sickness, 'wrapped and sealed by sickness', as if they had been parcelled for dispatch away from the ordinary routine of life by the ordeal of suffering.

However, the harsh reality of sickness and old age is also recognised: 'We knew they could not carry for long.' Just as the cloud grows bigger as it absorbs moisture, finally dissolving into rain, so did the poet's loved ones buckle beneath the weight of their illness, under the 'piled weight of sleep'. **Ní Chuilleanáin finds constant reminders of her family's past in the natural world.** She uses a simple image of cloud-like shapes of pillows and bed-covers as they surrender to sickness. Characteristically, the thinking within the poem has progressed considerably. The poet has widened its scope, its spatial dimension, to include those external experiences to which she so eloquently pays witness. Indeed, the poem now stands as a monument to silence and time, absence and presence, past and present. The moment of stillness is evoked. This roadside location takes on a special importance. It marks the place where lost family members now reside. Ní Chuilleanáin's alliterative language is emphatic: 'This is the place of their presence.' They belong 'in the tree, in the air'. As in so many of her poems, Ní Chuilleanáin honours the invisible, unseen presence of other thoughts and feelings that – just like the bend in the road – lie waiting in silence to be discovered and brought to life again.

Writing About the Poem

'Eiléan Ní Chuilleanáin's poetry illuminates moments of perception in exact description.' Discuss this view in relation to 'The Bend in the Road'. Use suitable reference and quotation to support the points you make.

Sample Paragraph

'The Bend in the Road' is filled with accurate description. The opening lines pinpoint the exact place where 'the child/Felt sick in the car'. The ordinary conversational language, 'They opened the windows', 'Then he was better', brings me into this precise moment in time and place. I can see the dark, cool shadow of the house. I experience the tree, as if a child, through the almost cartoon-like simile, 'A tall tree like a cat's tail'. Yet, an otherworldly experience hovers as personification transforms the tree into a living being; it 'waited too'. And then it is displayed. The place has become a metaphor for the reality of being human. Everything in life changes. The poet suddenly realises that the child has now grown into a man, 'You are taller than us now'. Assonance subtly illustrates the changed house now overgrown with 'green creeper'. Another layer is added with the perception that the place has become suffused with the 'presence' of those 'faces never long absent from thought'. This still,

silent moment has allowed boundaries to be crossed as memories float 'like the one cumulus cloud/In a perfect sky'. I now began to understand that in a static moment, the distinctions between life and death, being and memory, all become blurred. The past now lives again, 'in the tree, in the air'. Through carefully observed, precise description, this poet transports readers into a different place, to an understanding that many experiences, 'all that went on in those years', can be savoured in various forms, 'softly packed like the air'.

EXAMINER'S COMMENT

This is a top-grade personal response that addresses the poet's interest in transience and memory. Apt, accurate quotes provide good support for developed discussion points which range effectively through the poem. There is some highly impressive focus on aspects of the poet's distinctive style. Expression is also excellent throughout, e.g. 'The place has become a metaphor for the reality of being human'.

N.B. Access your eBook for additional sample paragraphs and a list of useful quotes with commentary.

Class/Homework Exercises

1. 'Space in Ní Chuilleanáin's poetry is used as an expression of one's experience of the world and is a metaphor for the linking together of self and the world.' Discuss this statement, with particular reference to 'The Bend in the Road'.
2. 'The evocative power of a specific location is central to Ní Chuilleanáin's "The Bend in the Road".' Discuss this view, supporting your answer with reference to the poem.

Summary Points

- **Key themes include memory, family, transience, loss and grief.**
- **Symbolism used throughout the poem to suggest meaning.**
- **Effective use of assonance and alliteration to create atmosphere.**
- **Recurring references to sickness add unity to the poem.**

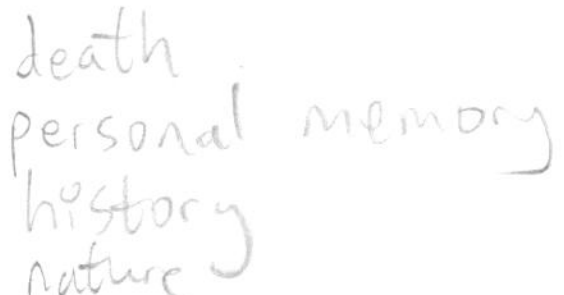

11 On Lacking the Killer Instinct

One hare, absorbed, sitting still,
Right in the grassy middle of the track,
I met when I fled up into the hills, that time
My father was dying in a hospital –
I see her suddenly again, borne back
By the morning paper's prize photograph:
Two greyhounds tumbling over, absurdly gross,
While the hare shoots off to the left, her bright eye
Full not only of speed and fear
But surely in the moment a glad power,

Like my father's, running from a lorry-load of soldiers
In nineteen twenty-one, nineteen years old,
Such gladness, he said, cornering in the narrow road
Between high hedges, in summer dusk.
The hare
Like him should never have been coursed,
But, clever, she gets off; another day
She'll fool the stupid dogs, double back
On her own scent, downhill, and choose her time
To spring away out of the frame, all while
The pack is labouring up.
The lorry was growling
And he was clever, he saw a house
And risked an open kitchen door. The soldiers
Found six people in a country kitchen, one
Drying his face, dazed-looking, the towel
Half covering his face. The lorry left,
The people let him sleep there, he came out
Into a blissful dawn. Should he have chanced that door?
If the sheltering house had been burned down, what good
Could all his bright running have done
For those that harboured him?
And I should not
Have run away, but I went back to the city
Next morning, washed in brown bog water, and
I thought about the hare, in her hour of ease.

hare: mammal resembling a large rabbit.
absorbed: engrossed, immersed, preoccupied.

absurdly: ridiculously, nonsensically.
gross: disgusting, outrageous.

coursed: hunted with greyhounds.

frame: picture, enclosure.

labouring: moving with difficulty.

Personal Response

1. Who, in your opinion, lacked the killer instinct in this poem? Was it the hare, the soldiers, the greyhounds, the father, the poet? Refer closely to the text in your response.
2. The poet alters time and place frequently in this poem. With the aid of quotations, trace these changes as the poem develops.
3. Did you find the poem's conclusion satisfying or mystifying? Give reasons for your response, referring closely to the text.

Critical Literacy

'On Lacking the Killer Instinct' is part of Eiléan Ní Chuilleanáin's *The Sun-fish* collection. A sunfish is so-called due to its habit of basking on the water's surface. Ní Chuilleanáin often presents daily life with a sense of mystery and otherworldliness as the poems move between various realms of experience. Each scene lies open to another version of the narrative. She blurs the distance between past and present in this three-part poem. History, which is something of an Irish obsession, always informs the present. This poet discovers and remembers. As she herself has said, 'In order for the poem to get written, something has to happen.'

The title of the poem immediately intrigues and unsettles. The opening lines focus on a stationary hare, silent, engrossed, 'absorbed', at rest. It is a vivid picture. Why is this hare preoccupied? The sibilant alliterative phrase, 'sitting still', captures the motionless animal in 'the middle of the track'. This **naturalistic setting** and image is brought into high resolution as the poet recounts that her own journey 'up into the hills' caused her to meet this creature. Ní Chuilleanáin juxtaposes the stillness of the wild hare with her own headlong flight from the awful reality, 'that time/My father was dying in a hospital'. In describing this terrible experience, her tone is remarkably controlled – detached, yet compassionate.

Another narrative thread is introduced in line 6 when the poet recalls the 'morning paper's prize photograph'. Here the predators are presented as ungainly, almost comical characters incapable of purposeful action: 'Two greyhounds tumbling over, absurdly gross.' The broad vowels and repetition

'While the hare shoots off to the left'

of 'r' highlight the hounds' unattractively large appearance. Irish coursing is a competitive sport where dogs are tested on their ability to run and overtake the hare, turning it without capturing it. It is often regarded as a cruel activity that causes pain and suffering to the pursued creature. From the start of the poem, **readers are left wondering who exactly lacks the killer instinct**. Do the dogs not have the urge to pounce and kill? Has the hare got the killer instinct, running for its life, showing the strong will to survive against all odds? The rapid run-on lines mimic the speed and agility of the hare exulting in 'glad power'.

In line 11, the **reader is taken into another realm** – a common feature of Ní Chuilleanáin's interconnected narratives. In this case, she recalls another pursuit. Her father was a combatant in the Irish Civil War in 1922 and was on the run. Like the hare, he fled, 'cornering in the narrow road/Between high hedges, in summer dusk'. Both are linked through 'gladness' as they exult in their capacity to outrun their pursuers. For her father, this was a 'lorry-load of soldiers' – the compound word emphasising the unequal odds against which the poet's father struggled. This is similar to the hare's predicament against the 'Two greyhounds'. The precise placing of 'The hare' tucked away at the end of line 15 suggests the animal's escape. Ní Chuilleanáin comments that neither the hare nor her father should ever have 'been coursed'. She is happy to think that on some other occasion, the hare is likely to outwit the 'stupid dogs' and will 'spring away out of the frame', nimbly escaping her pursuers. In Irish coursing, the hare is not run on open land but in a secure enclosure over a set distance. The heavy, panting exertions of the pursuing dogs is illustrated in the run-through line, 'all while/The pack is labouring up'.

Ní Chuilleanáin returns to her father's story in line 22, imagining a moment of danger from his time as a fugitive. The scene is dominated by the threatening sound of a lorry, 'growling' like a pursuing hound. The repetition of the adjective 'clever' links her father and the hare as he too made his escape. Intent on surviving, 'he saw a house/And risked an open kitchen door'. **The enemy soldiers go through the motions of pursuit cursorily, seemingly lacking the killer instinct** when they 'Found six people in a country kitchen'. Ní Chuilleanáin is characteristically ambivalent about why the rebels were not challenged, reminding us of the contradictory attitudes among the various combatants of the Civil War.

For whatever reason, the fugitives ('one/Drying his face, dazed-looking') were not arrested and their deception worked. The poet's father is allowed refuge: 'The people let him sleep there.' Throughout Ireland's troubled history, 'safe houses' existed that sheltered those on the run. In her mind's eye, the poet pictures her father emerging in triumph the next day 'Into a blissful dawn' (line 29). In a **series of questions**, she considers his crucial decision to stand his ground and feign innocence. In retrospect, anything might have happened to affect the outcome at 'the sheltering house'.

Ní Chuilleanáin emphasises how chance has played such a significant role – not just in her father's life, but in Ireland's history.

The poet concludes by returning to the opening scene. Having observed the hare and remembered her father's encounter during the Civil War, she now realises that she should never have run away from her dying father. Her decision to return is seen as a mature one – almost like a religious ritual in which the poet cleanses herself, 'washed in brown bog water'. Is this a form of absolution to remove her guilt for running away? Typically, she uses this unifying symbol to gently draw the poem's three narratives together. After the common experience of the turbulence of the run, all three (the hare, the father and the poet herself) have entered a new state of being – calm composure. Ní Chuilleanáin reflects on 'the hare, in her hour of ease', the soft monosyllabic final word gently conveying a sense of peace and reconciliation. The poem closes as it began, with the **beautiful silent image of the hare**, self-possessed and serene after all the turmoil of the chase.

Writing About the Poem

'Eiléan Ní Chuilleanáin is a quiet, introspective, enigmatic poet.' Discuss this statement with particular reference to 'On Lacking the Killer Instinct'.

Sample Paragraph

I thought 'On Lacking the Killer Instinct' moved effortlessly, mysteriously weaving three different narratives: the story of the hare and greyhounds, the detached family history of her father's escape in 1921 and her own headlong flight from the city. Ní Chuilleanáin celebrates resilience, the hare's 'bright eye' is full of 'a glad power'. Similarly, her father exulted in his cleverness, 'never/Such gladness' as he out-manoeuvred the 'lorry-load of soldiers'. The poet also faced up to the unpalatable fact of death and 'went back to the city/Next morning'. Her impressionistic style is similar to watching a photograph as it slowly develops before our eyes. At first there are vague unconnected shapes, but as the order establishes itself, the meaning becomes clear. The reader is effortlessly guided through different times and places as the focus of the poet's gaze shifts from the hunt of the hare in coursing to the hunt of her father in his role in the Civil War, 'In nineteen twenty-one, nineteen years old'. She then quietly reflects on her own flight and concludes that running does not solve problems, 'what good/Could all his bright running have done'. In the end, this poet poses questions that resonate. Does she too lack the killer instinct, the capacity to seize and capture rather than suggest? The long monosyllabic word 'ease' suggests that staying calm is more effective than running. Yet who lacked the killer instinct, the hare, the greyhounds,

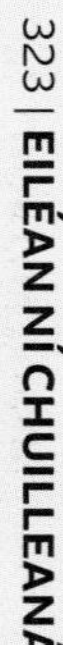

the father, the soldiers, the poet? Is the killer instinct worth having? This enigmatic, introspective poet leaves us with an image of quiet stillness to ponder.

N.B. Access your eBook for additional sample paragraphs and a list of useful quotes with commentary.

EXAMINER'S COMMENT

This lengthy paragraph offers a very clear and focused response to a testing question. Interesting critical discussion – aptly illustrated by accurate quotations – ranges widely, tracing the subtle development of the poem's various narrative threads. Impressive use of language throughout adds clarity to the key points. The questions posed towards the end round off the discussion effectively in this excellent top-grade answer.

Class/Homework Exercises

1. 'Eiléan Ní Chuilleanáin's poems elude categories and invite and challenge the reader in equal measure.' Discuss this statement with particular reference to 'On Lacking the Killer Instinct'.
2. 'Ní Chuilleanáin is capable of blending multiple narratives with great skill in her poetry.' To what extent is this the case in 'On Lacking the Killer Instinct'? Support your answer with reference to the poem.

Summary Points

- **Interwoven stories: hunting the hare, her father's death and Ireland's Civil War.**
- **Effective use of rhythm and contrast – movement and stillness.**
- **Subtle blending of past and present, time and place.**
- **Alliterative and sibilant sound effects echo related ideas throughout.**

To Niall Woods and Xenya Ostrovskaia, married in Dublin on 9 September 2009

When you look out across the fields
And you both see the same star
Pitching its tent on the point of the steeple –
That is the time to set out on your journey,
With half a loaf and your mother's blessing.

Leave behind the places that you knew:
All that you leave behind you will find once more,
You will find it in the stories;
The sleeping beauty in her high tower
With her talking cat asleep
Solid beside her feet – you will see her again.

When the cat wakes up he will speak in Irish and Russian
And every night he will tell you a different tale
About the firebird that stole the golden apples,
Gone every morning out of the emperor's garden,
And about the King of Ireland's Son and the Enchanter's Daughter.

The story the cat does not know is the Book of Ruth
And I have no time to tell you how she fared
When she went out at night and she was afraid,
In the beginning of the barley harvest,
Or how she trusted to strangers and stood by her word:

You will have to trust me, she lived happily ever after.

Title: An epithalamium is a poem (or song) in celebration of a wedding. Eiléan Ní Chuilleanáin has included this poem (to her son Niall and his bride, Xenya) as the introductory dedication in her poetry collection *The Sun-fish*.

sleeping beauty: European fairy tale from 'La Belle au bois dormant' (Beauty of the sleeping wood) by Charles Perrault and 'Dornröschen' (Little Briar Rose) by the Brothers Grimm.

the firebird: Russian fairy tale; 'Tsarevitch Ivan, the Fire Bird and the Gray Wolf' by Alexander Afanasyev.

the King of Ireland's Son: Irish fairy tale; 'The King of Ireland's Son' by Padraic Colum.

Book of Ruth: religious story from the Old Testament.

Or how she trusted to strangers: In the Bible story, Boaz owned the field Ruth harvested. He was a relative of the family and by law could 'redeem' her if he married her now that she was a widow. He wished to do so because he admired how she had stood by her mother-in-law, 'For wherever you go, I will go'.

Personal Response

1. Do you think the references to fairy tales are appropriate on the occasion of Eiléan Ní Chuilleanáin's son's marriage? Give one reason for your answer.
2. In your opinion, what is the dominant tone of voice in the poem? Is it one of warning, reassurance, hope, consolation? Briefly explain your response with reference to the poem.
3. Write your own short personal response to the poem, highlighting the impact it made on you.

Critical Literacy

'I write poems that mean a lot to me' (Eiléan Ní Chuilleanáin). This particular poem is dedicated to her son, Niall, and his new bride, Xenya, on the happy occasion of their marriage. Folklore is central to this poet's work. Her mother, Eilís Dillon, was a famous writer of children's stories. Fairy tales allow Ní Chuilleanáin the opportunity to approach a subject from an oblique, non-confessional perspective. It gives distance. Story-tellers rarely comment on or explain what happens. They simply tell the tale. In this poem, Ní Chuilleanáin refers to folklore and a well-known Bible story as she addresses the young couple.

The first stanza opens with **warm advice** from a loving mother as she gives the young man leave to set out on his own journey through life with his new partner. Run-on lines contain a beautiful, romantic image of a harmonious vision: 'you both see the same star.' Personification and alliteration bring this natural image to radiant life, 'Pitching its tent on the point of the steeple', suggesting the new home which the young couple are about to set up for themselves. **Ní Chuilleanáin's gaze is one of relentless clarity and attentiveness.** She illuminates details. She also counsels that it is the right time to go, 'to set out on your journey' when you are prepared ('With half a loaf') and with good wishes ('and your mother's blessing'). She combines colloquial and fairy tale language. The tone is warm, but also pragmatic – offering practical advice to the newlyweds to make the most of whatever they have to start with: 'half a loaf is better than none.'

Stanza two begins with the imperative warning: 'Leave behind.' The mother is advising the couple to forget 'the places that you knew'. Is 'places' a metaphor for their actual homes or their cultural environments? Or does it refer to values the young people hold sacred? She consoles them that past experiences can still be found 'in the stories'. Ní Chuilleanáin now weaves an intricate web of such stories from many different sources. The first tale is that of 'sleeping beauty in her high tower'. This classic folk story involves a beautiful princess, enchantment, and a handsome prince who has to brave the obstacles of tall trees that surround the castle and its sleeping princess.

Is Ní Chuilleanáin illustrating that the path to true love is filled with difficulties and that only the brave will be successful? The extended run-on lines suggest the hundred years' sleep of the spellbound princess, who can only be awakened by a kiss. The poet also makes use of another familiar element of fairy tales – talking animals. In this case, the 'talking cat' probably refers to Irish folklore, and the King of Cats, a renowned teller of tales. Ní Chuilleanáin is able to link the basic characteristics of the animal with human behaviour. The cat slumbers with the princess, 'Solid', stable and dependable, beside her feet. Despite the poet's realism, however, this fairy tale allusion is primarily optimistic.

In stanza three, Ní Chuilleanáin imagines the cat awakening and telling stories in both 'Irish and Russian', a likely reference to the young couple's **two cultural backgrounds**. The poet has said that in her work she is trying 'to suggest, to phrase, to find a way to make it possible for somebody to pick up certain suggestions ... They might not be seeing what I am seeing.' The poet continues to set her personal wishes for Niall and Xenya within the context of folktales, turning to the Russian tradition: 'Tsarevitch, the Fire Bird and the Gray Wolf.' Again, the hero of this story is on a challenging mission, as he attempts to catch the 'firebird that stole the golden apples ... out of the emperor's garden'. The assonance of the broad vowel 'o' emphasises the exasperation of the repeated theft. As always in folklore, courage and determination are required before the hero can overcome many ordeals and find true happiness.

Ní Chuilleanáin introduces the Irish tradition with the story of the King of Ireland's son, who must pluck three hairs from the Enchanter's beard in order to save his own life. On his quest, he gains the hand of Fedelma, the Enchanter's youngest daughter. But he falls asleep and loses her to the King of the Land of Mist. **Is the poet simply advising her son and daughter-in-law that love must be cherished and never taken for granted?** Throughout the poem, she draws heavily on stories where heroes have to fight for what they believe in. All of these tales convey the same central meaning – that lasting love has to be won through daring, determination and sacrifice.

In the playful link into stanza four, Ní Chuilleanáin remarks that 'the story the cat does not know is the Book of Ruth'. This final story is not from the world of folklore, but from the Bible (although the poet has commented that 'a lot of religious narrative is very folkloric'). The Book of Ruth teaches that **genuine love can require uncompromising sacrifice**, and that such unselfish love will be well rewarded. This particular tale of inclusivity shows two different cultures coming together. The Israelites (sons of Naomi) marry women from the Moab tribe, one of whom is Ruth. She embraces Naomi's people, land, culture and God. This is very pertinent to the newly married couple, as they are also from different lands and cultures. Not surprisingly, the biblical tale is one of loving kindness – but it also includes a realistic

message. After her husband's death, Ruth chooses to stay with her mother-in-law and undertakes the backbreaking farm work of gleaning to support the family. This involves lifting the grain and stalks left behind after the harvesting of barley. The metaphor of the harvest is another reminder that married couples will reap what they sow, depending on the effort and commitment made to their relationship.

The poem's last line is placed apart to emphasise its significance. Ní Chuilleanáin tells the newlyweds that they 'will have to trust me' – presumably just as Ruth trusted her mother-in-law, Naomi. For doing this, she was rewarded with living 'happily ever after', as in the best tales. The poet's quietly light-hearted approach, however, does not lessen her own deeply felt hopes for Niall and Xenya. **All the stories she has used are concerned with the essential qualities of a loving relationship** – and share a common thread of courage, faithfulness and honesty as the couple journey to a happy future. Tales and dreams are the shadow-truths that will endure. Ní Chuilleanáin's final tone is clearly sincere, upbeat and forward-looking.

Writing About the Poem

'The imagination is not the refuge but the true site of authority.' Comment on this statement in relation to the poem 'To Niall Woods and Xenya Ostrovskaia, Married in Dublin on 9 September 2009'.

Sample Paragraph

I feel that Ní Chuilleanáin's poem has subtle messages which only become clear after several readings. I think the poet is counselling her son and his new bride, Xenya, that stories, 'the imagination' are where truth, 'the true site of authority' lies. Stories are not escapism, although we may scoff in this modern age at 'Once upon a time'. The stories she chooses, 'sleeping beauty in her high tower', 'the firebird that stole the golden apples' and the 'King of Ireland's Son and the Enchanter's Daughter' all suggest that perseverance and sincerity win the day. Nothing worthwhile is won easily. While the language, 'half a loaf and your mother's blessing', and imagery seem to be from children's fiction, they resound with good sense. I thought the inclusion of the story of Ruth was very apt as it involved two cultures which is relevant to the couple's Irish and Russian origins, but also to many other situations in this time of immigration. People in this new era will have to 'trust to strangers'. I understood that Ní Chuilleanáin is showing that no matter where these imaginative tales come from, Europe, Russia, Ireland or the Bible, obstacles have to be overcome in life through resolution and perseverance. This is a tough message, there is no hiding here. I thought the poet was clever because by putting this insight into the realm of a fairy story, it does not sound like preaching which the young couple might resent, yet the message rings true throughout time from this 'site of authority', the kingdom of storytelling.

N.B. Access your eBook for additional sample paragraphs and a list of useful quotes with commentary.

EXAMINER'S COMMENT

A sustained personal response showing genuine engagement with the poem. The focused opening tackles the discussion question directly. This is followed by several clear points, e.g. 'perseverance and sincerity win the day', 'Nothing worthwhile is won easily', 'obstacles have to be overcome', tracing the development of thought throughout the poem. Accurate quotations and clear expression ensure the highest grade.

Class/Homework Exercises

1. What impression of Ní Chuilleanáin do you get from reading 'To Niall Woods and Xenya Ostrovskaia, Married in Dublin on 9 September 2009'? Write at least one paragraph in response, illustrating your views with reference to the text of the poem.
2. 'Ní Chuilleanáin's poems are often seen as challenging, but ultimately rewarding.' To what extent is this true of 'To Niall Woods and Xenia Ostrovskaia, married in Dublin on 9 September 2009'? Support your answer with reference to the poem.

Summary Points

- **The advice to the young couple is couched in the language of a fairy tale.**
- **Recurring references to Bible stories and legends.**
- **Effective use of personification, alliteration and sibilance.**
- **Ending is sincere, sympathetic and optimistic.**

Leaving Cert Sample Essay

'Eiléan Ní Chuilleanáin's extraordinary poetic world reveals compelling narratives which never cease to captivate readers.' Discuss this view, supporting your answer with suitable reference to the poems on your course.

Sample Essay

(Ní Chuilleanáin's extraordinary poetic world reveals compelling narratives which captivate readers)

1. To me, Eiléan Ní Chuilleanáin's lyrical world thrives on the creeping rustlings and barely noticed stirrings of life. Enthralling stories are quietly let slip to bewitch and enchant her readers in a wide range of variety, from hopeful poems such as 'All for You' to the family stories of 'Fireman's Lift' and 'To Niall Woods and Xenya.'

2. 'The Bend in the Road' takes a normal event, a child becoming car-sick, and transforms it with arresting images from the surreal, ominous world of the fairy tale, 'A tall tree like a cat's tail'. The poet links together selected memories from various times and places and so mesmerises the reader with the resonance from this 'bend/In the road'. The family all point, on subsequent journeys, to 'Where you were sick on the way to the lake'. Ní Chuilleanáin's intent gaze reminds us that a bend in the road, which is cleverly emphasised by its line placement, prevents seeing what is around the corner. Now the poet interjects another memory into the story, the death of loved ones 'Piled high, wrapped lightly, like the one cumulus cloud/In a perfect sky'. This place now becomes 'the place of their presence'. They live now 'in the tree, in the air' because this is where they are remembered.

3. The driving narrative of the young girl in 'Following' as she attempts to keep up with her father on a hectic fair day holds the readers who are pulled into this world by the unusual description of 'beasts packed solid as books'. The explosive 'b' links 'beasts' and 'books' and I can really picture the crammed animals standing in lines as they await sale. Other stories are woven into the poem, as the image of the dead father appears, 'Gliding' as the girl crosses the 'shivering bog'. He is now sitting in 'the library where the light is clear'. The poet is challenging us to engage and 'push ... open' the poem, just as the 'crushed flowers', an evocative image for past shared memories, force the book open. The girl's suffering is represented by 'The square of white linen'. It is not 'shelved', never to be thought of or experienced again. It will emerge, 'crack/The spine open'.

MARKING SCHEME GUIDELINES

Candidates are free to agree and/or disagree with the given statement. The poet's treatment of themes and subject matter should be addressed, as well as her individual approach, distinctive writing style, etc. Reward responses that show clear evidence of genuine engagement with the poems. Expect discussion on how Ní Chuilleanáin's poetry appeals/does not appeal to readers.

INDICATIVE MATERIAL

- Poet's views on life/ relationships.
- Recurring optimistic themes on life and rebirth; the continuous past.
- Fragmented narrative; innovative narrative blending.
- Collapse of time and place.
- Atmospheric detail; artistic and architectural references.
- Dispassionate, detached tone of storyteller.
- Focus on uniquely Irish phenomena.
- Biblical, historical and mythical references.
- Mystical/spiritual experience.
- Layered and interwoven nuances challenge the reader, etc.

4. Ní Chuilleanáin recounts a story in the poem, 'On Lacking the Killer Instinct', which her father had told her about running away from the Black and Tans when he was a young man. The reader is submerged into the Ireland of 1922. He seeks refuge in a 'safe house'. The relief of the escape is graphically conveyed in the detail, 'he came out/Into a blissful dawn'. In my opinion, the reader is delighted at the father's breath-taking escape. It is similar to the escape of the hare, recounted in the earlier part of the poem, 'her bright eye/Full not only of speed and fear/But surely in the moment a glad power'. Narratives are blended together seamlessly as the poet relates her own flight from the awful reality of her father's final illness, 'I fled up into the hills, that time/My father was dying a in hospital'.

5. 'Fireman's Lift' deals with the harsh truth of her mother's death. They had both visited Parma Cathedral once and their close relationship is clearly caught. 'I was standing beside you looking.' The strong verbs, 'spiralling' and 'heaving' capture the huge effort of the angels as they lifted Mary from her earthly life. The hands of the angels act as a 'crane and support' for Mary. 'Their heads bowed to reflect on her/Fair face' reminded the poet of the nurses who tended her mother in her final illness. Readers become immersed in the poem's storyline when the poet comments, 'This is what love sees, that angle'. The poet is coming to terms with the harsh reality that life has a natural cycle, 'The crick in the branch loaded with fruit'. The reader stands with mother and daughter marvelling as 'The Virgin was spiralling to heaven'. Now it is time for the poet's mother to go too.

6. Although Ní Chuilleanáin tells a story from an oblique, non-confessional perspective, this detachment does not prevent her engaging her reader. In 'To Niall Woods and Xenya' she intricately weaves Russian and Irish stories as she celebrates the two diverse cultures of the young couple. She also uses the story to gently pass on her advice on their new life together. I thought the phrase, 'you both see the same star', showed how she understood that the young couple had a shared vision of life. But Ruth's story from the Bible was most fascinating. She had to show courage to succeed as she trusted to strangers. The young people will also need these qualities if they are to succeed in the best tradition of the fairy tale to 'live happily ever after'.

7. For me, Ní Chuilleanáin has opened a poetic world in which she intertwines stories from her own family life, 'poems that mean a lot to me', with those from many other sources. The reader stands fascinated by a bend in the road, a hare 'sitting still', 'The sleeping beauty in her high tower', the Virgin Mary as 'she came to the edge of the cloud', a 'key still in your pocket', all thanks to the gaze and skill of a remarkable poet.

(approx. 870 words)
(45–50 minutes)

EXAMINER'S COMMENT

This is a top-grade personal response that shows clear engagement with Ní Chuilleanáin's poems. Effective use is made of accurate quotations and detailed reference to support perceptive critical discussion. For example, in paragraph 3: 'The explosive "b" links "beasts" and "books" and I can really picture the crammed animals standing in lines as they await sale.' This clearly organised essay is very well written and highly impressive.

GRADE: H1
P = 15/15
C = 14/15
L = 15/15
M = 5/5
Total = 49/50

Sample Leaving Cert Questions on Ní Chuilleanáin's Poetry

1. **'Ní Chuilleanáin's intriguing poems emerge from an intense but insightful appreciation of human experience.' Do you agree with this assessment of her poetry? Write a response, supporting your points with reference to the poems on your course.**
2. **'Eiléan Ní Chuilleanáin is a truly original poet who leads us into altered landscapes and enhances our understanding of the world around us.' To what extent would you agree with this statement? In your response, refer to the poems on your course.**
3. **'Eiléan Ní Chuilleanáin's demanding subject matter and formidable style can prove challenging.' Discuss this statement, supporting your answer with reference to the poetry of Eiléan Ní Chuilleanáin on your course.**

First Sample Essay Plan (Q1)

'Ní Chuilleanáin's intriguing poems emerge from an intense but insightful appreciation of human experience.' Do you agree with this assessment of her poetry? Write a response, supporting your points with reference to the poems on your course.

Intro: Ní Chuilleanáin's innovative treatment of a broad thematic range – Irish history, myth, transience, memory, relationships, loss, religious life, the dispossessed, etc.

NOTE

As you may not be familiar with some of the poems referred to in the sample plans below, substitute poems that you have studied closely.

Exam candidates usually discuss three or four poems in their answers. However, there is no set number of poems or formulaic approach expected.

Key points about a particular poem can be developed over more than one paragraph.

Paragraphs may also include cross-referencing and discussion of more than one poem.

Remember that there is no single 'correct' answer to poetry questions, so always be confident in expressing your own considered response.

Point 1: 'Fireman's Lift' – compelling treatment of her mother's death. Importance of dramatic setting as a context for personal experiences/ memories. Poet's sympathetic tone, atmospheric detail, artistic references.

Point 2: 'Translation' – perceptive account of the Magdalene laundry workers. Sensitive approach to women victims. Use of effective symbols. Collapse of time. Silence and understated meanings. Imaginative and interwoven nuances affect readers.

Point 3: Dispassionate, detached tone of storyteller – 'Deaths and Engines', 'Kilcash'. Underlying sense of the poet's compassion. Interlinked layered narrative threads entice the reader.

Conclusion: Poetry can challenge/excite responses – Ní Chuilleanáin's mesmeric exploration of universal themes invites readers to unravel the secrets of her work.

Sample Essay Plan (Q3)

Develop **one** of the above points into a paragraph.

Sample Paragraph: Point 2

'Translation' offers an intriguing account of a dark period in Irish history. Ní Chuilleanáin's dramatisation of the Magdalene laundry victims begins in Glasnevin Cemetery, with an unnerving description: 'soil frayed and sifted evens the score.' This image is typical of the poet, suggesting both the communal grave and the horrifying injustice. In death, these women have become 'ridges under the veil' of the earth. The reference also conveys a sense of the strict Magdalene nuns who are also viewed as victims of an unchristian era. Time and places blend throughout the poem. The poet's concentrated vision of the laundries is associated with their exploitation – 'where steam danced/Around stone drains'. She contrasts the girls' youthful spirit with the cold conditions around them. Without a trace of sentimentality, 'Translation' movingly recalls a whole generation of women whose lives were ruined. Generously, the ending focuses on the authoritarian figure of an unnamed nun who is envisioned in death and who finally understands the tragedy – 'Allow us now to hear it, sharp as an infant's cry'. This line suggested the communal suffering shared by the nuns and the unmarried mothers who were separated from their babies. The poet's intense depiction of the Magdalene experience is highly compelling, allowing me to relate to this truly regrettable 'cloud over my time'.

EXAMINER'S COMMENT

As part of a full essay, this is a strong, top-grade paragraph that shows clear engagement with the poem. The discussion relating to Ni Chuilleanáin's dense imagery is particularly impressive. Apt – and accurate – quotations are used effectively. Language use is also excellent throughout.

N.B. Access your eBook for additional sample paragraphs and a list of useful quotes with commentary.

Second Sample Essay Plan (Q3)

'Eiléan Ní Chuilleanáin's demanding subject matter and formidable style can prove challenging.' Discuss this statement, supporting your answer with reference to the poetry of Eiléan Ní Chuilleanáin on your course.

Intro: Ní Chuilleanáin – addresses universal concerns (change, the exploration of one's identity and search for self). Exhilarates with vast canvas of people, places, voices, times and images. Weaves complex references into third-person narratives (historical, religious, philosophical, feminist, mystical, classical). Demands readers to pay close attention to details of isolated moments caught in the unrelenting clarity of the poet's gaze. Pushes reader into self-enclosed worlds of poems.

Point 1: 'Street' – unnerving, dramatic poem draws reader and would-be lover into surreal world. Cinematic close-ups reveal a tangible world ('white trousers/Dangling a knife on a ring at her belt'). Interesting characterisation of girl operating in a man's role. Run-on lines mimic the slanting lane of the 'shambles'. Intriguing image of 'half-open' door invites and bars. Ambivalent threshold scene filled with menace ('marked with the red crescent'). Gaps in narrative tantalise the reader.

Point 2: 'The Second Voyage' – through the use of the Greek myth of Odysseus, the poet explores the human problem of wanting the impossible and not appreciating what is possessed. Imaginative description breathes fresh life into the old myth.

Point 3: 'Lucina Schynning in Silence of the Nicht' – compelling, eerie setting. Ominous silence ('Moon shining in silence of the night'), fragmentary images ('a sour candle', 'the crazed window') lead the reader back into Ireland's troubled history. Nightmare sequence of revolting images ('plague/Of mice, plague of beetles/Crawling') conjures past scenes of misery, disease and famine. Change of tone reflects contrasting harmonious image of present-day Ireland (the hare 'sitting still', the 'chirp of the stream running'). Reader left to unravel poem's veiled meaning.

Conclusion: Ní Chuilleanáin – presents elusive vision in potent poetry. Subtle messages unfold through multiple readings. Transformative poet, breaks down barriers between shifting realms. Fragmented narratives

open many doors into multiple worlds. Transports readers into luminous scenes of great visual beauty through impressionistic style. Like the poet, the reader is led to ask, 'Do I really believe this, do I really feel this?'

Sample Essay Plan (Q3)

Develop **one** of the points on the previous page into a paragraph.

Sample Paragraph: Point 2

Ní Chuilleanáin's, 'The Second Voyage' addresses the contrast between those who constantly travel and still life pictures of everyday scenes. Ní Chuilleanáin uses the classical myth of the alpha male Odysseus who fears stasis. His relentless battle with the sea is portrayed through a stylised feminine image, 'ruffled foreheads of the waves/crocodiling and mincing past'. Yet in vain does he stamp the 'simmering sea' with his masculine authority, failing to 'name them as Adam had the beasts'. The sea could not be mastered no matter how hard he 'rammed/The oar between their jaws'. So Odysseus retreats to the other world of land. Order reigns, 'herons parcel out the miles of streams'. Odysseus plants his oar in a gesture of conquest, 'I'll plant you for a gatepost'. But Odysseus is not satisfied, 'His face grew damp with tears'. He yearns for the freedom of the boundless sea, 'frying under the ship's side', which he cannot conquer. Life on land has boundaries, but lacks allure, 'Housekeeping at the roadside in brown trickles floored with mud'. The reader is challenged to consider the very human dilemma – what we want we cannot have, what we possess, we do not desire.

EXAMINER'S COMMENT

As part of a full essay answer to Q3, this clear response uses the poem effectively to address the question. Good use is made of apt and accurate quotations that are integrated well into the developed commentary. The poet's challenging style is suggested through key references 'classical myth', 'stylised feminine image'. Language use is impressive throughout. An assured high-grade standard.

Class/Homework Exercise

1. **Write one or two paragraphs in response to the question: 'Eiléan Ní Chuilleanáin's demanding subject matter and formidable style can prove challenging.' Discuss this statement, supporting your answer with reference to the poetry of Eiléan Ní Chuilleanáin on your course.**

Revision Overview

'Lucina Schynning in Silence of the Nicht'
Powerful monologue addresses themes of exploitation, loss and resistance.

'The Second Voyage'
Dramatic presentation of theme of transience. Innovative use of mythical Greek hero's love/hate relationship with sea.

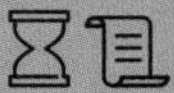

'Deaths and Engines'
Themes of memory, loss and death. Blending of two narratives (plane and father's death).

'Street'
Intriguing oblique narrative of falling in love. Central puzzling enigma.

'Fireman's Lift'
Vivid memory poem explores themes of death, regeneration and love.

'All for You'
Intricately layered broken narrative depicts theme of transience through analysis of the challenges and rewards of religious life.

'Following'
Themes of power of memory and unjust balance of power through metaphor of journey.

'Kilcash'
Translation of Irish lament addresses theme of impact of change on Irish society, past and present.

'Translation'
Belated acknowledgment of wrongs perpetrated on Irish women in Magdalene laundries.

'The Bend in the Road'
Blended autobiographical events express transience and loss. The continuing existence of memory is acknowledged and honoured.

'On Lacking the Killer Instinct'
Interwoven introspective narratives bridge past and present. Enigmatic examination of theme of powerful and powerless, through illustrations of hunter and hunted.

'To Niall Woods and Xenya Ostrovskaia, Married in Dublin 9 September 2009'
Celebratory epithalamium blends folk tales and biblical stories. Theme of sacrifice needed for success.

Last Words

'There is something second-sighted about Eiléan Ní Chuilleanáin's work. Her poems see things anew, in a rinsed and dreamstruck light.'
Seamus Heaney

'Ní Chuilleanáin's eccentric poems uncover hidden dramas in many guises, and she continually holds us captive by her luminous voice.'
Molly Bendall

'Inspiration comes from everywhere, from the places I go and the things I do. I never write unless I have an idea that seems really interesting to me.'
Eiléan Ní Chuilleanáin

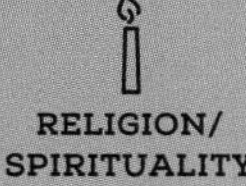

Adrienne Rich (1929–2012)

'Poetry can break open locked chambers of possibility, restore numbed zones to feeling, recharge desire.'

Poet, teacher, critic, political activist and women's rights advocate, Adrienne Rich once said that 'poems are like dreams: in them you put what you don't know you know'. Born in Baltimore in 1929, Rich was to become one of America's most successful and influential poets. Her themes explore issues of identity, sexuality and politics. A graduate of Radcliffe College in 1951, she was awarded the Yale Series of Younger Poets Award, a prize that led to her first publication, *A Change of World*. However, it wasn't until her third collection, *Snapshots of a Daughter-in-Law*, in 1963 that she received popular recognition. Widely read, and anthologised, Rich went on to publish numerous volumes of poetry and several books of non-fiction prose. She sought to include 'non-poetic' language into poetry and her distinctive writing style is noted for its speech rhythms, enjambment and irregular line and stanza lengths. Throughout her distinguished career, Adrienne Rich dared to make poetry out of the prosaic, humdrum, and sometimes secret events of women's lives. Years after her death at the age of 82, her poems still retain their extraordinary power.

Investigate Further

To find out more about Adrienne Rich, or to hear readings of her poems, you could search some useful websites such as YouTube, BBC Poetry, poetryfoundation.org and poetryarchive.org, or access additional material on this page of your eBook.

○ **1 'Aunt Jennifer's Tigers' (OL)**
The poet explores the theme of power by contrasting the imaginary tigers with the oppressed life of their creator, Aunt Jennifer, who was trapped in an unfulfilled marriage.
Page 338

○ **2 'The Uncle Speaks in the Drawing Room' (OL)**
This poem considers aspects of social unrest while addressing the nature of patriarchal power and its effects.
Page 341

○ **3 'Power'**
Celebrating the life of Marie Curie, the poem contrasts the different ways in which power can be used.
Page 345

○ **4 'Storm Warnings'**
Powerlessness and change are central themes in the poem. Just as people are at risk from approaching storms, they are also vulnerable to their own changing emotions.
Page 348

○ **5 'Living in Sin'**
The poem contrasts ideal romantic relationships with the more mundane experiences of everyday reality.
Page 352

○ **6 'The Roofwalker'**
Using the extended metaphor of a builder at work, the poet raises interesting questions about alienation and personal decision-making.
Page 356

○ **7 'Our Whole Life'**
The poem is an exploration of the failure of language to adequately communicate human experiences.
Page 360

○ **8 'Trying to Talk with a Man'**
Set in a remote desert location where nuclear tests are taking place, the poem traces the breakdown of a couple's relationship.
Page 363

○ **9 'Diving into the Wreck'**
This thought-provoking poem combines the description of an amateur dive to investigate a shipwreck with an exploration of social/political history and change.
Page 367

○ **10 'From a Survivor'**
The poem focuses on a failed marriage and on the broader issue of changing male-female relationships.
Page 373

*(OL) indicates poems that are also prescribed for the Ordinary Level course.

1 Aunt Jennifer's Tigers

Aunt Jennifer's tigers prance across a screen,
Bright topaz denizens of a world of green.
They do not fear the men beneath the tree;
They pace in sleek chivalric certainty.

Aunt Jennifer's fingers fluttering through her wool
Find even the ivory needle hard to pull.
The massive weight of Uncle's wedding band
Sits heavily upon Aunt Jennifer's hand.

When Aunt is dead, her terrified hands will lie
Still ringed with ordeals she was mastered by.
The tigers in the panel that she made
Will go on prancing, proud and unafraid.

prance: walk with exaggerated, bouncing steps.
screen: surface on which an image is formed.
topaz: semi-precious stone, yellow or light blue.
denizens: inhabitants, occupants.
sleek: glossy, smooth, shiny.
chivalric: behaving in a formal, courteous way.
ivory: hard, white bony substance that forms elephant tusks.

ordeals: painful or difficult experiences.

'The massive weight of Uncle's wedding band'

Personal Response

1. This poem illustrates the power of a symbol. Comment on Rich's choice of symbols.
2. 'Rich challenges us with her ideas on relationships.' To what extent is this true in 'Aunt Jennifer's Tigers'?
3. Would you regard the ending of the poem as positive or negative? Explain your answer with reference to the text.

Critical Literacy

'Aunt Jennifer's Tigers' was published when Adrienne Rich was just 21. It appeared in her first volume of poetry, *A Change of World*. Rich wrote: 'It was important to me that Aunt Jennifer was a person as distinct from myself as possible, distanced by the formalism of the poem, by its objective observant tone.' The tigers represent an aspect of Aunt Jennifer's personality that she herself is not at liberty to display.

This formal lyric with its rigorous three-quatrain structure and rigid rhyme (*aabb, ccdd, eeff*) depicts the aunt in a **confined and restricted situation. She is forced to create an alternative world in order to express her innermost thoughts. The fierce noble tigers of the first quatrain** are a symbol of the aunt's imagination and creative force. Her embroidery speaks volumes in an oppressive world that forces her to remain silent. The tigers are shown as being energetic and playful, signifying great vigour, assertion and fearlessness. Strong verbs, 'prance' and 'pace', vividly sketch these proud dynamic creatures: 'They do not fear the men beneath the tree.' Ironically, they have been hunted by humans almost to the point of extinction. Their bright colours are exotic and unrealistic. The term 'chivalric' is interesting as it has its origins in Medieval history when powerful knights had a reputation for honourable behaviour and for the respect they showed to women. Is this what is missing from the aunt's relationship with her husband?

Throughout the **second quatrain**, Aunt Jennifer is portrayed in sharp contrast to the beautiful jungle animals. Exhausted and insecure, **she seems to be overwhelmed** with life. The poet's use of alliteration ('fingers fluttering') suggests a fragile, sensitive person who struggles with simple tasks, finding 'even the ivory needle hard to pull'. As a dominated wife, she suffers acute emotional pressure, highlighted by 'The massive weight' that 'Sits heavily'. Yet her fear is never fully articulated. Is she afraid of her husband, society, the Church? A ring usually symbolises union; here it stands for confinement and domination. Does she – unlike the tigers – fear men? All through the stanza, there is a palpable sense of the absent 'Uncle'. His presence is particularly underlined by the forceful tone and strict iambic pentameter in the line: 'The massive weight of Uncle's wedding band.'

While the first quatrain described the tigers and the second gives us a picture of Aunt Jennifer and the missing uncle, the **third quatrain** moves to **the future**, to a time when 'Aunt is dead'. But even here she is still experiencing distress and every part of her is fearful, 'terrified hands'. The striking description, 'ringed with ordeals she was mastered by', highlight the poet's resentment of the subjugation of women. Although Rich's poetic voice is trenchant, the poem ends on a positive note as the tigers, symbols of the aunt's imaginative powers – her inner life – achieve a kind of artistic immortality. These stunning creatures will go on, 'prancing, proud and unafraid'. The timid aunt's gesture of defiance through her needlework

creations (a craft usually associated with women) will live on forever. Is this her victorious rebellion against patriarchal culture?

Writing About the Poem

'Some critics claim that Adrienne Rich's poems are gloomy and downbeat.' Discuss this view with particular reference to 'Aunt Jennifer's Tigers'.

Sample Paragraph

My reaction to Rich's poems is positive not negative. I definitely don't think her poems are gloomy. How can critics say that about 'Aunt Jennifer's Tigers'? Especially when the tigers are described using exotic colours of 'topaz' and green shining from the embroidered screen she is creating in silent, yet powerful protest against the confinement she finds herself in, 'The massive weight of Uncle's wedding band'? All of us in our lives are bound in by powerful forces beyond our control, but Rich shows us how it is possible to 'speak' even though we are like the Aunt, 'terrified'. Is this not upbeat? In the final lines, in defiance of all her suppression and defeat, 'terrified hands', it is the tigers, symbolising Aunt Jennifer's repressed desires, which will go on 'prancing, proud and unafraid'. Sometimes we speak most powerfully when we are silent. With such a strong uplifting ending, how could anyone suggest that Rich's poems are gloomy?

EXAMINER'S COMMENT

This lively high-grade response is generally well focused and aptly supported. The paragraph shows a good sense of engagement with the poem. Expression is reasonably fluent, though over-reliant on questions. More thorough analysis of the poet's attitude and subtle tone would have raised the standard.

Class/Homework Exercises

1. 'Adrienne Rich challenges us with her ideas on marriage.' To what extent do you agree with this statement? Discuss with reference to 'Aunt Jennifer's Tigers'.
2. Comment on the effectiveness of Rich's choice of verbs throughout this poem.

Summary Points

- **Central themes include marriage and male–female relationships.**
- **Effective use of vivid imagery and symbolism.**
- **Contrast between the powerful and the oppressed.**
- **Varied tones (objective, ironic, didactic) convey the poet's view.**
- **Ambiguous ending – art endures but inequality also continues.**

2 The Uncle Speaks in the Drawing Room

I have seen the mob of late
Standing sullen in the square,
Gazing with a sullen stare
At window, balcony, and gate.
Some have talked in bitter tones,
Some have held and fingered stones.

These are follies that subside.
Let us consider, none the less,
Certain frailties of glass
Which, it cannot be denied,
Lead in times like these to fear
For crystal vase and chandelier.

Not that missiles will be cast;
None as yet dare lift an arm.
But the scene recalls a storm
When our grandsire stood aghast
To see his antique ruby bowl
Shivered in a thunder-roll.

Let us only bear in mind
How these treasures handed down
From a calmer age passed on
Are in the keeping of our kind.
We stand between the dead glass-blowers
And murmurings of missile-throwers.

Title: Drawing Room: room where visitors are entertained.

mob: disorderly crowd.
sullen: surly, resentful.

follies: foolish actions or ideas.

frailties: physical or moral weaknesses.

crystal: clear and brilliant glass.

missiles: objects or weapons aimed at a target.

grandsire: old-fashioned word for grandfather.
aghast: overcome with amazement or horror.
ruby bowl: red glass bowl.

in the keeping of our kind: in the care and charge of people like us.
glass-blowers: people who make glass objects by shaping molten glass.

Personal Response

1. The voice in the poem belongs to 'The Uncle'. What type of man do you think he is? Consider what he says and how he speaks.
2. Choose two symbols or metaphors that are used in the poem and briefly explain what you think each represents.
3. In your view, what do you think is the central theme or message in the poem? Refer to the text in your answer.

Critical Literacy

'The Uncle Speaks in the Drawing Room' is part of Rich's poetry collection, *A Change of World* (1951). While these early poems had formal structures and elegant formats, they often addressed disturbing themes, including issues of social class divisions and fears about nuclear war. In this poem, the persona is a man who is the representative of high-class culture.

The **opening stanza** introduces a world of **order, wealth and refinement**. This is established in the title phrase, 'Drawing Room'. The choice of the definite article to describe 'The Uncle' suggests that he is distant and aloof. Who is he addressing in this beautiful, privileged setting? Does the uncle's tone seem condescending, patronising? Look at the use of the word 'mob'. Is it a dismissive term? Notice the alliteration in the line, 'Standing sullen in the square', as it describes the suffocating atmosphere of threat from the people gathered outside.

The uncle is certainly speaking from an advantaged position of authority in his residence with 'balcony and gate'. Would you view him as an image of old-fashioned conservative values? Consider how the regular rhyme scheme (*abbacc*), the controlled seven-syllable line and the strict structure of six-line stanzas all stress the orderly world of the poem's speaker. **This formal style suits the persona** of the conservative uncle. Meanwhile, the crowd 'talked in bitter tones' and 'fingered stones' in an intimidating manner. Are they an obvious symbol of discontent and menace?

In **stanza two**, the uncle's **arrogant tone** is evident as he states that the mob's ill-advised threat will soon 'subside'. He disparages the crowd's grievances as mere 'follies'. However, he is also concerned that his much-prized material possessions, the 'crystal vase and chandelier' might be damaged during these uncertain times of social unrest. To him, they are vulnerable treasures, 'frailties of glass'. Could this also be a reference to the fragility of accepted social values? What does this suggest about the uncle? Does he simply represent the 'haves' and the crowd the 'have-nots'?

The smug reassurances of the uncle continue in the **third stanza**, 'Not that missiles will be cast'. There is a certain bravado in his voice as he again dismisses the notion of danger, 'None as yet dare lift an arm'. But the hint of trouble is still present in the phrase, 'as yet'. He reminisces about a former

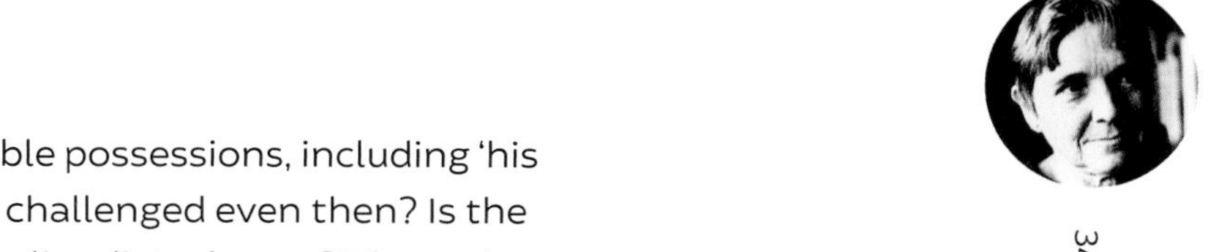

upheaval when 'our grandsire' lost some valuable possessions, including 'his antique ruby bowl'. Was the ruling order being challenged even then? Is the 'thunder-roll' a foreboding metaphor for an earlier disturbance? The verb 'Shivered' suggests both the shattering of glass and the cold blast of revolution. Rich's onomatopoeic effects vividly convey the **violence of social upheaval and its chilling consequences**.

In the **closing stanza**, the speaker seems to assume that readers will agree with all his assertions. This is indicated by his use of the plural first-person pronoun 'us' in the line, 'Let us only bear in mind'. The uncle is equally confident that he is speaking to people of like class ('our kind'), those who are used to wealth and privilege. He is also proud that he and his class are **maintaining the old order, the status quo**, 'these treasures'. Once more, he resorts to the notion of tradition as a means of protecting power. He clearly sees it as his duty to stand as custodian between those who have created this world of privilege, 'the dead glass-blowers' and the 'missile-throwers' who seek to destroy it.

The uncle's concluding comment is to sneer at the 'murmurings' of the restless crowd, perhaps hoping that their mumbling incoherence (vividly captured in the broad assonant sounds) will inevitably fail. However, **his tone appears to lack conviction**. Is it possible that beneath all the empty rhetoric, he realises that his generation might be the last line of defence between his great ancestors and the unruly mob that will destroy the life of privilege he has known?

Writing About the Poem

Rich once wrote that a reader could be 'fairly encoded in poetry'. What do you think is the code or hidden message of 'The Uncle Speaks in the Drawing Room'? Support your answer with reference to the text.

Sample Paragraph

'The Uncle Speaks in the Drawing Room' is a clever poem which both by its use of symbols and tone has a subversive message. The uncle symbolises traditional conservative values, 'treasures handed down' which 'are in the keeping of our kind'. His wealth and privilege are eloquently conveyed by words such as 'Drawing Room', 'balcony', 'crystal vase'. It's ironic that the uncle is intent on keeping the 'mob' outside, 'We stand between', as he speaks in the drawing room, a room which was designed for receiving visitors. The structure of the poem surrounds the uncle with the mob in the first line, 'the mob of late' and in the last line, 'missile-throwers'. He is both physically and metaphorically under threat. The mob represents those who want the old social order swept away. They speak in 'bitter tones'. But to the uncle, their 'murmurings' are unintelligible. This gulf between the classes is the poem's hidden message. The resentful underclass are 'missile-throwers' threatening violence, 'fingered stones'. The uncle's ruling class, represented by possessions, is fragile and likely to be shattered, 'Shivered'. This is a powerfully coded poem about one of the most fundamental elements of life.

EXAMINER'S COMMENT

This top-grade focused response offers a sensitive reading of the poem and is well-rooted in the text. The opening sentence introduces the response effectively. This is followed by a coherent discussion, identifying the central theme of class warfare and tracing the development of thought (particularly Rich's use of symbols) within the poem. Supportive quotes are effectively integrated and the expression is clear and impressive.

Class/Homework Exercises

1. 'Rich draws on vivid language to create thought-provoking poems.' Discuss this statement with particular reference to 'The Uncle Speaks in the Drawing Room'.
2. In your view, what does this poem suggest about the personality and views of Adrienne Rich? Support your response with reference to the text.

Summary Points

- **Central themes include unrest and instability in a class-divided society.**
- **Rich addresses key issues of power – its use and abuse.**
- **Formal writing style, controlled four-stanza structure.**
- **Central tone is pompous and arrogant.**
- **Effective use of symbols, alliteration, assonance and sibilance throughout.**

3 Power

Living in the earth-deposits of our history

Today a backhoe divulged out of a crumbling flank of earth
one bottle amber perfect a hundred-year-old
cure for fever or melancholy a tonic
for living on this earth in the winters of this climate

Today I was reading about Marie Curie:
she must have known she suffered from radiation sickness
her body bombarded for years by the element
she had purified
It seems she denied to the end
the source of the cataracts on her eyes
the cracked and suppurating skin of her finger-ends
till she could no longer hold a test-tube or a pencil

She died a famous woman denying
her wounds
denying
her wounds came from the same source as her power

1974

backhoe: mechanical digger.
flank: side.
amber: orange-yellow.
melancholy: deep sadness.

Marie Curie: (1867–1934) pioneering scientist.
radiation sickness: illness caused by damaging radioactive rays.
bombarded: attacked.

cataracts: medical condition causing blurred vision.
suppurating: festering.

Personal Response

1. Briefly explain what you understand by the first line of the poem.
2. From your reading of the poem, what image do you get of Marie Curie?
3. Describe the dominant tone in the final stanza. Refer to the text in your answer.

Critical Literacy

Written in free verse and using a stream of consciousness technique, this wonderful, thought-provoking poem is overtly a portrait of the famous female scientist, Marie Curie. It also invites readers

to consider the nature, use and abuse of power. When Adrienne Rich wrote 'Power' in 1974, the study of women's historically marginalised contributions to society was still taking shape.

The **opening line** ('Living in the earth-deposits of our history') seems almost like the poem's subtitle in highlighting the importance of understanding the past. **What does history teach us?** In **stanza two**, the speaker connects past and present by focusing on the unearthing of a perfectly-preserved 'hundred-year-old' medicine bottle that might have been sold once as an all-purpose 'cure'. The image of the backhoe excavating 'a crumbling flank of earth' suggests a divided and disharmonious world. We can only imagine the suffering of past generations whose efforts to survive ('living on this earth') made them easy targets for exploitation. The extended spaces separating key words interrupt the rhythm and reflect the idea of time passing in fragmented segments.

Stanza three focuses on the life of Marie Curie. This eminent scientist, who dedicated her life to advancing medical research, embodies the positive use of power. The initial word ('Today') echoes line 2 and sharply contrasts Curie's indisputable contribution with the bogus cure-alls of earlier times. The tone is appreciative and sympathetic: 'she must have known she suffered.' What seems to fascinate the speaker most is **Marie Curie's courage and selflessness** as she continued to take life-threatening risks – 'her body bombarded for years' – while working with dangerous radioactive materials.

The speaker also notes the **tragic irony** of the scientist's life; the radium she struggled to purify eventually killed her. Shocking images of Curie's illness, especially 'the cracked and suppurating skin' highlight her obvious lack of self-pity and her refusal to allow herself to be diverted from her life's work. The **last stanza** repeatedly emphasises how she went to her death 'denying her wounds'. The tone seems to waver between admiration and regret. This final view of Curie as 'a famous woman' refusing to acknowledge that her suffering resulted 'from the same source as her power' makes her an enigmatic figure, a universal symbol of endurance.

Curie gave her whole life to addressing and overpowering the challenges she herself encountered. In committing herself wholeheartedly to what she believed in, she demonstrated her own individual power in improving other people's lives. Is Rich implying that such example should inspire us all to take a principled stand on contemporary issues, such as racism, sexism and other injustices? In the end, this poem revisits history to reconstruct **two contrasting views of power**. The poet leaves readers free to consider the differences between cynical opportunism and genuine devotion to work. The final phrase ('her power') is optimistic, suggesting the potential within people to change the world for the better.

Writing About the Poem

'Adrienne Rich's poem, "Power", challenges readers to revise traditional attitudes regarding the roles of women in society.' To what extent do you agree with this view? Support your answer with reference to the poem.

Sample Paragraph

Rich's poem 'Power' made several interesting points about the subject of power. It told two stories and showed that power can corrupt or help, depending on how it is applied. Marie Curie, the heroine of the poem, had both the determination and vision necessary to succeed in helping people through her research into radioactivity as a cure for cancer. The poet shows how Curie was ironically killed by the destructive power of her own discovery because she could not accept that 'her wounds came from the same source as her power'. However, she was a truly motivating figure – for both idealistic women and men alike – who used power for our common good. On the other hand, the amber bottle that the backhoe turns up has sinister implications. The poet seems to be saying that medical power has been abused throughout history. She does not lecture us on the misuse of power, instead she allows us to think about the enormous contribution made by Marie Curie during her lifetime. The poem concludes on a hopeful note with a tribute to Curie as a pioneering chemist who selflessly dedicated herself to others. Curie was the first woman to win a Nobel Prize – and this in itself speaks volumes about our patriarchal world. I found her to be inspirational.

EXAMINER'S COMMENT

This high-grade personal response presents a consistent view of how the theme of power is explored in the poem. The point about the amber bottle would have benefitted from some more clarification. Overall, references are used effectively to support discussion points. Expression is clear and assured throughout (e.g. 'sinister implications', 'self-sacrificing use of power').

Class/Homework Exercises

1. What impact did the poem, 'Power', have on you? Refer to the text in your response.
2. Comment on Adrienne Rich's use of sensual imagery throughout the poem.

Summary Points

- **Central themes focus on aspects of power – personal and public.**
- **Anecdotal style; various tones – detached, reflective, ironic, didactic.**
- **Reference to Marie Curie's research effectively used to illustrate the poet's viewpoint.**
- **Innovative layout; effective use of alliteration and assonance.**

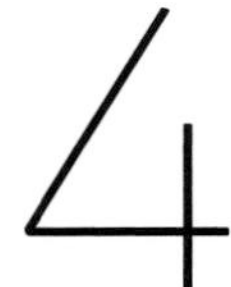

Storm Warnings

The glass has been falling all the afternoon,
And knowing better than the instrument
What winds are walking overhead, what zone
Of gray unrest is moving across the land,
I leave the book upon a pillowed chair
And walk from window to closed window, watching
Boughs strain against the sky

And think again, as often when the air
Moves inward toward a silent core of waiting,
How with a single purpose time has traveled
By secret currents of the undiscerned
Into this polar realm. Weather abroad
And weather in the heart alike come on
Regardless of prediction.

Between foreseeing and averting change
Lies all the mastery of elements
Which clocks and weatherglasses cannot alter.
Time in the hand is not control of time,
Nor shattered fragments of an instrument
A proof against the wind; the wind will rise,
We can only close the shutters.

I draw the curtains as the sky goes black
And set a match to candles sheathed in glass
Against the keyhole draught, the insistent whine
Of weather through the unsealed aperture.
This is our sole defense against the season;
These are the things that we have learned to do
Who live in troubled regions.

glass: barometer.

boughs: branches.

core: centre.

undiscerned: unseen.

prediction: forecast.

averting: avoiding.

elements: weather.

sheathed: enclosed, protected by.

aperture: opening.

Personal Response

1. With reference to the opening stanza, comment on Adrienne Rich's description of the developing storm.
2. Choose one image from stanza four that you consider particularly interesting and briefly explain your choice.
3. In your opinion, what does the poem suggest about people's attempts to control their lives? Support the points you make by quotation or reference.

Critical Literacy

In everyday conversation, we often use the weather as a metaphor for our moods – 'up bright and early', 'feeling fine', 'under the weather', etc. 'Storm Warnings' is one of Adrienne Rich's earliest published works. She described it as 'a poem about powerlessness'. Characteristically, the poet raises interesting questions about attitudes to the world around us and about how much control human beings actually have over how they live.

The poem opens dramatically as unsettled weather closes in. The speaker senses the approaching storm 'better than the instrument'. The ominous atmosphere in **stanza one** is illustrated by the disturbing personification of the winds 'walking overhead' and the image of the gathering clouds ('gray unrest') which are 'moving across the land'. The speaker's **restlessness adds further tension** as she walks 'from window to closed window'. The alliterative 'w' and sibilant 's' sounds suggest growing unease: 'Boughs strain against the sky.'

The gathering storm causes the speaker to 'think again' as she considers the impact of weather and time. The **distinction between nature and human nature becomes increasingly blurred** in **stanza two**. As the winds strengthen, the speaker becomes more passive – 'a silent core of waiting'. **Lines 12–14** draw a direct parallel between weather conditions and human experience ('weather in the heart'). Human beings are fated to endure both, 'Regardless of prediction'. In a symbolic way, the encroaching thunderstorm allows the

'gray unrest'

speaker to recognise all the other unwelcome forces ('secret currents') that can affect our fragile lives in 'this polar realm'. The image of the stranded individual at the mercy of the freezing elements is an unnerving one that foreshadows the reference to 'troubled regions' at the end of the poem.

Stanza three begins with a clear emphatic statement: knowledge and preparation ('foreseeing') are essential for survival. But such 'mastery of elements' is difficult. The speaker acknowledges the limitations of humans to endure storms of any kind. We are reminded of our place in the world: 'Time in the hand is not control of time.' Rich's stark image of the 'shattered fragments of an instrument' emphasises the ironic tone as the speaker acknowledges the reality that 'the wind will rise'. All she can do is retreat and protect herself as best she can. She also knows that her own experience is shared by others: 'We can only close the shutters.' **Powerlessness is a universal experience.** The plural pronoun and measured rhythm highlight our shared need to resist uninvited change and injustice by taking positive action.

This realisation seems to offer some encouragement and the poetic voice is much more purposeful in **stanza four**: 'I draw the curtains as the sky goes black.' Like the delicate candle-flame under glass, the speaker avoids the changing weather for the time being. It is an expedient solution of sorts, based on an understanding of the actual threat she faces. **The poem ends on a quietly resilient note** as the speaker faces up to the reality of damage limitation: 'These are the things that we have learned to do.' The tone is typically dignified and sympathetic to every individual under pressure 'in troubled regions'.

Writing About the Poem

In your view, what is the central theme or message in 'Storm Warnings'? Support your answer with reference to the poem.

Sample Paragraph

On the surface, I think the poem simply describes the way people try to protect themselves. Especially when faced with a storm. The opening atmosphere is edgy. The theme is a wake-up call. People are not all-powerful. The narrator moves nervously about the house checking the temperature and looking out at the clouds. She senses the danger 'better than any instrument'. This makes me think that the storm outside is simply a symbol of her inner fears. The whole poem is based around this comparison. Adrienne Rich is suggesting that people can do little to control their lives. So many forces are outside our control. But the message is far from negative. The key sentence for me is 'We can only close the shutters'. This sums up the human situation very well. Fate and

fortune may be powerful, but we have the power to make our own luck as much as we can. For me, there is some redemption in the upbeat final stanza – 'I draw the curtains as the sky goes black'. The main message appears to be a realistic one – we do whatever we can to survive life's bad times.

EXAMINER'S COMMENT

This high-grade paragraph includes some incisive discussion and personal engagement with the poem. Relevant quotations are used effectively. Although the opening section is note-like, the writing is lively and coherent throughout. A more developed analysis of the point about redemption would have improved the grade.

Class/Homework Exercises

1. Identify the dramatic elements in 'Storm Warnings' and comment briefly on their effectiveness.
2. Write your own personal response to the poem, referring closely to the text in your answer.

Summary Points

- **The idea of human vulnerability under pressure is central to the poem.**
- **Effective use of the extended storm metaphor.**
- **Impact of vivid visual imagery and dynamic sound effects.**
- **Personification of the wind adds a dramatic quality to the scene.**

5 Living in Sin

She had thought the studio would keep itself;
no dust upon the furniture of love.
Half heresy, to wish the taps less vocal,
the panes relieved of grime. A plate of pears,
a piano with a Persian shawl, a cat
stalking the picturesque amusing mouse
had risen at his urging.
Not that at five each separate stair would writhe
under the milkman's tramp; that morning light
so coldly would delineate the scraps
of last night's cheese and three sepulchral bottles;
that on the kitchen shelf among the saucers
a pair of beetle-eyes would fix her own—
envoy from some village in the moldings ...
Meanwhile, he, with a yawn,
sounded a dozen notes upon the keyboard,
declared it out of tune, shrugged at the mirror,
rubbed at his beard, went out for cigarettes;
while she, jeered by the minor demons,
pulled back the sheets and made the bed and found
a towel to dust the table-top
and let the coffee-pot boil over on the stove.
By evening she was back in love again,
though not so wholly but throughout the night
she woke sometimes to feel the daylight coming
like a relentless milkman up the stairs.

studio: one-room studio flat with small kitchen and bathroom.

heresy: deviation from what is socially acceptable.
vocal: noisy.

picturesque: pleasant to look at, forming a picture.

writhe: twisting, painful movement.

delineate: show by outlining or drawing.
sepulchral: gloomy, melancholy.

envoy: messenger.
moldings: skirting boards.

demons: voices, evil spirits.

relentless: persistent, uncompromising.

'the scraps of last night's cheese'

Personal Response

1. 'Living in Sin' is not an expression that is often used today. What did this phrase originally mean? Has society's views on this matter changed? How?
2. Comment on Adrienne Rich's use of imagery and language throughout the poem. Support your answer with reference to the text.
3. In your view, is this an optimistic or pessimistic poem? Give a reason for your answer, supporting your response with reference to the text.

Critical Literacy

'Living in Sin' was published in 1955 when the view of society at that time was to disapprove of unmarried couples living together. This 26-line single-stanza poem captures the contrast between a young woman's romantic notions and the disenchantment she feels towards her partner and her domestic arrangements.

The poem's title prompts the reader to question why any person is judged to be 'living in sin'. Beginning with a flashback, the female speaker recalls how she once imagined living with the man she loved. The **opening lines** effectively convey her naivety, 'She had thought the studio would keep itself'. Dreaming of a fairy tale relationship, she had convinced herself that they would share an ideal life together, 'no dust upon the furniture of love'. Might this also apply to the couple's relationship? This perfect domestic scenario is deftly sketched, like a photographic display in a glossy home magazine, 'A plate of pears,/a piano with a Persian shawl'. Almost inevitably, such **idealised views** seem too good to be true.

Indeed, the reality proves to be very different. The **contrasting picture of everyday life** is seen through the poet's clever selection of details: the heavy sound of the 'milkman's tramp', the cold 'morning light', the leftovers of a late meal, 'scraps/of last night's cheese and three sepulchral bottles' (**line 11**). Rich's disenchanted tone matches the sad truth that the couple's day-to-day routine has become tedious. The situation gets even worse as the woman is faced with an infestation of insects, wryly described as 'a pair of beetle-eyes would fix her own'. Their hidden world is captured in the phrase 'envoy from some village in the moldings'. Despite her disappointment, however, she does not feel that she can complain. It would be a form of betrayal, 'Half heresy'.

The woman's partner emerges, seemingly oblivious to the unsatisfactory domestic situation. His indifference is sharply contrasted with the speaker's keen awareness. He yawns while attempting a few notes at the piano – and quickly 'declared it out of tune' (**line 17**). Making no attempt to conceal his apathy, he simply shrugs his shoulders and goes off to buy cigarettes.

Everything about him suggests that he is entirely self-absorbed and lacking in commitment. **He does not engage with the woman.** Is this why 'living in sin' has lost its allure? Is the woman, 'jeered by the minor demons', now being forced to act as a dutiful housewife? Ironically, she sets about making the studio a more appealing place, but the coffee-pot boils over. Is this indicative of the minor frustrations of life which take the gloss from a relationship?

Despite all this, the woman is not prepared to give up on her dream, 'By evening she was back in love again' (**line 23**). Yet there is a subtle difference, 'though not so wholly'. Does the final image suggest a relationship growing cold? The speaker has revived only some of her feelings – but these are far from certain: 'throughout the night/she woke sometimes to feel the daylight coming/like a relentless milkman up the stairs.' The cover of night seems to temporarily hide the reality of her relationship, allowing the woman to **relive her fantasy** – for the moment.

Written in **free verse** (without regular stanzas, line length or rhyme), the poem relies on sustained steady rhythm to convey its central tone of disillusionment. Does the measured pace suggest the disappointing monotony of real life? Look at the repetition of the 'milkman'. What does this suggest? Does this free verse underline the free living of the young couple? Or does it hint at the disorder of their apartment?

The poem is also in the tradition of an **aubade**. Such poetry often describes young lovers at dawn, parting after a night of passion with expressions of undying love. A famous aubade occurs in Shakespeare's play, 'Romeo and Juliet'. Is this the type of daring romance the young woman was expecting?

Writing About the Poem

Comment on Adrienne Rich's use of contrast throughout the poem. Support your answer with reference to the text.

Sample Paragraph

Rich is an intriguing poet who uses contrast to highlight modern dilemmas and to raise interesting questions. Having read 'Living in Sin', I felt I could really sense the woman's growing dissatisfaction with her lover and her living situation. This is eloquently expressed in the contrast between 'a plate of pears', 'a Persian shawl', and 'the scraps of last night's cheese and three sepulchral bottles'. The exciting life she had hoped to lead is echoed in the alliteration of the repeated letter 'p'. Everything was supposed to be perfect, glossy, exotic. Instead, 'that morning light so coldly' reveals the reality. The ugly leftover food, graphically described as 'scraps' – even the sound of the word is repulsive – and the three sad bottles spoke volumes to me. The image of the young girl's boyfriend is the direct opposite to her fantasy figure. What a contrast is here as her lover appears, unshaven, yawning, dying not for her but for a cigarette! These contrasts vividly speak of the gap existing between the idealised, romantic version of life the young woman expected, and the mundane reality as it really is. The romantic illusion of 'living in sin', in youthful freedom, is shattered by these carefully crafted contrasts.

EXAMINER'S COMMENT

This perceptive top-grade response sensitively explores key contrasts in the poem, and successfully shows how they illuminate the poem's central theme. Apt quotations and references reflect a close understanding of both the subject matter and the poet's language use (e.g. alliterative effects). Expression is lively and confident.

Class/Homework Exercises

1. Comment on the significance of the line, 'By evening she was back in love again'. In your opinion, what point is the poet making?
2. Write a personal response to 'Living in Sin', referring to both its central theme and the poet's language use. Support your answer with reference to the text.

Summary Points

- **Key themes explore romantic love and the contrasting expectations of the sexes.**
- **Informal structure (free verse) adds immediacy and makes the poem accessible.**
- **Effective use of narrative style, metaphor, vivid imagery.**
- **Variety of tones – frustration, rejection, disillusionment, etc.**

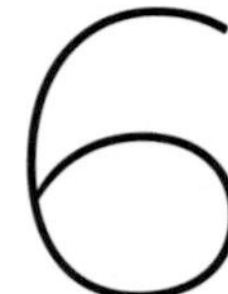

The Roofwalker

– For Denise Levertov

Dedication: Denise Levertov, post-war Anglo-American poet and activist.

Over the half-finished houses
night comes. The builders
stand on the roof. It is
quiet after the hammers,
the pulleys hang slack.
Giants, the roofwalkers,
on a listing deck, the wave
of darkness about to break
on their heads. The sky
is a torn sail where figures
pass magnified, shadows
on a burning deck.

I feel like them up there:
exposed, larger than life,
and due to break my neck.

Was it worth while to lay—
with infinite exertion—
a roof I can't live under?
—All those blueprints,
closing of gaps,
measurings, calculations?
A life I didn't choose
chose me: even
my tools are the wrong ones
for what I have to do.
I'm naked, ignorant,
a naked man fleeing
across the roofs
who could with a shade of difference
be sitting in the lamplight
against the cream wallpaper
reading—not with indifference—
about a naked man
fleeing across the roofs.

pulleys: wheel and rope device for lifting weights.

listing: leaning.
deck: floor of ship.

infinite exertion: non-stop effort.

blueprints: plans, models.

Personal Response

1. Comment on the choice of adjectives in the first stanza. What do they suggest about the poet's state of mind?
2. Choose one interesting visual image from the poem and comment on its effectiveness.
3. In your opinion, is there a definite conclusion reached at the end? Would you regard the poem as optimistic or pessimistic? Support your answer with reference to the text.

Critical Literacy

'The Roofwalker' was published in Adrienne Rich's collection, *Snapshots of a Daughter-in-Law* (1963). The poem focuses on Rich's struggle to live her life the way she chooses. It also shows that our personal lives have public consequences – and that people can sometimes waste a great deal of time and energy creating lives for which they are not suited. When the poem was written in 1962, Rich was reassessing her personal life and political views.

The poem **opens** as darkness is beginning to descend on a building-site. A group of roofers are finishing up their work, 'the pulleys hang slack', after all the ferocious effort and strain of the day. Rich describes the roofwalkers as 'Giants'. Do they see themselves as important? **Does society regard them as impressive?** They are working on an unstable rooftop, 'a listing deck'. Is this an effective metaphor for trying new and hazardous things? A building site is traditionally associated with men. But the site is 'half-finished'. Does this

'on a listing deck'

incompleteness suggest that new skills are needed? What else was a male preserve during the early 1960s?

From ground-level, the roofwalkers look as though they are on a tilting ship. The metaphor is extended to suggest that nightfall is about to descend on them like waves. The sky is a 'torn sail' **(line 11)**. We can imagine the workers silhouetted against the ragged dusky clouds. The men are seen as insubstantial ('shadows'). They are also described as being in an increasingly risky position ('a burning deck'). But while there is **a disturbing sense of imminent danger**, the men seem unconcerned about the precarious position they are in and that they might be in danger of a fall.

Lines 13–15 introduce the personal pronoun 'I', the interior world that the speaker is experiencing. **She now identifies directly with the roofwalkers**: 'I feel like them up there.' All of them are vulnerable to sudden change, they are all 'exposed'. Each is trying to do an impossible job against the odds ('larger than life'). Notice how the three lines stand on their own, apart from the rest of the poem, mirroring the silhouetted roofwalkers. The speaker also feels apart. Like the roofers who are risking physical injury, she is beginning to make radical changes in her personal life. For her, the roof is dangerous, but it is also a vantage point, providing a larger vision.

From **line 16** onwards, the **building metaphor is developed** further. The speaker reflects on the enormous amount of sustained energy used to create something which she is preparing to leave behind, 'with infinite exertion'. She wonders if it was of any benefit to construct a roof that she can no longer live under. We are left to wonder about what the roof is actually sheltering. What exactly is she challenging that was so carefully crafted, 'blueprints … measurings, calculations'? The speaker is adamant about one thing, however. She feels that she was forced into the role she now occupies: 'A life I didn't choose/chose me.' Does she need to escape from the constraints of marriage, motherhood and patriarchal culture?

While the speaker equates the building of the roof with the reconstruction of her own life, she admits that she is not equipped to deal with this: 'my tools are the wrong ones.' In the **nightmare scene** that follows, she envisions herself as 'a naked man fleeing/across the roofs' **(line 27)**. The frantic tone reflects her sense of isolation, of feeling 'ignorant'. In particular, the repetition of 'naked' emphasises the speaker's defencelessness. If things were slightly different, she could be secure 'in the lamplight/against the cream wallpaper', reading sympathetically about someone else attempting change and in danger, instead of experiencing these things herself.

Although she associates herself with men in this deeply personal poem, it is obvious that the speaker **no longer views maleness as power**. However, the turmoil of the roofwalker is the motivation that leads her to define herself on her own terms and in alliance with other women.

Writing About the Poem

Comment on Adrienne Rich's use of metaphors throughout 'The Roofwalker'. Support your answer with reference to the text.

Sample Paragraph

Rich's metaphors are central to this poem. The building site, traditionally a man's world, becomes a metaphor for patriarchal traditions. The site had 'blueprints' and 'calculations'. It had even thought of closing 'the gaps'. Nothing new was getting in. I think this could refer to any institution which was historically male-dominated. But it is now an endangered place, 'the wave of darkness' is about to be unleashed. Rich's emerging feminist views are evident throughout. The roofers are now in an unsafe place, 'a burning deck', facing uncharted waters. They are seen as insubstantial, 'shadows'. The 1960s was a time of radical social progress when women dared to demand equal rights. The macho male 'roof' society would no longer survive in its present form. Rich's poem not only refers to the breaking down of oppressive male strongholds, but it can also refer to any change in society, as new ideas arise. Those who are involved in social change can feel 'naked', 'ignorant'. They often wish they were not leading the charge, but 'sitting in the lamplight' – a symbol of comfort – rather than trying to activate change. Had Rich accepted the status quo, she would have been safe under the 'roof'. Rich's metaphors convey a powerful, universal message. 'I feel like them up there.'

EXAMINER'S COMMENT

A clear and insightful response to a challenging question, offering a wide-ranging interpretation of the poem's metaphors and explaining how they convey the poem's central themes. Excellent expression throughout and comments are backed up with judicious use of suitable quotation. A top-grade standard.

Class/Homework Exercises

1. Would you regard Rich's poem, 'The Roofwalker', as optimistic or pessimistic, overall? Support your answer with reference to the text.
2. In your opinion, what image of Adrienne Rich herself emerges from this poem? Support your response with suitable reference to the text.

Summary Points

- **Central themes include human personal responsibility, vulnerability and alienation.**
- **Effective use of the sustained builder image.**
- **Variety of tones – personal reflection, confusion, determination, etc.**
- **Impact of repetition, detailed description, metaphorical language.**

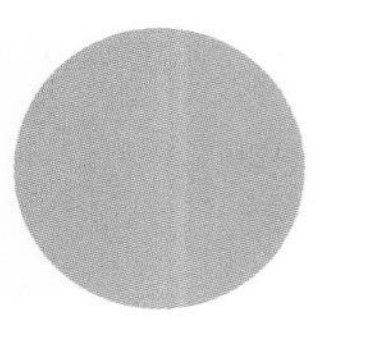

7 Our Whole Life

Our whole life a translation
the permissible fibs

and now a knot of lies
eating at itself to get undone

Words bitten thru words

meanings burnt-off like paint
under the blowtorch

All those dead letters
rendered into the oppressor's language

Trying to tell the doctor where it hurts
like the Algerian
who walked from his village, burning

his whole body a cloud of pain
and there are no words for this

except himself

translation: interpretation.
permissible fibs: acceptable untruths.

blowtorch: fuel-burning tool for removing paint.

dead letters: useless words; undelivered mail.
rendered: turned into.
oppressor's language: words used by tyrants.

Personal Response

1. The poet mentions 'fibs' and 'lies' in the opening lines of the poem. What do you think she really means by this?
2. How would you describe the poet's tone in lines 3–7? Give reasons to explain your response.
3. Write your own personal response to this poem, highlighting the impact it made on you.

Critical Literacy

Communication breakdown is often the cause of conflict and suffering in the world. The abuse of language has been part of propaganda and oppression throughout history. It is still used to disempower minorities, racial groups, women in society and entire nations. From a feminist viewpoint, Rich's poetry combines an impassioned poetic imagination and an engagement with political issues. In 'Our Whole Life', she addresses important aspects of language and communication.

The poem begins with a series of dramatic claims, all of which reflect Rich's dissatisfaction with the **limitations of language**. Life is reduced to 'a translation'. Her frustration is evident in the derisive phrase, 'permissible fibs', suggesting a certain compliance by those who are victims of everyday language. The opening statement ('Our whole life') is unclear. Is the poet referring to people in general or to any marginalised group whose voice is ignored?

In **lines 3–7**, the tone becomes more urgent as the speaker uses a number of violent images to highlight the distortion of language. It is 'a knot of lies/ eating at itself'. Its chaotic effects are reflected in the aggressive phrase, 'Words bitten thru words'. The sense of harshness associated with the abuse of language is heightened in the vivid comparison, 'meanings burnt-off like paint/under the blowtorch'. **Searing onomatopoeic effects** emphasise the intensity of the painful lies that cause untold pain within relationships.

The poem's central viewpoint is found in **lines 9–11**: 'All those dead letters/ rendered into the oppressor's language.' Traditionally, men have controlled language in patriarchal societies. As a result, language is worthless for those adversely affected and subjugated by misinformation. The hopelessness of the oppressed to find ways of articulating the truth about their lives is similar to a child 'Trying to tell the doctor where it hurts'. This **simple comparison** manages to combine angry frustration with agonising sympathy for the victim.

The poem's most **startling image** occurs in the **final lines** where the failure of language is likened to an Algerian war victim 'who walked from his village, burning'. For Rich, the horror of his experience is almost beyond description

– 'there are no words for this'. Nothing can adequately communicate the man's tragedy 'except himself'. The language used throughout this short poem has itself been stripped largely of punctuation and precise grammar. This produces a much more forceful and dramatic impact that reflects Rich's passionate feelings.

Writing About the Poem

Comment on Adrienne Rich's use of imagery throughout 'Our Whole Life'. Support the points you make with reference to the poem.

Sample Paragraph

Rich uses powerful imagery in 'Our Whole Life'. One of the poem's main themes is the way language fails to communicate the truth when people talk to each other. She suggests the way people tie themselves in knots by comparing everyday language to 'the knot of lies'. This image is developed further. She suggests how we keep trying to explain what we really mean to say. But the 'knot of lies' ends up 'eating into itself'. It shows how liars can tie themselves up. Many images are to do with burning. Such as when Rich describes the words we use as damaging, 'under the blowtorch' burning off old paint. There is something very violent suggested here. This suggests the destructive power of language. Mainly by those who want to oppress other people. The most memorable image is of the desperate Algerian victim – 'his whole body in a cloud of pain'. I've seen some disturbing photographs of war victims and they are also beyond words. This is the most effective image. To me, it suggests the horror of man's inhumanity to man.

EXAMINER'S COMMENT

A reasonably good personal response that engages with the text and generally focuses well on the effectiveness of imagery. The discussion ranges over the whole poem. Language control is uneven – too note-like in places – and the verb 'suggests' is overused. There are also minor errors in some of the quotations. Overall, a solid middle-grade standard.

Class/Homework Exercises

1. In your opinion, what is the central theme or message in 'Our Whole Life'? Refer closely to the text in your response.
2. Comment on Rich's use of emotive and disturbing language in this poem.

Summary Points

- **Poet focuses on the ways that language has been used to control people.**
- **The female experience has been largely lost in translation.**
- **Effective use of vivid symbols and dramatic imagery.**
- **Variety of tones – didactic, frustrated, angry, etc.**

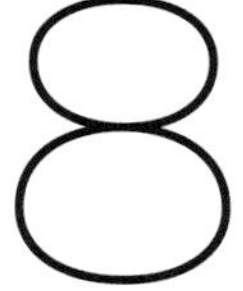

Trying to Talk with a Man

Out in this desert we are testing bombs,

that's why we came here.

Sometimes I feel an underground river
forcing its way between deformed cliffs
an acute angle of understanding
moving itself like a locus of the sun
into this condemned scenery.

What we've had to give up to get here—
whole LP collections, films we starred in
playing in the neighborhoods, bakery windows
full of dry, chocolate-filled Jewish cookies,
the language of love-letters, of suicide notes,
afternoons on the riverbank
pretending to be children

Coming out to this desert
we meant to change the face of
driving among dull green succulents
walking at noon in the ghost town
surrounded by a silence

that sounds like the silence of the place
except that it came with us
and is familiar
and everything we were saying until now
was an effort to blot it out—
coming out here we are up against it

Out here I feel more helpless
with you than without you
You mention the danger
and list the equipment
we talk of people caring for each other
in emergencies—laceration, thirst—
but you look at me like an emergency

desert: the Nevada Desert where nuclear weapons were tested during the 1950s.

deformed: misshapen.

acute angle: angle less than 90°.
locus: position.

condemned scenery: poisoned landscape.

LP collections: long-playing music discs.

succulents: desert plants, cacti.

laceration: flesh wound, gash.

Your dry heat feels like power
your eyes are stars of a different magnitude
they reflect lights that spell out: EXIT
when you get up and pace the floor

talking of the danger
as if it were not ourselves
as if we were testing anything else.

magnitude: size, measure.

Personal Response

1. Based on your reading of lines 8–14, what was the couple's relationship like in the past?
2. Choose one image or symbol from the poem that you found particularly effective. Briefly explain your choice.
3. Write a short personal response to the poem, explaining its impact on you.

Critical Literacy

Adrienne Rich wrote 'Trying to Talk with a Man' in 1971. The poem focuses on a woman and man who try to salvage their relationship by isolating themselves in the desert. Its title clearly indicates that lack of communication is threatening to end the couple's relationship. The poem also reflects people's anxiety over the testing of nuclear weapons. Characteristically, Rich questions traditional thinking about issues of gender and power.

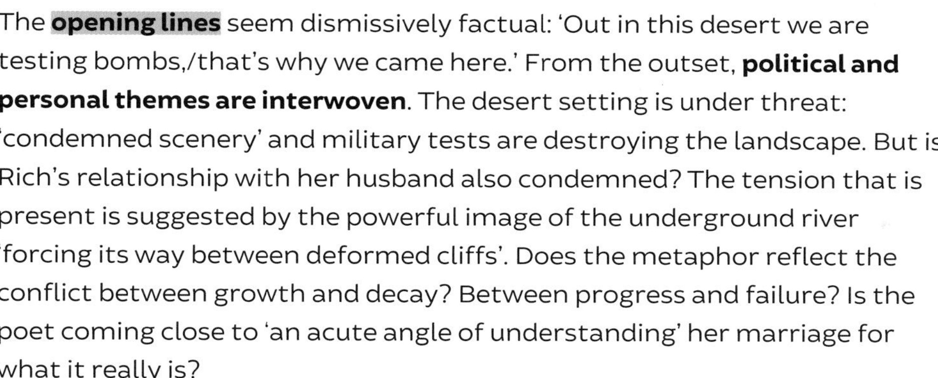

The **opening lines** seem dismissively factual: 'Out in this desert we are testing bombs,/that's why we came here.' From the outset, **political and personal themes are interwoven**. The desert setting is under threat: 'condemned scenery' and military tests are destroying the landscape. But is Rich's relationship with her husband also condemned? The tension that is present is suggested by the powerful image of the underground river 'forcing its way between deformed cliffs'. Does the metaphor reflect the conflict between growth and decay? Between progress and failure? Is the poet coming close to 'an acute angle of understanding' her marriage for what it really is?

Imagery from the couple's domestic life is juxtaposed with the arid location. **Lines 8–14** offer an insight into their early years together: 'What we've had to give up to get here.' The **tone is ambiguous, both nostalgic and resentful**. Most of the memories listed refer to the conventional moments of a romantic relationship: 'whole LP collections, films we starred in.' But the romance is abruptly undermined by the disturbing reference to 'the language of love-letters, of suicide notes'. The poet faces up to the tragic reality of the past. Were all the written expressions of love a dreadful mistake? Did the couple deceive themselves all along?

In **lines 15–25**, the desert wasteland ('surrounded by a silence') becomes a more evocative metaphor for their misguided relationship. The desolate setting is highlighted by the repetition of 'silence' and the haunting image: 'walking at noon in the ghost town.' Rich recognises the **symbolism** for herself: the silent desert 'is familiar', signifying the emptiness of a doomed marriage. She is compelled to accept the truth ('we are up against it') that all meaningful communication has ended. The frank admission that she feels 'more helpless/with you than without you' marks a crucial turning point – a daring admission of failure.

On the edge of nuclear destruction, the poet recognises that military and interpersonal violence echo each other as the couple become distant figures, 'talking of the danger/as if it were not ourselves'. The tone becomes increasingly frustrated as she voices her deepest fears: 'Your dry heat feels like power' **(line 33)**. **Dramatic tension builds** as her husband – now seen as a destructive force – remains in denial: 'you get up and pace the floor.' Nevertheless, the end of the relationship is also clearly reflected in his eyes as 'lights that spell out: EXIT'.

The **last three lines** sum up the poet's feelings of relief. The journey into the desert has clarified her view of the disintegrating marriage. To a great extent, the focus has moved away from the danger of nuclear experiments, 'as if we were testing anything else'. The ending is poignant and moving. Once again, the tone seems to reflect **feelings of loss and sadness** with a bittersweet understanding of what might have been. As in so much of her

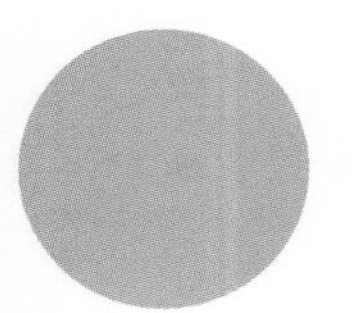

work, Rich exposes power imbalances between the sexes. In this case, she succeeds in connecting the risk of 'testing bombs' with the personal danger of one couple's miscommunication.

Writing About the Poem

In your view, what is the dominant atmosphere in 'Trying to Talk with a Man'? Support your answer with reference to the poem.

Sample Paragraph

I found this to be quite a disturbing poem. The atmosphere is tense. The title itself implies dissatisfaction. The narrator is angry and frustrated – 'Trying to talk'. The mood at the beginning is also intimidating. The narrator and her lover have gone into the desert as tourists to view the US Army bomb sites. However, it soon becomes clear that this uneasy background is really a context for their own danger-filled relationship. Deserts are lonely places where nothing grows. This makes the whole poem disturbing and intimidating. The narrator sees 'condemned scenery' and 'deformed cliffs' all around – symbols of her own feelings about a hopeless love affair that is on the brink and about to fall apart. The poem is written using nervous rhythms, in broken fragments, using very little punctuation – 'Your dry heat feels like power' is typical of the disappointed tone. This adds further tension to the atmosphere. The poem concludes on a reflective note when the narrator faces up to the tragic fact that she can no longer communicate with her lover. This is symbolised by the 'EXIT' sign she imagines. The final atmosphere is pessimistic. The couple have no future together.

EXAMINER'S COMMENT

This paragraph focuses effectively on the tension within the poem. Discussion points are coherent and quotes are integrated effectively into the critical commentary – with interesting reference to stylistic features, such as rhythm and symbolism. Apart from some repetition and a tendency towards short sentences, the expression is varied and lively. A good high-grade standard.

Class/Homework Exercises

1. 'Adrienne Rich's poems are often concerned with tensions.' To what extent is this the case in 'Trying to Talk with a Man'? Refer to the poem in your answer.
2. In your opinion, what points does this poem make about modern-day society? Support your response with reference to the text.

Summary Points

- **Lack of communication and the failure of relationships are key themes.**
- **Vivid images and symbols illustrate the couple's fraught relationship.**
- **Varying tones – frustrated, regretful, realistic, pessimistic, etc.**
- **Effective use of everyday conversational language.**

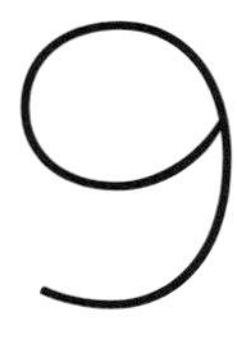

Diving into the Wreck

First having read the book of myths,
and loaded the camera,
and checked the edge of the knife-blade,
I put on
the body-armor of black rubber
the absurd flippers
the grave and awkward mask.
I am having to do this
not like Cousteau with his
assiduous team
aboard the sun-flooded schooner
but here alone.

myths: ancient tales, folklore.
body-armor: wet-suit.
Cousteau: Jacques Cousteau, French underwater explorer and filmmaker.
assiduous: methodical, professional.

There is a ladder.
The ladder is always there
hanging innocently
close to the side of the schooner.
We know what it is for,
we who have used it.
Otherwise
it's a piece of maritime floss
some sundry equipment.

schooner: sailing ship.
maritime: naval, seafaring.
floss: thread.
sundry: varied, miscellaneous.

I go down.
Rung after rung and still
the oxygen immerses me
the blue light
the clear atoms
of our human air.
I go down.
My flippers cripple me,
I crawl like an insect down the ladder
and there is no one
to tell me when the ocean
will begin.

immerses: surrounds, overwhelms
atoms: basic elements, particles.

First the air is blue and then
it is bluer and then green and then
black I am blacking out and yet
my mask is powerful

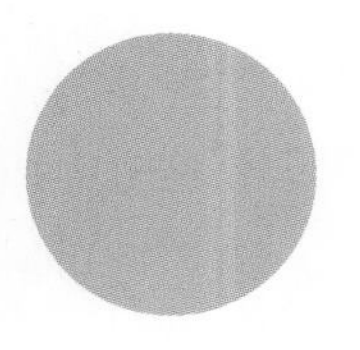

it pumps my blood with power
the sea is another story
the sea is not a question of power
I have to learn alone
to turn my body without force
in the deep element.

And now: it is easy to forget
what I came for
among so many who have always
lived here
swaying their crenellated fans
between the reefs
and besides
you breathe differently down here.

I came to explore the wreck.
The words are purposes.
The words are maps.
I came to see the damage that was done
and the treasures that prevail.
I stroke the beam of my lamp
slowly along the flank
of something more permanent
than fish or weed

the thing I came for:
the wreck and not the story of the wreck
the thing itself and not the myth
the drowned face always staring
toward the sun
the evidence of damage
worn by salt and sway into this threadbare beauty
the ribs of the disaster
curving their assertion
among the tentative haunters.

This is the place.
And I am here, the mermaid whose dark hair
streams black, the merman in his armored body
We circle silently
about the wreck
we dive into the hold.
I am she: I am he

crenellated: having ridges or notches.
reefs: outcrops of jagged rocks.
prevail: survive.
flank: side.
threadbare: worn, shabby.
tentative: unsure, timid.
haunters: divers who repeatedly explore wrecks.
mermaid: mythical sea creature (part-woman and part-fish).
merman: male version of a mermaid.

whose drowned face sleeps with open eyes
whose breasts still bear the stress
whose silver, copper, vermeil cargo lies
obscurely inside barrels
half-wedged and left to rot
we are the half-destroyed instruments
that once held to a course
the water-eaten log
the fouled compass

We are, I am, you are
by cowardice or courage
the one who find our way
back to the scene
carrying a knife, a camera
a book of myths
in which
our names do not appear.

vermeil: precious metal, gilded silver or gold.

log: day-to-day ship's record.
compass: instrument showing direction.

'bluer and then green'

Personal Response

1. Describe the atmosphere in the opening stanza. Support your view with reference to the text.
2. Choose two striking images from the poem that you find particularly effective. Briefly explain your choice in each case.
3. At one level, this poem is about a shipwreck. In your view, what else is the speaker exploring? Refer closely to the text in your answer.

Critical Literacy

The poem (written in the first person) narrates the speaker's quest as she explores a sunken ship. She dives deep to investigate the cause of the disaster and to salvage whatever treasures remain. The sea is a traditional literary symbol of the unconscious – and to dive is to probe beneath the surface for hidden meanings, to discover submerged desires and emotions. The poem's title raises several questions. What is the history of the wreck? What is the speaker's connection with it? Like the diver, readers will be rewarded by repeated explorations of this provocative poem.

In the opening lines of **stanza one**, the speaker addresses the reader directly, as if recalling her initial interest ('having read the book of myths') in this forgotten shipwreck. (Is this also a likely reference to the historic view of women in patriarchal societies?) The tone is observational and detached. There is a sense of nervous anticipation as the speaker makes military-style preparations (she sees her wet suit as 'body-armor') before her adventure. At times, she can almost laugh at her own amateurish appearance in 'absurd flippers' and 'awkward mask'.

Stanzas two to four focus on the underwater experience. As in many of Rich's poems, **the setting acts as an extended metaphor** for exploring other issues, such as gender roles. Armed with stories of what might have happened to the wreck, the speaker uses the ladder on the side of the schooner to begin her descent. On a metaphorical level, of course, the dive represents a journey of self-discovery. The ladder (or opportunity for finding truth) 'is always there' – but only for those who choose to use it.

Moving steadily downwards, the diver experiences a variety of sensations: helplessness ('the oxygen immerses me'), exhilaration ('the clear atoms') and pain ('My flippers cripple me'). The uncontrollable descent is suggested by the short lines, rapid rhythm and hypnotic repetition of the phrase, 'I go down'. The **sense of alienation and insignificance** increases: 'there is no one/to tell me when the ocean/will begin.' Fear of the unknown is also emphasised in the stark admission: 'I crawl like an insect down the ladder.' However, deep down in this startling deep-sea world, the speaker manages to reach an understanding of how she can survive and triumph in this anonymous environment 'I have to learn alone/to turn my body without force'.

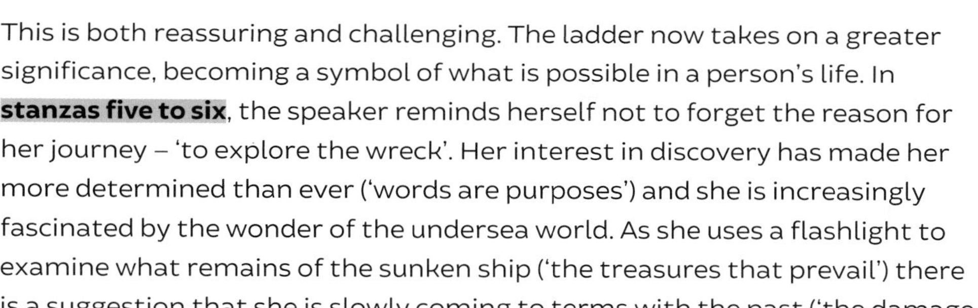

This is both reassuring and challenging. The ladder now takes on a greater significance, becoming a symbol of what is possible in a person's life. In **stanzas five to six**, the speaker reminds herself not to forget the reason for her journey – 'to explore the wreck'. Her interest in discovery has made her more determined than ever ('words are purposes') and she is increasingly fascinated by the wonder of the undersea world. As she uses a flashlight to examine what remains of the sunken ship ('the treasures that prevail') there is a suggestion that she is slowly coming to terms with the past ('the damage that was done').

Throughout **stanza seven**, **the mood is more resigned and faintly beautiful**. Gentle assonant sounds ('the drowned face always staring/toward the sun') add a note of poignancy. Whether applied to a tragic shipwreck, an individual's life, or social and political history over the centuries, nothing can alter the 'disaster' of past generations. Yet, even within the wreck of history, there exists a 'threadbare beauty' that can still be appreciated.

The poem becomes increasingly dreamlike in **stanzas eight to nine**. The diver imagines herself as a fabled mermaid or merman. Does this androgynous (genderless) creature emphasise the common experiences of all human beings who search for meaning in their lives? But the persona quickly turns into a more compelling figure 'whose drowned face sleeps with open eyes'. **Roles become blurred** as the speaker is identified closely with the shipwreck: 'we are the half-destroyed instruments/that once held to a course.' Ironically, the damage done to the drowned ship has corroded equipment that might once have guided the way. Nevertheless, the fact that lost treasure ('silver, copper, vermeil cargo') still lies hidden in the wreck offers the possibility of future rewards.

In **stanza ten**, the sunken ship is depicted as a **symbol of the traditional female role in society**: 'our names do not appear.' The challenge to 'find our way' and discover the truth about established social structures involves everyone. Although the wreck demonstrates disaster, much can still be salvaged. This is characteristic of Rich's feminist perspective that social structures need to improve – particularly regarding issues concerning human rights and gender equality. The final lines are realistic, forecasting that people will come 'back to this scene' and explore the wreck of history. The poem ends as it began, with a flashback to the earlier preparation for the dive, another reminder that planning and organisation are essential elements of any journey or movement.

Writing About the Poem

Comment on the poet's description of the underwater world in 'Diving into the Wreck'. Support your answer with reference to the poem.

Sample Paragraph

In her poem, 'Diving into the Wreck', Rich uses colour images to make the water appear vivid. She seems overwhelmed by the beauty and stillness of 'the blue light' and 'the clear atoms'. The new environment seems infinite. She tells us that she feels lost as there is nobody to tell her where the ocean 'will begin'. The deeper she dives, the more the colours change – 'it is bluer and then green'. To her, it is a strange and frightening world. As the waters get darker, she almost blacks out. From the contrasting colour images, I can sense the strangeness of this eerie sea world. Rich also gives us a clear idea of the freedom underwater. The swimmer has to learn to avoid awkward movements. Everything is different close to the ocean floor – including the fish who have their natural habitat there. The poet describes them swaying 'between the reefs'. Throughout the poem, the imagery and rhythm succeed in conveying the fluid movement and strangeness of this alien world – 'the sea is another story'. The absence of punctuation combined with run-on lines add to our understanding of the free movement in this beautiful undersea world.

EXAMINER'S COMMENT

This is a reasonably well-controlled response that attempts to directly address the question. The extended discussion on the use of colour imagery is supported by apt reference. The final point about rhythm is very good, but deserves further development and illustration. Overall, a solid mid-grade standard that shows some engagement with the poem.

Class/Homework Exercises

1. 'Diving into the Wreck' is typical of Adrienne Rich's poetry in that it is layered with hidden meaning. Discuss this view, supporting your answer with reference to the poem.
2. In your opinion, is this ultimately an optimistic or pessimistic poem? Explain your response, supporting the points you make by suitable quotation or reference.

Summary Points

- **Poet explores aspects of society, particularly male–female roles.**
- **Extended metaphor of the exploratory sea dive sustained throughout.**
- **Stunningly vivid imagery, symbolism and personification reinforce themes.**
- **Effective use of assonance, alliteration and sibilance.**

From a Survivor

Survivor: someone who exists after a difficult experience or who lives after the death of another.

pact: formal agreement.

The pact that we made was the ordinary pact
of men & women in those days

I don't know who we thought we were
that our personalities
could resist the failures of the race

Lucky or unlucky, we didn't know
the race had failures of that order
and that we were going to share them

Like everybody else, we thought of ourselves as special

Your body is as vivid to me
as it ever was: even more

since my feeling for it is clearer:
I know what it could and could not do

it is no longer
the body of a god
or anything with power over my life

Next year it would have been 20 years
and you are wastefully dead
who might have made the leap
we talked, too late, of making

which I live now
not as a leap
but a succession of brief amazing moments

each one making possible the next

Next year it would have been 20 years: reference to the 19 years the poet and her husband spent together.
wastefully: without achieving.

'we thought of ourselves as special'

Personal Response

1. Why do you think the poet uses '&' between 'men' and 'women' in line 2? What does this suggest to you?
2. Do you think the poem's ending is optimistic or pessimistic? Give a reason for your response.
3. Write your own personal response to the poem, supporting the points you make with reference to the text.

Critical Literacy

'From a Survivor' was written in 1972. Rich had begun dating her poems from 1956 so that her readers could see 'my sense of being engaged in a long continuing process'. This intensely personal poem is a considered reflection on the beginning and the aftermath of Rich's own failed marriage. The tone varies from reminiscence to sorrow, wistfulness, acceptance and quiet optimism.

The title suggests that this is a message from someone who has lived through a difficult experience. In **line 1**, the word 'pact' is an unusual way of referring to marriage vows. The term is more usually applied to a formal agreement between warring factions. What might this indicate about relations between men and women? The adjective 'ordinary' implies that getting married was the conventional thing to do at that time. While the use of the ampersand symbol '&' joining 'men & women' might reinforce the idea that heterosexual marriage was taken for granted, the abbreviation could also suggest that such a general presumption should have been much more carefully considered.

The poem's **fragmented appearance** on the page gives the impression of Rich's tentative stream of thought as she seeks to come to terms with her feelings. The tone is almost derogatory: 'I don't know who we thought we were' **(line 3)**, linking the poet and the reader in an intimate way. She now realises that she and her young husband were naïve, that they assumed they would have a happy married life together where others had been unsuccessful. Conversational language gives the poem a wonderful sense of immediacy, 'our personalities/could resist the failures of the race'.

Looking back on the marriage, Rich is still not sure whether it was good or bad luck that they were unaware of the pitfalls that lay ahead, 'failures of that order', or that they were going to be part of them. She reminds us of the intense feelings that exist in the early stages of romantic relationships, 'Like everybody else,

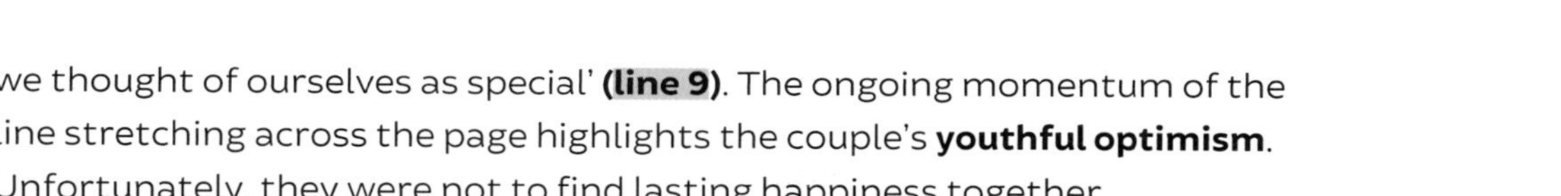

we thought of ourselves as special' **(line 9)**. The ongoing momentum of the line stretching across the page highlights the couple's **youthful optimism**. Unfortunately, they were not to find lasting happiness together.

Despite the tensions of their marriage, the poet's affection for her late husband endures. Rich's tone is affectionate as she remembers his physical presence, 'Your body is as vivid to me/as it ever was' **(line 11)**. Time has passed and her 'feeling' has become 'clearer', free from doubt and confusion. She now knows that the man she married was an ordinary human being who had abilities and limitations. Significantly, the poet no longer views him as a 'god', who has 'power' over her life. Social and cultural changes (brought about largely by the feminist movement) give Rich a more informed perspective on how her marriage disempowered her.

In **lines 16–20**, the poet reflects on the passing years and on what might have been. Her former husband is 'wastefully dead'. The description underlines Rich's deep sense of compassion over the tragic loss of someone who had so much to offer. As in all relationships, of course, there is **an element of mystery**. What did he not achieve? What was the 'leap' he could have made? Was this a challenge he could have taken on? Why was it 'too late' when they 'talked' about it?

The tone through **lines 21–24** is much **more positive**. Rich feels that her success in life has been a sequence of small steps ('brief, amazing moments'). But these have a charged momentum of their own, 'each one making possible the next'. The poem ends without a full stop, suggesting that this movement will continue. The survivor is progressing onward.

Writing About the Poem

How has the order and structure of 'From a Survivor' helped you to understand the poem? Support your answer with reference to the text.

Sample Paragraph

I was very struck by the disjointed, almost ragged appearance of the shape of the poem, 'From a Survivor'. It was very like everyday life itself, uneven and unpredictable. As I read the poem, structured with flowing run-on lines and little punctuation, I felt as if Rich was speaking to me in a stream of consciousness as she remembered and reflected on the innocence of the young couple before marriage, 'we thought of ourselves as special'. I liked the longest line, 'Like everybody else, we thought of ourselves as special'. It summed up the ambition and energy of young lovers as it extended right across the page. Love conquers all. But the tone becomes more regretful and nostalgic as the poet faces the harsh realisation that the couple will have no wedding anniversary. This was suggested by short lines, such as 'and you are wastefully dead'. I also liked the way the poet structured the ending, as it concludes with gentle optimism. Life is good, there is no need for the 'leap'. Instead, there are just small 'steps', each creating a steady forceful rhythm. The lack of a full stop at the very end emphasises the idea that life goes on, particularly for a survivor.

EXAMINER'S COMMENT

This solid high-grade response successfully tackles a challenging question. Discussion points about line length are focused well and aptly supported. The paragraph explores the format of the poem, touching on aspects such as layout, punctuation and rhythm. Points are clear and the expression is confident. Some good personal engagement also.

Class/Homework Exercises

1. Relationships are an important theme in Rich's poetry. Discuss this statement with particular reference to the poem 'From a Survivor'.
2. In your opinion, what is the central or dominant tone in this poem? Briefly explain your response.

Summary Points

- **Female–male power structures and failed relationships are central themes.**
- **Absence of punctuation creates an uninterrupted fluent rhythm.**
- **Simple conversational language makes the poem accessible.**
- **Various moods – personal, reflective, regretful, optimistic, etc.**

Leaving Cert Sample Essay

'Rich's powerful poetic voice is often focused on the need for social change.' Discuss this view, supporting your answer with reference to the poetry of Adrienne Rich on your course.

MARKING SCHEME GUIDELINES

Reward responses that show clear evidence of personal engagement with the poetry of Adrienne Rich.

INDICATIVE MATERIAL

- Challenges stereotypical feminism.
- Addresses issues of power politics.
- Frequently confronts patriarchal society.
- Uses powerful images and symbols.
- Forceful tones: confessional, persuasive, didactic, etc.

Sample Essay
(Rich's powerful poetry is focused on social change)

1. The American poet Adrienne Rich is best known for her feminist themes. Yet her poetry is also associated with vibrant language and symbolism through which she tackles a variety of social tensions. It's well known that Rich struggled early in her career to find a voice for herself and those who were disenfranchised. She eventually found it in such poems as 'Aunt Jennifer's Tigers', 'Living in Sin', 'Diving into the Wreck' and 'Power'.

2. In 'Aunt Jennifer's Tigers', Rich cleverly uses strict iambic pentameter to mirror the confined constriction of the aunt's marriage. The timid title character, 'fingers fluttering through wool', is clearly downtrodden. Yet she creates the antithesis of her oppressed situation through her decorative craftwork – the proud 'tigers' who 'prance across a screen'. They are unlike the browbeaten aunt beneath the 'massive weight of Uncle's wedding band'. The vibrant animals represent everything the aunt is not. Symbols of power, the tigers lead independent lives. Most of all, they are not controlled. This dramatic poem is making a stark statement about power and gender roles. Even though the aunt in death seems to be subjugated (her hands are 'terrified') yet the exotic tigers will live on, 'proud and unafraid'. The poet's concern is clearly directed at achieving women's rights in marriage.

3. The harsh truth of unbalanced relationships is also dealt with in 'Living in Sin'. Many young women today move in with their boyfriends believing in an ideal image of 'love' which has been sold to them in the media, 'A plate of pears,/a piano with a Persian shawl'. It is like a scene from an American sitcom, charming but false. The reality is reflected in the striking imagery as we see the 'scraps of last night's cheese'. This is real life. Somebody has to clear up and do the housekeeping. Rich is obviously frustrated at the way society still expects women to be supportive of men. In this case, the girl learns the harsh truth, as she encounters 'a pair of beetle-eyes' from some creepy-crawly creature. The 'studio' does not 'keep itself'. So, where is the partner? Rich sketches him, leaving 'with a yawn'. This is unacceptable oppression of a different kind - indifference. As in so many of her poems, Rich presents a feminist perspective to highlight her concern for women everywhere. With a few precise details, the poet

focuses on a familiar drama, the unequal relationship. But this is not only about the unending war between the sexes, it is about all people who are taken for granted, and who come back for more.

4. Again in 'Diving into the Wreck', Rich presents a strong argument for social change. On a simple level, the poem is about an exploratory dive at sea, but the poet is using this metaphor to encourage individual self-discovery. The poet was keen on individuals transcending their given roles in society and using all possible means to find fulfilment. She presents the wreck as a symbol of the traditional female role: 'our names do not appear.' The poet argues that it is essential to 'find our way' and avoid being oppressed by society's expectations. Her vigorous tone suggests that society can improve on the past – suggesting necessary changes regarding issues of human rights and gender equality. The final lines are hopeful, indicating that people will come 'back to this scene' and salvage what they can from history.

5. Rich's poem 'Power' made a huge impact on me. It gave an impressive picture of the great scientist Marie Curie, who was refused permission to study in her native Poland simply because she was a woman. The words are often spaced unusually with gaps in the poem's layout and this suggests that Marie Curie was herself a broken woman who struggled to develop the power of radium. The graphic language which describes Curie's pain is horrifying. The scientist puts her own welfare beneath the welfare of others who she wanted to help. 'Power' is the title and the last word of the poem. Ironically, Curie achieved power and died a famous woman who won the Noble Prize for Chemistry, 'a tonic/for living on this earth'.

6. Adrienne Rich is frequently concerned with the powerlessness of women and the need for social change. The characters in her poems often struggle to be heard – whether it is the terrified Aunt Jennifer, the young love-struck girl or the famous scientist. The poet's didactic voice is emphatic and her poems are often intensely compelling – aided by her use of form, imagery and symbolism. Rich demanded gender equality and her poetry gives a voice to those who struggle to survive 'in the winters of this climate', in this harsh and unfair world.

(approx. 780 words)
(45–50 minutes)

EXAMINER'S COMMENT

The essay showed a genuine engagement with Rich's poetry. There is evidence of clear understanding throughout, with most points firmly rooted in the texts of the poems. The response also benefits from the effective introduction and conclusion. Paragraphs 2, 3 and 4 address the question with confidence, using apt quotation. The focus drifts into general comment in the fifth paragraph where the reference to 'graphic language' needs to be developed and illustrated. Overall, this is an impressive top-grade response which interacted closely with Rich's prominent themes and powerful writing style.

GRADE: H1
P = 15/15
C = 13/15
L = 14/15
M = 5/5
Total = 47/50

Sample Leaving Cert Questions on Rich's Poetry

1. **'Adrienne Rich's poetry is interesting both for its universal themes and its effective language use.' Discuss this statement with reference to the poems on your course.**
2. **'The poems of Adrienne Rich are carefully crafted to expose dark themes of disappointment and resilience.' To what extent do you agree or disagree with this view? Support your answer with reference to the poetry of Adrienne Rich on your course.**
3. **'Rich makes effective use of symbols and metaphors to explore personal experiences and offer perceptive insights about history and society.' To what extent do you agree or disagree with this statement? Support your answer with reference to the poetry of Adrienne Rich on your course.**

NOTE

As you may not be familiar with some of the poems referred to in the sample plans below, substitute poems that you have studied closely.

Exam candidates usually discuss three or four poems in their answers. However, there is no set number of poems or formulaic approach expected.

Key points about a particular poem can be developed over more than one paragraph.

Paragraphs may also include cross-referencing and discussion of more than one poem.

Remember that there is no single 'correct' answer to poetry questions, so always be confident in expressing your own considered response.

First Sample Essay Plan (Q1)

'Adrienne Rich's poetry is interesting both for its universal themes and its effective language use.' Discuss this statement with reference to the poems on your course.

Intro: Rich – personal anger/frustration expressed through interesting images, traditional portrayal of women in a patriarchal society, compassionate philosophical insights portrayed through striking symbols and innovative language use.

Point 1: 'Living in Sin' – aubade with a difference, common experience of unfulfilled young women in modern relationships ('She had thought'), use of symbolism of light ('morning light/so coldly would delineate'), inventive verbs ('stalking', 'writhe', 'fix'), realistic, resigned conclusion ('back in love again,/though not so wholly').

Point 2: 'The Roofwalker' – addresses the role of a woman worldwide, effective use of extended building metaphor ('my tools are the wrong ones'), common dread of exposing oneself to ridicule ('I'm naked, ignorant,/a naked man fleeing').

Point 3: 'Power' – interesting exploration of the nature of power in the world, conversational tone accessible to the reader ('Today I was reading about'), Marie Curie is a paradoxical symbol of the good and bad aspects of power throughout history ('suffered', 'denied'), erratic spaces in layout used to emphasise theme.

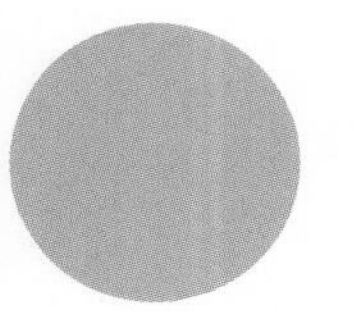

Point 4: 'Storm Warnings' – shared experience of individuals through troubled times ('These are the things that we have learned to do/who live in troubled regions'), use of extended storm metaphor ('weather abroad/ And weather in the heart'), structure of poem mirrors movement of the storm.

Conclusion: Rich rewards readers by expressing engaging universal themes in a fresh way, using vibrant imagery and rich symbolism to explore life's difficulties.

First Sample Essay Plan (Q1)

Develop **one** of the points on the previous page into a paragraph.

Sample Paragraph: Point 2

In 'The Roofwalker', Rich deals with the modern dilemma of the role of women in a patriarchal society. 'Over the half-finished houses/night comes. The builders/stand on the roof.' A building site, traditionally 'a man's world', becomes a metaphor for a past tradition forever renewing itself. However, Rich pictures an imminent revolt, transforming the image of the construction site into that of a 'burning deck'. This changing imagery pattern suggests to me a rushed voyage into a newly liberated society and the destruction of the old carefully built values, 'closing of gaps,/measurings, calculations'. There is a sharp change in the short three-line stanza as she envisages herself in the precarious position of a roofwalker, 'I feel like them up there:/exposed'. The act of walking on an unstable roof is, I think, a very interesting metaphor for Rich's experience of being a female writer. She is operating in a male-dominated world of literature where there has not been an equal place traditionally for the female voice. Rich said all literary effort requires risk, 'I'm naked, ignorant,/a naked man fleeing/across the roofs'. She was prepared to take that risk.

EXAMINER'S COMMENT

As part of a full essay answer, this clear response uses 'The Roofwalker' effectively to illustrate Rich's distinctive writing style in exploring her themes. Carefully chosen quotations show close engagement with the development of thought within the poem. Impressive expression (e.g. 'she envisages herself in the precarious position') and assured personal interaction with the poem contributes to the top-grade standard.

Second Sample Essay Plan (Q3)

'Rich makes effective use of symbols and metaphors to explore personal experiences and offer perceptive insights about history and society.' To what extent do you agree or disagree with this statement? Support your answer with reference to the poetry of Adrienne Rich on your course.

Intro: Rich – struggled to find a voice for herself and those who were disenfranchised. Experimental language, vivid images, striking symbols offer insightful views of key themes – particularly relating to social structures.

Point 1: 'Our Whole Life' – limitations and distortion of language, mocking tone ('permissible fibs'), unnerving personification of cannibalism ('knot of ties/eating at itself'), violent similes ('meanings burnt off like paint/ under the blowtorch'), revealing concluding image of Algerian victim.

Point 2: 'Trying to Talk with a Man' – interwoven political and personal themes addressed in this tense, disturbing poem about lack of communication. Desert nuclear test site becomes powerful metaphor for couple's failing relationship. Negative symbols ('condemned scenery', 'deformed cliffs') expose poet's pessimistic frame of mind.

Point 3: 'Storm Warnings' – incisive exploration of human vulnerability and the harsh realities of everyday life ('in troubled regions'), poet's developed storm metaphor ('weather in the heart') suggests that people must endure emotional turmoil and learn to deal with tragic situations.

Point 4: 'From a Survivor' – perceptively personal and reflective poem examining different stages of a relationship. Fragmented appearance of poem mirrors style of stream of thought. Troubling change of perspective, no longer regards husband as 'god', now describes as 'wastefully dead'. Defiant attitude – poet continuing on with life, in small 'steps'.

Conclusion: Rich is unafraid to confront the difficulties of modern life through unusual images and symbols, innovative use of structure, drawing on deeply personal experiences. She gives a voice to those who don't have one in this unforgiving world, 'in the winters of this climate'.

Sample Essay Plan (Q3)

Develop **one** of the points on the previous page into a practice paragraph of your own.

Sample Paragraph: Point 3

'Storm Warnings' uses form to emphasise its central message. Using the metaphor of a developing storm, the poem is mainly concerned with facing up to change and disorder. Rich's long opening sentence runs through twelve lines, with all the relentless energy of the gathering rainstorm. This symbolises an interior emotional state, 'Weather abroad/ And weather in the heart', and neither can be controlled. The lighting of candles reminds me of a power failure caused by a storm. When a storm breaks, all the comforts of modern civilisation seem weak and helpless against the force of the elements, 'shattered fragments of an instrument'. We have all felt powerless in situations beyond our control, whether facing an exam, or waiting on the results of hospital tests. Rich captures the unease we experience in these situations, as she moves restlessly about, 'I leave the book'. She calmly states how people have learned to deal with tragedies, 'These are the things we have learned to do/Who live in troubled regions'. Weather has been effectively used as a metaphor for our everyday human moods.

EXAMINER'S COMMENT

As part of a full essay answer to Q3, this is a good high-grade response that focuses well on the poem's central metaphor of the storm. The personal engagement is slightly overdone, but there is general engagement with the text and accurate quotations support discussion points. Expression is clear and controlled throughout.

Class/Homework Exercise

1. **Write one or two paragraphs in response to the question: 'Rich makes effective use of symbols and metaphors to explore personal experiences and offer perceptive insights about history and society.' To what extent do you agree or disagree with this statement? Support your answer with reference to the poetry of Adrienne Rich on your course.**

Revision Overview

'Aunt Jennifer's Tigers'
Themes of power, oppression and revolution, female/male relationship and contrasting roles in society.

'The Uncle Speaks in the Drawing Room'
Addresses key themes of power, powerlessness between rich and poor.

'Power'
Exploration of use and abuse of power between men and women.

'Storm Warnings'
Themes of the power balance between humans and nature.

'Living in Sin'
Aubade, love poem examines romantic love and disenchantment, woman's position in life.

'The Roofwalker'
Central themes of personal responsibility and public consequences, woman's place in a patriarchal world.

'Our Whole Life'
Theme of broken communication leads to disenfranchisement. Harsh visual and aural imagery depicts limitations and distortion of language.

'Trying to Talk with a Man'
Presents themes of communication difficulties, the breakdown of relationship between man and woman.

'Diving into the Wreck'
Revealing focus on theme of male/female roles in society. Traditional female role represented by metaphor of shipwreck.

'From a Survivor'
Presents recurring themes of male/female roles in society, broken relationships.

Last Words

'All her life she has been in love with the hope of telling utter truth, and her command of language from the first has been startlingly powerful.'
W. S. Merwin

'Adrienne Rich's poems speak quietly but do not mumble ... do not tell fibs.'
W. H. Auden

'What is possible in this life? What does love mean, this thing that is so important? What is this other thing called "freedom" or "liberty" – is it like love, a feeling?'
Adrienne Rich

POWER

RELATIONSHIPS

CONFICT

NATURE

LOVE

SUFFERING

HISTORY/ MEMORY

William Wordsworth 1770–1850

'The world is too much with us.'

William Wordsworth was one of the most influential of England's Romantic poets. Like his friend, the poet Samuel Taylor Coleridge, he explored the inner self and looked for knowledge through the imagination. As a young man, Wordsworth developed a profound love of nature, a theme reflected in many of his poems. He believed that poetry was created from 'emotion recollected in tranquillity'. In 1799, he and his sister, Dorothy, settled in Grasmere in the Lake District, and it was there that he wrote his most famous poem, 'I Wandered Lonely as a Cloud', in 1804. His masterpiece is generally considered to be *The Prelude*, a lengthy semi-autobiographical poem of his early years which the poet revised many times. Wordsworth was England's Poet Laureate from 1843 until his death in 1850.

Investigate Further

To find out more about William Wordsworth, or to hear readings of his poems, you could search some useful websites such as YouTube, BBC Poetry, poetryfoundation.org and poetryarchive.org, or access additional material on this page of your eBook.

Prescribed Poems

*(OL) indicates poems that are also prescribed for the Ordinary Level course.

1 To My Sister

It is the first mild day of March:
Each minute sweeter than before,
The redbreast sings from the tall larch
That stands beside our door.

There is a blessing in the air,
Which seems a sense of joy to yield
To the bare trees, and mountains bare,
And grass in the green field.

My sister! ('tis a wish of mine)
Now that our morning meal is done,
Make haste, your morning task resign;
Come forth and feel the sun.

Edward will come with you; and, pray,
Put on with speed your woodland dress;
And bring no book: for this one day
We'll give to idleness.

No joyless forms shall regulate
Our living calendar:
We from today, my Friend, will date
The opening of the year.

Love, now a universal birth,
From heart to heart is stealing,
From earth to man, from man to earth:
– It is the hour of feeling –

One moment now may give us more
Than years of toiling reason:
Our minds shall drink at every pore
The spirit of the season.

Some silent laws our hearts will make,
Which they shall long obey:
We for the year to come may take
Our temper from today.

redbreast: common name for the robin.

Edward: Wordsworth and his sister were taking care of a friend's son whose real name was Basil Montague.

And from the blessed power that rolls
About, below, above,
We'll frame the measure of our souls:
They shall be tuned to love.

Then come, my Sister! come, I pray,
With speed put on your woodland dress;
And bring no book: for this one day
We'll give to idleness.

And from the blessed ... above: a similar idea is found in lines 100–102 of 'Tintern Abbey'.

'The redbreast sings'

Personal Response

1. Describe the dominant mood in this poem. Support your answer with reference to the text.
2. What does the poem reveal to you about Wordsworth's own personality? Use reference to the text in your response.
3. In your opinion, do the views expressed by Wordsworth in 'To My Sister' have any relevance to our modern world? Give reasons to support your response.

Critical Literacy

A bright spring morning will almost certainly lift our spirits and make us feel glad to be alive. 'To My Sister' was written in 1798, when Wordsworth was living near the beautiful Quantock Hills in Somerset. The scene is a March morning at the start of a mild English spring. All the poet does is ask his sister to wear her warm outdoor clothes, bring the young boy they were caring for and join him in taking the day off. The poem is made up of ten four-line stanzas, each with a regular abab rhyme scheme.

In the first two stanzas, Wordsworth uses simple and direct description to convey a vibrant sense of the new spring season – 'the first mild day of March'. Vivid images of the 'redbreast' and the 'green field' are evidence of his closeness to nature. The poet's **conversational language** is engaging and his enthusiastic tone ('Each minute sweeter than before') increases as he acknowledges 'a blessing in the air'. It seems as though nature itself, in all its god-given wonder and beauty, is inviting him to embrace this great 'sense of joy'.

Wordsworth is obviously **keen to share his feelings** with his sister, Dorothy, to whom he seems devoted. In stanza three, he urges her to forget about work and hurry outside to 'feel the sun'. The emphatic tone of the exclamation ('My sister!') echoes his sense of urgency. She should also dress for the outdoors ('your woodland dress') and 'bring no book'. The run-on line ('for this one day/We'll give to idleness') adds to the energetic rhythm and emphasises Wordsworth's eagerness that they should seize the moment while they can. It's clear that the poet feels there is a great deal more to be learned out of doors than from any book. For him, life's sensual pleasures (the sights and sounds of the great outdoors) are what matter most.

From stanza five onwards, the poet reflects on the intimate relationship between people and nature. He dismisses the restrictive routines of daily life as 'joyless forms' and looks forward to a new 'living calendar'. For Wordsworth, the mysteries and delights of nature will be both **an emotional and spiritual experience**. Springtime is a new birth, an astonishing stirring of 'universal' love. This 'hour of feeling' will bring him into harmony with a greater love, a cosmic force that enriches the whole of creation – nature and human nature – 'From earth to man, from man to earth'.

The poet develops this idealistic theme of **nature's positive influence** in stanzas seven to nine by contrasting the limitations of people's 'toiling reason' with the limitless delights on offer in our natural surroundings, which 'Our minds shall drink at every pore'. Wordsworth is equally convinced of nature's beneficial effects, not just in allowing us to get in touch with our feelings, but in humanising society's 'laws' and transforming all our lives so that 'They shall be tuned to love'.

In the final stanza (almost identical to stanza four), the poet again asks his sister to join him in enjoying the pleasures of nature. The relaxed tone, brisk rhythm and regular end-rhymes leave us in no doubt about Wordsworth's increasingly cheerful mood. Throughout the poem, he has used simple, everyday language to **celebrate the beauty of creation**. It is ironic that planning a whole day of 'idleness' could produce such worthwhile lessons for the poet – especially the belief in the way our senses can recognise the 'blessed power' of creation.

Writing About the Poem

It has been said that there is a vitality to Wordsworth's language. Do you agree that this quality is evident in 'To My Sister'? Give reasons for your answer, illustrating your points with reference or quotation.

Sample Paragraph

'To My Sister' is typical of much of Wordsworth's poetry. The writing is colloquial, especially the opening verse where he sets the scene on a fresh spring morning – 'It is the first mild day of March'. But immediately he fills in the scene with lively images of the robin singing and the 'tall larch' outside his door. The simplicity of his language is what gives it life. The tone becomes more enthusiastic and imperative in stanza three, where Wordsworth persuades Dorothy to accompany him on a day of idleness. 'My sister!' and 'Make haste' reflect his excitement at the thought of exploring the great outdoors. The dynamic rhythm also gives the poem energy and there is a vigorous balance in some of the lines – 'From earth to man, from man to earth'. There are also a number of upbeat images, such as when he describes nature as 'Our living calendar'. There is additional energetic repetition – for example, when he mentions the 'blessed power' that exists 'About, below, above'. To a large extent, the strength of Wordsworth's writing is its simplicity. His use of language keeps the poem moving along at a strident pace, making his enthusiasm for nature infectious.

EXAMINER'S COMMENT

A well-focused top-grade response that addresses the question directly. Selected key quotations are handled with assurance to illustrate the energy and originality of Wordsworth's writing. Language use is impressive throughout, with varied sentence lengths and controlled expression (e.g. 'more enthusiastic and imperative', 'dynamic rhythm', 'strident pace').

Class/Homework Exercises

1. Wordsworth set out to use 'language actually spoken' by ordinary people. In your view, did he succeed in doing this in 'To My Sister'? Support your answer with reference to the text of the poem.
2. Trace the pattern of varying tones used by Wordsworth over the course of this poem, commenting on the impact they make. Support your answer with reference to the text.

Summary Points

- **Wordsworth's close relationship with his sister is a central theme.**
- **Emphasis on the strong spiritual benefits of the natural world.**
- **The personal beliefs of the poet are in keeping with those of the Romantic Movement.**
- **Effective use of repetition, blend of nature imagery, variety of tones.**

A slumber did my spirit seal

A slumber did my spirit seal;
   I had no human fears:
She seemed a thing that could not feel
   The touch of earthly years.

No motion has she now, no force;
   She neither hears nor sees;
Rolled round in earth's diurnal course,
   With rocks, and stones, and trees.

slumber: sleep.
spirit: soul, consciousness.
seal: close up.

motion: movement.

diurnal: daily.

'With rocks, and stones, and trees'

Personal Response

1. Choose one interesting aural image or sound effect from the poem and comment on its effectiveness.
2. In your opinion, is the poem's focus on stillness or movement? Explain your response, using textual support.
3. Write a short personal response to the poem, highlighting its impact on you. Refer to the text in your answer.

Critical Literacy

This poem is part of the collection known as the 'Lucy poems' and was regarded by Coleridge, a close friend of Wordsworth's and fellow Romantic poet, as a 'most sublime epitaph'. An elegy is usually written for someone famous who has achieved great things in his/her life. This elegy is written for the unknown Lucy, whose importance was her effect on the poet. The poem suggests Lucy's qualities and how Wordsworth was affected by her death.

The 'Lucy poems' cannot be related to one specific person, although it is often thought that Wordsworth's sister Dorothy, with whom he had a very close relationship, may be the inspiration for these poems. But it is not clear if they actually refer to a real person or someone imagined. The opening image in the first stanza is one of the poet falling into a pleasant sleep. The alliteration of the soft 's' sound induces a relaxed feeling. The poet is now in another state, one of **suspended animation**, where there are no 'human fears'. He is beyond considerations of passing time, loss and death. The use of the past tense shows that this is a recollected incident. 'She' suggests a mystery. We are given no details except that she is beyond the reach of time: 'could not feel/The touch of earthly years'. It appeared ('seemed') as if she did not grow old. We are left wondering if this is a delusion.

In stanza two, the change of tense unsettles: 'No motion has she now.' Time has touched her. There has been a radical change in her condition. Lucy is incapable of action or strength. But now we are left with another enigmatic mystery: although she herself is incapable of ordinary physical movement, she is 'Rolled round'. **Now she is part of the great force of nature.** She is no longer an individual. The alliteration of 'r' and the word 'diurnal' (the only word in the poem that has more than two syllables) add to this feeling of continuous movement of the earth as it spins on its axis. Lucy has been able to connect with nature in a way that the poet cannot.

Wordsworth believed that if a poet's 'works be good, they contain within themselves all that is necessary, to their being comprehended and relished'. In that case, the identity of 'She' is irrelevant. The poet ends with an **acceptance that transience is inevitable and natural**, yet also mysterious and ambiguous. The punctuation of the final line causes the reader to pause and reflect on life and death. This little lyric is deceptive, as contained within its eight lines is a complex exploration of life, transience, mortality and eternity. As the earth revolves on its axis, so the poem revolves on two musical words, 'slumber' and 'diurnal'. This short lyric poem is haunting in its simplicity. By narrating the story of Lucy's immortality, Wordsworth seems to desire the same peace Lucy has found after becoming part of nature.

Writing About the Poem

'Wordsworth's poems move from personal relevance to universal relevance.' In your reading of this poem, would you consider this statement to be true? Support your response with references from the text.

Sample Paragraph

'A slumber did my spirit seal' explores the poet's response to loss and his acceptance of change. This simple poem, with its regular eight lines and even rhythm, deals with huge themes, transience and death. In the first stanza, 'She' is above the march of time, 'could not feel/The touch of earthly years'. There is a false sense of security, 'I had no human fears'. She is not real, a 'thing' which does not age. The change occurs in the second stanza as she can no longer move. She has no energy, no 'force'. She is no longer aware, 'neither hears nor sees'. She is not a conscious individual, but part of the bigger picture of the world of nature as she is 'Rolled round'. The alliteration emphasises the fact that as the earth goes through its daily course she is moved, as are the 'rocks, and stones, and trees'. The interconnectedness of all things is being stressed, as all move around according to the laws of nature. The use of the present tense encourages the reader to view her as part of nature's grand plan of continuity. She is nothing, yet she is part of everything. The highly personal feeling of loss felt by everyone at some point in their lives is translated into a universal acceptance of transience.

EXAMINER'S COMMENT

A mature top-grade answer to a challenging question. Good engagement with both theme (the personal leading to universal significance) and style (sound effects, present tense, etc.). Points are clearly stated and effectively supported. The accomplished final sentence rounds off the discussion effectively.

Class/Homework Exercises

1. 'A slumber did my spirit seal' is an example of a poem that is both sad and uplifting at the same time. Discuss with reference to the text.
2. Comment on the poet's use of language throughout the poem. Support your answer with reference to the text.

Summary Points

- **One of several 'Lucy poems' recording Lucy's life and death.**
- **Wordsworth uses characteristically simple language.**
- **Some effective imagery and metaphors.**
- **Range of tones – emotive, reflective, gloomy, etc.**

3 She dwelt among the untrodden ways

She dwelt among the untrodden ways
  Beside the springs of Dove,
A Maid whom there were none to praise
  And very few to love:

A violet by a mossy stone
  Half hidden from the eye!
– Fair as a star, when only one
  Is shining in the sky.

She lived unknown, and few could know
  When Lucy ceased to be;
But she is in her grave, and, oh,
  The difference to me!

untrodden: remote; unspoiled.
Dove: an English river.

Maid: young girl.

'But she is in her grave'

Personal Response

1. Choose one image from the poem that you find particularly effective. Briefly explain your choice.
2. From your own reading of the poem, what is your impression of Lucy?
3. Comment on the tone of the last two lines. Is it optimistic or pessimistic? Give reasons for your answer.

Critical Literacy

'She dwelt among the untrodden ways' is the best-known of Wordsworth's short series of 'Lucy poems'. These were probably written during the winter of 1799 when he was living in Germany. This short poem combines the beauty and simplicity that is the hallmark of Wordsworth's work. It is written with a sparseness that captures Lucy's plain character and natural way of life. While Lucy remains an enigmatic figure, it seems clear that the poet is deeply affected by her death.

In the opening stanza, Wordsworth chooses very **simple language** (mainly one-syllable words) to describe the isolated area where Lucy lived. Her anonymity is emphasised from the start – she is 'A Maid whom there were none to praise'. No details are given. Instead, her sincerity and gentleness are suggested. Although she is a solitary figure and somewhat unappreciated, she is one of nature's children. The poet also highlights her loneliness – she had 'very few to love'. He himself admires her rustic simplicity and seems to believe that more sophisticated people can learn a lot from her.

The second stanza explores Lucy's innocence and beauty through **contrasting images**. Wordsworth sees her as a 'violet by a mossy stone' in harmony with her rustic world. However, he balances this view of a simple country girl with a more forceful simile. She is also 'Fair as a star, when only one/Is shining in the sky'. These vivid comparisons are both drawn from nature to highlight Lucy's modest charm and striking individuality. They might also reflect Wordsworth's own deep sense of the mystery in all of creation.

This idea is developed further in the third stanza with a renewed **focus on Lucy's 'unknown' life**. While Wordsworth is clearly affected by Lucy's life and death, we are left to guess about his own thoughts and feelings. The final lines are emphatic, perhaps suggesting pain and loss at her death. However, the poet does not clarify the 'difference' Lucy's passing has made. Is the tone mournful or celebratory – or both? Is he simply reminding us that we can never fully know another person?

'She dwelt among the untrodden ways' contains several features associated with traditional folk ballads and fairy tales, which often told unhappy stories of young girls in a dramatic style. Tragic tales of such young lives were also a common feature of the Romantic poets. Wordsworth's account of Lucy is much more restrained (she simply 'ceased to be') and concentrates on his own reaction to her death. The use of regular rhyme along with a quietly dignified rhythm contributes much to the poem's **attractive musical qualities** – and to the mysterious appeal of Lucy herself.

Writing About the Poem

'"She dwelt among the untrodden ways" closely identifies human beings with the natural world.' Discuss this statement, supporting your answer with reference to the poem.

Sample Paragraph

I would agree with this view of Wordsworth's poem. Lucy is the central figure and she is portrayed as a personification of nature. She is described as living in the unspoiled wilderness 'among the untrodden ways'. Wordsworth celebrates her closeness to the earth – she grows up alongside the riverbank – 'the springs of Dove'. Lucy is likened to a violet, one of nature's unimportant but beautiful flowers. There is a childlike quality to Wordsworth's writing which links the simplicity of his language to the humble life Lucy led. But Lucy is also compared to a single star 'shining in the sky'. The word 'shining' suggests the vivid beauty of her life and the impact it has made on the poet. This comparison also shows her uniqueness. She is the 'only one' in the sky. This suggests that every human life is equally important as part of God's creation. Wordsworth believed in a shared spirit throughout all of nature. In her grave, Lucy has returned to this universal spirit. In both life and death, she is part of nature.

EXAMINER'S COMMENT

A well-focused high-grade paragraph that makes clear points in response to the question. Quotations are used effectively throughout. The style is a little note-like (with an over-reliance on short sentences) and repetitive in places, but the final point is confidently expressed.

Class/Homework Exercises

1. In your opinion, is 'She dwelt among the untrodden ways' still relevant today? Give a reason for your answer.
2. How effective is Wordsworth's use of monosyllabic language, regular rhyme and the features of fairy tales in capturing Lucy's character in this poem? Refer closely to the text in your response.

Summary Points

- **Emphasis on harmonious, universal world of nature.**
- **Simple language captures Lucy's innocence.**
- **Contrasting natural imagery.**
- **Regular rhyme, rhythm, gentle musical effects.**

4 Composed Upon Westminster Bridge

3 September 1802

Earth has not anything to show more fair:
Dull would he be of soul who could pass by
A sight so touching in its majesty:
This City now doth, like a garment, wear
The beauty of the morning; silent, bare,
Ships, towers, domes, theatres, and temples lie
Open unto the fields, and to the sky;
All bright and glittering in the smokeless air.
Never did sun more beautifully steep
In his first splendour, valley, rock, or hill;
Ne'er saw I, never felt, a calm so deep!
The river glideth at his own sweet will:
Dear God! the very houses seem asleep;
And all that mighty heart is lying still!

fair: beautiful; fine.

doth: does.

towers, domes, theatres, temples: the panoramic view of London, including the Houses of Parliament, Westminster Abbey and the dome of St Paul's Cathedral.

steep: soak; saturate.

'The beauty of the morning'

Personal Response

1. Which one of these words best describes the poet's tone in the opening line: emphatic, reflective, sentimental, persuasive? Brefly explain your response.
2. Choose one image from the poem that you find particularly interesting. Give a reason for your choice.
3. Does the ending of the poem suggest uneasiness or calm? Does the poet feel that this moment will soon be gone or that it will always remain?

Critical Literacy

Written, according to Wordsworth, 'on the roof of a coach' as he set out for France to visit his daughter Caroline and her mother, the poet succeeds in capturing the freshness and beauty of a city before the day's rush begins. His sister Dorothy accompanied him and wrote of the scene in her journal: 'The City, St Paul's, with the River and a multitude of little boats, made a most beautiful sight as we crossed Westminster Bridge.' Wordsworth uses the strict form of the Petrarchan sonnet as he meditates on the scene, which Dorothy describes as having 'the purity of one of nature's own grand spectacles'.

The poem opens with the confident assertion that the world has no sight more beautiful than this early-morning scene of London: 'Earth has not anything to show more fair.' The strong **monosyllables underline the statement** and create a note of expectancy in the reader. The poet goes on to claim that only a person who was lacking in spirit would not find this scene emotionally moving. Although the poem is set in a particular place and time – London on 3 September 1802 – the scope of the poem, like the city, moves beyond its boundaries to celebrate the beauty of nature.

The word 'majesty' suggests that the scene has the grandeur of both king and God. In line 4, the focus of the poem moves from the general to the particular, signalled by the word 'This'. The city is given a capital letter, as if it were a person, and further **personification** is used to show how London assumes this beauty: 'This City now doth, like a garment, wear/The beauty of the morning.' People wear magnificent clothes to create an impression, but clothes are changed frequently and this suggests that the beauty of the city is only temporary, as it can be cast aside like an item of clothing.

Wordsworth did not like cities; he regarded them as dehumanising places full of noise. Notice how the adjectives used reinforce this idea: 'silent, bare.' The panoramic sweep of the cityscape from Westminster Bridge is impressive: 'Ships, towers, domes, theatres, and temples.' These 'lie/Open' – the city has the capacity to expand, bringing in its surroundings, the 'fields' and the 'sky'. The poet shows us the interconnectedness of city and nature.

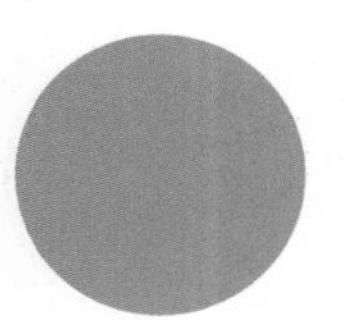

Even the buildings appear 'bright and glittering'. The air is 'smokeless'. Why? The capital is quiet before the morning rush of people, factories and transport turn it into the ugly, chaotic place Wordsworth disliked. He regarded the 'hum of cities torture'. This is why the image of the 'garment' is so apt. **Unlike the beauty of nature, which is permanent, the beauty of the city is transient.** This concludes the octet of this fourteen-line Petrarchan sonnet.

In the sestet, the poet compares the perfection and attraction of early morning London to a country scene, where the sun saturates 'valley, rock, or hill' with its bright light, as if it were the first day of the world: 'In his first splendour.' He is **reacting positively** to his surroundings, and the use of the present tense throughout adds to the sense of immediacy. As a Romantic, he delights in the world around him. The exclamation marks show Wordsworth's surprise at this experience. Here he uses the first-person personal pronoun 'I' as he emphatically states 'Ne'er saw I, never felt, a calm so deep!' The river echoes the peaceful state, as it is undisturbed by its busy traffic at this early hour in the morning.

The gentle rhythm and the assonance of the slender vowel sound 'i' allow the reader to experience this serenity: 'The river glideth at his own sweet will.' The emotional intensity of the phrase 'Dear God!' is at odds with the calm. Is Wordsworth realising how temporary this beauty is? The personification continues as he describes the silence of the houses that 'seem asleep'. Again, appearance is stressed by the use of the word 'seem'. The final image encompasses both the buildings and the inhabitants: 'all that mighty heart is lying still!' **This is how Wordsworth prefers the city, when it most closely resembles nature.** He does not passively observe – the sight raises questions within him which he shares with us.

Writing About the Poem

'Wordsworth's choice of the sonnet form enriches the subject matter of his poem, "Composed Upon Westminster Bridge".' Discuss this statement, supporting the points you make with close reference to the text.

Sample Paragraph

'Westminster Bridge' celebrates the city of London in its quiet moments, before the hustle and bustle of its everyday frenzy. The poem's sonnet structure (fourteen lines consisting of an octet and sestet and including a strict rhyming scheme of *abba abba cdcdcd*) creates a soothing effect. For Wordsworth, a city is an alien place, but here the regular rhythm and assonance contribute to the 'deep calm' experienced by the poet. His

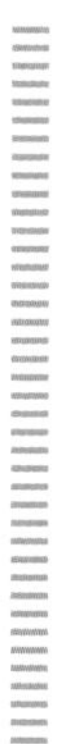

response is enthusiastic, 'Dull would he be of soul who could pass by/A sight so touching in its majesty'. This creates a fresh immediacy in the poem. The rhyme scheme reinforces the subject matter as Wordsworth states that the city is 'fair' because it is deserted and 'bare', without the presence of people. All the sights around him 'lie/Open … to the sky'. So the great city is able to operate at its 'own sweet will' because it is 'lying still'. The formal sonnet structure is ideally suited to the serene, orderly city at dawn.

EXAMINER'S COMMENT

This well-informed response shows a depth of analysis of the poem's structure which is combined with a real sense of personal engagement. Clear understanding of the sonnet form throughout. An interesting and developed examination of the rhyme scheme is effectively supported with apt quotations. Expression is also impressive. An assured top-grade standard.

Class/Homework Exercises

1. 'Wordsworth is often described as a poet of intense emotion.' Discuss this view with particular reference to 'Composed Upon Westminster Bridge'.
2. Wordsworth's subject matter comes from 'incidents and situations from common life'. Having studied this poem, would you agree or disagree with this statement? Refer closely to the text in your answer.

Summary Points

- **Petrarchan sonnet celebrating the city of London.**
- **Emphatic tone reflects poet's enthusiasm.**
- **Effective use of personification and onomatopoeia.**
- **Colloquial expression, detailed description, use of comparison, etc.**

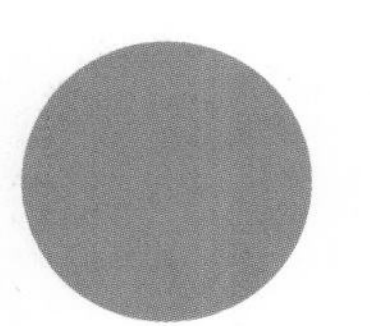

5 It is a beauteous evening, calm and free

It is a beauteous evening, calm and free,
The holy time is quiet as a Nun
Breathless with adoration; the broad sun
Is sinking down in its tranquillity;
The gentleness of heaven broods o'er the Sea:
Listen! the mighty Being is awake,
And doth with his eternal motion make
A sound like thunder – everlastingly.
Dear Child! dear Girl! that walkest with me here,
If thou appear untouched by solemn thought,
Thy nature is not therefore less divine:
Thou liest in Abraham's bosom all the year;
And worshipp'st at the Temple's inner shrine,
God being with thee when we know it not.

Dear Child: Caroline, the daughter of Wordsworth and Annette Vallon.

Abraham's bosom: biblical reference for heaven.
Temple's inner shrine: the holiest place.

Personal Response

1. Select two images from the poem that effectively show the harmony and perfection of nature. Give reasons for your choice in each case.
2. In your view, what is the poet's attitude towards the 'mighty Being'? Support your answer with reference to the text.
3. From your reading of the poem, what is your impression of the young girl? Support your answer with reference to the text.

Critical Literacy

'It is a beauteous evening, calm and free' is thought to have originated from the reunion between Wordsworth and his estranged nine-year-old daughter. The poem was written after their visit to a beach near Calais in the autumn of 1802. It is a typical Petrarchan sonnet, consisting of an octave (eight lines) and a sestet (six lines). The form was popularly used by Petrarch, a 14th-century Italian writer. Other types of sonnets have less intricate rhyme patterns. The octave (or octet) usually describes a problem, while the sestet offers the resolution to it. The term 'sonnet' itself derives from the Italian 'sonetto', meaning 'little song'.

In the opening lines of 'It is a beauteous evening', Wordsworth is watching the sun set over the ocean. The evening is beautiful and calm, inspiring a mood of religious wonder, like 'a Nun/Breathless with adoration'. The explicit religious simile reflects the **poet's own intimate, spiritual relationship with nature**. There is an obvious emphasis on the reverential silence ('calm', 'quiet', 'gentleness') of the setting. This is further enhanced by the use of assonance, particularly the broad vowel sounds ('holy', 'adoration', 'broods') and by the measured rhythm of the early lines. In the midst of such tranquillity, Wordsworth's attention shifts and he suddenly notices the sound of the waves. The noise, 'like thunder', shows that the ocean is awake and its unceasing motion brings thoughts of eternity to the poet's mind.

In lines 6–8, we see the poet's **mystical view of nature**. The exclamation 'Listen!' signals his recognition of a mystical presence. The 'mighty Being' may refer to God or nature – or to God manifested through nature. At any rate, this indefinable force is in 'eternal motion' and 'everlastingly' omnipotent, making 'A sound like thunder'. Is it paradoxical that such a deafening spiritual insight should occur within the stillness of this sublime setting?

In the final six lines, Wordsworth addresses the young child ('Dear Child! dear Girl!') who walks with him by the sea. The repetition of 'dear' clearly suggests his great affection for her. Although she seems untouched by the 'solemn thought' that he is gripped by, this does not make her 'less divine'. He recognises the natural sanctity of childhood as a time when she 'worshipp'st at the Temple's inner shrine'. In other words, **she is always in the presence of God**. Is Wordsworth simply celebrating the child's instinctive spirituality? Or might he also be envious of her innate closeness to God?

The poem's conventionally Christian message is similar to the central theme of 'Composed Upon Westminster Bridge'. The religious references and biblical language ('beauteous', 'doth', 'thy') are in keeping with the **dignified tone** throughout the sonnet. In the reverential final lines, Wordsworth seems to link the young girl's spiritual beauty with the evening itself, 'calm and free'. It is as though he senses that Heaven is touching the earth and the child is as sacred as the beautiful sunset.

Writing About the Poem

What is the poet's attitude to nature in 'It is a beauteous evening, calm and free'?

Sample Paragraph

William Wordsworth is extremely positive about nature. The picture he paints is of a very hushed evening scene along the seashore. It is 'calm and free'. He associates nature with religion all through the poem. This is seen where he says the evening is a 'holy time'. Wordsworth finds great comfort in the stillness and tranquillity of nature. The beautiful image of the 'gentleness of heaven' over the sea creates a reassuring atmosphere. I can imagine the beauty of this peaceful moment when he gets a chance to think about life. Wordsworth seems to believe that nature and childhood are both divine. There is a common energy or power in the world of nature and in the young child who is accompanying him on his walk. He refers to this natural force as a 'mighty Being'. The same power is present in the child – 'God being with thee'. Although the poem is quite short, it is clear that Wordsworth finds intense spiritual significance in the natural world.

EXAMINER'S COMMENT

A solid high-grade response, supported by suitable reference and quotation. Some further comment on how the poet's style (especially tone and rhythm) reflects his appreciation of nature would have enhanced the answer. However, the final succinct sentence rounds off the paragraph effectively.

Class/Homework Exercises

1. How would you describe the dominant mood of this sonnet? Support your answer with reference to the text of the poem.
2. Comment on the impact of Wordsworth's use of sensuous language throughout this poem.

Summary Points

- **Petrarchan sonnet expressing the poet's feelings for his daughter.**
- **Descriptive octave followed by meditative sestet.**
- **Vivid imagery ranges from nature to religion.**
- **Effective use of varying tones – heartfelt, reflective, emphatic, etc.**

The Solitary Reaper

Behold her, single in the field,
Yon solitary Highland Lass!
Reaping and singing by herself;
Stop here, or gently pass!
Alone she cuts and binds the grain,
And sings a melancholy strain;
O listen! For the Vale profound
Is overflowing with the sound.

No Nightingale did ever chaunt
More welcome notes to weary bands
Of travellers in some shady haunt,
Among Arabian sands:
A voice so thrilling ne'er was heard
In springtime from the Cuckoo-bird,
Breaking the silence of the seas
Among the farthest Hebrides.

Will no one tell me what she sings? –
Perhaps the plaintive numbers flow
For old, unhappy, far-off things,
And battles long ago:
Or is it some more humble lay,
Familiar matter of today?
Some natural sorrow, loss, or pain,
That has been, and may be again?

Whate'er the theme, the Maiden sang
As if her song could have no ending;
I saw her singing at her work,
And o'er the sickle bending; –
I listened, motionless and still;
And, as I mounted up the hill,
The music in my heart I bore,
Long after it was heard no more.

Behold her: look at her.

Yon: that.

melancholy strain: sorrowful melody.
Vale profound: deep valley.

chaunt: sing.

Hebrides: islands off the west coast of Scotland.

plaintive numbers: sad verses.

lay: song.

theme: meaning, type of song.

sickle: curved blade used for cutting grass or grain.

Personal Response

1. Comment on Wordsworth's use of tone in the first stanza. In your response, consider his choice of verbs and use of punctuation.
2. The poem is rich in imagery. Choose one image (visual or aural) and comment on its effectiveness.
3. In your opinion, why did the song have such a lasting impact on the poet? Refer to the text in your answer.

Critical Literacy

On a tour of Scotland with his friend, the Romantic poet Coleridge, and his own sister Dorothy, Wordsworth came upon a lone girl reaping and singing a sad song in Erse, a type of Gaelic dialect. Although he could not understand what she was singing about, the sound of the song made such an impact on the poet that he composed this poem about it two years later, as part of his collection *Lyrical Ballads.* The girl sings of events long ago, the poet remembers the girl's song and now we remember the song also. This is 'emotion recollected in tranquillity'.

Wordsworth **addresses the reader directly**, 'Behold her ... O listen!' in the opening. This creates a sense of immediacy and intimacy between the poet

and the reader. The use of the present tense adds to the freshness of the scene: 'she cuts and binds ... And sings.' This freshness challenged the poets of the time, the Augustans. The Romantic poets believed in using the 'language of conversation' in their work, unlike the poetic diction that was the fashion. They were also obsessed with solitude – here, the girl is described as 'solitary', 'single', 'Alone'. The reaper is alone with nature. These poets focused on individual experience. The liberal use of exclamation marks adds energy to the scene. When he offers the choice of stopping to listen or of 'gently' passing, the poet is suggesting that to move on would show a lack of spirit, as the music is so enticing.

The second stanza, which **deals with Wordsworth's reaction to the scene**, uses the imagery of birdsong. The nightingale singing in the heat of the desert ('Arabian sands') conjures up an exotic, magical place. The Romantics revelled in the allure of foreign places. The cuckoo is then described singing in a completely different scenario – the cold, hostile, windswept North Atlantic, 'the farthest Hebrides'. The singing causes a reaction in the listeners; the nightingale's song is full of 'welcome notes to weary bands'. The cuckoo breaks the 'silence of the seas' as it signals the return of spring. In hostile settings, the birds bring relief, comfort and hope. Does the 'Highland Lass' do the same? And for whom – the reader, Wordsworth or both?

In the third stanza, we are brought back to the actual scene. Wordsworth's conversational tone invites us to **ponder what she is really singing about**: 'Will no one tell me what she sings?' Again, the focus is on the listener rather than the song, which is sung in traditional Erse. Perhaps she sings of 'old, unhappy, far-off things'. Others might hear a haunting song, telling of secrets hidden in the mists of time, a favourite topic of the Romantics. Although the song's subject matter is imperfectly understood, the mood is sensed: 'sorrow, loss, or pain.' The use of rhetorical questions invites us to join Wordsworth in wondering about the meaning of the song.

Finally, in the fourth stanza, the poet concludes that it doesn't matter what the young girl is singing about ('Whate'er the theme'), it is how she sang that stays with him. She sings in a free-flowing manner, 'As if her song could have no ending'. This might refer to the unfamiliar Gaelic tunes which give a haunting and inconclusive sound. The lack of an ending also symbolises that this song will reverberate down the generations, both passed on through the oral traditions of the area and also because **it remains in Wordsworth's memory** and is then made into a poem that is passed onto the us: 'The music in my heart I bore,/Long after it was heard no more.' The poem concludes in the past tense. The beauty and mystery of the scene surpasses time.

Writing About the Poem

Wordsworth stated that poetry should 'treat of things not as they are, but as they appear; not as they exist in themselves, but as they seem to exist to the senses'. Discuss this view with reference to 'The Solitary Reaper'.

Sample Paragraph

In my opinion, it is not the actual event of hearing the girl alone in the fields singing which is the focus of this poem, but rather Wordsworth's reaction to the incident, and subsequently our response to his reaction. The impact this girl's song had on his senses is all-important, 'I listened motionless and still'. Wordsworth uses the imagery of birdsong to explain the lasting impact of this young woman's voice. His imagination takes him from the 'Vale profound' to a song in the heat of the 'Arabian sands', and then to the 'farthest Hebrides', as he explains through the imagery of birdsong, how comfort and hope is brought to listeners. But nothing is 'so thrilling' as the 'Maiden's song'. He prefers the human voice. So the emphasis in this poem is on the impact the music had on the poet's senses ('The music in my heart I bore') and its reverberations in his memory. Although Wordsworth describes the girl vividly in stanza one, 'Alone she cut and binds the grain,/And sings a melancholy refrain', it is when he is reflecting and speculating on the song that really remains with the reader. 'A voice so thrilling ne'er was heard.' This enigmatic song, recollected in memory, stays with the poet and the reader 'Long after it was heard no more'.

EXAMINER'S COMMENT

This mature high-grade response offers a clear personal opinion that is considered and articulate. Wordsworth's emphasis on speculation and remembrance is aptly illustrated with relevant quotation. Apart from some repetition, expression throughout is well controlled and vocabulary is varied (e.g. 'reverberations', 'reflecting and speculating', 'enigmatic song').

Class/Homework Exercises

1. Comment on Wordsworth's attitude to nature in 'The Solitary Reaper'. Support your answer with reference to the text.
2. In your own words, describe the impact of the girl's song on Wordsworth. Support your answer with reference to the poem.

Summary Points

- **Memory and nature are central themes.**
- **The poem blends detailed description with personal reflection.**
- **Effective use of vivid comparisons and contrasts.**
- **Sibilant and alliterative effects add a musical quality to the poem.**

from *The Prelude*: The Stolen Boat

The Prelude is Wordsworth's longest poem. It is largely autobiographical and contains much of the poet's own ideas on poetry and on life.

One summer evening (led by her) I found
A little boat tied to a willow tree
Within a rocky cave, its usual home.
Straight I unloosed her chain, and stepping in
Pushed from the shore. It was an act of stealth
And troubled pleasure, nor without the voice
Of mountain-echoes did my boat move on;
Leaving behind her still, on either side,
Small circles glittering idly in the moon,
Until they melted all into one track
Of sparkling light. But now, like one who rows,
Proud of his skill, to reach a chosen point
With an unswerving line, I fixed my view
Upon the summit of a craggy ridge,
The horizon's utmost boundary; for above
Was nothing but the stars and the grey sky.
She was an elfin pinnace; lustily
I dipped my oars into the silent lake,
And, as I rose upon the stroke, my boat
Went heaving through the water like a swan;
When, from behind that craggy steep till then
The horizon's bound, a huge peak, black and huge,
As if with voluntary power instinct
Upreared its head. I struck and struck again,
And growing still in stature the grim shape
Towered up between me and the stars, and still,
For so it seemed, with purpose of its own
And measured motion like a living thing,
Strode after me. With trembling oars I turned,
And through the silent water stole my way
Back to the covert of the willow tree;
There in her mooring-place I left my bark, –
And through the meadows homeward went, in grave
And serious mood; but after I had seen
That spectacle, for many days, my brain
Worked with a dim and undetermined sense
Of unknown modes of being; o'er my thoughts
There hung a darkness, call it solitude
Or blank desertion. No familiar shapes
Remained, no pleasant images of trees,

her: nature.

unswerving: straight.

elfin pinnace: small boat.

bound: boundary.

As if ... instinct: as though it had special powers.

covert: shelter.

bark: boat.

undetermined: uncertain.

unknown modes: mysteries.
solitude: alienation.

Of sea or sky, no colours of green fields;
But huge and mighty forms, that do not live
Like living men, moved slowly through the mind
By day, and were a trouble to my dreams.

mighty forms: terrifying dreams.

Personal Response

1. What impression of nature is given by the images in lines 1–11 of the poem?
2. A significant change of tone occurs after line 21. Briefly explain the change. How does Wordsworth convey this change through his use of language?
3. Write your own personal response to the poem. Your answer should make close reference to the text.

Critical Literacy

Taken from Wordsworth's long autobiographical poem, *The Prelude*, this extract narrates a childhood experience dominated by fear. Written in blank verse (unrhymed with a regular iambic pentameter rhythm), the poem recalls a memorable occurrence on a tranquil summer evening. In many of his poems, the poet seemed to be happiest when he had only nature for company. However, in 'The Stolen Boat', Wordsworth projects his own feelings onto a hostile landscape and discovers that nature is enforcing a moral lesson that was to affect him for the rest of his life.

The poem opens with a few well-chosen **narrative details** ('summer evening', 'little boat', 'rocky cave') that recreate this memorable scene from early boyhood. Wordsworth remembers being captivated by the beauty of nature ('led by her') and it first seems that he is casually recalling a nostalgic moment from his past. However, the mood changes in line 5: 'It was an act of stealth.' The underlying sense of wrongdoing is emphasised by the phrase 'troubled pleasure', a further admission of disquiet.

Any guilty feelings are quickly replaced with a vivid description of the exquisite surroundings on that magical evening. The image of the child alone in the boat is powerfully evoked through vivid details, such as 'I dipped my oars into the silent lake' and 'Small circles glittering idly in the moon'. There is an increasing sense of the poet's close **affinity with his natural surroundings** as he grows aware of the 'sparkling light' all around him. By line 12, he imagines himself as a young romantic hero and thinks of the boat as 'an elfin pinnace' being spirited over the water. He is conscious also of his own strength confidently guiding the small craft. The simile ('heaving through the water like a swan') effectively captures all the delicacy and naturalness of the movement.

However, this sublime experience is dramatically interrupted in lines 21–22 with the appearance of 'a huge peak, black and huge' towering before him. The child imagines it as a monstrous figure that 'Upreared its head'. **His terror grows out of his guilt**, which in turn causes him to invest the cliff with awesome, primitive powers. Ironically, the insistent repetition of 'I struck and struck again' underscores the boy's powerlessness. He is compelled to recognise nightmarish forces that he cannot control. Indeed, the more he tries to escape the 'grim shape', the more the mountains seem to shadow him.

The disturbing sequence is relieved with the child's shameful return to 'the covert of the willow tree'. But the menacing experience ('That spectacle') continues to haunt him and he tries to understand its significance 'for many days'. Through the rest of the poem, Wordsworth attempts to clarify his vague understanding ('a dim and undetermined sense') of the moral relationship between human beings and the natural world. He feels as if nature has punished him for his earlier wrongdoing in stealing the boat. An **uneasy mood of guilt and uncertainty** dominates lines 39–44. This is emphasised by a series of negatives ('no pleasant images of trees', 'no colours of green fields'). There is little doubt that the poet still finds difficulty coming to terms with such a traumatic event from his past. Only in composing the poem many years later does Wordsworth recognise the way such episodes have shaped his life. He can finally acknowledge that the experience was sublime.

Writing About the Poem

How does Wordsworth present nature in 'The Stolen Boat'? Does it seem beautiful, benevolent, intimidating or mysterious?

Sample Paragraph

Wordsworth is usually described as a great lover of nature. This is true of many of his poems. But it is not the case with 'The Stolen Boat'. At first, he presents what looks like a harmless childhood memory. He 'found' a little

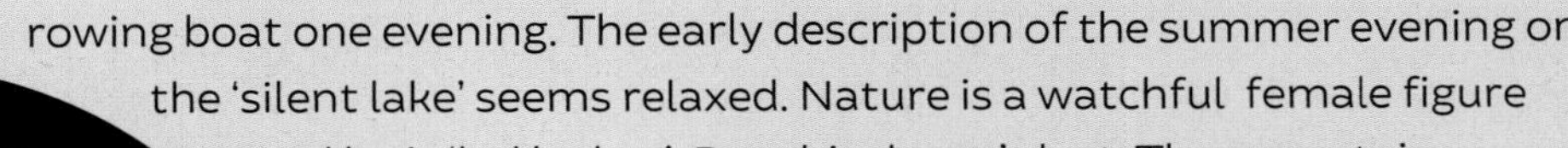

rowing boat one evening. The early description of the summer evening on the 'silent lake' seems relaxed. Nature is a watchful female figure and he is 'led by her'. But this doesn't last. The mountain overlooking the lake suddenly seems threatening – described as a 'craggy steep'. To his innocent mind, it becomes a 'living thing' looming over him. He is soon terrified. He retreats back to the shoreline where he tries to come to terms with stealing the small boat. His own guilt-ridden conscience is now like nature itself – 'a darkness'. The whole incident has taught him a lesson. Human nature is part of the natural world. Wordsworth believes that there is a definite link between our human moral laws and the harmony of nature. What he did as a young lad was wrong – the theft of a boat. In the end, he seems troubled by all that has happened and more respectful of nature.

EXAMINER'S COMMENT

This is an admirable attempt at quite a difficult question. There is a clear, cogent response, tracing the varying views of nature throughout the entire poem. Effective use is also made of apt reference and quotations. A solid high-grade standard despite the tendency towards short, note-like sentences.

Class/Homework Exercises

1. 'The Stolen Boat' has been described as a highly dramatic poem. Do you agree with this view? Give reasons for your answer, supporting the points you make with reference to the text.
2. In your own words, trace Wordsworth's changing emotions over the course of the poem. Support your answer with reference to the text.

Summary Points

- **Poet's boyhood experience brings him closer to the wonders of nature.**
- **Detailed language and vivid imagery of the natural world.**
- **Effective use of personification, repetition, varying moods.**
- **Wordsworth draws some moral strength from the dramatic incident.**

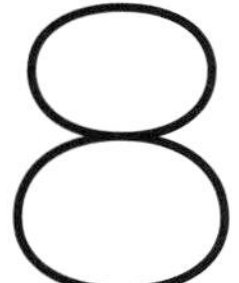

from *The Prelude*: Skating

And in the frosty season, when the sun
Was set, and visible for many a mile
The cottage windows blazed through twilight gloom,
I heeded not their summons: happy time
It was indeed for all of us – for me
It was a time of rapture! Clear and loud
The village clock tolled six, – I wheeled about,
Proud and exulting like an untired horse
That cares not for his home. All shod with steel,
We hissed along the polished ice in games
Confederate, imitative of the chase
And woodland pleasures,– the resounding horn,
The pack loud chiming, and the hunted hare.
So through the darkness and the cold we flew,
And not a voice was idle; with the din
Smitten, the precipices rang aloud;
The leafless trees and every icy crag
Tinkled like iron; while far distant hills
Into the tumult sent an alien sound
Of melancholy not unnoticed, while the stars
Eastward were sparkling clear, and in the west
The orange sky of evening died away.
Not seldom from the uproar I retired
Into a silent bay, or sportively
Glanced sideway, leaving the tumultuous throng,
To cut across the reflex of a star
That fled, and, flying still before me, gleamed
Upon the glassy plain; and oftentimes
When we had given our bodies to the wind,
And all the shadowy banks on either side
Came sweeping through the darkness, spinning still
The rapid line of motion, then at once
Have I, reclining back upon my heels,
Stopped short; yet still the solitary cliffs
Wheeled by me – even as if the earth had rolled
With visible motion her diurnal round!
Behind me did they stretch in solemn train,
Feebler and feebler, and I stood and watched
Till all was tranquil as a dreamless sleep.

rapture: wonderful excitement; bliss.

exulting: rejoicing.

shod with steel: wearing skates.

games/Confederate: playing in groups.

din: loud noise.

Smitten: struck by.

precipices: steep cliffs.

melancholy: deep sorrow.

Glanced: moved.

tumultuous throng: noisy crowd of skaters.

reflex: reflection.

glassy plain: smooth ice.

diurnal: daily.

train: line.

Personal Response

1. 'It was a time of rapture!' How is the boy's feeling of 'rapture' conveyed throughout the poem?
2. What impression of Wordsworth himself as a young boy do you get from reading 'Skating'?
3. What picture of nature emerges from this poem? Support your answer with reference to the text.

Critical Literacy

This extract from *The Prelude* is a fond memory of Wordsworth's schooldays. The poem describes an evening's ice-skating on the frozen surface of Esthwaite Water in the north-west of England. It was getting dark and the lights in the cottages plus the chiming of the clock reminded him that he should be indoors. However, his desire to continue skating with his friends was so strong that he decided to take no notice of time. For Wordsworth, the centre of this extraordinary experience is the way in which people and landscape are so closely interrelated.

In the opening lines, the poet invites us into the special world of his boyhood with a simple description of a memorable winter scene – 'the frosty season'. His personal narrative has a richly **nostalgic tone and the vivid imagery immediately sets the scene**: 'The cottage windows blazed through twilight gloom.' As the poet begins to relive the moment, his language reflects the intense sense of delight and freedom that he felt during that 'happy time'. The repetition and run-on lines emphasise the tremendous excitement he recalls: 'for all of us – for me/It was a time of rapture!'

Wordsworth goes on to describe the thrilling experience of skating in lines 7–14. What is most noticeable is the **vitality of the language**, particularly the dynamic verbs ('wheeled', 'hissed', 'flew'). Acutely observing the movement, he makes use of both the urgent rhythm and a powerful simile to capture his exhilaration: 'I wheeled about,/Proud and exulting like an untired horse.' The comparison is developed further when he describes the skaters as seemingly 'shod with steel'. Musical sibilance reinforces the importance of the memory: 'We hissed along the polished ice.' Caught up in the moment, the children imagine themselves as wild hounds pursuing a hare: 'The pack loud chiming.' Onomatopoeia ('We hissed along') conveys the fast movement. Speed is more obviously shown by the use of the verb 'flew'.

Indeed, **sound effects are used successfully throughout**, including lines 15–22, where the poet continues to bring the noisy scene to life: 'with the din/Smitten, the precipices rang aloud.' The activity ('uproar') is in contrast with the 'silent' landscape surrounding the skaters. Wordsworth remembers leaving 'the tumultuous throng' to seek out a quieter area where he skates round and round. When he stops, he feels the earth is still spinning on 'her diurnal round' and for a brief moment he feels connected to the wider universe surrounding him. Fascinated as always by the vast solitude, he takes time to reflect on the

mysterious relationships between people and nature. The underlying sense of sadness is never explained. Perhaps the assonant phrase 'alien sound/Of melancholy' reflects the reality of time passing and that even echoes die.

After all the dramatic exuberance, the mood becomes subdued and reverential in the eloquent final lines. Overcome by the beauty and majesty of 'the shadowy banks on either side', Wordsworth tells us that he simply 'stood and watched'. Although the boy does not realise that he is learning about the transience of life, the adult poet does. 'All was tranquil as a dreamless sleep' might refer to the dying of day, just as other images (the sun setting and the child spinning in circles on his skates) signified the harmonious movement of the universe. To a large extent, the poem is about the passage of time, which is in itself a difficult concept. In the skating episode, the child Wordsworth is simply playing on a lake with his friends. However, such life-shaping memories (he later called them 'spots of time') made him see **nature as a formative force that enriches our understanding of life**.

Writing About the Poem

From your reading of 'Skating', would you say that Wordsworth is a writer of great descriptive power? Support your answer with reference to the text of the poem.

Sample Paragraph

I think 'Skating' is remarkably descriptive. Wordsworth uses contrast to describe the cottage windows, which 'blazed through twilight gloom' and skilfully weaves these with revelations about his own exited emotions – 'It was a time of rapture!' He really gives me a sense of the actual sensation of what it was like to be skating on ice. The feeling of moving gracefully at speed and yet being close to danger is suggested through lively phrases like 'I wheeled about', 'We hissed along' and 'sweeping through the darkness'. Wordsworth builds up a vivid picture of the landscape around the lake at dusk. There are 'leafless trees', an 'orange sky' and 'solitary cliffs'. He also uses comparisons to show the recklessness of the children playing. They are like a pack of wild dogs chasing 'the hunted hare'. Such descriptive details really bring out the excitement of the scene.

EXAMINER'S COMMENT

A focused high-grade response, very well supported by useful reference and quotations. The expression is varied and controlled. While some mention of sound effects would have been welcome, there is a convincing sense of engagement with how Wordsworth's descriptive power creates a pervasive mood of exhilaration within the poem.

Class/Homework Exercises

1. Comment on the effectiveness of rhythm and movement in 'Skating', supporting your answer with reference to the text.
2. In your opinion, is this a realistic childhood memory? Or is it nostalgic and sentimental? Support your answer with reference to the poem.

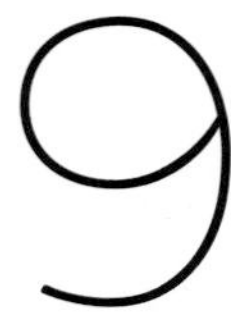

Tintern Abbey

Five years have past; five summers, with the length
Of five long winters! and again I hear
These waters, rolling from their mountain-springs
With a soft inland murmur. – Once again
Do I behold these steep and lofty cliffs,
That on a wild secluded scene impress
Thoughts of more deep seclusion; and connect
The landscape with the quiet of the sky.
The day is come when I again repose
Here, under this dark sycamore, and view
These plots of cottage-ground, these orchard tufts,
Which at this season, with their unripe fruits,
Are clad in one green hue, and lose themselves
'Mid groves and copses. Once again I see
These hedge-rows, hardly hedge-rows, little lines
Of sportive wood run wild: these pastoral farms,
Green to the very door; and wreaths of smoke
Sent up, in silence, from among the trees!
With some uncertain notice, as might seem
Of vagrant dwellers in the houseless woods,
Or of some Hermit's cave, where by his fire
The Hermit sits alone.
These beauteous forms,
Through a long absence, have not been to me
As is a landscape to a blind man's eye:
But oft, in lonely rooms, and 'mid the din
Of towns and cities, I have owed to them,
In hours of weariness, sensations sweet,
Felt in the blood, and felt along the heart;
And passing even into my purer mind,
With tranquil restoration: – feelings too
Of unremembered pleasure: such, perhaps,
As have no slight or trivial influence
On that best portion of a good man's life,
His little, nameless, unremembered, acts
Of kindness and of love. Nor less, I trust,
To them I may have owed another gift,
Of aspect more sublime; that blessed mood
In which the burthen of the mystery,
In which the heavy and the weary weight

Five years have past: Wordsworth is now revisiting the ruins of Tintern Abbey and the River Wye, which he had first seen five years earlier on a walking tour.

sycamore: large shady tree.

orchard tufts: small groups of fruit trees.

hue: colour.

groves and copses: wooded areas.

vagrant dwellers: wandering gypsies.
Hermit: loner, recluse.

sublime: exquisite, awe-inspiring.

burthen of the mystery: the weight of the wonder of life.

Of all this unintelligible world,
Is lightened: – that serene and blessed mood,
In which the affections gently lead us on, –
Until, the breath of this corporeal frame
And even the motion of our human blood
Almost suspended, we are laid asleep
In body, and become a living soul:
While with an eye made quiet by the power
Of harmony, and the deep power of joy,
We see into the life of things.
If this
Be but a vain belief, yet, oh! how oft –
In darkness and amid the many shapes
Of joyless day light; when the fretful stir
Unprofitable, and the fever of the world,
Have hung upon the beatings of my heart –
How oft, in spirit, have I turned to thee,
O sylvan Wye! thou wanderer thro' the woods,
How often has my spirit turned to thee!

And now, with gleams of half-extinguished thought,
With many recognitions dim and faint,
And somewhat of a sad perplexity,
The picture of the mind revives again:
While here I stand, not only with the sense
Of present pleasure, but with pleasing thoughts
That in this moment there is life and food
For future years. And so I dare to hope,
Though changed, no doubt, from what I was when first
I came among these hills; when like a roe
I bounded o'er the mountains, by the sides
Of the deep rivers, and the lonely streams,
Wherever nature led: more like a man
Flying from something that he dreads than one
Who sought the thing he loved. For nature then
(The coarser pleasures of my boyish days,
And their glad animal movements all gone by)
To me was all in all. – I cannot paint
What then I was. The sounding cataract
Haunted me like a passion: the tall rock,
The mountain, and the deep and gloomy wood,
Their colours and their forms, were then to me
An appetite; a feeling and a love,
That had no need of a remoter charm,
By thought supplied, nor any interest
Unborrowed from the eye. – That time is past,

affections: feelings; sensations.
corporeal frame: body.

fretful: uneasy, distressed.

sylvan: tree-lined banks of the River Wye.

half-extinguished thought: memories that are half-forgotten.

roe: deer.

cataract: waterfall.

And all its aching joys are now no more,
And all its dizzy raptures. Not for this
Faint I, nor mourn nor murmur; other gifts
Have followed; for such loss, I would believe,
Abundant recompense. For I have learned
To look on nature, not as in the hour
Of thoughtless youth; but hearing often-times
The still, sad music of humanity,
Nor harsh nor grating, though of ample power
To chasten and subdue. And I have felt
A presence that disturbs me with the joy
Of elevated thoughts; a sense sublime
Of something far more deeply interfused,
Whose dwelling is the light of setting suns,
And the round ocean and the living air,
And the blue sky, and in the mind of man:
A motion and a spirit, that impels
All thinking things, all objects of all thought,
And rolls though all things. Therefore am I still
A lover of the meadows and the woods,
And mountains; and of all that we behold
From this green earth; of all the mighty world
Of eye, and ear, – both what they half create,
And what perceive; well pleased to recognise
In nature and the language of the sense
The anchor of my purest thoughts, the nurse,
The guide, the guardian of my heart, and soul
Of all my moral being.
Nor perchance,
If I were not thus taught, should I the more
Suffer my genial spirits to decay:
For thou art with me here upon the banks
Of this fair river; thou my dearest Friend,
My dear, dear Friend; and in thy voice I catch
The language of my former heart, and read
My former pleasures in the shooting lights
Of thy wild eyes. Oh! yet a little while
May I behold in thee what I was once,
My dear, dear Sister! and this prayer I make,
Knowing that Nature never did betray
The heart that loved her; 'tis her privilege,
Through all the years of this our life, to lead
From joy to joy: for she can so inform
The mind that is within us, so impress
With quietness and beauty, and so feed
With lofty thoughts, that neither evil tongues,

murmur: complain in a quiet, continuous way.

recompence: compensation.

A presence: an unseen being or influence.

interfused: filled with.

both what ... perceive: both what is taken in by the senses and transformed by the imagination.

my dearest Friend: Dorothy, the poet's sister. She accompanied him on this walk when the poem was composed.

Rash judgements, nor the sneers of selfish men,
Nor greetings where no kindness is, nor all
The dreary intercourse of daily life,
Shall e'er prevail against us, or disturb
Our cheerful faith, that all which we behold
Is full of blessings. Therefore let the moon
Shine on thee in thy solitary walk;
And let the misty mountain-winds be free
To blow against thee: and, in after years,
When these wild ecstasies shall be matured
Into a sober pleasure; when thy mind
Shall be a mansion for all lovely forms,
Thy memory be as a dwelling-place
For all sweet sounds and harmonies; oh! then,
If solitude, or fear, or pain, or grief,
Should be thy portion, with what healing thoughts
Of tender joy wilt thou remember me,
And these my exhortations! Nor, perchance –
If I should be where I no more can hear
Thy voice, nor catch from thy wild eyes these gleams
Of past existence – wilt thou then forget
That on the banks of this delightful stream
We stood together; and that I, so long
A worshipper of Nature, hither came
Unwearied in that service: rather say
With warmer love – oh! with far deeper zeal
Of holier love. Nor wilt thou then forget,
That after many wanderings, many years
Of absence, these steep woods and lofty cliffs,
And this green pastoral landscape, were to me
More dear, both for themselves and for thy sake!

intercourse: social activities.

exhortations: entreaties, urgent appeals.

pastoral: rolling rural.

Personal Response

1. What is the dominant mood of the poem's opening section (lines 1–22)? What words and images are used to create this mood?
2. Which of these words would you use to describe the tone of the second section (lines 22–49): quiet, intense, contemplative, nostalgic, reverent? Choose two and explain your choice.
3. Write a short personal response to the poem, highlighting the impact that it made on you. Support your answer with reference to the text.

Critical Literacy

'Tintern Abbey' comes at the end of Wordsworth's collection, *Lyrical Ballads.* It is an intensely personal poem and shows a new preoccupation with the poet's inner life, as it is explicitly autobiographical and contains Wordsworth's ideas about nature, perception and spiritual growth. It is a reflection on the importance of the natural world to the poet and the way in which his relationship with nature has changed since boyhood. The urge to explain his own life gave rise to his greatest poetry. Wordsworth wrote this poem at the age of 28 in one day as he left Tintern Abbey: 'Not a line of it was altered ... and not any part of it written down till I reached Bristol.'

The opening (lines 1–22) describes the present moment when **the scene at the River Wye was revisited**. At first this seems to be a pictorial account of a landscape in the conventional 18th-century manner. However, on looking closer we realise that this description of the rural scene is **a projection of the poet's own mood of tranquillity**. The repetition of 'I' reminds us of his presence: 'I hear', 'I behold', 'I again repose'. The landscape is a symbol of the unity Wordsworth perceives in nature, as everything merges seamlessly: 'clad in one green hue, and lose themselves.' The tranquil mood is emphasised by the 'quiet of the sky', the 'soft inland murmur' of the river and the wreaths of smoke 'Sent up, in silence'. The **simple language** used records experience in a vivid, clear manner rather than embroidering it, as was the fashion of the times. Wordsworth uses language in ebbs and flows as speech moves in natural conversation: 'These hedge-rows, hardly hedge-rows.' This was a dramatic move away from the formal poetic diction of contemporary poets.

The second section (lines 22–49) shows us **what the place meant to him** in the intervening years between his two visits. The memory of this landscape has been a 'tranquil restoration', as it has had a therapeutic effect on the poet in 'hours of weariness' in city life. It also had a moral influence on him as it encouraged acts of 'kindness and of love'. It gave him the 'gift' of 'that serene and blessed mood' which enabled him to 'see into the life of things'. In this state of heightened perception, he becomes aware of an inner force which permeates the natural world and also himself. Wordsworth becomes

less aware of his bodily self, 'our human blood/Almost suspended'. The world then stops being oppressive and problematic: 'the weary weight .../Is lightened'. This 'blessed mood' is a state of suspension where insight occurs in a period of tranquillity. Wordsworth discovers a feeling of the unity of the universe and of being part of that unity: 'become a living soul.'

In lines 50–57, **the poet expresses doubts**: 'If this/Be but a vain belief.' The use of natural language speaks to us from the heart as moments of certainty give way to hesitation, pauses to reflect or doubt. He is not sure whether he has really seen into the 'life of things'. There is a desperate need to believe so that he can grasp the meaning of a world that is otherwise 'unintelligible' to him. The repetitions and movement between past and present allow us to feel that we are following Wordsworth's thoughts as he tries to clarify and evaluate what nature has meant to him.

The phrase 'And now' returns the reader to the present, in lines 58–111, to stand alongside the poet as he remembers how this place sustained him in the past, how he is enjoying it now and how he realises that this view will sustain him in the future: 'there is life and food/For future years.' Thus past, present and future are fused together in this great harmony. He **recreates his 'boyish days' and traces his relationship with nature**, recalling his unthinking, physical enjoyment ('glad animal movements') and reliving the intense emotional and sensory delights ('aching joys' and 'dizzy raptures'). That is gone: 'That time is past.' Now he is aware of **an invisible force that unifies and drives nature**, a 'motion', a 'spirit' that 'rolls through all things'. The phrase 'I would believe' hints again at his uncertainty. Is he almost forcing himself to believe? Is his adult response to nature (the 'sense sublime') sufficient? Is it really an 'Abundant recompense' for losing 'thoughtless youth'?

In the final section, lines 111–159, **he examines his sister's relationship with nature** and dedicates his prayer for her. Dorothy is like a reincarnation of Wordsworth's former self – her 'wild eyes' and 'wild ecstasies' remind him of the 'aching joys' and 'dizzy raptures' of his youth: 'May I behold in thee what I was once.' He prays that nature will be a restorative force for her, helping her to deal with what life is: 'the dreary intercourse of daily life.' His sister's relationship with nature will change as his has done into a 'sober pleasure'. He now anticipates his own death as he looks into the future and hopes that he will live on in Dorothy's memory, 'on the banks of this delightful stream/ We stood together'.

The poem ends on a **religious note**. Wordsworth describes himself as 'A worshipper of Nature' and one capable of 'holier love', as he declares how 'this green pastoral landscape' meant so much to him for its own sake and also for Dorothy's sake. The reader is left with the landscape of the River Wye bound up with its impact on the poet and his responses to it. We view this place through Wordsworth's eyes forever.

Writing About the Poem

'Growth is a central preoccupation for Wordsworth.' Discuss how Wordsworth explores the growth of his relationship with nature in the poem, 'Tintern Abbey'.

Sample Paragraph

Wordsworth was very interested in his changing relationship with nature, how it influenced him at various points in his life, and how his awareness of it changed. After describing the scenery of the Wye valley, and the influence this has had on him, the poet reaches back into the past and recollects his younger self, 'when like a roe/I bounded o'er the mountains'. Here Wordsworth distinguishes between two phases in his relationship with nature. He describes 'the coarser pleasures' of his boyhood when enjoyment came from physical activity. He traces the emotional intensity of his love of nature at this time, 'To me was all in all'. He responds to the 'colours' and 'forms' of the landscape, but his intellect was not engaged. In the second phase, he includes people in his adult response, 'the still sad music of humanity' and now he realises the essential unity in all things. He becomes aware of a dynamic, living force which 'rolls' through everything. This adult response to nature is reflective. But there is a note of regret for this 'remoter' response. He wonders if it is sufficient reward for losing the 'dizzy raptures' of youth. But he is not certain. Although he is saying that this more 'sober' response to nature is superior to his 'former pleasures', yet it is the 'sounding cataract' which has 'haunted' him 'like a passion'.

EXAMINER'S COMMENT

A commendable top-rate response to a challenging question. Clear engagement with the poem and some informed commentary on the various phases in Wordsworth's changing relationship with nature. Supportive quotations and references are interwoven throughout the answer. Expression is assured and very well managed.

Class/Homework Exercises

1. Seamus Heaney wrote that Wordsworth established how truly 'the child is father to the man'. Discuss how Wordsworth shows that our early life determines our adulthood. Support the points you make with reference to 'Tintern Abbey'.
2. Based on your reading of 'Tintern Abbey', outline briefly what nature means to Wordsworth. Support your answer with reference to the text.

Summary Points

- **Key theme is the central significance of nature in Wordsworth's life.**
- **Sensuous appeal of youthful experience contrasted with a deeper mature understanding.**
- **Poet openly expresses his high regard for his sister Dorothy.**
- **Recurring religious imagery reflects the spiritual importance of nature.**
- **Characteristic use of simple language, colloquial speech, varying tones.**

Leaving Cert Sample Essay

'In Wordsworth's richly sensuous poems, there is a vivid evocation of both the natural world and the mind of the poet.' Discuss this view, supporting your answer with reference to the poetry of William Wordsworth on your course.

Sample Essay
(Sensuous poetry evokes nature and the poet's mind)

1. Throughout his poems, Wordsworth seems mainly preoccupied with celebrating the beauty of nature. But it is not just the sights and sounds of nature that delight him. He also presents nature in a much deeper spiritual way – as a creative and comforting force for good. Like other nature poets, Wordsworth's engagement with the natural world allowed him to develop insights into the meaning of life. His sensuous and most passionate poetry is also concerned with the relationship between human beings and nature.

2. In 'Tintern Abbey', Wordsworth tries to re-live his past feelings about a part of the English countryside he had visited five years before. The overall feeling he has is one of peace, 'The day is come when I again repose' and also one of being able to appreciate beauty, 'beauteous forms,/Through a long absence'. Although the opening appeals to our senses with a beautifully evoked pastoral landscape – a 'soft inland murmur' – it is the effect of the landscape on the poet that is the main focus. Wordsworth is overwhelmed by the tranquillity of the River Wye Valley. Broad assonant sounds convey the 'soft inland murmur' and the lively 'waters, rolling from their mountain-springs'. The poet reveals that treasured memories of this scenic place have comforted him in times of trouble, 'in lonely rooms, and 'mid the din/Of towns and cities'.

3. It is obvious that nature is not just a beautiful experience, it also has tremendous healing powers, filling Wordsworth's mind with 'tranquil restoration'. His deep connection with the natural world also has a moral effect, making him a better person, capable of 'unremembered acts/Of kindness and love'. Wordsworth's close relationship with nature was therefore rooted not only in great appreciation for nature on the surface, but also for the comfort it provided in his mind. 'Tintern Abbey' includes recurring religious imagery ('blessed mood', 'prayer', 'holier love') which reflects the mystical significance of the natural environment for this 'worshipper of Nature'.

MARKING SCHEME GUIDELINES

Candidates are free to agree and/or disagree with the statement. However, the key terms ('richly sensuous poetry', 'vivid evocation of both the natural world and the mind of the poet') should be addressed. Reward evidence of genuine engagement with the prescribed poems of William Wordsworth.

INDICATIVE MATERIAL

- Compelling relationship with nature.
- Subject matter comes from interesting 'situations from common life'.
- Fresh, sensuous imagery, vivid description, varying tones.
- Challenges poetic diction of the time, uses simple language effectively.
- Nature as an aesthetic, moral and spiritual force.
- Appealing autobiographical element, etc.

4. The poet's longing for peace – even in noisy cities – is described in 'Upon Westminster Bridge' as he praises the beauty of London 'worn' briefly like a precious garment. The scene is just before the hustle and bustle of people and transport disrupting this 'calm so deep'. Wordsworth captures the stunning serenity of the early morning in the rich, flowing line: 'The river glideth at his own sweet will' as he describes the mighty Thames River gently rolling at nature's pace. The emphatic tone echoes the enthusiasm he feels for this majestic place: 'all that mighty heart is lying still!'

5. Wordsworth continues to praise the rustic lifestyle in 'The Solitary Reaper'. He valued imagination and feeling more than reason and intellect, always favouring the poetry of sensation. This poem beautifully sets the atmosphere for introducing a young girl in the Scottish highlands, reaping the corn and singing a sad song. Wordsworth is struck by the sad beauty of her song. A variety of onomatopoeic features, including alliteration ('silence ... seas') and sibilant effects ('lass', 'silence', 'listened') provide a musical context throughout. The reader has been allowed to hear the young girl's 'plaintive' voice just like the poet, 'Long after it was heard no more'. Wordsworth is indeed the great Romantic poet who puts the emphasis on feelings – poetry which 'thinks into the human heart'.

6. In his wonderful poem 'Skating' (from *The Prelude*), Wordsworth recalls a boyhood experience on a frozen lake at nightfall. It was a time that transcended everyday reality. The natural world was suddenly a source of inspiration for poetry. The imagery is vivid and powerful. The sky is 'orange' and 'the twilight blazed'. The sounds are 'clear and loud' with the skaters 'hissing' on the ice and 'bellowing' like a pack of hounds. The poet feels not just happiness, but 'rapture' – and he conveys his childhood sensation of exhilaration and limitless energy by comparing himself to 'an untired horse'. Wordsworth's excited response to nature becomes more reflective towards the end when he felt 'tranquil as a dreamless sleep'. His delighted tone is reflected in such compelling words as 'rang', 'exulting' and 'sparkling'.

EXAMINER'S COMMENT

A convincing and deeply felt response, showing good engagement with, and knowledge of, the poetry of Wordsworth – both subject matter and style (especially sound effects, tone, rhythm). The focused discussion ranges widely over several key poems. Use of accurate, supportive quotations is particularly impressive. While some of the critical comments (e.g. in Paragraph 6) are note-like, undeveloped and slightly disjointed, language use is good overall. Fluent and varied expression ('recurring religious imagery', 'emphatic tone' 'echoes the enthusiasm', 'sensation of exhilaration') adds to the top-grade standard of the essay.

GRADE: H1
P = 15/15
C = 13/15
L = 13/15
M = 5/5
Total = 46/50

7. As in so many of his poems, Wordsworth makes good use of aural devices – particularly the sibilant 's' effect ('polished ice', 'precipices') – to create the authentic sound of ice-skating. Run-through lines and the use of steady iambic pentameter also create flow and rhythm in the poem. As a result, the poet's youthful excitement is always evident. But Wordsworth is not just a poet who feels strong emotions. He is also meditative and thought-provoking, constantly inviting us to consider our relationship with nature.

(approx. 770 words)
(45–50 minutes)

Sample Leaving Cert Questions on Wordsworth's Poetry

1. **'Wordsworth's distinctive poetic voice brings personal memories to life.' Discuss this statement, supporting your answer with reference to the poems by Wordsworth on your course.**
2. **'While aspects of transience and death are addressed in Wordsworth's heartfelt poems, these are generally balanced by the poet's own exuberant sense of life.' Discuss this view, supporting your answer with reference to both subject matter and style of the poems by William Wordsworth on your course.**
3. **'Wordsworth uses striking imagery and accessible language to show that nature is central to his poetic world.' Discuss this statement, supporting your answer with reference to the poems by William Wordsworth on your course.**

NOTE

As you may not be familiar with some of the poems referred to in the sample plans below, substitute poems that you have studied closely.

Exam candidates usually discuss three or four poems in their answers. However, there is no set number of poems or formulaic approach expected.

Key points about a particular poem can be developed over more than one paragraph.

Paragraphs may also include cross-referencing and discussion of more than one poem.

Remember that there is no single 'correct' answer to poetry questions, so always be confident in expressing your own considered response.

First Sample Essay Plan (Q2)

'While aspects of transience and death are addressed in Wordsworth's heartfelt poems, these are generally balanced by the poet's own exuberant sense of life.' Discuss this view, supporting your answer with reference to both subject matter and style of the poems by William Wordsworth on your course.

Intro: Wordsworth – provocative poet, idolised and dismissed. Believed poetry to be 'the spontaneous overflow of powerful feelings' which pursued the truth of man's knowledge of himself and the worlds around him. Passionate exploration of the beauty and tragedy of life.

Point 1: 'To My Sister' – the poet urges his sister to celebrate the natural beauty of a new day ('Put on with speed your woodland dress'). Underlying sense of transience and mortality. Human beings have the opportunity to be at one with the natural world which has a spiritual meaning for Wordsworth: 'blessed power.' Vivid imagery, vigorous tone and rhythm reflect his intense feelings. Nature's divine quality treated similarly to 'Tintern Abbey'.

Point 2: 'A slumber did my spirit seal' – lyrical elegy examines transience and death. Repetition of 'r' ('Rolled around in earth's diurnal course') mimics the continuous movement of the earth spinning on its axis. Soft sibilance creates the impression of gently falling asleep ('A slumber did my spirit seal'). Repetitive negatives ('No motion', 'no force', 'neither') reflect Lucy's changed state of lifelessness, now part of nature.

Point 3: 'She dwelt among the untrodden ways' – childish monosyllabic words describe Lucy's environment ('the spring of Dove'). Beautiful metaphor ('A violet by a mossy stone/Half hidden') describes Lucy as personification of nature. Appreciation of unique beauty of nature and Lucy ('fair as a star when only one/Is shining in the sky'). Regular rhyme *(abab, cdcd, efef)* creates a soothing mood.

Conclusion: Wordsworth – delight in nature, yet realistic awareness of passing time and mortality addressed in poetry of engaging imagery and simple diction. Regards the mind as 'white paper void of all characters'. Fills it with the great force for good – nature to be a powerful moral guide for humanity.

Sample Essay Plan (Q2)

Develop **one** of the above points into a practice paragraph of your own.

Sample Paragraph: Point 1

It is probably a cliché to say that Wordsworth found God in Nature, but many of his poems illustrate his deep spiritual relationship with the natural world. In 'To My Sister', he invites Dorothy to enjoy a free day idling in the countryside ('Put on with speed your woodland dress'). His excited tone ('make haste') reminds us that there is not a moment to be wasted. For Wordsworth, being absorbed in nature has spiritual significance – 'There is a blessing in the air'. He refers to the 'universal birth' – showing his belief that nature is a uniting force, connecting 'heart to heart'. The poem's run-through lines and energetic rhythms also suggest the joy he feels – and there is an optimistic feeling right

through the poem –'for this one day/We'll give to idleness'. The urgency to enjoy life clearly suggests that Wordsworth is deeply aware of the passing of time and the inevitability of death. The poet acknowledges the power of the natural world. Nature brings him in touch with a universal consciousness. In simple terms, he believes that it will lift the spirits of his sister and himself: 'We'll frame the measure of our souls.'

EXAMINER'S COMMENT

As part of a full essay answer, this is an assured top-grade response that displays a close understanding of the poem. Insightful discussion focuses on Wordsworth's spiritual bond with the natural world. The exploration of the poet's style is impressive. Expression is varied and fluent. Suitable references and quotations support key points throughout.

Second Sample Essay Plan (Q3)

'Wordsworth uses striking imagery and accessible language to show that nature is central to his poetic world.' Discuss this statement, supporting your answer with reference to the poems by William Wordsworth on your course.

Intro: Readers coming to Wordsworth's poems expecting a simple visual representation of nature's sights and sounds will be surprised. He is much more interested in the fundamental workings of nature and the relationship between man and nature.

Point 1: 'Tintern Abbey' – poet uses simple, accessible language and vivid religious imagery in this meditation on the growth of his personal relationship with nature, detailing physical, emotional and contemplative response; sees nature as a process of continual growth, the past enhances the present.

Point 2: 'The Stolen Boat' and 'Tintern Abbey' – Nature as a powerful moral guide, effective personification, detailed description.

Point 3: 'A slumber did my spirit seal'/'Tintern Abbey' – awareness of ultimate unity of all living things. Sensuous natural imagery. Nature seen as healer and consoler.

Point 4: Engaging poetic style – 'speaking from the heart', 'a man speaking to men'; blank verse, varied tones, etc.

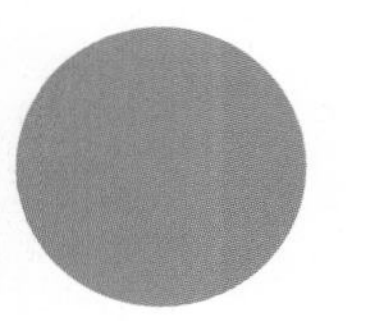

Conclusion: We enjoy Wordsworth's poetry for its original treatment of nature. He makes our 'eye quiet by the power of harmony' so that 'We see into the life of things'.

Sample Essay Plan (Q3)

Develop **one** of the points on the previous page into a paragraph.

Sample Paragraph: Point 3

In the second stanza of 'A slumber', Lucy is dead, unable to hear, move or see. Buried in the earth, she is as dead as the rocks or stones. Wordsworth is acutely aware of the impersonal forces of nature which control the universe. They cannot be stopped in their course. Death is part of the natural cycle of things. Nothing escapes, not even Lucy, although he deludes himself that she is a 'thing that could not feel/The touch of earthly years'. The word, 'diurnal', conveys the reality of passing time. Lucy is now free of human restraints and is at one with the dynamic forces of the universe, 'Rolled round'. As in 'Tintern Abbey', Wordsworth is conscious of an inner life that is part of the natural world. He 'sees into the life of things' because of the 'blessed mood' which nature's beauty bestows on him. He gains an understanding of the ultimate unity of the mysterious universe – and of being part of that great natural unity, 'the motion of our human blood/Almost suspended, we are laid asleep/In body'. Wordsworth clearly believes that nature teaches us of the 'power of harmony', the interconnectedness of everything, 'connect/The landscape with the quiet of the sky'. The poet is exploring the workings of nature and their relationship to man, rather than simply describing pretty images.

EXAMINER'S COMMENT

As part of a full essay answer, this informed response shows a genuine understanding of Wordsworth's preoccupations. The paragraph is clearly written and focuses on the insight to be gained from a mature perception of the significance of nature to the poet. Good use of cross-referencing, demonstrating close engagement with two poems. Accurate and well-integrated quotations support discussion points, further enhancing the top-grade standard.

Class/Homework Exercise

1. **Write one or two paragraphs in response to the question: 'Wordsworth uses striking imagery and accessible language to show that nature is central to his poetic world.' Discuss this statement, supporting your answer with reference to the poems by William Wordsworth on your course.**

 Revision Overview

'To My Sister'
Explores themes of close relationship with people and nature, and nature as a force for good.

'A slumber did my spirit seal'
Elegy for unknown Lucy. Themes of loss/death and the effect on poet.

'She dwelt among the untrodden ways'
Addresses themes of loss and death and impact on poet.

'Composed Upon Westminster Bridge'
Exploration of themes of transient beauty and its impact on poet.

'It is a beauteous evening, calm and free'
Addresses nature's beauty and contrasting responses.

'The Solitary Reaper'
Lyric ballad examines theme of recollection through girl's song and remembered event.

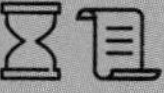

from *The Prelude*: 'The Stolen Boat'
Theme of nature as a moral guide for good. Recollection of important moment – trip taken in small boat.

from *The Prelude*: 'Skating'
Themes of transience and interconnectedness of people and place.

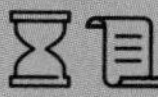

'Tintern Abbey'
Lyrical monologue. Theme of importance of nature and its relationship with the narrator.

Last Words

'Wordsworth's poetry still has the ability to engage, provoke, even entertain.'
John L. Mahoney

'Wordsworth's poetry is inevitable ... Nature not only gave him the matter for his poem, but wrote his poem for him.
Matthew Arnold

'Poetry ... takes its origin from emotion recollected in tranquillity.'
William Wordsworth

RELATIONSHIPS

NATURE

DEATH

TIME

BEAUTY

CHILDHOOD

RELIGION/ SPIRITUALITY

The Unseen Poem

'Students should be able ... to read poetry conscious of its specific mode of using language as an artistic medium.'
(DES English Syllabus, 4.5.1)

Note that responding to the unseen poem is an exercise in aesthetic reading. It is especially important, in assessing the responses of the candidates, to guard against the temptation to assume a 'correct' reading of the poem.

Reward the candidates' awareness of the patterned nature of the language of poetry, its imagery, its sensuous qualities, and its suggestiveness.

SEC Marking Scheme

In the Unseen Poem 20-mark question, you will have 20 minutes to read and respond to a short poem that you are unlikely to have already studied. Targeted reading is essential. **Read over the questions** first to focus your thoughts and feelings.

In your **first reading** of the poem:

- Aim to get an initial sense of what the poet is writing about and think about why the poet is writing about that particular subject.
- What is happening? Who is involved? Is there a sense of place and atmosphere?
- Avoid wasting time worrying about any words that you don't understand. Instead, **focus on what makes sense** to you.

Read through the poem **a second time:**

- Who is speaking in the poem? Is it the poet or another character?
- Which themes or issues is the poet exploring?
- What point is the poet making?
- What particularly do you notice about the **poet's language use**?
- How does the poem make you feel? Trust your own reaction.

Check the **'Glossary of Common Literary Terms'** (page 441)

- **Imagery** (includes similes, metaphors, symbols and personification)
- **Sound (aural) effects** Often referred to as omomatopoeia. (Includes alliteration, assonance, sibilance, rhyme and repetition.)
- **Tone** (sad, nostalgic, happy, optimistic, etc.)
- **Mood** (atmosphere)
- **Rhythm** (slow, even, quick, jumpy, etc.)
- **Contrasts**
- **Structure and layout**

REMEMBER!

'This section [Unseen Poetry] was often not answered, resulting in a loss of 20 marks. Omitting questions or parts of questions has a deleterious effect and is often due to poor time management.'

Chief Examiner's Report

Underline **interesting words or phrases** that catch your attention.

Unseen Poem – Practice 1

Read the following poem by Seamus Heaney from his collection, *Door into the Dark*, and answer **either** Question 1 **or** Question 2 which follow.

1 The Peninsula

When you have nothing more to say, just drive
For a day all round the peninsula.
The sky is tall as over a runway,
The land without marks, so you will not arrive

But pass through, though always skirting landfall.
At dusk, horizons drink down sea and hill,
The ploughed field swallows the whitewashed gable
And you're in the dark again. Now recall

The glazed foreshore and silhouetted log,
That rock where breakers shredded into rags,
The leggy birds stilted on their own legs,
Islands riding themselves out into the fog,

And drive back home, still with nothing to say
Except that now you will uncode all landscapes
By this: things founded clean on their own shapes,
Water and ground in their extremity.

Seamus Heaney

1. (a) In the above poem Seamus Heaney recommends driving 'all round the peninsula'. Based on your reading of the poem, explain why you think the poet recommends undertaking such a journey. (10)

(b) Choose two images from the poem that appeal to you and explain your choice. (10)

OR

2. Discuss the effectiveness of the poet's use of language throughout this poem. Your answer should refer closely to the text. (20)

Sample Answer 1

1. (a) (Reasons why Heaney recommends driving 'all round the peninsula'.)

Heaney recommends driving all round the peninsula for a number of reasons. He sees it as a good break from normal work and an alternative to talking, 'When you have nothing more to say'. A long drive around this beautiful coastal area will act as words. Conversation won't be needed as you drive because 'now you will uncode all landscapes'. It is obvious that the landscape is a scene of natural beauty.

Stanza 3 gives several images of all the sights the poet sees and is able to 'recall'. I think he sees the landscape as an easy way to relax. We all need to take time out. You aren't really going anywhere. You will pass through. You will be there, but not stop. Then you will keep going and head for home. I think this is the appealing thing about this journey of Heaney's.

EXAMINER'S COMMENT

This solid mid-grade response makes a reasonable attempt at exploring the possible reasons to explain the poet's recommendation. Closer engagement with the poem would raise the overall standard, e.g. by further considering what 'uncode all landscapes' might mean. The expression in the second paragraph is repetitive, but the central point lacks supportive reference from the text.

Sample Answer 2

1. (a) (Reasons why Heaney recommends driving 'all round the peninsula'.)

I think Seamus Heaney urges 'driving all round the peninsula' as a way of raising a person's spirits. Nature has a way of rediscovering wonder – especially when viewing the landscape from a different perspective. Heaney regards the leisurely drive as a substitute for small talk, 'when you have nothing more to say'. I felt the poet was reflecting on the experience of running out of ideas, of being inarticulate, of having an empty silence within himself.

This long narrow piece of land projecting out into the water is 'clean', 'without marks', so you can see it as it really is. It is not a destination in itself, but 'skirting landfall', a journey. The poet details all the strange sights the visitor can experience here, immersed in these surroundings, 'Islands riding themselves out into the fog'. The journey ends in a circle on the 'drive back home'. The driver will be transformed by the journey, recalling its sights and so is empowered to 'uncode all landscapes/By this'. He had discovered secret symbols by which he can get closer to unlocking nature's wonders.

EXAMINER'S COMMENT

This top-grade response includes much more thorough interaction with the poem. Perceptive points show a good understanding of the development of thought in the poem. All three paragraphs are organised effectively and comments are aptly supported by quotations. Expression is impressive throughout (e.g. 'a rich visual, emotional and mental treasury of images').

Heaney now has a reference point, this landscape, where things were 'founded clean on their own shapes'. There is only water and ground here at their most intense, 'in their extremity'. This quiet place provides the driver with a rich visual, emotional and mental treasury of images. This is why I believe Heaney recommends driving 'all round the peninsula'.

Sample Answer 3

1 (b) (Two appealing images from the poem.)

The first image that appeals to me is
'At dusk, horizons drink down sea and hill,
The ploughed field swallows the whitewashed gable/And you're in the dark again'.

I think this is a beautiful image of how night falls in a coastal area like this. The poet effectively uses personification to suggest the dramatic nature of how the darkness comes and 'swallows' up the surrounding landscape. It is a vivid and clever image. Contrasting shades ('whitewashed' and 'dark') add to the visual quality and give a sharper impression of the scene.

The second image that appealed to me was
'The sky is tall as over a runway,
The land without marks, so you will not arrive
But pass through'.

EXAMINER'S COMMENT

Some excellent analysis of the poem, showing great understanding of the chosen images. The energy and subtlety of Heaney's language is explored effectively. The critical commentary is also highly impressive ('adds to the visual quality', 'a dense evocative image') and in keeping with the top-grade standard.

Once again, this is a dense evocative image. The simile comparing the overhead sky to a wide airfield gives a sense of space and openness. The run-on lines suggest the movement of the car journey. I get the impression that the landscape goes on forever. It is a 'land without marks' so you can just relax, you don't have to concentrate. The poet creates the idea of freedom, of being uncontrolled.

Sample Answer 4

2. (Effectiveness of the poet's language use.)

'The Peninsula' describes driving all day around the peninsula until dusk floods the landscape. The first image which appealed to me was the voracious landscape drinking and swallowing, 'At dusk, horizons drink down sea and hill,/The ploughed field swallows the whitewashed gable/and you're in the dark again'. I found the poet's use of personification very effective in describing the sudden arrival of the overwhelming darkness. The alliteration of the deadening 'd', 'drink down', suggested to me the thirsty gulp of the horizon as sea and hill are shrouded in the evening's gloom. The run-on line also emphasises the engulfing night. These are the aspects of the landscape which can be experienced if driving on the peninsula.

EXAMINER'S COMMENT

Overall, this succinct answer includes several insightful points and displays a nuanced appreciation of the poet's language use. Some of the points and references (e.g. in the opening paragraph) were effectively developed in greater detail, with an emphasis on the powerful sound effects in Heaney's language. Expression is clear and controlled. A solid high-grade standard.

Details bring the scene to life – and some of the metaphorical description gives a real sense of the waves crashing onto the shore – 'breakers shredded onto rags'. Even the rough 'r' sound suggests the sea water washing up on the rocks. I also liked the humour of the image, 'The leggy birds stilted on their own legs'. I thought it vividly captured the clumsy walk of the seabirds on land. They were bumbling like clowns on stilts, even though they were walking on their own legs. They were out of their natural environment of air and sea where their movements are easy and graceful. The line, I thought, read awkwardly, with its use of the repetition of 'leggy' and 'legs'. Its unnatural rhythm mimicked the awkward posture of the birds.

REMEMBER!

In a poem, every word counts.

Unseen Poem – Practice 2

Read the following poem by Liz Lochhead and answer **either** Question 1 **or** Question 2 which follow.

2 Poem For My Sister

My little sister likes to try my shoes,
to strut in them,
admire her spindle-thin twelve-year-old legs
in this season's styles.
She says they fit her perfectly,
but wobbles
on their high heels, they're
hard to balance.

I like to watch my little sister
playing hopscotch, admire the neat hops-and-skips of her,
their quick peck,
never-missing their mark, not
over-stepping the line.
She is competent at peever.

I try to warn my little sister
about unsuitable shoes,
point out my own distorted feet, the callouses,
odd patches of hard skin.
I should not like to see her
in my shoes.
I wish she could stay
sure footed,
sensibly shod.

Liz Lochhead

peever: a Scottish word for the game of hopscotch

callouses: hard thickened areas of skin

1. (a) What do you think is the central theme or message in the poem? Explain your answer with reference to the poem. (10)

(b) Identify the dominant mood or feeling in the poem and explan how the poet creates that mood or feeling. Support your answer with reference to the text. (10)

OR

2. Discuss the appeal of this poem, commenting on its theme and the poet's use of language and imagery. Refer to the text in support of your answer. (20)

Sample Answer 1

2. (Appeal of poem – theme, language use, imagery.)

I found the poem very appealing. It reminded me of my own sister running around the house in my mother's high heels. I thought it was realistic because little girls do wobble about in heels and sometimes fall over. I thought it was nice looking at the little girl playing hopscotch. This was a nostalgic approach to describing my own childhood. In the second verse, the older sister warns the child not to take risks. This shows me the emotions of concern and love. 'I warn my little sister.' I find the tone is concerned and loving.

The main theme of the poem is that the poet doesn't really want the little girl to grow up. I think she wants her to be a little girl forever always wearing sensible shoes. The older sister regrets her life and wearing high heels that have hurt her feet. Her tone here is regretful. 'I would not like to see her in my shoes'. I get the impression that she has had unhappy experiences in her life. This is because her language and imagery describe 'callouses and old patches of hard skin'. I think this is a very appealing poem with a strong message about growing up.

I liked the poem because no one is completely happy when they lose their childhood. The images in the poem are contrasting happy times with older experiences. The whole poem is nostalgic and really celebrates the joy of being young, but also decribes the sadness of growing older.

EXAMINER'S COMMENT

There are some potentially good points in this basic mid-grade answer – particularly in the second paragraph. Paragraph 1 is largely unfocused, however, and overly relies on personal response. Further discussion of the final point could have been possible by referring closely to the poet's language. Expression is also repetitive and some of the quotes are inaccurate.

Sample Answer 2

2. (Appeal of poem – theme, language use, imagery.)

This engaging poem explores the eternal problem for humans – transience. A charming picture of the poet's little sister tottering about in her elder's sister's shoes is presented. She is on the verge of womanhood. The monosyllabic verb 'strut' cleverly depicts the confident grown-up stance the little girl is attempting to mimic. Then she is shown comfortably inhabiting her simple childhood world, 'playing hopscotch'. The repeated references to the image of the 'high heels' is effective in portraying the surface glamour and hidden cruelties of adulthood, 'callouses', 'hard skin'.

The poet uses line length in an innovative way. The long line, 'admire her spindle-thin twelve-year-old legs in this season's styles', pokes out

awkwardly from the body of the poem. The image mirrors the ungainly wobbles of the little girl attempting to 'balance' in her sister's high heels. She is trying to find her way into the next stage of life. The disfigurement of the elder girl's feet by her high heels is vividly portrayed, reminding the reader how the hard knocks of life mark and wound the grown-up. Run-on lines are used to show the effort the young girl is making while she attempts to walk in her sister's shoes, 'but wobbles/on their high heels'. Going from childhood to adulthood can be difficult.

A series of compound words describe the little girl, 'spindle-thin twelve-year-old', 'hops-and-skips'. This suggests how the little girl is at a complex stage of life. She is also aware of the boundaries of her familiar world. The poet is uneasy, concerned for her little sister and painfully aware of life's dangers, 'I try to warn', 'I should not like to see'. Her wish is for her sister to remain in childhood forever. The concluding line's soft sibilance presents the simple childhood world, 'I wish she could stay/sure footed, /sensibly shod'. The poem ends on a sad note. The child will soon have to leave her innocent world behind and enter the merciless world of adulthood.

EXAMINER'S COMMENT

An insightful and focused top-grade response that shows genuine engagement with the central theme in the poem. The perceptive commentary on the poet's language use (imagery, compound words, sibilance, etc.) is commendable. Apt quotations provide good support and the expression is impressive throughout.

REMEMBER!

Use quotations to support your points.

Unseen Poem – Practice 3

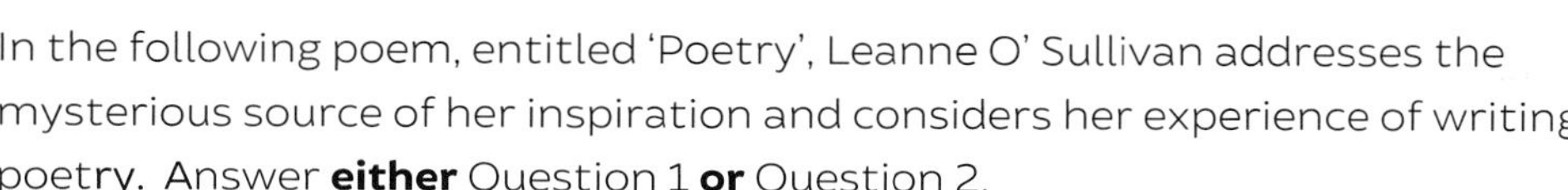

In the following poem, entitled 'Poetry', Leanne O' Sullivan addresses the mysterious source of her inspiration and considers her experience of writing poetry. Answer **either** Question 1 **or** Question 2.

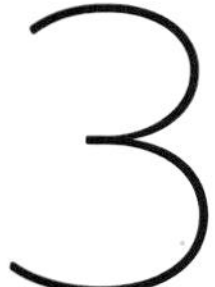

Poetry

I can never find a pen when you come,
when you snap me up on your lizard tongue,
and wrap yourself around me as if I were a spool.
Vague as metaphors you tease, trawling
your shadows as feathering clouds do,
shedding infant vowels in your vaporous image.
You will never be perfected,
and while you are half-born I will never sleep.

In picking ink I preserve all your fruits;
perhaps you are a prophecy,
a mouthing of the boundless,
or some God or other Minerva* festering
like secrets in empty lines.
Years gone now, labouring to drain
the reddest blood from your throat, and I am none the wiser.

Leanne O'Sullivan

Minerva: Goddess associated with artistic creativity

1. (a) Comment on one emotion expressed by the poet in this poem. Refer to the text in your answer. (10)

(b) Choose a line or phrase from the poem that impressed you. Explain your choice. (10)

2. Write a personal response to this poem. Your answer should make close reference to the text. (20)

Sample Answer 1

1. (a) (Comment on one emotion expressed in the poem.)

EXAMINER'S COMMENT

This basic grade reponse identifies one emotion, but there is little or no attempt to explain how the poet creates this emotion or its effect. A much closer engagement with the poem would be expected in order to improve the standard. Expression throughout is repetitive and there are some grammatical errors.

The poet is very unhappy. She can't find a pen and has no ideas. Her poems are just not good enough. It is as if she has spent ten years writing poetry and she doesn't know any more about anything at the end of it all. Leanne cannot sleep well because her poems are only festering. She is none the wiser, as she says herself.

She addresses the mysterious source of her inspiration. Her experience of writing the poems is one of being unhappy and without any fun in life. The emotion in the poem is this feeling of feeling imperfect. In the second paragraph, there are violent imagery. This is a painful experience and the main reasons for her being so unhappy with her life as a poet that cannot write.

Sample Answer 2

1. (a) (Comment on one emotion expressed in the poem.)

Leanne O'Sullivan expresses deep frustration in her poem, 'Poetry'. At the moment creativity strikes, 'when you snap me up on your lizard tongue', she is unable to find a pen to write it down. Sharp verbs, such as 'snap' and 'wrap', vividly express the poet's negative feelings towards the tenuous process of actually writing poetry. She feels as if she cannot quite seize the inventive impulse when it appears, 'Vague as metaphors you tease'.

For her, the poetic thought is as insubstantial as 'feathering clouds', glimpsed, but impossible to catch. O'Sullivan feels that her poems are never entirely finished, 'You will never be perfected', so she always remains dissatisfied with her efforts, 'while you are half-born I will never sleep'. The personification of poetry is used to show how the elusive presence of inspiration constantly teases and irritates the poet. Like so many artists, O'Sullivan is exasperated.

EXAMINER'S COMMENT

An exceptionally good response, clearly focusing on the feeling of frustration. This is then developed through a coherent exploration of the poet's experience, based on close interaction with the language of the poem. Expression is excellent (particularly the concluding sentence). An assured top-grade answer.

Class/Homework Exercise

Write your own 1. (b) Sample Answer.

I have chosen the impressive phrase 'Years gone now, labouring to drain/the reddest blood from your throat'...

Write the rest of the answer to the question above. You may use some of the points in the Prompt section below. (Allow 10 minutes.)

PROMPT

Shocking image ('to drain/the reddest blood from your throat') suggests the vampire-like activity of the poet as she strains to draw ideas.

Ambiguous tone ... startling, ironic, desperate, etc.

Broad-vowelled assonance ('gone now') highlights the lenghty expanse of time spent writing poetry.

Run-on line ('labouring to drain/the reddest blood ...') accentuates the exertion expended in writing.

Placing of onomatopoeic verb 'drain' at end of line illustrates the act of squeezing every last drop from the creative process of writing poetry.

NOTE (based on the Chief Examiner's Report)

High marks were rewarded for

- The ability to analyse and evaluate the language and concepts they encountered.
- Appreciating how meaning was shaped.
- Shaping their own writing in the appropriate register and genre.

Recommendations

- Guard against overly literal interpretation of language.
- Realise language is rich and nuanced.
- Re-read to appreciate suggestion, inference and meaning.
- Students should show an appreciation of 'the power of language to move beyond the concrete to more expressive levels'.

Unseen Poem – Practice 4

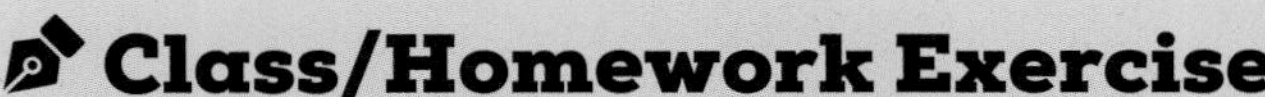

Class/Homework Exercise

Read the following poem by Imtiaz Dharker and answer **either** Question 1 **or** Question 2 which follow. (Allow 20 minutes to complete the question.)

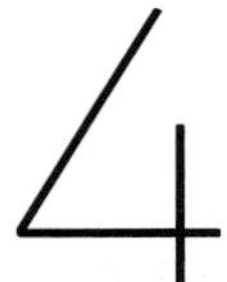

This Room

This room is breaking out,
Of itself, cracking through
Its own walls
In search of space, light,
Empty air.

The bed is lifting out of
Its nightmares
From dark corners, chairs
Are rising up to crash through clouds.

This is the time and place
To be alive:
When the daily furniture of our lives
Stirs, when the improbable arrives.
Pots and pans bang together
In celebration, clang
Past the crowd of garlic, onions, spices,
Fly by the ceiling fan.
No one is looking for the door.
In all this excitement
I'm wondering where
I've left my feet, and why

My hands are outside, clapping.

Imtiaz Dharker

1. (a) In your opinion, is the dominant mood in the poem positive or negative? Explain your answer with reference to the poem. (10)

(b) Comment on the poet's use of personification throughout the poem. (10)

OR

2. Discuss the appeal of this poem, with reference to its theme and the poet's use of language and imagery. Refer closely to the text in support of your answer. (20)

Glossary of Common Literary Terms

alliteration: the use of the same letter at the beginning of each word or stressed syllable in a line of verse, e.g. 'boilers bursting'.

assonance: the use of the same vowel sound in a group of words, e.g. 'bleared, smeared with toil'.

aubade: a celebratory morning song, sometimes lamenting the parting of lovers.

blank verse: unrhymed iambic pentameter, e.g. 'These waters, rolling from their mountain-springs'.

conceit: an elaborate image or far-fetched comparison, e.g. 'This flea is you and I, and this/Our marriage bed'.

couplet: two successive lines of verse, usually rhymed and of the same metre, e.g. 'So long as men can breathe or eyes can see,/So long lives this, and this gives life to thee'.

elegy: a mournful poem, usually for the dead, e.g. 'Sleep in a world your final sleep has woken'.

emotive language: language designed to arouse an emotional response in the reader, e.g. 'For this that all that blood was shed?'

enjambment: the continuation of a sentence without a pause beyond the end of a line, couplet or stanza.

epiphany: a moment of insight or understanding, e.g. 'Somebody loves us all'.

free verse: unrhymed and unmetred poetry, often used by modern poets, e.g. 'but the words are shadows and you cannot hear me./ You walk away and I cannot follow'.

imagery: descriptive language or word-pictures, especially appealing to the senses, e.g. 'He was speckled with barnacles,/fine rosettes of lime'.

irony: when one thing is said and the opposite is meant, e.g. 'For men were born to pray and save'.

lyric: short musical poem expressing feeling.

metaphor: image that compares two things without using the words 'like' or 'as', e.g. 'I am gall, I am heartburn'.

onomatopoeia: the sound of the word imitates or echoes the sound being described, e.g. 'The murmurous haunt of flies on summer eves'.

paradox: a statement that on the surface appears self-contradictory, e.g. 'I shall have written him one/poem maybe as cold/And passionate as the dawn'.

persona: the speaker or voice in the poem. This is not always the poet, e.g. 'I know that I shall meet my fate/Somewhere among the clouds above'.

personification: where the characteristics of an animate or living being are given to something inanimate, e.g. 'The yellow fog that rubs its back upon the window panes'.

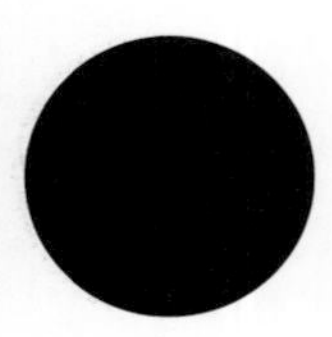

rhyme: identical sound of words, usually at the end of lines of verse, e.g. 'I get down on my knees and do what must be done/And kiss Achilles' hand, the killer of my son'.

rhythm: the beat or movement of words, the arrangement of stressed and unstressed, short and long syllables in a line of poetry, e.g. 'I will arise and go now, and go to Innisfree'.

sestina: a complex 39-line verse form which can be traced back to 12th-century France. The sestina relies on end-word repetition in place of rhyme. It consists of six sestets (six-line stanzas) followed by a concluding tercet (three-line stanza). The six words at the end of each of the lines of the first stanza are repeated in a different order at the end of lines in the subsequent stanzas. These six words are also included in the closing tercet.

sibilance: the whispering, hissing 's' sound, e.g. 'Singest of summer in full-throated ease'.

sonnet: a 14-line poem. The Petrarchan or Italian sonnet is divided into eight lines (octave), which present a problem or situation. The remaining six lines (sestet) resolve the problem or present another view of the situation. The Shakespearean sonnet is divided into three quatrains and concludes with a rhyming couplet, either summing up what preceded or reversing it.

symbol: a word or phrase representing something other than itself, e.g. 'A tattered coat upon a stick'.

theme: the central idea or message in a poem.

tone: the type of voice or attitude used by the poet towards his or her subject, e.g. 'O but it is dirty'.

villanelle: a five-stanza poem of three lines each, with a concluding quatrain, using only two end rhyming words throughout, e.g. 'I am just going outside and may be some time,/At the heart of the ridiculous, the sublime'.

Critical Analysis Checklist

Leaving Certificate examination questions in the Prescribed Poetry section usually refer to the poet's subject matter and style. You will be rewarded for showing genuine engagement with the poetry.

When discussing a poem, you will be expected to demonstrate an understanding of the poet's themes or ideas. Some poems reveal the poet's personal views or concerns.

It is also important to interact with the language in the poem. The poet's distinctive style refers to how language is used to communicate themes and ideas.

Subject Matter (What the poem is about)

Look beyond the surface meaning of the poem and remember that there is no 'perfect' or 'correct' meaning. However, your interpretation must always be rooted in the text of the poem.

When examiners read your responses, they will be assessing your own use of language and will reward fluent and controlled expression as well as fresh, insightful ideas.

Useful critical phrases include:

The poet is suggesting ...
This stanza indicates ...
The reference reveals that ...
The poet's final lines hint at ...
This might well signify ...

Stylistic Techniques

Look closely at the language used in conveying the poet's meaning. Nouns, adjectives, verbs, adverbs, etc., are all chosen for a purpose. Consider why the poet preferred that word, and why it was selected. Is the poet using contrast, exaggeration, modern/archaic terms, personification, alliteration, similes, imagery, metaphors, assonance, onomatopoeia, etc.? What is the effect? Does a particular image engage you? Why?

Other Useful Questions

- Does the poet use repetition, lists, short/long sentences, commands, questions, etc.? Why?
- Is the poem written from a particular viewpoint (first, second, third person)? Why?
- Is it written in free verse? Or is rhyme used?
- Is there a definite rhythm? Or contrasting rhythms?
- Does the poet use end-stopped or enjambed lines?
- Is a particular form used (e.g. sonnet)?
- Is a line placed apart from the main body of the poem? Why?
- How does the poem start? How does it conclude?
- In all cases, consider why the poet has decided on that particular language technique.
-

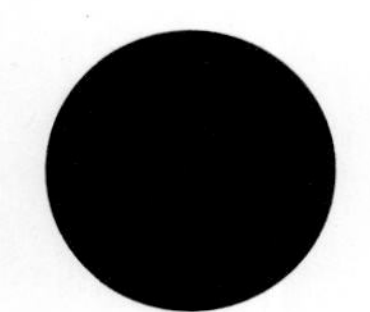

Acknowledgements

'The War Horse', 'Child of Our Time', 'The Famine Road', 'The Shadow Doll', 'White Hawthorn in the West of Ireland', 'Outside History', 'The Black Lace Fan my Mother Gave Me', 'This Moment', 'The Pomegranate', 'Love', by Eavan Boland © Eavan Boland, *New Selected Poems*, Carcanet Press, 2013.

'There's a certain Slant of light', 'I felt a Funeral, in my Brain', 'A Bird came down the Walk', 'I Heard a fly buzz–when I died', 'The Soul has Bandaged moments', 'I could bring You Jewels–had I a mind to', 'A narrow Fellow in the Grass', 'I taste a liquor never brewed', 'After great pain, a formal feeling comes', by Emily Dickinson. *The Poems of Emily Dickinson: Reading Edition*, edited by Ralph W. Franklin, Cambridge, Mass.: The Belknap Press of Harvard University Press, Copyright © 1998, 1999 by the President and Fellows of Harvard College. Copyright © 1951, 1955 by the President and Fellows of Harvard College. Copyright © renewed 1979, 1983 by the President and Fellows of Harvard College. Copyright © 1914, 1918, 1919, 1924, 1929, 1930, 1932, 1935, 1937, 1942 by Martha Dickinson Bianchi. Copyright © 1952, 1957, 1958, 1963, 1965 by Mary L. Hampson.

'The Tuft of Flowers', 'Mending Wall', 'After Apple-Picking', 'The Road Not Taken', 'Birches', 'Out, Out–', 'Spring Pools', 'Acquainted with the Night', 'Design', 'Provide, Provide' from *Collected Poems* by Robert Frost. Published by Vintage Classics. Reprinted by permission of The Random House Group Limited © 1930.

'Lucina Schynning in Silence of the Nicht', 'The Second Voyage', 'Deaths and Engines', 'Street', 'Fireman's Lift', 'All for You', 'Following', 'Kilcash', 'Translation', 'The Bend in the Road' by Eiléan Ní Chuilleanáin, from *Selected Poems*, by Eiléan Ní Chuilleanáin, 2008. 'On Lacking the Killer Instinct' and 'To Niall Woods and Xenya Ostrovskaia, married in Dublin on 9 September 2009' by Eiléan Ní Chuilleanáin, from *The Sun-fish*, by Eiléan Ní Chuilleanáin, 2009. Reproduced by kind permission of the author and The Gallery Press, Loughcrew, Oldcastle, Co. Meath, Ireland.

'Aunt Jennifer's Tigers', 'The Uncle Speaks in the Drawing Room', 'Power', 'Storm Warnings', 'Living in Sin', 'The Roofwalker', 'Our Whole Life', 'Trying to Talk with a Man', 'Diving into the Wreck', 'From a Survivor', from COLLECTED POEMS: 1950–2012 by Adrienne Rich. Copyright © 2016, 2013 by the Adrienne Rich Literary Trust. Copyright © 2011, 2007, 2004, 2001, 1999, 1995, 1991, 1989, 1986, 1984, 1981, 1967, 1963, 1962, 1961, 1960, 1959, 1958, 1957, 1956, 1955, 1954, 1953, 1952, 1951 by Adrienne Rich. Copyright © 1984, 1978, 1975, 1973, 1971, 1969, 1966 by W. W. Norton & Company, Inc. Used by permission of W. W. Norton & Company, Inc.

'The Peninsula', by Seamus Heaney. Copyright © Seamus Heaney, Door into the Dark, Faber and Faber Ltd.

'Poem For My Sister' by Liz Lochhead from *Dreaming Frankenstein and Collected Poems, 1967–1984*, Polygon Books 1984. Copyright © Liz Lochhead. Reproduced with permission of Birlinn Ltd via PLS Clear

'Poetry' by Leanne O'Sullivan. Copyright © Leanne O'Sullivan, *Waiting for My Clothes* (Bloodaxe Books, 2004).

'This Room' by Imtiaz Dharker. Copyright © Imtiaz Dharker *I Speak for the Devil* (Bloodaxe Books, 2001).

The authors and publisher have made every effort to trace all copyright holders, but if any have been inadvertently overlooked we would be pleased to make the necessary arrangement at the first opportunity.